Jazz Singing

America's Great Voices from Bessie Smith
to Bebop and Beyond

Will Friedwald

DA CAPO PRESS

Library of Congress Cataloging in Publication Data
Friedwald, Will, 1961–
  Jazz singing: America's great voices from Bessie Smith to bebop
and beyond / Will Friedwald.—1st Da Capo ed.
    p.   cm.
  Originally published: New York: C. Scribner's Sons, c1990. With
updated discography.
  Discography:
  Includes index.
  ISBN 0-306-80712-2 (alk. paper)
  1. Jazz vocals—History and criticism. 2. Singers—United States. I.
Title.
ML3508.F74   1996
782.42165'092'273—dc20   96-23837
                                                                         CIP

This Da Capo Press paperback edition of *Jazz Singing* is a
republication of the edition published in New York in 1992, with a
new discography substituting for the old. It is reprinted by
arrangement with the author.

4 5 6 7 8 9 10   02 01 00 99

Published by Da Capo Press, Inc.

A member of the Perseus Books Group

Manufactured in the United States of America

*In memory of Sarah Vaughan, 1924–90,
and in memory of those who contributed
immeasurably to this book but didn't live
to see it published: Maxine, Woody, Wally,
David, Elliot, Vet, Annette, and Herb.*

*"These People don't give up, Maggie,
they just go on forever."*
—*Thornton Wilder,*
The Skin of Our Teeth

*And also to Babey, who I hope will stick
with me for a few dozen books more.*

Contents

Preface

Definitions

●————————————————————————

Definitions confuse as much as they illuminate. Take the movie *The Jazz Singer*, for instance. Its very title has significance to millions who've never seen it, yet its place in the history of popular art is a mass of mythology and assumptions that can be dismissed with the phrase "contrary to popular belief. . . ." It was neither the first talking picture (sound films go back to the very beginning of movies) nor the film that put talkies on the map (that best describes Al Jolson's subsequent feature, *The Singing Fool*), nor was it even the first film appearance of Jolson (he had made a talkie short subject a few months previously). An equally improbable series of events had previously led author Samson Raphaelson to change the title of his short story "The Day of Atonement" to *The Jazz Singer* when he reworked it into a play in 1925, as did Warner Bros.'s selecting of said story as the basis for their experimental partial-sound film, and then again to the casting of Al Jolson in the lead (he was actually their third choice, after George Jessel, who had played the role on Broadway but wanted too much money to do the film, and Eddie Cantor, who didn't think anyone would go to see a talking picture).

How fitting that the art form that takes its title from this picture should also be such a mass of contradictions. Titles and definitions are at once irrelevant and important to this music because everyone who performs it or listens to it forms his own set, while critics endlessly argue its finer points. In the twenties black instrumental jazz soloists regularly appeared on blues vocal records, while white jazzmen just as often backed singers as sympathetic as Cliff Edwards or Annette Hanshaw or as antijazz as Kate Smith and Ruth Etting. Yet by the end of the decade, Louis Armstrong had appeared, trumpet in one hand and handkerchief in the other, leaning forward into the microphone to half-croon, half-scat the same basic pop tune repertoire as the leading white singers; almost simultaneously, Bing Crosby would demonstrate how the innovations of Armstrong, mixed in with a few of his own, could serve as a foundation for a whole new kind of pop music.

The major problem with defining the music was that its scope constantly changed. From the perspective of the mid-twenties it looked like a pretty meager art, the classic blues (with the exception of Bessie Smith) struck many at the time and since then as a base vaudevillization of the older folk blues, and the first batch of dance-band vocalists had even less flair for hot music than the Broadway belters of the day (at least Jolson had heard of syncopation). Armstrong and Crosby brought an end to all that, but by the end of the thirties, Billie Holiday, Leo Watson, and the Boswell Sisters had expanded the music to the point where it required new definitions. So had Frank Sinatra and Sarah Vaughan a decade later; not long after that it would be Anita O'Day and Mel Torme, and one of the things I like about the contemporary Bobby McFerrin is that what he does requires still another rewrite of the jazz singer's dictionary.

There are enough similarities among these styles to justify my claim that they're all the same music, but we'll probably never come up with a word that accurately describes them all. "Jazz singing," for what it's worth, will have to do as I doubt that something better will come along. In the early forties the British critical fraternity, in trying to define a frame of reference for such a rapidly expanding music, had used the term "vocal jazz" as the title for a pamphlet (largely concerned, again, with definitions) covering the work of Crosby, Bessie Smith, Hoagy Carmichael, Lee Wiley, and others (they had apparently not yet discovered Holiday). The term "jazz singer" really began to come into use with the widely read syndicated columnist Ralph J. Gleason, who spent endless interviews and reviews dickering as to whether the vocalist in question deserved the title.

So why spend so much time arguing who is and who isn't a jazz singer if the term is so vague that it really doesn't tell us anything? Remember the college student who, holding a handful of verses and a letter of introduction, presented himself to Robert Frost as a poet. "The term 'poet' is a gift word, son," Frost told him. "You cannot give it to yourself." "Jazz singer" has also assumed gift word status. As Gary Giddins sarcastically pointed out when asked to draw lines between jazz and nonjazz, "If you like it (and you're a jazz fan) it's jazz"—the same sort of antilogic that Ionesco's characters use to prove that cats and dogs are the same animal in *Rhinoceros*. The word shouldn't be an automatic compliment. Most rock fans I know freely admit that most of that music is worthless, and science-fiction author Robert Bloch once said that 99 percent of anything is junk. But jazz, and especially jazz singing, doesn't have any budget for mediocrity. Still, looking at it as objectively as I can, there are plenty of awful singers (Dianne Schurr, for one) who meet the definition of authentic jazz vocalist no less than Sarah Vaughan; at the same time, there are many completely jazzless singers who have more to say *to* jazz as a whole than most jazz singers, such as Mabel Mercer and Edith Piaf.

Part of the problem lies in jazz's close relationship with the blues and pop singing. From the twenties onward, the three musics have benefited from a mutual trade agreement, each taking what it needs when it needs it from one or both of the others, as well as occasionally borrowing from other sources, such as nonblack folk music and the European art music heritage. The main thrust of this work is the interaction of jazz and pop singing, from the pure, undisputedly jazz kind (Armstrong) to the sort where it's difficult to tell if the gift word applies (Crosby).

The other great source for jazz singing is, naturally, instrumental jazz. The tiptoes you have to walk on when comparing the two typify the delicate balance the artists themselves must maintain to sing credible jazz. The best jazz singers borrow ideas from instrumental jazz, and often belong to the same schools of thought (swing, bop, cool), but if you borrow too much and start merely imitating horn techniques, then you've kind of lost sight of what singing is all about. Again, the line between influence and imitation is a thin and subjective one. Though scatting (I use the term to describe any wordless performance, generally an improvised one) is an essential part of jazz singing, in sixty years I doubt that we've come up with even ten artists who ought to be permitted to scat for a mere thirty-two bars. Then there's the matter of drama and lyrics: While many outside jazz think of its singers as being more interested in the musical rather than the emotional aspects of singing, in looking at the total picture of this music, I find that jazz far more frequently operates as a key to lyric interpretation. Only Ella Fitzgerald and Anita O'Day can successfully perform a song without giving any particular attention to the words, and even they don't try it all the time.

To leave it right there would be to make the same mistake that ill-informed singers do when they assume that ignoring the lyric gives them a jazz instrumental sound, for who's to say that the great jazz soloists are unconcerned with the words that belong to the music they play? Besides the encouraging statements of Thelonious Monk and Sonny Rollins concerning the uses of melody (apart from its harmonic foundation), many of jazz's finest soloists have been equally informed by the literary and the melodic content of the songs they play, an idea that has been part of jazz from the beginning and was most eloquently expressed by Lester Young. The vocal aspects of instrumental jazz come through most strongly in ballads and blues, even as the instrumental aspects of vocal jazz come through in improvisation.

Another tendency of vocal jazz in which it's easy to put too much stock is the use of repertoire and accompaniment. Certain vocal records may be jazz records—or, at least, worthy of inclusion in a jazz discography (the standard guide to premodern jazz, Brian Rust's *Jazz Records, 1895–1942*, lists millions of these)—even if we can't call the vocal portions of them jazz singing. As Mel Torme once told Leonard Feather, Eddie Fisher doing Feather and Benny Golson's "Whisper Not" would not be jazz singing, any more than Judy Garland with Bob Crosby or Frankie Laine with Buck Clayton,* but Billie Holiday with Gordon Jenkins's army of strings is, and so is Sarah Vaughan arpeggiating her way through the most tepidly antiswinging of Sondheim opuses. Setting makes a difference *only* with pop singers out of the band era who, having reached musical maturity in such close contact with jazz (and appreciating it themselves), could go either way depending on what the occasion called for—witness Jo Stafford with Johnny Hodges and Ray Nance or Dinah Shore with Gerry Mulligan and Ben Webster.

Neither improvisation, however, nor setting nor material provides precisely the key to the relationship between vocal and instrumental jazz. There are many related uses of tonal qualities,

---

* Good accompaniment doesn't necessarily make a weak singer look any better either: Nelson Riddle's dull but slick arrangements for Linda Ronstadt only accent her amateurishness; the Count Basie Orchestra's subtle swing makes Dianne Schurr's screechy posturing appear all the more uncool.

ways to apply vibrato, methods of coloring pitch that go in and
out of fashion (after Crosby hit in the early thirties band ensembles and soloists began to lower their tonal colors to approximate
his baritone sound, even as singers did), and uses of dynamics.
But the secret at the heart of all jazz is rhythm, and vocal jazz
that depends so heavily on nonjazz source material makes a
standard practice out of rhythmic superimposition. You take a
song written in a given time signature and superimpose a jazz
beat over it, with jazz syncopation, jazz accenting, and, most
importantly, swing. Keeping in time, in jazz, is even more important than keeping in tune—explaining why so many jazz musicians double on voice. The way a singer or player hears the
beat, more than anything else, determines the way they interpret a piece of music.

The central thesis of this book is an examination of jazz's
effects on popular singing, thus drawing the parameters around
what I could and could not include here. And because I was
looking at all of "pure" vocal jazz as well as at a great deal of pop,
the scope had to remain pretty wide, as vocalists range far beyond those traditionally identified as "jazz singers." This has
taken me as far away from the jazz mainstream as Perry Como—
don't look so surprised, Billie Holiday once named Como as a
favorite of hers and he actually kept up his end in a duet with
Louis Armstrong, on a blues piece no less.[*] You see what I
mean? Because of the incredibly broad nature of the jazz-pop
relationship, even in limiting it to vocal music, I've had to im-
pose certain restrictions on this text. My original outline included a great deal more about the blues, but considerations of
space and narrative flow gradually made it plain that the blues—
both in and of itself and in its interactions with jazz and pop—
required a book of its own. I hope to write it, as I would not be

---

[*] Sharing a microphone with Armstrong makes for a reliable criterion of any jazz
versus nonjazz judgment; after all, neither Eddie Fisher nor Barbra Streisand could do
it.

able to do justice to either jazz-pop or blues by cramming them all in here.

In assembling a history of this music, I have to ask the reader's indulgence on a couple of points because of the way I, you might say, hear the beat. First, I've had to presume some knowledge on the reader's part concerning the general history of jazz, as delving deeply into the development of jazz as a whole would take too much space away from the vocal end. I can recommend James Lincoln Collier's *The Making of Jazz*, Martin Williams's *The Jazz Tradition*, and Dan Morgenstern's *Jazz People* as probably the three greatest overall histories of the music.* Second, I've also let the criticism come before the history (if Gene Lees is right, then young people should never write histories anyway) in that I include biographical information on an artist only when it strikes me as appropriate, and I also have tried to avoid rehashing overly familiar life stories (Billie Holiday and Frank Sinatra, for example) unless I can use this information to make a new point. Third, I hope I have succeeded in getting ideas across in layman's language without resorting to too many technical terms, and I've had a distinct advantage in this area in being a layman myself. I've also picked up a trick from Ross Russell's *Bird Lives* in that you'll find the acknowledgments at the end rather than the beginning. I'd just as soon have you read all the way through and decide for yourself if there's anything here worth acknowledging.

Lastly, I've tried not to couch everything in the traditional narrative set of progress and advances—after all, the history of music, and jazz in particular, though usually seen as linear, may also be perceived as cyclical, and the token cause-and-effect this-led-to-that approach doesn't always apply. In general, I pre-

---

* If you want more, I offer Gary Giddins's *Rhythm-a-Ning* and *Riding on a Blue Note* as the best essay anthologies; Alan Lomax and Jelly Roll Morton's *Mr. Jelly Roll* and Art Pepper's *Straight Life* as the best autobiographies; and Stanley Dance's *The World of Swing*, Ira Gitler's *Swing to Bop*, and John Leitweiler's *The Freedom Principle* as the best genre histories.

fer to think of the work of each major figure in this music (among them a few nonsingers, such as Duke Ellington, Benny Goodman, and Nelson Riddle) as an "expansion" rather than a "progression." As we'll see shortly, thanks to Bessie Smith and Cliff Edwards, "jazz singing" was a worthwhile, valid, and, in many ways, complete art even as early as 1926. That was the year that the two-headed juggernaut of Armstrong and Crosby set this music in radical motion, and with it the world.

Jazz Singing

Forebears

The Birth and the Blues

• ────────────────────────────────

"I can't tell my future, so I'm going to tell my past."
—Ma Rainey, "Last Minute Blues"

"Honey, don't play me no opera,
Play me some blue melodies."
—Marion Harris, "Paradise Blues"

When Cole Porter observed that black was white in 1934, he was right: Black was becoming white as fast as white was becoming black. Yet though he sarcastically submitted this observation as evidence that the world had gone mad today, the black-ing of white and the white-ing of black was, in retrospect, a natural, inevitable, and even desirable occurrence. It could not have helped happening once you gathered a number of people of European descent (in other words, Americans) around enough people of African descent (in other words, Americans).

This trend figures most importantly in American music. "Why the United States produced no considerable composers in the nineteenth century," the classical music critic Joseph Kierman has written, "when we produced such painters as Mary Cassatt and Winslow Homer and such writers as Herman Melville and Emily Dickinson, is of considerable interest."* As pop music historian Russ Sanjek has said, and this is borne out by the biographies of the first generation of great American songwriters (especially Irving Berlin and Jerome Kern), nobody had as yet figured out a way to make any money in developing an indigenously American tradition of art or pop music. And unless there was money in it, the capital of capitalism would just as soon import songs and shows from Europe.†

At the same time the American music business community discovered the untapped resources of the black tradition, which began to occur in a big way in the second decade of the twentieth century, and the slowly emerging black middle class began to work toward the creation of black popular music (as opposed to earlier black folk music). The white songwriters, producers, and publishers saw money in the union, as did their black equivalents; the black intelligentsia, however, also saw a possible means of integration.

"Jazz" is the catchall phrase that has come to refer to all music born out of the black-white union. While all jazz depends on both halves, *how* they work together is subjective. It's easy enough to think of the European harmonic tradition aligning itself with the equally sophisticated African heritage of rhythm, but we could never have the blues without black or "blue" notions of harmony. And Western "blank verse" rhythm has also played a part in the development of jazz. Ian Carr, in his biography of Miles Davis, has argued that the two cultural backgrounds constantly war with each other. While that may take the point a little too far, they've never produced the kind of com-

---

* The one important pre-jazz American composer was Charles Ives. Importantly, much of his music was not performed until forty years after it was written, and it, too, flirts with improvisation.

† This situation roughly parallels England in the years before the emergence of Gilbert and Sullivan's indigenously British operetta; then, too, imported shows (mostly Offenbach's) captured far more attention than the local product.

pletely harmonious musical miscegenation that made Southern colonels upchuck their mint juleps. The "opposing" factions assert themselves in the music of different individuals (the Modern Jazz Quartet's "Milano" versus John Coltrane's "Dial Africa") and movements ("white" cool jazz and "black" hard bop, each of which, however, involved players of both colors), which in certain ways is what was happening in the mid-twenties.

Black and white elements came to the surface in the music of both races, instrumentally and vocally. By the middle of the decade jazz had reached a level where it could become more than the popular sounds of two cultures impacting upon each other; it was ready to grow into an art form as great as any that had been produced by either faction. The years 1925 and 1926 are the best starting point from which to examine its development: 1925 marked the first successful and widespread use of the new electric recording technique, which would greatly affect our perception of the human voice, and, more importantly, Louis Armstrong's first recording sessions as a leader, which feature his singing from the beginning; 1926, though no one noticed it at the time, saw the recording debut of Bing Crosby. From the vantage point of these two years, we can most easily look forward and backward at the constantly changing elements beginning to fall into place in jazz, or black-white music.

The music of blues singer Bessie Smith, which stands at the exact halfway point between black and white traditions, represents the highest peak ever reached by black pop of the twenties. This style, also known as the "vaudeville blues," developed on a pattern of a gradually decreasing connection with both jazz and "genuine" blues. In its ever-increasing "whiteness," its evolution parallels that of the ancient Greek comic theater. Both grew steadily more and more genteel over the course of three distinct stages. Ma Rainey could stand for "old comedy," the classic blues style at its roughest and, to use terminology to which historians have applied both positive and negative connotations, most primitive. The five unrelated singers named Smith—beginning with Mamie, whose hit record "Crazy Blues"

(1920, OK/Phonola) generally gets credit with launching the classic blues as a commercial movement; Clara, who had the prettiest voice of the bunch; Trixie; Laura; and Bessie—exemplify the middle period as well as the apogee of classic blues as an artistic whole. The singers of the "new" period—Ethel Waters, Edith Wilson, Eva Taylor, Alberta Hunter, and others—though their music (of these four specifically) was no less excellent, show the movement moving farther and farther away from indigenous black style and becoming increasingly albino. Greek comedy, however, developed over hundreds of years, while the classic blues as a fad lasted no more than a decade; thus it's important to remember that artists in all three "periods" were performing at the same time.

But even among the few women in this group who had a direct connection with the blues, you don't get any guarantee of quality. Most of their records are "of interest" today, says Brian Rust (the leading discographer of prewar jazz), only because of the musicians who had accompanied them. Lillie Delk Christian, who recorded for the Okeh label's "race" series between 1926 and 1928, provides the most extreme example: For six decades, jazz fans have been forced to suffer through her ear-piercing, dog-whistle squeals (which might have served as the inspiration for Alvin and the Chipmunks) because she used Jimmie Noone and Louis Armstrong in her backup groups. But most so-called classic blues records don't necessarily have anything more to offer than the white personality and dance records of the twenties, which just as frequently offer solos by respectable jazzmen.

None of which applies to Bessie Smith. She doesn't need the presence of Armstrong and his colleagues to justify our listening to her music sixty years after it was recorded. Smith was, in fact, the one classic blues artist to outlive the genre, the one artist whose work justifies the entire style. As her biographer, Chris Albertson, tells us in his definitive *Bessie*, Smith had been born in Chattanooga, Tennessee, in 1894, at a time when performing represented virtually the only alternative to sharecropping and manual labor* for the poor and black, and for most, the working conditions it entailed were not much of an improvement. Smith's brother, Clarence, had preceded her into show business and arranged for Bessie to join the troupe that he danced in. Ma Rainey also sang with this particular troupe, and she and Smith worked in this and other companies simultaneously for almost a year. In the ten years between her first professional work and her "discovery" by Frank Walker, Clarence Williams, and Columbia Records in 1923, Smith worked up and down the East Coast, slowly and steadily building up a following.

The classic blues craze happened to reach its peak just when Smith was ready to be recorded. Fortunately for her, the label that signed her, Columbia, could do much more for an artist than the ordinary "race records" company that reached only the black population. Even if, in themselves, her records did not make her a lot of money, they made her a star and allowed her to draw large crowds and to be rightfully billed, as Albertson reports, as "the Greatest and Highest Salaried Race Star in the World." Her ten years of experience made her well prepared to put together her own show and take it on the road, but like many who were uneducated and born poor, she could not handle suddenly being able to have virtually anything she wanted: possessions, alcohol, good times, or people. Already something of a manic depressive, her personal problems (as Sidney Bechet described it, the trouble "inside her") increased along with her fortune and worsened even more when her career deteriorated with the end of both the classic blues fad and the twenties recording boom in the aftermath of the depression. She faced tough times in the thirties but never quite reached bottom, and her career was on the upswing at the time she was killed in a car crash in 1937.

To return to the notion that Smith's music defines a halfway point between black and white styles, look at the way she takes

---

* Ethel Waters came to showbiz only as an escape from the grimiest of scullery work.

on thirds of the scale, which are a traditional hot spot of black harmony. Even on the occasions when she doesn't sing an out-and-out blue third, she'll give a major or minor third a distinct blue feeling. Rhythmically, Smith also encompassed a tantalizing mixture of what was past and what was to come. On one level, her against-the-grain feeling would fall into disuse after Armstrong popularized his more "modern," streamlined 4/4 swing—in fact, Albertson notes that Smith and the classic blues in general fell out of fashion first in Harlem, where Armstrong's rhythmic innovations first took hold. At the same time, however, Smith's vertical (as opposed to horizontal or melodic) approach would continue to have a place in jazz no matter how tangential. Smith-derived rhythmic feeling turns up in the work of Mildred Bailey, is in turn suggested by Billy Eckstine in the forties, and, through Mr. B., has continued to affect musicians as diverse as Tony Bennett and John Coltrane.

These were only the building blocks of a style and do not explain why Smith's music should have so profoundly moved so many people in her day and since, or how her records have changed the lives of individuals as diverse as Billie Holiday, Mezz Mezzrow, James Baldwin, and Edward Albee—who have all written movingly about what Bessie Smith meant to them. Smith sings with a quality of harshness and at the same time with great passion but never with irony or sarcasm. With Smith, the two seemingly incongruous attitudes are compatible, a sort of tender invective. Smith sings about love without a trace of sentiment, and of sex without guilt. She has an amazingly realistic attitude toward life and love, and even in moments of heightened, not to say suicidal, despondency ("[Judge! Judge!] Send Me to the 'Lectric Chair!" [1927, Columbia]) has a sober, realistic view of life, devoid of self-pity. I don't know about early classical recording artists other than Caruso, but as far as jazz, blues, and popular music are concerned, Smith was the first fully three-dimensional recording artist, the first to use the new medium to express a complete personality.

Smith's music, much of which has been available continuously since it was first issued, went beyond the limits of the classic blues genre in the twenties, and in the last years of her life, long after the movement's glory years, she remained virtually the only classic blues artist to keep active. To use the black slang of the day, the spotlight had shifted away from the "haincty," or gully-low, rough, and comparatively primitive types (like Rainey and the Smith girls), and on to the "dicty," sophisticated, polished, urban, and urbane likes of Ethel Waters, Alberta Hunter, and Eva Taylor, who were taking black music out of the cotton-field and into the cabaret, while Josephine Baker, Elizabeth Welch, and Adelaide Hall (in her post-Ellington career) polished up the rougher aspects of the black tradition so much that they were actually acceptable to white society—European as well as American.

Hunter, Taylor, and Waters deserve singling out. Ultimately (with the possible exception of Waters), they must be judged no less guilty to the charge of blues dilettantism than any of the dozens of now-forgotten pseudo-blues recording stars of the twenties who, like them, had been singing other kinds of music both before and after the twenties blues craze. At the start of her career, "I had not heard anything remotely resembling [the blues]," Hunter told Chris Albertson. "The first songs I learned were 'All Night Long' and 'Where the River Shannon Flows,' and they were about as far removed from jazz as 'God Bless America.' " However, besides bringing positive media attention to the black woman, for the first time the craze also enhanced the capabilities of these three ladies as artists. At the time the fad ended, Hunter was in London with the musical *Showboat*, and though she had not recorded prior to the craze (beginning in 1921 for W. C. Handy's label, Black Swan), it's safe to say that the close contact to jazz and blues enriched her art immeasurably.

Hunter, the only artist from this period to continue performing into the eighties, became one of the first to demonstrate that the blues could supplement a more conventional pop style. In the twenties Hunter used a lot of vaudeville declamation, laced with frantic quavers that gradually calmed down to a kind of sophisticated singspiel in which she more or less talks the lyric through, but generally to a traditional jazz beat. Hunter represents one of the few figures in this music for whom the term "personality"—generally used to cover up an artist's inability to sing—does not represent a cop-out. She had the advantage of being able to perform in our lifetime, true, but on all of her recordings—going back to the dark premicrophone days and on through her days in "legit" musicals, cabarets, clubs, dance bands, and other venues—Hunter's motherly concern and love of the human race equally permeates both the most sentimental of ballads and the bluest of blues.

Eva Taylor's singing has just about zero connection with genuine blues style, and one doubts she would have ever recorded at all had she not married Clarence Williams. A much-maligned dynamo of twenties blues record activity, Williams composed dozens of blues-related songs and organized hundreds of the very best race records sessions, on most of which he also played reasonable piano. But even holding obvious charges of uxoriousness against her, Taylor fits remarkably well into these records. Williams generally wrote three kinds of lyrics: thinly disguised erotic metaphor patterns (generally involving dirty mistreaters and misbehaving deacons); dance instructions ("Come on people, do the whatever-it-is!"); and naive "poor little pickaninny" songs ("Pickin' On Your Baby"). As a whole, Williams and Taylor's classic blues have little of the epic tragedy of Bessie Smith's "Poor Man's Blues" or Eubie Blake's harrowing "Black and Blue." Instead, bandleader and vocalist saw eye to eye on an upbeat sound performed on jugs and washboards and expressed with unabashed "pep" that was so very much in keeping with the white dance bands of the twenties that it helped Williams accomplish his life's work of making a popular music out of jazz and blues.

Ethel Waters has equally valid ties to both black and white pop, both the traditional kind of loud-mouthed vaudeville associated with the early twenties and earlier, and the modern jazz-influenced pop that came after Armstrong and Crosby. I'm hardly the first to drop Waters's name as a possible equal to these two. Jimmy Rushing, when asked by Leonard Feather to name his favorite singers, mentioned all three. Waters herself broadcast to the world the importance of Armstrong to her music when she recorded "West End Blues" (with Clarence Williams on piano) in 1928 for Columbia. Waters used Armstrong's version of the tune, only two months old and already a classic, as her point of departure (rather than the tune, written by King Oliver, as published), incorporating Armstrong's famous scat sequence in the center. Apart from being the earliest recorded example of what has come to be known as "jazz repertory," she showed an understanding of the shape of vocal jazz to come—meaning Armstrong—almost as astute as Crosby's.

But there's a paradox where Waters is concerned. While "West End Blues" doesn't exactly constitute the sole example of Waters looking forward, her singing just as often seems limited by the past. To cite a specific technique, Waters skillfully employs playful embellishments in the second choruses of many of her tunes, just as Connee Boswell and Lee Wiley (who also cited Waters as a favorite and an influence) would do ten years later, but these variations generally emit from a pre-Armstrong sensibility (just as her heavily rolled r's suggest pre-Crosby tendencies). Admittedly, it's a distinction for semanticists. Far from being obnoxious, Waters's dated mannerisms more often add to the charm of her records. In fact, for many of her pinnacle performances Waters very effectively juxtaposes the high-brow past and the low-brow present. On "Harlem on My Mind" in particular, although Waters and composer Irving Berlin intended the scene in which she sang it in the Broadway show *As Thousands Cheer* (and recorded for Columbia in 1933) as a parody of Josephine Baker, Waters gets full mileage out of a lyric that parallels her own personality: She's not only refined; hell, she's *"damn refined!"*

Smith, Hunter, Taylor, and Waters constitute the best singers in a style that would have direct ramifications on what would later be considered jazz-pop singing proper. And as black was becoming whiter, white, over the course of decades, was becoming blacker as white fascination (though not respect) for black culture steadily increased, climaxing in the emergence of jazz shortly after the European war. As early as 1871, says Marshall Stearns in *The Story of Jazz,* blacks had been singing a heavily Caucasianized version of their religious music in white concert halls. According to Jim Haskins in *Scott Joplin,* by 1903 blacks could get away with performing European operas in America. In the mid-twenties Roland Hayes and Paul Robeson became the first black concert stars, their repertoires including plantation songs as well as arias and lieder.

But, importantly, only in the more commercial areas of music did blacks find wide acceptance. The minstrel show, which dates back to the 1840s and was based on the idea of caricaturing black music and humor (by both whites and blacks in blackface), had been America's first contribution to both world theater and music. The American musical comedy, which has roots in minstrelsy as much as it does in European operetta, had a place for blacks from the beginning: In 1914, *Watch Your Step* incorporated Irving Berlin's interpretation of ragtime (à la "Alexander's Ragtime Band") and Broadway welcomed it with open arms at the same time the high-browed opera-company operators were rejecting Scott Joplin's ragtime opera *Treemonisha.* Black musical comedian Bert Williams had been a star with white audiences going back to the 1910 *Ziegfeld Follies.* By the time *Shuffle Along of 1921* opened, an all-black show could score a major hit on the Great "White" Way. The stage, and not only musicals, would achieve full integration long before, to name two other areas, professional sports and the armed forces.

The teens and early twenties belong to Al Jolson. His singing may have been no more genuinely black than the burnt cork on his face, but he summed up everything both positive and negative concerning the evolution of modern vocal style during these years. Exciting and boring, charming and repulsive, all-knowingly funny and pretentiously serious, Jolson is a transitional figure on many levels: from minstrelsy to Broadway musical comedies and revues; from strictly live performances to the big three of mass media coming together in the twenties (records, radio, and talking pictures—all of which admittedly captured only faint echoes of Jolson); taking the mainstream of popular singing from an operetta-derived style to something if not quite black or jazz, at least which deserves credit for suggesting that black music would be an influence on American pop.

We have to wait for Crosby for the perfect and seamless infiltration of genuine jazz into mass-market music, but Jolson hints at what that might sound like. His syncopation, though rudimentary and crude, offers the idea that something new can be done with the beat. Bombastic, unsubtle, and loud, his very raucousness approximates that of the earliest recorded jazz.[*] Jolson can be most easily appreciated straight down the middle: When he tries to get really "hot" he comes off like a goofy uncle amusing a baby with childish noises, while at the other extreme he never applied his ur-jazz approach to "straight" ballads. In succeeding decades, Crosby, Armstrong, and Benny Goodman, three of the men most responsible for making a pop music out of jazz, would achieve this largely because they refused to divide their programs into "straight" and "hot" numbers. Applying jazz toward ballads and nonjazz material served a crucial integrating function. For Jolson, this would have entailed giving up his heavy-handed sentiment, which he could no more do than he could stop breathing.

Significantly, two of the three greatest minstrel-style entertainers, Jolson and Eddie Cantor (the third was Bert Williams), were Jewish. As greenhorns in the New World, they found they could achieve automatic identity and acceptance when they stepped in front of the footlights in burnt cork. It also supplied a license for silliness and lack of inhibitions, so much so for

* The Original Dixieland Jazz Band sort, not the King Oliver–Jelly Roll Morton sort.

Jolson that he couldn't confine his pseudo-Negro chutzpah to the stage and had to come bouncing out into the audience (sometimes unexpectedly, as in the play *Show Girl*). Jolson's hyperactivity in itself provided a point of reference for his contemporaries. Bert Williams did just the opposite of Jolson, and underplayed everything to the hilt as if he could hardly be bothered to move. Cantor, too, developed his own blend of kinetic energy (Jolson jumps back and forth, Cantor jumps up and down) and played on the idea of the masculine black as sexual predator: His dicty Negro is a coy, urbane lad who wears heavy glasses and shies away from lascivious females.

In many ways, Cantor has weathered the generations far more effectively than Jolson. Today we laugh at Jolson as much as with him, and part of his charm lies in the camp, unintentional humor exuded by his mastodon ego: He really thought he was God's gift to the human race, that he was doing the black man a favor by aping his physiognomy and mannerisms, and that his endless marathons of maudlin mammy songs could never fail to make crowds bawl like babies. Though Cantor, like Jolson, devoted at least one number per show or film to blackface, he refused to take either it or himself all that seriously. He also avoided Jolson extremes of overt "jazz" and sentiment, and considered himself strictly a comic, especially in his earlier films. Today his *Yiddishkite* aesthetic has never lost its ethnic hipness. From a strictly musical point of view, Cantor's two 1924 (Columbia) sides with the Georgians win the cigar. His energetic wailing jibes perfectly with the acoustic brashness and jerky rhythm of this pivotal white jazz group. "If You Do—What You Do," a tune that Bessie Smith might have done on one of her more pop-oriented sessions, suggests that he might have someday worked up to straight-ahead blues. Apart from setting the trend for combining name bands with star singers, the Cantor-Georgians disc demonstrates why many black performers were so enamored of Cantor. "We black people are not stupid," black entertainer Avon Long told Gary Giddins when asked if Cantor's blackface routine disturbed him. "We, too, can appreciate genius."

Marion Harris never became a showbiz legend like Cantor, Jolson, or Sophie Tucker, yet she was an incredibly big star in the teens and twenties and is quite easily the best white singer of this prehistoric period. Like Jolson, her career illustrates various transitions—from vaudeville to Broadway shows to cabaret—and her music also reflects a Jolson-era minstrel sensibility, but one devoid of Jolson's inflated sense of self-importance. With Harris, it's not so much a matter of authenticity or inauthenticity as it is a matter of stylization and interpretation. She isn't imitating black style so much as interpreting it, much the same way Ellington would base a piece of music on his impression of a given culture (*The Far East Suite*, for instance) rather than strictly re-create the sounds he heard there. She has the bombastic zest and punch of Jolson and Cantor, but for her these elements are still congruous with taste and subtlety. In Harris, Tin Pan Alley found the perfect performer for its dozens of numbers with the words "jazz" or "blues" in the title, her exuberant galavantin' especially suitable to the comparatively authentic works of W. C. Handy. In doing so many tunes that reflect some aspect of the vaudeville jazz/pseudo-Negro tradition,* and in doing them so well, Harris makes an art out of coon-shouting.

As seeds of modern vocal style began to sprout, so, too, were those of a form that would serve as both rival and ally to all singers for a quarter century, the modern jazz-oriented dance band. The early band arrangers set about devising ways to adapt the rough, polyphonic textures of early jazz to the orchestral format, and almost from the start, vocalists had a place among the brass, reed, and rhythm sections. In 1918, Joseph C. Smith's orchestra recorded "Mary" with a vocal refrain by the trio of Harry McDonough, Charles Hart, and Lewis James. In 1920

* To drop the names of a few titles, "There's a Lump of Sugar Down in Dixie" and "Mammy's Chocolate Soldier" (both 1918, Victor). Harris also invented what would later be known as "vocalese" with her 1934 "Singin' the Blues" (English Decca) in which she sings lyrics to jazz solos originally improvised by Frank Trumbauer and Bix Beiderbecke, as King Pleasure would later do for James Moody (see Modernism 1).

vaudevillian bandleader Ted Lewis sang his theme song for the first of many times on records, "When My Baby Smiles at Me" (Columbia), and Art Hickman, another of the very first leaders of anything that can be considered a dance band in the modern sense, recruited headliners Frank Crumit and Nora Bayes as guest stars for two of his own Columbia records.* These were hardly precedent-setting events; however, two years later, when the two biggest-drawing bandleaders of the twenties, Paul Whiteman and Vincent Lopez,† started bringing in established singers for brief "vocal refrains," that was something to pay attention to, even if it was only on records.

Plainly, in 1925 popular singing on both the black and white sides of the fence was in a state of flux in terms of both form and content. And then somebody invented the microphone. Recording technology itself has since influenced not only just the way we hear a given voice but the very way voices are chosen for recordings. In the days before the mike, as Jimmy Rushing told Stanley Dance, "Unless you could overshadow the horns, they wouldn't let you sing. You had to have a good pair of lungs—strong!—to reach out over the band and the people in the big dance halls." Herb Jeffries was fired from a singing spot in a ballroom in the early thirties because his voice couldn't fill the hall, the owner said, and he couldn't afford "one of those new-fangled microphones."

In making quiet voices audible, the mike forever altered our perception of the human voice, but its positive ramifications

---

* "In Old Manila" and "I Could Have You," respectively.

† The British had recorded dance-band vocal refrains as early as 1919, and Aileen Stanley sang "Away Down East in Maine" with Lopez in September 1922 (Columbia). Less than four months later, Billy Murray, who'd been making records since 1903, joined Whiteman's orchestra for "Mr. Gallagher and Mr. Shean," a famous vaudeville duet that obviously cried out for at least one singer, and in September, Murray participated in Whiteman's second recording to use a vocal, as a member of the American Quartet, on "Last Night on the Back Porch" (both 1923, Victor). Other ancient recording studio vets employed as band vocalists at this early stage included Billy Jones and Irving Kaufman.

have been greatly overstated. Only the influence of jazz made modern pop singing possible, and initially the microphone proved more of a hindrance than a help. The singers who became famous in the earliest days of electrical microphone recording today come off as far more antiquated and unlistenable than their acoustically recorded predecessors: Gene Austin, Ruth Etting, Kate Smith, Whispering Jack Smith, and Vaughan DeLeath (who, according to legend, had been using "mike" techniques in her singing on the radio long before record companies picked up on electrical pickups). Their rhythm is atrocious, their prowess as interpreters practically nil, and their ability to say anything to a future generation nonexistent. Of this early electric bunch, only Rudy Vallee would stay in the public eye into the thirties and forties, and he more because of his gifts as a comedian and character actor than as a singer.

In the relatively new area of dance-band record vocal refrains, the ancient vaudevillians like Billy Murray, Irving Kaufman, and Billy Jones were replaced by what were then considered more "natural" sounding vocalists.* High-pitched and effeminate, this new breed of band singer—Scrappy Lambert and Smith Ballew were the most prolific—had a lot in common with the new kinds of leading men popular in Hollywood in the years before and after the electrical recording process had been applied to the movie industry.

On the whole, the initial postmike bunch seems far less "modern" than the singers of the teens. While Cantor and Jolson simply continued doing what they had always done without altering their styles to suit the new equipment (therefore, as John McDonough has written, rendering themselves anachronisms doomed to forever rehash earlier triumphs), Marion Harris became the one major acoustic pop star to alter her approach come the revolution. Electrical recording cramped her style, quieted

---

* The change from acoustic to electric was not overnight but gradual; acoustic recordings continued to be made by some of the smaller companies as late as 1930, and on these Kaufman and his contemporaries continue to supply the singing.

her down, and deprived her of the damn-the-torpedoes abandon of her earlier records. Harris's sides from 1927 on (made largely in London) suggest the day after the circus leaves town.

Electrical microphones shook up the record business almost as much as they shook up the film industry. As various film historians have pointed out, the silent comedians were, as a whole, most upset by the change. But just as Laurel and Hardy simply affixed voices to their screen personas and proceeded to get each other into audible fine messes in the talkie era, Cliff Edwards represents the one major pop singer to stand equally tall in both the acoustic and electric dynasties—perhaps because Edwards had the strongest ties to the instrumental jazz tradition.

This comes through most immediately in Edwards's use of scat singing and in the fact of his being, if not the inventor of the technique then certainly the first to use scatting (wordless vocal improvisation) as a cornerstone of his style. According to Larry Kiner (compiler of *The Cliff Edwards Discography,*[*] the most complete compendium of information on Edwards), Edwards's scatting has pre-jazz origins. In the early teens Edwards got his first musical job in a cinema, where he accompanied the silent movies with his ukelele as well as with singing, vocal sound effects, and "eefin' "[†] (the word Edwards used before anyone had thought of "scat"). At the very beginning of his recording career, Edwards anticipates the contemporary Bobby McFerrin by creating a whole band by himself: singer, horn solo, and background accompaniment. He introduces his very first record proper, James P. Johnson's "Old-Fashioned Love," with scat phrases that could have been played by trumpeter Joe Smith on a Bessie Smith record, and in between his two verbal choruses, scats an interlude instead of using an instrumental soloist. On this 1923 (Pathe) side, Edwards only scats the melody, but by 1924 he had moved up to creating fully improvised choruses,

---

[*] Bridgeport, Conn., Greenwood Press, 1987.

[†] The term also occurs in "Hi Lee Hi Lo," a mock-oriental epic by the Happiness Boys (1923, Gennett) which describes "eefin' " Chinese men.

and the breaks he devised for Gershwin's "Fascinatin' Rhythm" (Pathe) suit the song better than the ones Gershwin wrote for it.

Yet scatting represents only the beginning of the ways Edwards used jazz. One of the earliest white folks to understand the blues, Edwards can even create a solid blues solo based on only marginal blues material, as he does on "The Hottest Man in Town" (1924, Pathe). Edwards may also be the first to suggest how hot techniques can inform ballads: His embellishments on "The Lonesomest Girl in Town" and "Dreaming of a Castle in the Air" may be tamer than those of his rhythm tunes, like "Say, Who Is That Baby Doll?" (all 1925, Pathe), but the funky aroma of Dixieland hangs in the air along with the castle. "Remember" (also 1925, Pathe) contains the crème-de-la-crème example of Edwards rejecting Jolsonian sentiment. After singing one chorus of the Irving Berlin waltz almost painfully straight, Edwards starts into the second even stiffer, but reveals that he's been pulling our legs when he answers himself in "female" falsetto with hysterically dumb commentary. He: "Remember you vowed . . ." She: "Oh, I vowed?" He (stoically): "Yes. You vowed by all the stars above you . . ." She: "What stars?" He (angry): "Those stars up in the sky!" She: "Oh, up there!"

Born in 1895 in Hannibal, Missouri, Edwards left home in his early teens, Kiner tells us, to try to break into show business. He had almost no "school" learning, but just the same he was not a self-taught man so much as an untaught man who never quite mastered the skills it takes to control either a career or a life. Edwards was an alcoholic, a womanizer, a gambler, a junkie, a chronic debtor, and did just about everything awful that it was possible for a person to do to himself in those days before crack, AIDS, and heroin (and some people say he even did *that!*). In short, Edwards was completely unable to manage *any* aspect of his life except his music. His talent attracted fame and riches though he had no idea what to do with either. In the teens he worked his way up the show-business ladder with a number of partners, including "Ja Da" composer Bobby Carleton, comics Lou Clayton and Joe Frisco, and dancer Pierce Keegan, with whom he broke into his first Broadway show, *Ziegfeld's Mid-*

night Follies, in 1919. Five years later, Edwards, along with his co-stars Fred and Adele Astaire, became a bona fide headliner with the thundering success of *Lady Be Good*—as Astaire later wrote, Edwards "stopped the show with his specialty ('Fascinatin' Rhythm')." After that, for a long time it was strictly up.

Edwards remained one of the biggest names on Broadway and probably MGM's most employed comic-singer long into the thirties, his career not impeded by changing fashions but by his own foibles. Edwards's infamy overshadows his performances: bankruptcies, divorces, long periods of obscurity, and the inability to take advantage of potential breaks, as when his vocal portrayal of Jiminy Cricket in Walt Disney's *Pinocchio* (1939) and the song "When You Wish Upon a Star" earned him a shot at a second career. Unbelievably, he lived until 1971, when he died in a home for destitute has-beens in Hollywood.*

In contrast to Jolson's clumsy, left-field sense of time, Edwards was the first pop star to display genuine jazz rhythmic virtuosity. Besides constructing scat solos that predict Leo Watson and Ella Fitzgerald, Edwards had a remarkable gift for using jazz techniques to make a lyrical point—the ultimate ideal of twentieth-century vocal music. On the above-mentioned 1924 "Fascinatin' Rhythm," he drops a heavy downbeat accent onto the first syllable of the title phrase, and thereby makes the rhythm that much more *fas*cinating. On the second chorus of "How She Loves Me Is Nobody's Business" (1925, Pathe), Edwards gets more swing out of the rhythmic configuration of the main phrase by ever-so-briefly pausing in between the two words "Nobody's . . . business" and singing the second on kind of a postafterbeat that, abstractly, anticipates what Sinatra would do with "Summer Wind" more than forty years later.

Edwards also makes remarkable use of space, first on two

---

* Contemporary actor–performance artist Jeff Weiss does a monologue concerning the last days of Cliff Edwards that's far more meaningful than Edward Albee's play *The Death of Bessie Smith*.

series of recordings made for Pathe between 1923 and 1928. His earliest sides most resemble Bobby McFerrin, with "Ukelele Ike" (a stage nickname) performing largely solo, except for his own uke, occasionally with a wise pianist who knows enough to stay in the background out of Edwards's way—and Edwards exploits the open space around him magnificently.

Any kind of solo voice, whether horn, rhythm, or vocal, varies between orchestral and horn concept—for instance, Jelly Roll Morton approximating a full band with his piano in comparison to what Earl Hines called his trumpet-style piano. Edwards can't be limited to any one of these concepts, and as other instruments are introduced on his sessions, he shifts among them. First they beef up Edwards's treble lines with basses, either brass (Joe Tarto's tuba) or reed (Adrian Rollini's bass sax), and he responds by flying into higher keys and getting even farther off the ground in his improvising.

When Pathe decided to record Edwards with a six-piece band, far from cramping his style (as with McFerrin), Edwards gets into some terrific interplay with the hot soloists in the all-star bands with which they supplied him—as on "Dinah" (1925), wherein he bests cornetist Red Nichols in a "chase" chorus. Nichols plays a few bars, Edwards scats a few more bars in return, then Nichols, then Edwards, and so on for thirty-two bars (one chorus). Edwards also chases down Adrian Rollini's bass saxophone on "I Don't Want Nobody but You" (1926).

After the hot combination sides, we then have to wait a long time before Edwards's last great series of records. In 1928 he switched from Pathe to Columbia, and from 1932 on his recording sessions became increasingly sporadic, first for the American Recording Corporation's lower-priced labels, then Decca and others. He made plenty of swell sides in these years, his gift for comedy coming to the fore in "The Hunkadola" (a parody of Fred Astaire's mock-Latin dance spectaculars "The Cariocha," "The Continental," and "The Piccolino" [1935, ARC/Melotone]) as well as a series of down-and-dirty "party" records that included "I'm a Bear in a Ladies Boudoir" and "Give It to Mary

with Love,"* but on the whole, the post-1928 sides have far less
to offer than the Pathes. Someone at Columbia tried to do to
Edwards what had already been done to Marion Harris—that is,
to hold him down in keeping with the listlessness of late twenties
microphone-singing style and ground his jazz-powered flights of
fancy. Even when he tries scatting in these years, instead of a
hot combination or his own uke to egg him on, Edwards receives
only the unsympathetic support of a rather blasé studio orchestra.

In the early forties, when it looked as if Edwards's recording
career was finished and his primary employment consisted of bit
parts in Killer Gorilla B-movies, Edwards got in on the wartime
and postwar nostalgia boom that inspired a million MGM and
Fox period musicals and also rediscovered Jolson. Edwards's
primary activity at this time was no longer records but syndicated radio: Three transcription services produced regular programs starring Edwards in 1943 and 1944 alone. The first two,
for C. P. MacGregor and Lang-Worth Feature Programs, consist of Edwards and his ukelele but are drastically disappointing,
giving the idea that on all of his post-twenties recordings the
enthusiasm so crucial to his work has dissipated into a stale,
hung over lethargy. Edwards proves this impression false with
the third series, recorded by the Tower Transcription Service in
1944. The strictly oldies repertoire of the first two shows didn't
change, but far from having gone downhill, Edwards had actually improved since his glory years. However, like the best of
the New Orleans "revival" players who were "discovered" at
around the same time, his style had evolved in a manner only
tangential to the mainstreams of pop and jazz.

Everything fits on these tunes, which were, according to re-
searcher Morton Miller, selected and worked out at the actual
sessions. Edwards not only came up with the songs themselves,
but his bag of tricks contained one choice little arrangement

---

* Here's a sample of the under-the-counter lyrics: " 'Cause you see I'm so bashful
and shy / I'm afraid that she'll get it from some other guy." Not exactly Cole Porter or
Clarence Williams or even Dwight Fiske, but effective.

after another, whether simply following an out-of-tempo verse with a straight-ahead refrain (on "K-K-Katy" he transforms the chorus's first two lines into an ad hoc verse), or making ingenious forays into the patter choruses of "Shine," "Shakin' the Blues Away," and "Everybody Step" (in which Edwards literally dances in and out of tempo). These loose routines perfectly suit the instrumentation, a xylophone-piano-guitar-bass combo that could have been fronted by either Benny Goodman or Red Norvo and belongs far more to the forties than the twenties. The tempos may be blisteringly fast, the arrangements (though short) deceptively complex, and there's no drummer to help them with the time (although on "Hang on to Me" somebody either pulls out a washboard or bangs on a suitcase), yet Edwards came to *swing*, and swing he does.

If Edwards was this on-target, one wonders, why did he become a tangent and not the center of jazz-influenced pop singing, as Crosby did? For one thing, his approach predated Louis Armstrong, and post-Armstrong style would quickly blot out the memory of everything else as if it had never existed. But more importantly, Edwards was thought of strictly as a comic, always playing the hero's best friend or comic relief in his films and shows. His particular sense of humor immediately dates him. The hero of the jazz-pop movement would have to be a leading man—in other words, he had to be able to offer uncompromised romance (stronger than mere sentiment) as well as hot jazz.

There was one vastly important element that had developed in the years prior to the introduction of the microphone and that was "form." In fact, with exceptions such as the Boswell Sisters, Irving Berlin, and Mel Tormé, the song forms developed by the end of the teens would remain unchanged for the duration of this art. American popular song had, by the end of the teens, pretty much codified itself into what we call the thirty-two-bar AABA form: each section lasting eight measures—the first, second, and fourth more or less using the same piece of melody and only the bridge being anything significantly different—and the whole piece usually introduced by a sixteen-bar verse. These AABAs were then organized into two other forms, "vocal with accompaniment" and "vocal refrain." The first pertains to "solo" singers, in which two-thirds of the recording is given to the vocalist, and the band (or a soloist from the band) plays an interlude in the middle. The second applies largely to dance music, and here the band takes up two-thirds of the record and the singer gets only one chorus (or refrain) in the middle. In other words, singer-band-singer versus band-singer-band.

Blues form, which means, among other things, a shape in which vocal and instrumental portions repeatedly alternate, would also be prominent, but the classic blues itself had left behind one idea that would pertain to all singing done with either a jazz or blues affiliation: the obbligato. Simply put, the term describes an isolated instrumental line that follows a vocal.* The obbligato is a marvelously useful device for jazz purposes. It can be harmonic when the different voices simultaneously hit notes that form chords. It can employ counterpoint when the two lines fill in each other's gaps. It can create polyphony when the lines are separate enough to play distinct melodies, heterophony when the lines are so very close but never quite touch, or antiphony when the voices call and respond to each other. The obbligato was so much a part of jazz literature that, in the fifties, singing musicians as diverse as Louis Armstrong and Chet Baker overdubbed their own obbligatos behind their vocals.

So, at the dawn of electrical recording in 1925 and 1926, all the elements were in place to produce one of the most significant ramifications of the black-white explosion, namely, jazz-oriented popular singing. The technology to record it was there (although, as we have seen, the new devices were by no means a panacea), the influences were there, and the people and climate were finally there. Edwards, Smith, and the others had laid a foundation; now it was up to Armstrong and Crosby to build.

---

* While usually used to describe a voice and a horn, it can also refer to two instruments or two voices, as on the Bessie Smith–Clara Smith duets like "Far Away Blues" (1923, Columbia).

Mr. Satch
and Mr. Cros

Louis Armstrong and Bing Crosby

●

"I was in the spirit on the Lord's Day, and heard behind me a great voice, as of a trumpet."

—*Revelations 1:10*

"Oh, melody! Oh, memory!"

—*Louis Armstrong, spontaneous interpolation to "Star Dust" (1931)*

BING: Now, folks, I'd like to present an old friend of mine and an old friend of yours, too. In fact, this fella's a friend of everybody that really gives a hoot about music. This man here is at least 99 and 44/100ths percent *pure* music. Ladies and gentlemen, the mighty Louis Armstrong! [applause] Louis, that's quite a write-up I saw about you. I was reading *Esquire* magazine this month; you're in there big, ain't you?

LOUIS: Yeah, Pops! Thanks very much.

BING: I dug it, and I wanna tell you that your description of the jazz music and the jazz musicians of the twenties was a tremendously interesting item, Lou.

LOUIS: Well, we were all jumpin' pretty high then, Daddy.

BING: You still jump pretty good, I think.

LOUIS: Thanks, Daddy, but I ain't really been off the ground in years!

BING: I was thinkin' of some of those old records you made in those days, the twenties, for Okeh. Gee, they were really wild! Those songs had some titles, didn't they?

LOUIS: Yeah, we took tunes like "Potato Head Blues" . . .

BING: "Potato Head Blues"! Yeah, that was a gasser . . .

LOUIS: "Chicago Breakdown," "Struttin' with Some Barbecue" . . .

BING: "Cornet Chop Suey," "Hotter Than That" . . .

LOUIS: "Heebie Jeebies" . . .

BING: "Heebie Jeebies"! That's the record where you dropped the music and you had to scat.

LOUIS: We had to keep goin', yeah.

BING: Scattin' first started there, wasn't it 1926?

LOUIS: Scattin' started right there, because we dropped the music and the man in the booth said [falsetto], "Go ahead! Go ahead!"

BING: So you made with the re-bops, huh?

LOUIS: Yeah!

BING: Well, they were killers, all those recordings, every one of 'em. You know, lots of those records are collector's items now, Lou.

LOUIS: Yeah, but when us boys made these records, we was collector's items, too, you know!

BING: You were?

LOUIS: Of course, the collectors never caught up with us.

BING: I see what you mean, Louis, 'cause I was with a band once myself.

LOUIS: Yeah, but when you went into the band business, you joined Paul Whiteman, and that was very high class.

BING: I should say it was, we had our own special bill collector. . . . What are you doin' in Hollywood this trip, Louis? You making a picture or something?

LOUIS: I'm working on a picture out at MGM called *Glory Alley*. It's a story about New Orleans.

BING: I read about that picture, *Glory Alley*. I understand that you have a very, very dramatic part in the picture.

LOUIS: Yeah [laughs], this old cat has gone legit there!

[After Louis sings "I Get Ideas"]

BING: I don't think you've become a legitimate actor; you've become
a legitimate singer!

LOUIS: No, Daddy, no, that's your racket!

BING: That's not my racket! I don't want to complain or anything,
Louis, but now that you and I and Ella [Fitzgerald] have gotten
together on the same show, don't you think we oughta head
South and see if we can pick up a few blues for the folks, pick up
a few beats down there?*

Louis Armstrong and Bing Crosby, the two most important
figures in jazz-derived popular singing, both went to their graves
without the world knowing when they were born. Only in a 1988
Village Voice article did Gary Giddins, author of *Satchmo* (New
York: Dolphin, Doubleday, 1989), the finest study of Armstrong
yet, reveal that the date of Armstrong's birth was August 4,
1901, and only in the eighties did Ken Twiss, president of the
Bing Crosby Historical Society, prove beyond all doubt that
Crosby was born on May 3, 1903 (baptismal certificates held the
answer in both instances).

We know also that both came from poor families—
Armstrong's hardly a family at all. In the late forties, when
Crosby was seen as the ultimate American everyman, the writers of his broadcasts and his press releases tried to create a
middle-class background for him. Ironically, this was the one
stratum to which he had never belonged. Raised at near-poverty
level in Tacoma, Washington, he became one of the wealthiest
men in show business before he was forty. Crosby's father, when
he worked, held down a job in a brewery and was barely able to
support his wife, seven children (of which Bing—originally
Harry—was the fourth), and the various other relatives who
lived with them. Crosby later admitted that while his father
succeeded in feeding and sheltering them all, the children had
to work for everything else, including clothes, shoes, and school-
books. Armstrong's upbringing was even bleaker. He was raised

---

* From Bing Crosby's radio show, broadcast on November 28, 1951, and recently
issued on LP: Sounds Rare 5010.

in the most squalid, desolate area of New Orleans—it would make a contemporary black ghetto seem like Shangri-la by comparison—by a mother who was barely around. His father wasn't there at all.

Both men became attracted to music and entertainment early on and each grew up determined to make it his career. In New Orleans' Negro red light district, where Armstrong was born and raised and where diversions of every sort were the principal trade, even danger (to use Armstrong's metaphor) "was *dancing* all around you then." "Little Louis" sang in a vocal quartet in his early teens; no casual affair this, since there was money to be made by poor boys on the Storyville streets and almost no place else. Armstrong's group faced much competition and had to rehearse and make an informal study of harmony and part-singing. "He could sing real well, too," remembered Peter Davis, bandleader in the Colored Waif's Home where the teenaged Armstrong learned to play cornet, "even though his voice was coarse."

From the beginning, Armstrong's interest in singing and songs equaled his enthusiasm for the cornet and instrumental jazz, the music he more than anyone else would turn into a international art form. Shortly after leaving the orphanage, in fact, Armstrong composed what would later become the popular standard "I Wish I Could Shimmy like My Sister Kate."* Still, for the next dozen or so years of his life, singing took a backseat to the trumpet.

His rise to the top of the New Orleans music scene, though not overnight, occurred quickly, and over the next few years he played with virtually all the major bands in the city, including Fate Marabel's riverboat groups and Kid Ory's. In 1922, Armstrong's mentor, King Oliver, invited him to work with his Cre-

---

* "When I was young and very green, I wrote that tune, 'Sister Kate,' and someone said that's fine, let me publish it for you. I'll give you fifty dollars outright. I didn't know nothing about papers and business and I sold it outright." (Armstrong, quoted in *Hear Me Talkin' to Ya* by Nat Shapiro and Nat Hentoff [New York: Dover Press, 1955.])

ole Jazz Band in Chicago, and after playing and recording with Oliver for over a year, Armstrong moved into what, thanks largely to him, would become the most important early-jazz big band, Fletcher Henderson's Orchestra. Armstrong had recorded dozens of discs as a sideman with Oliver, Henderson, Clarence Williams, and a dozen or so blues singers (including the greatest, Bessie Smith) by the time he began his most important series of records in 1925. Collectively known as the Hot Fives, a term that refers to all the small-group sessions under Armstrong's leadership between 1925 and 1928, these are by general consensus the most influential of Armstrong's accomplishments and quite likely the most significant body of work in all jazz.

Here he changes the face of jazz on every conceivable level: Rhythmically, he establishes the soon-to-be standard 4/4 "swing" tempo; structurally, he solidifies use of the theme-solos-theme format; conceptually, he defines the idea of jazz itself with the soloist at the center, from playing short, simple "breaks" of slight melodic embellishments to fully improvised chord-based solos of a whole chorus or longer. And in the strategy he describes as progressing from the melody to routine-ing the melody to routine-ing the routine, he sets down the basic model as well as the vocabulary most, if not all, jazz soloists would use from then on. Even before 1928, Armstrong's achievements begin to elevate from a purely musical plane to a social one, as he launches the shifts in the music that would enable it to become both a high-brow art form and an international pop entertainment. To use Lester Bowie's phrase, Louis Armstrong created "jazz as we know it."

How to top an act like that? For Armstrong, the logical next step after reinventing jazz was to reinvent popular music in his own image—to apply his discoveries as a jazz musician to mass-market pop. To speak diagrammatically, from 1929 onward Armstrong works just as hard at expanding *out*wardly as a performer as he had at growing *up*wardly from 1925 to 1928, the years of the Hot Fives. The opinion of some of his critics to the contrary, this expansion did nothing to lessen the internal content of Armstrong's art; it altered his music only in terms of its outward manifestations in three specific areas: On records especially, Armstrong now works almost exclusively with big dance bands as opposed to Hot Fives and Sevens; he concentrates more on popular songs instead of original compositions and material out of the jazz tradition; and he gives equal time to singing.

To be sure, Armstrong had sung quite a bit on his earlier small-band records, his vocals on these coming off more like a direct extension of his horn work than the other way around (as was actually the case). On "Hotter Than That" (1927) and "West End Blues" (1928),* for example, Armstrong experiments with transposing the functions of the voice and the trumpet: He trades call-and-response phrases with another musician, but sings back his answers where you expect him to play them. Armstrong also sings a trumpet-style obbligato behind Lillie Delk Christian, the main vocalist on "Too Busy" (1928).† Many Hot Five sides also contain stop-time breaks sung instead of played, but the most revealing glimpses into the future occur on Armstrong's longer scat choruses. As we have seen, Cliff Edwards had been the first to apply scat to pop singing,‡ and he had done as much as it was possible to do with the technique in the pre-Armstrong world. Armstrong not only brought scatting into his universe, he de-

---

* All Armstrong records discussed on this and the next few pages, unless otherwise noted, were originally recorded for the Okeh label and were reissued by American and/or European CBS.

† Unfortunately, he doesn't sing it loud enough, as Miss Christian is still audible.

‡ There are, however, a few isolated examples of the technique being used in a jazz or pop context that undoubtedly precede any form of literate communication; the vaude-villian Gene Green incorporated a half chorus of mock-Chinese scatting into his 1917 "From Here to Shanghai," and jazz saxist and arranger Don Redman scats on Fletcher Henderson's 1924 "My Papa Doesn't Two-Time No Time" (Columbia). We can even find earlier, though not as absolutely substantiated examples, such as Leadbelly's allegedly pre-blues performance style and Jelly Roll Morton's testimony that "Most people believe that Louis Armstrong invented scat singing. I must take that credit away from him because I know better. Tony Jackson and I were using scat for novelty back in 1906 and 1907 when Louis Armstrong was still in the orphan's home." (Actually, he wasn't even *there* yet.)

vised new contexts for it. "Heebie Jeebies" (1926), the most celebrated of his vocal improvisations, transliterates patterns Armstrong had conceived for instrumental music very directly into vocal terms, starting with lyrics, then modulating into scat phrases, and returning to the words at the conclusion, which all lends credence to the trumped-up tale of the record's scat sequence not being deliberate (as rehashed by Armstrong and Crosby in the broadcast excerpt at the beginning of this chapter). No one could make such a claim with Armstrong's two equally remarkable 1928 scat vocals, "Basin Street Blues" and "Squeeze Me"; so in place of an extra musical explanation, Armstrong "excuses" his scat episodes by having two other members of the band hum in harmony behind him—as if to somehow normalize them. In doing so, Armstrong unearths the folk origins of each tune, investigating what they might have sounded like before W. C. Handy and Clarence Williams codified them into song form.

Other indications of things to come can be found on his more or less conventional vocal refrains. There's the monumental sense of humor that produced the comic duet of Mr. and Mrs. Lil Armstrong (then also his pianist) on "That's When I'll Come Back to You," and the mastery of the blues in spirit and form on "I'm Not Rough" (both 1927), which contains the single most powerful blues ever sung by a man (or anyone besides Bessie Smith) in this period, authenticated by the presence of blues guitarist Lonnie Johnson, here serving as guest accompanist.

By 1929, Armstrong had all the elements necessary to become a great singer. The next move in the evolution of jazz-influenced popular singing would then be a matter of integration. Fortunately (as Armstrong once later said of cornetist Bix Beiderbecke), Bing Crosby happened to be "working on the same thing."

The story of Crosby giving up law school to play drums and sing in a jazz band ("I'd rather sing than eat," he reportedly told his disappointed parents) and the one about his trip from his native Washington to find big-time showbiz in Los Angeles in a beat-up old jalopy, are as much a part of the mythology of popular music as the tale of little Louis Armstrong firing a gun and winding up in the orphanage is to that of jazz.

A few months after Armstrong cut "Heebie Jeebies" in 1926, Paul Whiteman, who had been one of the first popular bandleaders to show an interest in jazz and, as we have seen, in vocalists, hired Crosby and his partner, Al Rinker, as the industry's first full-time recording band singers. The mere act of signing on someone who did nothing but sing seemed strange enough in those days, but the choice of Crosby proved to be nothing less than radical. Crosby did not fit into either of the two molds that had been established for nonclassical singers by this point. He was not a noisy Jolson clone like Billy Murray or Irving Kaufman. Nor did he act like the equally affected zombies of the early postmicrophone period, like Ruth Etting, Whispering Jack Smith, and Gene Austin, who overdid the understatements to such a degree that they were even farther away from jazz than the belters had been. Even his voice, a steadily deepening baritone with a husky rasp and an occasional trill, sounded as far removed from the popular tenors and falsettos of the time as Armstrong's vocal gravel pit.

The pop music world must have wondered what Whiteman saw in Crosby. My guess is that Whiteman realized that Crosby had the potential ability to accomplish one of the basic functions of an artist, one that was particularly germane to what Whiteman himself aspired to: to recognize what was valid in contemporary popular music, to preserve the best parts of it, and to integrate them all into a cohesive whole by filtering them through his own personality. Integration, in fact, represents the single most important element of Crosby's accomplishments. In this sense, integration means more than a union of African and American elements; it means art as a whole being, as a series of connections, of making seemingly disparate forms fit together in new ways. And in the traditional sense, integration signifies the single most crucial element of American music, the very basis of its existence.

In Crosby's earliest recordings, made with the Whiteman orchestra, Crosby puts together the various ingredients as if they were pieces in a jigsaw puzzle; but in each case, what Crosby adds of his own is equally important. The classic blues singers, especially the phonetically correct but no less blue Ethel Waters (who, in turn, would learn a thing from both Armstrong and Crosby), had already adapted blues feeling to the harmonic practices of Western music, but not, as Crosby did, to the American pop song. Jolson and Marion Harris provided a model for energetic charisma and the concept of black imitation, but Crosby would firstly remove all traces of the minstrel show. Etting and Austin and the other early microphone singers demonstrated how the new electric recording technique could be used, but left it to Crosby to prove that subtlety didn't have to mean somnambulance. Edwards had demonstrated the relevance of scatting to pop singing but never really developed it as Crosby and Armstrong would, simultaneously taking the technique forward into the new world of post-Armstrong rhythm. Most importantly, Crosby absorbed the new instrumental soloists, especially Armstrong and, to a lesser extent, Beiderbecke: their approach to melodic organization, their use of rhythm, and their concept and vocabulary of improvisation.

Crosby's greatest accomplishment—the result of all this alchemy—was the application of jazz to the music of Tin Pan Alley. The significance of "hot" music to ballads, in particular, had been a nut that no one had been able to crack, especially vocally. Certainly Crosby's assimilation of Armstrong's rhythmic advances gave him a major jump on the competition. On Whiteman's records of "I'm Afraid of You" (1928, Victor) and "T'aint So, Honey, T'aint So" (1928, Columbia), he introduces the device of holding notes at the end of phrases as a means of playing with the time. On "Make Believe" (1928, Victor), Crosby goes even farther, leaving his colleagues in the orchestra behind. To reduce the risk of the elephantine Whiteman entourage getting in his way, the strings and the horns lay out while Crosby takes his chorus with just the rhythm section. And not even all of them: The piano, banjo, and drums keep fairly quiet while Crosby performs what amounts to a duet with the band's New Orleanian string bassist, Steve Brown. While the piano, banjo, drums, and Whiteman's other bass (tuba actually) churn out dated oom-pah chunks, Crosby and Brown genuinely swing and at times they even ease into surprisingly modern 4/4 time. (Brown later described this time signature as one of the cornerstone elements of "modern" jazz.)

The success of the other half of Crosby's achievement, his use of lower pitches, can't be explained in strictly musical terms. The twenties were great years for "naturalism," but their idea of natural differed drastically from any that has come since—and Crosby represents the line of demarcation. He was the one who came up with the kind of "natural" that worked: the warm B-flat baritone with a little hair on it, the perfect balance between conversational and purely musical singing, the personality and the character. Crosby was the first singer to truly glorify and exalt the American popular melody, and his deep, perfectly in-tune resonance gave American music the wherewithal at last to compete with (and, in my ears at least, surpass) opera and the European art-song tradition. It became the sound that defined generation after generation of pop singing, largely because of its jazz origins: The single most identifiable characteristic of Crosby's style, in fact, was as a jazz device, namely, the use of trills and what classical music crit Henry Pleasants describes as mordents or satellite notes, which serve as grace notes* or syncopes employed to break up the time.

This takes us ahead of our story but not by all that much. Once Crosby had conquered the new rhythm, all the other elements began to fall into place; after 1929, both he and Armstrong could finally perform jazz-ballads that meet all the requirements of both sides of the hyphen. While Crosby's ear-

---

* Don Cherry once described Johnny Hodges's glissandi as "microtones"; I wonder if he'd make the same claim for Crosby.

liest solo outings (outside dance-band refrains and vocal groups), such as "Till We Meet" (1929, Columbia), reveal a not-surprising apprehension about how he's going to fill all two hundred seconds by himself, his later vocal refrains, like "Oh! Miss Hannah," "Waiting at the End of the Road" (both with Whiteman [both 1929, Columbia]), and "It Must Be True" (with Gus Arnheim's Coconut Grove Orchestra [1930, Victor]) show considerable progress and characteristic confidence.

Simultaneously, Armstrong's 1929 recordings, especially "I Ain't Got Nobody" and "I Can't Give You Anything but Love" (Okeh), show that interpreting lyrics is gradually becoming as important to him as scatting, though at this early stage his vocals still serve as mere interludes between more crucial trumpet solos. Armstrong's 1930 "I'm Confessin' " (Okeh), selected by Gary Giddins as the Armstrong record that most strongly reflects Crosby's reciprocated influence,* represents a milestone of the latest stages of the new art's development. Armstrong gives out with as many Bing-ish trills and extended line-ending notes as he does his own devices, like roars, repeated phrases, and personal interjections, playing off the guitar accompaniment in the same manner that Crosby had done with his guitarist, Eddie Lang. (Armstrong's November 1931 "Star Dust" includes a line of "boo-boo-boo"-ing inspired by Crosby's May 1931 record of "Just One More Chance.")

The early thirties saw the Crosby and Armstrong styles at their most convergent, although their individual personalities were strong enough to pull them away before too long. Nevertheless, they would retain enough of their mutually developed bag of tricks to make their later performances together high points of both careers. More importantly, now that they had put all the pieces together, no man could tear them asunder, and hundreds and hundreds of singers, arrangers, and songwriters

---

* It was also selected by Dizzy Gillespie as the most primal Armstrong vocal for his homage, "Pops Confessin'," which combines this tune with the format from "Laughin' Louis." Well! What do you know about that?

would use the vocabulary developed by Armstrong and Crosby in the late twenties and early thirties. The spread of the new language was hastened by the rising popularity of each man in two of the only cases in Western history where an artist's fame and fortune came to equal his talent. They were so perfectly a part of their time and culture. By the mid-1930s all of the problems had been solved.

Crosby's improvisations on three standard tunes—"Sweet Georgia Brown," "Some of These Days," and "St. Louis Blues" (all Brunswick)—make clear how far his ability to spontaneously create melodies had developed by 1932. The jazz content is extraordinarily high even on the "straight" melody statements (the first choruses), and in time we will value these even more than the scatted portions. He embellishes each melody with the full stock of stop-time breaks and passes, grace notes, passing tones (a device he would not be fully comfortable with for a few more years), syncopes, and irregular and middle-of-bar entrances.

But more than melodic and rhythmic ingeniousness, there's a sense of just plain rightness to everything he does, from the way he states the lyric and tune and makes you feel the meaning of each deep inside, without being maudlin or hammy, to the amazing architectural skill he displays—clearly he has learned Armstrong's lessons well—in the way he organizes an improvisation. The scat on "Sweet Georgia Brown" swings with a vigorous up-and-down motion from the very first syllable. Around the sixteenth bar he produces a catchy five-note lick that sounds so good he repeats it five times, drifting lower and lower each time. When he finally hits bottom, he springs back by climbing up on a more complex figure that he had introduced previously at around bar eight. It turns out to be only a partially scatted chorus, but this is no loss as he climaxes the performance by coming down real hard on the words "Sweet!" and "Georgia!" in strong, staccato fashion, with an attention-grabber of a pause between them. Then, in complete contrast, he concludes with a superfast topper, "They call her sweet Miss Georgia Brown!"

The structure of this ending could not have been conceived before Armstrong, but Crosby has personalized it completely.

All the more remarkably, "Sweet Georgia Brown" does not mark an especially high point in his career; he made dozens of records that are equally satisfying or more so. In contrasting, "St. Louis Blues" was destined to be a masterpiece for its teaming of Crosby with Duke Ellington's Famous Orchestra. There hadn't even been many name band–pop star teamings at all yet, and here was the idea multiplied exponentially: the ultimate jazz–pop singer with the ultimate jazz orchestra. In the twelve-inch 78 rpm, four-and-a-half-minute affair we have time for Cootie Williams, Tricky Sam Nanton, and Johnny Hodges to solo in addition to two vocal refrains by Crosby. In the first refrain, Crosby uses Handy's melody as a point of departure, and he sings both the major and minor strains in a slow, authentically gully-low meter, backed by Ellington's piano and Barney Bigard's clarinet. The second vocal takes place in double time and wordless syllables, but it's the first refrain that we remember. We know he can scat like it's going out of style, especially at double time (it would have aroused greater interest and been reminiscent of Armstrong's "West End Blues" if Crosby had scatted in slow blues time), but who knew he could sing a blues lyric with such authority? "St. Louis Blues" triumphs in the way it manages to be Ellingtonian, Crosby-esque, and genuinely the blues all at the same time.

Crosby recorded "Some of These Days"—just about the greatest of his earlier, jazz-styled performances—in Chicago about a month after "Sweet Georgia Brown," using a small group of Whiteman men directed by Lennie Hayton. In a way, the side predicts the later sides by Billie Holiday with Teddy Wilson's band in that the human voice stands as an equal with the other instruments of jazz without having to imitate them or sacrifice the qualities that make it special. Crosby's solo precedes statements of equal length by Eddie Lang, Mannie Klein, and Frank Trumbauer. He builds the first sixteen bars, which include some of the fastest scatting ever put on vinyl, out of pairs of notes rather than individual ones. Apart from creating a mood of poly-rhythmic superimposition (2/4 over 4/4, or is it the other way around?), this instills a marvelous feeling of momentum as these syncopated units not only swing by themselves but as cells in the phrases he builds out of them.

For the rest of the chorus, Crosby alternates between these two note patterns and conventional single notes. In fact, only once in any of these three pieces does anything reminiscent of the composer's original melody appear—toward the end of the A-take of "Sweet Georgia Brown"—but it is just a fragment, and one that Crosby does not use in the B-take. Remarkably, though Armstrong and Crosby had brought scatting—vocal improvisation—into "modern" (post-Armstrong) jazz only a few years earlier, by the mid-thirties they had exhausted all of its possibilities, and it wasn't until the bop era that anyone really found something new to do with it (though Leo Watson and Ella Fitzgerald gave it a good try).

Armstrong's "Basin Street Blues" (1933, Victor), one of the most thrilling records of the decade, shows the singer taking the scat technique to its limits. It owes little to the melody Handy wrote (or transcribed) and even less to the limits of the blues. Armstrong had recorded the piece five years earlier in a small-group version that serves as a blueprint for this 1933 big-band masterpiece, passing on to it its relaxed tempo, tinkly celesta introduction, scat vocal with background voices, and overall structure. The arranger (probably Budd Johnson) has divided the piece into five sections with stop-time breaks running throughout. The first of these, which follows the celesta vamp (here played by Teddy Wilson instead of Earl Hines), has trombonist Keg Johnson playing the melody and a clarinet break halfway through. Louis takes most of the remaining four sections for himself, and on these alternates between playing and singing.

The two vocals here bespeak Armstrong's mastery of the human instrument for two separate, though related, reasons. Armstrong sings on top of a choir of sidemen who hum the harmony line, an effect he tried in the 1928 version but couldn't quite pull off with only two hummers. The effect he gets of voice-over-voices has metaphoric counterpoints that stretch across the whole history of jazz, from its church roots to the parallel of big-band swing, where a soloist plays in front of a choirlike ensemble of horns (Herschel Evans's chorus in Count Basie's "Blue and Sentimental" [1938, Decca] being the most vocal I can think of). Equally important, Armstrong scats both vocal refrains. Why is scatting so appropriate here? Because Louis Armstrong has tapped into his own core of emotion, gone back and released feelings so deep, so real, and so full of meaning that they can't be verbalized. To try to connect them with lyrics would only change them. We receive these messages the same way Armstrong transmits them; they bypass our ears and our brains and go directly for our hearts and souls.

At the end of the side, Armstrong voices aloud what surely must be going through the heads of everyone listening: "Yeah, man!"

Crosby and Armstrong would go on perfecting their craft until their deaths, but by 1935 most of the dragons had been slain. And it's from this point on that they do their best and most consistently exciting singing—here the mature period in the lives of each man begins.

The single most important event that marks the mid-thirties as the halfway point in the recording careers of both men is that they now came under the control of Jack Kapp. Joe Glaser, Louis's manager, had also begun encouraging him in Kapp-like directions, and Crosby had worked with Kapp since 1931, but it was not until 1935 that Kapp had both men under contract and complete freedom to carry out all his ideas on his own label.

Jack Kapp is possibly the most controversial figure in all of popular music. He is revered in as many histories of the record business as he is vilified in histories of jazz. At the same time, he is the ultimate philistine, forcing artists to record material that critics charged was trashy and beneath them, and the ultimate high-brow snob, going bananas when anyone tried to jazz up the classical repertoire. Kapp was the crook to end all crooks; he was the man who shamelessly cheated the young Count Basie as he twisted his arm to record inane novelty tunes while simultaneously acting the benevolent patriarch who was the first to give Billie Holiday a royalty check. He was also indirectly responsible for Holiday's "Lover Man" and "Good Morning Heartache." You can credit Kapp with such innovations as the girl band singer (all three of the first great canaries—Mildred Bailey, Connee Boswell, and Lee Wiley—ran up against him at one point or another) and also justifiably accuse him of a short-sighted point of view that was directed, in the main, against jazz. As Lee Wiley said, "At Decca they had a sign above the door that said, 'Sing the melody.' " But whatever you think of him, you have to admit that, as far as Bing Crosby and Louis Armstrong are concerned, his ideas were 100 percent dead on target.

Realizing that in Armstrong and Crosby he had the two founding fathers of modern pop music, Kapp devised a way for them to expand both their musical horizons and their popularity, turning them into all things for all people, covering all musical genres. Under Kapp's aegis, the two men continued to record current mainstream popular songs (and Armstrong continued with jazz instrumentals), but between the two they also took on country and western (then called "hillbilly") music, sacred music, Hawaiian harmonies, rhythm numbers, novelties, French *chansons,* folk songs, nostalgic "good-old-good-ones," cover versions of other artists' hits (including each other's), light classics, kiddie ditties, comic pieces, and a limitless number of duets with other singers and vocal groups as well as team-ups with popular name bands. In the midst of this ocean of vinyl, which nearly drowns us in sheer variety, Armstrong and Crosby tackled a fair amount of small-group jazz performances of the kind that had initially made both reputations.

The Kapp principle worked for each man for different reasons. It worked for Crosby because, as it turned out, he really *was* the ultimate musical everyman, and he and Armstrong were able to use this overwhelming plethora of performance modes to convey the full range of human experiences. Slowly, a persona evolved out of the records, and the writers of Crosby's radio shows and movies gradually fashioned an everyman character for him. Whether or not this actually was the case isn't important, for he played it so well for so long that it must have had some ring of truth to it. No one ever found a limit to the kind of songs he could sing. Unlike Frank Sinatra, his only rival to the title of the century's most identifiable voice—though not in intonation—Crosby (or was it Kapp) believed there was no such thing as a bad song, and he could prove it, too. Whether singing "Just a Kid Named Joe," "The Hut Sut Song," or "Aloha Oe," he could leave you touched.

The Kapp principle worked for Armstrong because, as it turned out, he was a genius. The only other improviser in all of music who truly deserves this accolade, Charlie Parker, also proved that geniuses are simply above such "mortal" considerations as repertoire and accompaniment. Armstrong was the only singer who ever lived who didn't care anything about material or backing.

One point mentioned over and over again concerning Armstrong is how he "makes gold out of mere sentimental dross." If Armstrong can make gold out of a second-rate pop tune, then he ought to be able to get something even better from an immortal, beloved standard. But he doesn't. Armstrong makes "Red Cap" sound just as good as "Love Walked In," because the Satchmofication of a piece of music is an equalizing process, and the innate quality of the notes and chords before Armstrong gets to them has absolutely no effect on the quality level of the music he makes.

Which isn't to say that all of his bands were worthy of him— Dexter Gordon once complained that the Armstrong orchestra in which he held the tenor chair (around 1943–44) was pretty square, and even Anita O'Day, listening to Armstrong Deccas in the throes of passion, was moved to gripe about the lousy musicians "Louis inevitably chose to accompany him." And I won't pretend that my stomach doesn't turn as fast as yours when I hear Gordon Jenkins's sickly sweet choir of strings behind Armstrong on the especially banal "Indian Love Call" (1951). But it really doesn't matter, Louis transcends all of it. Nothing, whether bad tunes, hack orchestrations, or even the bowel troubles that occasionally find their way into ad hoc lyrics, can stop him from making wonderful music.

Of course Armstrong does sing about his favorite laxatives ("Red beans and rice and Swiss kriss in the morning!"); on "Baby, It's Cold Outside" (1951, Topline), he jokes about his "bay window"; while singing "That's My Desire" (a 1944 Italian film), he grimaces wildly in reaction to Velma Middleton's cleavage; and on "You're Driving Me Crazy" (1931, Okeh), he pokes fun at speech impediments ("Now you got me talkin' all that chop suey!"). On his earliest flat-out comedy record, the hysterical and nearly existential "Laughin' Louis" (1933, Bluebird), he parodies his own trumpet style, singing, and even physiognomy. In time, Armstrong came also to be attacked for the streak of racism—"Uncle Tomming"—present in his work, a quality that depends more on the listener than on the performer. Dizzy Gillespie once wrote in *Esquire*, "I violently disagree with [Louis Armstrong] because of his Uncle Tom–like subservience—nowadays no cat should be a Tom." But Billie Holiday countered, "Of course Pops toms, but he toms with class."

Some writers attacked Louis for singing songs like "Little Joe" (1931, Okeh), a typical though somewhat extreme mammy song that refers to kinky-headed babies, little pickaninnies, and colored sonny boys, but also contains lines like "Although your color isn't white, you're more than mighty like a rose to me." As Dan Morgenstern says, "If that's not black-is-beautiful, I don't know what is." Whatever the case, Armstrong would leave his sense of humor as a legacy for jazz's other great clowns (to use Morgenstern's term, in the Elizabethan sense) like Fats Waller, Gillespie, and Sun Ra, who said that Armstrong "always had a sense of humor so lacking in many musicians of today. He is part of my destiny."

In the art of Louis Armstrong, humor connects rather directly with religion; the shortcomings of mankind forever underscore the perfection of the divine. He makes the point with both reverence and irreverence: Collection-conscious clerics provide ripe targets for ribbing, but the Almighty Himself is not to be jived with. On the first recording of "The Saints" ("Oh, When the Saints Go Marching In" [1938, Decca]), the spiritual that Satchmo took out of the Sunday services and into the Dixieland canon, and on "Bye and Bye" (1941, Decca), Armstrong introduces trombonist J. C. Higginbotham and other soloists between strains and plays and sings jubilantly with the band, which doubles as choir (according to Rex Stewart, when Armstrong sang this type of number in person his audiences filled this function). A professional chorus backs Louis on his first "legitimate" sacred recordings (four from 1938, Decca), including the sublime "Shout All Over God's Heaven" and "Nobody Knows the Trouble I've Seen," and he doesn't even need to take his trumpet out of the case. None of these would have been made without Jack Kapp.

Taken another way, the religious sides illustrate the evolution of Armstrong (like Crosby) from a revolutionary to an establishment figure. On his first church-styled record, "The Lonesome Road" (1931, Okeh), he ruthlessly lampoons down-home deacons with lines like "Thank you for your contributions, Sisters and Brothers. It could've been bigger, two dollars more would have got my shoes out of pawn!" But by 1958, when Armstrong had made his ultimate religious statement in the classic *Louis and the Good Book* (Decca), he no longer satirizes preachers. Instead, he has become one of them: the Reverend Satchelmouth. He plays both roles, the saint and the sinner, to the hilt.

Louis and the Good Book may just be, along with the moving *Musical Autobiography* (1957, Decca), the homage *Satch Plays Fats* (1955, Columbia), and the rhapsodic *Louis Under the Stars* (in which arranger Russ Garcia proves that Satchmo-with-strings and standards doesn't have to be vomitous [1957, Verve]), the most satisfying of all of Armstrong's long-playing record projects. There is more of a modern gospel feel to it as opposed to the old-time spiritual flavor of his 1938 sacred sides, supplied mainly by the presence of Louis's All-Stars, an electric organ, and a ten-voice choir masterminded by Sy Oliver in what may be the greatest of the arranger's post–Tommy Dorsey efforts.

Louis's relationship with God superseded Sunday visits, and as extreme as it may sound, I like to think that He gave us Louis Armstrong as the ultimate proof of Divine existence. As Lewis Carroll wrote in one of his letters, "Do you think that He cares to see only kneeling figures and only to hear tones of prayer— and He does not also love to see the lambs leaping in the sunlight, and to hear the merry voices of children . . . ? Surely, their innocent laughter is as sweet in His ears as the grandest anthem that ever rolled up from the dim religious light of some solemn cathedral."

If Louis Armstrong's sacred music (and his modulation from the sacrilegious to the sacral) can serve as a microcosm for his entire career, then Crosby's mature work can be summed up by the many jazz records he made after 1935. Crosby had taken scatting as far as he could in the early thirties, and, as "St. Louis Blues" revealed, he crammed so much jazz feeling into his "straight" vocals that the scat itself was becoming obsolete. This suited Jack "Sing the Melody" Kapp fine, but didn't mean that Crosby didn't take advantage of every opportunity to work in a jazz setting.

From 1936 to 1939 especially, Crosby waxed dozens of incredibly bouncy, rhythmic sides, first with Jimmy Dorsey's band when Dorsey served as Crosby's "house" accompanist, and then with Dorsey's replacement, John Scott Trotter, the ex–Hal Kemp arranger who became Crosby's musical director in 1937. When Trotter began to slow the tempi, around 1939–40, he created the milieu for Crosby's most successful ballad performances, among them "Somebody Loves Me," "Maybe" (both 1939), and "Day Dreaming" (all of which use Victor Young's Orchestra [1941, Decca]). As jazz figured less and less in the bulk of Crosby's records, he compensated for the loss by launching a series of exclusively hot sessions with small groups.

One typical date, June 10, 1940, used many of the musicians who played in the Trotter orchestra for Decca and on Crosby's Kraft Music Hall radio show, including trumpeter Andy Secrest, originally Beiderbecke's stand-in, who, by this time, had adapted the Bix idiom both to swing-era requirements and his own temperament, and Abe Lincoln, the fine trombonist associated with the California Ramblers bands. Four horns and four rhythms all told, they back Crosby on four tunes: Two are up-beat numbers from his current film, *Rhythm on the River*, the title cut and "That's for Me." Next Crosby does a remake of one of his early, pre-Decca hits, "I Found a Million Dollar Baby," which outdoes the original. Finally, he puts out with the definitive version of "Can't Get Indiana Off My Mind," an excellent though obscure song by his old drinking buddy, Hoagy Carmichael. All are terrific.

In addition to the sessions with Trotter's small groups, Kapp and Decca A&R (artist and repertoire) man Milt Gabler assembled many sessions with better-known attractions from the hot circuit. Crosby made six sides with black pianist Eddie Heywood and his small band (Vic Dickenson was there on the trombone); Eddie Condon, Wild Bill Davison, Bud Freeman, and their great 1946 "orchestra" played behind three Crosby vocals; he made two surprisingly compatible duets with Louis Jordan and His Tympany Five in 1944; 1952 saw a virtually overlooked reunion session with one of the major trumpeters of the Beiderbecke epoch, Red Nichols; there were also many dates with Woody Herman and Bob Crosby, both their orchestras and their small bands (the Woodchoppers and the Bobcats, respectively). This isn't crooning, groaning, boo-boo-booing, or any of the other unfortunate adjectives that attached themselves to Crosby's work. The only term that fits is jazz singing.

Not to be Pollyanna about it, Crosby didn't bring complete enthusiasm and perfect pipes to every recording date, especially on the hundreds of bread-and-butter affairs with strings, choirs, and run-of-the-mill fodder. His voice sounds as thin as his hair around the mid-forties (though considerably better on airchecks than on the Deccas), and during the late forties and early fifties much of his material is so far beneath him he can't sing for all the stooping. The 1946 pairing with Lionel Hampton's great orchestra disappointed on both sides as, on one side, Crosby attempts to re-create Pine Top Smith's spoken monologue on the classic 1928 piano solo "Pine Top's Boogie Woogie" and, on the other side, a well-arranged "Sunny Side of the Street" has Crosby cracking in the most gruesome fashion on the first high note. It was irresponsible of Decca to ever issue the record and of Crosby not to insist on a remake. Crosby's long-awaited collaboration with Count Basie (*Bing and Basie* [1972, Daybreak]) can also be written off as a loss because of poorly chosen contemporary songs and low spirits.

You might think that Crosby would have been finished by the late fifties because of the new kiddie pop, which, apart from its musical deficiencies, undermined both the values of familial togetherness and American individuality that Crosby stood for. On the contrary, the latter half of the Eisenhower decade brought forth Crosby's most consistently wonderful work. In some ways the loss of the youth market freed Crosby of any responsibility for hit-or-miss current tunes, and after reaching the big five oh, Crosby turned increasingly to the more idiosyncratic music that had been his first love: jazz. He sang well on a Verve album, *Bing Sings While Bregman Swings* (1956), made apparently as an answer to the hyperhard swinging sessions of Sinatra with Nelson Riddle or Billy May, although thirty years later Crosby sounds considerably hipper than the overrated Bregman. With pianist (and sometimes organist) Buddy Cole and his spiffy trio, Crosby transcribed hundreds of combo cuts for his radio show, some of which came out commercially on the albums *Some Fine Old Chestnuts* (1955, Decca) and *New Tricks* (an aging basset hound adorns the cover [1957, Decca]). Other CBS-recorded trio tracks were subjected to overdubbed orchestras and strings after Crosby's death in 1977, which, though lamentable, ultimately seems a better fate than what befell the remaining cuts, which have been left to languish unheard in the vaults.*

In 1957, Crosby made his grooviest record ever, *Bing with a Beat* (Victor), a perfectly realized collaboration with Bob Scobey and his Frisco Jazz Band. Although the Frisco men had originally modeled themselves after New Orleans "primitives" like Bunk Johnson and George Lewis, on this particular disc Matty Matlock, the arranger and clarinetist best known for his work with Bob Crosby, reconceives Scobey's band sound as an extension of the Bobcats. As we've seen, Bing Crosby was probably the first pop singer to work in Armstrongian 4/4 time; however, both he and his bandleading kid brother, Bob, had an atavistic fondness for earlier two-beat jazz à la King Oliver and Jelly Roll Morton, the younger Crosby's band being built around New Orleans–born players. Many of Crosby's late thirties and early forties small-group sides fall on that cusp between swing and Dixieland, and the *Beat* album exploits this to maximum effect, not only in the rhythm but in the texture of arrangements and instrumental solos. The effect can be compared to Benny Carter soloing on one of his own arrangements—background and foreground alike reflect the same musical logic. Matlock and Crosby open up each of these ancient songs. First, they restore the verses and score them in such a way as to insist that verses don't have to be tempoless and draggy, then they rewrite the codas ("Along the Way to Waikiki," for instance) and throw in all sorts of especially congenial bits of musical business for both the singer and the band. "Mack the Knife" contains a newly composed countermelody that suggests Armstrong's "Coal Cart Blues," while "Exactly like You" gains a little more musical meat be-

---

* The overdubbing is tasteful and, having been done by Ken Barnes and Pete Moore, the producer-arranger team responsible for Crosby's last "living" records, probably would have been approved by Crosby, but it's still not as good as the original untampered tracks. It's like trying to justify computer-colorizing Crosby's old movies by hiring an ex–Paramount art director to participate—the best possible way to do something awful. It also strikes me as the traditional British phobia of electric organs carried to bizarre extremes.

cause of a new strain, first introduced as a backdrop to the
chorus but then picked up by the singer for a scat sequence.

The arrangements and mise-en-scène depend on the singer
even more than the singer depends on the arrangements. Com-
municating the obvious joy the music arises in him, Crosby fairly
oozes with charming insouciance above and beyond even the call
of Crosby, expressed in semispoken asides and lyric alterations.*
It all contributes to the remarkable duplicity that Crosby and
Armstrong were the first to bring to popular music: You can
follow the narrative of the story they're telling, but you still don't
have to suspend your disbelief that these people aren't pop
stars—the same sort of having your cake and eating it that made
Hollywood movies great.

But after *Louis and the Good Book* and *Bing with a Beat*,
their most rewarding performances were made together. The
friendship of Armstrong and Crosby probably goes back to the
late twenties, when the Whiteman orchestra played through
Chicago and *all* visiting musicians made a point of going to hear
Armstrong. There were undoubtedly reunions later in New
York, and in Los Angeles in 1930. "When you were at the Coconut Grove, and I was at the Cotton Club in Culver City,"
Louis later quipped on one of Bing's radio shows, "you showed
up more nights at the Cotton Club than you did at the Grove."

When Armstrong became a hero to blacks across the nation
and "There wasn't a jukebox in Harlem that Louis wasn't scatting on," as Mezz Mezzrow reports, the only other artist whose
records were permitted on Harlem jukes was Crosby (we'll see
the effect he had on black singers later on). In 1936, Crosby
worked Louis into his movie *Pennies from Heaven*, which
launched Armstrong's career as a motion picture performer, and
Armstrong probably guested on Crosby's radio shows at this
point at well. Paramount Pictures filmed an Armstrong sequence
for Crosby's flick *Doctor Rhythm* (1938), but their editing of it

* On "Last Night on the Back Porch" he switches both "But last night Maw went
shoppin' . . ." and "Last night gave her my frat pin . . ." for the title phrase.

from the release print became no real loss as the song they gave Armstrong, "The Trumpet Player's Lament," was no great masterpiece. Armstrong went into the Decca studios in 1939 to cut a special private recording of "Happy Birthday" for Crosby's thirty-fifth, and it shows that even then he called him "Papa Bing."

It is important to note that in none of these early ventures did Mr. C. and Mr. A. sing together—undoubtedly fear of the dread color line kept them apart. But between 1949 and 1951, when Armstrong had broken the line with top-ten hits like "Blueberry Hill," he made no less than eight appearances on Crosby's program, sang with him in Frank Capra's comedy *Here Comes the Groom*, and made one hit record with him, "Gone Fishin'."

A lot of time is wasted on these shows; they were, after all, not made for connoisseurs who remembered "West End Blues," and they constantly remind us of the sacrifices jazz had to make to remain a popular music. But they also feature some of the most heart-warming, crowd-pleasing entertainment either man was ever to produce. Their duets, "Lazy Bones," "Blueberry Hill," "Gone Fishin'," "You're Just in Love," and "Kiss to Build a Dream On," do not fit within the prescribed notions of what "music" and "comedy" ought to be, but are examples of *pure*, undiluted entertainment that simply and utterly move us.

"Kiss to Build a Dream On" had originally been written for the 1935 Marx Brothers movie *A Night at the Opera*, but lingered unsung till Armstrong introduced it in *The Strip* (1951). The radio version starts out as a solo for Crosby, who unexpectedly entreats Armstrong to join him, and then the two spend the first chorus trying to figure out just who will sing what. On the second round, Papa and Pops pick up on each other's mannerisms with humor and love. When Satch substitutes "chops" for "lips" (he did this regularly on "That's My Desire") in the last eight, the crowd gets ecstatic. When Bing repeats the device in chorus two, they nearly fall out of their seats en masse. How could they not? "If you don't like Louis," said Mahalia Jackson, "you're not human!"

Though the 1949–51 period saw the most heavily concentrated amount of tandem activity between the two, they would combine frequently right up to the end. Cole Porter's "modohip" tune "Now You Has Jazz," though no one could have predicted Porter would turn out to be such an expert on the subject, gave Armstrong and Crosby an excellent excuse for a duet, which they did in the 1956 picture *High Society* and even better in numerous TV appearances from the same period. But their one full-length album collaboration, the 1960 *Bing and Satchmo* (MGM), has only a few good moments, due to overdubbing and overarranging (why does Billy May have to throw in background voices, even if he did have the panache to transcribe Armstrong's lovely 1931 trumpet solo on "Lazy River" for the choir?).

Their work, together and apart, did not triumph so much because of their similarities as because of their differences. Each took up where the other left off, and this allowed them to create virtually the entire vocabulary of twentieth-century vocal music. Armstrong, who had grown up virtually parentless, had only the family he created for himself out of the millions of people who loved him and his music. Crosby grew up seeking individuality and inner strength in a family where the family was all-important, and eventually became the musical patriarch of the entire world. Armstrong's great strength was his freedom and ability to express emotion, and the key to the success of Crosby's singing is the way in which he controlled emotion. It was said that Crosby never invited Armstrong (and hardly anyone else) to his house, but the same way that Louis sang the glories of God in a way that counted for more than his going to church each week, their relationship and their empathy transcended that consideration. In Crosby's personal life, he lived the words of the poet Percy MacKaye: "Because he never wore his sentient heart / For the crows and jays to pick, oftimes to such / He seemed a silent fellow."

"Like everyone else, Louis loved my father," Gary Crosby told Ross Firestone. "Between shows he'd tell me endless stories about him. 'Your old man is the greatest singer,' he'd say.

'Really, he can wail.' Then he'd go on to reminisce about all the funny things that happened when they crossed paths in the old days, and how much he enjoyed working Dad's radio show and being in his movies. 'Well, Dad loves you, too, Louis.' And that was so, Louis was always one of his favorites."

Though we didn't know the birth dates of either Bing Crosby or Louis Armstrong, we were painfully aware of their deaths. When each died the news was carried by every form of media on the planet. Two days after the death of Louis Armstrong, on July 6, 1971, Bing Crosby served as pallbearer at his funeral. Six years later, on October 14, 1977, Crosby joined him.

> *"Bing's voice has a mellow quality that only Bing's got. It's like gold being poured out of a cup."*
> —*Louis Armstrong,* Time

> *"No question about it, the happiest times in my recording career were the days I worked with Louis Armstrong . . . just being in the same room with this fella when he's comin' on is a complete joy and inspiration."*
> —*Bing Crosby,* A Musical Autobiography

> *"I'm proud to acknowledge my debt to the Reverend Satchelmouth. He is the beginning and the end of music in America."*
> —*Bing Crosby,* Downbeat

The First Generation

The Late Twenties and Early Thirties

● ─────────────────────────────────

"Annette Hanshaw . . . was once the sole proprietor of a music shop in the hills of Westchester. That the enterprise failed is no fault of hers. When a customer asked to hear a certain piece of music, Annette, who cannot read notes. would sing and play it by ear, imbuing her rendition with unusual notes and clever interpolations of her own. After taking the music home, the purchaser would return the next day with the complaint that it didn't sound the same as when she sang and played the tune."
—Unidentified clipping (probably a press release, verbatim),
circa 1930

≡ **Y**our mental soundtrack of the twenties doubtlessly contains more roaring than singing, but it's not difficult to imagine those speakeasy-cabarets employing singers from two of jazz's fringes, musical comedy and the blues. The mainstream of pop singing that flows from these years emanates from a stream with as much connection to instrumental traditions as it has to vocal ones. Crosby and Armstrong lit the spark, but it had to travel down a long fuse. By 1935, Armstrong and Crosby had transformed all popular singing. By 1945, Armstrong and Crosby–derived pop singing had become the dominant mode of all pop music. The years from 1925 to 1935 mark a crucial decade of dissemination, a gradual transformation of singers and their public.

The evolution of vocal music pivoted upon the development of the other central medium of interwar pop, the jazz-influenced dance band, and the two forms grew up as nonidentical twins in the jazz family. The great movers and shakers of jazz orchestral style were mostly black (Fletcher Henderson, Duke Ellington, Don Redman) with a few exceptions (Bill Challis, Ferde Grofé, Gene Gifford); however, that part of the big-band idiom that involved singing, the vocal refrain format, came out of white conventions.[*]

Before the swing era made stars of bandleaders, singers, and occasionally instrumentalists, the dance-band business relied a great deal on genericness and anonymity; a few stars existed, but enormous numbers of dance records were produced by contractors (the most prolific being Ben Selvin, Sam Lanin, Fred Rich, Nat Shilkret, and Ed Kirkeby) and arrangers (Victor Young) who assembled bands only for studio sessions, usually putting a pseudonym (clever or otherwise) on the disc label. Furthermore, well-known leaders recorded under similar noms de plume as often as they did under their own names, and all used the same small stable of four or five vocalists whom they now began to consider important (as opposed to the strictly instrumental dance-band record of a few years earlier), according to "Smoke Willoughby" in *Young Man with a Horn*, because the principal audience for records is little girls who want to learn the words.

Apart from Whiteman, Fred Waring, and Ellington, bands had no interest in developing an identity through their vocal departments, and thus had no complaints that the same four singers were turning up on everybody's records. Singers were such an afterthought that no one ever bothered with the minor wording changes needed on many a period love song originally

---

[*] Sure, Tommy Dorsey's "Marie" concept, which paid a lot of bills for him, had been inspired by a black band, but it still seems more white than black. Anyhow, as if to repay the loan, Cab Calloway uses Dorsey's "Sentimentalist" formula (à la TD's "I'll Never Smile Again") on his own "I'll Be Around" (1942, Okeh).

intended for one specific gender. Since their voices were so high and effeminate to begin with, it sounds doubly hilarious to hear, for instance, English bandleader Jack Hylton's record of "Ten Cents a Dance" on which tenor Patrick O'Malley sings about the pansies and rough guys, tough guys who tear his gown.

But the coming of Crosby bettered the business of vocalizing, both stylistically and socially. Electric recording put a gradual end to the careers of the very earliest generation of band singers, the Billy Murrays and the Irving Kaufmans. The singers who followed still sound dated in the light of Crosby and Armstrong, but they fit their period perfectly and represented a major improvement on their predecessors: Smith Ballew, Scrappy Lambert, Chick Bullock, and Dick Robertson. All four had experience with vaudeville, and within a short time each had forsaken performing in front of flesh-and-blood audiences to all-but-live in the recording studios. They worked as many as three or four sessions a week at the height of the twenties recording boom, with every band that passed through, hot or sweet, black and white, famous and obscure, touring or studio-only.

Lambert had the purest and most serious twenties-style tenor, and could evoke perfectly a slave on the plantation singing "Away Down South in Heaven" (with Nat Shilkret's Victor in-house dance orchestra) in a sort of indirectly black-style falsetto, yet could completely miss the point of the sillier novelties assigned to him, inspiring unintentional humor on a record like Frank Trumbauer's "Borneo" (1928, Okeh) ("When you see them do that Borneo / You'll just put your shoes in pawn-eo . . ."). Smith Ballew offers a strong western twang, which ultimately led to a brief career as a B-western star, tempered with some of Rudy Vallee's nasality. He fares best as the center of attention on a group of sides produced by Ed Kirkeby under the pseudonym of "Ted Wallace and His Campus Boys" and "His Singing Boys" (for Columbia in 1929) where his vocals have an unmistakable ring of sincerity and even charm, two elements not to be taken for granted among twenties vocalists. Dick Robertson was the most vaudevillian of this group, and often alternated between different voices (one a baby-boy equivalent of Helen Kane, the infamous boop-oop-a-doop girl) to suit the material. Best of all was Chick Bullock, who had a far gutsier baritone and a genuine sense of the blues, heard to full power with Bunny Berigan on "Underneath the Harlem Moon" (1932, Conqueror). Both Robertson and Bullock lasted into the forties, by that time mainly doing sessions under their own names with small jukebox-oriented bands not all that different from Billie Holiday's nominal records.

If these four constitute the mainstream, much of the rest of the vocal music of the era falls under the category of personal taste. Many collectors enjoy the country-influenced singing of Lee Morse, but no matter how hard I try to like her, she always comes off as an irritating yodeler who makes no sense, musical or otherwise. But take Red McKenzie: This record-biz raconteur, who made his reputation with the briefly popular Mound City Blue Blowers (leading the group and "blue-blowing" on a comb covered with wax paper), was by no stretch of the imagination a heavyweight vocalist, and doubtless puts many modern listeners to sleep, but has always struck me as a wonderfully amiable putz. Rudy Vallee, who was actually considered a rival to Crosby,* is hopelessly fey on his twenties recordings, but he saves some of them with his sense of humor (he made a far better character actor than leading man) and his peppy backup band, the Connecticut Yankees. Yet he stayed active far longer than the others and developed into a worthwhile singer for a short time in the late thirties, at which point some of his records (the best being "Good Night My Love" [1937, English Columbia]) actually betray a slight tinge of masculinity. One could never make such a statement about either Gene Austin or Segar Ellis, who make Vallee at his wimpiest look like Billy Eckstine by comparison.

---

* For a short while there existed a triumverate of superstar crooners, Crosby, Columbo, and Vallee. We'll get to Columbo in a later chapter.

Cab Calloway lasted far longer than any of them, and while no one can deny that he made a great bandleader (in terms of both picking the players and giving the downbeats) and was certainly something to see—with his bizarre ballet choreographed out of the visual actions of vocalizing and baton-waving—whether or not one enjoys his singing makes more of a statement about the listener than the performer. He's treaded the line between good taste and bad for nearly sixty years now, and not carefully like a tightrope walker either, but swaying wildly from one side to the other like an inebriate failing a drunk test. He leans to one side, and he comes up with in-the-groove rhythm numbers (somehow the period term "novelties" doesn't do justice to the best of them), like "Hi-De-Ho Romeo" (1937, Variety), "A Chicken Ain't Nothin' but a Bird" (1945, Columbia), and "Minnie the Moocher" (first recorded for Brunswick in 1931), the signature hit that not only put Calloway on the map but made "Hi-De-Ho" a household word.

Yet Calloway often sways over to the other side and dishes out examples of outrageous bad taste: an exhibitionistic sideshow of pure tonsils and the ability to hit superhigh highs, low lows, and long longs (both he, singing, and Carmen Lombardo, playing trumpet, choose to hold notes forever on "St. Louis Blues," indicating a mutual fondness for unmusical gimmicks). Calloway is often just too much. He'll push his killer vibrato just a hair more than it ought to be pushed, and he'll talk over too many good solos for us to remain patient (which he counterbalances by rewarding his faithful with wonderful instrumentals on the level of "Moon Glow" [1934, Victor, and then subtitled "I'm Living in the Past"] and "Ghost of a Chance" [1940, Okeh]).

Still, Calloway sometimes indulges in tackiness on such a grand level he almost passes through the other side; as a Hollywood beatnik turned on to Nietzsche would say, "Man, that cat's so out, he's in!" Some of his endless cycles of post–"Minnie the Moocher" call-and-response numbers levitate to existential levels of consciousness. On the 1933 remake of "Minnie the Moocher" (Victor), and the 1947 "Hi-De-Ho Man" (Columbia),

Calloway, in the middle of calling out phrases for the band to sing back at him in unison, indulges in a "Cantor on the Sabbath" type chant; consider his unkosher davening repayment for all the Jewish entertainers who found acceptance in blackface.

At the start of his career, Calloway's only claim to fame lay in being the younger brother of Blanche Calloway, a very with-it though undistinguished singer-entertainer who had tagged along with all phases of black showbiz in the twenties and thirties—the classic blues craze, the early all-black revues, and her own big band. Cabell Calloway, born in Rochester on Christmas 1907, originally got work only through his more famous sister, but his popularity quickly eclipsed hers. Fronting territorial bands in search of national exposure, the Missourians, the Alabamans, and the Missourians again—soon to be Cab Calloway and His Orchestra—he gave these units identity and personality, and they provided him with the perfect vehicle for his talents. Like Ellington, Calloway used the Cotton Club as home base for a series of increasingly successful tours, under the management of Irving Mills. Calloway's detractors argue that no one would listen to his records if he didn't have that wonderful orchestra, which is akin to claiming no one would watch Busby Berkeley movies if they didn't have the musical numbers. The fact is, Calloway had the orchestra, and vice versa, and who's to say who made what great?

At his most musical, Calloway likes to stretch words and phrases to their limits, though his scat choruses (excepting the early and Armstrongian "Devil and the Deep Blue Sea") are less notable for their improvisational content than the singer's own irreverent personality. In fact, straight-out "pure" ad lib solos don't measure up to "The Scat Song" (1933, Victor) or "Mama, I Wanna Make Rhythm" (1937, Variety), in which the nonsense episode gets written into the narrative of the lyric and therefore rationalized.

As the only simultaneously great bandleader and great singer (Billy Eckstine would like to have been the second to succeed at both), Calloway, in most of his records, blurs the distinction

between vocal refrain and vocal accompaniment formats. Billie
Holiday minimalized these boundaries on many of her small-
group records of the late thirties, in which her voice gets no
more attention within the context of the arrangement than each
horn soloist. Most vocal refrains, especially by the likes of Martha Tilton or Edythe Wright, seem an intrusion on an otherwise
swinging disc, but Holiday takes her chorus on equal terms with
the hornmen, and her hornlike voice so in-abruptly precedes the
voicelike horns of her colleagues (the best of all being Lester
Young) that it never hits you over the head with its vocal-refrain-
ness.

But where Holiday and Calloway jumble the accepted formats, Ellington had already succeeded in jettisoning them
altogether—or at least sidestepping them. Ellington conceived a
whole new way to use the human voice in jazz: not for putting
over lyrics of popular songs, despite much artistic satisfaction in
the long run, in what was basically a commercial concession, but
the human voice as part of the orchestra proper. A tenet of both
instrumental vaudeville acts and jazz had been the playing of
instruments so that they sounded like voices; Ellington, who had
already perfected this procedure in collaboration with Bubber
Miley, the growling "singing" trumpet star of that first great
band (a period of Ellingtonia tagged "The Jungle Band"), simply
reversed it. It worked because Ellington maintained the primacy of the human instrument. He may abandon lyrics and the
conventional band-vocal-band arrangement, but he keeps the
singer at the center of attention and gives her the main melody
of the piece to carry. The rest of the band, therefore, doesn't
accompany her in the traditional sense, but travels alongside
her. Furthermore, "Creole Love Call" (1927, Victor), the first of
the two vocals on this record, dwells in the realm of the ethereal
and airy like the operatic exercise of vocalism, but when singer
Adelaide Hall returns for the second, she modulates from the
high brow to the low brow with bluesy growling directly inspired by Bubber Miley—a voice imitating a trumpet imitating
a voice.

"Creole Love Call" plays on Rudolf Friml's "Indian Love Call" (from a hit operetta of only three years earlier, *Rose Marie*) not only in title but in concept, as in each an exotic race implies an exotic use of the voice as an expression of musical passion. Appropriately, to solidify the idea of voice as instrument, Ellington found the melody for the vocal part on a 1923 King Oliver (a heavy influence on Miley and Ellington in the area of voice-instrument relations) record, "Camp Meeting Blues" (Columbia), played by clarinetist Jimmie Noone.*

At the time, no one picked up on the "Love Call" format as an alternative to the vocal refrain—least of all Ellington himself. On the same date, he recorded "Blues I Love to Hear" with Hall scatting over the orchestra in a more conventional blues pattern, and not long after that made "The Mooche," which, though a mysterious female apparently named "Baby Cox" vocalizes, seems more like an example of Ellington fooling around with ideas from the Louis Armstrong Hot Five sides: taking two instruments new to his palette, the voice (Cox) and the guitar (Lonnie Johnson, the guest star who filled the same role on the Armstrong sessions), and bouncing them against each other. Ellington dabbled again in wordless singing twenty years later, when the classically trained diva Kay Davis canaried on such compositions as "Transbluency," "Minnehaha," "On a Turquoise Cloud," and new performances of the original "Creole Love Call," and did even better another twenty years later with the simultaneously soulful and ethereal Swedish pop singer Alice Babs.

The "Love Call," however, returned significantly in the sixties in two striking reinterpretations. Ellington himself rescored it strictly as an instrumental, with Cootie Williams replacing Bubber Miley. Roland Kirk, the multi-instrumental visionary who explored the avant-garde future simultaneously with the traditionalist past, reconceived the "Love Call" in accordance

---

* Some discographies say the clarinet soloist is Buster Bailey.

with an old idea reiterated for the sixties by Ornette Coleman: that horns should speak with a human voice. Of the forty years of "Love Call"s, Kirk's is the most erotic. First stating the melody on two instruments simultaneously, Kirk improvises on clarinet and then tenor sax, his exceedingly warm, Ducal vibrato (à la Ellington's Johnny Hodges and Ben Webster) gradually climaxing in free jazz orgasms.

The original "Mooche" (with Johnson and Cox) and "Creole Love Call" point to two separate schools of thought concerning scat singing: "The Mooche" refers to Armstrong and the line of scat improvisers that continued, in the classic era, with Bing Crosby (occasionally), Leo Watson, and Ella Fitzgerald. "Love Call" inaugurates a parallel stratum of auteurs who used scat singing as an extension of composing. Like so many of Ellington's ideas, it remained only a tangent to the mainstream of jazz-pop arranging and composing, which used the vocal refrain and vocal-with-accompaniment as its basic formats for singers. But perhaps because of the reverence accorded Ellington in every era of jazz history, his idea of compositional scatting refused to die, and has seen revivals at the hands of Stan Kenton ("June Christy" [1950, Capitol]) and Sarah Vaughan, singing Alfred Newman's movie theme "Pinky" (more a composition than an improvisation [circa 1950, Columbia]), as well as various vocal groups and multivoice experiments, from the Boswell Sisters to Charlie Ventura's Bop for the People Band to Charles Mingus's "Weird Nightmare" (1960, Mercury) and Sonny Rollins's "Don't Stop the Carnival" (1962, Victor)—all of which are subjects for other chapters. Importantly, the two schools of scat, improvisational and compositional, finally came together in the work of Mel Torme, a confessed Ellington "idolator," and have since been jointly explored by Betty Carter, Jeanne Lee, and others—but that, too, we'll cover later on.

All this underscores a mysterious failing of the twenties: plenty of seeds planted for later generations, but what is there of its own that we can enjoy in the context of the period? Crosby and Armstrong wouldn't hit their stride until later on. And though Jimmy Rushing's earliest records (with Walter Page's Blue Devils and Bennie Moten's Orchestra) struck people as excellent in 1929 and 1930, when he began recording in earnest with Count Basie in 1937 he immediately devalued his earlier work.

The twenties have precious little they can call their own. Anyone who can appreciate, say, Frank Sinatra can also, at least, understand Louis Armstrong or Lee Wiley or Bobby Darin or Helen Forrest, or any vocalist of any post-twenties era, simply because they all share common values of music and lyric interpretation even if the actual meat of the given stylistic differs. Even singers of the Jolson era make sense, and we can forgive them their transgressions of post-Crosby ideals simply because they are pre-Crosby. The singers of the early electric years aren't so easily fathomed; it's never clear just exactly where they're coming from. Only Annette Hanshaw used the musical idiom of the twenties in a creative, modern way, just as Anita O'Day used the musical idiom of the forties and Abbey Lincoln did of the fifties. Because there's really no one else in twenties music to compare her to, Hanshaw is best described as the Louise Brooks of jazz. Imagine watching a faded print of some ancient silent movie where the decor, the costumes, the co-stars, and the story are all hopelessly dated, yet Brooks's face speaks out to you so strongly she obliterates the inherent stylization of silence as well as the six decades between her generation and yours.

Annette Hanshaw has that same kind of appeal; no matter what the setting or the song, she comes off as immediately modern. Hanshaw intuitively mastered those jazz rhythmic nuances that could apply to pop songs and expressed them with the subtlety required for the microphone. Far from interfering with her ability to communicate the meaning of a set of lyrics, the jazz feel provides the key to interpretation, helping her to get under the skin of both the words and music of her material. Hanshaw arrived at these conclusions without the stars of Armstrong and Crosby to steer by, her style having been virtually perfected as of her earliest recordings in 1926, considerably before she could have heard either man.

It's all important, then, that Hanshaw was born wealthy and became a recording star relatively easily: No two-bit manager ever cracked the whip and tried to Svengali her into sounding like everybody else, no financial necessity ever forced her to give up the daring, innovative qualities that might have prevented her from getting work in many situations. At the same time, she had little or no ambition. She became a star through her records, yet despised the trappings of celebrity-hood as well as the pressures of being responsible for the careers of a battery of agents, musicians, arrangers, and others. Furthermore, audiences *terrified* her. So, ultimately, the same mind that was capable of making such original musical decisions also arrived at the dead-ended conclusions that the only way out was to chuck the whole bit. Other artists ran up against this problem or something like it; their greed, their egos, or their love for their art forced them to overcome it. Hanshaw simply chose to avoid the heat by getting out of the kitchen. She retired permanently at age twenty-eight and lived happily ever after until her death in March 1985.

In her eight years of recording, Hanshaw produced the period's most consistently excellent series of female vocal records outside the blues idiom. If anything, her rare misfires make clear how remarkable her triumphs are: When she ends "Forgetting You" with a corny near-yodel, it reminds one that such cornball, unmusical gimmicks were the basic vocabulary of most singers of her generation (Lee Morse). When her record company pressured her to record some impersonations of the godawful Helen "boop-oop-a-doop" Kane, it makes us all appreciate all the more a singer for whom the rule is tasteful, thoroughly felt and thought swing—and the exception is faddish drivel.

Hanshaw uses a "black" of medium-slow, very sincere ballads, and a "white" of swingy up-tempo rhythm tunes, but also any number of subtle gray tones in between. She saturates

"Ready for the River"* and " 'Cause I Feel Low Down" (both 1928, Pathe) with the morbid passion of the blues, sharing elements of their specific vocabulary—namely, the use of the fast tempo to convey a desperate though aggressive attitude and, even more so, the clear-eyed directness of their expression. As the title suggests, "Little White Lies" (1930, Harmony) is considerably more Caucasian, yet Hanshaw proves this sound needn't be any less effective in putting across a similar feeling. Instead of tearing into the transgressor (or as Clarence Williams would say, a "mistreater"), Hanshaw here sounds as if it takes all the gumption she can summon up merely to bare her wounded soul. One by one she meets each possible kind of world outlook and masters them all, both on their terms and hers, even the imitation Irish "Sweetheart Darlin' " (without Hanshaw, 'twould surely be a crock o'baloney now) and the mock-Chinese "Sing a Little Low-Down Tune." Who else could instruct someone to wink their blinky almond eyes and not make it sound ludicrous? Or find a note of melancholy in Harold Arlen's "Let's Fall in Love"?

Her career can be summed up in terms of gradually getting into showbiz, making her way close to the top, and then gradually getting out of it. Born in 1910, Hanshaw became enamored of singing and of the phonographic medium early on. "At that time, everyone sang very straight," she told David Tarnow a few years before her death, "and anyone who had the slightest bit of difference in their singing always fascinated me." Among these she listed Frank Fay (the comic actor who later married Barbara Stanwyck and immortalized Elwood P. Dowd in Mary Chase's play *Harvey*), Sophie Tucker, and, not surprisingly, Marion Harris. Her father, in the hotel business, indulged her, buying her a music shop and then arranging for her to sing at his hotels and parties. At one of these, an A&R man (though the term had not

---

* Brian Rust's discography in *Jazz Records*, probably going on Hanshaw's recollections thirty years later, claims that the alto sax soloist between Hanshaw's two choruses is Jimmy Lytell. To me he sounds like Frank Trumbauer.

yet been coined) named Wally Rose heard her and arranged an audition for Pathe Records. She quickly became one of the label's biggest attractions, and as some of her ukelele-and-scat work on these early sides suggests, a sort of female counterpart to Pathe's own Cliff Edwards. When the firm was absorbed into the Columbia family of labels, she began appearing on some of their dime-store discs because, she remembered, of an offer Columbia couldn't refuse from Ruth Etting's gangster sweetie,* who demanded that only his Ruthie should get billed on the prestigious main Columbia logo.

If Hanshaw and Etting were rivals, Etting's career at first galloped ahead because of her eagerness to do show and film work, whereas Hanshaw, preferring only to record, steadily turned down those offers. But within a few years, Etting's star began to fade as Hanshaw latched on to one hit radio series after another, and with a new contract from the ARC Corporation (Banner, Melotone) she began making the best records of her career. About this time she began to back out. She stopped recording in 1934, the year she married her agent, Wally Rose, and then left her successful radio show, "The Camel Caravan," the following year. For a few years she remained in the studios making syndicated transcriptions for various sponsors. Finally, she retired altogether in 1938. She lived to meet a new generation of fans and eventually remarry, but she did not sing again.

Hanshaw preserved her well-being at the expense of our aural pleasure, leaving us to imagine what an Annette Hanshaw–Gil Evans collaboration would have sounded like, or what she could have done with "Lush Life" or "Guess Who I Saw Today?" As John Hammond, an admirer who knew her from childhood, put it, "I don't think she realizes how good she is."

Neither did a lot of other people, as Hanshaw proved too unique a stylist to be absorbed into the jazz and pop main-

* Affectionately known as "The Gimp," he couldn't match Jimmy Cagney for anti-hero warmth any more than Etting could sing a tenth as well as Doris Day.

streams. Her records lay unreissued until the early seventies in England, which was appropriate as she'd had her greatest influence there forty-five years previously. The best and (according to Brian Rust) the most popular of British canaries, Elsie Carlisle, sounded a lot like Hanshaw, although she added a British accent and substituted worldly wisdom for Annette's naïveté. Reversing the usual pop singing career, Carlisle had been well known as a solo act for some time before joining Ambrose and His Orchestra in 1932; she'd already introduced "What Is This Thing Called Love?" in the revue *Wake Up and Dream* and had made a reputation doing risqué double-entendre records (including a few from Bessie Smith's repertoire) that she had to live down once she began working with Ambrose.

Carlisle's male counterpart in the Ambrose band, Sam Browne, had similarly started with Scrappy Lambert's sound and did more to improve upon the original, gradually moving from tenor to baritone, and developing far more muscle both vocally and emotionally. The busiest of English band singers, Browne recorded with virtually every band going on that side of the pond (as well as a soloist) from the thirties into the fifties, The English even had their own counterpart to Adelaide Hall in Ella Logan. Then they got the real thing just as we landed their version, as Hall settled in the U.K. at about the same time Logan migrated to Hollywood.* At first, Logan was too much the little fish in a big pond. She's hip as hell with Jack Hylton (especially on "Moanin' Low") and Ambrose ("Shoo the Hoodoo Away" [both 1930, HMV]), but was clearly in over her head with Leo Watson on the Spirits of Rhythm ("It's a Long Way to Tipperary" [1941, Epic]).

Though America remained the capital of the world for show business as well as jazz, the band scene in interwar England was indeed a jolly old jumping one. The Brits not only loved to

---

* The greatest benefit of this relocation was the child Logan brought with her, Annie Ross, but once again we'll have to wait for a later chapter to get into that.

dance, they had a nationalistic gift for smart and snappy, jazz-tinged dance music. They certainly danced *more* than anybody else; according to Vic Bellerby and the *Melody Maker* (the major British music mag), "89% of factory workers, 93% of office workers and 84% of shop assistants make dancing their favorite hobby," while in America, radio sit-coms and movie double features commanded a larger slice of the diversions pie. The early thirties signified, in fact, the only time Brits were able to keep pace with American pop, as come 1935 they couldn't handle flat-out swing à la Benny Goodman or Count Basie, and after the band era died down had no real heavyweight vocalists. The big four of thirties British dance music—Hylton, Ambrose, Lew Stone, and Ray Noble (the latter two being innovative arrangers as well as leaders)—created pop music up to the level of any of the white American bands. Britain boasted a number of inspired soloists (anticipating the flowering of Brit jazz in the fifties, albeit one polarized into twin schools of trad and bop) and a few more great arrangers (none who had real lasting influence as the band era didn't really continue after them), but the greatest musical talent to come out of this era was, paradoxically, a singer, Al Bowlly. And though he came to regard England as his home, he was neither American nor English nor even European, and neither really black nor white.

Born in South Africa sometime around the turn of the century, Bowlly's parents were half-Greek and half-Lebanese. In the days of the Empire, they would have described Bowlly's complexion as "swarthy," and his cross-continental treks similarly suggest a good yarn by Kipling, albeit with a banjo and microphone rather than pith helmet and musket, and searching for Third World dance bands to croon with rather than heathen wogs to suppress. Bowlly started in Johannesburg, where he grew up surrounded by African music as well as that imported from the civilized West, and sang and played banjo with Edgar Adeler, the pianist who led one of South Africa's earliest jazz-dance groups, which took Bowlly on a tour of the continent's eastern coast. After a fight with Adeler, Bowlly next turned up working with Jimmy Lequime, who led the swankiest modern dance band in Calcutta, India, which recorded for HMV in their Dum-Dum studios and which played for a year in the Raffles Hotel, Singapore. Then Bowlly headed for Europe, where he worked with two groups led by black American jazzmen Noble Sissle in Paris (with Sidney Bechet) and Arthur Briggs in Berlin. His first record was "Song of the Wanderer." (His last, made shortly before his death, was "When That Man Is Dead and Gone." I'm not making any of this up.)

In 1929, Bowlly finally settled in London, where, apart from a later fling in the United States, he was to live for the remaining twelve years of his life. His career as a British band singer begins in tandem with another émigré, the Spaniard Fred Elizalde, an intellectual, progressive-minded composer infatuated with the Whiteman-Beiderbecke-Gershwin school, who staffed his orchestra with refugees from the American California Ramblers band. Bowlly made his greatest records with two less far-out but more farsighted arranger-bandleaders, Ray Noble and Lew Stone (and the latter's predecessor at the Monseigneur Restaurant, Roy Fox). At their best, Stone's and Noble's stylish and elegant yet still jazz-influenced dance music equals or surpasses any of the pre-swing white American bands (with the possible exception of the Casa Loma and Isham Jones, though Bowlly certainly out-classes any of their singers).

Noble initially led the studio-only house band for HMV Records, yet his records with Bowlly proved so popular that he not only organized a band for in-person dancing but became the first English bandleader to take on America. Bowlly's star at first ascended with Noble's, and for a time their record sales rivaled Crosby's in England; Bowlly also being tapped for radio and the movies. The American sojourn and the coming of the swing era, unfortunately, upset his career equilibrium and he never recovered. He never quite figured out where he fitted in on the American scene, and found the same problem waiting for him when he returned home. Too big to be a boy vocalist, the world (especially the dance-happy English) wasn't ready to accept a singer as a solo attraction. Ideally, he should have led his own band, but the necessary business acumen and foot kissing were beyond the reach of his rather limited social graces. When his career was at low ebb, he was killed in a Luftwaffe blitz of London.

The swing era disrupted only Bowlly's career, not his music. The main reason we listen to Bowlly today is because, in fact, he swings. He has soul. He sounds for real. Bowlly had a warm, gray voice that sounds congruous with the Crosby era as well as with gravelier singing musicians like Armstrong and, more specifically, Jack Teagarden. But like Tony Bennett, he had a phonogenic personality and was a virtuoso of heart. And that combination of high rhythmic style and infectious charisma makes Bowlly one of the great singers of his generation.

In saying that he knew how to swing, I mean that Bowlly can get tremendous effects out of the most subtle beat manipulations—dropping behind the pulse puts that extra spin on the ball for a ballad, racing ahead of the band makes an up-tempo number that much hotter. On some charts, Noble places Bowlly directly on the beat while he has the ensemble lope slightly behind with sort of an "echo" pulse. Bowlly also gets turned on by minor and blue-tinged intervals, songs with Yiddish origins like "A Brivele De Mame"/"A Letter to My Mother" (1934, Decca) and "Bei Mir Bist Du Schoen" (1937, HMV). None of his records is harder to resist than "Mama, I Wanna Make Rhythm" (1938, Decca), a combination of cantorial wailing and tonality with a solid-four up-tempo that Bowlly handles even more deftly than its inspiration, Cab Calloway.

And yet his greatest gift is his attitude: Bowlly is so remarkably on the level he knows that you can't mess with corn. You've got to look it straight in the eye and say, "Work, darn ya!" And it works. He can read a libretto like "Hang Out the Stars in Indiana (to Light My Way Back Home to You)" (1931, HMV) and make you believe it. He can get cute and cuddly on a kiddie tune ("This Little Piggy," yech!) or one of Herman Hupfeld's always suspect lyrics, and can leer salaciously on the dirty-minded, blues-tinged "Who Walks In When I Walk Out?" (1934, HMV). The hardest to take of Bowlly's numbers may well be his megamaudlin maternal melodies; even worse than Jolson's Jewish-cum-colored mammy songs, Bowlly does goyish "granny" songs ("Grandma Said," "Granny's Photo Album"), but unlike Jolie, Bowlly sounds like he loves his mammy more than himself. When Bowlly sells a song, you can't help buying.

He was a good salesman because he stood behind his merchandise—literally. Bowlly may be the only singer before Billie Holiday for whom lyrics can constitute an absolute reality. As Ray Noble remembered, "I've often seen him turn away from the microphone with tears in his eyes." Holiday (and Sinatra after her) makes the lyrics real by singing them as if they applied to the real world, but Bowlly makes them resound with such absolute conviction it's as if he believes the real world has some connection to the world Tin Pan Alley describes. It's got nothing to do with the period. If anything, the depressed thirties were a more cynical decade than the fantasy-oriented eighties; it has everything to do with Bowlly. Holiday supplies moral fortitude, but understanding the world Bowlly paints so vividly won't help you to deal with reality. Just the opposite. Just as Sam Raphaelson had loosely based *The Jazz Singer* on Jolson's life, Dennis Potter used Bowlly as his model for *Pennies from Heaven*,* his story about a song "seller" who's unable to deal with life when it doesn't work out the way it does in the songs. Perhaps that's ultimately what happened.

The period would be a far poorer one without him; he and Hanshaw provide much-needed evidence that the immediate post-Crosby era produced valid music and not merely nostalgia. Though their voices were silenced nearly fifty years ago, they still have something to say to us today. Time doesn't stand still for Bowlly and Hanshaw; it just doesn't exist.

---

* The original BBC-TV serial with Bob Hoskins being superior to the American movie version with Steve Martin.

Cult of the White Goddess

Mildred Bailey, Connee Boswell, and Lee Wiley

• _____

"You sing the way Bix played."
—Bud Freeman to Lee Wiley (as reported by Wiley in an interview with Richard Lamparski)

W hite goddesses were as essential to the big-band era as brass, reed, and rhythm sections. They decorated the fronts of swing bands like the figureheads on a ship, and no bandleader who wanted to fill dance halls or sell records dared go on the road without one.

As late as 1929, however, no such creatures existed. Men sang on dance-band records and you might go through two dozen sides before you found one with a girl singer. A few vocalists in the late twenties used small, sometimes hot bands to back them, but of these only Annette Hanshaw herself sang anything resembling jazz. The classic blues singers would eventually influence later generations of singers (and Bessie Smith was even making a comeback shortly before her death), but as a genre, they were never deader than they were in the early thirties. The double onslaught of Crosby and Armstrong had pushed women aside, and the earliest ones to assimilate the new style were men.

How, then, did it get to the point where it is now—where singing has become women's work almost exclusively, where female musicians are inevitably asked if they sing and male singers are expected to also play an instrument? One feminist point of view suggests that women who had an interest in music were forbidden by the dominant patriarchy to play instruments and were instead encouraged to sing. (The only instrument deemed acceptable for women was the piano. There were so many lady pianists in New Orleans; as Jelly Roll Morton remembered, "When a man played the piano, the stamp was on him for life, the femininity stamp." Although it's ridiculous to suggest that Billie Holiday, Carmen McRae, and Peggy Lee are nothing more than thwarted trombonists, this makes more sense than Jimmy Rushing in a backless evening gown.)

The real harbinger of the species of female jazz-and-band singers was the virtually simultaneous appearance of three women, the Three White Goddesses, who invented and defined the canary tradition in the early thirties: Mildred Bailey, Connee Boswell, and Lee Wiley.

The age of the girl singer began on September 15, 1931, when Jack Kapp put Mildred Bailey in front of the Casa Loma Orchestra for four songs. Kapp was then developing the theory that would later put Decca Records on the map, that of combining names—or good band plus good singer equals a doubly strong record and extra sales. Two other major vocalists appeared in the same year: Lee Wiley recorded her first vocal refrain with Leo Reisman's very-much-listened-to society orchestra in June, and two months later, Connee Boswell, who had only recently become the dominant voice in the Boswell Sisters trio, began recording as a soloist both on her own releases and in tandem with name bands.

Then, a record called "Rockin' Chair," by Mildred Bailey with a group of Paul Whiteman sidemen, became one of the year's major records and established the band canary for all time. Though Whiteman's name wasn't on the label, bookers, agents, and other bandleaders knew it was a "Whiteman Production" and started aping it. If Whiteman, still the central figure in American popular music, had scored a hit using a spoon player, doubtless all the other bands would have gone out and hired spoon players. As it happened, they started hiring girl singers.

Immediately, the status of Boswell and Wiley went up along with Bailey, and with them a new flock of songbirds suddenly began turning up on band records. Helen Rowland sang with Fred Rich's band in 1931, and then joined Freddy Martin in 1933. Jean Bowes fills up thirty-two bars with the Dorsey Brothers studio group in 1932, and when the Dorseys took to the road they brought along Kay Weber in the chirping department. Ben Pollack, whose bands will always be remembered for their excellent jazz musicians, modulated from hot to sweet by adding a skirt to the payroll, and similarly, Hotel Taft bandleader Georgie Hall knew his unit could never hit the big time unless they were behind the behind of a "chantootsie" (Earl Wilson's term), and always made sure he had one who had one. Most importantly, Duke Ellington annexed Ivie Anderson—temporarily jettisoning his "female voice-as-orchestral instrument" concept—to His Famous Orchestra in 1931, and Benny Goodman, in premiering his ground-breaking white swing band in 1934, brought along Helen Ward. After the following summer, when Goodman made white swing the prevailing mode of popular music, the waves of new bands that modeled themselves after BG made these gowned, bejeweled creatures as inevitable a part of the scenery as batons and music stands.

It's ironic that the woman most responsible for the whole phenomenon should be Mildred Bailey, and as we'll see, irony is the stuff of Mildred Bailey's life. Both her career and her music are shot through with it, like a Cole Porter lyric. It's the comic irony of the big woman who wants nothing more than to be perceived as dainty and petite; it's the dramatic, almost tragic

irony of the artist who never really learned who she was and
what she wanted, so instead she spends her life in a fruitless
pursuit of what Artie Shaw calls $ucce$$, love, money, fame,
and popular approval, which continually elude her like the Lost
Chord.

At the time of "Rockin' Chair" in 1932, the twenty-nine-year-
old Bailey was on the verge of her third marriage, husband
number two having given her the name Bailey. Born Mildred
Rinker in Spokane, Washington, she shared an early passion for
hot music with her three brothers (all of whom wound up in the
music business: Al in vocal groups and then as a radio producer,
Charles in song publishing, and Miles as a booking agent) and
Bing Crosby, then a local lad who hung around with brother Al.
Bailey's mother died when she was fourteen, and she went to
live with family in Seattle, later working as a song demonstrator
and singer in Los Angeles. When Al and Bing gained some local
success as a vocal duo, Bailey encouraged them to come to Hollywood and obtained work for them through the same agency
she dealt with (Crosby later credited Bailey with giving him his
"start"). Bailey went to work on radio station KMTR at about the
same time Crosby and Rinker joined Paul Whiteman. Fortunately, not long before they left the Maestro's entourage, they
were able to help Mildred on to the bandstand of the "King of
Jazz."

Though Whiteman would later get the credit for using the
first steady girl band singer, he very nearly missed the boat
where Bailey was concerned. Even though he brought her along
on tours and occasionally gave her a spot on his broadcasts, he
didn't take her seriously enough to use her on any of his records
for two whole years—and probably never would have recorded
her at all had Kapp not first shown Whiteman her potential. (She
did appear on records by two satellite bands of Whiteman per-
sonnel, Eddie Lang's and Frank Trumbauer's.)

When she finally did record with the Whiteman band proper,
in the last ten months of her tenure with "Pops," the result was
twenty of the limpest entries in her entire discography. White-

man's 1932–33 orchestra played far less jazz than his earlier bands with Beiderbecke, Trumbauer, and Crosby, or his later ones with Berigan and then the Teagarden Brothers, so it's not surprising that her ten sides with this elephantine orchestra should be so stiff and unswinging (although she does get a little funky on "We Just Couldn't Say Goodbye" and toward the end of the bridge of "Can't You See?"). The other ten—made with Mildred feted by small though not especially hot groups of Whiteman men—fare little better: "Too Late" has an unbelievably corny (in both arrangement and performance) bridge, and when she tries to phrase a little farther out in the last eight bars of "Lies" and "Dear Old Mother Dixie," an intrusive vocal group defeats her purpose. Of the Whiteman-era performances, only "Concentratin'," with its adventurous though unsure rhythmic liberties, and the remarkable "Rockin' Chair" (which would be replaced by a superior remake) can be called satisfying.

Bailey sings "I'll Never Be the Same Again" on one of her last Whiteman sides, and sure enough, when she resumed recording a few months later—this time under the aegis of Jack Kapp—everything changed. "Harlem Lullaby" and "Is That Religion?" reveal the oversize Whiteman organization as the culprit holding Bailey back. These two art-deco minstrel numbers, one a mammy tune and the other a mock hymn, call for Bailey to rock, moan, and preach, without the timidity and self-consciousness that mar her earlier work. Bailey's nine sides with the Dorsey Brothers (1933) not only prove that she had solved most of her rhythmic problems (they would never go away completely), but that she's working on her tone as well. The early voice sounds uncomfortably dark and deep, influenced in equal portion by the classic blues singers and the white belters of the acoustic twenties. Typically, when we describe a singer as achieving tonal maturity, as in the case of Crosby, Armstrong, and Sinatra, we mean their voice shifts from the light whimpers of their first recordings to the lower, fuller sound of their grown-up work. In Bailey's case, we mean the opposite. As she got better her voice grew lighter and lighter until it became delicate and paper-thin but nevertheless solid. Bailey apparently figured it was easier to swing a clarinet than a tuba, and later told *Time* that "I couldn't sing *big* if I wanted to."

In addition to her work with Kapp, Bailey began working with jazz-oriented producer John Hammond. Hammond's idea was that you were not a "jazz singer" until you recorded with Negroes, so he organized a date for Mildred and an early Benny Goodman band with Coleman Hawkins, and then a series of small-band sessions, one of which used the inspired idea of recording her without a drummer in the classic blues tradition. These four numbers, made with Berigan, Johnny Hodges, bassist Grachan Moncur III, and Bailey's favorite accompanist, Teddy Wilson, thankfully did not attempt to re-create the Clarence Williams Blue Five idea but rather to update it, with some modern prefigured background riff scoring and a less formalized interaction between all five participants. Though Hammond accurately assessed these four tracks as "among the most beautiful that I ever made," he never got greedy for seconds. Instead, over the next four years, he put Bailey in front of a series of semiorganized jam sessions. These records bounce amiably and boast a colorful supporting cast (especially Chu Berry and Roy Eldridge). But her recorded legacy would be so much poorer if it consisted *only* of these.

The best thing that ever happened to Mildred Bailey was Red Norvo, her third and last husband and her most important collaborator. They met in Whiteman's ranks (he played vibes behind her on "Rockin' Chair") and were married in 1933—the same year Kapp stupidly prevented Norvo from putting his advanced ideas on wax—and organized a touring band together in 1936, appropriately christened "Mr. and Mrs. Swing." Together with the young arranger Eddie Sauter, they created three years' worth of the most beautiful vocal records ever produced, each a perfect blend of written ensemble passages, vocal refrains, and instrumental improvisations and each a minor classic of shading and dynamics that would have a profound influence on many singers, including Frank Sinatra, and even more arrangers. Making these years all the more remarkable for Bailey was the fact that she still did the small-group dates for Hammond. The two radically different kinds of records, the earthy blowing sessions on the one hand, the masterfully scored orchestral works on the other, compliment each other beautifully, in much the same way Duke Ellington alternated between big- and small-band sessions throughout his career.

On Sauter's superior 1937 remake of "Rockin' Chair," Bailey's now mature and secure, featherlight voice emotes for two slowly rocking choruses over a choir of saxophones that suit her far better than any "genuine" vocal group ever did (such as her 1931–32 Victors with the King's Jesters and her 1941–43 efforts with the Delta Rhythm Boys). "Smoke Dreams," another 1937 triumph, represents the three-way collaboration at its zenith: The arranger second-guesses the future with a dissonant, amelodic ensemble of brass and reeds; Bailey speaks for the past with her highly individual rhythmic patterns; and Norvo's vibes both lead them and hold them together as the dominant voice in the score.

Quixotically, Sauter did not develop into a great jazz arranger, although he was much praised by critics who confused his classical leanings for what they called "progressive" jazz. Sauter's charts for Benny Goodman today sound cold, hollow, and occasionally pretentious, and his later Sauter-Finegan Orchestra disavowed jazz (and, one might say, music) entirely (to give him credit though, his last significant work was *Focus*, a stunning album-length creation for strings, rhythm, and Stan Getz's tenor). Sauter's later work with Bailey brings home dramatically that the Bailey-Sauter combination signified nothing without Norvo.

Unfortunately, Mr. and Mrs. Swing did not get along as well financially and personally as they did musically. Their band broke up in 1939 and their marriage followed early in 1940. Bailey, suffering from one of her first serious illnesses (brought on by constant touring), which had contributed to the disintegration of the band, looked around for something new to do. She tried chirping with Benny Goodman's band on a few cold-sounding Sauter arrangements that were not up to her classic collaborations with either man. She indulged a penchant for commercialism by Europeanizing her accompaniments, first using a pretentious chamber octet piloted by Alec Wilder (which also backed her on a season of Bob Crosby's radio show), and later with a pitiful pitfull of pseudo-symphonic strings. She made a series of sides for Decca with the Delta Rhythm Boys and others, which went nowhere.

Finally, in 1944, she got her last break. CBS put her in front of one of the major jazz radio shows of the war era in which she performed a mixture of ballads, up-tempos, and blues with Paul Barron's sympathetic swing band, which, though not as idiosyncratically perfect for Bailey as the Norvo group, suited her fine nonetheless. Importantly, a roster of big-league players from the jazz world came with the package as guest stars.

Too bad there were only thirty-four shows and only a handful of the aircrecks have ever been released, because apart from one last good session with Hammond for Majestic, which resulted in two terrific takes of "Lover, Come Back to Me," and numerous novelties and dates with strings, and a good, completely overlooked Victor session, that was about it for Mildred Bailey. Illness had been a serious problem for her since 1938, and she was hospitalized then and again in April 1943 and yet again in 1949, after which she went into retirement on a farm she owned in Poughkeepsie, New York. She made it to Los Angeles in the spring of 1950 for a final recording session and a long-overdue appearance on the Bing Crosby show (their duet was a marvelous "I've Got the World on a String"). Back in New York, she did a Saturday morning radio show with the dreaded Morton Downey, Sr., and in the fall of 1951 played Detroit with Ralph Burns as accompanist. Becoming seriously ill around Thanksgiving, she checked into the Poughkeepsie Hospital, where she died on December 12, 1951.

The first of the canaries was dead. The tragedy wasn't her death but that in life she was only able to produce her greatest art by accident when the circumstances were right, with the same kind of chance results that define jazz itself. From the evidence of those who knew her, she had little idea of what made her special. "Mildred thought that the big-band sound, often with choirs, was essential for popular appeal," said John Hammond, and when he proposed the Berigan-Hodges-Moncur-Wilson session, "Mildred thought I was crazy." According to Bucklin Moon, she considered her *Time* review (of a gig at Cafe Society) a major triumph even though the anonymous critic was an ignoramus who not only made several insulting remarks about her "mountainous girth," but went on to insinuate that the only thing she could sing was "Rockin' Chair."

But the most revealing description of Bailey's personality comes from her close friend and fellow artist, Lee Wiley. "In going out" of Wiley's apartment, she told Richard Lamparski, "Mildred fell on the floor and by God I really talked her into living, because she apparently [wanted to be] dead. Well, what I did was to use some of her own language. I said, 'Mildred! Now you get your _____ off of this floor! You can't go on being like this! Stop! Get up your _____ !' Or something like that, and do you know that pretty soon a smile came over her face [and] she got up."

Rhythmically, Bailey comes out of the classic blues approach, specifically Bessie Smith's a cappella phrasing, and this in spite of Bailey's sweet and unblue tone. Norvo has spoken of Mildred's friendship and adoration of Bessie, and Eddie Condon reported that when Smith played one of her final shows in New York, Mildred was present but refused to follow her, such was her respect for the empress. As it happened, she never outgrew the twenties approach to rhythm, and never fully absorbed the new rhythmic language of Crosby and Armstrong. By 1935, when the official coming of swing made 4/4 *the* standard time of popular music and jazz, Mildred must have seemed increasingly anachronistic.

Today, if the 1960s has taught us anything, it's not to be concerned with what time signature (or lack of it) a performer picks out for himself so long as he "swings" within that idiom. But in the late forties Mildred had a tough time finding critics and audiences—not to mention accompanists—who knew what she was going for. For her entire life Mildred would never be truly comfortable with the "four heavy beats in a bar and no cheating" (the words are Count Basie's) that characterize swing.

The most recent standard in Bailey's repertoire, "Almost like Being in Love" (recorded with a string orchestra in 1947 on Majestic), makes her rhythmic thinking crystal clear, and is accentuated by a shortness of breath caused by illness and middle age. She takes the tune as written, in standard post-Crosby ballad time (that is, legato), and staccato-izes it into little tiny pieces, breaking it down into the strong/weak pulses characteristic of Dixieland. To try to capture her meter on the typewriter: "*What* a *day* (pause) / *This* has *been* (pause)."

Armstrong might have given these notes equal weight, probably pausing just before and not after that last syllable, "been." Crosby would have filled in what Armstrong only suggests, extending the last note and likely throwing in one of his characteristic satellite notes halfway through this last word to break up the time a little. Frank Sinatra, who recorded "Almost like Being in Love" two months before Bailey, also fills in the pauses within the line (only taking a breath between lines) but would never use one of Crosby's grace notes here, thereby only according the most minute difference in the weight of each note.

All this helps explain why Mildred needed Norvo so badly. As the man who brought the xylophone* to jazz, Norvo had to master every jazz rhythm style, his career serving as an outline of the history of the music. From the 2/4 of Whiteman-era dance bands to the 4/4 of swing, from the double time of bebop (he led one of the pivotal Charlie Parker sessions in 1945) to the free time of his collaborations with third-streamers and prototypical

---

* As Norvo played it, the xylophone was a tunable percussion instrument that belonged in the front line as much as it did in the rhythm section.

avant-garde men like Bill Smith, Jack Montrose, and Charlie Mingus, there is nothing that Norvo didn't play. Both as a great musician and as her husband, Norvo knew exactly how to make Bailey comfortable, what kind of backing would produce the most from her. She suffered without him in more ways than one, and was fiercely envious of his second, successful marriage to Shorty Rogers's sister Julia.

Sadly, that dainty and delightful powderpuff bounce (bounce as distinct from straight swing) that makes her so special today came across as antiquated in her own life. No wonder she resented Bing Crosby so much; although Crosby (as John Hammond has confirmed) repeatedly bailed her out of rough financial waters, she never came close to equaling his chameleonic rhythmic mastery, which allowed him to fulfull Jack Kapp's prophecy of the ultimate pop music patriarch. She could never, as Crosby did, land a Hawaiian hit in 1937 and a country-western bestseller six years later; instead, she struggled vainly to keep her career and life together. That she and Crosby were born a few months and a few miles apart, and grew up with the same influences and advantages (and the same Guinness book achievements, the first full-time male and female singers with a band, the same band no less), must have really made her gnash her teeth. Forty years since her death it seems ironic, but then "ironic" is a word that pops up quite a bit when the subject is Mildred Bailey.

On the other hand, being born in New Orleans doesn't ensure jazz greatness, but the Crescent City's musicians have traditionally enjoyed a rhythmic advantage over those from other locals. Importantly, the only major popular singer (after Armstrong, Louis Prima and a few other doubling instrumentalists) to come out of New Orleans was Connee Boswell, who was so much a part of that city, and vice versa. Though we hear a considerable amount of Bing Crosby in her work, and something of Bessie Smith and a few of Caruso's techniques, the overwhelming influence is that of Louis Armstrong and, going deeper into the roots of both Boswell and Armstrong, New Orleans itself. But

Boswell had the most commercial success of the three original White Goddesses—in spite of her unswerving allegiance to the great New Orleans jazzmen, sharing their wildly swinging beat; a raw, earthy voice; and her delightful disrespect for "proper" enunciation. Boswell epitomizes the New Orleans musician's directness and open emotionality.

Born in 1907 in Kansas City, Missouri, Connee, a cripple since early childhood, grew up the most musical child of one of the most musical families in the most musical city in the world. She studied several instruments, primarily cello, and later claimed to have a classical background, which is likely since we don't know how much Negro jazz a middle-class white girl would have been able to hear. "We liked jazz music and swing music and even some of the ragtime music that they played in those days," she told Rich Conaty later. "But we bought virtually every type of record that came out. . . . I loved Caruso and the way he used to be able to take a deep breath and then sing on that deep breath. But also I used to listen to Mamie Smith and then to Bessie Smith."

There'll be a history and analysis of the Boswell Sisters vocal group in a later chapter, but for now keep in mind that this group didn't go anywhere until Connee emerged as the trio's dominant voice and mind in 1930–31. Probably not coincidentally, this happened at about the same time they began to work for Jack Kapp and started to really sell records. Their new boss also insisted on recording the middle Boswell as a solo act right from the beginning of their association.

Apart from the previously mentioned Dixie rhythm style, Boswell structures her 1931–35 Brunswick recordings according to the New Orleanian tradition as codified by Armstrong. The first chorus is sung relatively straight, the second turns much looser, and if there is an instrumental break, the out chorus (or half-chorus) will be wilder still, climaxing and then resolving the performance. Even on these "straight" first choruses Boswell gets endearingly playful: On a tune with a basic three-line construction, for instance, she'll drop way behind the beat on the first two lines and then jump back on top of it on the third—an elaboration of an idea from the Armstrong-Crosby vocabulary that no one ever did as well as Boswell. She does it to make the harmony, which will generally resolve to the tonic chord at this point, the rhythm, and she "resolves" back to the top of the beat, and drama, which "resolves" as the title line is repeated, all parallel to each other.

Kapp believed that Boswell's frisky embellishments would deter sales (he told the same thing to Crosby) and you can almost hear Kapp shouting "sing the melody" at the top of his lungs in the recording booth. He temporarily conventionalized both Connee's and the trio's work and, as Connee put it, "Those records just didn't come out right."

These disappoint at first, because songs like "Clouds" and "Chasing Shadows," which have relatively little melodic development, require Connee's deluxe treatment to make them special. But without rhythm to play with and without the opportunity to do her own arrangements (as she always preferred to do), Connee focuses our attention on her tone—and what a tone it is! Unlike Bailey's thin, delicate wisp, which, though charming, represented a coy middle-American attitude toward sex, Boswell's is a more directly sensual, genuinely vaginal instrument, something else she picked up in New Orleans. That ain't fur on her voice, honeychile, that's pubic hair. Bailey may elaborate on Bessie Smith's rhythm, but Boswell picks up on her attitude.

When Goodman legitimized swing music and made it marketable, Kapp no longer had any excuse to hold Connee to straight numbers. She waxed a lot of sides with a Crosby-derived schottische beat, and also got to work with jazz units such as Woody Herman's, Ben Pollack's, and a rhythm section that followed her through four jazzed-up ballads (two standards, "Nobody's Sweetheart" and "Dinah," and two new songs destined to achieve that status, "Blueberry Hill" and "The Nearness of You").

However, nothing matched the empathy she shared with the

homeboys in Bob Crosby's Bobcats. They had already made one satisfactory session together (which produced the fine "You Started Me Dreaming") when, on the heels of Maxine Sullivan's hit "Loch Lomond," they reteamed to swing four other ancient numbers, the folk "Home on the Range," two Victor Herbert operetta pieces—"Gypsy Love Song" and "Ah! Sweet Mystery of Life"—and another "Ah!" number, "Ah! So Pure," from von Flotow's *Martha*. Kapp, who at first wanted to cash in on another label's hit, showed a middle-brow streak about a mile wide. In an interview with Michael Brooks, Boswell said Kapp "nearly fainted at the playback. Said von Flotow would turn over in his grave." He considered the Boswell-Bobcats record, which they called "Martha," a desecration, or at least a mean parody of the semiclassical stuff he was raised on. Actually, Boswell consummated a perfect marriage of jazz and the Euro-pop tradition, realigning von Flotow's melody to the demands of swing but retaining its recitative/aria structure to alternate Connee's vocal passages with choruslike chanting by the band and superb solos by Eddie Miller's hard swinging tenor and Yank Lawson's trumpet. It worked beautifully.

But Kapp was livid. "He wouldn't issue it at first and only consented after I said if the record didn't reach a certain number of sales I'd take full-page ads in *Variety* absolving him and the company from any blame." (If he was willing to "betray" the music he loved to make a buck, why should we be shocked at what he did to music he didn't particularly care about—meaning jazz?)

Anyhow, "I didn't need to place the ads," Boswell concluded, since "Martha" quickly became her biggest seller. In the late thirties she headlined at least one major New York nightclub, spent a season of singing overdone Meredith Willson charts on the big-money *Maxwell House Good News* show, and, then a more musically satisfying year as the first regular femme thrush on Crosby's radio program, and, in spite of her handicap, an off-and-on movie career that sustained itself deep into the television era. The years leading up to the war became rewarding ones for Boswell, and not only career-wise: Her voice grew deeper, her rhythm freer, her abilities as an arranger more skillful, and her command of a lyric more mature.

Next to none of Boswell's postwar performances have been made available in my lifetime, but the few I've heard (mostly airchecks) indicate that just as Annette Hanshaw's postretirement disc of "You're a Heavenly Thing" reflects a more modern Connee Boswell influence, Boswell's own later work shows that one of her own disciples, Kay Starr, was rubbing off on Connee, leading to a more "mannish," harder-swinging approach. But other vocalists, emerging in the postband era, among them many Boswell "students" such as Ella Fitzgerald, Doris Day, and Starr, gradually usurped the older woman's popularity. The big-time appearances became fewer and fewer until she retired in the late fifties, by then a victim of rock 'n' roll. She claimed later that her husband-manager's sickness had caused what she described as her "temporary retirement."

But there were to be a few more records with Bing Crosby (specifically "That's A-Plenty"), a few LPs for minor labels, and two important albums. Sy Oliver's small-band arrangements on *Connee* (1956, Decca) demonstrate a common failing of Boswell's later work, that of being too tightly arranged. Without enough blowing, the idea of Connee singing a standard melody over an Oliver riff works for a couple of songs and then becomes predictable. (Only "Lullaby in Rhythm," which started life as an Edgar Sampson riff, seems suited to its quasi-R&B setting.)

But after the partial success of the Oliver album, Boswell created her last important work, the apex of her entire career: *Connee Boswell and the Original Memphis Five in Hi-Fi* (1956, Victor). It began as a project to record the ailing jazz giant Miff Mole. "He was a great trombonist of the twenties," she told Rich Conaty; he "had been very sick and they didn't expect him to live. Finally, he got a little bit better and [Victor] finally decided . . . to call and ask me if I'd like to do this Dixieland album. They were going to get as many [of the Original Memphis Five] as they possibly could."

They decided on a format of half Boswell vocals and half band instrumentals, which consisted of the three remaining active Memphis Fivers, clarinetist Jimmy Lytell, pianist Frank Signorelli, and Mole, filled out by the great trumpeter Billy Butterfield, bassist Gene Traxler, and Tony Sparbaro, the New Orleans drummer who'd been there on the first jazz records ever made. "It was up to me which tunes I wanted to do and all that," Connee reminisced, "When I did 'Say It Isn't So,' I didn't write out a solo for Miff to play. I said, 'I want you to play a solo on this.' He said, 'I don't think my lip will hold out.' So I said, 'Miff, come on and try it.' And so I talked him into it. Miff played the solo on that, and if you listen to the solo he does, it's really very beautiful."

In addition to the lovely ballads ("Say It Isn't So") and jazz standards ("All of Me" and "The Saints"), the album's pinnacle is Boswell's very worthy sequel to "Martha," a jazz adaptation of Rudolf Friml's "Giania Mia." Instead of the usual solos from her sidemen—there are plenty of those on the other tracks—Connee re-forms the Boswell Sisters through overdubbing and shows her Ukelele Ike roots with a vocal trumpet imitation. Again, her translation of classical effects into the jazz idiom, such as the substitution of a perfectly timed rest for the original's high-note climax, makes it work on a level beyond parody.

The rightness of the total album that makes it a classic, the perfect balance between vocals and instrumentals, the fast and slow numbers, the solos of Boswell and the musicians underscore another difference between Boswell and Mildred Bailey: Connee instinctively knew what would work for her and what wouldn't, while Bailey's own judgment did her more harm than good and she floundered like a fish out of water without worthy collaborators, a Norvo or a Hammond. In a telephone conversation shortly before his death in 1972, Jimmy Lytell said that of the thousands of records he'd made, "that one with Connee Boswell" was easily his favorite.

After this final triumph, a 1958 B-movie called *Senior Prom*, in which she sang "The Saints" again, was her last major gig. She

always spoke of a comeback, but those who knew her in her
sixties describe her as having gotten quite silly in her last years.
She died in 1976, within a year of two other stars of the Kraft
Music Hall, Bing Crosby and bandleader John Scott Trotter.

Boswell's pairing with the Memphis Five was only one of the
records that made the late fifties the richest period in the history
of vocal jazz. Not only were the giants associated with that era
doing their greatest work (Frank Sinatra's *Only the Lonely, Mel
Torme Swings Shubert Alley*) and newcomers making significant
debuts (Carmen McRae and Betty Carter), but many major artists of the thirties created their most satisfying efforts, like the
Boswell album, Crosby's *Bing with a Beat*, Armstrong's
Satchmo: A Musical Autobiography, Jimmy Rushing's *The Jazz
Odyssey of James Rushing, Esq.*, and perhaps the best of all,
Lee Wiley's *West of the Moon*.

Even before Wiley opens her mouth on the first song of *West
of the Moon*, the rocking first notes of Ralph Burns's introductory vamp let us know that we're in for something special. Then,
when Wiley enters on the first few bars of the neglected Irving
Berlin tune "You're a Sweetheart," we know at once that she and
Burns will make good that promise. Never on any of the twelve
songs on this album does either one let us down. *West of the
Moon*, like the other records I've mentioned, still astounds me
with its natural perfection, translucent mist atmosphere, flaw-
lessly selected (and sequenced) tunes, and tasteful organization—all of which display the highest possible level of
craftsmanship.

But Wiley herself elevates *West of the Moon* into a work for
the ages by being simply the most naked of all singers. There's
a muscular, internally strong quality to Crosby, Armstrong, and
Sarah Vaughan that allows them to be vulnerable yet never
leaves them completely defenseless. Even Billie Holiday, who
learned a thing or two from Wiley, will respond to pain with
invective and the sharp-edged wit of the blues. Bailey and
Boswell find protection in rhythm, but Wiley extends no defenses, no walls, no barriers between her heart and her audience.

Where Boswell swings hard and Bailey bounces, Wiley blows smoke rings, each note a puff that melts into wisps of vibrato. Rhythm is second to tone here, her burnished, bittersweet instrument dominating where the beats will fall in a much freer way than had ever been done before. Bud Freeman told her, "When you sing, you remind me of the way Bix played." Although she didn't agree, the comparison suggests why she had to wait until the "cool" fifties to find her most perfect accompanist in Ralph Burns, the modernist arranger associated with Woody Herman's Lester Young–influenced band, and indirectly points up Wiley's similarities with Holiday, who had also picked up on the Beiderbecke influence by way of Lester Young.

In fact, Burns gives the entire orchestra a Wiley sound by emphasizing the slightly spacey intervals she loved, and by creating a floating, tranquil ensemble sound that makes you think Wiley is somehow playing all the instruments herself. Unlike many arrangers who'll try to sweep a singer's shortcomings under a carpet of distractions (strings, choirs, loud brass), Burns's writing is as honest as Wiley herself. Realizing that a woman in the thinnest of negligees is sexier than one completely nude, his strings don't cover Wiley but further expose her nakedness (a lesson Nelson Riddle learned on Sinatra's *Close to You* and Marty Paich on *Torme*).

The story of Wiley's life and career would be easier to tell if it were one of triumph after triumph leading up to 1956's *West of the Moon*, but that masterpiece climaxes nearly fifty years of stops and starts. Like Boswell and Bailey, she lied or let others lie about her age, claiming 1915 as a birth date when the maturity of her voice in 1931 (and Vince Giordano's discovery that she recorded a demo for Victor in the late twenties) points to a date a few years earlier. Her brother recently admitted 1910 to Gus Kuhlman. (Wiley was also supposed to be part Indian, something they used to say about Bailey, Kay Starr, Keely Smith, and even Jack Teagarden, even though his sister flatly stated that there was never one drop of Indian blood in their veins.) Like Boswell, Wiley had an instinctual sense of what would work for her musically and what wouldn't, and her talent for songwriting (she always claimed to have written "Ghost of a Chance") paralleled Boswell's gift for arranging. Unfortunately, like Bailey, Wiley allowed herself to be the victim of her own destiny rather than the master of it, like the heroine of a forties film noir like *Detour:* "Someday, fate or some mysterious force can put the finger on you or me for no reason at all."

Originally from Oklahoma (born in Fort Gibson, although John Hammond remembers her as being from Muskogee, raised in Tulsa), Wiley discovered the blues early on. "I used to sit in school and dream about being a singer," she told Richard Lamparski many years later. "I had a boyfriend who would skip school with me and we would go over to the local store and play records . . . they called them 'race records,' and they were sold only in a certain part of town, the colored part . . . like Bessie Smith and Clara Smith, but especially Ethel Waters." She added, "Mildred Bailey used to come on WPW every night around dinnertime. It was so wonderful, I couldn't wait until she would come on." To hear Wiley tell it, her life was a rags-to-riches story from the Tony Bennett record: As a teenager she sings on an Okie radio station where a music publisher hears her and says there's a big future for her in New York. So, not yet twenty, she runs away to the big town (working at station KNOX in St. Louis en route) where big-time bandleader Leo Reisman signs her immediately for his broadcasts and Victor recordings. From the band she graduates to her own program, "The Pond's Cold Cream Hour Starring Lee Wiley," and her own records—once again, Kapp—backed by the Dorsey Brothers, Casa Loma, and Johnny Green's orchestras. At this time she also guest stars with Paul Whiteman and appears on the covers of radio fan magazines.

Suddenly the first of several serious illnesses hit her and shook her off her perch at the top. "I got out of the doctor's office and I walked down Central Park West . . . crying all the way," she said. The hospital suspected she had a touch of tuberculosis, and even though they turned out to be wrong (fortunately), she had to stop singing and recuperate in Arizona for a year. The scenario was repeated sometime later: Shortly before she was scheduled to do a screen test in Hollywood she caught an eye disease that left her temporarily blind and disfigured. Still, she carried on—or off-and-on. After the public deserted her, the jazz community took her under its wing. In 1963 a TV executive made Wiley's life into a telefilm with Piper Laurie playing the lead and Benny Carter directing the music.*

Wiley's early "popular" sides interest us more for archeological reasons than musical ones. Though Leo Reisman claimed to dislike jazz, he didn't let that keep him from such great hot musicians as Bubber Miley, Max Kaminsky, Adrian Rollini, and Wiley, and his band has a rhythmic lilt that complements its musical comedy affiliations. On Wiley's own song, "The South in My Soul," the band substitutes concert aggrandizing for black feeling (Don Redman recorded it with Harlan Lattimore, "The Colored Crosby," handling the refrain), but with her help they pull it off with conviction. Don't mind that she didn't have everything down pat during this prelude to her fifteen minutes of fame, but rather be amazed that she shows any trace at all of her later advanced style so early on.

When Wiley stepped up from canary to chanteuse and the selective audience replaced the mass one, everything about he work improved, not just her voice itself but the caliber of he sidemen and repertoire. In a phenomenon we'll explore i greater detail later on, Wiley may have been the one to intro duce the idea of the "standard." In the thirties performers di. whatever tunes music publishers hoped would sell, there being such a limitless flow of good and sometimes great songs that it never became necessary to do anything that was even six months

* In an as-yet-unpublished memoir by a sideman of Fats Waller, one musician of the period offers the following account of how Wiley was cast out from paradise. According to this fellow, Wiley and Kapp had an argument which climaxed in Wiley's insulting Kapp with an anti-semitic remark, which seems strange as no other person who ever knew Wiley has ever reported that she had any kind of racial or ethnic hang-ups. In any case, Kapp is said to have had her blacklisted at the time, which explained why she didn't record again for years (and only then for small labels), and why she lost her radio spot.

old. The only exceptions were jazz musicians, who, much to the song plugger's chagrin, frequently recorded old numbers out of the New Orleans or blues tradition or that Louis Armstrong had transformed into jazz perennials. But Wiley made a series of sessions for Liberty, then a high-class music shop that catered to an upper-crust clientele of sophisticated showgoers, in which she waxed albums of the works of Cole Porter, Rodgers and Hart, and the late George Gershwin. (Recently, Merritt Records issued one of the Porter sessions complete with breakdowns and alternate takes, providing a fascinating window into Wiley's creative process.)

With their all-star accompaniment (Bunny Berigan, Fats Waller, Pee Wee Russell), these sides and Wiley's five-year marriage to pianist Jess Stacy (their union consummated musically in a Commodore recording) served as her ticket into the semiunderground world of jazz. First the musicians and then the critics picked up on her, even more than they had Mildred Bailey, who once said to Wiley, "You know, Lee, it's an interesting thing about you and me. We have certain audiences and they seem to be the same type of people." Wiley played Wendy to that ragtag group of drunkards, geniuses, and lost boys whose Peter Pan was Eddie Condon. Though this combination resulted in only a few recordings—and those marred by Jack Kapp—she was given at least one specialty at each Condon concert or broadcast, and dozens of excellent live performances have been preserved on tape.

Finally, Mitch Miller of Columbia saw fit to give her one final shot at the big-label big time and, by way of the songbook package, reacquaint her with the musical comedy crowd. They used twin piano backing to steal some of Mabel Mercer's thunder, which, to my ears, wears pretty thin after one or two songs (and she committed no less than eighteen songs to wax with this accompaniment). The record bombed, but the idea worked. Wiley became virtually the only artist in history to be equally admired by devotees of both Louis Armstrong and Bobby Short; the combination of jazz and cabaret patronage made one of her albums, the 1950 *Night in Manhattan,* go legitimately gold after thirty-five years in record-shop racks.

Night in Manhattan, the best of the two CBS albums, combines two ten-inch LPs, one with the proto-Ferrante-Teicher-type pianos, the other with an extension of Bessie Smith's cornet-piano-voice format. Wiley had first experimented with this instrumentation on her Commodore disc and then added bass and drums on her Berigan–Cole Porter date for Liberty to modernize the idea for her own needs without sacrificing its vitality. *Night in Manhattan* goes a step farther, covering Wiley, trumpeter Bobby Hackett, and the rhythm section with a shimmering silk stocking of strings. Wiley's "I've Got a Crush on You" remakes Sinatra's rendering of that Gershwin classic from three years earlier, using the same arrangement and the same scrumptious Hackett introduction, obbligato, and solo.

The two Victor albums, *A Touch of the Blues* and *West of the Moon,* followed an underpar group of Rodgers and Hart numbers for George Wein's Storyville label (with the same instrumentation and Ruby Braff assuming Hackett's role). The charts are generally overbaked on *A Touch of the Blues*—except for an exquisite "Melancholy Baby" with that great trumpet and rhythm idea, this time it's Billy Butterfield—but thankfully only a temporary lapse of taste for arranger Al Cohn. The previously mentioned *West of the Moon,* however, is great enough for two albums; my only regret is that it's over too quickly and that Wiley and Ralph Burns didn't make another fifty albums together. Like Boswell, she chose to let these Victor albums close her third act, and thereafter retired—coming back only briefly, on the insistence of Johnny Mercer, to do a final album for Monmouth-Evergreen. She died on December 11, 1975.

The three women had more in common than that long walk down the thirteen miles of bad road that too often separates musical artistry from commercial marketability. For one thing, there was the relationship with Crosby: Bailey being a home-town friend, Wiley recording with him on Decca, Boswell sharing his mike on countless discs and programs. Even more

important, each exerted an important influence on Billie Holiday, an influence that revealed itself more in each of the three
white goddesses of the immediate post-Holiday generation—
Peggy Lee, Kay Starr, and Anita O'Day—than in Holiday's own
work. Though all three have their deepest roots in Holiday, the
only thing in jazz that foreshadows O'Day's vibratoless tone is
Bailey's; what Starr gleaned from Boswell has already been mentioned. Peggy Lee's debt to Lee Wiley may be the greatest of
all.

As Bill Borden, producer of Lee Wiley's last album, put it,
"Decades in jazz are generations as the classicists count." Lee
sings the way I like to think Wiley would have had she been
born ten years later: a notch or more free in her rhythm and
fluffier in her tone. Think of Wiley's phrases as jagged lumps of
sugar floating in dark coffee—sharp but sweet nonetheless. With
Lee, the edges are softer and more streamlined, and the liquid
flows right along with the lumps. On Lee's best record, the
well-titled *Black Coffee,* she uses Wiley's favorite setting—
voice, trumpet, and rhythm. The Wiley influence so pervades
Lee's "Call It a Day" (mid-fifties, Capitol) that it's hard to believe she wasn't trying to copy Wiley's 1933 performance of the
song—the kicker is that Wiley's was unissued (rejected by Kapp
because of harmonic noodling in the climax), and there's no way
Lee could have heard it.

What Mildred Bailey, Connee Boswell, and Lee Wiley added
to the jazz vocabulary would vastly outlive their own careers;
though each was more than a torch singer, each died with the
knowledge that the torch had been passed on.

Sing Me
a Swing Song!

Canaries of the Hellenic Era

"Working with a good band in those days was the end of a rainbow for any singer who wanted to make it in this profession."

—*Frank Sinatra*

Duke Ellington, that classically minded Renaissance man, used the term "beyond category" only when he wanted to bestow the highest possible praise. As the classical historian H. D. K. Kitto once observed, "The modern mind divides, specializes and thinks in categories. The Greek instinct was the opposite, to take the widest view, to see things as an organic whole." However, if we accept the idea of categories as a valid one, where do we begin to draw the dividing lines in jazz? The first ideas that come to mind are between classic (pre-1945) and modern (post-1945) jazz, between jazz recorded for either 78 or long-playing record release, or between any kind of jazz that uses metered rhythm and tempered notes and is completely "free."

While all of these points are useful, the most obvious demarcating point has less to do with the creation of music than with the way it is received by its audience: jazz as entertainment versus jazz as art. To look at the excesses of each rather than their common ground, those who treat jazz like any of the high arts (musical or otherwise) are willing to bear with a great deal of sounds that are unpleasant or difficult to listen to (as Arnold Schoenberg once informed movie mogul Irving Thalberg, "I don't write lovely music"). Conversely, those who approach jazz as a popular music have their own share of indulgences and must endure a disproportionately large share of nonjazz mixed in with the real thing; at times the sacrifices of vitality and charisma that jazz must make in order to be marketplace are no longer worth it.

The swing era (generally regarded as 1935 to 1945, though Ellington had anticipated the whole schmeer as early as 1932 with his song, "It Don't Mean a Thing [If It Ain't Got That Swing]") saw entertainment and art at their most convergent. Still, the compromises jazz made to maintain that status proportionately equaled its mass popularity.

For most jazz-oriented band buffs at the time, vocalists were one of those compromises. You sat through the vocal group's dreary rendition of the latest plug tune—paying more attention to the figure on the blonde than her musical attributes, while you waited for the tenor player to squeeze in his eight-bar "solo" and the flagwaver (jazz instrumental) you hoped would follow. And that's not counting the long minutes of novelties, comic routines, and production numbers that they would all too often throw in the middle of jazz sets. No wonder that those who came to jazz in the more art-oriented and socially conscious fifties and sixties have a difficult time admitting that swing-era music, especially by the white bands, is jazz at all.

But take into account what jazz *gained* in these years. It's commonly realized that any number of legitimate artists (Basie, Ellington, Goodman, Herman) became genuine stars and celebrities for the rest of their lives, but there were thousands of other musicians who had an opportunity to grow, to experiment, and to advance their art (in 1989 most jazz players can't even find enough work to earn a real living). It's doubtful that modern jazz would ever have been born without the swing bands to incubate it. Think of the hundreds of important jazzmen who started with the big dance orchestras—either as sidemen or listeners—who were first attracted to jazz by hearing this music on the radio and jukeboxes. Now think of the millions of record buyers, movie-goers, dancers, and radio owners who became jazz fans because of the swing bands. You come to realize that jazz-at-large was still benefiting from the positive effects of the swing era at least fifteen to twenty years after it ended.

For band vocalists, it's easiest to think of these years as the "Hellenic Era"—not only as a parallel to the flowering of art and culture in ancient Greece but because virtually all of the major singers of the period happened to be named Helen. (Benny Goodman quickly gave up keeping track of his canaries and simply called all of them "Pops.")

Fletcher Henderson, Don Redman, Duke Ellington, and the other black bandleaders and arrangers developed the idea of orchestral jazz by means of juxtaposing improvised solos with prescored ensemble passages, and we've seen how Paul White-man and the white bands established the vocal refrain formula. At the same time, Louis Armstrong made the soloist the most important man in jazz, and in tandem with Bing Crosby, worked out a system for pure jazz and popular music to interact, each as a basis for the other. Lastly, we traced how the three White Goddesses built on the Armstrong-Crosby foundation and re-claimed the role of singer-with-the-band as woman's work. Benny Goodman, then, may not have been able to contribute purely musical innovations on the order of Jelly Roll Morton or Thelonious Monk, but his creation, the swing dance band, is still among the most important in Western music. He provided the final step of jazz's evolution into a popular music, the logical culmination of all the innovations that had come before him, by playing music from the jazz tradition, original pieces (often riff-based flagwavers) and, most importantly, current pop tunes and ballads in the modern swing idiom, with jazz-influenced canaries to sing them.

Though the first of the Hellenic dynasty was actually Helen Rowland (aka Helen Daniels), who sang on records by Fred Rich, Freddy Martin, Ben Selvin, and others (and stylistically belonged in Ruth Etting's croonette club), Helen Ward toured with Benny Goodman's ground-breaking first band and thus became the archetype of the early canaries. Born in New York City on September 19, 1916, Ward began fooling around with the piano at age three; at sixteen she joined the then-aspiring songwriter Burton Lane, whose aunt played bridge with Ward's mother, in a piano-vocal act. Not long after leaving high school she joined Nye Mayhew's dance orchestra (a band noteworthy only in that it once had Ward as its vocalist), which led to a string of stints with other sweet groups, among them Eddy Duchin, Enric Madriguera, David Rubinoff (with boy singer Bob Crosby), Will Osborne, and Roxanne's Orchestra on her own show on station WOR in New York. Goodman hired her in October or November 1934, thereby putting the finishing touch on the band that would inaugurate the swing era nine months later.

Clearly, Goodman, his rabbi John Hammond, and his agent Willard Alexander wanted Ward because she specialized in those 4/4 rhythms at medium to fast tempi at which the band played virtually everything, even ballads. Ward comes across so sure and so right at quarter notes and diatonic intervals that if you take her away from these—as on a 1935 aircheck of the "personality" number "You're Not the Only Oyster in the Stew"— she sounds uncomfortable. Ward basically is a streamlined Lee Wiley, sharing the older woman's way with diatonic lines and trimming Wiley's smokey vibrato just as Count Basie trimmed Fats Waller and giving a terrific lift to the whole band.

At age twenty, Ward retired to marry Albert Marx, in December 1936, opening the door for a succession of Wiley-Ward types: The best known was Martha Tilton (a star at Goodman's Carnegie Hall concert); Louis Tobin (the first Mrs. Harry James), who later did some fine singles for MGM and live dates with Stan Hasselgarde, and, when last heard from, was co-running a nightclub in downtown Denver with her current husband, Peanuts Hucko; Jane Harvey; Marilyn Moore; Barbara

Lea (the last of the BG canaries); and, an artist with even stronger ties to Wiley, Peggy Lee.

Ward's own retirement was never more than semi: Just as Wiley became the official vocalist of the Condon gang, Ward served as canary on call for Goodman alumni (a role also filled from time to time by Mildred Bailey). Five months after quitting, she unretired herself to help BG out on a broadcast; she pitched in for Gene Krupa on his first session before he had located his own steady chirper. Ward guest starred on one of Teddy Wilson's small-group dates in the spot normally taken by Billie Holiday; she helped out Harry James on his cover of Sammy Kaye's hit "Daddy" when James's only regular singer was Dick Haymes (already enough of a sexually surreptitious, not to mention Nabokovian ditty to start with) and then did a few months on the road with James in 1941. Ward also did a V-Disc date with Red Norvo's Overseas Spotlight Band in 1943, and toured with Hal McIntyre's orchestra. During 1946 and 1947 she worked the other side of the mike, producing radio shows for WMGM (including Vic Damone's), but came closest to a genuine comeback in 1953 when she and BG hit the road together for the last time, and, after twenty years in the business, made her first record as a solo act. On these performances, as well as her mid-fifties appearance with Larry Clinton and Wild Bill Davison and also on recent albums, it's clear that the more she sounds like Lee Wiley, the more she sounds like herself.

By virtue of the role she played in the Goodman success story, Ward became the model for virtually all mid-thirties canaries; her exuberant, toe-tapping approach affecting not only her successors and counterparts in other bands, but even those who had come before her, like Duke Ellington's Ivie Anderson. The two singers who owed the most to Ward never gave her reason to worry. At the time, publicists described both Martha Tilton, Ward's replacement with the Goodman band from 1937 to 1939, and Edythe Wright, the singer with Tommy Dorsey's first band for four pivotal years, as "song stylists," a term conceived to hide their considerable failings as musicians.

Although the singing of both improves over time (Wright

doesn't sound bad by 1939; Tilton turned out some surprisingly swell solos for Capitol, among them the Mel Torme–penned hit "Stranger in Town" from 1946), their vocal duties took a backseat to their glamour chores: filling those sequined gowns, decorating bandstands, and giving the gal jitterbugs reason to get sore at their pubescent boyfriends.

Jazz people never considered Wright one of their own, and for this reason it's impossible to learn anything about her other than that she came from Bayonne, New Jersey, and, according to Dorsey confidant Jack Egan, had a long-running affair with her very-married bandleader. In contrast to Wright, who did nothing in music after leaving TD in 1939, Tilton used her band tenure as a stepping-stone to a career of solo (and occasionally band) gigs on records, movies, USO tours, and hundreds of radio shows.

While the discographies of Wright and Tilton are enormous, consider three excellent singers, second only to Ward herself in the finger-snapping bounce department, who were fated to record only a handful of sides with bands that never got off the ground. Kathleen (aka Kitty) Lane and Gail Reese each sang with Bunny Berigan and Glenn Miller's ill-fated first (and thoroughly unsoppy) band, as did Kathleen Long with Berigan and an unsuccessful early Charlie Barnet group. Lane will be best remembered by George Simon's description of her as "A gorgeously proportioned girl who, for my dough, sang better than any girl singer Glenn [Miller] ever had"—an observation born out both by photographs and her few recordings.

But if you're looking for mountains of unrealized potential, you can't do any better than Teddy Grace. After a few promising sessions and one film appearance with Mel Hallett, Grace became the only vocalist with Bob Crosby to be truly worthy of that great hot band, including the leader himself. At the same time, Jack Kapp recorded her as a soloist (all her records were on Decca) with a terrific series of small jazz groups both black and white, doing blues and standards with blues affiliations—two rarities for the supercommercial Kapp. On these she proves herself the blackest white singer who ever lived, displaying a propensity for the blues greater than that of most colored canaries of the period. Had it not been for her disappearance in the early forties (if anyone knows where she is, let me know),* and then the coming of Kay Starr, there's no doubt that we'd be celebrating Teddy Grace as the definitive white blues singer.

On the positive side, Bea Wain and Ivie Anderson represent the relatively few canaries in whose cases talent translated into productivity. Wain has such a distinctive sound that it's surprising to learn she started singing in radio vocal groups, one of which served as Kate Smith's background choir (not that the humongous Smith ever needed any more background than she already had), where blandness rates as an asset. Besides her Ward-era sense of swing and her occasionally adventurous use of time (hear how she doubles the tempo at the right moments in "Dipsy Doodle" and in the last four bars of "Whistle While You Work"), you can't mistake Wain for any other singer because she has the thickest New York accent in jazz or any of its fringe areas. This makes it difficult for her to handle Americana, whether ersatz, like "It's a Lonely Trail," or real, like Willard Robison's "Old Folks," but adds to the sophistication of "You Go to My Head" and gives a touch of J.A.P.-iness right where it belongs on "My Heart Belongs to Daddy." Nothing like Wain was ever heard in pop music until Frank Sinatra captivated the country with his hearty Hobokenisms a few years later.

At nineteen, in 1937, Wain graduated from the chorus (those of Fred Waring, Kay Thompson, and Ted Straetter) to the canary perch in veteran Gene Kardos's dance band (her best side there being "A Gypsy from Poughkeepsie") and from there she went on to the gig that made her a national name, one year with Larry Clinton and His Orchestra. Clinton, a very intelligent,

---

* Someone did. Collector David McCain located Grace, now 86 but alive and well, in a senior citizens' home in La Mirada, California. It turned out that Grace had joined the WACS early in the war, and was put on a rigorous schedule of recruiting shows for that organization. The schedule was so rough on her throat that she lost before the war was over, and never sang professionally again.

musically minded man, made some strange decisions. He didn't form his own band until after he had masterminded the sounds of both Tommy Dorsey's band and that of the Casa Loma Orchestra in the mid-thirties, so his own band never sounded like anything other than an imitation of either group. Also, Clinton chose to lead an "arranger's band"—that is, he made his own writing more important than hiring any worthwhile jazz players—at a time when even Glenn Miller (whom Woody Herman once described as "a real smart guy about business") employed Bobby Hackett and Ernie Caceres. Ultimately, the only reason we listen to Clinton records today is Bea Wain.

When Clinton and Wain are on a roll, the results can be terrific. The same way Clinton's arranger's ear attracted him to as idiosyncratic a singer as Wain, it also helped him build the most extraordinary of band books in an era when pop tunes and flagwavers dominated. Clinton and Wain took "Martha," which in the hands of Connee Boswell and the Bobcats had been a strictly New Orleans affair, and brought it uptown to New York. And as they made an honest woman out of "Martha," they sullied a phrase from Debussy, adding lyrics and bringing it down to earth, creating the pop standard "My Reverie," and did even better with an aria from Saint-Saëns's *Samson and Delilah*, "My Heart at Thy Sweet Voice." The impeccable Wain never fails to captivate us as Clinton's brassmen play natty little curlicues around her, and is no less compelling on a short series of sides made apart from Clinton with her in the spotlight.

After leaving Clinton in 1939, she concentrated on radio work (starring on "Your Hit Parade" for years) and recorded rarely. To this day she and announcer/husband Andre Baruch remain a permanent fixture on the airwaves, Wain unfortunately not singing but spinning other people's records. When she does perform—usually at multistar gatherings that spell "nostalgia" with a capital N—she proves that she's lost none of her chops and power and is still pronouncing the word "clear" (in "Our Love Is Here to Stay") as "cle-ah."

Even before Ivie Anderson joined Duke Ellington's Famous

Orchestra in 1931, she had proved herself a singer who could appeal to black and white audiences alike, and she came aboard Ellington's bandwagon just as he was about to achieve the international recognition for which he and manager Irving Mills had worked long and hard. Anderson, born to a couple named Smith in a small town outside Oakland, California, on July 10, 1905,* learned to sing at a convent. In 1922 the hoofers-turned-bookers Fanchon and Marco "discovered" Anderson and sent her out to dance on their white vaudeville circuit in a unit headlined by Mamie Smith. Before the twenties were over she would sing on both coasts and even in Australia, her better gigs including both the New York and Los Angeles Cotton Clubs, and the Mark Hopkins Hotel in San Francisco, where she became the first black vocalist to work with a white band, Anson Weeks and His Orchestra. After doing specialties in front of numerous black bands and in her own Fanchon and Marco package, she settled down to a year-long engagement in Chicago's Grand Terrace with the house band there, Earl Hines and His Orchestra. In February 1931, Duke Ellington came to town to play the Oriental Theatre, caught Hines's show at the Grand Terrace, and, according to legend,† asked Anderson to go on the road with his band immediately. She accepted only after repeated assurances from Hines that she was good enough.

Previously, Ellington had explored his own unique approach to the use of a voice in the orchestra, and though he occasionally used vocalists in the conventional way, he never took it seriously enough to sign on a steadily working singer (using instead studio freelancers, his own musicians, and even his agent). Anderson made her first records with the band a year after she joined (some months after Whiteman began recording with Bailey).

Even so, in Anderson he had caught no ordinary canary. She must have reminded him just slightly of Adelaide Hall and some

---

* This date is according to Chilton. Feather and other sources list 1904.

† Set down in the *Pittsburgh Courier* on January 7, 1950.

of the other "sophisticated" black ladies of the twenties, like Ethel Waters, Josephine Baker, and Eva Taylor, and others who grew in popularity as the blues craze faded. But along with a touch of Hall's arty trilling, Anderson also shared her facility to launch effortlessly into a growling, bluesy scat routine. Even more important, she could also adjust to the economically swinging style that became triumphant in 1935 with Ward and Goodman, though Anderson was always warmer and more expressive than any of Ward's comparatively "cool" followers.

Anderson introduced any number of major Ellington compositions—from her first record, "It Don't Mean a Thing (If It Ain't Got That Swing)" (1932), in which Ellington achieves a balance between wordless vocals and lyrics, to "I Got It Bad (and That Ain't Good)." But we remember her mainly for the dozens of unimportant and wonderfully insignificant little songs that seemed to exist only for Anderson to sing; since many were in fact written by Ellington, this could well have been the case. Every Ellington buff has his own favorites; my own are Ivie's uniquely convincing version of one of the all-time great dumb metaphor songs, "Love Is like a Cigarette," and the old-timer "When My Sugar Walks Down the Street," which she makes sound like "meshuga," and two minor pieces of Ellingtonia, the optimistic "Oh, Babe, Maybe Someday" and "The Chocolate Shake"* (a dance with historical lyrics along the lines of "Rhythm Saved the World" and "Some Like It Hot"), which she makes into Ducal classics.

She sang "Stormy Weather" with the band on a record, in a movie short, and most significantly at the London Palladium during the band's first overseas tour where, by all accounts, she stopped the show. An unnamed critic described her as "a coloured lady who sings 'Stormy Weather' as you'll never hear it again," and Ellington himself remembered, "The audience and

---

* Stanley Dance tells me Helen Humes once named "I'm Satisfied" (1933, Brunswick) as her favorite Anderson record.

all the management broke down crying and applauding. . . .
Ivie did the most believable performance ever." She did the
same for "All God's Chillun Got Rhythm," a movie tune that
gave Anderson her first record under her own name and her
only featured appearance in a major film, and in turn Anderson
gave it a permanent place in the jazz repertoire. (Along with "I
Got Rhythm," "All God's Chillun" became one of the foundation
chord sequences of the entire bebop movement.) A comparison
of Anderson's definitive version with the young Judy Garland's
cover for Decca illustrates the very meaning of swing: Garland is
stiff as a board from note one, and having no idea which beats to
emphasize, just chomps down on all of them. Even in her attempts to scat (which were doubtlessly written out and not improvised), Garland is the very stuff of anti-swing and comes
across like a square at the fair.

The Los Angeles musical show *Jump for Joy* marked Ivie
Anderson's last important appearance with Duke Ellington; she
left the band in the summer of 1942, partly because the chronic
asthma that would eventually kill her made it impossible for her
to sing full-time. From this point on she performed only sporadically, in California and Mexico City, and recorded rarely,
none of her later sides capturing the splendor of her Ellington
years. Though she died very young—at age forty-five—and long
out of the limelight, she was far from impecunious at the time of
her death. With the help of her first husband, Marques Neal,
she made a success of an L.A. eatery called the Chicken Shack,
and then in real estate with her second husband, Walter Collins.
She left no will when she died on December 28, 1949, and both
men went into a legal battle over her estate. I never heard how
it came out, but obviously her most important legacy was her
eleven years with Duke Ellington. "They still talk about Ivie,"
he wrote years later, "and every girl singer we've had since has
had to try to prevail over the Ivie Anderson image."

At first listen, or even first two or three, Helen O'Connell
sounds like anything but a central figure in the bandsinger hall
of fame. She's never really flat, well not *all* the time, not by

much anyway, but she can't handle more than, say, five or six notes, and she never has enough wind to hold anything for more than a couple of beats at the most. Jazz fans hated O'Connell: To them the novelties she did with Jimmy Dorsey's band took time away from his straight-blowing charts like "Dusk in Upper Sandusky" and "Long John Silver." And to a certain extent their animosity was justified: At the peak of the band era, Helen O'Connell was a pretty sour singer. But O'Connell was the first "comedienne" canary, a breed that became more and more popular as the thirties (and the depression) ended, and dozens of chirpers aped her daffy mannerisms (even the young Anita O'Day, then with Gene Krupa, covered O'Connell's hit "Green Eyes").

Certainly no one could ever accuse O'Connell of being a vocal athlete; Sarah Vaughan's football and Ella Fitzgerald's basketball-of-the-larynx are not for her. Instead, O'Connell's navigation of the notes she can and cannot hit reminds me of miniature golf, and there are times when one is in the mood for miniature golf. As Bob Eberle, the other half of Jimmy Dorsey's vocal section, told George Simon, O'Connell's limited range forced her to swerve toward notes that were always just an arm's length away. She *has* to work harder, and though she may, especially in the early Dorsey years, overdo it, each line she sings is carefully and intelligently thought out beforehand.

Even if much of her work with Dorsey is as bad as her detractors said (a 1940 film, short in which she does an obnoxious "My Wubba Dolly" like Shirley Temple imitating Ella F., is the all-time nadir, her earliest solo sides for Capitol sound remarkably better. As her button-nose cuteness grew into a *Playboy* magazine kind of beauty, she recorded a pair of albums for Victor (and a set of transcriptions recently issued on Hindsight), by which time she was a truly fine singer in an age of fine singers. So much of the time O'Connell is silly and banal, but at her best she casts a spell over an audience that many singers blessed with superchops could never fathom.

Case in point: Marion Hutton, who fulfilled the same function with Glenn Miller's orchestra that O'Connell did for Jimmy Dorsey's, illustrates the dangers of chops without class. Where most of the bands use a songbird for the romantic ballads and a guy from one of the sections doing a Satchmo impression for the rhythm numbers, Dorsey and Miller employed crooners for the serious numbers and dizzy dames for the silly ones. In fact, just to make sure Hutton would never get near any halfway decent ditty, Miller gave all the better up-tempo numbers to his superb singing saxist, Tex Beneke, while Hutton got stuck with the muck. The good songs got through to her only by accident. Miller didn't want a diva; he wanted to give his jitterbug fans one of their own: a dancing, jiving chick who acted coy and made with the eyes. As a result, only a few of Marion Hutton's dozens of recorded vocals are worth listening to today ("Ding! Dong! The Witch Is Dead" and the aircheck of "Back to Back" are two). On many, her vocals destroy the momentum built up just as the band really starts to take off.

The same thing holds true for most of O'Connell and Hutton's male counterparts, even though nearly all the boy singers of the band era had a worthy archetype in Bing Crosby. "All the singers tried to be Crosbys," pointed out Englishman Sam Costa. "You were either a high Crosby or a low Crosby, and we all had that quaver in the voice." It's hardly surprising. Crosby was *the* popular singer before, during, and after the swing years, and many of the major white bandleaders (the Dorseys, Miller, Berigan, Goodman) had worked with him in their sideman days. During these years the Crosby-Armstrong approach was the only one for male singers, and Frank Sinatra attracted attention at first simply because he was not a Crosby imitator. When the Dorsey Brothers put together their first touring band, they even instructed their arranger (Miller again) to give the orchestra "a Crosby sound." But while the dance-band crooners approximated his baritone and "that quaver," none could touch him in range, emotional depth, or swing. Not all the Crosbys were white; at least three Negro crooners pegged themselves as "Black Bings" and "Colored Crosbys": Harlan Lattimore (with

Don Redman), Roy Felton (with Benny Carter), and Herb Jeffries (with Duke Ellington). Nor were they all Americans; the
list of Bing's international impersonators could make a good gag
for "Late Night with David Letterman": Dick Todd, the Canadian Bing Crosby (briefly with Larry Clinton); Denny Dennis,
the British Bing Crosby (with Roy Fox and later, on this side of
the pond, Tommy Dorsey); and Jean Sablon, the French Bing
Crosby (who sang like "Le Bing" affecting a phony French accent).

The best remembered of the bogus Bings would have to be
Jimmy Dorsey's Bob Eberle (older brother of Glenn Miller's
Ray Eberly), who, at the time Dorsey served as accompanist on
Crosby's "Kraft Music Hall" broadcasts, had the honor of
singing—though not recording— their special Crosby arrangements at the band's live appearances (an unusual example of a
band singer going longer than thirty-two or tops forty bars). My
own favorite of the breed, though, is Bob Carroll, a handsome-
voiced crooner who marched briefly in the long, long Charlie
Barnet parade of vocalists and also appeared with Jimmy Dorsey
and Glenn Miller's A.A.F. Orchestra. Like Dick Todd, Bob
Carroll tried to recapture the more intense, melodramatic
Crosby of the early thirties (what the singer once jokingly called
his "Brunswick key"). He came the closest on September 11,
1941, Barnet's only date with strings, producing the best
straight-as-written band version of the Raye-DePaul standard-
to-be "I'll Remember April." On this and other dates, Barnet
used Carroll as much, as we'll see, as Ellington used Herb Jeffries, counteracting the crooner's immaculate, smooth baritone
with his own more emotional soprano sax obbligati and any number of Duke-ishly growling trumpets and paper-tearing trombones. Though both Eberly (and Eberle, for that matter) and
Carroll faded with the band biz, for Crosby's three greatest
protégés—Buddy Clark (who sang with Benny Goodman and
others), Dick Haymes (with Goodman, Tommy Dorsey, and
Harry James), and Perry Como (with Ted Weems)—the end of
the band era signified only the beginning of their own careers.

By the time the bands began to fade, the reigning queen of the canaries was the third Helen, Forrest, whose sultry siren qualities reflected the seriousness of the war years even as the mid-depression called for solid-four hipchicks like Helen Ward and the end of that decade led to ding-a-lings like Helen O'Connell and Marion Hutton. Forrest summed up her whole idiom in one marvelously succinct quote that ran in a 1944 issue of *Look* magazine: "I try to sing so a guy can picture soft lights and his girl."*

But when she made her first recordings with Artie Shaw in September of 1938, Forrest could only hint at the ability to make anybody picture anything. During her fifteen months with that deservedly legendary aggregation she achieved a mastery of the thirty-two-bar vocal refrain structure rivaled by no one before or since. Still, no one listening at the time could have predicted how her style would develop. On her Shaw appearances, particularly the live ones captured on airchecks, Forrest unleashes far more excitement and emotional involvement than anyone from the Ward ward would, at times nearly screaming and shouting like a slightly toned-down Garland. Yet instead of curbing this tendency, she refines it and nurtures it until it dominates every note that comes out of her mouth. In conquering the single chorus refrain, Forrest learned to slightly exaggerate. She makes every emotion a tad bigger by making every high note a bit higher, every interval a notch bigger, and every pause a step more dramatic. Think of a blue note—that is, for our purposes, a step in a scale made more minor than it ought to be. Reverse that idea to where major steps sound even more major, and you have a pretty good idea how Helen Forrest sings. I've never heard her do either "My Funny Valentine" or "I Love Paris," but if she did I could easily imagine her singing the minor passages in major.

---

* Not counting a recently discovered audition disc made under the pseudonym "Bonnie Blue."

Luckily, this trick salvages most of Forrest's work with Benny Goodman, whose band she joined after Shaw broke up his own to cool his doggies south of the border. The Forrest-Goodman discs need rescuing because of the presence of Eddie Sauter, BG's chief arranger at the time, whose charts are heady, often hollow creations that were extremely difficult to play and not always worth the effort. But though their sterility impedes the chances of any good blowing, even that by the toasty-warm trumpeter Cootie Williams and the usually undauntable leader himself, Forrest's uppercase emotionalism is precisely what is called for to inject a little life into Sauter's dead pan. Forrest left Goodman for personal more than musical or career reasons, one of which was a charge also leveled at him by Anita O'Day, that BG's obbligatos behind singers were blatant attempts to hog the spotlight for himself.

How different in every way was her liaison with Harry James! Instead of constructing art out of radical and perhaps accidental juxtapositions, Helen Forrest and Harry James's Musicmakers were meant for each other. Here she was the gushy, sentimental singer with the big, sentimental band led by the strapping, sentimental trumpeter who rarely let on that he was one of the finest hot men in jazz. As such, the Forrest-James combination provided just what the doctor ordered for the romance-starved Americans of World War II, and side after side of theirs made it to the top ten. To give them even more sentiment, James gave them more Forrest, resulting in the gradual abandoning of the vocal refrain formula. Today, when bands feature singers, they largely follow the pattern of James and Forrest in using the vocal with accompaniment (singer-band-singer) rather than the band with vocal pattern (band-singer-band).

The change in structure helped Forrest at first—as it did all singers—but it turned on her in the long run. On the strength of her hits with James she went out as a solo act, getting, at first, the bookings and contracts that stars got. Unfortunately, her technique got in the way. That extra oomph that allowed her to cram so much into thirty-two bars was just too much when she expanded her role to seventy-two bars or more. But what's ironic is that although Forrest became sort of a walking jukebox of her biggies from way back, she sang these songs better in the fifties and sixties. By comparison, Helen O'Connell was a completely different artist in 1955; Forrest was the same artist, only better (as her wonderful last confrontation with *Harry James in Hi-Fi* [1955, Capitol] will attest). But she never figured out how to be interesting all by herself, and could only create something meaningful as a duet partner (to Dick Haymes) or a cog in the dance-band machinery.

Which points up the central failing of the band singer as a breed: They *all* had severe limits that were accepted as givens throughout the band biz and had little chance to expand beyond them. Hence, slotting them into Helen-related categories doesn't seem nearly as crude as it would for any other species of jazz artist. Bandleaders, especially those who had more than one vocalist on the payroll, would use them in different ways, much the same way as they'd use one trumpeter to play lead and another to solo.

Duke Ellington, that master of typecasting, once traveled with four singers: The contrived contralto Kay Davis did excessively straight numbers like "If You Are but a Dream," which apes Rodgers and Hammerstein's stolidity, as well as the reclassicalized wordless wailing on "Creole Love Call"; Joya Sherrill romped through "Kissing Bug"; Al Hibbler handled the blues; and Marie Ellington (billed only by her first name and no relation to Duke, although soon to be Mrs. Nat King Cole) got a few leftovers. And if that weren't enough, he'd often summon trumpeter and violinist Ray "Floorshow" Nance to the mike for a rhythm specialty like "(Otto Make That) Riff Staccato."

So band singing was a limited art, and even those whom I've praised most enthusiastically ran into constant dead ends. Furthermore, happy marriages between band and vocalist were as rare as cops in *Il Trovatore*, even at the pinnacle of band-dom. True, Forrest and James found each other, as did Doris Day and Les Brown, and the fine Mary Ann McCall managed to land gigs with the likes of Charlie Barnet and Woody Herman, whose bands suited her hip and lightly blue sound. But we'd listen to Bob Crosby's records a lot more today if he'd held on to Teddy Grace, and Bea Wain really deserved better and hotter than Larry Clinton (Hotel Taft bandleader George Hall gradually turned his band into a vehicle for his strongest attraction, the rhythmic belter Dolly Dawn, but that particular combination lacked a really sharp arranging mind—a Sy Oliver, a Ralph Burns—requisite for making music for the moment and the ages). Band instrumentals will always be more desirable than vocal numbers, which seems like a waste as there is nothing inherent in the band-singer combination that renders it any less jazzy.

However, none of these warnings apply to the three crucial artists who lauched their careers with Count Basie and His Orchestra, which made even Benny Goodman's and Duke Ellington's vocal departments fight for second place. By this I mean Helen Humes, Jimmy Rushing, and Joe Williams.

Helen Ward could get you to snap your fingers, Helen O'Connell could make you laugh, and Helen Forrest would move you to tears, but only Helen Humes, the greatest of the Helens, could wrap you around her little finger and get you to do exactly what she wanted. No singer ever covered as much ground as Humes, for despite the endless variety of the recordings of Rosemary Clooney and Bing Crosby, for example, only Humes left us with a half-dozen completely different bodies of work, each of which can stand on its own independent of the others. From the classic blues of the twenties to the rhythm and blues of the forties, and from the raucousness of the Jazz at the Philharmonic (JATP) bread and circuses to the smooth sophistication of the New York "niteries," Humes sang it all.

But this multistylistic accomplishment had its negative ramifications, too. If she couldn't be tied down to one milieu, then press and PR people had a tough time getting the public to remember her at all. She spent too much time in the shadows of other black female singers, for one thing, having replaced Billie Holiday in the Count Basie Orchestra in 1938 and Lena Horne at the Cafe Society in 1941. And though she toured with Norman Granz's JATP troupe for five seasons, not only did the impresario elect not to record her, but, apparently, only used her to warm up the seat for Ella Fitzgerald. Lastly, Humes's final comeback, in her mid-sixties, came about only partially because of her talent. Like Alberta Hunter and Maxine Sullivan, Humes had both outlived her competitors and had traded on the illicit thrill audiences enjoyed of hearing someone their grandmother's age singing about sex.

However, this marvelous and always tasteful use of what Preston Sturges called "Topic A" was always more than her strong point; it was the nexus between each of her myriad incarnations. Humes was our greatest master of the double entendre. Most blues singers, especially Bessie Smith, were interested in getting only one point across, but Humes milked the technique for everything it was worth. In reminiscing about her first sessions, made in 1927 when Humes was all of fourteen, she told Stanley Dance, "Of course I didn't know then what the words of the songs [i.e.; "Do What You Did Last Night"] really meant."

In listening to Humes—these prepubuscent blues performances and everything else—you can't be sure that she ever did learn. So just when she's got you absolutely convinced that *she thinks* that a lyric is as innocent as a Sunday school picnic, she'll throw you a knowing wink by lightly inflecting a certain syllable a certain way just to make certain you'll think again. She bridged all the generations of women's blues because she could play both the virginal kitten and the lewd minx at the same time, giving you an idea of what *Otello* would have been like had Desdemona been the Moor.

"They'll never want to film the story of my life," Humes told Leonard Feather in 1961. "I came from a happy family. . . . People don't like to hear about you when it's all happiness and contentment—you have to be drug [sic] through the mud and you have to be standing on the corner. But all I know is the good things in life." It doesn't matter if this statement, if not a bald-faced lie, has been literally doused in whitewash. Humes knew discrimination and not only in the South. Humes knew about good rye whiskey and had to have a fifth of it before each recording date;* Humes also knew the gambling bug—perhaps because she was raised so close to the Kentucky Derby in Louisville—and with it the humiliation of going broke at the track and being arrested in gambling raids. Humes knew what it was like to be forgotten by bookers and producers and to have to support oneself by labor both menial and manual. In short, Humes knew what it was like to be "drug through the mud," but she chose only to talk about "the good things in life."

After her 1927 sessions, Humes went back to school at her mother's insistence (though Okeh Records wanted to send her out on the road) and worked both in and out of music, as she would for the rest of her life. She made the transition from classic blues to band canarydom with tenor player Al Sears, first in Buffalo (she had gone there on a visit) and then in Cincinnati and New York, where Sears broke up his group but brought Humes and himself into Vernon Andrade's Renaissance Ballroom Orchestra. Count Basie, who wanted Humes for his band ever since he'd heard her with Sears in Ohio, got her on his payroll with the help of John Hammond. "We replaced Billie [Holiday] with Helen Humes as fast as we could," Basie wrote in his autobiography. "And we hung on to her as long as we could, which was for four years."

While the Okeh recordings prove Humes to be one of the all-time champs at the blues in general and the double entendre in particular, the twenty-six numbers she recorded during her stay with Basie showcase a completely different Helen Humes. This one has a light, diaphanous tone and shows time obviously spent listening to Mildred Bailey ("I just loved the way *she* sang," Humes told Dance), though Humes tempered Bailey's style with the rhythmic propulsion of the Ward era. The most interesting of the lot are four made with Basie's band under the direction and name of Harry James, wherein the pixieish Humes

* According to producer Bob Porter.

makes clear that she's a cherub in attitude as well as physiognomy, and on a very minor-sounding Basie version of Porter's
"My Heart Belongs to Daddy."

John Hammond and Basie got Humes out of the territory
bands and into the big time, and Leonard Feather helped her
into the next phase of her life. Feather had already written and
arranged a specialty number for Humes and Basie ("My Wan-
dering Man," one of her only blues with that band) and subsequently put together her first two post-Basie recording sessions:
the first with altoist Pete Brown on Decca, which included the
best of Feather's original compositions, "Mound Bayou"; the
second under Humes's own name for the smaller, black-oriented
label, Savoy Records. The material on this date more than su-
perficially resembles the genre that would come to be known as
"rhythm and blues," not least because of a tenor player who
sounds like he's trying to honk but succeeding only in blowing
his sax apart. This session established Humes as having a black
audience apart from Basie's, and when another independent
outfit, Aladdin Records, followed it with more sexually risqué
blues and jump tunes recorded at a date in 1945, Humes walked
out with a major hit in "E-Baba-Le-Ba" that brought her work on
the R&B circuit for the next ten years.

Feather ironically detested this phase of Humes's career, describing her singing in his *Encyclopedia of Jazz* as having "de-
generated . . . into a more commonplace blues-shouting
technique." Though this period may undoubtedly be her least
interesting phase (coinciding with her unrecorded JATP stint), it
did result in many worthwhile records. Double-entendre blues
dominated; Humes described them as "little cute blues . . .
little fun blues, something to make people laugh"; Jelly Roll
Morton might have called them "riffs so old they've got whis-
kers." For instance, take the only two numbers that stayed in
Humes's act until the end, "E-Baba-Le-Ba," a set of blues lyrics
set against eight-to-the-bar rhythm that Basie and Jimmy Rushing had recorded in 1937 as "Boogie Woogie (I May Be Wrong)"
and which Lionel Hampton still plays as "Hey Bop A Re Bop."

The other, "Million-Dollar Secret," extolled the virtues of young-old entanglements on varying sides, and got released as "Helen's Advice" and "New Million-Dollar Secret." But during these years she also created lovely readings of the Sinatra ballad "This Love of Mine," Cole Porter's "Laziest Gal in Town" (a nonblues double entendre for a change), and a terrific older song that would be forever associated with her, "Every Now and Then," a performance unjustly overlooked at the time because it came out on the B side of "E-Baba-Le-Ba." On these and on Benny Carter's hard-hitting "Rock Me to Sleep" she uses a heavier, more expressive sound than she or anyone else would have tried ten years earlier.

So even if she wasted her voice on a lot of junk in the forties and fifties, in the long run you could hardly call it degeneracy. For when Humes swam back into the jazz mainstream at the end of the fifties—first with Red Norvo (on a tour that began in Australia and ended in Hollywood and on an album for RCA) and then on three brilliant albums for Contemporary Records— she had obviously grown as a performer. By now she could combine the two characters she had played, the timid little girl of "Sub-Deb Blues" with the lascivious shouter of "Knockin' Myself Out," into one fully rounded, three-dimensional performer. Marty Paich, the arranger and conductor of the best of the three Contemporary albums, *Songs I Like to Sing*, built all twelve scores around Humes, not only as the central voice in the score but incorporating her modus operandi into their construction, modeling them on her standard "If I Could Be with You" (which she had first recorded in two takes with Basie in 1939 and performed hundreds of times thereafter, including a live version from 1950 and a film with Basie's Octet from around the same time). Paich explained that he let Humes sing "the first choruses more or less straight, and then as Helen got more into the tune, improvising her jazz choruses, I tried to create a little more excitement." Paich and Humes did eight tracks with a conventional fourteen-piece big band, featuring such unapologetically modern soloists as Art Pepper and Jack Sheldon and Paich's advanced scoring. Among the tracks are a terrific, gospel-like "I Want a Roof over My Head" and a great, fast run-through of Humes's favorite blues, the one from St. Louis. The remaining four titles posit Humes and a single horn—the immortal Ben Webster—against a string background, and the two soloists turn in definitive interpretations of the ballads "Imagination" and "Every Now and Then," a superior remake of the 1945 Aladdin version.

By this point, Humes must have figured that nothing in her career could last, and the "California Comeback" (with Norvo and Contemporary) gradually lost its momentum. She made several return trips to Australia and played a blues festival in Paris, but then, "I wouldn't hear from the agents for six months," she told Feather, actually speaking of a similar and frequently repeated predicament of a decade earlier. "So I'd just forget about it and go off to the racetrack and lose my good money." Finally, in 1967, after Humes's mother died, she chucked the whole music thing and went to work making gunpowder in a Louisville munitions factory and "didn't even hum" for six years. Fortunately this retirement lasted only until 1973, when a few old friends lured her back into the limelight: Stanley Dance got her into that season's Newport Jazz Festival; Barney Josephson gave her a very important booking at his swank New York club, the Cookery, in 1975; and that same year John Hammond produced her only album for a major label, CBS's *It's the Talk of the Town*. The following year the *New York Times* ran a story headlined, "HELEN HUMES DISCOVERED AGAIN AT 63."

Humes recorded more prolifically in her sixties than in any other period of her life, almost exclusively for English and French labels but also for two American independents, Audiophile and Muse. Despite the presence of the sublime accompanist Ellis Larkins and the guiding hand of producer Hammond, the one Columbia album suffers from George Benson's deliberately corny licks and frightfully unimaginative selections. Do we really need a third "Every Now and Then" or a three millionth "If I Could Be with You"?

As it turned out, two 1979 recording sessions organized by a producer far less idealistic than Hammond became in retrospect the best of her later albums. True, her voice doesn't impress you with its strength as much as it did forty—or even four—years earlier, and occasionally she'll run into dead ends where her voice won't do what she wants. But the album *Helen Humes and the Muse All-Stars* works. Starting with the natural though obvious choice of Buddy Tate, her colleague from the Basie days who also appeared on the CBS and other Humes discs, two other saxists with stronger blues affiliations also participate, Arnett Cobb and Cleanhead Vinson. The latter duets superbly with Humes on the comic blues, "Outskirts of Town," his squeaky roughness matched by her smooth and understated sauciness. The set also contains a typically great dirty blues ("Loud Talking Woman"), a novelty calypso ("Woe Is Me," an ancient joke that Jack Buchanan had recorded in 1933 as "Adapted from the French"), and four terrific ballads. Only one of them is a remake—Humes moves forward on *The Muse All-Stars*, instead of just reliving her own past.

We'll never know how much farther Humes might have gone, because even though she made a slightly lesser follow-up album for Muse and a third was being planned, she died before it could be recorded. That was in 1981. She was sixty-eight.

In September 1970, at a recording session that no one knew would be the final one for Jimmy Rushing—who went back even farther with Basie than Humes or Billie Holiday, and was two years older than the Count himself—the singer told producer Don Schlitten that this had been the best session of his life. Dan Morgenstern, who was present, remembers thinking that this wasn't showbiz hyperbole, not only because Rushing was not the sort of man given to saying things he didn't mean, but that the date consisted of exclusively popular standards and ballads, with only one blues, and Jimmy Rushing had been showing the world for over forty years that he was more than a blues singer. Perhaps this came out of the black bourgeoisie attitude that looked down on the blues, but more likely it was an uncommonly accurate and insightful self-assessment, for the blues are only a small part of what Jimmy Rushing does. "Anytime a person can play the blues, he has a soul and he has a 'lift' to play anything else he wants to play," Rushing said in the 1957 "Sound of Jazz" telecast. "It's sort of like the foundation to a building."

But Rushing couldn't have built at all unless the foundation was pretty strong to begin with—that is, unless he was, as many people (myself included) feel, our all-time greatest male blues singer. Born in Oklahoma City on August 26, 1902 (from his fifties onward he would push the date back a year),* Rushing first became aware of the blues as an entity in themselves in his teens. "It was at Douglas High School that I found the blues," he said in 1946. "My daddy was a fine trumpet player [in brass bands and parades] and my mother was the best church singer I ever heard." More importantly, his mother's brother, Wesley Manning, "used to play piano and sing in the sporting houses" and "was responsible for me singing the blues." The Rushings tried to get their boy to learn "respectable" music, first the violin, then the mandolin, then the piano, but, as Rushing remembered, "Man, I had to do more than that to get across what I wanted to say . . . the piano and I got along fine and I still like to mess with the keyboard, but my kicks came from singing." Rushing Sr. became even more upset when Uncle Wesley would come home with "handfuls," "hatfuls," and even "basketfuls" (depending on the interviewer) of money in tips from the red-light district, and taught "Little Jimmy" how to sing and play the blues. Even after Rushing became good enough to play professionally, he generally avoided the good-paying gigs in the "houses of ill repute" for fear of his parents. Even so, forty years later he still recalled to the letter one of his uncle's whorehouse songs, "Tricks Ain't Walkin' No More," a blue dialogue between a pimp and one of his employees, and recorded it, performing both voices (the trollop's in falsetto) and accompanying himself on piano.

But even as Rushing matured as an artist, he never let himself

---

* This from Phil Schaap, confirmed in the April 1946 issue of *Hollywood Note*.

entirely outgrow the blues, even when the form could never completely contain him. He didn't have to turn every song into a blues, as Big Joe Turner, Aretha Franklin, and, in the early stages of her career, Dinah Washington did. Instead, he informed everything he sang with blues honesty and passion. As Rushing's sideman Rudy Powell pointed out to Burt Korall in 1957, "Jim's biggest influence has been the funky feeling. He knows the blues; what they are; why they exist and where they come from; that's what makes him the Daddy."

Tellingly, when Leonard Feather asked Rushing to write down his "favorite musicians on [his] instrument," he listed three vocalists who, like him, could handle the blues but were by no means limited to them: Bing Crosby, Ethel Waters, and Louis Armstrong. The parallel between Rushing and Waters comes through most strongly in that the label of "blues singer" haunted both, though the combination of Crosby and Armstrong holds even more meaning in the light of Rushing's work. Like both men, Rushing communicates the notion of a heavy, rough voice that comes out smooth because of the way he uses rhythm and inflected accents; to achieve the smoothness he's after, Rushing has simply *got* to swing, or else it's no go, a lesson Coleman Hawkins taught his followers. Rushing's rough gentleness, along with his organizing of notes, beats, and accents, points to Crosby. On his two best band vocals, "I Keep Remembering" and "The You and Me That Used to Be" (the latter extant only as a radio aircheck), you can hear it loud and clear, as well as on the ballad coda to his 1947 blues "Little Girl, Don't You Want a Man like Me?" and his 1963 "Please Come Back." On "Remembering," he repeatedly rushes over the middle syllable in one key phrase —"keep *re*-mem-ber-*ing*"; "sweet-*est* mem-or-*y*"—so that the unstressed beat could almost be one of Crosby's syncopated grace notes. In fact, it's easy to imagine Crosby's voice singing Rushing's entire vocal on "I Keep Remembering," note for note, pause for pause, accent for accent, although Bing would add embellishments that Rushing, in the Kaycee-Basie style, has streamlined away.

Three of Rushing's first long-playing albums, *Goin' to Chicago* (1954, Vanguard), *If This Ain't the Blues* (1957, Vanguard), and *The Jazz Odyssey of James Rushing, Esq.* (1956, Columbia), were conceived as musical autobiographies, the first remaking many of the songs Rushing made jazz standards with Basie, the second put together along geographical lines, the point being that we can think of Rushing's life as one of constant traveling. "I liked to travel and roam around in those days," he told Frank Driggs in 1966. "You couldn't keep me in one place very long." This was largely because his parents never approved of what he did for a living, although they must have been pleased when he stopped moving long enough to matriculate at Wilberforce University. However, Rushing never had to produce his college degree to convince people that he was literate, learned, and articulate. Before reaching age twenty-five, he had made it as far south as New Orleans, southwest to Fort Worth, north to Chicago, and in 1921 he left for Los Angeles, where he stayed for five years working as a singer, pianist, accompanist, and drummer. "A lot of people don't know this, but there was a lot of jazz being played out West then," Rushing informed Driggs. "That's when I met all the New Orleans boys like Dink Johnson, Mutt Carey, Buddy Petit, and all of them." But Rushing reserved his fondest memories for Jelly Roll Morton, whom he described to Stanley Dance as "the greatest thing I ever heard." "Every time Jelly Roll came up we split the take half and half," he told Douglas Hague in 1958, "which was all right by me 'cause Jelly really brought in the money."

But on Feather's *Encyclopedia* questionnaire, when Rushing is asked to summarize his career, he makes it clear that he felt it really began when he joined Walter Page's Blue Devils in 1926–27. Rushing had returned from the coast the year before, leaving the music business to be a cook in his father's hamburger stand in Oklahoma City. Page had been part of a touring show orchestra, which he left in 1925 to front his own band. "By 1925 the Blue Devils were getting big in the state," Rushing remembered for Dance, "and when they heard me sing one night, I was gone again! We toured all over the Southwest and were recognized as one of the top bands." In 1927, Rushing called Page's attention to a twenty-three-year-old pianist with another touring show, Bill (not yet "Count") Basie, and brought him into the Blue Devil fold. "I didn't audition Jimmy," as Basie later told Dance. "Jimmy auditioned me."

Basie stayed only a short time, because he and Rushing were gradually absorbed into the most prestigious of Midwest dance bands, Bennie Moten's Kansas City Orchestra. With the addition of these first-rate soloists and of special arrangements by Easterners Benny Carter and Horace Henderson, Moten's band might have become a territory counterpart to Fletcher Henderson's Orchestra (especially with the presence of the Hawkins-influenced Ben Webster), though, in Rushing, Moten had a singer far greater than anyone who worked with Henderson—or any other band. When Moten died, Rushing joined Basie's new band at Kansas City's Reno Club. As Basie later said, "There were times in the early days of the band that I'd have given it all up but for Jimmy's urging to stick with it."

Rushing waxed one blues with the Page group and nine numbers with Moten, but we really don't get any chance to hear him as length until he made twenty songs with Basie on the Decca label between 1937 and 1939. Where Helen Humes, who got on board the Basie superchief halfway through the Decca period, came off like a little girl singing about adult themes, the Kapps would have you think of Rushing as a mature man who sang numbers deliberately infantile in conception. Known as "rhythm" or "jump" tunes long before either term related to R&B, these songs inevitably combined fast tempos with nursery-rhyme texts wherein the words "jump," "children," and "mama" frequently reoccur, as in "Do You Wanna Jump, Children?" and "Mama Don't Want No Peas an' Rice an' Coconut Oil." Though it may be hard to tell one of these from another, they're all a hoot. Take his very sarcastic "Boo Hoo." It may be juvenilia from Lombardoland that only Huntz Hall could interpret as it deserved (see the movie *Dead End* for details), but Rushing treats it with humor and irony. The same applies to an early forties film soundie of "Take Me Back Baby," in which Rushing portrays a slumbering Basie sideman who dreams of crooning to a colored chorine. On "He Ain't Got Rhythm," Rushing's sole appearance with the Benny Goodman Orchestra, he sings the praises of jumping children indirectly by describing in gory detail the sorrows of the man who has prodigious accomplishments under his belt (in the manner of the protagonist of "I Can't Get Started") but who finds life is meaningless because he ain't got rhythm. Rushing clues us to what this chap is missing not so much through Irving Berlin's witty lyrics but by using his voice as a working model of the rapturous possibilities open to the one who *has* got rhythm.

The Basie numbers that served Rushing best were the blues specialties built around him. His first record, "Blue Devil Blues," set the format for these, and his third, "That Too, Do" (1930), anticipates two later classics, "Good Morning Blues" (also predicted by Bessie Smith in her 1923 "Jail House Blues") and "Sent for You Yesterday" (1938). On the most celebrated Basie-Rushing side, the four twelve-bar choruses on the 1941 "Goin' to Chicago Blues," Basie and the band fete Rushing's terse, controlled vocal with wild, anguished shouts in between his phrases on the first and last episodes, a turgid, bottom-to-top riff behind him on the second, and an ecstatic, antiphonous response to one key word of the lyric ("to-mor-row!") on the third. Though both this number and "I Left My Baby" use the same band and singer in the same setting, they represent two very different shades of the blues. Rushing instills the first with not entirely serious scornfulness, while the latter affords him the opportunity to display sincere sorrow for the gal he left in the backdoor cryin', "sayin' 'Son, you've got a home as long as I've got mine.' " All Rushing blues blend together ancient folk lyrics with the singer's own, which became codified into their present form when Basie and Rushing made them hits (and still more so when Jon Hendricks wrote words to the entire disc arrangement of "Chicago," including the fills behind Rushing). He then whittles them down into compact and constantly mobile phrases built on quarter notes. "As I kept singing I tried to develop my own style," he said in *Goin' to Kansas City*. "I think I always had a sort of telegraph style. Tried to stay with the short-liners. Like those words, 'I sent for you yesterday, here you come today.' "

In having both Rushing and Humes in his band bus, Basie dealt with the traditional limits of band singers by assigning his two different vocalists different material. It may have been appropriate for other band singers, but it was not for Rushing and Humes, each of whom could express the full range of human experiences. In divvying up the tunes, Basie imposed unnecessary limits on two great artists. Humes complained that Rushing got to do "all the blues, and originals" and Rushing probably wanted some of the good new songs that Humes got. Humes and Rushing could respond only by striking out on their own, although each would reteam with the Basie Octet around 1950 (by which time Rushing was the only forty-eight-year-old boy singer around). After leaving the band, each transcended the limits of the band-singing genre: Humes by scoring hits in the blues idiom, Rushing in that almost all of his post-Basie triumphs involved pop standards.

Rushing's solo career began with a string of strictly blues singles and two years of leading his own sextet, and then his major series of LPs for Vanguard and Columbia. As you'd expect, Rushing does tremendouly with a set of numbers associated with the Smith girls, perennial favorites of his whom he always lauded in interviews. (He credited Bessie and Clara Smith as being "the greatest blues singers who ever lived. There ain't a human being alive who can touch 'em." In 1946 and in 1957 he told Burt Korall that "the real blues singers, Bessie and Mamie Smith, showed me the way. Listen to them and you'll hear the blues.") A teaming with the Dave Brubeck Quartet turned out far better than anyone might have expected, though he'd have been better served by Thelonious Monk and the Modern Jazz Quartet.

Five Feet of Soul, his 1963 album arranged by Al Cohn, tops the list of Rushing's big-band projects and also led to a working partnership with tenor immortal Zoot Sims, the two having been brought together by another Okie singer, Marilyn Moore, who was then Mrs. Al Cohn. Though the Rushing-Sims group went unrecorded (and it often was the Rushing-Sims-Cohn group), it worked steadily at New York's Half Note and formed the nucleus of Rushing's last record, the classic *The You and Me That Used to Be.* Here they augmented their working band with the very worthy Budd Johnson and Ray Nance for the all-standards program that Rushing had striven for all his life. That very high baritone of his may betray its sixty-eight years here and there, but Rushing's joy is so infectious that any signs of strain are hardly worth mentioning. It was a good high note to end on. Rushing died on June 8, 1972, two months short of his seventieth birthday. Been here and gone, his lyric went, been here and gone.

The total excellence of Rushing and Humes becomes especially apparent when you compare them to their contemporaries. It seems absurd now that Rushing's rivals were Dan Grissom and Pha Terrell of, respectively, the Jimmie Lunceford and Andy Kirk orchestras. These men dealt with the blues and jazz influences by replacing it with a sort of open-toothed sibilance drawn from the genuine but nonetheless obnoxious black tradition of falsetto singing that found a better place in the perversely misnamed "soul" movement of the sixties and seventies. Still, while jazz collectors (usually white) nicknamed these two Dan "Gruesome" and Pha (pronounced, appropriately, "Fay") "Terrible," they had their admirers—among them the young Earl Coleman, who said, "Pha wasn't no *corny* tenor like Bill Kinney" (of the Ink Spots)—and even made hits for their bandleaders, most notably the Kirk-Terrell "Until the Real Thing Comes Along," perhaps the biggest-selling black record made up to that time. Those who knew Terrell or saw him perform, including Kirk himself, are quick to describe him as "really tall." They point this out apparently because that voice would sound odd coming out of anyone larger than four feet. White bandleader Jan Savitt's black singer, Bon Bon Tunnell, had a lot more to offer, including a giant sense of swing, which inspired both Jon Hendricks and Mel Torme. Humes had to compete with June Richmond, of the Jimmy Dorsey and Andy Kirk bands, and

Louis Armstrong's femme foil, Velma Middleton. But neither gave her any sleepless nights. Richmond could outbelt Humes and Middleton could roll her eyes something fierce, but neither could convince you of anything the way Humes could.

Only one band singer could compete with Humes and Rushing, and justifiably he became their successor: Joe Williams. Unlike Rushing, who seemed to spring fully grown out of the head of Zeus, Williams was a late bloomer no one outside Chicago had heard of until he was pushing forty (most band vocalists became quick celebs in their teens) and didn't become a truly great singer until years later.

To listen to Williams's earliest recordings, made with two prominent Chi-town R&B orchestras, you have to concur with Whitney Balliett's thumbs-down assessment of Williams as "a loud imitation of a blues singer" (though the word "parody" fits in there better). On these early sides, Williams has barely enough wherewithal to squeeze through the meager "Detour Ahead"—one of those songs with a metaphor so thin, as Raymond Chandler would say, it's hardly worthy of the name—but on "They Didn't Believe Me," he resorts to a ludicrous Vaughn Monroe imitation (or was he too nervous to inform the arranger that the key was too low?), and on "Safe, Sane and Single," Williams and his whitewashed background singers would clearly rather be singing along with Mitch.

The gap between Williams's abilities to sing ballads and the blues would widen during his Basie years to the point where the two were truly polarized, resulting in good to excellent performances of the blues and only middling interpretations of standards. *Count Basie Swings—Joe Williams Sings* (1955, Verve) collects the best of the singer's early work—it's almost all blues—and to this day may be the definitive though not the best Joe Williams record. It opens with the marvelous Basie version of "Ev'ry Day I Have the Blues,"* which generates more excite-

---

* One of several definitive Williams performances of compositions by Memphis Slim, a writer whose work Williams glorifies as eloquently as Joan Sutherland does Verdi's.

ment than his earlier original Chicago version (which used an unnecessary echo chamber), the effortless momentum of the Basie piano and orchestra giving Williams no chance to get out of the groove. The singer quietly talks his way through the first few choruses of "The Come Back," and slowly builds from calmness to hysteria. On "All Right, Okay, You Win," he *rides* the orchestra like a cowboy on a bucking bronco, but instead of trying to pacify the beast he digs in his spurs to get it to keep kicking. "In the Evening" succeeds by giving Williams something to work against in a very unbluesy flute background and a comically Ducal "talking" trumpet that enters, appropriately, on the word "holler."

On his first album of nonblues, *The Greatest . . . Count Basie Plays . . . Joe Williams Sings Standards* (1956, Verve), he has to contend with the lackluster charts of Buddy Bregman when it must have been obvious that the scores written by his Basie colleagues Frank Foster and Ernie Wilkins (who arranged the blues album) suited him much better. And though at this point Williams can't deal with the overly lean rhythm section on *Memories Ad-Lib* (1958, Roulette), beefed up a bit by Basie's always welcome organ, the real killer here is a set of standards so standardized it would take a Louis Armstrong or a Lester Young to find anything new to say with them. Still, the blame for this quickly monotonous set rests with Williams, who, in coming from blues to ballads, uses the latter simply as a chance to sound wistful and pretty. The misconception is that you don't have to work as hard with thirty-two bars as you do with twelve, wherein one simply *has* to find ways of investing variety into a potentially monotonous series of repetitions from line to line and song to song.

Williams has run up against the same dead end: The bands were essential to his development, even as they were for hundreds of singers and players. With the exception of Tony Bennett, every major singer of the forties and fifties had big-band experience (Nat Cole's King Cole Trio, if not a big band, was no less a part of the swing era), even as late as Carmen McRae and Betty Carter. And ultimately, their moving on was equally inevitable.

Despite their hokey album titles, *Joe Williams Sings About You* (1959, Roulette), *Joe Williams with Songs About That Kind of Woman* (1959, Roulette), and *Jump for Joy* (1963, Victor) effectively introduce the modern, mature, post-Basie Joe Williams. You'd think that strings might be a complete turnaround from the kind of singing Williams did on the South Side of Chicago, but he finds their common ground and makes the transition easily. Of all the settings in vocal jazz, the string orchestra has the most in common with the blues band in that both are associated with given stylistic idiosyncrasies (tempos, etc.) and both can, in effect, establish a mood all by themselves. The soloist or singer then has to think carefully about how much he wants to say on top of the background without being redundant or working overhard to communicate a point that the setting has already made. It becomes a matter of knowing what *not* to sing, a skill Williams had already been exposed to in the streamlined, economical swing of the Basie organization. In his twenty-five years since leaving Basie, Williams has concentrated on this more than any other aspect of his craft, and age has not only purified his voice but increased his ability to concentrate on essentials.

Williams combines this economy with the most delightfully eclectic repertoire of any singer going. He'll throw in one of his band-era hits (the always welcome "Ev'ry Day") just like Helen Forrest would, but he'll also take on some songs just off the beaten track and just to the left of the standard repertoire, and then move on to some completely obscure ditties that no one does but Joe Williams, championing their composers in his intertune patter. It doesn't always result in instant classics—I can't believe some of the losers he's trotted on to "The Tonight Show"—but it means you'll always hear something new every time you hear Joe Williams, something I can say about few singers. Even in Williams's scatting, the least of his abilities, he's capable of creating something extraordinary.

But in some ways Williams, like Rushing, was an anachronism. Rushing and Basie had the longest vocalist-bandleader relationship in all of music (off and on for over twenty-three years), and in Williams, Basie had the last major vocal artist to come out of the band tradition. That Williams had to leave Basie to become a truly world-class singer signifies that the band singer era was finally over. As the great bands tumbled and fell, the conquest of the crooners was upon us.

Lady Day
and Lady Time

Billie Holiday and Ella Fitzgerald

"I cannot hide what I am: I must be sad when I have cause, and smile at no man's jest; eat when I have stomach, and wait for no man's leisure; sleep when I am drowsy, and tend to no man's business; laugh when I am merry and claw no man in his humour."
— *Shakespeare*, Much Ado About Nothing

"The whole basis of my singing is feeling. Unless I feel something, I can't sing."
— *Billie Holiday*, Lady Sings the Blues

$\equiv$ **B**illie Holiday's art is the kind that takes you deeper inside yourself and ultimately out again; Ella Fitzgerald's is the kind that takes you outside yourself and ultimately in again.

Holiday creates a five-senses reality out of the lyric to a song, yet her abilities as a musician equal or surpass any "pure" instrumental improviser to work in jazz. To some, the actual tonal quality of her voice sounds off-center and requires effort to fathom its miraculous beauty; Fitzgerald makes melodies, whether a songwriter's or her own, soar through skies of aural heaven, and creates a no less effective, no less emotional kind of drama through purely musical means. While her voice, even on first hearing, is quite the loveliest in all music, it takes time to appreciate its depth.

Both are capable of slapstick comedy and epic tragedy* and all the gradations of feeling that fall between. Being true daughters of jazz, both can sing the blues, and both can swing—interpreting these foundation elements of the music no less personally than they do an individual song.

The swing era serves as a convenient nexus for both careers (who wouldn't trade in their CD players to have been there on that night in 1939 when Chick Webb "battled" Count Basie at the Savoy Ballroom in Harlem, with Fitzgerald and Holiday as competing canaries?). Fitzgerald, born in Virginia in 1918, the first important victor of an Apollo Theatre amateur show, enjoyed a longtime collaboration with one of the most crucial of black bandleaders, Chick Webb. With Webb she landed a career-establishing hit ("A-Tisket, A-Tasket") very early on, and she even led the band for two years after Webb's death in 1939.

Holiday, born in Baltimore in 1915 (or earlier), worked on the fringes of the big-band epoch, although she toured with both Count Basie and Artie Shaw for just under a year apiece. The bread-and-butter recording work of her early career—when she worked with bands that were not big, did not tour, and did not necessarily exist outside the studio—came through her original rabbi, John Hammond. He had first heard Holiday singing at a small Harlem club in 1933 and arranged for her debut session (vocal refrains with Benny Goodman's pretouring studio band); her long-running series of small-group dates under Teddy Wilson's leadership began two years later.

Apart from being the year in which Goodman discovered that large numbers of people would pay to dance to big-band swing, 1935 is also significant as the year, according to Frank Driggs, that saw the invention of the modern jukebox, a contraption that was to have great ramifications for jazz, the recording industry as a whole, and Billie Holiday in particular. Studio-only bands had

---

* I disagree with Martin Williams's assessment that Fitzgerald is incapable of tragedy.

produced acres of jazz and more conventional dance music in the twenties, though with the depression only a few sweeter in-house bandleaders carried on. The jukebox provided a shot in the arm for small bands just as Goodman launched the boom for big ones, and the "combo" records made largely for juke consumption differed from most jazz small-group recordings of other times (and other considerations, such as Artie Shaw and Goodman's band-within-a-band records) in their heavy emphasis on current pop tunes and vocals. They featured either a singing instrumentalist (Red Allen, Lionel Hampton, Wingy Manone, Louis Prima, Fats Waller, or, in England, Nat Gonella); an occasional band warbler (Fitzgerald, Helen Ward) on a small-group holiday along, perhaps, with some of her fellow sidemen; or in-house studio vocalists including three holdovers from the early electric years, Dick Robertson, Chick Bullock, and Red McKenzie, and relative newcomer Billie Holiday, either just on the date or getting top billing on the label.

For the rest of her career, Holiday raved about producer Bernie Hanighen for making possible for her the transition from "with vocal refrain by Billie Holiday" to "Billie Holiday and Her Orchestra," which made more of a career difference than a musical one. Except that her vocal usually comes first, Holiday was apparently only minimally more in charge than on the Wilson dates. As she explained in a 1955 interview with disc jockey Gordon Spencer, "I didn't lead, honey, we just sort of went in the studio. And here's Cozy Cole, here's Roy Eldridge, here's Billie Holiday, here's Teddy Wilson, here's Ben Webster, or here's Lester Young, and we got four sides to do. Now, the man that's running the studio says, 'I want a blues, I want a sweet tune, I want something that moves.' So I think, let's do 'Man I Love,' let's do 'All of Me,' let's do some blues in E flat. And that's the way it went, and we did it. No music, nobody's worried from nothin'. We'd get the beat and I'd say, 'Ben, you make this introduction,' or 'Lester, you make the introduction,' or 'Teddy, you make the introduction,' and we get the tempo and we're gone!"

That the song publishers largely controlled the repertoire of these sessions has led many an ignorant commentator (most being far greater hacks than the songwriters they put down) to complain that the songs Holiday sings are unworthy of her. The jazz press has always tended to view the pop mainstream as an enemy, and while I can see doing this within one's own generation, to extend this pejorative judgment back fifty years is ludicrous—there are almost as many derivative critics who claim that Holiday, or Pops or Fats, turned "dross into gold" (a favorite phrase of Brit crits who can't quite comprehend American pop) as there are witless reviewers who think it droll to quote the opening line of Holiday's autobiography. In many ways, this is the same dog-brain logic that led as otherwise sensible a body as the Chicago AACM to ban all but original music from their performances—from Cole Porter to Sonny Rollins.

But listen, folks, those one-shot songs that Billie Holiday does are *wonderful*. Even party-line purists who don't care for pop, big bands, Broadway, or Busby Berkeley have to admit that Tin Pan Alley, at least before its standards were corrupted by the likes of Mitch Miller and Allen Freed, was one of the greatest friends jazz ever had, no less than the blues. Sure, Holiday improves on them, but no more than she does "They Can't Take That Away from Me" (1937, Vocalion) or "The Man I Love" (1939, Vocalion) or the way she turns standard blues material into performances as special as "Billie's Blues." What's more, these songs are precisely what this young singer needs to polish her chops. A few of the rhythm novelties, like "Swing, Brother, Swing" (1939, Vocalion) and "One, Two, Button Your Shoe" (1936, Vocalion) suggest Fitzgerald-style concentration on the riffish melodies while giving little attention to the somewhat minimal lyrics. But on a few very early quasi-ballads ("A Sunbonnet Blue" [1935, Vocalion]) she acts equally unconcerned with the narrative. Holiday grows out of this quickly, and the transition is something to hear. By 1936 she can make the most out of a parallel between a descending melody line and story line on "You Let Me Down" (literally!, Brunswick); by 1937 she's mastered conversational directness, making tune and libretto sound like a natural extension of speech on "It's Too Hot for Words" (again, an idea suggested by the song title, Brunswick). By 1938 she effortlessly communicates screwball comedy chutzpah in "Here It Is Tomorrow Again" (Brunswick).

Hammond, Hanighen, and Morty Palitz, who produced most of Holiday's jukebox-period records (for the ARC Corp.: Vocalion, Brunswick, and Okeh) from 1935 to the early forties, were already known as A&R men, meaning artists and repertoire men. While it's common critical currency to knock the "R," the "A" involved in these dates has long been accepted as one of their chief attributes. I've mentioned how her voice, sandwiched between instrumental solos, challenges the vocal refrain concept— in which everything else stops while the canary indulges herself—by desegregating players and singers. You might call her voice hornlike, but I think it's more a matter of sharing common concepts of rhythm and phrasing (how melodies are divided up into breath-sized chunks) with her fellow musicians. Trumpeter Buck Clayton, trombonist Benny Morton, and tenor man Ben Webster all share Holiday's warm and very human vibrato, and their improvisations on the chord changes are just as valid dramatically as Holiday's melodic and dramatic embellishments make sense musically (her extension of the interval between "of" and "you" in "The Way You Look Tonight," for instance [1936, Brunswick]). "In the good old days of Billie," Joe Williams explained to Leonard Feather, "the soloists would wait until there was a space and play something that would corroborate the vocal statement." As Holiday asserts in "Getting Some Fun Out of Life" (1937, Vocalion), when she wants to sing, she sings.

The musicians on these sides function as collaborators more than sidemen, none more so than Lester Young. "Lady Day . . . is the last word," Jimmy Rushing once told Burt Korall. She admired Lester Young so [much] that she used to play his records over and over to get the phrasing." The ninety minutes or so of recorded sound they produced together stands as a milestone in Western music, from Bach to Mozart to Ornette. Holiday's round, chubby voice (which matches the zaftig young Billie captured in contemporary snapshots) and her off-center way of attacking the beat so perfectly matches Young's feathery alto-tenor (his own term) tone, strikingly original melodic concept, alternately languorous legato, and ferociously up-tempo use of time. You can sense they had an understanding of each other far beyond what musical terminology or metaphoric imagery can describe. It's beyond mere obbligato, even on the level of Armstrong and Bessie Smith, beyond matched vibrato, a level of understanding of which I can find no counterpart, which happened only this once. Almost everyone who knew them has taken pains to assure us that they were not lovers, including Holiday herself. "Lester likes to eat good home cooking, so I took him home to Mom one night," she told Gordon Spencer. "So, Lester moved in and he was like her son." (But, like John O'Hara on the death of Gershwin, I don't have to believe that if I don't want to.) Like "The Chink and the Child" in D. W. Griffith's *Broken Blossoms*, Holiday and Young were two miraculously kindred souls who found in each other shelter from a world of violence and brutality.

After taking the art of collaboration to its zenith, it's no wonder Holiday's next series of recordings, made for Milt Gabler's Commodore label from 1939 to 1944 (which began because of ARC's refusal to record the controversial "Strange Fruit" and dovetailed with her last few years under contract to that corporation), reinstate her voice at the center of attention, demoting the musicians back to humble accompanists. Beginning with the overdramatic but startlingly effective "Strange Fruit" (1939, Commodore), Holiday experiments with slightly suppressing her melodic embellishment as a means to turn lyrics into personal videos of the mind. If you're in the right frame of mind, any reasonably competent singer can make you sad with a tender ballad or spiteful with a vindictive blues, but only Holiday can take Jerome Kern's rather stately "Yesterdays" (1939) and make it swing gently while at the same time retaining its drama, and only Holiday can take Oscar Hammerstein's deliberately archaic (full of backward constructions) and somewhat pompous lyric (forsooth!) and make it breathe; only she can make you visualize the waterfront she covers in search of the one she loves, only she can implant in your mind the horrifically powerful image of lynch mob victims hanging from the trees like so much strange fruit. One word from Holiday is worth a thousand pictures.

In the early forties Holiday put the finishing touch on her art of the miniscule. Even the tiniest of nuances assumes epic grandeur; the lightest of inflections takes on tremendous significance (and films and TV appearances reveal that she moved no more physically). Her mastery of time grew stronger, as she had perfected the dramatic effect of dropping behind the beat for a disconcerted off-balance feeling and then shifting back on top of it, and maintaining control at superslow tempi. As early as parts of 1936's "Pennies from Heaven" and "The Way You Look Tonight" (both Brunswick), and by the Commodore recordings, she worked some ballads in half time, making the audience hang on to every syllable. "How Am I to Know?" becomes simultaneously a heavy and a light dirge, Dorothy Parker's poignant question going unanswered by the horns in the background, who sidestep conventional harmonic support to sort of comment softly on the action like a Greek chorus.

Though Gabler ran the pure-jazz Commodore label out of his own pocket, by this time he had a "day job" at Decca Records where he was trusted to bring potential hits to their attention. Already having a good track record with Holiday's big seller for Commodore, "Fine and Mellow" backed with "Strange Fruit," Gabler smelled money in the song "Lover Man" and brought both it and Holiday to the big label, which was better able to afford Holiday's then-surprising request for a string section. Gabler's instincts proved correct, and both he and Holiday remained at Decca for six years.

As the informality of the jukebox years deferred to the high drama of the Commodores, the stark, open spaces of the Commodores would soon be filled by strings and occasional choirs;

you'd think they'd curtail Holiday's creativity, but she finds
sweet uses of adversity in any situation. To my ears, she gets
friskier when the strings behind her ensure a serious tone,
whereas on the earlier "I'll Be Seeing You" (1944, Commodore)
she seems compelled to take the tempo as slow as she can possibly stretch it without stopping altogether and to restrict her
melodic playfulness for fear of breaking the spell (she didn't have
to worry, but Gabler was the good witch who let her find out for
herself).

In spite of a few middle-brow misfires, largely brought on by
the presence of arranger Gordon Jenkins, who simultaneously
put the anal in banal but also the taste in tasteful, Holiday's
forties sessions mark the most entertaining and polished in her
whole career. Surprises abound in this underappreciated period, appearing along with the Holiday trademarks she's taught
us to expect, just as her playful, melodious lines are both interrupted and accentuated by her emphasizing dramatically appropriate words in offbeat ways: Never has the word "cute" sounded
legitimately cuter or "flirting" more flirtatious than on "Them
There Eyes" (the soft vowel squeezed like a mustachioed night-
clubber getting fresh with a cigarette girl), and the brisk, somewhat wacky tempo she and arranger Sy Oliver ascribe to it
typifies the period. Even most of the ballads ("What Is This
Thing Called Love?," "Crazy He Calls Me," "Good Morning
Heartache") come rolling out faster than anyone else could do
them and still touch you, "Solitude" surprisingly taking the original Ellington medium-retard tempo (and Ducal muted brass) as
a model. She reserves the more traditional real slow speeds for
the two least traditional numbers, her definitive "Porgy" and
"My Man," from her sole rhythm-section-only session for Decca
(1948). Both songs depict a woman looking for love (no amount
of pronoun substitution would render them suitable for a man to
sing), and neither uses the standard AABA structure, following
their twisting trails into unexpected new patches of melody;
both keep going where a conventional pop song just stops. She
travels (to quote another song by Gershwin) the music's bumpy

road to love way down into the dark depths on the flipside of romance's dizzy heights, beyond the blatant masochism—at once archaic and modern—of the lyrics, to unearth truths even bleaker and more unsettling.

In the second chorus of the above "Them There Eyes," Holiday's audacious mood puts on the gloves and goes a few rounds back and forth with Oliver's pugnacious, blustering ensemble (at times its roughness anticipates Lester Bowie's Brass Fantasy). The same brashness and exuberance pervades her blues-oriented numbers of the forties, practically the only ones in her career *not* to use her stock "Fine and Mellow"/"Billie's Blues" pattern. Both "Now or Never" and "Baby, Get Lost" could have been played by Lionel Hampton for their R&B-style rowdiness, invective lyric, and climactic stop-time episodes, and her mini-cycle of Bessie Smith homages in 1949 touches on this same raucousness. She "covered" (to use a rock 'n' roll term) four Smith classics: one pairing, "T'ain't Nobody's Business" and "Keeps on A-Rainin' " from 1923, the beginning of Smith's recording career; and another from the end in 1933, "Do Your Duty" and "Gimme a Pigfoot." Slight lyric modernizations update the specifics of these songs; in "Gimme a Pigfoot," what the folks up in Harlem do on a Saturday night is described by the bebop figure "Klook-a-mop" rather than "tut-tut-tut," and they're too busy doing "The Hucklebuck," a popular dance modeled on Charlie Parker's "Now's the Time," to be bothered by the arresting officers when the wagon comes (the old-fashioned reefers are omitted altogether—now they partake in unmentionable substances). However, Holiday shares Smith's jaunty defiance, underscoring her right to do as she pleases, whether that means something we can sympathize with sixty years after Bessie and forty years after Billie (sexual service in "Do Your Duty," hell-raising in "Pigfoot") or not (more masochism and wife-beating in "T'ain't Nobody's Business").

The forties also saw Holiday's greatest flowering as a songwriter, and considering that music has produced only a few individuals who can both sing and write (Mel Torme and Lee

Wiley are two others), it's unfortunate that this aspect of her work hasn't received more attention. After her first triumph with the socially conscious "Strange Fruit," she penned one of the most effective of all torch songs, "Don't Explain," and then "God Bless the Child." Not a religious song but a song about religion that's both sacred and profane, it describes, in poetically abstract fashion, how man's knowledge of God has no effect on his treatment of other men. Arranger Gordon Jenkins either thought it was a hymn or, knowing of his formidable (if not always well-applied) smarts, wanted you to think he thought it was a hymn, for in addition to backing her with a bleached-out Protestant choir, he put the ersatz-sacral "This Is Heaven to Me" on the disc's B side.

Along with the standout "Crazy He Calls Me" and her two scrumptious duets with Louis Armstrong, these signify her last days at Decca. After the death of Jack Kapp, the corporation demoted two of his producers, Gabler and Kapp's brother Dave, and dropped many of their black artists, including R&B stars Buddy Johnson, Louis Jordan, and Billie Holiday. She made no studio dates at all (excepting a one-shot session for Aladdin Records memorable for the only "official" version of "Detour Ahead") until going to work for Norman Granz in 1952.

The operative word for her last seven years is erratic. Too unpredictable an artist to provide those who would cop out critically with a simple cutoff date, Holiday does work that varies wildly from session to session (the same holds true for Tony Bennett and Frank Sinatra today, but, my God, they're twenty and thirty years older than Holiday!). The first Granz date in March 1952 sounds as if twenty years have passed, not just two, since the final Decca in March 1950, but the July 1952 session captures a vastly rejuvenated set of chops. On August 14, 1956, she's at her absolute peak, turning in a "Speak Low" that puts all other versions to shame (she's the only one who gets full effect from Ogden Nash's magnificent bridge, making "time" sound genuinely "old" and "love" truly "brief"), but on the next date, four days later she sounds as if she's spent the whole time on a sleepless bender. And then there are her three extant television appearances. Her masterpiece blues "Fine and Mellow" from CBS's "The Sound of Jazz" in December 1957 captures the fullest, most perfect Holiday you can imagine, while the two July 1958 "Art Ford Jazz Party" shows reveal a great artist in decline. The voice is thinner, but we don't notice it as much because we're too absorbed by her emaciated figure, her ribs fairly sticking through a loose summer dress. Bearing this in mind, as well as the knowledge that she died in July 1959, you'd expect Holiday to resemble a walking skeleton on her February 1959 BBC-TV performance. Instead, we get the full-voiced, full-control, full-figured Holiday of the old days. The skeleton, however, as photographed by bassist-historian Milt Hinton, returns on her last studio date (MGM) one week later: With zero windpower, every breath sounds like it might be her last. Not to say this album, *Billie Holiday*, isn't worth hearing, or worth hearing for reasons more substantial than Sinatra–*Only the Lonely*–like wrist-slashing nihilism, for Holiday interlaces the prevailing mode of despair with the most faintly discernible traces of defiance and even hope, flowers sprouting in a graveyard.

Many of Holiday's most sublimely perfect moments come from her last seven years. A&R-wise, she and Granz appropriately picked and chose from her own past, remaking the best of her previously recorded songs in definitive versions, and drawing upon both ARC-style small groups with heavyweight soloists as collaborator-accompanists on most of the Clef/Verves and strings on her last two albums (for Columbia and MGM), as well as any number of tempo gradations between the crawl speeds of the Commodores and the brisker ballads of the later forties. Instead of sandwiching her vocals between instrumental solos, here her beginning and ending choruses frame their statements, these being full two- or three-chorus LP-era outings as opposed to the terse thirty-two- or sixteen-bar one-liners of her thirties 78s. Though these four- and five-minute dramas all use the same script (usually vocal-solos-vocal) and the same cast (trumpet, sax, four rhythm) and the same ending (one note sliding down into another), never once do they get repetitious or fail to command our attention.

Granz deserves praise for assigning Holiday to do virtually all the classic American songs of the "Golden Years" from 1925 to 1945, though Holiday rarely ventured far afield from her rather small established repertoire on extant live performances (the same ten or so songs over and over!). Granz made a mistake in not including any of the worthwhile new tunes of the postwar era (what she could have done with "Teach Me Tonight" or "Along the Way") and also in not letting her record with Mal Waldron, the last of the great Holiday pianists (after Teddy Wilson, Bobby Tucker, and Jimmy Rowles), whose sensitive, post-Monk shadings of mood and time made her the perfect partner for Holiday's twilight years.

Still, there's morbidness in some of her later work, which developed partly out of her successful exploitation of her personal life. After the minor scandal that followed her arrest and internment on a narcotics charge, seekers of cheap thrills began to flock to her appearances (for the same reason that Robert Mitchum's star rose after the bulls caught him with cigarettes that had no printing on them). When writer William Dufty put together a brief biography, *Lady Sings the Blues,* based on interviews with Holiday, illegitimacy, prostitution, and inconceivably nasty abuse from husbands added to the mounting list of Holiday horrors (as a child she's forever trapped with corpses). To read it without knowing Holiday's music is to agree with Robert Reisner's portrait of Holiday as a "professional sufferer."

Yet even on the surface there's more than suffering in her work; laughter abounds as much as tears. As one of many wildly confessional autobiographies in jazz (not as fine a piece of literature as the more Augustinian *Mr. Jelly Roll* or *Straight Life*), it doesn't nearly depict her struggles with racism as vividly as her singing of her own lyrics to "Strange Fruit" or abusive husbands as well as "Don't Explain." Nonetheless, from its supermarket-tabloid shock value opening line to its more revealing closer (a quote from her oft-sung French Apache sop to masochism, "My

Man"), it's a compelling read, and perhaps even helped exorcise more traces of "poor me" attitude out of Holiday's system.

Holiday didn't *have* to suffer on either an amateur or a professional level; two in-depth studies, John Chilton's well-documented biography, *Billie's Blues,* and John Jeremy's mesmerizing BBC documentary, *The Long Night of Lady Day,** leave one with the impression that much of her pain was voluntary, that she had never worked to find a way of life that didn't include it (other remarks to the contrary, suffering is no more essential to great singing than heroin). Perhaps her agony was inflicted because of the unwritten laws she violated, a single all-important rule of popular music. Before Holiday, the pop song was a harmless medium. Even when its lyrics had acid in their veins and its melodies stinging wit, the form itself was escapist and unreal; originally, pop songsmiths felt compelled not to make their wares more complicated than amateurs could play or sing. Holiday changed all that. Armstrong had made great music with a pop foundation by transcending the songs, Al Bowlly made them work for him by fine-tuning his own naïveté to match theirs, but Holiday made her songs real by depriving them of their innocence. After Holiday, pop singing could never go home again.

When the newspapers, the same tabloids that kept their readers up to date on every Holiday bust, wanted to give their readers something juicy on Fitzgerald, they ran a press release along the lines of:

Portly Ella Fitzgerald was a bit late for a recording date last week when she was caught in the escape hatch of an elevator. The infernal machine stalled between floors, and Ella, already late for a recording date, endeavored to escape through a trap door in the top of the cage.

It took three strong men to rescue the 200-pound songbird.

---

* Mesmerizing if you get the right version: the one released commercially in Japan being more effective, with more music and less yammer-yammer than the one edited for American TV.

Any connections between musicology and biography decrease from vague to nonexistent in Fitzgerald, whose far-out scat lines have no parallel in her controlled and well-managed career. On the face of it, she has more in common with the life and art of her most immediate inspiration in this area, Leo Watson, the only scat singer of note between Armstrong and Fitzgerald. Personal descriptions of Watson range from Leonard Feather's "a mad genius" to just plain "flaky." The stories of his adventures out-zany those of any other figure in jazz, even certified cuckoos like the maniacal Jack Purvis and the perverse Joe Venuti. Nonetheless, in the long run, we'll remember Watson more for his singing than for his insanity.

People first heard of Watson, born in Kansas City in 1898, when his vocal-instrumental group, the Spirits of Rhythm, became so popular that they established not only themselves but the Onyx Club and all of 52nd Street in the early thirties. Otis Ferguson, who wrote the only important article on the group besides Feather, describes the Spirits getting started as "kids helling around with ukeleles," although John Chilton reports that they didn't come together until Watson had passed thirty. After the Spirits disintegrated, a number of major pop stars tried to help Watson on his solo career. Artie Shaw used a wordless Watson chorus on Cole Porter's "I've a Strange New Rhythm in My Heart" (1937, Brunswick), perhaps the first time anyone ever got away with scatting on a new plug tune in place of the usual vocal refrain. Gene Krupa hired him as a regular vocalist (concurrent with Jan Savitt's Bon Bon) for eight months, until Watson picked a fight with a Pullman porter and put his fist through a train window. The Andrews Sisters made their only significant contribution to music by persuading their contract company, Decca, to award Watson his first solo recording session. Slim Gaillard took him into his kooky combo as drummer, vocalist, and resident meshuggener in the funniest series of jazz programs ever broadcast. But these periods of productivity only amounted to intervals in a life of (unprovable) rumors of marathon drum solos that could be silenced only by the police, arrests for possession of illegal substances, spells outside music where he worked as a waiter and in a munitions plant, percussion accompaniment to race riots, naked sprints through hotel lobbies, and other causes for commitment. When Watson died in Los Angeles in 1950, the killer was officially pneumonia, but I suspect that he was just too crazy to live.

Only a superficial hearing would offer evidence that his seemingly nonsensical scat choruses betray a turbulent state of mind. Ultimately, the only time Watson *was* under control was when he was singing. His vocals, especially the scat choruses, reveal a marvelous sense of construction, symmetry, and interior logic. Even tranquility, as Dan Morgenstern suggests, citing his solo on "Way Down Yonder in New Orleans" (with Red McKenzie and the Spirits of Rhythm [1934, Decca]) as one of the earliest examples of the relaxed feeling Lester Young later brought to jazz, as does his markedly ungospel antiphonous second-to-last chorus of "I'll Be Ready When the Great Day Comes" (1933, Brunswick).

Watson made the first significant extension of the scatter's vocabulary since Armstrong and Crosby. Though voices had been imitating instruments since Cliff Edwards's time, Watson developed ways for singers to learn from horns without having to mimic them. Some of his admirers, like Jon Hendricks and writer Carlton Brown, mention his trombonelike approach, but Watson used long, smeary glissandi long before he actually learned to play the trombone (Feather says he picked it up—literally—for a date with the unzany John Kirby Sextet in 1937). On his great 1939 "It's the Tune That Counts" (Decca), Watson comes armed with short, percussive phrases that refer to his experiences as a drummer and with the guitar family. Watson also standardized another Armstrong technique that the trumpeter had never fully developed in his singing, the quote. In improvising, Watson's mind frequently lighted on fragments from older tunes, generally nursery rhymes and folk airs (this being before the body of American popular songs grew large enough to support its own circulating library of references), and he'd combine these extracts, sometimes with, sometimes without the accompanying lyric, with his variations on the original theme as well as completely improvised material, creating what George Simon called "singing in shorthand" and Leonard Feather dubbed a "vocal stream of consciousness." Watson's work was so complete that around 1939, when he met Eddie Jefferson, then a young dancer who told Watson of his desire to do something new in jazz singing, Watson told him that everything possible had already been done with scatting*—this before the mature Fitzgerald, Anita O'Day, Mel Torme, Betty Carter, and everyone else.

Watson had only a few opportunities to freeze his innovative sounds for posterity before he went to that big wangadoodle in the sky, but his ideas caught on quickly. His short burst of notoriety, combined with the longer stays in the spotlight of the considerably better-known Cab Calloway and Louis Armstrong, guaranteed that scat singing would be one of the more steadily demanded novelties of the swing era. The trumpeter-leader and occasional singer Bunny Berigan, who shared Watson's structural genius as well as his propensity for screwing up, fashioned an extremely Watsonian vocal on the quasi-nonsensical "Mama, I Wanna Make Rhythm" (1937, Victor), loaded with slurred phrases and hard *g* and *k* sounds.

In fact, to judge Fitzgerald on her Chick Webb–era sides alone, including the pre-1939 titles under her own name (she had just turned twenty-one at the time of Webb's death, having spent the last four years on the road with that great band), we might dismiss her scatting as simply the best to come along in the path of Watson and her ballads merely as the finest of Connee Boswell's heiresses. Throughout the years, Fitzgerald repeatedly scats along trails blazed by Watson, especially in her instrumental noises (the air-bass solos) and her method of quoting (especially the nursery rhymes). In her first modern masterpiece. Fitzgerald squeezes in the same "crazy over horses"

---

* This information from Jefferson's friend Ira Steingroot.

.lick that Watson played on "I Got Rhythm" (1933, Brunswick) and sang on "Junk Man" (1934, Decca).

Though Fitzgerald never completely escaped Watson, he still amounts to only one of her influences. She told Murray Kempton once that she "remembers everything, absorbs everything and uses everything," and continued, "I steal everything I ever heard." The singers she's studied go way beyond Watson and Boswell, as you can tell from her impressions. At a 1949 club date and other references that she drops as she recalled for George Hoefer a year later, while her bassist soloed on "Basin Street Blues," she hummed the lyrics behind him in a Louis Armstrong fashion. Her drummer, Lee Young, encouraged her to take it out front and the imitation became part of her act. When recording "Basin Street" in 1952, she worked in a whole chorus à la Armstrong. She used the bit as part of an introduction to "St. Louis Blues," and when sharing a bill with Satchmo at the Hollywood Bowl in 1956, did "I Can't Give You Anything but Love" like him for one chorus and like Rose Murphy for another (an imitation that went back to 1950). It remained a staple of her act for years: Fitzgerald, inimitable herself, creating impressions of female singers as uncannily accurate as Sammy Davis, Jr.'s imitations of male vocalists. One 1964 specialty number, "Bill Bailey," gave her the chance to do Sophie Tucker, Della Reese, Pearl Bailey, and Dinah Washington. With Mel Torme's arranger, Marty Paich, she borrowed the vamp Torme and Paich used to introduce "Lulu's Back in Town" for her own "If I Were a Bell" on *Ella Swings Lightly* (1958, Verve). *
This album offers Fitzgerald's tributes to Bon Bon Tunnell on "720 in the Books" and to Roy Eldridge in "Little Jazz."

Fitzgerald's earliest scat lines stay closer to home rhythmically, especially the 1-2-3 beat of "The Organ Grinder's Swing" (1936, Decca), than do Watson's high-flying phrases. In 1945, Fitzgerald recorded "Flying Home," and listeners forgot that

---

* Paich used the same figure to set the stage for Art Pepper's entrance on "Anthropology" on *Art Pepper + 11.*

anyone else had ever scatted. The first of hundreds of versions of "Flying Home" reveals as many differences from Watson's method as it does similarities, virtually all of which she would expand on later. She takes the piece at a more relaxed long-form approach, possibly learned from Holiday, which contrasts with Watson's compressed and manic outbursts, giving her greater opportunity to build up tension and then disperse it. She also incorporates well-known jazz solos and arrangements into her vocal improvisations, like the Illinois Jacquet "honk" climax of "Flying Home" and the shape of the Count Basie–Bill Davis chart of "April in Paris" into her own version of the piece (the latter from a 1957 Newport set issued by Verve). "Flying" also offers a link to Connee Boswell through a quote from her "Martha." This incorporation is more satisfying than the vocalese movement of Eddie Jefferson and King Pleasure.

Nonetheless, over the long haul, Fitzgerald was only revving up her engines in "Flying Home," and only really took off following her involvement with the bop movement a few years later. "These bop musicians have stimulated me more than I can say," Fitzgerald related at the time in *Ebony* magazine. "I've been inspired by them and I want the world to know it. Bop musicians have more to say than any other musicians playing today." Not only by absorbing modern jazz, but by publicly allying herself with the new music, she became its most identifiable figure at the height of the bop controversy. Only a handful of swing-era stars—Woody Herman, Coleman Hawkins, and Benny Goodman—and only one star singer—Fitzgerald—came out in support of bop, although a few others capitalized on its notoriety. Fitzgerald learned bop at the hands of its originators: during a tour with Gillespie himself. "I used to get thrilled listening to them when he would do his bebop," she later told Al Fraser. "That's the way I learned to what you call bop. It was quite a new experience and he used to always tell me, 'Come up and do it with the fellas. . . .' That to me was my education in learning how to really bop." In 1947, Fitzgerald married Ray Brown, the new music's leading bassist.

In the early forties Anita O'Day had experimented with increasingly shorter notes that anticipated bop's rhythmic style, but Fitzgerald dove headfirst into bop's harmonic maelstrom. Just to keep up with the chord patterns of swing improvisation took more musicianship than almost any singer had in the band era, and in the late forties only five or six perhaps fully understood the advanced bop changes. Fitzgerald, as Martin Williams has pointed out, took it even farther; her ability to make musical sense out of the spaciest intervals and harmonic patterns imaginable established her as one of the most important minds in modern jazz. Of the dozens of vocalists to try their tonsils at scatting, only Fitzgerald could keep an audience entertained with nothing else but this. Only Fitzgerald would never repeat herself, never grow monotonous. She's always had the showmanship never to try this for more than one or two numbers a set, to mix in scat features with familiar standards and current tunes at varying speeds and extraslow ballads—but she doesn't need it.

Perhaps because her improvising is the most accomplished in vocal music, she's never had to consider the context in which it appears as carefully as O'Day or Mel Torme, whose balance of preset form and improvisation resembles that of John Lewis and the Modern Jazz Quartet. In contrast, Fitzgerald uses the bonesimplest of patterns. Her classic set piece of "How High the Moon" (1947, Decca, and endless concert versions) utilizes a few relatively simple pegs: Each performance uses the same tempo, opens with a reading of the lyric, and then goes into some special material designed to introduce the improvisation ("We're singin' it, 'cause you asked for it . . ."). The scat itself inevitably includes loads of quotes (à la Leo Watson) both irrelevant—"Rockin' in Rhythm" and "Rhapsody in Blue" on her Decca *Flying Home;* and "Poinciana," "Deep Purple," "Love in Bloom," "The Peanut Vendor," Charlie Ventura's "Whaddya Say We Go?," "Did You Ever See a Dream Walking?," "A-Tisket, A-Tasket," "Heat Wave," and "On the Trail," "L'il Liza Jane," "Got to Be This or That," "Idaho," "Smoke [Sweat] Gets in Your Eyes," and others on a 1960 Berlin concert performance

(Verve)—and relevant—as on her third or fourth wordless chorus of each run-through of "Moon" when she goes into the melody of Charlie Parker's "Moon"-variation and bop anthem, "Ornithology." But though she follows these rules, Fitzgerald completely improvises the content of her vocal. Like John Ford getting to work on yet another western or Chuck Jones directing his twelfth "Roadrunner" cartoon, Fitzgerald uses formulas creatively, not only to precondition her audiences as to what they can expect, but to deliver the goods.

Two mid-fifties scat features, "Later" (1954, Decca) and "Ella Hums the Blues" (1955), make clear that Fitzgerald knows the musical elements of the blues, but her one full-scale attempt at conquering the Smith girls repertoire, *These Are the Blues* (1963, Verve), reveals that she lacks the gruff, hoarse passion that even the smoothest real blues singers (such as Joe Williams) have. This doesn't make her a lesser artist, any more than Bach was a lesser artist for writing about fugal variations in D minor or Vivaldi was for writing about the four seasons. Her deeper understanding of the medium's implications may be only as cursory as Joe Williams's scatting, but she does wonders with the purely musical aspects of the form on the above-mentioned improvisations and also when the blues spirit touches a pop song, especially "I've Got a Right to Sing the Blues" and others in *The Harold Arlen Songbook* (1960–61, Verve).

Her lack of blues passion affects her work with other kinds of music, leading some of her detractors to claim that fate chose badly when it selected Ella Fitzgerald to be the one singer to record definitive collections of the essential American songs, her *Songbooks*. It must have seemed especially ironic to theater buffs that the first singer to make extralong albums of the Broadway repertoire should be one who had absolutely nothing to do with the theater, either specifically or philosophically. As we've seen, Fitzgerald's career began and stayed, for a time, with rhythmic novelties. By 1950 the gap between singer and material was widening; she was getting better and what she sang was getting worse. She reacted by pressuring Decca to allow her to record an auspicious LP of Gershwin songs (only eight of them, as LPs were only ten inches back then) with solo piano accompaniment by the brilliant Ellis Larkins. Even at the pinnacle of her involvement with bop she insisted, "Despite the different kinds of songs I sing, I still consider myself a ballad singer. I suppose I'll always be that way."

That *Ella Sings Gershwin* signifies the high-water mark of her Decca period shouldn't be interpreted as meaning that the rest of her Decca sides are crass rubbish, though MCA (which, unfortunately, currently owns the Decca catalog) would have you think so by issuing only the worst of these selections on anthologies they perversely title her "greatest hits." When we think of Fitzgerald on Decca, the worst titles tend to automatically come to mind ("Molasses, Molasses," "A Guy Is a Guy") as do the Kapp-italist extremes, the duets with Louis Armstrong and Louis Jordan (but, strangely enough, not Crosby), and the insufferable vocal groups, like the unbearably square Ink Spots, who dig their toes into the ground through seven tracks while poor Ella tries in vain to force them into the groove. In fairness, she made just as many excellent records for Kapp and his successors: *Ella*, a hauntingly beautiful 1952 reunion with Larkins; *Lullabies of Birdland*, which collects all of her scat specialties; and *Listen and Relax*, an entertaining jumble of good songs and fair songs made acceptable by Fitzgerald's singing and Gordon Jenkins's tasteful arrangements. Several cuts here forecast the future musical comedy–oriented pieces, such as two *South Pacific* songs from 1949, issued first on a single and then on *Listen*. Could she have recorded "I'm Gonna Wash That Man Right Outa My Hair" for any other reason than to show off her rhythmic dexterity? Taking the central part of the refrain at a reasonably fast clip, she effortlessly dives into the bridge at double time. Like a rubber ball bouncing up and down in an empty room, put it into a smaller space and it'll go faster because the floor and ceiling are closer together. When Ella hits that stream of short lines in the release, she starts moving twice as fast, and the effect exhilarates.

As good as some of her Deccas are, her really great years are the Verve years, 1956 to 1966.* Legend has it that Norman Granz didn't want her to sing with his Jazz at the Philharmonic troupe at first, and only invited Fitzgerald on stage for one number as a favor to her husband and his bassist, Ray Brown. Subsequently, her relationship with Granz lasted much longer than either of her marriages. Granz had already been making records, but Fitzgerald was too important a star (selling 22 million Decca discs by 1954 and making the cover of *Life* the following year) for Granz to record until he inaugurated his major pop music label, Verve Records. Fitzgerald began making singles for the new label in January 1956. In March the new label announced that her first album for them would be a live set called *A Night at the Fairmont.* Though it was never released, her premier album for Verve—*The Cole Porter Songbook*—became one of the biggest-selling jazz records of all time. It made major powers out of both Verve (and Granz) and its arranger, Buddy Bregman, and if there had ever been an empty seat at a Fitzgerald club date or concert, such an animal now no longer existed.

The runaway success of *The Cole Porter Songbook* testifies more to the strength of the idea—Fitzgerald in an extended, thirty-two-song program of tunes by a single composer—than the quality of the record itself. For all the hoopla surrounding arranger Bregman in thirty-year-old liner notes, his work today comes off as routine and unimaginative, and this monotony also pervades the second Bregman-Fitzgerald outing, *The Rodgers and Hart Songbook,* also 1956, also Verve, also two records (thirty songs), and also difficult to endure without a break. The set begins to come alive when the conductor steps down and lets Fitzgerald tackle "Bewitched" with only her trio, but the singer makes too much of an effort to prolong the unorchestrated mo-

---

* Almost every album mentioned hereinafter comes from Verve, so in the parentheses following each record title you'll find only the year; you can assume the label is Verve.

ment by doing every single verse and refrain of Larry Hart's introspective soliloquy. She meant it to be moody and ballsy ("I got real sexy on that one," she said in a contemporaneous interview), but it winds up as rambling, a seven-minute track that argues for the restoration of the 78-era three-minute limit, and also for leaving extra choruses where they belong—on the musical comedy stage. Her 1958 songbook, *Irving Berlin*, fares better under the baton of the surer-footed Paul Weston.

The songbook series includes two inarguable masterpieces, each devoted to the works of composers who straddled the boundaries of jazz and popular music: George Gershwin, Tin Pan Alley's most celebrated songwriter, who introduced the idea of working genuine jazz and black music ideas into classical music, which in turn became a building block of the jazz repertoire; and Duke Ellington, who wrote music for a jazz orchestra and soloists that, with very little finagling, belongs just as much to singers and to the theater. Fitzgerald's art relates to both men as she never crossed between pop and jazz but always kept one foot in both, making her, in retrospect, the definitive jazz singer, since before the bottom dropped out of pop in the late fifties even jazz-oriented vocalists could appeal to popular audiences.

Ellington organizes his material for Fitzgerald in three ways. On pieces that already have a vocal part or a vocal refrain, he merely recasts Ella in the role of one of his own singers, rather like Jimmy Hamilton taking over a part originally written for Barney Bigard. On "Rockin' in Rhythm," though, Ellington overlays Fitzgerald's scatting right on top of his standard arrangement as Charlie Barnet had done ten years previously with scatting dancer Bunny Briggs (also recorded by Norman Granz). Third, for some works Ellington created entirely new shapes for Fitzgerald. The new "Caravan," for instance, refers to neither of the number's two previous well-known incarnations: as vehicle for its originator, valve-trombonist Juan Tizol; and as a best-selling piece of romantic exotica for Billy Eckstine. Bandleader and singer would reteam occasionally in the sixties, for a TV special, another Verve album, and a tour to promote a potential hit single, "Imagine My Frustration," but *The Duke Ellington Songbook* remains their definitive collaboration.

By virtue of the composer's presence, *The Ellington Songbook* had to be authentic, its departures from established molds of its material done by one in a position to make them legitimate. For *The George Gershwin Songbook*, Fitzgerald and Granz strove not for authenticity but topicality, recruiting the single greatest orchestrator in all of grown-up pop music, Nelson Riddle, and Fitzgerald and Riddle jettisoned the music's original purposes to make the songs work in a contemporary context. One of the most cloying tunes Gershwin ever wrote, "Aren't You Kind of Glad We Did?" (apparently George also thought it cloying as it went unperformed in his lifetime), had previously been best known as a duet between Dick Haymes and Judy Garland. The piece's overdone coyness inspires Garland to overact more than usual, though perhaps it's only the contrast with the restrained and subtle Haymes that makes her histrionics here unbearable. The normally cool Gene Kelly flies off the handle in "By Strauss," a comic relief number in the film *An American in Paris*, which sarcastically attacks Broadway music in mock support of nineteenth-century Viennese waltzes. Fitzgerald strips each of its camp and gushiness. Riddle scores the Strauss-mock homage with just the slightest touch of Teutonic oom-pah (it would be a different song without it), and while Fitzgerald doesn't rely on the "jazz waltz" idiom ("Bluesette," "Valse Hot," "Waltzing the Blue," et al.), she makes the piece swing in an understated ¾ time. On "Kind of Glad," she latches on to the music's gentle pulse and flows along on top of it gracefully, and gives the lyrics the same respect (or degree of respect) she affords to "Someone to Watch Over Me" or "The Man I Love" or any of the other great works in the Gershwin book.

Among other gifts, Riddle shared with Ellington a talent for making albums work as albums, which Ellington explored in classics like *His Mother Called Him Bill* and *The Far East Suite* and Riddle took to the limit in his work with Frank Sinatra. A songbook album has now a natural flow of its own; the juxtapo-

sition of ballads with comic turns and pieces written as background for dancers gradually turns the record into a musical
comedy itself. The five-record *George and Ira Gershwin Songbook* amounts to an opera, fifty-three songs[*] that cover the widest range of human situations. The early ten-inch *Ella Sings
Gershwin* stands to this monument as a Picasso sketch does to
his epic "Guernica."

If the Gershwin and Ellington packages are the most essential
collections of Fitzgerald's work, each has a close runner-up. Her
next greatest songbook, taped over 1960 and 1961, addresses
Harold Arlen, whose jazz-shaped songs reflect an even greater
understanding of black music than Gershwin, under the baton of
Billy May, an arranger as bodacious as Riddle is subtle. Fitzgerald sounds just as good with orchestras of Count Basie and
Bill Doggett as she did with Duke's. *Ella & Basie, On the Sunny
Side of the Street* (1963) and *Rhythm Is My Business* (1962)
demonstrate the most propulsive, impetuous, and catchy rhythmic motion (meaning swing) ever heard. On the hit instrumental "Shiny Stockings," arranger Quincy Jones reprised one
Ellington method by slipping the standard Frank Foster chart
behind Ella's singing of her own new lyrics. For Japanese television several years later, Fitzgerald devised a new small-group
version in which she hums parts of the Foster arrangement in
harmony with Roy Eldridge's muted trumpet in between her
vocal choruses, working in two other Basie standards, "Every
Day I Have the Blues" in Tommy Flanagan's piano introduction
and "April in Paris" through Ella's hollering, "One more once!"

Fitzgerald made loads of wonderful records for Verve besides
the attention-gathering songbooks and live albums, more than
could possibly be reissued and then kept in the catalog even
though she's one of Polygram's best-selling artists no less than

---

[*] Completists will also want "Somebody Loves Me" and "Cheerful Little Earful,"
two Fitzgerald-Gershwin-Riddle tracks (the latter only by Ira) that appear only on her
Get Happy album, as well as a 45-rpm of Riddle doing Gershwin's instrumental pre-
ludes, included only in the original box set and on a recent Japanese reissue.

Verve. Her two themeless sets with Riddle, *Ella Swings Gently with Nelson* (1961) and *Ella Swings Brightly with Nelson* (1962), are actually more consistently excellent sets than her last two songbooks with the swingin' Riddle, *Jerome Kern* (1963) and *Johnny Mercer* (1964). They gather many of the remaining great songs of the thirties and forties as do her heavily stringed ballad outings with the worthy Frank DeVol, including *Ella Fitzgerald Sings Sweet Songs for Swingers* and *Hello Love*. DeVol's Columbia albums with Tony Bennett tend to be overdone, while his work for Doris Day (and earlier for Peggy Lee at Capitol) leans toward the nondescript. However, since he knows he can't titillate and excite as consistently as Riddle, he compensates by adding two master tenor obbligatists to the mixture: Stan Getz on four tracks of *Like Someone in Love* (1957) and Zoot Sims on most of *Hello, Dolly!* (1964).

With the great modern jazz arranger Marty Paich, Fitzgerald made *Ella Swings Lightly* (1957), a jewel of a selection of big-band numbers which proved that even though she had moved up to the biggies like Gershwin and Rodgers, she could still do a great job with swing trivialities; and *Whisper Not* (1966), where top-echelon accompaniment excuses tunes like "Matchmaker" and "Wives and Lovers." Lastly, she left behind arrangements, horns, reeds, and strings altogether for two charming rhythm-section-only dates, the up-tempo *Clap Hands, Here Comes Charlie* (with pianist Lou Levy [1961]) and the lovely ballad-oriented *Let No Man Write My Epitaph* (with Paul Smith [1960]). And that's not even mentioning Fitzgerald's great live sets.

The reader will excuse me, I hope, for going on at such length about the ten years Fitzgerald recorded exclusively for Verve, but they contain so much of her best work that her earlier period seems like a mere prelude and her post-Verve years an afterthought. Since 1966, Fitzgerald has made quite a few mistakes, like a religious album, *Brighten the Corner* (1967, Capitol); a group of sacred Christmas songs, *Christmas* (1967, Capitol), which is not in the same league as her secular seasonal album,

Ella Wishes You a Swinging Christmas (1957, Verve) with Frank DeVol; and a long-awaited collaboration with Benny Carter wasted on piddling medleys. Mistakes are to be expected, but too much of her recent work seems redundant: live albums that add little to her earlier in-person recordings and a third Gershwin outing with Andre Previn, who isn't fit to polish Ellis Larkins's pedals. Compared to these, her few attempts to try something new seem ineffectual. On *Take Love Easy* (1973, Pablo), *Again* (1976, Pablo), and *Speak Love* (Pablo), she delves at length into the lyricism of voice and solo guitar, an idea she used on the verses only of "Nice Work If You Can Get It" and "They All Laughed" on *The Gershwin Songbook*, and on passages of the long "Spring Can Really Hang You Up the Most" on *Clap Hands, Here Comes Charlie.* Her double-length excursion into bossa nova, *Ella Abraca Jobim,* comes along too many years after the fact.

No one expected Fitzgerald to weather the decades all that successfully. A seventy-year-old Frank Sinatra, a Billie Holiday with a toe or two already in the grave, or a senile Mabel Mercer can get up there and still interpret a lyric meaningfully, but Fitzgerald's interpretations have always been of melodies and harmonies. No other singer depends so much on pure chops as she does. And for anyone but Ella, her recent voice would be enough. To add, or to subtract, from this, her improviser's wit and imagination may be fading as well. Those long scat lines lack the logical cohesion she once had. Again, it's too much to expect Fitzgerald to do at seventy what she could do twenty-five years ago.

As this is being written, Fitzgerald hasn't recorded—the longest period in her whole career—and one suspects that she has momentarily retreated to the wings to think carefully about her past and future. As Chick Webb's band singer, Fitzgerald perfected her pitch to the point where it was the envy of even such precise pitch-mongers as Jo Stafford. With the coming of bop she mastered modern harmony and rhythm, learning how to swing and improvise better than any other vocalist. On the 1950

Gershwin ten-incher, she conquered the slower tempi, adding new delicateness and grace to her realm of possibilities. With the 1959 Gershwin box, Fitzgerald reaches her limit. Now she can occasionally rough up her notes for effect, helping her to interject varying levels of mood (which isn't the same as emotion) into her work—mild irony, humor, and pathos.

Of her eight songbooks, she devoted only one to a lyricist, and this was that most down-to-earth of wordsmiths, Johnny Mercer. And this because, to Fitzgerald, the lyric is only something to swing on—as Claudius said in *Hamlet*, "Words without thoughts never to heaven go."

There are enough sultry saloon singers and balladeers in this world; we don't need to cry all the time. We need singers like Fitzgerald to remind us that our great songwriters wrote music as well as words. Ella's success with "Memories of You" (on *Hello, Dolly!* [1964, Verve]) owes nothing to "waking skies at sunrise" but to the diatonic obstacle course that leads her away from and ultimately toward the resolving five-note figure that concludes the melodic payoff. Our pulses race when Fitzgerald starts to scat. Will she follow the melody? For how long? Will a fragment of another tune momentarily pop into her head? Will she slow down the tempo, double it, or suspend the beat altogether? Will she do her crowd-pleasing "bass solo"? Will she trade fours with her accompanists, and will they be able to keep up with her endless inventiveness?

If this isn't drama, I don't know what is.

It's an enthralling experience, one, you could say, matched only by the thrill of hearing Billie Holiday interpret a ballad. They may travel completely different ways to the same destination, but the women whom Lester Young christened Lady Day and Lady Time can reach you and thrill you. That each influenced no end of other singers seems unimportant compared to the way each, when at full throttle, can still move an audience. The results make *Much Ado About Nothing* a speech that runs like iron through your blood.

Brothers and Sisters

The Early Hot Vocal Groups

"To Whom It May Concern:

I should like to know if the Boswell Sisters are white or colored.

I am asking you to settle a long [-standing] argument to the above question.

I'm thanking you in advance,

> Herbert A. Bailey
> Roxbury Mass.
> October 17, 1931"

"When you compare [the Boswell Sisters] with all the group singers and trios that were around in the twenties, and then when you hear when we came in—I don't say this boastfully, I say it gratefully, because I feel we contributed an awful lot to music."
—*Connee Boswell to Rich Conaty*

In 1930, Clarence Williams wrote "Shout, Sister, Shout," an unpretentious, semigospel affair consisting of a standard A-flat thirty-two-bar refrain with a bridge, preceded by a sixteen-bar verse in the relative minor key of F. The composer thought enough of the number's commercial possibilities to record it several times with his usual washboard groups, and even recruited the entire Bingie Madison big band for two additional versions issued as Clarence Williams and His Orchestra, and Clarence Williams and His Jazz Kings. On the latter disc, recorded on February 19, 1931, Williams sings the refrain accompanied by a male vocal trio. They hum along nondescriptly in the background, adding little to the performance besides retroactive camp. In 1931 that was as good as it got.

A little more than two weeks later, another vocal trio, one that shared Williams's New Orleans background, recorded "Shout, Sister, Shout." The Boswell Sisters' reading opens with a slow, minor-sounding introduction in the form of a duet by violinist Joe Venuti and guitarist Eddie Lang. When Arthur Schutt's piano and Chauncey Morehouse's marimba join in, the pace quickens in time for the singers' abrupt entrance. More remarkable than the unexpected surge in tempo, they avoid the words "Shout, sister, shout," which Williams placed at the end of each eight-bar "A" section, instead substituting a chord-based scat variation.

They perform the first of these passages in unison as Mannie Klein's muted trumpet joins in on the last two bars in what at first sounds like an obbligato. At the end of the second "A," immediately prior to the release, the three sisters start off together in the same variation. But instead of a trumpet playing on top of the vocal part, Connee Boswell leaves the other two sisters to handle the harmony line while she scats a blues-inflected lick in place of the horn. For contrast, Connee's brief solo here comes in short bursts while the two sisters' line is long and smooth. Together they cross the bridge in short, staccato steps, elongating notes at the end of every other line for emphasis. Again, at the final eight bars they end with the first of their two wordless lines as before; the second again is completely different. Here they slow down to introduce the next "movement" of the performance.

And then it dawns on us that we've heard only the first chorus. The last line of this chorus expands and slows down to set the mood not for another chorus just yet, but the verse. Though in minor and designed by Williams to set up a mood of gloom and tension, which he intended to dispel by modulating into major with the refrain (and cheerful lyrics to go with it), the Boswells contrastingly make it the most positive part of their arrangement. They sing it in unison at a relaxed and easy-to-follow march beat with Eddie Lang's steady, chunking guitar and Klein's bugle as fellow marchers.

Okay, so now you expect them to return to the swing tempo, right? Wrong. At this point they slow the proceedings down even further, crawling into a wordless interlude only marginally if at all related to Williams's tune (the motif that was already their theme song). Vet Boswell and Martha Boswell sing high and low harmony lines, and Connee then enters smack in the middle with eight bars of both the melody and the lyrics of the refrain. Now, for the first time, we hear the "tonic" phrase, which the sisters have been saving, the "Shout, Sister—Shout, Sister, Shout!" They even underscore it with an "Oh! Lawdy!"

Having finally dropped that other shoe, the sisters now dispense with all the lyrics *except* that line, flying into a double-time variation rooted in Williams's chord changes but completely new melodic highs and lows, the bridge's long lines breaking into unconnected dots and then slowing back down into a two-part "moaning" passage over which Connee sings the final eight bars, repeating the last word as Martha and Vet gently reiterate "Oh, Lord" behind her. Connee then joins in their hum as the three voices fade into the concluding notes of the marimba.

"Shout, Sister, Shout" has been analyzed here not because of its complexities—actually, by Boswell standards, it's a comparatively simple chart—but because it's one of the first of seventy-odd masterpieces by the greatest of all jazz vocal groups, the Boswell Sisters. It represents a high-water mark in that most misbegotten of musical forms, a pinnacle that singers had worked for years to attain and would, after 1935, never reach again.

Even conceiving of the vocal group as having potential for jazz may raise a few eyebrows. We can trace instrumental jazz to the blues and, if we choose, can practically overlook all sources of mainstream jazz singing besides the blues. However, in talking about vocal groups we can't gloss over middle-class white traditions, because they aren't just one branch but virtually the whole tree—nuts and all. A thumbnail sketch of jazz's beginnings would suggest that the new music took from Afro-Americans their advanced rhythm-and-blues tonality, adapting these gradually to the harmonic system developed over several centuries by Europeans. Jazz trumpeter Max Kaminsky once speculated that if whites had been slaves instead of the other way around, their Negro masters would remark on the white gift for harmony, just as in real life the white plantation owners had to admit that their black slaves possessed a remarkable gift for rhythm. The black gift for vocal harmony for some reason rarely surfaced in jazz, as we shall see; instead, it realized itself in such unfortunate forms as doo-wop and earlier in gospel and its predecessor, the spiritual, which Marshall Stearns once described as having "the most European and fewest African qualities of all American Negro music."

So where does the jazz vocal group come from? When we listen to the trios, quartets, and quintets of Bessie Smith and Cliff Edwards's generation, it makes the early triumphs of the Boswell Sisters seem all the more remarkable. The Revelers and the American Quartet are just as godawful as the Ink Spots and the Platters—you want to present each with a solid tin ear of corn. The Revelers, the most popular group of the early electric era, have a more direct counterpart in the Hi-Los in that each preferred obnoxious embellishments to swing, treating shallow vocal acrobatics as if they were ends in themselves.

To find the first group to effectively use jazz techniques, remember the following caveat: A great vocal group by definition needs to have at least one truly great singer. The Boswell Sisters had Connee Boswell, the Mel-Tones had Mel Torme, Lambert and Hendricks had Ross, and the first great jazz-influenced popular singer, Bing Crosby, came out of the first important jazz-influenced vocal group, the Rhythm Boys. Like virtually all groups, excepting the Boswells and Lambert et al., the Rhythm Boys wasted almost as much wax as they used creatively. Formed when Paul Whiteman annexed Tin Pan Alley *Wunderkind* Harry Barris to the team of Al Rinker and Crosby, the group made records that fall into two categories, each with its own failings. The sides made with the full Whiteman orchestra suffer from Whiteman's insistence on combining the trio with other vocal instrumentalists from the ranks of his entourage. Prior to hiring the Boys, the first unhyphenated, full-time vocalists in dance-band history, Whiteman had used trombonist Jack Fulton, violinist Charles Gaylord, and guitarist Austin "Skin" Young in a gruesome threesome known as the Sweet Trio; their total wimpiness made the strange sexual connotations of "Here Am I, Broken Hearted" all the more bizarre. Later, when Whiteman teamed them with the Rhythm Boys, these yodeling yokels force Crosby and Co. out of any groove they might get into, and the Sweet Trio muddy down many a potentially hot Whiteman chart like "I'm in Love Again" (1927, Victor).

The Rhythm Boys' other series of recordings (made sans Whiteman but with his name on the labels), with Barris and Rinker on twin pianos and Crosby summoning up his undeveloped talents for cymbal-ism, justify the charge leveled against them by their severest critic, Crosby himself. "We ignored [music] in favor of our new conviction that we were side-splittingly funny," Crosby later lamented. A casual listen to Rhythm Boys solo sides like "That's Grandma" (1927, Victor), which spotlights mediocre imitations of Coolidge-era radio personalities, and "Louise" (1929, Columbia), which offers a silly routine based on the act of record-making itself, will reveal more horsing around than singing.

Small surprise, then, that all this tomfoolery should obscure the substantial contribution the Rhythm Boys made to vocal music: They came up with the idea that singers and groups of singers had to follow new trends in jazz, even as instrumentalists and arrangers did. On the few records where the trio operates unfettered by additional voices and one-liners, we hear instrumental influences going beyond their colleagues (Beiderbecke and Trumbauer and associates, not bad colleagues at all) to Armstrong and the great black jazzmen. Influences that have been absorbed though, because anyone who thinks voices should imitate (rather than learn from) horns ought to hear the way the Rhythm Boys address the still-developing trap-drum kit: Barris reflects the high-hat cymbal's "Scha! Scha!," Rinker makes snarely little syllables, and Crosby assumes the role of the bass drum. His percussive "Bom! Bom! Bom!" on "Sweet Li'l/Ain't She Sweet?" (1927, Victor) leads to the "boo-boo-boo" on his 1931 breakthrough hit, "Just One More Chance" (Brunswick), a phrase destined to become a cliché forever associated with him, although he never uttered it again except in self-parody.

What might well be the most important idea they left posterity can be heard in "Changes" (1927, Victor), a record justly celebrated by Beiderbecke buffs as the first Whiteman outing to feature Bix, and one in which, though the Sweet Trio are present, Crosby and his men assume the dominant roles. After a typically top-heavy harmony chorus (albeit punctuated by Barris's cymbal-breaks), Gaylord, Fulton, and Young drop out as Crosby goes ahead into the sixteen-bar verse, backed by Rinker and Barris. Then an incredible thing happens: Beiderbecke plays a sixteen-bar solo as the Rhythm Boys continue humming behind him. In seeking to show the similarity of Crosby and Beiderbecke's approaches, arranger Bill Challis created the device of backing instrumental soloists with voices. So many important ideas came out of the pioneer jazz orchestrators of the twenties—Ellington, Redman, Henderson, Challis—that we shouldn't be surprised that history misplaced a few. In fact, when Mel Torme scored "singing backgrounds to instrumental solos" twenty years later the young singer-writer assumed he was doing it for the first time. That, after Torme, A&R hacks picked up on the trick to steer jazzmen like Sam the Man Taylor and Georgie Auld into middle-of-the-road elevators was no fault of either Challis or Torme. It could still be, as Ellington, Charlie Ventura, and Charles Mingus had to reprove, a legitimate jazz technique.

"Rhythm King," however, contains devices that had a far more immediate impact. Their most significant recording (1928, Columbia), it opens with a lightly minor verse sung in solo by Crosby, following which the trio goes through some "comedy" involving minstrel and falsetto voices that grows easier to take from the second hearing onward, after one knows what's coming. Once out of the comic dialogue, Crosby talk-sings the lyrics, so by the bridge he's really singing, and by the second chorus the trio makes it plain that they're no longer interested in juvenile jive—just good jazz. They embrace the bluesy melody with a nearly perfect harmonic blend, neither too close nor too dissonant, lagging not long after the beat with more cymbal noises from Barris. The pull between the written melody and lyrics and the Boys' desire to drift off into wordless variation results in a tension that reaches out and grabs you like no vocal group had been able to do.

As we've seen, other bandleaders appropriated Whiteman's ideas almost as soon as he could put them on records. That Ben Bernie chose to do his record of "Rhythm King" (1928, Brunswick) with a vocal trio, labeled "Ben Bernie and His Speed Boys," illustrates the general desire to keep up with Whiteman's trends. Bernie's singers take it at a more typical fox-trot bounce; obviously they couldn't sustain the slow bluesy mood the Rhythm Boys built, and their scat chorus sounds rudimentary by comparison.

Around the same time, Ed Kirkeby, leader of the various "California Ramblers" bands, built a recording unit called Eddie Lloyd and His Singing Boys around the nasal Smith Ballew, and the group took on some of the issues of multivoice dissonance raised by Crosby's Trio. Meanwhile, Don Redman and Benny Carter put together the most delightfully off-center vocal group yet for the Chocolate Dandies' disc of "Six or Seven Times" (1929, Okeh). They accurately captured the falling-down cadences of a bunch of drunks boasting of sexual accomplishments, framing this vocal with a sax section tap dancing lopsidedly and Redman's voice and Carter's alto chasing each other à la "West End Blues." Carter also sings as part of a minstrel version of Gershwin's "Somebody Loves Me" for Fletcher Henderson (1930, Columbia), joining the background to an "Amos 'n' Andy"–inspired singspiel by trombonist Jimmy Harrison.

But as influential as the Rhythm Boys were, and they lasted longer than their tenure with Whiteman (leaving him in 1930 to work with Coconut Grove bandleader Gus Arnheim and briefly with Duke Ellington), no one missed them after they broke up in 1931. In fact, long before Crosby, Rinker, and Barris went their separate ways, the formative sounds of their successors were being transmitted on airwaves across the South, the Victor Company was putting their first record into Louisiana shops, and vaudevillians who traveled through New Orleans were bringing rumors of their prowess as far north as Chicago. So quickly did the Boswell Sisters replace the Rhythm Boys that one suspects the three men disbanded just to avoid the competition.

Though Martha and Connee Boswell* were born in Kansas City, Missouri, in 1905 and 1907, respectively, and Vet in Birmingham, Alabama, in 1911, they all truly came from New Orleans, part of the same strain of Crescent City Italian-Americans that also produced Leon Rapollo and their childhood companions Tony Parenti and Leon and Louis Prima. The notion of familial harmony shaped them even earlier than most sibling acts, since their mother, aunt, father, and uncle (two sisters who had married two brothers) sang together in a quartet that the three girls tried to emulate, the lack of a fourth voice necessitating an approach to harmonic space that made their sound unique from the start. The whole family was musical. "My dad had a way of playing [piano] with that left hand that was something else," Connee told Rich Conaty. "Martha played like Dad in that way." Between the three girls they mastered banjo, violin, saxophone, cello, and piano, which Martha continued to play.

The three girls became even closer when a younger brother and sister died in childhood and an older brother was killed in World War I. After performing for years as an instrumental trio, they gradually began to consider what they could do with a vocal group and began the experiments with harmony and rhythm

---

*Almost all of my information in this section comes from two sources, David McCain, the "Boswell" of the Boswell sisters, who's spent most of his life researching their career, and Rich Conaty, who permitted me to transcribe the most rewarding interviews ever conducted with Connee and Vet Boswell.

that would in due course lead them to their trademark sound. They sang for kids in school and church, where Martha and Connee won their first amateur contest, and at jam sessions they'd hold at the Boswell residence. "Whenever there was a flood . . . they'd stick us on a truck and take us around to get donations for the flood victims," Vet remembered. "They'd have a little piano on the truck, and we'd have people like Tony Parenti on the truck with us." The highly regarded cornetist Emmett Hardy encouraged them to make the vocal group a career. Their chance to do this came in 1925 when an act canceled out at the Orpheum Theatre, the number-one variety house in New Orleans, and the Boswell girls took a week off from school to go on in their stead. So many of their friends turned out to see them, as their teachers obligingly held no classes one day, that the now-professional act broke the house record.

A local radio station got wise to them, and so did Edward King of Victor Records, then passing through town with a remote recording unit. King recorded five songs by the teenaged sisters, the two he issued giving us our first chance to hear the formative Boswell sound. As Connee remembered that unfateful first session, "Vet still had a squeaky little voice at the time and so did Martha; we had to sing about ten feet away" from the acoustic pickup horn. "Cryin' Blues," the side released under Connee's name, combines two Boswell sources, Mamie Smith, whose gutturality Connee tries to emulate in her solo (some of her trills also evoke Lee Morse's yodels), and Cliff Edwards, when a three-voice scat episode replaces the customary instrumental chorus. The Ukelele Ike–like noises take center stage on the other side, "Nights When I'm Lonely" (like its flip, a song of Boswell authorship), providing a welcome respite from two straight choruses chirped in irritatingly high bird voices. "It was a thin sound," Vet admitted, "because our voices weren't developed to the extent that they were later. But you can see, if you listen, that it's the same idea all the way through." Even in their fetal period, the Boswells have more to offer than the most polished groups of the twenties.

As their fame spread beyond the Delta, comedians Olsen and Johnson and novelty singers Van and Schenk tried to take them on the road with their acts, but as Connee said, "Our father didn't believe too much in girls going out and working and traveling and all that sort of thing." Finally, in 1928 a Chicago agent made them an offer even the protective Mr. Boswell couldn't refuse, and they left New Orleans. After a successful booking in Chicago, they moved on to Hollywood—presumedly to break into pictures but instead securing a radio spot at a Los Angeles station. The hour-long format gave the Bozzies room for further experimentation. They dragged out all their instruments, gave Martha solo piano spots and piano duets with Connee, let Connee sing by herself (as on "I'm on a Diet of Love"), and mainly worked on the vocal trio. For a time they assigned Martha the lead and solo vocal parts, which you can hear on "Good for You, Bad for Me," before concluding that Connee fit most naturally into that role.

A March 1930 trip into the Hollywood Victor studio with a local dance band brought two 78 sides (one unissued until 1982), both relatively straight vocal refrains cast in a typical Whiteman-era fox-trot, with Rhythm Boys–style breaks interspersed. However, fourteen songs recorded that summer on transcriptions by the Continental Broadcasting Co. give a more accurate accounting of the way the trio sounded in the clubs and on the air. The rhythms are stiff, the arrangements are plain, and the tunes ponderous, but occasionally you'll hear something that sounds like the Boswell Sisters.

We take it for granted that the Boswells used "Shout, Sister, Shout" as their theme song, but though they first recorded the theme that later introduced their broadcasts as part of their arrangement of Williams's tune, it appears in none of Williams's own versions. It turns out that the same phrase appears on one of the Continental discs nearly a year before they worked it into "Shout, Sister, Shout." Their transcription of "Song of the Dawn" ends with a riff that later became the basis of their arrangement of "Heebie Jeebies," the latter being one number out of four recorded for Okeh that October, which proves that the

Boswells came closer to mastery with every passing month. Though Vet told me that they didn't pick up the tune directly from Louis Armstrong (no one else had recorded it since 1926; the Boswells brought it back into the mainstream), that they had, instead, remembered it as a song popular in New Orleans, their scat sections clearly refer to Armstrong's. Their gradual shift to lower registers—"Mostly we liked to sing in the lower keys," Vet concurred in 1982, "because it's more mellow"—and steady use of time-breaking syncopes suggest another hardly surprising influence, Bing Crosby.

Finally, in early 1931 the Boswell Sisters arrived in New York to a contract with Jack Kapp and Brunswick Records and with Rudy Vallee's "Fleischmann's Yeast Hour" (coincidentally, their father managed Fleischmann's New Orleans branch and his daughters had performed for the company's brass as children), their first coast-to-coast airspot. Chesterfield cigarettes and Woodbury soap sponsored later radio runs. The October 1930 "Heebie Jeebies" and the March 1931 "Whadja Do to Me?" dispel all doubt that by the time of their apple jump they had honed to perfection two important cornerstones of their art, the "blend" and the "beat."

The term "blend" applies to the Boswells and really to no other vocal group, although Harry Mills of the Mills Brothers knew what he was talking about when he told the *New York Times*, "It's in the blood. The Boswell Sisters and the Mills Brothers had it, too. It's a family thing." Vet broached the subject in 1982: "Funny thing, we could be in different rooms in the house. I'd be in the bedroom, Martha'd be in the kitchen, and Connee in the living room, and we'd all start singing the same song at the same time in the same *key*. That's how in tune we were to each other." Though biography and musical quality rarely intermingle so purposefully, in vocal groups they jolly well have to. On top of other reasons, it provides one explanation as to why the Boswells were so much better than the Andrews Sisters. "We were not only sisters, we were friends. We had a wonderful time together." Vet continued, "I never knew

until I left home that . . . [some] sisters didn't like each other.
I couldn't fathom that. Like the Andrews Sisters, they never got
along."

The Boswells start with three gorgeous voices that sound even
better when raised together. If you listen to isolated bars of a
Boswell performance, you'll hear these three separate lines
whenever they want you to, while at other times they mesh into
one indistinguishable ensemble. The standard road map of their
voices, which makes the claim that Vet sang the high parts,
Martha the low ones, and Connee assuming the lead and solo
voices, doesn't always work since the blend is so flexible the
sisters don't have to stay in the same places.

They can move between the strict trio, the trio with Connee
firmly in the lead, Connee in solo while the other two do something else or drop out entirely, Connee with one of the other
sisters (such as Connee and Martha's give-and-take on "Whad'ja
Do to Me?," an even finer female duet than Bessie and Clara
Smith's "Far Away Blues"), and endless variations on these
ideas. Their shifting parts never jar the listener or sound anything less than completely natural, even when they revoice their
material to the point where they all but totally reharmonize their
songs. The harmonic substitutions often incorporate blue notes,
with one of the three girls hitting a minor third or an augmented
fourth that just wouldn't be there if they were paying the strict-
est attention to European harmonic theory (this at a time when
even most classic blues singers avoided the blue notes entirely).

Just as the "blend" takes in more than harmony, the "beat"
encompasses more than rhythm. It means dynamics, the finely
tuned ability to hit the same part of the beat at the same time
with the same degree of force and volume. It includes swing, a
quality forever impossible to define on paper and easier to illuminate with examples. The Boswell Sisters swing all the time
after 1930, the Mills Brothers do most of the time before 1934.
The Rhythm Boys swing on "Magnolia" but not on "C-O-N-
S-T-A-N-T-I-N-O-P-L-E." The Spirits of Rhythm always swing,
the Manhattan Transfer never does. That you've probably al-

ready disagreed with a few of the above contentions underscores the eternal subjectivity of this quality.

Just as the blend allows the Boswells to seamlessly move between one and three voices, the beat affords an equal naturalism to their frequent and abrupt shifts in tempo. This device, characteristic of their sound from the beginning, reaches its zenith with "Roll On, Mississippi, Roll On" from the second Brunswick session (1931), which works in no less than four dramatic time jumps and one crescendo climax in which the music gradually (but still quickly) increases in speed. Tempo shifts such as these had never found a place in jazz. Apart from the Boswells and extremely well-arranged exceptions like Gil Evans's chart of " 'Round Midnight" for Miles Davis and John Coltrane, the only place in jazz where you can hear this approach to rhythm is in classically influenced pieces such as Harry James's trumpet concerti, John Lewis's compositions for the Modern Jazz Quartet, or Mel Torme's rhapsody in "Blues in the Night." The Boswells most likely picked up the idea from their experience with European art music; according to Vet they had performed as instrumentalists with the New Orleans Philharmonic very early on. It wasn't so much a matter of classical influences specifically but that they frequently looked beyond the boundaries of jazz and pop to find what they wanted in their music.

For one thing, they went out of their way to use instruments that were not commonly part of a jazz orchestra: "Shout, Sister, Shout" exploits drummer Chauncey Morehouse's lifelong mania for tempered percussion and "Sentimental Gentlemen from Georgia" opens with an introduction played on flute by Larry Binyon.

Kapp eternally strived to literalize their Southern accents, and assigned them endless sessions of mammy masterpieces glorifying the antebellum South.* However, their quest for the new

---

* "An Ev'ning in Caroline," "Got the South in My Soul," "(Take Me Back to) Old Yazoo," "Down Among the Sheltering Palms," "Louisiana Hayride," "It's Sunday Down in Caroline," and the most Jolsonian of them all, "Swannee Mammy."

and the novel took them into musical domains hitherto un-
charted: They use Latin American rhythms for the first time, in
fact, on their premier Brunswick, "Whad'ja Do to Me?" from
March 1931, only a few months after Havana bandleader Don
Azapiazu introduced the rhumba to gringo ballrooms. Louis
Armstrong's "Peanut Vendor" and his glorious previous exposi-
tion of the traditional tango chorus in Handy's "St. Louis Blues"
made it permissible to jazz up material originally written with a
Latin accent; hardly anyone before the Boswells had ever Latinized a straight American pop song. The rhumba being such a
new immigrant to American shores, proper percussion instruments proved impossible to find, so Connee improvised by shak-
ing rice (accounts differ as to whether the rice was shaken in a
box, a tin can, or a wooden bowl). Four years later, Vet arranged
a Boswell "Darktown Strutter's Ball" so avant-garde that Kapp
refused to issue it in America, letting it languish in the hands of
Australian 78 collectors until it turned up on an American LP in
1986. Kapp undoubtedly objected to the second chorus in which
"the band starts to rhumba" and the girls harmonize on top of
what sounds like a whole section of rice-shakers with trumpeter
Mannie Klein making like a Tijuana brassman in a sort of
mariachi-cum-frahlicha.

The move to New York filled the last gap in their development, restoring to them what they had taken for granted in New
Orleans but couldn't get in Los Angeles: musical minds to corroborate their own. In fact, collectors of Benny Goodman, the
Dorsey Brothers, Glenn Miller, Bunny Berigan, Joe Venuti, and
Eddie Lang probably did the most to keep the music of the
Boswell Sisters alive, long after the showbiz community had
forgotten them. They searched out Boswell records for their
accompaniments, and most likely played them expecting to hear
hacks like Kate Smith and Ruth Etting, whom these future
bandleaders also accompanied before the band boom. Instead,
they discovered singing every bit as vital, every bit as swinging
as the solos of Berigan and Goodman. And no lack of instrumental features besides; as Connee told John Campbell in 1944, "My
motto was—let the guys alone!"

These men don't even have to solo to inspire their stars. Compare the first "Heebie Jeebies," the one made for Okeh in 1930 using only Martha's piano for support, with the Brunswick remake from nine months later with Klein, the Dorseys, and their favorite bassist, Joe Tarto, which crams infinitely more inspiration and excitement into the same three-minute chart. A third "Heebies" from a 1934 "Woodbury" radio program using the journeyman studio orchestra of Georgie Stoll (a few years before the great Eddie Barefield joined it) came out comparatively listless in spite of host Bing Crosby's introduction of them as "three little girls with but a single thought—harmony. And what harmony!" The same thing happened on their tours. Vet related, "A lot of the pit bands had good musicians but they just couldn't play our type of music. So we would just cut 'em out. Get a bass and drums and Martha would play the piano."

But all of these elements—the blend, the beat, the flair for unusual ideas, and the excellent soloists—wouldn't mean anything without a unifying concept to alloy them into musical creations that are, like the trio itself, greater than the sum of their parts. As an arranger, Connee Boswell anticipates Gil Evans (and as arranger-performer, Thelonious Monk) in that her arrangements differ so much from the original sources that they approach recomposition. In the twenties post-Armstrong jazzmen and singers had embellished melodies and improvised on their harmonies, and also used a third method, a combination of the two that Andre Hodier called "paraphrase."

Boswell reshapes her material from start to finish. "Sometimes the three of us would take a song that was a ballad. 'Blue Heaven' certainly wasn't a hot number," Connee said as she outlined her approach to Rich Conaty. "But we would take it and put a real Dixieland background to it. And we'd have fun doing that. Then we would take a swing number . . . a jazz number of some kind, something that was real good with a good solid beat. We would slow it down and maybe put the major tune in a minor and we would make almost a semiclassical number out of it." This proclivity for reversals comes through strongly in the already-analyzed "Shout, Sister, Shout" wherein the Boswells use the portions the composer set up to provide tension and release for just the opposite purposes. Take a tune by Duke Ellington and one by Harold Arlen: "It Don't Mean a Thing," a melody with the Boswellian device of having the scat lines written directly into the sheet music, and the fast, jazzy "Minnie the Moocher's Wedding Day." Boswell slows both down to a slow, bluesy crawl and finds strengths in each that the composers themselves might not have realized.

Like everyone else in Kapp's stable, the Boswells recorded a great number of one-shot songs for Brunswick, providing us with our only reason to listen to these songs today. On these, the Boswell recorded arrangements have superseded the published music as a basis for further interpretations. When the sisters waxed the cheery "We've Got to Put That Sun Back in the Sky," it struck contemporary performers as being so definitive that they retained the Boswell device of humming the first three notes of the rhyming first and third lines of the bridge (as did the choir of sidemen in the dance band Roane's Pennsylvanians); only the stodgy English bothered to reinstate the original words. On better-known tunes, like the two Dubin and Warren warhorse standards from *42nd Street*, the title cut and "Shuffle Off to Buffalo" (both 1933, Brunswick), the Boswell revisions of melody, harmony, and lyrics have the same startling effect they did in 1933.

What really makes the Boswells spiritual kin to Gil Evans involves their incorporation of indigenous material into charts of other people's music. They take a melody and, not content to reverse it, slow it down, speed it up, alter its harmonies (even its major or minor-ness), or reshape its melody till its own composer wouldn't know it (the composer of "Whad'ja Do to Me?" is supposed to have asked, "Whad'ja do to my song?"); they add original pieces of music that have absolutely nothing to do with the original composition. Nearly twenty-five years later, Gil Evans did the same thing with his new introduction to "Bess, You Is My Woman Now" on *Miles Davis—Porgy and Bess*.

Because the Boswells created so many scores—an act, for them, equivalent to writing new songs—in so short a time, we have at least one example of their reusing an original melody in two completely unrelated examples. In the summer of 1935, during their second tour of Europe, traveling apparently left them with little time to write new material. So when they had a record date with English Decca (the first under their contract with Kapp's new label), Boswell simply recalled her indigenous hot chorus from "Every Little Moment," recorded for Brunswick only a few months earlier, and grafted it on to "Fare Thee Well, Annabelle." The composer of "Moment" intended it to be a slow ballad, the author of "Annabelle" wrote a peppy fox-trot; that they both wind up the same way only underscores the Boswells' originality. A month later in Holland, Connee teamed with the Ramblers, the best local jazz group in the years before Dutch Swing went to College, to produce the bouncy "I'll Never Say Never Again Again" as a solo number. When a radio sponsor back in the States not long after demanded a trio version, Connee added Martha and Vet's voices to several key lines of her first chorus and then the three of them reprised part of "Way Back Home" (also just a few moons old) for the second thirty-two bars, rewording the jazzy break that went "*I'm* singin' my *song* of loneliness!" to go "*I* said I'd *ne*-ver do!"

The Boswell girls also reworked contemporary songs with a system they had inherited from their parents, whereby they could transform lyrics into seminonsensical syllables through a more complicated form of pig latin. By this process the word "boy" becomes "boggledoy," "swing" becomes "swiggleding" and a whole chorus of "Yes Sir, That's My Baby" sung in "Boggleswellese" can appear in "Everybody Loves My Baby" (1932, Brunswick). "We got onto it and put a lot of the gibberish in our songs, so nobody ever knew what we were doing," Vet remembered. "But we had a lot of fun with it, it gave us a different sound." The gag caught on briefly in the movies: Busby Berkeley's *Gold Diggers of 1933* opens with Ginger Rogers chirping "We're in the Money" in the more conventional pig latin; Hugh

Harman's 1938 short, *Swing Wedding*, offers a soundtrack in which Bill Kinney and the Ink Spots* swipe the Boswells' gibberish section from "It Don't Mean a Thing."

Most of the credit for their wondrous arrangements goes to Connee Boswell, but the other sisters also contributed their share, Vet creating at least one piece ("The Darktown Strutter's Ball") all by herself. In the early days, they would go over a few ideas the night or morning before the appointed recording session. Later, after they worked out the details of their vocal parts, Connee would notate the instrumental lines in collaboration with Glenn Miller. "I'd make the arrangement and Glenn would come in," Connee told Rich Conaty. "It was just like if you wrote a story and you called a secretary in and she took out her shorthand book and took down everything you said. So Glenn wrote 'em down for us and put 'em together." For another example of the same Boswell chart with and without instrumental parts, compare the commercially recorded "Fare Thee Well, Annabelle" and "Lullaby of Broadway" using a British rhythm section with the transcription versions of these tunes that use Victor Young's whole orchestra.

Perhaps because the Boswells recorded these numbers a few thousand miles away from Kapp they could take improvisational liberties that he had already begun to restrict on the sessions he supervised. When the sisters, like Crosby and many another act, switched from Brunswick to Decca, they had to do as Kapp said, and his interference pretty much killed the spirit of the Boswell Sisters. Kapp brought in a regular arranger, and Connee said, "It's like fish and fowl . . . and some of those records, they just don't come out right. Because he'd be writing with one heart and one ear and one feel, and we're writing with three hearts and a different way and three minds a different way and we never cared much for him." She continued, "Jack was a wonderful guy, he was a terrific commercial man. When he first

---

* Not credited on screen but so identified to me by the late Hugh Harman.

started hearing us, he liked us, but he wanted to rearrange us. He wanted us to sing differently, to stick a little closer to the melody. Which is great, nothing wrong with the melody. In many choruses I did the full melody, so that you got the beauty of the melody itself. But many times a melody would be good, and when the three of us put it together it wouldn't sound as good as when we kept the lyric but changed the melody." Not that it was possible for the Boswells to produce one note of inferior music, but had they stayed together recording for Decca they risked becoming as bland as the Mills Brothers and as banal as the Andrews Sisters, two other products of Kapp's machinations.

History provides a less embarrassing conclusion for the Boswell saga: marriage. It doesn't add up though, because while married women (especially middle-class ones) weren't supposed to work, the sisters had already broken an equally major taboo by taking to the road and singing professionally, and Connee kept right on working anyhow. Vet, the youngest, got hitched first, to a Canadian named John Paul Jones, and actually kept the wedding a secret from her sisters and the world for a year until Morton Downey, Sr. ("who had a dirty mind" no less than Morton Downey, Jr.), spotted the couple checking into a Toronto hotel. When Vet became pregnant they retired the trio, though she always intended the split to be temporary. Everything seems to indicate that Connee simply wanted to get on with her career as a soloist, much the same way Bing Crosby did when he left the Rhythm Boys. Both Martha and Connee married in the business: Connee wed her agent, Harry Leedy, and kept singing as long as she could find work (for about another twenty-five years); Martha middle-aisled it with George Lloyd, ex-RAF major and co-founder of Decca's English parent label, and she retired to Peekskill, New York, with him until her death "after a long illness" at age fifty-three in 1958. Vet moved to Peekskill, too, after the death of her husband and a few years before Connee died in 1976.

Mrs. Hevetia Boswell Jones lived there with her daughter,

Chica, until her death at seventy-seven in 1988. She made it down to Manhattan once in 1985 to catch another trio from New Orleans, a group called the Pfister Sisters, who base their act on Boswell arrangements. Similar Boswell re-creations were something of a trend in the mid-eighties. Apart from the Southern Pfisters and the British Sweet Substitute, who also have recorded, I've heard the Canadian Airwaves, the New York Jazz Babies, two male Boswell-inspired teams, the Disneyland-based Rhythm Brothers and the Manhattan Rhythm Kings, and my own favorite, the Sweet Hots, who appeared frequently at New York clubs like Paper Moon and the Angry Squire in the mideighties. They came closest to capturing the Boswell blend and beat, and they did two things exactly like the originals: They used the cream of New York jazzmen (Ken Peplowski, Spanky Davis) and they split up. Revivalists may introduce new listeners to this music, but none of them can ever touch the originals. The Boswell Sisters succeeded because they did as Johnson once demanded of another person named Boswell and cleared their minds of cant.

Too bad no group came along to succeed the Boswells as succinctly as the Bozzies took up where the Rhythm Boys left off. Too bad that in the fifty years since then no group has ever replaced them or beat them at what they did best. Too bad that the swing era couldn't inspire vocal groups as meaningful as its big bands and solo singers. Too bad most of the units associated with this period—specifically the Andrews Sisters—seemed content to repeat the same hackneyed clichés over and over, the same trite impressions of Martha Raye.

Two extremes characterize the thinking of group arrangers both before and after the Boswell breakup: monophonic and orchestral. The Revelers, the Hi-Los, and their ilk essentially did what a solo singer did, albeit in their cases a solo singer singing badly. The Mills Brothers came up with the idea of using multiple voices to mimic an entire orchestra. "There was a seven-piece band that performed in our hometown," Harry Mills told the *New York Times*. "They used to play this fast little tune that didn't have words. We found out it was called 'Tiger Rag.' That's how we got the idea of trying to sound like a band." This approach, perfected by 1931 when they began recording, takes the idea of replicating a seven-piece band quite seriously, as one brother does the work of a four-piece rhythm section all by himself by playing guitar and humming bass notes, and the other three become a trumpet and two saxophones.

At first glance, their collective career approximates that of the Boswells, chronologically at least. The four brothers—Harry, Herbert, Donald, and John, Jr.—born between 1910 and 1915, began working professionally in the mid-twenties, landed a gig on CBS Radio in 1930 and a contract on the Bozzies' own label, Brunswick, in 1931, and left that company to follow Kapp to Decca as soon as said contract would permit it. Nevertheless, the differences from the New Orleans trio outnumber their similarities. Their all too perfectly balanced four-part harmony grows tiresome a lot quicker than the Boswells' more spacious three-part blend, and none of the Mills quartet had a voice to match the superb pipes of any of the Boswell girls, as Harry Mills demonstrated when he recorded two solo vocal refrains with Andy Kirk's Orchestra in 1936 (but then, *anything* was better than Pha Terrell). The Mills Brothers also deviated from the Boswell Sisters in their concept of the relationship of voices and instruments in jazz. The Bozzies supplemented their sumptuous singing with the finest instrumental soloists; the Millses just cupped their hands in front of their faces and blew. And who would you rather hear: Bunny Berigan or some bozo trying to sound like a trumpet, even if he does it well?

The Mills Brothers, then, have an awful lot of disbelief to suspend, making it all the more remarkable when they actually do pull if off. In the early years they cut this particular mustard quite frequently, especially during their Brunswick tenure. "Coney Island Washboard" (1932), "Jungle Fever" (1934), and "Put on Your Old Gray Bonnet" (1934, all Brunswick) create enough centrifugal force to pull us along despite the frivolousness of the phony instruments idea. There's a kind of straightforward simplicity to their thirties records. It isn't important that their mixing wordless variations in with the given lyrics and melody doesn't match the Bozzies for richness, and since perfection counted for more than spontaneity, it doesn't bother anyone that they never improvise any of their scat segments—the different recordings of "Tiger Rag" made for Brunswick, Decca, and Paramount's *The Big Broadcast* (in 1931, 1934, and 1932) could almost be the same performance. The brothers shine the brightest on a series of Fleischer cartoons where their ace off-camera vocalizing provides a perfect counterpart to the animated action. Instead of photographed actors on the screen, we have highly stylized caricatures of human beings and anthropomorphic animals; instead of real instruments on the soundtrack, we have human voices creating an impression of instrumental sound, again, highly stylized. As a title card near the beginning of *I Ain't Got Nobody* (1932), *Dinah* (1933), and *When Yuba Plays the Rhumba on the Tuba* (1933) reads,

NOTE! The music throughout this cartoon is furnished by the Mills Brothers Quartette.
They employ no musical instruments of any kind—except the guitar.
There is no tuba, no trumpet and no saxophone.

Since the brothers had the more concrete and easily imitable gimmick, they inspired greater numbers of imitators than the Boswells. At least two of their ideas got picked up by other vocal groups—the first turning out to be a genuine sleeper. On their 1932 record of Hoagy Carmichael's "Old Rockin' Chair," John Mills, Jr., intoned the lyrics in a deep basso. The trick worked for one chorus of one record, and it probably never occurred to them to use it again. However, along came the Ink Spots, a newer unit that had begun promisingly with four acceptable sides for Victor. They took this device, not all that wonderful to begin with, and turned it into the most monotonous and repetitious of all formulas, using it on virtually all of their hundreds of Decca releases. They ran it so far into the ground that they struck oil, lucking into a commercial success that resulted in decades of big-time gigs and recordings by any number of "Ink Spots" groups—sort of a McDonald's franchise of bad music. Their obvious and easily imitable contrast of high falsetto and low basso made them an easy target for parodists as diverse as the Modernaires on their "Juke Box Saturday Night," Spike Jones on his "You Always Hurt the One You Love," and the great Hollywood cartoonist Tex Avery in his *Magical Maestro.* Hard to believe as it may be that anyone could ever take the Ink Spots seriously, they set off sincere imitators, too, like the British Issy Bonn. And as if to prove that there is no God, their gimmick survived long into the rock era, perpetuated and perpetrated by doo-woppers like the Platters who, if possible, made music even cornier than the Ink Spots. Even when Earl Coleman's career reached its lowest ebb, he steadily refused offers to join the Ink Spots; he said he'd rather starve than have to make music *that* corny.

The Mills Brothers also launched dozens more off-the-cuff quartets and quintets who made with the mouth-trumpets. The incredibly obscure Roland Smith Ramblers got into the studio to wax their arrangement of "Kickin' the Gong Around" (1933, Clanka Lanka). Far from the pallid and dicty tones of Les Frères Mills, the Ramblers use five rougher, more scabrous voices to evoke not only an entire orchestra but a hard-shell church choir as well, digging deep into the same folk-blues sources that the song's composer, Harold Arlen, drew on. A little of this stuff goes a long way, however, and it doesn't strike me as a real loss that only one disc by the R. S. Ramblers has surfaced. Remember, the Millses wisely brought their "Tiger Rag" in at under a minute and a half.

Criticizing the Mills' Brunswick work and that of their contemporary impersonators seems like carping, however, in light of the speed with which they went downhill after 1934, when they fell into the clutches of Kapp at Decca. Pitifully few of their Deccas deserve to be heard today or reissued, but then Kapp always expressed more concern for the present than the future, and who can blame him? Like their ancestors on the plantation, the Mills boys could make their peppiest music only when out of earshot of de massuh. One of the first black acts to regularly tour Britain, they showed up for eleven sessions at English Decca, all but the first after January 1936, when John Mills, Sr., replaced his dead son, John Jr., on bass voice and guitar. Under the supervision of Harry Sarton rather than Kapp, they waxed a succession of uncommonly swell sides like "F.D.R. Jones," which, due to some fortunate licensing agreements, have been consistently available in LP form.

While the Mills Brothers and the Roland Smith Ramblers took orchestral imitation to its limits, the Spirits of Rhythm and the Cats and the Fiddle conceived a more feasible alternative. Instead of straining their throats to connive audiences into believing that four boys could replace a full band (one French critic actually thought the Mills Brothers were a real band, according to Hector Stewart), these two groups considered it saner and more satisfying musically to pare the orchestra down to just the saxophone section. It took thoroughly musical minds to work out the mechanics of such a concept, and accordingly, almost all the members of each group played instruments, in both cases various members of the guitar family. The Spirits consisted of three tiples (sort of a bigger and more flexible ukelele), one proper guitar, and a drummer, four of whom sang, plus a bassist who played on their recordings; one tiple, two guitars, and a bass made up the Cats. The doubling of guitars and voices gave them two "sections," the balance and contrast between the two bringing out a limitless diversity of textures. For a topper, each of these groups also had one truly wizard player, the Spirits' Teddy Bunn and the Cats' Tiny Grimes. The Spirits also had a genuine mad genius innovator in Leo Watson.

For "My Old Man" (1933, Brunswick), the funniest of the Spirits of Rhythm's records, they invent a five-note introductory phrase out of the song's opening line and state it four times, twice on the guitar, twice on their voices ("My-My-My Old

Man"). They take the first chorus as a quartet, except the bridge; this Watson handles by himself. Since the composers, Johnny Mercer and Bernie Hanighen, have graciously written in a break for some scatting near the end of this release, Watson makes the most of it. As on most Spirits' records, a fine single-note guitar solo by Teddy Bunn follows, showing that guitars can also learn from horns. The Spirits add breaks to the sung third chorus, emphasizing the ends of the first and second A sections, and concoct an entirely different ending for the bridge, each of the five men entering one note at a time to arpeggiate the five pitches of a G_9 chord, which they top with a quick machine-gun lick. Watson gets the next sixteen bars (they wisely reserved space for him to improvise on most of these records, either vocally or instrumentally or both, as on "World on a String" and "I Got Rhythm"), and out of the chords he sculpts another of his warm and lush wordless originals. All of the Spirits come back together for the last eight bars, wrapping it up with the same original phrase that they used to introduce the whole enchilada.

Both the Spirits of Rhythm and the Cats and the Fiddle had a much stronger feeling for genuine improvisation than the Boswells and Millses, and if they fall a little short of the Boswells' rhythmic dexterity, they still had powerful and relentless swing and displayed it front and center on all their records. They revel in a distinctively black sound that owes as much to contemporary 52nd Street as it does to spirituals and the blues. The Spirits' two pseudo-religious numbers, "Shoutin' in the Amen Corner" (1933) and "I'll Be Ready When the Great Day Comes" (1934, both Brunswick), use antiphony and other gospel-inspired devices but in a completely up-to-date way. When the Cats do "I'd Rather Drink Muddy Water," Eddie Miller's adaptation of an ancient blues phrase associated with Jack Teagarden, they treat it like a blues *song*, handling the central theme in a high baritone very much in the Crosby idiom.

The Cats and the Fiddle make concrete the idea of four voices as a sax section on their very first record, the original tune "Gangbusters," which includes a vocal transcription of a chorus

written by Benny Carter for his reed section. All of the Cats'
records can't be the gems that the Spirits' are, but their discography includes "Killing Jive" (1939, Bluebird), "Public Jitterbug
No. 1" (1939, Bluebird), and other examples of vocal group jazz
at its most electric. Their "When I Grow Too Old to Dream"
(1939, Bluebird), like many of the best Boswell numbers, became part of the lexicon. Using double time and the standard
small-group theme-solo-theme format, they rewrite this Sig
Romberg aria with extra words and notes wherever they'll fit.
Some of this interpolated material comes from other songs—
"Old Rockin' Chair," "Old Folks at Home," "American Patrol,"
(the earliest King Cole Trio used this same quote this same way
on their "By the River St. Marie"), and "Christopher Colum-
bus." They expand the second line with a corker of a phrase, "I'll
have you *if you're not too big and fat* to remember" (italics
under new portion). When Rose Murphy recorded the song ten
years later, she retained the reference to the girth of the protagonist's ex, and also reiterated that same "big and fat" line at
the end of the side.

The groups discussed up to now worked independently of the
swing system, excepting Kapp's guest-star pairings like the
Boswell Sisters and Victor Young or Jimmie Grier's orchestras
and the Mills Brothers with Don Redman's Orchestra (forecast-
ing the day when they would abandon the "four boys and a
guitar" approach for actual brass and reeds). The groups that
recorded and toured with the major bands, like Tommy Dorsey's Pied Pipers and Glenn Miller's Modernaires, just didn't
have the goods as far as jazz or jazz-oriented pop was concerned,
the Modernaires (*not* the Ordinaires of the forties) having done
more credible work in their pre-Miller days with Charlie Barnet
and Paul Whiteman.

Though annexing trios and quartets to dance bands led to a
dead-end street; bandleader Jimmie Lunceford made his already
exciting records all the more terrific with vocal units drawn from
the ranks of his sidemen. The "Lunceford Singers" (my term)
initially appear on the ersatz spiritual "Chillun, Get Up" (re-

corded in 1934 for Victor and again the next season for Decca) and then on the mildly ribald "Unsophisticated Sue" (1934, Decca), which pivots around a blues-derived stop-time interlude. On "My Blue Heaven" (1935, Decca), "Muddy Water" (1936, Decca), and "Cheatin' on Me" (1939, Vocalion), these Lunceford-ettes do an about-face from the frenetic dot-doot-dah peppiness of virtually every other singing group of the thirties and, instead, achieve a luxuriously laid-back sonority. On "Me and the Moon" (1936, Decca) especially, they could be three guys on the corner smoking tea. And until Perry Como began recording for Victor a few years later, you just couldn't get any mellower. Lunceford and his head arranger, Sy Oliver, only blew it when they assigned solo ballad vocals to Dan Grissom—Oliver sounds better when he sang these refrains himself. Unfortunately, Lunceford's excep-tional "sections" of vocalists (and their offspring, like the vocal trio of Ellington bandsmen who back Ivie Anderson on the Duke's "I've Got to Be a Rug-Cutter" [1937, Master]) proved to be just that: exceptions.

Still, going back to the rule about good vocal groups needing at least one really strong singer, you could transform a middling unit into a top-notch one by teaming it with an outstanding soloist. Jack Kapp discovered this when he combined the Mills Brothers with Bing Crosby for two titles in 1932 and one in 1933.* A solid but unsensational trio, the Three Peppers, be-came something to really listen to when the powerful, Bessie Smith–influenced Sally Gooding became the fourth Pepper. The Modernaires never sounded better than when they harmonized with Jack Teagarden on a 1938 aircheck of "Christmas Night in Harlem" (with Paul Whiteman [Totem]).† The Mills Brothers

---

* The Spirits of Rhythm obviously had these Mills-Crosby discs on their minds when they tried to record "I've Got the World on a String," because an unidentified Spirit croons the first chorus à la Crosby.

† Teagarden's solo version of "Aunt Hagar's Blues" from a 1945 aircheck has it all over the recordings and broadcasts he made of the same arrangement with Whiteman and the Modernaires seven years earlier.

restore your faith when they collaborated with Ella Fitzgerald and Louis Armstrong, the latter combination leaving posterity a magnificent "Song Is Ended" (1938, Decca) in which the melody for once really does linger on. Even the Andrews Sisters stopped embarrassing themselves every time Bing Crosby stepped between them and the microphone, and ceased smelling up the screen when Gringo Bingo samba'd them through Harold Rome's raucous rhumba "You Don't Have to Know the Language" in the movie *Road to Rio* (1947, Paramount). Predictably, only the Ink Spots couldn't rise to the occasion when the real article shared their vinyl: In their excursions with Ella Fitzgerald they hang from her neck like a collective albatross, pummeling all the vitality out of her.

Crosby's own forties and fifties sides with backup singers don't live up to the potential of either the Rhythm Boys or a Bing solo, and for that reason everyone prefers Bing sans glee clubs. Nevertheless, he compensated for this by introducing to the record-buying public *the* seminal vocal group of the forties: Mel Torme and his Mel-Tones. Forty years later we can discuss this remarkable unit more easily in terms of what they *didn't* do rather than what they did. They developed a harmonic sound that gets as pretty as possible without becoming cloying, they spin completely natural embellishments that never become empty jive double-talk, and they never overstay their welcome. (On their Artie Shaw sides particularly, they know when to clam up and let the folks hear the band.) The late thirties left unfulfilled the promise of the Boswells' ideas and the swing-band format, but then along came Torme to bring these ideas two steps farther into modern jazz.

Most groups hung together only a short time, the Spirits of Rhythm leaving us just about enough to fill a single LP, the Cats and the Fiddle and the Rhythm Boys making enough for two, but only with some padding. Only the Boswells could fill three or four LPs with all good stuff. Not counting their 1960 reunion album (and some airchecks and interim revivals for Capitol and Coral), the Mel-Tones also require only one LP to preserve their essential recordings, including the six exquisite sides made as guest stars with the Shaw orchestra. (All their important pieces were recorded in 1946 for the independent label Musicraft.)

The Mel-Tones succeed on both a purely musical and a literal level. The side that reinvented the use of instrumental solos on top of human voices, "What Is This Thing Called Love?," seems just as remarkable today for its masterful mix of jazz-band brass, uncompromisingly European strings, and miniature choir. These previously uncombinable elements merge to produce variations and paraphrases both in music and words, swirling around solos from both Shaw's clarinet and Torme's high baritone, each taking mischievous delight in composer Cole Porter's unexpected blue notes (on his Verve remake, Torme went even farther out, substituting Art Pepper for Shaw and avoiding any direct reference to the melody for most of the track). "And So to Bed" acts out the song's plot with musical devices: Opening with a drowsy celesta (soon to be a favorite instrument of Torme's) immediately roused by a thunderous brass entrance, the band then plays the theme very, very quietly, occasionally disturbed by a Shaw solo and one loud note, as if to depict someone slowly waking up in the morning. Appropriately the 'Tones incorporate a yawn and a chiming clock into their vocal refrain, the clock striking first at its beginning and then behind Torme's solo on the bridge.

Their sides without Shaw don't share the same high batting average. "South America, Take It Away," for instance, lacks the showbiz panache of Bing and the Andrews dames. But at least two of their Shaw-less sides warrant attention, "It Happened in Monterey" and "That's Where I Came In." The first affords us our earliest real glimpse of Torme, the arranger who would assert himself a generation later here juxtaposing two harmonically identical ersatz Mexican waltzes by Mabel Wayne, "Monterey" and "Ramona." Torme ribs their melodramatic sentimentality and latent chauvinism, cementing two melodies and five voices into a cohesive whole. Again, he adds new thematic material so that his first important attempt at extended multisong structures renders the term "medley" obsolete. "That's Where I Came In" explodes with Parker-era rhythm and harmony, forming a perfectly realized balance of written composition and improvisation where any of five voices (and instrumentalists, too) can solo in unison, individually, or in any combination.

Predictably, the vocal group format could no more contain Torme than it could Crosby or Boswell. His concepts didn't lie totally unexplored after the Mel-Tones split up, but they had more positive relevance for Torme's art as a soloist than they did for any successive vocal group. Eventually, some of his ideas passed into the careless hands of the Hi-Los and the Four Freshmen, and what had in Torme's work been a snazzy set of berets and fedoras became a closet of old hats: unappealing voices, obnoxious overclose harmony, and stale ideas.

In 1947 tenor saxophonist Charlie Ventura inspired new hope for the use of multiple voices in jazz—as opposed to jazz vocal groups—by forming his "Bop for the People" band. Records like "Euphoria" (1947, Savoy) and "East of Suez" (1949, Coral) display a thoughtful synthesis of male (Roy Kral) and female (Jackie Cain) voices within the context of the modern jazz small band, using the singers as part of the ensemble at openings, closings, and transitions between instrumental solos. At the same time, Ventura's "Gone With the Wind" (1948, Savoy) and "Lullaby in Rhythm" (1949, Victor) capture a potentially promising solo canary in Jackie Cain. For a time it might have seemed as if the two singers deserved some of the credit for the great sound of the Bop for the People band, but when Ventura disbanded and Cain and Kral went out on their own to become "Jackie and Roy," they never again made music as satisfying. Ventura wisely never made them the center of attention, and used the duo pretty much only to introduce heavyweight musicians like Bennie Green, Conte Candoli, Boots Mussulli, and the leader himself. Like the 2,000-year-old man's description of Sigmund Freud's primary talent—basketball—they did better setting up the shots than actually taking them. Since leaving the tenorist,

Jackie and Roy grew increasingly plastic, until the point where they came to sound like Steve and Eydie accompanied by Bud Powell. Ventura needed them less than they needed him; his subsequent recordings with Betty Bennett (again, an unremarkable chantootsie whose work with Ventura, Shorty Rogers, and sweetie Andre Previn makes her look better than she was) shows he didn't miss Cain and Kral at all.

That about says it all for the jazz vocal group. It remained an anomaly, an aside, a footnote to the rest of the vocal genre. It never grew strong enough to form any discernible mainstream, never challenging either the solo singer or the instrumental group as an alternative format. Outside a few of the Boswell Sisters' very best pieces, it never produced any music as satisfying as, say, Duke Ellington's saxophone section chorus on "Midriff"; either Frank Sinatra, Nelson Riddle, or Milt Bernhart's contribution to "I've Got You Under My Skin"; or Ornette Coleman's "Ramblin'."

The good groups just couldn't stay together long enough: Either they couldn't get along or their best singers wanted—and deserved—to be stars in their own right. And even the jazz audience never got sharp enough to tell the genuine article from the hacks and phonies who stole, then perverted every good idea that came along. As the stock became increasingly diluted, the breed grew rarer and rarer until the early fifties, when it became almost completely extinct.

With one exception: A team eventually did come along who could give the story of the jazz vocal group a fitting conclusion. But Lambert, Hendricks, and Ross came out of a tradition totally removed from the sisters and brothers of earlier decades, as we'll see when we get to them in another chapter.

The Conquest
of the Crooners

Pop Singing in the Postwar Era

● ──────────────────────────────

"The voice of the turtle is heard in the land."
—The Song of Songs

≡ We fight our battles for world dominance at the same time we fight them for cultural supremacy. World War I, which established the United States as a power far outside its own hemisphere, began just after the struggle to found the American Society of Composers, Authors, and Publishers (hereafter ASCAP) and to guarantee royalties for composers, thereby inventing a new and distinctly American breed, the songwriter-businessman. In 1939, ASCAP's rebellion against the broadcasting industry for a larger piece of the pie coincided with Germany's gambit for a bigger chunk of the planet. Two years later, America's entry into the war preceded the American Federation of Musicians' (hereafter the AFM) strike for a piece of the action by only a few months.

Both ASCAP and the AFM, having already established that professional music makers deserved the same rights as other workers, used the same tactics as other labor unions: bans and strikes. ASCAP forbade the networks from airing songs by its members; the AFM prohibited its members from making records. Both fights ended the same way: The networks turned to a rival agency, Broadcast Music Inc. (BMI), to supply them with songs; the record companies went after music not controlled by the union.

Since ASCAP and the AFM allegedly represented artists (the underdog), our sympathies would normally go out to them. But their actions weren't those of white hats versus black hats so much as one greedy organization against another, doomed to fail because they could not conceive of how music they had never bothered with could possibly prove a threat to them. ASCAP claimed to represent all composers while it really fended only for Broadway, Hollywood, and Tin Pan Alley. The AFM acted as if it took care of all musicians, yet it actually worried only about the sidemen in the big dance bands, theater pits, and movie soundstages. Even as late as the war, the double whammy of the two idioms, Tin Pan Alley and the big bands, seemed unimpeachable.

The clash between record companies and the AFM had the most immediate impact, because both sides lost to a third faction, the A&R man. Previously, he was only the guy who got stuck with the unglamorous chore of working out the details of dates, studios, sidemen, and tunes, and he was entirely dependent on the song pluggers and the bandleaders for his sustenance; after the music wars this dark horse quickly became the front-runner of the industry. Soon the A&R men would be more responsible for hits than any artist or any record label, for they had found a way to control popular music that went far beyond merely following trends, as they had traditionally done. Within a decade of the ban, the A&R men had figured out how they could actually create public taste.

"It was a black day for good music when the bandleaders lost control to the A&R men," said singer Barbara Lea. The musicians had to lose out; they knew only music and musical values, while the new A&R boys knew business and balance sheets, power and money. With musical minds in charge of things, pop music had the same kind of floor as New Deal economics—things couldn't get much worse than a certain level. With moneymen running the show we have no such guarantee, making the worst dreck of the thirties look good in comparison with the kiddie pop of the mid-fifties onward.

The new faction seized power and put the bandleaders out of business with pop singers. It proved an unwise move for them in the long run. The best singers, especially those who were jazz-oriented, turned out to be as quirky and uncontrollable as the bands. Frank Sinatra balked at having to record what he considered to be dog tunes (literally, in one extreme case). So did Mel Torme—even worse, he actually wanted to arrange his own material, as if *he* knew what would sell! They all seemed to have this weird thing about quality. Rosemary Clooney almost didn't sing "Come On-a My House," she despised the song so much, and Columbia almost didn't sell eighty zillion singles. Obviously, the moneymen had to take steps against such anarchy with so much money at stake, and eventually replaced adult pop singers with a commodity completely removed from the standards (in both senses of the word) of Tin Pan Alley. In the meantime, post-band and post-ban singers had a few years at the top.

The A&R-AFM war even had its own Manhattan Project. It probably never occurred to Petrillo, the union's boss, that Decca, Columbia, and Victor could make records without using any musicians at all, and clearly, the labels really didn't want to try. It meant they had to get about three dozen singers and somehow coax them into sounding like an orchestra. No one knew how to arrange for such an ensemble; worse, modern recording techniques had been designed expressly to record big bands, and even the most accomplished engineers couldn't put these big a cappella choirs down on wax. So as the ban dragged on, the

labels held out as long as they could before resorting to pseudo-
orchestras. Dinah Shore, who had gotten a few steps up the
ladder to singing stardom in the years immediately prior to the
ban, and who put over the last unrecorded hit song in the early
months of the strike ("Tess's Torch Song"),* waited until January
1944 before taking a crack at recording with one of these elephantine glee clubs. Bing Crosby, who had stockpiled no less
than fifty-eight songs as the ban loomed in the spring of 1942,
waited until July 1943 to try two sessions; even then, he bothered only with surefire hit material: two highly received tunes
from *Oklahoma!*, Broadway's biggest hit of the decade, and two
from his latest picture, one being a genuine shoo-in, "Sunday,
Monday or Always."†

Kapp was right about the song. It became a hit all right, but
not for Crosby: for Frank Sinatra, then a young upstart fresh out
of the Tommy Dorsey band. (Crosby didn't mind. On the day
the ban ended for Decca, he and the Andrews Sisters waxed
"Pistol Packin' Mama," giving Bing his hit for the season.) If
Crosby could practically wait out the strike, Sinatra and the
other band graduates couldn't. Dick Haymes, who had left Dorsey about six months after replacing Sinatra with that band,
began his solo career and Decca contract with four choir-backed
vocals in late May 1943. A few weeks later, Perry Como, a
recent refugee from the Ted Weems Orchestra, recorded a typical wartime romance ditty for Victor ("Goodbye, Sue"), again
supported by choral ooh-ing and ahh-ing.‡

---

* This information courtesy of Miles Kreuger.

† Paramount agreed with Kapp, and not only opened the movie, *Dixie*, with Crosby
singing the number but had him reprise it halfway through, backed by a huge choir—just
like the one on the record (even though the movie studio musicians were *not* on strike).

‡ By the time of the second AFM ban in 1948, multitrack recording techniques had
reached the point where orchestral accompaniment tracks could be recorded overseas
and the vocal dubbed in later, which worked on Margaret Whiting's "A Tree in the
Meadow" (one of the biggest hits of the ban year that should have been a banner year)
and on some of Sinatra sound-alike Ronnie Deauville's Mercury singles.

Ultimately, Crosby and Haymes got the jump on their competitors when their parent label, Decca (along with Capitol), negotiated the earliest major-label agreement with Petrillo in August 1943. Meanwhile, at Columbia, Sinatra and the Bobby Tucker Singers struggled through "People Will Say We're in Love," which took three sessions to get an acceptable take, and at Victor, Como and Shore had to wait until November 1944 before they could record with legitimate orchestras again. Still, they all came out on top. As mentioned, Shore landed a hit with "Tess's Torch Song," sung by her in the Danny Kaye movie *Up in Arms* and on the radio but not on a record several years after the fact. With "Sunday, Monday or Always," Sinatra told the world he didn't need Dorsey to sell lots of discs, while two of Haymes's first solos, "You'll Never Know" and "Can This Be Wrong?" (incidentally, the two best of the pseudo-orchestral records), became major hits, and a few months after Victor came to an agreement with the AFM, Como's star status was assured by "Till the End of Time," its success partly a result of its Chopin-derived melody and piano part that could not have been recorded during the strike.

But even though the contenders landed a few hits here and there, no one sold more records than the all-time champ, Bing Crosby: The man who virtually invented modern popular singing in the late twenties still led the pack well into the fifties. "Accentuate the Positive," "Pistol Packin' Mama," "Swingin' on a Star," and "Don't Fence Me In" all hail from the mid-forties, when Crosby reached the mountaintop of international popularity. In these years he didn't just experiment with different genres, he created them—"San Antonio Rose" launched the country record industry and "White Christmas" made holiday music a major staple of the record business. Of the male singers who came out of the bands, only Sinatra did anything fundamentally different from Crosby, and in the forties he came to be regarded as the exception that proved the rule. Most of the fellahs who came up in that decade were strictly-from-Bing, and as such they split into categories in which musical qualities sync-up with ethnic backgrounds. Crosby inspired Irish-Anglo types like himself: Dick Haymes, David Allyn, and Bob Manning; Italian-Americans like the earlier Russ Columbo, Perry Como, and Dean Martin; and blacks (whom I'm saving for the next chapter), most strongly Herb Jeffries. "In 1940," Perry Como later said, "unless you sang like Bing and Columbo, you didn't eat."

Each of these men did nothing that Crosby hadn't done first and, to be cruelly honest, better. As so often happens, the original can haul off in whatever direction he likes while his followers have to limit themselves to trails that have already been blazed—witness Dick Todd in the early forties, aping the Crosby of a half-decade earlier. The good ones eventually found their own identity in the Crosby style, which came through a process of subtraction. Though they appropriated what they could of his mellow baritone and sophisticatedly syncopated rhythm, few of these men ever tried to scat or reshape melodies as Crosby did. Most also stuck with songs that might have been in Crosby's repertoire, basically ballads with the occasional up-tempo and rhythm number mixed in, with some variations: Haymes went for sentimental oldies, while Como and Martin did lots of novelties, Dino's ancient and Perry's current. The whole idea of so many singers patterning themselves on a single model may seem a little odd forty years later, but remember that all of them had grown up with Crosby as the Supreme Musical Patriarch, and his shadow loomed so large in every area that it left room for all.

In limiting himself to moony-voweled ballads and generally avoiding the faster tempos, Russ Columbo set the style for post-Bing vocalists for the next two decades. Dead at twenty-six, Columbo made only a handful of records (almost all for Victor), these being only slightly augmented by a few scattered airchecks, soundtracks, and band vocal refrains; no wonder his supporters more usually discuss what he might have done had he lived rather than what he actually achieved. Time has considerably weakened Columbo's appeal; especially compared to later Italian Crosby-ites like Como and Martin, he comes off as tense and humorless, with a slight nasal tremolo. There's nothing you'll hear on any of his records that suggests a serious rival to Crosby, even though he went after Bing's thunder by boo-boo-booing and covering his theme song, "Blue of the Night" (Victor, 1931). Still, no one ever topped Columbo's "Prisoner of Love," an uneven though sincere metaphor song that so perfectly matched his personality it became a mantra of his life and death. Since his death in 1934, Columbo's biggest boosters have been other crooners who've tackled "Prisoner" in tribute to him, among them Crosby, Sinatra, James Brown (yes, *that* James Brown), and most significantly, Billy Eckstine, who years later achieved what Columbo had strived for but was unable to complete in his short, romantic lifetime.

The Irish-American crooners had their founding father figure in Buddy Clark, one who deliberately adopted both Crosby's initials and his Anglo-Saxon identity, having been born Jewish and named, believe it or not, Samuel Goldberg. His melodious, pleasant baritone came the closest to Crosby, and unlike most of the other boy singers here, he worried little about developing an individual style. The only important singer after Crosby and Al Bowlly to start as a studio freelancer, Clark concentrated on Crosby-esque versatility. When Benny Goodman, not yet the King of Swing, produced some sweet band sides for blue Columbia in 1934, he brought in Clark to sound square-jawed and stoic, and then to be punchy and full of pep in a duet with Helen Ward on a 1935 aircheck, "Not Bad," where the two become a junior league Crosby and Lee Wiley. But he could also bring out a Bing-ish blackness on the Hendersonian medium-fast "Livin' in a Great Big Way" (Goodman's orchestra [1935, Victor]—in two takes!) and the Ellingtonian medium-slow "A Sailboat in the Moonlight" (Johnny Hodges's orchestra [1937, Variety]). To quote Sam Costa, "You were either a high Crosby or a low Crosby." Dick Todd fits securely into the latter spot, but for a "high Crosby," Buddy Clark acquits himself quite nicely, and more of his Okeh and Columbia 78s deserve to make it to CD. Like Columbo he turned out to be a martyr, dying in a plane crash at thirty-eight.

Though basically Bing-ish in conception, the perpetually intoxicated Dean Martin mixes in a few parts each of Louis Prima and Al Hibbler, chasing the cocktail down with a strong shot of Jolson. Everything about Martin shouts inconsistency, until he takes it so far it almost becomes a virtue. He'll commonly make one line very high and the next extremely low, or move from deep notes resonating from the back of his throat to tinny tones that seem to originate in the cracks between his pearly whites. Martin misses the methods in the madness of the best jazz singers, instead filtering everything through the sloshed spoonerisms of the comic drunk. Sammy Davis, Jr., might savage Tony Bennett with one of his vaguely hostile impressions, but he could never be more ludicrous than Martin in inebriate phrasing, diction, or constant falling down. For ten years Martin formed an ironic partnership with Jerry Lewis: a comedian who came to take himself too seriously to be funny and a romantic balladeer who acted too silly to be taken seriously. Still, Dean Martin was a bigger success on TV than either Crosby or Sinatra.

Television did even more for Perry Como, and vice versa. He served the same function for crooners in the medium's golden age that Milton Berle did for roughhouse comics. Como first made the hit parade with heavy, Chopinesque numbers like "Till the End of Time" (1945, Victor) and "I'm Forever Chasing Rainbows" (probably also 1945). But once on top, he switched over to the most idiotic novelties of the pre–Mitch Miller era, beginning with "Hubba Hubba" (which he sang in the 1946 Fox flick *Doll Face*) and continuing through "Chi-Baba Chi-Baba" (1947), "N'Yot N'Now (The Pussycat Song)" (1948), "Bibbidi Bobbidi Boo (The Magic Song)" (1949), "Zing Zing Zoom Zoom" (1950), the awful "Chincherinchee" (195?), "Pa-Paya-Mama" (195?), and the monster hit "Hot Diggety-Dog Diggety" (1955–56),* most sung with the sappiest vocal groups this side of doo-wop. Nevertheless, when we think of Como we don't dwell on

---

* Compared to these, Como's " 'A' You're Adorable" (which after all encourages kiddies to read) seems a most literary ditty indeed.

material so much as style. The most relaxed character in all of pop, Como came to be described by Bing Crosby himself as "the man who invented casual." A much-aired "Second City TV" spoof showed a line of chorus girls propping up the pooped, "Como-tose" crooner, who sings while lying perfectly horizontal in between the sheets. Como doesn't just sing behind the beat, he makes you feel he has yet to catch up with the *previous* beat. To maintain the horizontal mode, Como makes his lines as even as possible by minimalizing every interval and making the harmonic distance from one note to the next seem shorter. Compared with pep boys like Sammy Davis and Eddie Cantor, Como would never impress anyone as a high-energy performer.

Reclining as he may be, when you get Perry Como away from the vocal choirs and the dumb songs, you can coax some good singing out of him. Most of his dreck never got on to the LPs that Victor filled with his singles, as they reserved this space for his renditions of standards and the better new Broadway tunes. Como does especially well by Rodgers and Hammerstein, where his minimalization technique helps to cut such grandiose texts as "If I Loved You" and "Some Enchanted Evening" down to size, and fits perfectly such smaller-scale airs as "All at Once You Love Her." The bulk of Como's albums—like *Sing to Me, Mr. C, So Smooth, A Sentimental Date with Perry Como* (one of his two great early twelve-inch "broad" covers), and the inevitable *Relaxing with Perry Como*—consist of good songs sung well, but one shouldn't listen to too many of them in a *row*.

Too bad they can't all be like *We Get Letters* (1957), perhaps the one absolutely essential Como record. Now, *Como Swings*, his own *Swingin' Lovers*, fails for the same reasons as Martin's *This Time I'm Swingin'*, as Como's natural sense of swing has nothing in common with Sinatra's. The disc seems too heavy, too deliberate, and besides, how could any male vocalist even consider swinging "I've Got You Under My Skin" without Sinatra mopping up the floor with him (musically, I mean)? The delightful miniatures of *We Get Letters* take Como away from glee clubs and all the orchestra sections, except the rhythm, 'natch, and musical director Mitchell Ayres (in his most inspired work) even slices up those four pieces pretty good. Varying the instrumentation from track to track, a guitar takes the place of the piano a lot of the time, and on side one, track one's "Swinging Down the Lane," bongos, guitar, and trumpet take over—a format that must have seemed the very farthest reach of the avant-garde to Como fans. For once we get instrumental solos between vocal choruses instead of choirs (can that be Dave Pell on "Angry"?), and Mr. C. establishes beyond doubt that he doesn't need to sound excited himself to excite his audiences. It may be true that Como sings out of his nose, but you've got to admit that his nose makes prettier noises than most singers' throats.

When we talk about Dick Haymes, now, we're talking about a genuinely superior artist and easily the best of the post-Bing generation (outside of Billy Eckstine, anyway). Martin and Como relied on gimmicks to a large extent; Haymes captures our imagination through his utter lack of same. He could even afford to ignore that veritable staple of adult pop—variety. You can listen to Haymes records for hours and hear only medium-slow ballads, and still be interested enough to keep right on listening. We've spoken of high and low Crosbys; Haymes stayed firmly in the middle, avoiding the Old Groaner's long, rangy strolls from the basement to the roof of his voice. He developed a voice so fine and pure, and had a gift for interpreting love songs so convincingly and meaningfully, that the blasé arrangements Decca gave him never mattered, and his personality even rendered his accompaniments a nonconsideration.

Russ Columbo left behind one worthy impersonator when he died, Jimmy Ray,[*] along with dozens of lounge acts that perform for his unsatiated followers. During the height of his career, Dick Haymes had to compete with two carbon copies of himself, Bob Manning (a "high Haymes") and David Allyn (a "low

---

[*] Ray recorded over fifty sides for Bluebird in the thirties, mostly vocal refrains with dance bands under his own and other names.

Haymes"), either one of which could fool a listener on the car radio. Though Manning made a fine version of "The Nearness of You" (Capitol), which nearly made a star out of him, I can honestly only recommend his albums to Haymes collectors who already have everything by the man himself and crave something incredibly similar to listen to. Parodoxically, almost all of Allyn's[*] records deserve a hearing today, as he took the Haymes approach into contexts, usually involving jazz arrangers and soloists, that Haymes himself rarely worked in—which is much the same reason we listen to other "derivative" musicians like Sonny Stitt and Bireli Lagrene. Allyn limited his popular appeal, as you might expect, in singing almost exclusively with jazz groups. True, the fence between jazz and pop didn't have barbed wire on top of it then the way it does today, but how could anyone have thought that such characters as Jack Teagarden or Boyd Raeburn might lead commercially successful dance bands?

Allyn didn't give us a collection of recordings that take up pages and pages in the discographies, but, as Spencer Tracy would admit, "what's there is cherce." Most pop singers recorded acres of forgotten and forgettable tunes, while Allyn never sang anything worse than "Blue Echoes," a Latinate Chihuahua tune that, when you listen to it two or three times, kind of grows on you with its interesting rhythmic motif of a dotted half note and two eighths. Otherwise Allyn did only the good standards and came upon one otherwise neglected Kern song, "Sure Thing,"[†] that he sang so masterfully that he and it became inseparable. Even if Allyn's career turned out to be anything but a sure thing, what other singer can boast of having virtually everything he ever recorded in print—and deservingly so?

---

[*] Allyn even recorded Haymes's hit "This Can't Be Wrong" at one of his first solo sessions (1949, Jewell), but the best rendition is neither the Haymes nor the Allyn record, but a 1945 Haymes radio performance issued in 1985 on the Ballad label.

[†] It can be found on his best album, *Sure Thing* (1957, World-Pacific). Allyn told Dr. Jack McKinney that the original mono issue contained different and better takes than the stereo reissue (WPM-408 versus DS-900).

Haymes himself had few opportunities to sully his recorded output. He may have scored nine[*] gold records during his Decca decade (1943–52), but by 1952, when Mitch Miller's campaign of crap against Sinatra, Rosemary Clooney, and Tony Bennett had reached its nadir, Decca let Haymes go. Battles with the IRS over money and Columbia Pictures godfather Harry Cohn over women (specifically Mrs. Rita Hayworth Haymes) didn't help his career any either. Then, in 1957, when his star had truly fallen, he quixotically made his best though least commercial album. Haymes's *Moondreams* matches Sinatra's *Close to You* for unsettling introspection, as Haymes extracts *melos* (the Greek word for music, relevant here also because it has become associated with melodrama) out of the remorseful "You Don't Know What Love Is" and even finds pathos in the normally cheerful "The Way You Look Tonight." On the hit-making Deccas, Haymes came off as assured and even-tempered; here, he's just a little bit trembly and mussed up, exactly the mood that Ian Bernard's offbeat stylized scores require. Bernard uses only a small string section and a handful of horns, among them the kinky clarinet of Jimmy Giuffre, paying homage to both Pee Wee Russell and Lester Young, as well as a two-finger pianist who's been listening closely to Thelonious Monk. Haymes recorded infrequently in the twenty years before his death, but never disappointed the small and intense coterie of admirers who supported him to the end. "He caressed the lyrics of a love song better than anyone," said Helen Forrest. "In my mind, no one ever sang a love song better than Dick. Not Sinatra, not anyone." On the day Haymes died, Mel Torme, giving a concert at Carnegie Hall that evening, announced that the evening's performance would consist entirely of ballads, "Because the world lost a great ballad singer today."[†]

How telling that so great an artist should score nine major

---

[*] The number is from Allan Dell. Milt Gabler says the actual number is more like six.

[†] This information courtesy of Ron Sarbo.

sellers in that many years and then for the rest of his life be relegated to the underground. It reflects more on the period than it does on Haymes. Lee Jeske dates the beginning of "The Vocal Era" to January 19, 1942, the date that Sinatra made his first records as a soloist and a few weeks after America's declaration of war and a few months before the Petrillo strike that would kill off the big bands. Actually, producer Harry Meyerson and arranger-conductor Axel Stordahl had nothing so earthshattering in mind when they ushered the nervous young crooner into the Victor Studio that winter day. As we have seen, Victor made a practice of recording some of the better band vocalists (Lena Horne, Bea Wain, Maxine Sullivan) in solo "vocadance" settings, issuing the results on their lower-priced Bluebird label. People wouldn't be willing to pay as much for Sinatra solo as they would for Dorsey and Sinatra together, they figured, and at this point in the Sinatra saga (he still had another nine months to stay with TD), they were right.

Then, during the ban and the war, newer-thinking minds began to conceive of new ways to market singers. Enterprising record companies have traditionally sprung up just in time to catch new trends: Remember how Jack Kapp, fully a year before Benny Goodman officially launched the swing-band boom, signed up virtually all of the major black bands (except Ellington), and when adult pop seemed ready to take a Fort Apache–like last stand against kid stuff in the early sixties—Sinatra rallied most of the important singers around him on his Reprise label. Capitol Records came along just in time to get in on the ground floor of the vocal era, having been founded in 1942 by Johnny Mercer, Glenn Wallichs, and Buddy DeSylva.

At the very start, Capitol had only a few flyweight singers like Ella Mae Morse and Andy Russell, and the new label made its most interesting music with bands (Paul Whiteman, Benny Carter, Stan Kenton) and Dave Dexter's ingenious jazz series, though some important acts turned up on these in the vocal refrain capacity: Billie Holiday, Jack Teagarden, and Peggy Lee. Capitol, along with Decca, beat the ban early and in 1943 landed its first chart-toppers with Freddie Slack's "Cow Cow Boogie" and a surprise hit by a newly signed act, the King Cole Trio's "Straighten Up and Fly Right." Before 1943 ended, Capitol had found its house style in the partnership of Tommy Dorsey veterans Paul Weston and Jo Stafford.* Weston's creamy arrangements, string-laden and full (pounds heavier than the John Scott Trotter–Bing Crosby tracks that set the norm for the thirties and early forties, but a dollop lighter than those Axel Stordahl wrote for Sinatra at Columbia), would dominate the sound of the era and the label at least until the end of the decade. When the Weston-Stafford partnership switched to Columbia, Pete Rugolo filled his shoes; then, not only did scads of major modernists get recorded (Miles Davis, Tadd Dameron) but Kenton-like (or Rugolo-like, actually) progressivism became the order of the day (as in the bop bands of Benny Goodman and Charlie Barnet). Eventually the label returned to more commercial though no less worthy stylists like Nelson Riddle and Billy May for their "house" sound.

Jo Stafford exemplifies the postwar era more than any other songbird. Of her most important contemporaries—Doris Day, Dinah Shore, and Margaret Whiting—all but Whiting had big-band experience and all but Day found their way over to Capitol at some point (and all but Whiting also worked for Columbia). Stafford's singing speaks, you should forgive the expression, for the whole era: intonation that approaches Fitzgerald and Torme but doesn't strive toward their ideal of improvisation and recomposition; a middle-range low soprano suggestive of a female Haymes, however, never trying to achieve his warmth or his involvement. Stafford provides a respite from other styles by providing so little of her own, and she sounds particularly great on the radio, particularly if the previous singer, say Billie

---

* This date is from Mark Greenfield. The best document of the Capitol style is *201 Vocal Standards*, a ten-record set issued by EMI's Japan affiliate, consisting almost entirely of Capitol vocal records from the forties and fifties.

Holiday or Sinatra, has just challenged your heart, or your ears, say Judy Garland or Ethel Merman. The lack of style is in itself a style, and Stafford's cool melo-tones are infinitely preferable to the flocks of mike-moths who dub themselves "song stylists" to excuse their complete lack of voice. Stafford only really lets us down on her "covers" of folk and country tunes; Southern accent or not, she shows so little empathy for "Jambalaya" and "Shrimp Boats" (which have been included in her *Greatest Hits* albums, so maybe *I'm* wrong) that she and the pasty-faced choir behind her trying to whoop it up like son-of-a-gun Cajuns might as well be in blackface.

Whiting's straight-down-the-middle tones suggest a Yankee Stafford, and, in her knack for humanizing Rodgers and Hammerstein, emerges as a female version of the forties Perry Como. Like many another warbler, it took age—not to mention years of hard work—for her to acquire real character: an angle, a point of view, an attitude that makes her more than a voice. Too many of her forties Capitol singles lack personality, but by the end of the fifties, when she briefly switched to the more jazz-oriented Verve label (though specific improvisational ingredients in her work would have been superfluous), she's got it. "Make Someone Happy," her solo feature on an otherwise disappointing set of duets with Mel Torme, and her entire two-record collection of Jerome Kern songs with Russ Garcia (which I would recommend over even the Fitzgerald-Riddle-Kern songbook), as well as more recent outings like *The Lady's in Love with You* (1985, Audiophile), reveal a voice as Simon-pure and Maggie-nificent as always, but tempered with the greater depth of expression that maturity and hard work bring.

Stafford, Day, Shore, and Whiting all made their livings in high-class pop, but they also lived by Huxley's dictum that "The natural rhythm of human life is routine punctuated by orgies," meaning that they interspersed straight-ahead jazz albums into their studio rosters. These could be team-ups with well-known musicians. In her small-group jazz set, *Young Man with a Horn* (1950, Columbia), particularly in "Too Marvelous for Words,"

Day sizzles atop a trio arm in arm with Harry James, each proving that while pop paid their bills, neither had lost their affinity for the harder stuff. On *Dinah Sings Some Blues with Red* (Capitol) Shore[*] makes good on her love of Red Norvo's music, a predilection she shared with Sinatra, Torme, and a generation of singers who grew up listening to the great Bailey-Norvo band. Shore and Day each made an album with the Andre Previn Trio, respectively, *Dinah Sings—Previn Plays* (subtitled *Songs in a Midnight Mood* [Capitol] and *Duet, Doris Day with Andre Previn* [Columbia]). As accompanist or soloist, Previn is no Hank Jones (hell, he ain't even a Joe Castro or a Bob Corwin), but his name gave commercial weight to projects that the A&R fellows wouldn't ordinarily have let their star canaries get involved with. The liner notes of each album insist that they labored hard for spontaneousness, Shore and Previn having actually selected their material on the spot, and Day and Previn not even meeting until work on the album began, and each record a more persuasive looseness and freeness than on any other record they made.

Johnny Mandel did the math for *Jo + Jazz*—Stafford's only purely hot record and easily the finest effort of her career—and supports one of the least emotional voices in pop, Stafford, with two of the most emotional voices in jazz, Ben Webster and Johnny Hodges, and also their fellow Ellingtonian, Ray Nance. The equation works out beautifully as Mandel adds two other superior trumpeters (whom he was used to working with), Don Fagerquist and Conte Candoli, and a rhythm section that includes Mel Lewis and two alternating pianists, Russ Freeman and Jimmy Rowles. Together they egg the steadfast Stafford into colors less monochromatic than usual, her honey-dipped y'alls very nearly evoking Connee Boswell.

So the late forties, and Capitol in particular, produced a lot of bad music. But from the standpoint of the mid-eighties, it's

---

[*] Dan Morgenstern spotted Shore in the old Metropole, where Charlie Shavers went out of his way to show off for her.

overwhelmingly obvious that the good outnumbers the bad. We have fine pop singers (and bandleaders also) who could make good jazz albums when the occasion called for it, and even the unjazziest jukebox music proves the pop-music floors were still strong. Nat King Cole and Kay Starr alone would be enough to justify not just the era but all of adult popular music. Capitol virtually discovered both artists, nurtured them, fed and clothed them, and ultimately all but strangled them. Neither could have come out of any other time.

Nat Cole had recorded for other labels (including fifteen unspectacular sides plus the promising "This Will Make You Laugh" for Decca) before coming to Capitol at the end of the ban with his King Cole Trio, first formed five years earlier. Significantly, the three instrumental (non-Cole trio) dates that would do the most for his reputation as a jazz pianist—the 1942 Lester Young session, the 1944 premier concert of Jazz at the Philharmonic, and the 1945 Sunset All-Stars date—would not reach the stores until 1945, long after Cole and the Trio had already established themselves as one of the record industry's biggest-selling acts. The thought of recording an already perfect group may seem untypical of Capitol, the label that invented the concept of the "house sound," but it did occur to them, too. Only a few years after Cole signed with the Hollywood and Vine corporation, its A&R department began putting him in front of orchestras and string sections; by the mid-fifties the Trio was just a memory.

Cole sold unbelievable quantities of records as a solo vocalist "with orchestral accompaniment": most of them very good, a few absolutely terrific, and a tiny few (do the name "Belford Hendricks" strike a familiar note?) unspeakably mediocre. When Cole phased out the Trio the world suffered the loss of Cole the pianist and arranger. During his forties Trio period, the rare dates away from the King Cole Trio proved him a first-rank jazz improviser, and the Trio's instrumentals ("The Man I Love" and "Body and Soul," both 1944, to name just two) make the point that Cole could have been a very marketable pop instrumentalist. Of the four major postwar cocktail pianists—Erroll Garner, Oscar Peterson, George Shearing, and Ahmad Jamal—only Garner could conceivably "cut" Cole as a piano player. Cole even anticipates the devices for which most of them became famous. On the first chorus of the 1943 "It's Only a Paper Moon" (the Capitol version, that is, and not on any of the noncommercial ones that have since been released), Cole plays block chords that out-Shearing Shearing's 1949 hit, "September in the Rain" (MGM) (Cole would later cut an album with that master of monotony). The Trio—Cole, Oscar Moore and later Irving Ashby on guitar, and Johnny Miller and later Joe Comfort on bass—make far more successful use of trio interplay than Jamal later got credit for. And while it's easy to outdo formula hacks like Shearing and Jamal, the Trio's instrumentals "Prelude in C-Sharp Minor" (1944, based on Rachmaninoff) and "Laugh, Cool Clown" (1949, based on *Pagliacci* by Leoncavallo) alloy European and American traditions so successfully they abolish the gimmick of "jazzing the classics" and, in fact, if you substitute vibes for guitar, "Clown" could have been played by the Modern Jazz Quartet. Cole's single-line solo over Jack Costanza'a bongos would have done John Lewis proud.

The description of Cole the pianist may seem irrelevant to Cole the vocalist, but his greatest strength was singing like a refugee from the rhythm section. In those days it seemed nervy enough to dawdle behind the beat, but Cole makes that not yet acceptable idea look like mere kid stuff. Instead, he hugs the beat and matches it pulse for pulse. The 1943 "Embraceable You" finds Cole building to a miniature climax at the end of the release, wherein he throws away the tempo by pushing the line's highest note ("Gyp-sy") just a little higher and then reshuffling the melodic sequence on the other side into a lighter, bouncier pattern that, in the hands of a lesser mortal, would break the mood of the ballad. Cole constantly invents new things to do with rhythm. On "Paper Moon" he uses the idea of reexpanded contractions to add grace notes. By adding an "is" in between "it" and "only" instead of "It's . . .," Cole gains a whole extra beat to play with.

Cole and his chief collaborator, Nelson Riddle, put together a miracle of rhythmic dexterity called "Papa Loves Mambo."* Any singer who didn't happen to be one of the world's great rhythm men would be a lame duck in this dangerous shooting gallery of Billy May–style slurping saxes and Prez Prado–inspired pauses and grunts. But Cole effortlessly jumps over conclaves of claves, dodges barrages of bongos, and gets out of the way of one scorching brass attack after another. The protagonists of the lyric don't fare nearly as well: One goes left, the other goes right, and the two lunging Latin lovers pas de deux in a mambo counterpart to the nearsighted swans described by Danny Kaye in his ballet extravaganza "Pavlova." But Cole, however, escapes unscathed.

Cole's penchant for exotic rhythms, along with his vaguely oriental appearance (those arched eyebrows combined with that jet black skin would have secured him a regular role on "Star Trek" had he lived a few years longer), led to Capitol's filling his sessions with all sorts of exotica. The trend climaxed with the hit "Nature Boy" (1948), a minimally melodied piece of phony philosophy (you can almost hear Eddie Lawrence asking, "Is that what's bothering you, Bunky?") swiped from an old Second Avenue Yiddish theater song by a so-called swami. It also included "Haji Baba," "Land of Make Believe," "Land of Love," "The Ruby and the Pearl," "Return to Paradise," "Song of Delilah," and dozens more that exploited the ethereal, alien quality of his voice—all around the same time that Capitol's new rival, MGM, assigned Cole's rival, Billy Eckstine, loads of similar "enchanted land" opuses. Capitol also discovered what Cole could do with overblown mock-religious epics like "Answer Me, My Love" (translated, Wouldn't You Know?, from the German), "Faith Can Move Mountains," and "Make Her Mine." What a relief to hear Cole sing a simple blues, even if he had to temporarily leave Capitol and wait for *Metronome* magazine to give him an

---

* Were Cole trying to appeal to nineties audiences he'd have to title it "Papa Loves Rambo."

award and team him with their all-stars and June Christy to do it on "Nat Meets June" (1946, Columbia).

But bear with all this grandiosity for just a minute. Because had Cole not recorded all of it, Capitol might never have let him do "Lush Life" (1949), and the world would be a sadder place indeed. According to Don George, carousing buddy of Duke Ellington, and the song's composer, Billy Strayhorn, the song had been kept under wraps for over a decade until Strayhorn found the perfect voice to sing it. Those familiar with later recordings of "Lush Life," especially those of Chris Connor (1954, Bethlehem) and Johnny Hartman (1963, Impulse), which use very spare quartet backings, will find Pete Rugolo's orchestral arrangement for Cole a revelation. Full of Latin percussion, it balances strings and pizzicato harps with bongoed counterrhythms, underscoring Cole's narrative as if it were the background for a Shakespeare soliloquy. The contrast of light (flute, solo piano) and heavy (the whole brass section) accompaniment points to, and at the same time surpasses, the entire jazz-and-poetry movement of the fifties, even Charlie Mingus's "Scenes in the City" (1957, Bethlehem). Cole finds more music in the song than any of its other interpreters; his is the most luscious of all lush lives.

Even in 1939 Cole was a more interesting vocalist than, say, either Eberle or Eberly or most of the musicians who sang with the bands, and ten years later, when he was about ready to retire the Trio, he had acquired sufficient vocal wherewithal to go out on his own as a world-class solo singer. More importantly, he had become a complete singer. Previously he had reserved certain ideas for the keyboard; now he had to learn how to express everything he wanted to say with just his voice. Accordingly, that voice grew in depth and range to match his ever-sharpening interpretive abilities.

Still, fifties and sixties Cole can be a harrowing experience. Capitol and radio stations alike conspired to keep Cole's worst records—his hits—in front of the masses. You just can't get any worse than "Ramblin' Rose" (1962) or "Those Lazy-Hazy-Crazy

Days of Summer" (1963) or the albums Cole made with the unlikely named Belford Hendricks, a talentless hack whom Capitol assigned the task of converting Cole into a country-western star. As with Kay Starr's hit singles for Capitol and Victor, it seemed like the worse these records got, the better they sold.

But Cole made so much excellent music between 1955 and 1965 that no one who values good singing can afford to skip his later work. As you'd expect, the discs made with Nelson Riddle, the greatest vocal orchestrator in all music, win the prize as Cole's best post-Trio efforts. *Nat King Cole Sings for Two in Love* (the one with the painted white couple on the cover [1953]) contains twelve exceptional standard ballads, among them the definitive "Handful of Stars," sung convincingly enough to worry even Sinatra or Haymes, while *To Whom It May Concern* (1958) digs up completely unknown tunes and comes up with a few Cole classics—specifically, "You're Bringing Out the Dreamer in Me" and "Too Much." Riddle guided Cole through loads of albums and singles as well as his short-lived TV series, where he sang the great "Crazy, but I'm in Love," and singlehandedly saves the 1960 *Wild Is Love*, an all-original concept album,* which Cole also made into a TV special. The format and songs are predictable from the git-go, and the megatacky choral introduction makes thirty seconds seem like twelve years at hard labor, but Riddle and Cole increase the excitement by running the high risk of camp—and just narrowly avoid it in numbers with titles like "Hundreds and Thousands of Girls" and "The Pick-Up." Nobody listening could fail to guess exactly how the title number is going to go as its description of love moves from the general to the specific, but Cole sweeps its shortcomings under the rug by attacking it straight on: with his commanding, unsentimental approach.

The Cole-Riddle collaboration could easily stand on one al-

---

* Around the same time, June Christy made *This Time of Year*, an all-original Christmas concept album, also for Capitol.

bum alone, the essential *St. Louis Blues* (first issued in 1958 as
the only beneficial by-product of Cole's one starring film, the
dreadful *St. Louis Blues*). Like Stafford's "Jambalaya" here's an
artist traveling into unfamiliar territory, W. C. Handy's blues
songs of the teens and twenties, but instead of embarrassing
artificiality, Cole (like Crosby) shows adult pop's method of absorbing and synthesizing new, or in this case old, influences, if
given enough creative forethought, can make them work. Handy
had adapted folk material to the song forms popular around the
time of the First World War; Cole and Riddle now adapt Handy's
adaptions to all the possibilities that pop music had to offer at its
zenith in the late fifties. Without even going beyond Handy,
they explore twelve very different kinds of blue: from the
haughty and defiant "Joe Turner's Blues" to the mournful
"Friendless Blues," from the grandiose semisymphonic jazzed
"St. Louis Blues" to the folksily simple "Chantez-les Bas," from
the down and dirty "Beale Street Blues"* to the hopeful and
completely unblue "Morning Star."

Cole made two other LPs that readdress his relationship with
jazz, and it tells us a lot about his development that *After Midnight* (1957), which uses the small-group format Cole had first
come to fame with, works far less successfully than *Welcome to
the Club* (1959), which captures Cole in the swing-band format
he'd spent the decade mastering. The slick, posed jacket of *After
Midnight* perfectly illustrates the slick, posed record within,
whereas the falsely spontaneous vocal-instrumental solo-vocal
formula (sometimes intermixed with obbligatos) gets done to
death. None of the original Trio records ever got this boring; in
fact, when Cole added a fourth man to the group it actually
decreased the variety of sounds they could achieve. But *After
Midnight* repeats itself too quickly, indicating that Cole
shouldn't make an *effort* to be spontaneous. Even when soloing

* Cole's "Beale Street Blues" is the only record of the Handy tune that really challenges Jack Teagarden, which is only fitting as Teagarden's version of "The Christmas
Song" is the only performance to rival Cole's.

on the piano, Cole (like Tatum) does best with a loose but set routine as on both the Capitol and live versions of the Trio's instrumental "Body and Soul," where he goes into a line of "Lullaby in Rhythm" a few measures before the coda. Cole needs a creative, individual arrangement to inspire him, whether for three men or thirty. He gets this and more in *Welcome to the Club*, because they give him the entire Count Basie Orchestra, though not Basie himself or his name (for legal reasons Gerry Wiggins takes his place at the piano),* and with it the chance to get into more blues and swingers.

Cole made plenty of other monster-swingers in the late fifties—the best being two dynamite Riddle charts of very obscure songs, "Can't Help It" (on *To Whom It May Concern* [1958]) and "I Just Found Out About Love" (on *This Is Nat King Cole* [1957])—and in the sixties he perfected his fullest and hardest-swinging voice. When Riddle followed Sinatra to Reprise, no one could replace him (as Ellington once said of Johnny Hodges), but Capitol then paired Cole with a better arranger than anyone had a right to expect, Ralph Carmichael. Carmichael made sure Cole's sixties albums would never be embarrassed by the earlier discs with Riddle. Their partnership had only one real disappointment: the pointless *Nat King Cole Sings My Fair Lady*. Too many of these songs have no life outside the stage; on "The Rain in Spain," all the Cole, crumpets, and castanets can't help this turkey of a tango that's tired where it should be torrid.

Of all the stages that Cole's voice passed through, I like his sixties voice best. By this time he had developed a remarkably resilient instrument, full of energy and feeling. In the Trio years, Cole left a lot to the imagination, suggesting where he wanted to take his voice rather than actually going there. Twenty years later, he could and did. Even so, he left intact all the more

---

* *I Gotta Right to Swing* does the same for Sammy Davis, Jr., and I've always suspected that *Blues Cross Country* fills the need for Peggy Lee: the Basie band without its contractually obligated leader.

endearing and enduring traits of his early singing. At the ends of phrases, for instance, when he wants to use an extended note, he usually sings it softly. When he wants to cap a line with a loud note, chances are it will be short and staccato.

On up-tempo pieces, "My Kind of Girl" and "Three Little Words" on *L-O-V-E* (1965, Carmichael), he still embraces the beat; in fact, now he pounces on it like a big cat. He comes down so hard he leaves a resounding "ah" after syllables that end on consonants, showing how much singers as diverse as Carmen McRae, Buddy Greco, and Della Reese have learned from him. Cole knocks us out even more with ballads, doing the best of these on his first full-length effort with Carmichael, *The Touch of Your Lips* (1960). Who could have predicted that this once ugly-duckling "musician's" voice could grow into a sound so lovely, so full of bottom and top, expressing a passion so eloquently and tenderly? Cole stops us from worrying whether he's believable or not. Archibald MacLeish once said, "A poem should not mean but be." Nat Cole simply *is*.

And he was never more so than in his last recordings, made right up to the hospitalization that preceded his death in February 1965. Cole's biographer, Jim Haskins (from whom most of these dates were cribbed), paints a discouraging picture of Cole the man. He grew up poor and made a fortune not for himself so much as for the IRS; he broke down color barriers in white neighborhoods and white theaters only to be called an Uncle Tom by militant black leaders. He helped a small, new record company grow into a world conglomerate, but because he was black he never came close to fulfilling his dream of singing in the movies and television. He died when he was forty-five, but thank God he lived as long as he did. Thank God there was a Nat King Cole.

The same pressures Cole faced also forced Kay Starr out of the record business just when she seemed ready to make records that, judging by her final Capitol albums (especially the sublime *I Cry by Night*), would have really made your hair stand on end. In 1962 it seemed unbelievable that only fifteen years earlier Capitol had considered Starr the perfect singer for their label.

Had they first discovered Starr in the late fifties, for example, they might have tried to turn her into an electric hillbilly like Elvis Presley. (As it happened, RCA signed Presley on the strength of Starr's hit after Starr had tested the rock 'n' roll waters by waltzing through them rather than the other way around.) Ten years after that they would have cast her as a beehived Nashville nightingale like Tammy Wynette or Loretta Lynn (though Capitol's signing of Starr in 1947 roughly coincides with MGM's taking on Hank Williams).

Starr isn't blues-ish. Starr isn't blues-y. She's *thoroughly* blue. Bluer, in fact, than you'd think any white woman has a right to be. Because she injects so much blues feeling into whatever she sings, for her to drop the other shoe and sing a straight-ahead twelve-bar blues sometimes seems like a case of overkill. Instead, Starr extracts the most oomph with blues songs that skirt the edge of blues tonality and structure but that also use bridges and verses.

Nobody can stretch a note like Starr, especially the long and high ones. Cole's best manipulations relate to the jazz ideal of highly developed syncopation (and its descendants). Starr's melismata come out of jazz's parents and its siblings: gospel, the blues, and white folk and country music. She naturally leans to a kind of highly individualized stop-time, a device her arrangers throw in whenever they get stuck for an idea. On "He's Funny That Way" (on *In a Blue Mood* [1955, Capitol]), the tempo starts and stops so frequently that you'd swear you were listening to a march. Her producers also loved obbligatos, even on straight pop albums, and Starr had more growling trumpets on her tail than any songbird since Bessie Smith.

I'm hardly the first to compare Starr to Smith; almost from the instant reviewers heard Starr they made the connection between the hard, gripping, and intense sound that both singers share—even Lester Young pointed it out in an interview with Chris Albertson. Connee Boswell also meant a lot to Starr. While Ella Fitzgerald started with the soft, yielding Connie of the thirties that she heard when she was coming up, Starr knew better the hard, Smith-ish Connee of her generation, and had plenty of time to study her when Boswell toured on the same bill with Charlie Barnet's Orchestra at the time when Starr sat in Barnet's canary perch. George Avakian, virtually the only jazz writer *not* to go crazy over Starr, dismissed her right off the bat as a mere "Boswell imitation."

Starr herself spoke of her fondness for her contemporary Dinah Washington, the best of all postwar blues singers. Washington could, in fact, get into a blues with the same ferocity as Starr, though she couldn't touch the Oklahoma gal on standard material. Starr admitted having Washington in mind when she cut "Everybody's Somebody's Fool" in 1950 (Capitol), and Washington returned the compliment with her single of "Wheel of Fortune" a year and a half later. You can also hear some of Billie Holiday circa 1937 in Starr, and more than Lady Day herself, you can find reference after reference to the band that Lady Day toured with that season, Count Basie's.

"She used to come down and hear us all the time in the old days," Jimmy Rushing said to Burt Korall. Plenty of singers might do "Night Train," or even "Goin' to Chicago," as Starr does on *Movin'* (Capitol), but who besides a died-in-the-wool Basie-ite would have even heard of "What Goes Up Must Come Down," which Basie and Rushing did in 1939 and Starr reprised in 1946 (Crystallite)? Or "Song of the Wanderer" (also on *Movin'*)? Or "Evenin' " (*In a Blue Mood* [1955, Capitol])? And no babe who didn't know her Basie-ana could ever take one of the Count's most appropriate records, "Blue and Sentimental" (on *Blue Starr* [1955, Victor]), and rethink it from a band instrumental to a vocal number, with the singer stating the theme instead of the ensemble, leaving in the featured tenor sax solo (the anonymous studio saxist doing a credible Herschel Evans) but replacing the instrumental choir behind it with a vocal one.* "Slow Boat to China" (on *Movin'* [1959]) quotes Basie's

---

* *In a Blue Mood* also contains homage to obscure Connee Boswell and Ella Fitzgerald in, respectively, "Don't Tell Him What's Happened to Me" and "The Spring Fever Blues."

"April in Paris"; "Just in Time" (on *Movin' on Broadway* [1959–60]) darn near becomes "Moten Swing"; and her hit blues "Kay's Lament" (on *The Hits of Kay Starr*) pays particular homage to Jimmy Rushing; on it she works in one of Rushing's most famous and oft-repeated lines, the one raising the theory that though the protagonist has not overruled the possibility that he may in fact be incorrect, this is not necessarily a permanent situation. Small surprise, then, that so many members of that first great Basie band went out of their way to say nice things about Starr, especially Lester Young and Helen Humes. Jimmy Rushing paid her the ultimate compliment when he said, "Kay Starr, she's got so much soul!"

In addition to the heavy Basie influence in everything she does, you can't underestimate the importance of country and folk music in Starr's work. "All my tricks," she told Harry Cronin in 1953, "come from that hillbilly singing on and on, yodeling and jumping octaves." Four years earlier she had said to Barbara Hodgkins, "I've run the gamut from hillbilly to jazz to just plain modern music to ballads, and though I might not sing them all well, I feel them. And if I sing them well, I attribute that to the fact that I have sung hillbilly stuff. Contrary to what people say, it's a hard style to sing, and it made my voice flexible enough so that I'm able to have my own style." Only Starr could have so miraculously merged her early country background with the disciplines she learned in the jazz and band tradition; give credit to Joe Venuti for spotting this talent in Starr when he first heard her singing with a hillbilly band on WMPS out of Memphis, Tennessee, in 1937 or 1938.

Born Katherine LaVerne Starks in Dougherty, Oklahoma, on July 21, 1922, the young Starr and family moved to Dallas three years later. Before she was ten, Starr was winning amateur shows, some of which were broadcast on Dallas' WRR. At age twelve, shortly after her folks moved to Memphis, she earned her own regular program on WREC and then WMPS. Joe Venuti heard the sixteen-year-old Starr on that "hillbilly" show and took her on the road with his band, one of the many Venuti ensembles that never recorded. Then history repeated itself. Gil Rodin, manager of the Bob Crosby Orchestra, heard her on the air with Venuti while the Crosby band was playing through Memphis[*] and hired her for a string of dance dates as the band one-nighted its way east, arriving in New York in June 1939. We get our earliest surviving glimpse of Starr from the Crosby orchestra's first "Camel Caravan" show, broadcast on the last Tuesday of that month, where she turns in a "Memphis Blues" so promising that one really wishes Mother Starks hadn't dragged her back home to Memphis and higher education before the second show (or so she says today; in 1946 she told the *Hollywood Note* that "the radio sponsor let me go"). Luckily, a month later Glenn Miller wired Starr to fly back and fill in for his own thrush, Marion Hutton, who had been temporarily knocked out of circulation by nervous indigestion and exhaustion (the fate of the touring-band canary), and Starr made her first records, "Baby Me" and "Love with a Capital You," for Bluebird on July 26, 1939.

They would have been her last, too, had not somebody told Charlie Barnet about her. After graduating from high school, she rejoined Venuti, but the fiddler's new band did no better than any of his others, and when he broke it up in the early days of the war, Starr rehearsed (and eventually recorded)[†] with Wingy Manone's group and auditioned for Barnet, who, upon hearing her, realized that here was the girl singer he'd been looking for throughout his entire career as a bandleader. The Petrillo ban prohibited her from recording extensively with Barnet, but one of the five commercial sides they made, "Share Croppin' Blues" (1944, Decca), gained Starr her first step toward a hit. She stayed with Barnet for about three years, leaving briefly to help saxist-arranger Dave Matthews out with his unsuccessful big band, and reuniting with Barnet for a theater date at the New

---

[*] This data is from John Chilton's *Stomp Off, Let's Go.* According to Will Warner's liner notes on the Bob Crosby Camel Caravan Series (which includes Starr's "Memphis Blues" on Giants of Jazz 1032), Rodin heard Starr with Venuti in Detroit.

[†] The very rare "If I Could Be with You" on ARA.

York Strand in August 1945. Then, what happened to Marion Hutton in 1939 happened to Starr: After all those months battling Barnet's blaring brass, her voice gave out.

The time had come to leave the band game anyhow, and the brief respite gave her the chance to go out as a single. The West Coast jazz community began to pay attention to her at the Streets of Paris, a Los Angeles jazz club, at the end of 1945. A number of small independent labels expressed interest in recording her, resulting in about two dozen generally lovely sides that have come out on no end of labels with names like Lamplighter, Crystallite, and (Ben Pollack's) Jewell. Using name jazz musicians (Venuti, Barney Bigard, Willie Smith, Vic Dickenson, Zutty Singleton) for sidemen and jazz-oriented standards for repertoire ("Honeysuckle Rose," "All of Me," "The Dixieland Band," and so on) these cracklingly noisy surfaces offer the first real proof of Starr's potential. In "There's a Lull in My Life," Starr, accompanied by a violin-guitar-piano combination that suggests a Venuti-Lang-Signorelli trio circa 1930 (excepting an out-of-place one-finger keyboard solo), builds more gradually to the high dramatic notes near the end of the bridge than she would a few years later, but she doesn't squeeze nearly as much juice out of them as she would on Capitol. On "Sunday" she virtually assumes the role of a rhythm section, holding down the melody and the beat while the instrumentalists noodle around her—and well they should, for she provides a perfect focal point for their improvisations. "Betcha I Getcha" could easily be Louis Armstrong circa 1929–32, as evidenced by Starr's fondness for ramming words together till they push into subsequent measures and lines and by a wordless scat sequence that suggests Lester Young's introductory solo on "When Dreams Come True" while at the same time making it clear that Starr feels freer with words than she does without them. "Where or When" offers a rare example of Starr experimenting with soft sounds, as if she were inhaling some of Peggy Lee's smoke and pixie dust.

Which is exactly what Capitol didn't want Starr to do when their jazz A&R head, Dave Dexter, signed her to the rapidly expanding label in 1947 (President Mercer had already worked with Starr on the Bob Crosby radio show eight years earlier), since they already had the original Lee. In fact, Capitol didn't quite know what to do with Starr, other than Dexter's limited-market jazz things. As Starr tells the story today, Capitol already had in the can versions of all the current songs of the season by their other female vocalists, and they wanted Starr to get some sides in before the next Petrillo ban, which would prevent virtually all recording for 1948. At a loss for tunes, Starr turned to an old colleague of Venuti's, Red Nichols, then getting his career as a trumpeter and bandleader back in gear. Nichols steered her to a peck of numbers from his generation that had never made it to the "jazz standard" level. Even during her late pre-Capitol period, Starr had done "You Gotta See Mama Every Night" and "Mama Goes Where Papa Goes," and now she made a specialty of good, rocking twenties songs with a jazzy feel, among them "Too Busy" and Irving Berlin's spiritual "Waiting at the End of the Road." In 1950, Starr went back as far as "Flow Gently, Sweet Afton" as the basis for a Dixieland disc with Nichols.

In the meantime, something nobody expected was happening. The excitement generated by the Capitol recordings and the publicity the label's PR wing turned out had begun to get her work—lots of it, in increasingly important clubs. Around the time her third Capitol single was released in February 1948, Starr was playing a distinctly nonjazz Hollywood venue, Slapsy Maxie's (Rosenbloom), on the same bill with Danny Thomas. As spring came around, Starr's popularity seemed strong enough to justify some bookings farther east. In April she headlined at the Hotel Sherman in Chicago, and on the second of May she cracked New York, opening at the Cafe Society, staying through June and then splitting a bill with the King Cole Trio at the New York Paramount in August.

The records had started to sell accordingly. Realizing that they had a potential hit-maker already under contract, Capitol took Starr out of Dexter's hands and let their more conventional A&R minds figure out how Starr could make some real dough. It

would be a shame to overlook the market she had built up for old
songs, since apparently a lot of people went for them. It would
also be too bad if they couldn't cash in on her country tinge,
since three big sellers of 1949—Bing Crosby's "Dear Hearts and
Gentle People" (Decca), Frankie Laine's "Mule Train" (Columbia), and Capitol's own "Careless Hands" by Mel Torme—
proved there was an audience for that sort of thing. In 1950 they
came up with the answer, a Pee Wee King tune called "Bonaparte's Retreat," and they recorded it right smack on the border where Dixieland meets the Old West, hot horns emitting
countrified moans as Creole cowboys square danced to a Dixie
two-beat. It sold a million copies and made Capitol very happy.

"Bonaparte's Retreat" was that great rarity, a swell record and
at the same time a natural hit. Its only unpleasant side effect
became obvious, as you might expect, when Capitol and Starr
tried to come up with another hit. And then another one after
that, and so on. Capitol started to gimmick-up her records with
increasing nerve and decreasing taste. For example, somebody
got the bright idea of putting doo-wop-type male choirs behind
her—Hey! Doo-wop is selling, so why the hell not?—so on
record after record we have to bear with hordes of chanters
cooing behind Starr, from the single "I Waited a Little Too
Long" to entire albums, even the jazz-ish *Rockin' with Kay*, *Blue
Starr*, and *The Jazz Singer*. And then it got even worse: A dozen
white doo-woppers got multiplied into the ultrabland mixed chorus behind Starr on "Half a Photograph" and "Allez-vous-en Go
Away."

Starr's multitrack voice discs win the prize for both sales and
bad ideas done to death, starting with the 1952 "Wheel of Fortune," a cartoonish melodramatic song that Johnny Hartman had
recorded for Victor seven months earlier but that had never
been released (it was the overdubbed all-Starr choir that put it
over anyhow), and proceeding with two records that would have
been swell if not for those corny dub tracks, "The Man Upstairs"
and "Side by Side" (1953). You want to talk about camp? You
can't get any more of it than on "Kay's Lament." A few years

earlier it would have been a wonderful, simple, up-tempo blues, and it still is at heart, but behind Starr's intense statement you get a hodgepodge of trends corny enough in themselves that acquire the sheen of absolute awfulness when alloyed: bongo drums, electric guitar, and six idiots chanting "Sing it, Sister Katie!"

In a 1946 article called "Kay Isn't Commercial," Starr said, "I am trying not to be affected by anybody or anything, and I hope I won't change." In 1950 she told *Downbeat*, "It's my style of singing that has changed. You can't make money as a jazz singer, and with a little daughter to support and bring up I've had to get commercial. Am I happy? Now, what do you think? I was brought up to be a jazz singer but I could never make any money doing that. Do you think I like to sing a song like 'Hoop-De-Doo'?" But if she was singing the blues to a jazz press reporter, she was neither singing them on records nor at the bank. By 1953 she had sold over 3 million Capitol singles, "Bonaparte" and "Wheel of Fortune" accounting for at least a million each. At the end of her first year at Capitol, she reportedly received a check for $100 in royalties; at the end of the last year of that contract they paid her $100,000. When she switched to Victor in January 1955, her agreement with that label stipulated a guarantee of $250,000 against royalties for five years.

Starr's Victor output illustrates the dichotomy that adult-pop singers began experiencing with the advent of ten-inch (eight song) and twelve-inch (twelve song) LP records at this time. Her new bosses still expected her to make big-selling pop singles, and with her megahit, "The Rock and Roll Waltz," she exceeded their expectations to such an unfortunate degree that they went out and got themselves an unwaltzing rock 'n' roller named Presley.[*] But in the beginning the labels presumed that albums would be bought by adults and not baby boomers, a suspicion confirmed by the promising sales of such mature efforts as the early Sinatra theme albums (especially the extralong *Wee Small*

---

[*] As Starr told Gary Giddins in 1986.

Hours and Ella Fitzgerald's multidisc *Songbooks*). Thus, when RCA issued their first Starr album, *Rockin' with Kay*, they could justifiably claim in a press release that "Her true fans might refer to it as the old Kay Starr." They gave her twelve beat-full old chestnuts, among them the only version of "Lover Man" that the world really needs after Billie Holiday's, though they still insisted on saddling her with the male choir.

That choir becomes appropriate on Starr's last Victor album, a long-awaited collection of "swingin' spirituals" called *I Hear the Word* (1959). It occurred to Starr and conductor Bill Stafford how much they could do with percussion even without resorting to such exotica as Latin instruments. Most of the disc assumes the rockish and heavy Panama Francis–Atlantic Records–style beat that became standard for Starr around this time, as on "I Shall Not Be Moved" and "Rock-a-My Soul." But on "Oh! What a Wonderful Feeling," Stafford has the drummer make do with just a snare, as might a pan-banger in a down-home hardshell church who couldn't afford (or fit) a full kit. For "Jezebel" he dispenses with the kit entirely, and supports Starr and her male foursome (who do a reasonable Golden Gate Quartet) with nothing but what sounds like a suitcase (filled with mashed potatoes, no doubt). Other than that piece of luggage and her gentlemen friends, Starr takes it completely a cappella and infuses it with more gin-yew-wine gospel passion than any full-time sacred singer I've ever heard. Stafford also uses an organ and thoughtfully took the role of Starr's chief obbligatist away from the customary trumpet and gave it to a trombonist, perhaps Ray Sims, who knows his Jack Teagarden ("Sometimes I Feel like a Motherless Child") and Tricky Sam Nanton ("Go Down, Moses") as well as Starr knows her Connee Boswell and Bessie Smith.

After about four albums and numerous singles at Victor, Starr returned home to Capitol on July 2, 1959. Of the six albums she made under the new contract (the first, *Movin'*, released on October 19, 1959) two are fine pop pieces, *Just Plain Country* and *Losers, Weepers*, while the remaining four, *Movin'*, *Movin' on Broadway*, *The Jazz Singer*, and *I Cry by Night* are so terrific as to give the impression that Starr knew her option wouldn't be renewed and wanted to end her stay at the top with four of the most colossal jazz vocal sets ever recorded.

Starr at last gets to go choirless on *Movin'* and *Broadway,* which, along with *The Jazz Singer* and *Losers,* were arranged and conducted by the gifted veteran Van Alexander, Starr's own equivalent of Ralph Carmichael. Though shows like *Can-Can* and *My Fair Lady* may seem out of Starr's hillbilly-cum-Harlem milieu, she sings the bejeebers out of them on the *Broadway* set. What she loves best about Cole Porter is his minor to major modulations; when she reaches that point in "I Love Paris" she fairly springs from the old key to the new. A few years earlier she'd had a hit with another *Can-Can* song, "Allez-vous-en Go Away," and here, too, she makes Porter's mock French come out like Louisiana Cajun, topped off with a new double-time patter chorus on "Paris" that makes no bones about belonging more to the square dance than the can-can.

Starr and Alexander get into metaphors on *Movin'.* They may open with the fastest "Slow Boat to China," but on "Night Train"—the best of all vocal versions of the hit Basie instrumental—her voice makes like the night train's whistle and tears your heart in two, and on "Ghost Riders in the Sky" the trombone section portrays the devil's herd that thunders along behind Starr's cowboy protagonist. Dem dry bones walk around throughout the whole album, playing a fully developed countermelody and a solo transcribed for section on "Indiana," conversing with her on "Lazy River," grunting after her in the bass on "Around the World," and setting up a call-and-response pattern with her to help desentimentalize "Sentimental Journey."

Starr ended her second Capitol contract with *I Cry by Night,* a collection of ballads that signifies her only all-small-group album. Somebody insisted on the static kind of rock harmony prevalent in post-fifties pop, and also that the normally astute pianist Gerry Wiggins play one-finger Roger Williams Muzak, but other than that we have here a powerful bunch of songs with no less a master than Ben Webster to serve as Starr's instrumental foil. As opposed to the soap-operatic "Half a Photograph" or "Three Letters," there's nothing the least bit melo about this drama—she puts our hearts and souls through the wringer on "Baby, Won't You Please Come Home?," "More Than You Know," and most of all on a "Lover Man" even more gripping than her earlier reading on *Rockin' with Kay*. I've heard few performances more moving or more thrilling. My reaction was tears; Capitol's was to not renew her contract.

Though not her last album chronologically, the few she made after hardly live up to its standards. After twenty years of homage to Basie, the collaboration they finally got together on (*Kay Starr and Count Basie* [1968, Gold Star]) somehow fell into the ill-chosen hands of arranger Dick Hyman and disappointed almost as many people as the later *Bing 'n' Basie* misfire. Starr, who had been headlining in Vegas practically since the day the town opened, gravitated toward the nostalgia circuit and wound up reprising "Wheel of Fortune" and "Rock and Roll Waltz" for bleary-eyed gamblers and, record-wise, grinding out a few ill-advised attempts at corralling the Nashville market.

She exceeded all expectations when she played a New York nightclub for the first time in years in 1985, revealing that the old Starr still shined and that she has an awful lot to offer the world. Tono Records taped one of her sets at Freddy's,[*] and if she ever does make a record as good as that club set, Kay Starr will easily be the rediscovery of the nineties.

The old-school floor concept held solid for both Cole and Starr, despite either "Ramblin' Rose" or any one of Starr's million-selling stinkeroos, and the bad never completely eradicated the good. Still, the temptation to make lousy music when you are capable of doing good has grown considerably since the forties, and it was bad enough then. The situation worsened because of a certain kind of corruption that popular art must continually risk.

"Music is music," Irving Berlin once said, "and there are only two kinds that I know of, good music and bad." At different times, Louis Armstrong, Igor Stravinsky, and Duke Ellington are all supposed to have said the same thing. Fair enough, if the

---

[*] Unreleased as of early 1990.

world of good music can have its Berlins, Armstrongs, Stravinskys, and Ellingtons, then bad music should also be allowed to have its own genius par excellence.

It found it in Mitch Miller.

Incredibly, Miller, a classical oboe virtuoso, got his foot in the pop music door thanks to Alec Wilder, who recruited Miller to play oboe in the chamber "octet" he assembled in the late thirties to, among other things, accompany Mildred Bailey. (As an instrumentalist, Miller also played behind Charlie Parker— another artist whose ideals represented the antithesis of Miller's.) Two of America's most important musical minds, Miller and Wilder were each determined to change the shape of popular music in their own image but to very different ends. Wilder apparently didn't think the pop music of his generation was good enough for the serious thinker. He sought to raise its sights by high-brow methods, most significantly by writing half-pop, half-classical, all-boring works for groups such as the aforementioned chamber ensembles as well as more conventional, though still very self-consciously arty, popular songs.

Miller took the opposite tack, showing the world that his brow was even lower than Wilder's was high. "The thing to remember about Mitch Miller is that he truly hated popular music," observed Barbara Lea, a friend of the late Wilder, "and did everything possible to cheapen it and destroy it." As anyone with half an ear can tell, he succeeded. Miller served as A&R boss at the most important record label, Columbia, at the most crucial decade in the history of popular music, the fifties, a time and place that put him in perfect proximity—like an assassin secluded atop a building across the street from a political rally—to kill adult pop music.

Because even though Miller claims not to like rock 'n' roll, his concepts—badness per se, and the idea that the producer was more important than the artist, and the production supreme over the performance—did more to assure its permanence than even his like-minded followers who at least admitted their preferences, like Alan Freed and Phil Spector. His career seems like something out of *The Manchurian Candidate*, that old Laurence Harvey post–cold war thriller, wherein a rabid red-baiting McCarthy-like senator turns out to be a paid agent of the Soviet Union. To give Miller the benefit of the doubt, he might have been like Reagan at the height of the Iran-contra scandal, either slightly evil or slightly blind or just moronic, or like the late unlamented Henry Luce of *Time* magazine, whose efforts to run the Reds out of China succeeded only in handing the country over to Mao Tse-tung on a pu-pu platter.

For years (certainly until the arrival of rock 'n' roll proper), Miller exemplified the worst in American pop. He first aroused the ire of intelligent listeners by trying to turn—and darn near succeeding in turning—great artists like Sinatra, Clooney, and Tony Bennett into hacks. Miller chose the worst songs and put together the worst backings imaginable—not with the hit-or-miss attitude that bad musicians (Lawrence Welk, Guy Lombardo) traditionally used, but with insight, forethought, careful planning, and perverted brilliance. He didn't have to force it down anyone's throat: Each time he took music lower, his sales went higher. Then, not surprisingly, when given the chance to make records under his own name in the "Sing Along with Mitch" series, Miller created music so ingeniously bad that there was no way it wouldn't sell millions upon millions of copies and also earn Miller his own TV show, the original MTV: a national arena for tacky music of the most offensive kind.

Defending the inventor of rock 'n' roll mentality by arguing that his music sold into the seven and eight figures and reestablished Columbia as one of the all-time biggest multimedia superpowers can be likened to defending Mussolini with the old cliché that Il Duce did, after all, make the trains run on time. As Francis Davis pointed out, Miller proved that no one would ever go broke underestimating the taste of the American public—even if he occasionally erred in the cause of what he believed in, as when he denied Peggy King, one of the canaries in his cage, the chance to sing the only-slightly sophisticated "Cry Me a River" and the hit went to Julie London on Liberty, thereby making both the lady and the label. Miller's successors in the rock era learned his lessons well: The producer (A&R man) is all, the ledger sheet is all, there are no standards, no floors. Forget about individuality, forget about the artist's freedom, and most of all forget about taste.

Which is precisely what most of the singers of the Miller era did, whether under his direct imprimatur or not. At the end of the forties, Sinatra fell from public favor, and gradually Crosby no longer maintained the grasp on their fancy that he had a few years earlier. Who would replace Sinatra? Capitol thought it might be Mel Torme, and though he came across with a couple of hits ("Blue Moon" and "Careless Hands") he was too unwilling to follow orders, too quick to desert major-label money for a miniscule indie where he could pick and choose what he was going to record. MGM bet on Billy Eckstine, but like Cole on Capitol, he was black, so that was definitely out. Mercury came up with Ronnie Deauville, a talented Sinatra clone whose career was bound to plummet along with the original FS (and whose career, though not his life, was ended by an automobile smash, according to expert Chick Wilson), and then Vic Damone, who would never be good enough or bad enough to climb to the top of that heap of jewels and junk that was the early fifties. Columbia's Guy Mitchell had raw talent, but Miller milked him quickly and efficiently as a one-gimmick wonder (with pseudo-folk material) that, not surprisingly, quickly petered out. Instead, we got stuck with singers who exemplified the Miller ideal of absolute badness: Frankie Laine (the only one of this bunch who, early in his career, revealed the potential to become a half-decent pop artist), Johnnie Ray (the first true rock 'n' roller—a white imitation of black R & B style), Eddie Fisher, Andy Williams, and later Johnny Mathis. They had their female equivalents, too, in Patti Page, Teresa Brewer, and others even worse.

With no-talents like these in front of the microphone and an evil genius like Mitch Miller on the other side, could things get any worse? Of course they could, and did. But jazz-derived adult pop still had a few blazes of glory left to go out in.

Modernism I

Sing a Song of Bebop

● ─────────────────────────────────

"Any time you hear people singing out of companionship and high spirits, you're in on a vocal jam session. Well, I've never gotten over the desire to join a vocal group if their stuff comes from the heart."
—Buddy Stewart

"I believe that where there is a sound, there is a mood which can be interpreted into words—at least in a general way. And it is my ambition to interpret a full band arrangement into words, with individual voices replacing individual instruments[,] expressing into words what the instruments expressed in mood."
—*King Pleasure to Leonard Feather on* Encyclopedia of Jazz
questionnaire

≡**B**ebop was an instrumental music. No singer could have conceived it. Charlie Parker forever altered the fundamental relationship between voices and instruments as it had existed up to that point. Horn players still had to breathe and so they had to base their phrases on the duration of the human breath, but no longer did they need to limit what they played to the boundaries of the voice. They played faster, way beyond what any human voice could articulate with clarity, and they played melodies that were never meant to be sung. Bop never came as naturally to the voice as it did to Parker's alto saxophone and Dizzy Gillespie's trumpet and then to the other instruments. The new music may have reasserted many of jazz's basic principles, especially the primacy of the blues, but it was almost exclusively a player's music.

Or was it? At face value, certainly. Those who tried to adapt
bop for the voice just as J. J. Johnson had brought it to the
trombone (possessing J.J.'s legendary musical acumen would
have helped) got nowhere. A few tried. After all these years I'm
still trying to determine exactly what the point of Babs Gonzales
(1919–80)* was. Basically a comedian, a professional hipster
(Capitol Records published his *Boptionary* of forties slang to
promote their two Gonzales singles), and a music businessman
(in Paris he ran a jazz club appropriately called the Maison
d'Idiots [Insane Asylum]), Gonzales occasionally stepped in front
of a microphone to sing and it never bothered him that he didn't
have the slightest ability to carry a tune. Gonzales loved to say
things like "It's crazy that you've come up to dig my Bops and a
Bip, man, and I'm sure crazy to be back in this crazy town.
People [here] dig the modern cool sounds and, man, that makes
everything real crazy." He also thought it was like wow to put
down singers who weren't in his clique but were inevitably more
talented than he.

Musicians apparently loved Gonzales: Billie Holiday sang at
his parties; Johnny Griffin still dedicates songs to him; Tadd
Dameron not only played piano but sang as one of his aforementioned Bops and a Bip; Bennie Green and others brought him in
to sing individual tunes on their dates. Gonzales eventually
wrote a book and published it himself under the title *I Paid My
Dues.* To him, "paying dues"—hanging around with jazzmen
and sharing their bad habits—counted for more than any kind of
musical talent. Gonzales claimed that his mission was to popu-
larize the new music, telling Val Willmer that his "Oop-Pop-A-
Da" (which Dizzy Gillespie also recorded) sold an unbelievable
45,000 copies for Blue Note, but ultimately he seems to have
done more than anyone else to keep bebop an impenetrable
cult. Crazy.

---

* The 1919 birth date comes from Feather. Other dates that have been given for
Gonzales include 1917, 1918, and 1921.

Since singing the new music didn't come as naturally as playing it, modern jazz had no equivalents to Louis Armstrong or Jack Teagarden, each of whom could do both on an equally remarkable level. Gillespie came closest, but with all that arranging, bandleading, composing, and, most importantly, trumpet playing, he had little time to work on his singing. Instead, he hired vocalists such as Kenny "Pancho" Hagood and Joe Carroll (1915–81) whose voices were only slightly more polished versions of his own. (Of Gillespie's band singers, only Johnny Hartman could establish anything resembling a reputation out of Diz's aegis.)

During his turn in the spotlight, Hagood was lousy on both ballads and scat features (his was one of the voices on Dizzy's "Oop-Pop-A-Da"). He had the misfortune to be completely out of place on his two most famous appearances, "I Should Care" by the Thelonious Monk Quartet (1948, Blue Note) and "Darn That Dream" with the Miles Davis Birth of the Cool Nonet (1950, Capitol). (Until very recently, LP compilers exhibited understandable reluctance to reissue these two tracks, even on "complete" collections of Monk's and Davis's sessions.) The four tracks Hagood made in late 1967 (issued on Spotlite) with the Jazz Crusaders rhythm section, however, mark one of the more satisfying surprises in all of this music, as they capture a fine balladeer (especially on two takes of "But Beautiful") with a loose, post-Eckstine voice and a good sensibility for scat; his career would have been different had he sounded this polished twenty years previously.

On the other hand, Joe Carroll could always do one thing well: scat. He made an essential contribution to the Gillespie big band's theater dates, pleasing the crowd with novelties like Mary Lou Williams's "In the Land of Oo-Bla-De (The Bop Fairy Tale)" (1949, Victor) and wearing an exaggerated parody of the standard bopper's outfit (beret, flashy cravat, and lapels big enough to ski down) that inspired as much mirth as his performance. Carroll viewed himself as a bop equivalent of the great Leo Watson, and captured some of Watson's feeling though never his

maniacal genius. Career-wise he amounts to more of a bop version of Helen Forrest, being too much of a band vocalist to make
it on his own. Because he can only handle up-tempo numbers
with scat passages, on the few albums that he made, the best
being *Joe Carroll with the Ray Bryant Quintet* (1956, Epic),
Carroll very quickly exhausts the listener's attention. He
couldn't sustain interest or come up with any worthwhile material outside the tunes he did in the band era and party pieces like
his "Lady Be Good" (the one that begins "Oh lovey dovey . . .").
Unlike Forrest and Harry James, when Gillespie pared down to
a small band and gave Carroll the sack, audiences soon discovered
Diz could do Carroll's shtick even better than he could.

Buddy Stewart (1921–50) and Dave Lambert (1917–66) deserve the honor of being the first to create a valid, vital music out
of the combination of vocals and bop. The mass audience de-
tected an element of insanity in both modern jazz and the older
tradition of scatting, and when you put them together it sounded
doubly crazy. Ella Fitzgerald got away with it because she could
be written off as cute and childlike; Gillespie's singers incorporated the nuttiness into their comedy, but Lambert and Stewart
vocalized with such precision, technique, and panache that you
had to take them seriously even though their music was rife with
humor.

It worked because Stewart and Lambert each had a passion
for vocal groups and a feeling for jazz, as well as voices handsome
enough to put over a ballad but flexible enough to make with the
rebops, and they put it all together in Gene Krupa's great band
of 1945. Stewart (born Albert James Byrne, Jr.) had been born
into show business; his parents, Al and Mamie Byrne, had been
a dance act. Both his sister, Beverly, who later married Stan
Getz, and his first wife, the former Martha Wayne, who appeared on many an armed forces radio show and in many a
B-movie musical, also sang professionally under the name Stewart. Buddy went on the circuit at eight with an act called Fitz
and Murphy Brothers, and stayed in vaudeville until he was
fifteen. The move from the greasepaint grind to the band bus

was a common one in the thirties, and Stewart accomplished it by playing banjo and singing tenor parts with a dance orchestra led by Jerry Livingston and then at the Arcadia Ballroom with Bobby Day's band. In 1940, Claude Thornhill heard Stewart at the Arcadia and invited him to organize a vocal group for the orchestra he was putting together. *

Originally, Thornhill and Stewart called the group The Pair of Pairs (one of the pairs being Mr. and Mrs. Stewart), but after Thornhill's composition "Snowfall" became the band's signature theme, he renamed the quartet the Snowflakes, and Stewart stayed with them into 1942 (beyond March), when he was drafted.

David Alden Lambert, by contrast, had been a professional drummer but had never really hit the big time before the war; he had even gotten out of music for a few years and worked as a tree surgeon. But after his discharge from the paratroops early in 1944, Lambert sold some arrangements to Johnny Long's Orchestra and soon after joined the band as a rhythm singer (Helen Young handled the ballads), which meant he took part in Long's hip (for its day) glee-club arrangement of "A Shanty in Old Shanty Town." Lambert and Stewart met in the Gene Krupa Orchestra, which Stewart joined after his discharge in 1944 and Lambert a short time later. A few months earlier in the summer of 1944, Krupa, not long out of prison after beating a trumped-up drug charge, had tried to clear up his tainted reputation with the dancing public by going out with an overtly commercial orchestra that contained a nine-piece string section and a four-voice vocal group called the G-Noters (among them Lambert and Stewart). When it didn't go over, Krupa swung radically to the opposite direction, switching from sweet to very hot with a "progressive" band that, Krupa let it be known, was receptive to

---

* Feather reports that Stewart worked in one of Glenn Miller's vocal groups before joining Thornhill, but this is unconfirmed by George Simon, the master maven on all matters Miller. Similarly, Curtis Jerde once wrote that Lambert also sang with Harry James, but I've been unable to substantiate this.

modern jazz. Essentially, he dropped the violins and reduced the voices to just Lambert and Stewart. Lambert left a year or so later, shortly before Anita O'Day rejoined the band.

Krupa made them neither an adjunct to the band's sound, as violins had traditionally been in swing orchestrations, nor the center of attention, as voices had usually been. "We'd always ask the arrangers to write for us, just as if there were another section in the band," Stewart said. "There'd be the rhythm, the brasses, the reeds . . . and us." Arranger Budd Johnson[*] and Lambert devised a chart that took the two voices in wordless unison over a roller-coaster ride through the new band's modern harmonies and fast, bop rhythm, and titled it with the question, "What's This?" (1945, Okeh). What's this? indeed; it became one of the more sensational records of the year,[†] reestablishing Krupa's position on the first tier of bandleaders and showing the music world what Lambert and Stewart could do—not to mention proving that a bop-oriented record could sell.

After Lambert had left Krupa, the two men continued to work together when they could find work. Their most famous non-Krupa session, the 1947 date for Keynote, teamed them up with Red Rodney and an all-star rhythm section of first-generation boppers: Al Haig, Curley Russell, and Stan Levey; put their new unison voicings to work in a small band; and, most importantly, restored the one element missing from "What's This?": improvisation. On all four titles, one of the two singers improvises a solo immediately after the trumpeter, while on "Charge Account," a variant on "All the Things You Are" introduced by Haig's quote from "Bird of Paradise" (Charlie Parker's title for the Kern song), Lambert exchanges fours with Rodney. "Cent and a Half," another numismatic title, eventually became part of Anita O'Day's repertoire (Miles Davis told O'Day that he wrote it).

---

* Dan Morgenstern says Budd Johnson, other sources identify Ed Finckel.

† The King Cole Trio even jumped on the "What's This?" bandwagon with their own bop scat epic, "That's What."

In 1948 the team did a date for the smaller Sittin' In With
label in which they dabble with a proto-cool sound provided by
another modernist out of the Krupa ranks, arranger Gerry Mulligan. On "Deedle" (aka "Static") and "In the Merry Land of
Bop," Lambert and Stewart experiment with instrumentation
somewhere in between the Rodney Quartet and the full Krupa
big band, adding a third voice, Blossom Dearie (verging on the
later Lambert, Hendricks, and Ross sound), and two horns,
Bennie Green and Allen Eager, with whom they trade scat
phrases like the Mel-Tones do in "That's Where I Came In." In
February 1949 they reached the zenith of the bebop aristocracy
when they broadcast with the new music's premier band, the
Charlie Parker Quintet.

In May of 1946, *Downbeat* ran a clip announcing that Buddy
Stewart was deliberating over whether or not to leave Krupa, as
so many other singers, hit records under their arms, were leaving the bands that spawned them. But then "What's This?" had
been no ordinary hit, so Stewart made the slightly offbeat decision, late in 1946, to strike out with Charlie Ventura's small band
rather than completely on his own. Another ex-Krupa sideman,
Ventura came out of Coleman Hawkins in his tenor saxophone
style and also shared both Hawk's and Krupa's affinity for the
new music, using his new band as a testing ground for some of
these new ideas. With the Ventura group on "Synthesis" and the
original, pre–Jackie and Roy "East of Suez" (both 1947, National/
Savoy), and with a group under his own name (with Wardell
Gray subbing for Ventura) on "Shawn" (1948, Sittin' In With),
Stewart does pretty much what he and Lambert had done with
Krupa, blending his baritone in with the horns to add weight to
the ensemble and scat in the front line. He had achieved a
continuation of the concepts Duke Ellington had first touched
on in "Creole Love Call" (which Ellington had dusted off in 1944
for his annual Carnegie Hall concert). In January 1948, Stewart
at last went out under his own name, again not as a solo act but
as co-leader of a new small group in partnership with Ventura's
trombonist, Kai Winding. They never recorded, but on paper

their trumpet-trombone-tenor-voice front line makes them sound very much like the Ventura band, a notion supported by two titles made with Al Haig and issued as the Five Bops (1948, Sittin' In With), which would seem to be by the Stewart-Winding group minus Red Rodney and Tiny Kahn.

In the meantime, Stewart also recorded "conventional" lyric vocals on three Ventura records, "Soothe Me," "Baby All the Time," and "Pennies from Heaven" (all 1947, National/Savoy). His very pretty voice and method of reconciling modern harmonic and rhythmic considerations with traditional ballad interpretation suggests a slightly thicker Mel Torme, while his early death sets him up as a sort of Russ Columbo to Torme's Bing Crosby. He might also have found the bigger audience beyond the jazz world, too, as he did get to make one straight-ahead solo session—all by himself with no other voices; doing words instead of "heeboobapoodaboo"—that produced three lovely sides: the plaintive "If Love Is Trouble"; "Hee Haw," a song about as good as its title implies, concerning a jackass (and presumedly written by one) but which Stewart makes the most of with some dazzling, dancing modulations, thus creating a silk purse out of the donkey's ear; and "Laughing Boy Blues." Fred Robbins, an important New York disc jockey, featured this last number extensively on his broadcasts, and as other djs followed his example, "Laughing Boy Blues" became a minor success.

Apart from Stewart, Lambert still concentrated on multiple-voice experiments—though as his friend Bill Crow explained in a warm, hilarious memoir in *The Jazzletter,* opportunities just to work were but tiny islands in a sea of years of scuffling. He joined the cast of an already running Broadway show called *Are You with It?,* which needed a quartet, and a few years later interested Pete Rugolo of Capital Records in his work. Early in 1949 he recorded two singles for Capitol with his Dave Lambert Singers (twelve voices doing two standards, "Always" and "When the Red-Red-Red Robin," and two pieces of exotica, "Hawaiian War Chant" and "Beban Cubop," in wordless bop syllables, backed by three great Parker vets for rhythm, Al Haig,

Curley Russell, and Max Roach), released by the label as part of
their premier modern jazz package, eight singles in their
57-60000 series.* Capitol also used Lambert's Singers in Stan
Kenton's vocal group, the Pastels, and to back some of their own
contract vocalists, specifically Mel Torme and Jo Stafford, in
curate's egg sessions that work for very different reasons. The
Torme–Pete Rugolo–Lambert numbers, especially "Lullaby of
the Leaves," repaint a familiar picture in bold new colors: Essentially the format is crooner, orchestra, and choir (like on a
million Haymes or Sinatra records), but it's a bop crooner, a bop
band, and a bop vocal group—a threesome you just don't expect
to hear. Paradoxically, the Stafford sides, especially one with a
nonverbal Anthony Braxton-esque title, succeed precisely because Stafford has absolutely no affinity for what Lambert is
trying to do and the conflict between the two purposes makes for
a campily enjoyable disc.

Rugolo also encouraged Charlie Barnet to record some sides
for Capitol in the "progressive" jazz style, and again they brought
in Lambert and also recruited Stewart. The Buddy Stewart–Kai
Winding band had not been a success—as George Hoefer wrote,
"People didn't accept it"—so Stewart went west to join Barnet.
It led to a surprise success for Barnet and Capitol: "Bebop Spoken Here." More than an update of "What's This?," this time
Lambert and Stewart use song form to frame their always terrific
unison vocalizing. After introducing the piece with a grand and
elaborate series of cadenzas, scatted alternately by each man
with dissonant brass screaming behind him, leader Barnet, playing a "square," enters and demands, "Wait a minute! What are
you guys talkin' about?" To explain bop lingo to the outsider,
Lambert and Stewart begin the song, a series of zany nonsense
phrases linked together by descriptive albeit absurd lyrics. To
hear Lambert and Stewart sing about it, the land beyond the

---

* 57-60001 was Lambert's "Hawaiian War Chant" and "Always" while 60015 was
Tadd Dameron's Orchestra, and 60000 and 60012 went to Babs Gonzales.

door opened by Parker and Gillespie is a wonderful place, as natural and inviting as any other musical domain, whose inhabitants make with a lingo that's drenched in hip humor and very easy to learn. After their first refrain and a Dick Kenney trombone solo, our boys return for exciting scat solos, not sung in unison but with each man simultaneously improvising a line of his own. Bebop isn't just spoken here, it's lived.[*]

Stewart then went on the road with Barnet, touring with him at least until Barnet broke up the bop band in October 1949. A few months later, Stewart had gotten a gig as a single at a club on the West Coast. He planned to drive crosscountry from New York, meeting his wife, Jerry, and baby in Deming, New Mexico. Somewhere along the border of February 1 and 2, 1950, on the outskirts of Deming, Stewart was killed in a car crash.[†] His Capitol contract not renewed after Pete Rugolo left his executive spot (they "decided bop was not going to be the next novelty craze," remembers Bill Crow), Lambert had more years of scuffling ahead, and continued to write and think. Within two years of Stewart's death, Lambert heard a record that would not only change the course of his career but signify one of the few examples in jazz where a single record would launch an entire move-

---

[*] Decca also wanted a ride on the pop-bop wagon and got Bing Crosby, an old colleague of the song's composer Matty Malneck, to record a duet with Patty Andrews on "Bebop Spoken Here" (1949). Here they return to the notion of the bebopper-as-cuckoo, most of all when the supersquare Andrews goes into a particularly unconvincing pseudo-scat and Crosby inquires, concernedly, "Are you feeling well, dear? Can I get you something?" Columbia and Frank Sinatra had already tried this the year before with "Bop Goes My Heart."

[†] As a footnote, his wife and child were left penniless at the time of his death, and Charlie Barnet started an emergency fund to help them out. It led to a benefit memorial for Buddy Stewart and Birdland on March 24, and among those who performed (besides Ella Fitzgerald, Charlie Ventura, Stan Getz, Tony Scott, Al Cohn, Billy Byers, Lester Young, Lennie Tristano, Harry Belafonte, J. J. Johnson, and Oscar Pettiford) were Charlie Parker and Dizzy Gillespie, performing together for almost the last time. (And as a footnote to this footnote, one of the last photos taken of Parker and Gillespie together—reproduced in Collier's *The Making of Jazz*, Driggs and Lewine's *Black Beauty, White Heat*, and Giddins's *Celebrating Bird*—was taken at the memorial, and it includes John Coltrane, then the tenor player with Gillespie, in the background.)

ment. The record was called "Moody's Mood for Love," released as a single on Prestige 924. The lyricist was an ex–tap dancer named Eddie Jefferson. The singer was a past and future everything who called himself King Pleasure. The movement was called "vocalese."

What is vocalese? Penguin's *New Dictionary of Music* describes voca*lise* as "a wordless composition for solo voice, whether for training purposes or concert performance." Jazz writers often use the term to describe any extended scat singing, such as Anita O'Day's or Ella Fitzgerald's. Eddie Jefferson meant something far more specific, something quite the opposite of improvisation. "Moody's Mood" began as "I'm in the Mood for Love," a pop standard originating from the 1935 movie *Every Night at Eight*, an Alice Faye–George Raft–Swannee Sisters epic today remembered primarily because it contains that song. James Moody, a saxophonist closely associated with Gillespie and then living in Sweden, recorded a jazz solo on the piece using, as most improvisers did, the song's chord changes as a basis for a spontaneous melody of his own. Jefferson then used Moody's improvisation as a basis for a new song, which, like the solo itself, occasionally referred back to the Fields-McHugh original. Instead of a wordless scat, Jefferson and Pleasure verbalized every note that Moody played, matching him inflection for inflection, and did the same for the only non-Moody interlude in the record, a piano solo, sung on that self-same Prestige 924 by Blossom Dearie.

The idea did not begin with either Jefferson or Pleasure. Vaudevillians Bea "The Shimmy Queen" Palmer and Marion Harris each recorded lyricized versions of Bix Beiderbecke's most famous solo, "Singin' the Blues," as Beiderbecke scholar Richard Sudhalter has discovered, although of the two, only Harris's record was released, and that only in England. The next two examples of this technique also refer to Beiderbecke: Bing Crosby's spontaneous annexation of lyrics to the concluding phrase of Bix's "Way Down Yonder in New Orleans" as the climax of his own "Someday, Sweetheart" (1934, Decca) and the

Modernaires' wordless chorus of "I'm Coming, Virginia" (1938, Aircheck) behind Jack Teagarden with Paul Whiteman's Orchestra. Then there's the Cats and the Fiddle singing a Benny Carter sax ensemble passage on "Gangbusters" and the Delta Rhythm Boys taking Duke Ellington's " 'A' Train" (or, rather, attaching words to the Strayhorn arrangement). But early examples of vocalese amount to pre-Columbus discoverers of America—Jefferson and Pleasure brought it to the fore and, for better or worse, made it part of the jazz singer's vocabulary.

When, in 1953, "Moody's Mood" became one of the biggest-selling records of the year (for lack of a category they classified it under "rhythm and blues"), Jefferson and Pleasure hardly had what could be described as your usual lyricist-vocalist relationship. Jefferson also fancied himself a singer, and as such wanted the hit record for himself. Pleasure wrote lyrics, too, and even claimed to have written these. In fact, although today we accept that Jefferson authored "Moody's Mood," Pleasure made such an impact with his recording that, had Jefferson not been given fifteen years after Pleasure's disappearance to tell his side of the story, we might never believe him; Pleasure even receives composer credit on Jefferson's own 1959 record of "Mood" (Inner City). But although Jefferson justifiably resented Pleasure for the plagiarism, there's no way Jefferson's technique, and subsequently his career, would have gotten off the ground without him. Jefferson, as we'll see, was a singer only by default—he had even put examples of vocalese down on wax three years before "Moody's Mood" and absolutely no one paid any attention. Pleasure, on the other hand, had exactly the kind of angular, haunting voice necessary to put the technique across. "Yeah, he copped those lyrics," Jefferson told Ira Gitler, "but in a way it opened up for me."

Like Buddy Stewart, Eddie Jefferson had a showbiz background. Born on August 3, 1918, in Pittsburgh, he was dancing professionally before the age of fifteen, and in the years prior to "Moody's Mood," he worked in various song and dance acts and played at least three or four instruments. He liked to tell about the time he met Leo Watson in 1938, relating to Carol Crawford how Watson and he "were talking about scat singing. He had taken that about as far as it could go, and advised me to sing lyrics. You know, like you could still improvise, but do it with lyrics." According to Jefferson's friend Ira Steingroot, Jefferson and partner Irv Taylor had begun fooling with lyricized jazz solos such as Chu Berry's "Ghost of a Chance" and Lester Young and Herschel Evans's on "Taxi War Dance" for their own kicks. "They only played short solos, you know, sixteen bars or so," Jefferson told Sudhalter about a month before his death, "and I got to learnin' 'em and puttin' in my own words to 'em. All in private, for my own pleasure." They started using the gimmick in their act in 1939, when he and Taylor were dancing on the same bill as Coleman Hawkins and at about the same time that Hawk's "Body and Soul" was on the jukeboxes. However, "I was strictly a dancer in those days," he told Leonard Feather, "and I did those things [vocalese singing] strictly for kicks." In 1950 it looked as if Jefferson might make the big time when, as half of Billie and Eddie, he appeared with Sarah Vaughan and made the first recordings of modern vocalese: "Beautiful Memories," based on Lester Young's improvisation on "I Cover the Waterfront" and "Bless My Soul," which came out of "Parker's Mood."

Not long after, the story goes, Jefferson was working at the Cotton Club in Cincinnati, singing, among other things, his lyrics on James Moody's recently recorded "Mood for Love;" the bartender was a twenty-eight-year-old aspiring singer from Tennessee named Clarence Beeks (who always claimed to have come across the idea on his own, starting with Lester Young's "DB Blues"). Beeks was never heard from again, but King Pleasure turned up at the Apollo Theatre in Harlem, where Prestige Records' A&R man Foch Allen heard him win their famous amateur talent competition with "Moody's Mood," which he then arranged for Pleasure to record. We know little else about Beeks, other than the tall tales that musicians tell about how he acquired the "Pleasure" nom de plume. When "Moody's Mood" took off, Pleasure went back in the studios four more times for

Prestige, further delighting label owner Bob Weinstock with the sales of "Red Top" (1952). Then he disappeared—twice—with just as much mystery as his career would lead you to expect.

At the time of Pleasure's first comeback in 1956, he cut some singles for Aladdin and Jubilee, telling Bill Coss in a *Metronome* interview that three years earlier he "didn't do too well with audiences . . ." and that he wasn't ready "artistically and emotionally" for the success that was nearly his; however, "an astute manager [Jeanne Burns]" was now grooming him for a comeback. When he re-reappeared four years later to do albums for Hifijazz and United Artists, Pleasure told Ralph J. Gleason, "I've got to thank Lambert, Hendricks and Ross and Eddie Jefferson for keeping me alive all these years I've been out of show business. . . . I'm going back into the business now, and you watch and see what I do. You tell 'em Pleasure's back." And that was the last anyone heard of King Pleasure. Those who know what happened to him aren't telling. Jon Hendricks has refused to explain "just why Clarence Beeks has not given us Pleasure for lo these many weeks, and towards what pursuit he has occupied himself these months past, nor must I speak further of such pursuit, lest I infringe on what should remain secret." Pleasure himself may have given us a clue in his lyrics to Stan Getz's "Diaper Pin," itself a reworking of "That Old Black Magic," when he opened and closed with, "I'm so afraid of where I'm going / And so in love with where I've been."

Pleasure's sole function, then, was to get the vocalese ball rolling—not that it had very far to roll. Both Eddie Jefferson and James Moody, who met while sharing the bill at the Apollo in 1953, had the good sense to capitalize on the success of "Moody's Mood" and they joined forces for a decade. Even more important, each of the future members of the greatest musical unit to work with vocalese—Lambert, Hendricks, and Ross—heard "Moody's Mood" and it changed their lives. Not coincidentally, each sought out Pleasure and recorded with him: Lambert and his singers backed Pleasure on two of his Prestige sides, taking the part of Slam Stewart's bass on Pleasure's reworking of Lester

Young's "Sometimes I'm Happy" and of Erroll Garner's piano on Charlie Parker's "This Is Always." Jon Hendricks came to a Pleasure date expecting to portray Lars Gullin to Pleasure's Stan Getz on "Don't Get Scared" (actually called "Don't Be Afraid" on the original Getz Metronome issue and the first in Pleasure's Getz cycle), but when he asked for his lyrics, Pleasure instructed him to write his own. " 'I wrote mine,' he said. 'Now you write yours,' and exited laughing, striding away with a combination of the Hastings Street Strut and the L.A. Getaway. Pleasure definitely had style, to the core. Nobody walks away like *that* anymore." Hendricks played the same part on the 1962 remake of "Don't Get Scared" for United Artists, and Annie Ross, uncredited, sang the Thore Swanerud piano part on Pleasure's 1960 remake of "Moody's Mood" for Hifijazz.

Jefferson had the showmanship and the idea, but Pleasure had the voice. Jefferson didn't have much range, and his voice got thin and stretchy, and often irritatingly screechy very easily. It grew on you the more you listened and the older he got, as on his seventies albums *Things Are Getting Better* (1974, Muse) and *The Main Man* (1977, Inner City), but it also grated on you more and wore you down. Neither Jefferson nor Pleasure nor Hendricks could have made it as a straight singer either, but Pleasure's voice was unusual, hypnotic, and strangely attractive, with exactly the sort of catchy appeal necessary to become a one-hit wonder in the fifties.

The shortcomings of vocalese, however, had nothing to do with vocal quality, but with faults inherent in the form. Limiting the voice to what an instrumental soloist had already done all but eliminated the freedom of choice of singer. Plus there was an inherent lack of inspiration as to what to sing about. Jefferson and most vocalese lyricists took it on themselves to preach. Usually they sang about the actual musicians who created the solos, and too often his lyrics come off like a recitation of a jazz reference book—a bad one at that, laden with cliché-heavy amateur criticism. On Bob Dorough's "Yardbird Suite" (1956, Bethlehem), for instance, he takes Parker's exquisite melody and reduces it to shoddy proselytizing for the jazz cause. Some might argue that this sort of thing does, indeed, bring new converts to jazz, but as with the recent movie 'Round Midnight, listeners who are already jazz fans don't need to be told while those who aren't will have no idea what's going on. Eventually Dorough found a niche where this approach was perfectly appropriate, writing jingles for a series of Saturday morning cartoons designed to teach children how to write and count. There already are two sets of lyrics to "Body and Soul," and while neither would qualify it as a great song and a jazz classic without its marvelously rich melody and harmonic progressions, both are preferable to Jefferson's stiff musical PR for Coleman Hawkins's musicianly prowess. When they weren't singing press releases, their love song–oriented lyrics had an overstated simplicity. It's one thing to use the same old "Baby, I dig you" words when you're doing a short twelve-bar blues, but Jefferson and Pleasure were trying to expand the length of time a vocalist stood in front of the microphone, and wound up with a repertoire full of numbers about five times as long as any Cole Porter song without a tenth of Porter's wit. They want us to listen to them longer but don't give us any good reason why we should. Vocalese was hot in 1952 and 1953, but by 1955 it was old hat.

Incredibly, the man who saved vocalese in 1957 was the same man who saved conventional bop singing in 1945. Dave Lambert had kept up his search for uses for the voice after Buddy Stewart's death, and, in addition to backing King Pleasure in 1953, had worked with bandleaders Georgie Auld (creating a five-voice choir to accompany the tenorist on eight sides for Coral in 1951) and Neal Hefti, singers Carmen McRae and later Tony Bennett, had also scored the one Lambert Singers session best left forgotten, the "Charlie Parker with Voices" (1953, Clef) travesty masterminded by Gil Evans.

In 1953, Lambert met Jon Hendricks, the new collaborator who would not only help him to realize the dreams he had been working toward all his life, but to go far beyond them in ways that neither could have ever conceived of at the time. Hendricks

Mr. Cros: Reconciling rhythm with romance, circa early thirties. (Wayne Knight Collection)

Pops Is Tops!

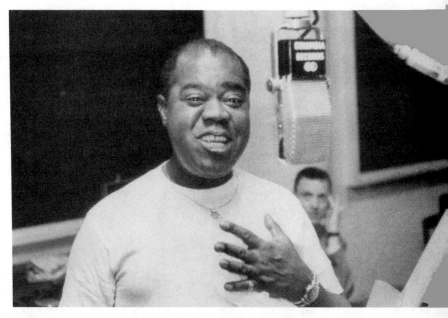

The man with the Star of David, recording one of his masterpiece sets in the late fifties for produ[...] George Avakian and Columbia. (CBS, courtesy of the Institute of Jazz Studies, Rutgers University)

Satchmo's Swingin' Session, circa 1940: The only sidemen that have been identified are "Big Chief" R[...] Moore, trombone (*far right*), and "Moon" Mullins, trumpet (*second from left*). (Hugh Turner Collectio[...]

Turning on the human light bulb, circa 1938. (Baron Timme Rosenkrantz, courtesy of the Institute of Jazz Studies, Rutgers University)

Cab Calloway: A James Kriegsman publicity photo in multiple images of the Hi-De-Ho man parallel the antiphonous music that was—and still —his trademark.

Images of Lady Day

As a "Decca Recording Star," mid- t
late-forties. As *Look* magazine said,
"She sings about as close as anybody
will come to a personal appearance
records." Decca may have been pus
that idea, since Holiday was prohibi
from making personal appearances
during the year and a day of her
incarceration, beginning in June 194
Thanks to that and the second AFI
ban, Holiday made no records betv
February 1947 and December 1948
(Institute of Jazz Studies, Rutgers
University)

Images of Ella

Presumedly taken in the early forties with her own band. The original caption tells us, "Loew's State, week of July 6," although it doesn't say what city or year. Also on the back of the print somebody, probably a PR writer, has written, "She can't resist and swings the ballad just a little". (Institute of Jazz Studies, Rutgers University)

er into the sixties, the
e of the "Dean Martin
w" and "Can't Buy Me
Dig that crazy "'do."
stitute of Jazz Studies,
Rutgers University)

Pop Music's Girth Stakes

Mildred Bailey: That old microphone's got me, early thirties. (NBC, courtesy of the Institute of Jazz Studies, Rutgers University)

"Little" Jimmy Rushing: Lean and low and built up from the ground. (Isador Seidman, courtesy of the Institute of Studies, Rutgers University)

Images of Sass and B

Acres of silk and satin still ain't as lush as her voice. (CBS, courtesy of the Institute of Jazz Studies, Rutgers University)

At work and in a semiconscious hi-fi reverie, circa 1950. (CBS, courtesy of the Institute of Jazz Studies, Rutgers University)

Back when Louis Armstrong and Nat Cole stayed mainly with the blues and novelties, Billy Eckstine was the first black to offer uncompromised eroticism. (Betty Page Collection)

Piano-Singing: The Two Masters

Fats Waller: A style even louder than his tie, a voice with more tones than his shoes, and an infectious rapture even more colossal than his pedal extremities. Victor recording session, July 13, 1942. (Institute of Jazz Studies, Rutgers University)

"Flash, Bam, Alakazam!" The King Cole Trio on stage with Stan Kenton and His Orchestra. Prominent are the KC3's Oscar Moore, guitar, and Johnny Miller, bass, and the SKO's Shelly Manne chopping wood on drums. Watch out for flying glass. (Institute of Jazz Studies, Rutgers University)

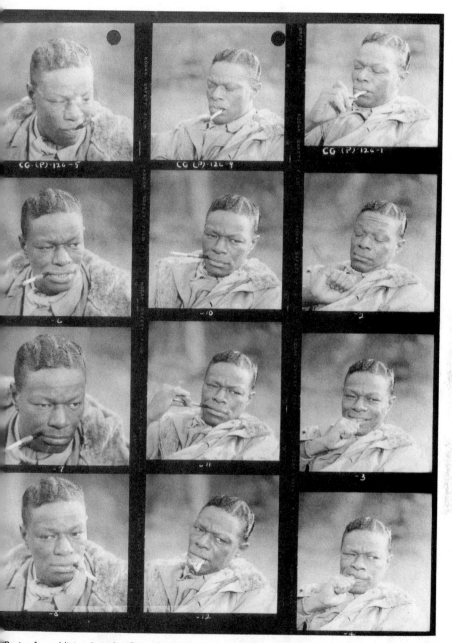

Posing for publicity shots for *China Gate*, a film from a combination even less likely than King Cole and Dean Martin: Nat Cole and Sam Fuller. (Wayne Knight Collection)

"You've got a million bucks worth of talent, but no class!" said Joe Glaser, who knew from no class, to O'Day in the brief period when he managed and tried to glamorize her. The jacket over her arm ties in with the come-hither look on her puss: Is Anita inviting us to kimono her house? (James Kriegsman, courtesy of the Institute of Jazz Studies, Rutgers University)

Mel Torme: Sinatra popularized bow ties among crooners, but, as Billie Holiday observed, everything else about Torme is his own. The Mel-Tones, which he headed around the time this publicity photo was taken, eventually lead to his adapting many of the vocal group's ideas to the solo voice. (Author's Collection)

Kay Starr: Swinging seduction. (Capitol Records, courtesy of the Institute of Jazz Studies, Rutgers University)

Chris Connor: A startlingly spare "Lush Life." (Institute of Jazz Studies, Rutgers University)

Peggy Lee: The high priestess of neoclassical, pan-cultural alternative music. (James Gavin Archive)

Dick Haymes: High-romance style, which, in the late fifties matured into fine jazz-tinged ballad singing. (Courtesy of Dan Singer)

Perry Como: How'd he get in here? Read chapter 8 and you will believe a nose can swing. (Courtesy of Dan Singer)

Tony Bennett: A virtuoso of heart and the perfect gladiator to fight the barbarians gathering at the gate. (Courtesy of Dan Singer)

Bobby Darin: So hip he won't even eat a square meal. (Courtesy of Dan Singer)

Vocalese Rogues Gallery

Eddie Jefferson. (Institute of Jazz
Studies, Rutgers University)

King Pleasure. (Institute of Jazz Studies,
Rutgers University)

When Jefferson joined with James
Moody's seven-piece band for a few
years, the two joined forces as kindred
souls who had been ripped off by
Clarence "King Pleasure" Beeks: Moody
had created a solo, Jefferson wrote
lyrics to it (and solidified that concept,
in fact), but the gold-toothed Mr.
Pleasure not only had the hit (and was,
in fact, a better singer than Jefferson),
he even claimed authorship. In poetic
though not necessarily musical justice, it
was Pleasure who disappeared
mysteriously and Jefferson who went on
to become a grand old man of jazz
singing (until he was murdered, no less
mysteriously).

Lambert, Hendricks, and Ross singing the original song of Basie, this photo proving that there were only three singers on the date (believe it or not!). "What are you, stupid?" (Aileen Armstrong, courtesy of the Institute of Jazz Studies, Rutgers University)

mbert, Hendricks, and Ross: Where ferson formalized vocalese and asure popularized t, Dave Lambert, n Hendricks, and nnie Ross gave it both significance. bert created the sound, Hendricks nned the words, 1 Ross gave them oth class and sex. (Institute of Jazz Studies, Rutgers University)

Betty Carter: Whose wardrobe of shmattes is exceeded only by her endless melodic invention. (Institute of Jazz Studies, Rutgers University)

"Baby pictures" of Mark Murphy: A smorgasborg of techniques, which add up to one of the most complete vocal artists in jazz.

was born in Newark, Ohio, in 1921, and grew up singing, eventually in show business but first in the African Methodist Episcopal church where his father ministered. Just as Lambert had been obsessed with the possibilities of multiple human voices, Hendricks was eternally curious about how the limits of the popular song form could be extended. "When I was first singing, I would forget the words and then make up ones I thought would fit and I got to the point where when I put in my own words, I found out that as long as they rhymed people didn't know the difference," Hendricks told Ralph Gleason in 1959, and in 1984 continued to Stanley Crouch, "I would [also] immediately write my own words if the original ones sounded dumb. For example, a song like 'It's the Same Old Dream' [1947]. It had a line like, 'I see a [crowded] steeple / Surrounded by people.' So I would wonder, what are they doing—standing on stilts?"

But Hendricks listened more to jazz musicians than to singers and songs, and would later name Art Tatum, a friend and mentor from childhood, and Charlie Parker, whom he first met when the bop sage played through Ohio in 1950, as his primary influences. After lots of amateur work, singing around with his own and others bands and vocal groups, and disastrous encounters with racial prejudice in the army and in college, Hendricks came to New York in the early fifties. It didn't take him long to get work as a lyricist in the rhythm and blues field. Louis Jordan, who only rarely recorded songs other than his own, took Hendricks's "Feed Me" into his act as well as "I'll Die Happy," which earned Jordan *Cashbox*'s award for the R&B Record of the Year, and his "I Want You to Be My Baby" gave Lillian Briggs a million-seller. Pretty soon jazz composers came to him for lyrics, among them Benny Golson with "Out of the Past" and Gigi Gryce with "Social Call," which both Ernestine Anderson and Earl Coleman recorded successfully.

Hendricks had admired Lambert for years, saying recently, "The early scat singing Keynote recordings he made with Buddy Stewart made me feel a lot less crazy in my hometown of Toledo, where I was scatting also." He sought out Lambert (first in a letter, according to some sources) and proposed a partnership, since the two had individually been working on the same idea. They experimented for the first time together on a release for Avalon Records, a recording company run by black bandleader-pianist-raconteur Teacho Wiltshire. Adding Butch Birdsall and Harry Clark to the team of Lambert and Hendricks and billing themselves on the label as "Jon [no comma] Dave Lambert and Singers," they put together a "crazy madrigal club" version of a well-known jazz instrumental. "Four Brothers," the Jimmy Giuffre composition that had named Woody Herman's greatest band. Lambert arranged for the quartet to sing the ensemble orchestral sections, and each of the four sang one of the four tenor saxophonists' solos (to be specific, Hendricks sang Al Cohn and Stan Getz; Birdsall, Serge Chaloff; Lambert, Zoot Sims; and Clark, Woody Herman) while Hendricks wrote continuous lyrics that established a scenario explaining the relationship between each of the brothers. Almost all the ingredients for their future success are there, but the team feared that their radical idea wouldn't have any chance at all if they sang too fast for listeners to understand the words, so they slowed the three-minute instrumental into a five-minute, two-sided vocal that, in the light of both earlier and later work, drags and drags—and drags. Lambert and Hendricks corrected the tempo mistake when recording the piece in a one-sided version for Decca in May 1955, relying on Hendricks's R&B track record for the flip side, which they based on the blues hit "Cloudburst," releasing the pairing as by "Jon Hendricks and the Dave Lambert Singers." Again it didn't make any noise, but they kept at it.

About this time they came up with the idea for a long-playing album of vocalized Count Basie pieces. Hendricks wrote out words for twelve Basie charts, in some cases writing around the lyrics of the records that already had vocal refrains ("Ev'ry Day," "Goin' to Chicago"), and Lambert conceived of the project as one for a twelve-voice choir of the sort that he had used at Capitol in 1949. Still they had no takers until, Hendricks said, "At ABC-Paramount Records we found a producer who was just getting started in the business [Creed Taylor]. He thought our ideas were great and agreed to record us." Annie Ross told Gene Kalbacher what happened next: "Dave had hired twelve singers for the session, six female and six male. I was called in merely to coach them—specifically, to coach the women how to sing with more of the Basie feel. That's something you really can't coach. They were wonderful in terms of knowing the right notes to hit. They were great sight-readers, but they didn't have the feel. . . . They didn't swing." Hendricks expounded to Crouch, "They couldn't swing at all. It was awful. They couldn't do it. We sent all the singers home and were at a loss. In my characteristically blunt way, I said, 'I think we'd better get some Negroes. No offense, but these people couldn't swing if you hung 'em.' "

They didn't realize it yet, but they already had the answer in Annie Ross. She was the one missing ingredient that would allow Lambert and Hendricks to find the sound they were looking for to restore the jazz vocal group to the plateau it had fallen from when the Boswell Sisters broke up twenty years earlier. Ross had moved to this country from her native Surrey, England, at the age of four and immediately started making the child-star rounds when she settled in Hollywood. There she was raised by musical comedienne Ella Logan, who, according to some accounts, was her mother but is usually described as her mother's sister. Logan and her husband loved jazz (though her American records show that she had little idea how to sing it) and exposed Annie to the music through records as well as musician friends. Ross sang professionally at age eight, doing an adorably cute miniature Scotsman in the "Little Rascals" short *Our Gang Follies of 1938*. She appeared as Judy Garland's kid sister in *Presenting Lily Mars* at twelve, and at sixteen went to the American Academy of Dramatic Arts. Differences between herself and Logan encouraged her to leave the country not long after, and following a disappointing reunion with her family in Scotland, Ross settled in London, where she got work as an actress in the West End and as a singer in the jazz clubs. Then she played American in Paris for five years, doing some singing and acting, but mostly palling around with expatriate jazzmen, sharing their lives, their music, their drugs, and, in at least one case, their love, and also cut her first record with an appropriately Franco-American jazz combo that included James Moody.

Back in the States for a few months in 1952, she did her first session under her own name, using the Modern Jazz Quartet with her current boyfriend, Kenny Clarke, on drums, and one-time partner Blossom Dearie in for John Lewis on piano, for Dizzy Gillespie's short-lived DeeGee Records (later acquired by Savoy). In October she made the records that probably first brought her to the attention of Lambert and Hendricks, "Twisted" and "Farmer's Market," which Bob Weinstock of Prestige marketed as a successful follow-up to "Moody's Mood for Love" in the vocalese stakes. It sold, and might have been the basis for a solo career, but by the time it picked up steam Ross had already beaten it back to Europe as Lionel Hampton's thrush. It was a catastrophic tour that ended with Ross and other sidemen quitting halfway through. In Stockholm she made another single, using some of Hamp's men as well as the leading European jazzman, Lars Gullin, but more importantly, on returning to London, she went to work on her first LPs as well as her first big theatrical hit in the West End revue *Cranks*. "Annie Ross makes a sensational success in new revue," one reviewer wrote. "At last someone has realised the many and varied talents of Annie Ross . . . the best musical comedy bet Britain has to offer today."

This, then, was the Annie Ross that Lambert and Hendricks hired (perhaps on the recommendation of Teacho Wiltshire, who accompanied Ross on her Prestige date) to coach their choir shortly after she arrived back in New York for a run at a cabaret called The Upstairs at the Downstairs in 1957, a maze of contrasting abilities that added up to a great artist. She brought to the trio a theatrical flair for showmanship combined with jazz feeling, and also combined the English old-school teamwork ideal with American star appeal. More than anything, though, she had a *real* voice, and gave Lambert the arranger and Hendricks the lyricist someone to write for and balanced their scratchy, "musician's" voices with one that needed no hyphen, strong and pretty in all registers, not to mention an appearance to go with it, her leotarded body, jeweled pumps, and shapely gams being the chief attraction of the original *Song of Basie* album cover.

It took the three of them time to discover this, however. When they realized that they had used up their $1,250 budget and had nothing to show for it, someone gave them the idea of overdubbing—perhaps it was Don Elliott, who had recently created an artificial vocal quartet album for ABC-Paramount by laying down four tracks of his own voice. If Elliott could turn one voice into four, couldn't they turn three into twelve? They had to do all the recording and mixing in the wee small hours, so producer Creed Taylor wouldn't know they had blown the real choir date, on a back-breaking series of sessions that began on Hendricks's thirty-sixth birthday and ultimately put him in the hospital. It worked out better mathematically than musically, since on the finished product the hash of three voices trying to sound like twelve trying to sound like an instrumental jazz orchestra sounds as muddled as it reads. Only when one of the three is soloing, which thankfully is a lot, are the results listenable. However, *Sing a Song of Basie* did reach the salesmark Taylor hoped for, and quickly Roulette Records, which had Basie under contract and doubtlessly didn't like the idea of anyone else making money on his name, brought in the trio to do an album of twelve more Basie tunes, this time with the Count's orchestra *and* his vocalist, Joe Williams. Neither this record, *Sing Along with Basie,* nor MGM Records' attempt to horn in on the idea, *Sing a Song of Goodman,* which uses Randy Van Horne's big choir in tandem with a group of horn soloists, works any better than the original overdubbed *Song of Basie.* Lambert, Hendricks, and Ross could replicate a whole band all by themselves, so to back them with another orchestra amounts to two Count Basie bands playing at once.

Jon Hendricks, then recuperating in the hospital from the stress of the first album, came up with the idea that would finally work. It turned out to be far simpler than any of them had predicted: Instead of messing with choirs, multitracking, and full orchestras, why not just use the three voices and a three-piece rhythm section? Booked by Willard Alexander, Basie's manager, and accompanied by Gildo Mahones, Lester Young's onetime pianist, they took to the road, and for four years were one of the most consistently popular attractions in jazz. In October 1957, while the first album was still at work, Richard Bock of World Pacific Records signed Annie Ross to an exclusive contract, and recorded the first of three solo albums even before the trio did their Roulette/Basie. In March 1959 they recorded the first pure Lambert, Hendricks, and Ross album (not counting a 1958 single of Horace Silver's "Doodlin' " and "Spirit Feel"), *The Swingers* for World Pacific; later in the year they began a contract with Columbia Records that lasted for three records, *The Hottest Group in Jazz* (1959, available now as *The Best of Lambert, Hendricks and Ross*), *Lambert, Hendricks and Ross Sing Ellington* (1960), and *High Flying* (also 1960). Though they also appear on a few odd tracks on *The Real Ambassadors* (1961), that botched collaboration with Louis Armstrong, Carmen McRae, and Dave Brubeck as authored by Mrs. Brubeck, and the anthologies *Giants of Jazz* and *Jingle Bell Jazz*, which contains their homage to Walt Kelly and *Pogo*, "Deck Us All with Boston Charlie," it's the four all–L, H & R albums that constitute the main body of their work, and therein lies some of the most sensational jazz ever sung.

Examples of Jon Hendricks's virtuosity as a lyricist abound. Mel Torme and Gordon Jenkins, June Christy and Pete Rugolo, and Tony Bennett and Ralph Burns would each find their own different ways for singers to break down the thirty-two-bar pop song boundaries, but once Hendricks found his method there was no stopping him. "Jon writes lyrics as easily as most people write a letter," Ross tells her audiences today. During his L, H & R years, Hendricks never wrote jazz commercials like Eddie Jefferson, and also refused to cop out by turning jazz instrumentals into conventional love songs, as Tin Pan Alley had made "A

Night in Tunisia" into "Interlude" and "Frahlicha in Swingtime" into "And the Angels Sing." Instead, he thought up a story for each song as suggested by the title, perhaps not corresponding at all to what the original composer and soloists had in mind, but a narrative inspired by the flow of the ensemble and each individual statement. Jazz fans on the "inside" will find plenty to amuse them in Hendricks's delightful scheme of compounded internal rhymes, as on Stan Getz's entrance in "Four Brothers" where he entreats listeners to "dig my Long Island sound," referring to a 1949 Getz record titled "Long Island Sound." Just the same, lay listeners won't feel left out.

Apart from the Count Basie book, which they returned to again and again, Hendricks penned his best lyrics to the melodies of Horace Silver, the central composer-bandleader of the late-fifties hard-bop movement. The L, H & R version of Silver's "Doodlin' " follows up Annie Ross's earlier "Twisted" as a depiction of the bop singer as ultimate meshuggener, while in "Home Cookin' " and "Cookin' at the Continental" Hendricks cooks three courses of fun playing with Silver's obsession with soul food and kitchen metaphors. "Come on Home" may be the single most representative cut of Hendricks in full flight, as he takes a typically eloquent and earthy Silver blues line, and decorates it with words that make something personal and special out of oft-used verbal blues ideas the same way that Silver does with oft-used musical blues ideas. Likewise, the way each of the trio offers a slightly different set of reasons why whoever it is should "come on home" parallels the way each of the three instrumental soloists (trumpeter Blue Mitchell by Dave Lambert, tenor champ Junior Cook by Jon Hendricks, and pianist Silver by Annie Ross) improvises a personal musical statement based on Silver's melody. Hendricks effortlessly matches every note of the ensemble parts and solos, capturing the mood, the cadence, and the idea of each phrase while at the same time maintaining the continuity of the overall narrative. Even if he had any real competition, Hendricks's work would still be the greatest argument for the artistic integrity of the vocalese lyric.

Lambert, back when he wrote for himself and Buddy Stewart, had learned to create breathtakingly complex and exhilarating sounds from the combination of two voices; in the years that followed, he tried to build up, experimenting with choirs of eight or twelve voices and then overdubbing even more. But once he and Hendricks got wise to the fact that they could achieve every effect they wanted with a mere three voices, Lambert masterminded the most remarkable vocal group sound heard in twenty years. The most popular multivoice units of the fifties had favored an annoyingly overclose kind of harmony, especially the Hi-Los and the Four Freshmen (the Mel-Tones get the blame for bringing very close vocal harmony into modern jazz, but they at least used it tastefully). Lambert instead devised distant harmony, three voices hanging together in a way that recalled some of the very loose black blues and jazz groups of the twenties and thirties, like the Hokum Boys and various Lonnie Johnson–Spencer Williams duets. Most of the time, Lambert's arrangements sound relatively simple in terms of score structure, as they start with the basic jazz head-solos-head formula. His brilliance lies in their horizontal organization, the way he uses the three voices to outline or suggest different chords. On the *Ellington* album, Lambert gets to play with vertical shapes as well, because where Ellington puts clarinets on top of trombones and baritone saxophones, Lambert puts voices on top of voices (sometimes with three different simultaneous lyric lines), maintaining the master's genius for balance and space and in general doing him proud. Where other vocalese acts could merely sing Ellington's praises, Lambert, Hendricks, and Ross pay him the greater tribute by singing his music.

Annie Ross supplied the trio's real vocal muscle. She makes the difference between a mere improvement on Jefferson-Pleasure style that only a few insiders might get off on and a group that could appeal to everybody. Besides having a beautiful voice in the fifties and sixties, Ross comes equipped with buckets of charm and genuine presence. At her most convincing, she strikes one as, like Abbey Lincoln, an updated Billie Holiday.

Each of the trio made solo albums, but Hendricks's *A Good Git-Together* (1959, World Pacific) uses the lyricist's voice only to introduce solos by Pony Poindexter and Wes Montgomery, and Lambert's album, which he intended as a one-man over-dubbed quintet, got goofed up by United Artists, which released it as *Swing/Sing Along with Dave Lambert* (1959) when Lambert had only recorded the first of five voices. Ross made three albums during the L, H & R years: *Annie Ross Sings a Song with Mulligan** (1958) *Gypsy* (1958–59), wherein conductor Buddy Bregman works hard to escape the stigma of mediocrity and the Styne-Sondheim score tries equally hard to prove that Broadway isn't going downhill; and *A Gasser* (1959), in which Ross never really catches fire despite the encouragement of Zoot Sims. But it's the first, *Annie Ross Sings*, that demonstrates what gets Ross going: unusual settings like the Gerry Mulligan quartet with baritone, trumpet, and no piano (inspiring collaborators like Mulligan, Chet Baker, and Art Farmer), offbeat ideas like speeding up "How About You?" (praising "Billy Eckstine's looks" instead of Franklin Roosevelt's) so that the beats fall in all kinds of unexpected places, and reconfiguring "I Feel Pretty" into a swinging kind of baroque harmony. With Ross, ideas like these count for more than songs.

With the trio, Ross uses the female voice as creatively as Lambert uses the vocal group and Hendricks uses words. Ross normally sings in the alto range, but she had the chops to go much higher when the occasion called for it, and from time to time could do a whole number in an ethereal "air" voice, such as "Skylark" on the British *Annie by Candlelight* (1956, Pye). When called upon to play the role of a trumpet or a piano, then, Ross uses the opportunity to go as high as she likes. The very looseness of Lambert, Hendricks, and Ross takes into account a pitfall you can't avoid when singing jazz solos: Many notes will

---

* One further Ross-Mulligan track, "The Lady's in Love with You," turned up on the anthology *The Genius of Gerry Mulligan*.

have to be too high or too fast to be clearly understood. Ross can't be bothered to stand still long enough for lesser beings to figure her out. In singing Miles Davis's solo from Charlie Parker's "Now's the Time" (on *The Swingers*), she gets higher and higher until she's just short of screaming, by which point we've long since lost track of what she's singing—and she gets her point across just the same. "Come on Home" (from *High Flying*) has Ross digging into one of Horace Silver's masterful but slightly frightening piano solos, tempered with a touch of dissonance. To match Silver's finger-popping up and down the keyboard, Ross radically shifts between high and low voices and keeps her cool in a remarkably "Twisted" call-and-response conversation with herself.

Ross proved to be such an important part of the trio that there was nothing worth saving after she left it. Ross was weary from too many years of touring; some have said she was doing too many drugs and no longer got along with Hendricks as well as she once did (as she told Leslie Gourse). It added up to the old vocal group's curse: Any good jazz group has to break up after three or four years, while the Ink Spots and the King Sisters go on forever. Lambert and Hendricks tried to find a suitable replacement, and after a few dates with Ann-Marie Moss (later partner and wife of Jackie Paris, who turned their act into "Lambert, Hendricks, and Moss") they settled for Yolande Bavan. Why, I couldn't tell you. They must have realized that they'd never find anyone with both the showbiz panache and the sexy swing of Ross, but it beats the heck out of me why they settled for someone who had neither. As "Lambert, Hendricks, and Bavan" they did three forgettable albums for RCA before breaking up for good in 1964. Any chance the trio might have had at reuniting got lost in 1966 when Lambert, who in 1964 had tried putting together yet another vocal group and also emceed many a jazz concert, was killed. Like his first partner, Buddy Stewart, Dave Lambert lost his life in a highway accident.

Surprisingly, neither Hendricks nor Ross achieved anything individually that compared with their triumphs as a trio. As you'd expect, Ross has since gone back and forth between America and England many times, and so has Hendricks. Ross fronted one very entertaining group for a short time, in partnership with the fine singing saxist Pony Poindexter and his Berlin All-Stars (including fellow expatriates Carmell Jones and Leo Wright) for a 1966 MPS album, *Annie Ross & Pony Poindexter*. She's gotten more attention for her film and theater work,* and today her nightclub sets are an engaging mixture of the very stuff of swing (Count Basie and Wardell Gray) with the very stuff of anti-swing (Stephen Sondheim).

Besides fronting many editions of his own Hendricks and Co. groups, Hendricks has worked a lot in theater. Reflecting the increasingly didactic leanings of his work, Hendricks invested much of his energies in a show called *The Evolution of the Blues,* which he first recorded for Columbia in the early sixties. At present it looks as if Hendricks's career and the vocalese movement will wind up where it started, in the pop bins, or so it seemed when Joni Mitchell covered Ross's "Twisted" and the Manhattan Transfer, restless after proving they hadn't the charm, wit, or professionalism to sing one Hendricks lyric after another, went and hired him to write a whole album of them, *Vocalese*, which only a few years later seems like the one major embarrassment of Hendricks's whole career. When Hendricks and Ross did get together for a mid-seventies public television show, in the company of the ever-hoarse Eddie Jefferson (only a few years before his murder in Detroit) and the inane yodeler Leon Thomas, it seemed as if their intention had been to prove that their art was long dead.

Not so when the two teamed up again at New York's Blue Note for the first time in twenty-three years, using the worthy Bruce Scott in place of Lambert, whom, Hendricks said, "had another gig." You still wouldn't want to hear Hendricks on a

---

* Most folks prefer *Superman III* or *Pirates of Penzance*, but my favorite is the obscure *Oh, Alfie!* for the simple reason that Ross goes topless in one scene.

conventional ballad, but his raggedy chops sound great as ever on his perennial "Goin' to Chicago." Furthermore, his "Monk Cycle" (besides being a close friend of Thelonious Monk, Hendricks also sang on the Genius of Modern Music's Columbia album *Underground*) showed he has good lyrics left in him, and his set comic routines, like Dizzy Gillespie's "I'd like to introduce the guys in my band" bit, continue to crack you up no matter how many times you've heard them.

Ross has lost her marvelous upper register, which, unfortunately, didn't stop her from screeching, but still has the presence, style, and Annie Ross–ness that launched a thousand wanna-be's, mainly attitude-heavy harridans like Bette Midler and Joni Mitchell and the assorted Manhattan Transfer broads, none of whom ever caught on that Ross has both swing and style that go way beyond her basic ballsiness.

Scott rightfully didn't try to assume Lambert's kinky authority but instead displayed a smoother tone and diction just as good as his predecessor's, with an impressive gift for articulating clearly on sixteenth and thirty-second notes as on "Four." As a trio they stayed mostly with the old L, H & R Basie and Silver pieces, breaking no new ground but feeding the bears of jazz repertory and giving my generation the chance at last to hear these masterpieces live by the only people who can sing them. Perhaps if Hendricks, Ross, and Scott do it again in the nineties they'll get around to some of Hendricks's choicer works of the last two decades, like his homage to Louis Armstrong's "Stardust." We have that to look forward to.

Modernism 2

Ballads, Baritones, and B.

"They weren't ready for black singers singing love songs. It sounds ridiculous, but it's true. We weren't supposed to sing about love, we were supposed to sing about work or blues or some dumb crap."
—Billy Eckstine to Lee Jeske, 1984

The black baritone tradition, like vocalese, grew up with modern instrumental jazz. Both movements also share the same periods of germination, going way back in jazz's classic era, and the same future, as today the fate of each style seems limited to new performances by past masters. However, it's hard to be optimistic about the style that Jefferson and Pleasure wrought, as their art had few followers at the most, and, if not for the work of one single exponent—Lambert, Hendricks, and Ross—wouldn't be worth bothering with at all. At its peak, the black baritone school affected hundreds of singers in and around jazz, at least a half dozen of whom were excellent, and gave us two of the greatest musicians of all time in Sarah Vaughan and Billy Eckstine.

Like so many aspects of jazz and pop singing, the movement began with Bing Crosby, who may have influenced even more black singers in the thirties and forties than he did white Italo- and Irish-Americans. Herb Jeffries, acting as spokesman for the movement in *Ebony* magazine (which certainly wasn't going out of its way to print nice things about white artists), went so far as to say, "Crosby is the biggest influence on American popular singing. Before Bing there was no baritone in the popular field, only tenors. Crosby made America baritone-conscious and popularized the rich deep tones that move people so much. Crosby revolutionized modern singing." Jeffries then summarized Crosby's importance to his art by calling him the "Daddy of Sing."

Crosby achieved all this largely from his own absorption of black style, and served a function of such importance to the development of Afro-American vocal music partly because he returned to blacks what was rightfully theirs. Around the time of Crosby's emergence, more showbiz blacks mimicked whites than the other way around: Avon Long and George Bias each took Eddie Cantor for a model, and when black bandleaders didn't use the stock white vocalists of the day (Dick Robertson et al.) they brought in blacks like Orlando Robison, whose stratospheric tenor made him a screaming Mimi like Donald Novis or Dick Powell.

Things changed when Crosby, after years of thirty-two-bar refrains and small-print billing, finally broke through to the top in the early thirties, his rise being roughly concurrent with that of Louis Armstrong. The two men had already learned so much from each other that no one could tell which mannerism had begun with which man, and as Mezz Mezzrow tells us, their records mutually flooded the jukeboxes of Harlem and, presumedly, of other black communities across the country. In November 1932 the movie fan magazine *Photoplay* published the following "letter"—in authentic Amos 'n' Andy dialect—to Crosby from an unidentified "colored boy 'down South' ": "Dear Mr. Croz Bee, I declare, times is gettin' that good I jus' naturally can't get over it. My gal, she jus' keeps in such a good humor all the time wif your singin' and all, that we ain't had no fights fer a long time." For both black and white bands everywhere a pattern became clear: Instrumentalists who wanted to sing rhythm numbers patterned themselves on Armstrong; band vocalists who longed to sing ballads based their crooning on Crosby. The real Armstrong could still sing ballads and Crosby could still get hot whenever the occasion called for it, and shout when it hit him, yes indeed, but their imitators rarely showed such flexibility.

Harlan Lattimore, the first of the "Black Bing"s and "Colored Crosby"s, sang with Don Redman's Orchestra. At that time it seemed a safe bet that Redman, a brilliant arranger responsible for the success of both the Fletcher Henderson Orchestra and the superb McKinney's Cotton Pickers band, would soon be as popular as Cab Calloway or Duke Ellington if given the chance to lead his own dance band. It was also assumed that Lattimore, with his light good looks, smooth hair, and smoother voice, would take the radio and record biz by storm. Neither happened. Redman, unable to lead a successful band of his own after nearly ten frustrating years, retreated to arranging for other bands, both black and white, while Lattimore, who nearly became one of the first black entertainment celebrities, became instead one of the first celebrity drug addicts and spent much of his life in prison. His habit was only part of his problems, and gave an excuse to the racist community to jail him for a far more serious crime: that of a black man who dares to sing of love, especially when white women might be listening.

Lattimore, born in Cincinnati in 1908, played guitar in addition to singing and possessed that great rarity among thirties blacks, a college degree. He first appears on records in February 1932 doing the vocal refrain with Redman on Lee Wiley's song "Got the South in My Soul" (Melotone), using Crosby-isms enough to more than justify his claim to black Bing-hood. Between 1932 and 1936 he made some twenty sides with Redman's band, some of which were released under Lattimore's own name, and in addition to doing two sessions with Fletcher Hen-

derson, also sang vocal refrains with the white dance bands of
Isham Jones and Victor Young. On "If It's True," from that same
first session, Lattimore finds plenty of opportunities to warble
Crosby-esque trills in Redman's lyric, which is full of "oo"
rhymes. Like most early Crosby imitators, Lattimore sounds far
more restrained than the often unpredictable original, with a
tight, pinched voice that suggests he has to work hard to sound
relaxed. Billy Eckstine, talking about Lattimore in 1947, referred to him as "one of the guys who inspired me." True, he'd
never threaten Crosby or Al Bowlly, but he comes across as far
more listenable than any other male band singer of the early
thirties.

Similarly, Roy Felton, the next entry in the roster of black
Bings, sang better than any other boy vocalist of the late thirties
excepting Sinatra and Haymes. Addictions also plagued his career. "He was a big drinker," said Dick Ables, a band road
manager and friend. "Every chance he'd get he'd be at the bar."
Comparing Felton's personality with Eckstine's, Earl Coleman,
who knew both and also sang with Benny Carter, described "the
difference between the two. [Roy] didn't have the bulldog tenacity that it took. Because there was no place for blacks to be
heard, like radio. In other words, his dedication wasn't what it
should have been." As a result, his total output consists of only
nine vocal refrains with Benny Carter's Orchestra on Vocalion,
Decca, and Bluebird, but they rank among the most superb
collaborations of bandleader and band singer ever recorded in
the band era, Felton's silken tones mixing magnificently with
Carter's elegantly dancing brass and reeds. "There, I've Said It
Again" (1941), the last of the nine, shows that black baritones are
moving deeper into the throat and growing less concerned with
vertical, melodic shapes than the deep richness of each individual note. "What you heard on record, he went and got up and
did that right out of a nap." Felton would be asleep in a corner
of the control booth, Carter would nudge him, and, Coleman
continued, "Benny said, 'All right, kid.' He'd yawn, take a
smoke, and sing."

Neither Lattimore nor Felton had what it took to make it. Inevitably "it" required more than talent to get ahead in show business, and to be a black ballad singer at this time you had to be something akin to a civil rights leader besides. The quality of your singing impressed people less than the nerve it took to dare to suggest that blacks were capable of feeling the same things white folks were and, consequently, able to sing the same songs. Louis Armstrong, Bill Robinson, Stepin Fetchit, and Ethel Waters had made a start by proving that black entertainers, if they didn't stray too far from the white preconception of how blacks were supposed to act, could be accepted by whites and even become wealthy and famous. No one minded if Little Jimmy Rushing sang a blues with Basie, if Pha Terrell went through his campy parody of crooning, if Cab Calloway hi-de-ho'd, or if Ivie Anderson expounded on how all God's chillun had rhythm, but no black man dared attempt a "straight" love song.

Things began to look up in 1939. Toward the end of this year, two of the most prestigious black bandleaders in the country— Earl Hines, known at that time as having Chicago's number-one orchestra, and Duke Ellington, who had already broken out of the Cotton Club to a never-ending series of national and soon international road tours—mutually decided to take on male vocalists. As Stanley Dance has described it, Ellington and Hines had an agreement regarding the exchange of musicians, and most of Ellington's best singers had worked first with Hines, including Ivie Anderson, her replacement Betty Roche, and Ray Nance. As Ellington's son and sometimes assistant, Mercer, remembered, Ellington and Hines had decided on two excellent black ballad singers: Herb Jeffries, who had worked on and off with Hines since 1934; and Billy Eckstine, whom Budd Johnson, Hines's ace arranger and tenor man, had raved about enthusiastically. Ultimately, Eckstine went with Hines and Jeffries joined Ellington. Within just a few months their idea started working: "Flamingo" (Victor), recorded by Ellington and Jeffries in December 1940, signified the first time a black man created a hit record with a straight-ahead ballad. Considering that Eckstine and Nat Cole's first hits ("Jelly, Jelly," 1940; and "Straighten Up and Fly Right," 1943) fit into the more acceptable blues and novelty patterns, "Flamingo" represented a new beginning.

Jeffries had an advantage over the very black Eckstine and Cole in his light, only marginally colored skin, as his mother had been Irish and his father a combination of French, English, Native American, and black. "Imagine," he said to Barry Ulanov in 1948, "if a few drops of Negro blood, besides all that white blood, make me a Negro, imagine how valuable Negro blood must be." Jeffries, who was more than light enough to pass for whatever color he wanted—once a real estate agent refused to sell him a home in an all-white Los Angeles neighborhood because he assumed Jeffries was Jewish, and once a pushy California broad called him a "dago"—simply chose to be black, and to rise to the top of the black showbiz world before "crossing over," as they say today, to the larger white audience. He had been born in Detroit in 1914, and in talking about his life thirty-seven years later for *Life*, said that he grew up feeling out of place and not sure who he was until he moved to Harlem in the early thirties and found his true identity as a Negro. "I decided some time ago," he told Richard L. Williams in 1951, "that the Negro people need all the good, intelligent, unbelligerent representatives they can get in this world, and I'm trying to become one."

Though he may have found himself in Harlem, he found his first musical successes in Chicago. There he landed the boy singer spot in Erskine Tate's Vendome Orchestra and then in Earl Hines's Grand Terrace Orchestra, with which he waxed two songs for Brunswick in 1934, "Just to Be in Caroline" and "Blue (Because of You)." His interpretation of Crosby's method struck his employers as radical, and Howard Bunt, whom Jeffries sang with at the Greystone Ballroom in Detroit, fired him because his voice wouldn't "fill the hall and I can't afford one of those new-fangled microphones." One of Hines's sidemen told him, "Look, I don't think you're going to make it, singing like a girl. You've got to lower that voice—if you possibly can." He kept on the move, and in Los Angeles in 1937 and 38, he starred in three all-black movie westerns, *The Bronze Buckaroo, Harlem on the Prairie,* and *Two-Gun Man from Harlem.* Jeffries made a tour of personal appearances at theaters showing these features and in Detroit ran into Duke Ellington, who had known "the Bronze Buckaroo" since childhood. Ellington offered him the first male vocalist's chair in His Famous Orchestra.

He first recorded with Ellington in March 1940 (a broadcast exists from two months earlier) on the premier side of the Duke's new contract with Victor,* "You, You Darlin'." At the same time he switched record companies, Ellington had also changed his management and started his own music publishing firm. The new company's first hit song, ironically, turned out to be "Flamingo," a song written by Ellington's friend Edmund Anderson and arranged by Ellington's collaborator Billy Strayhorn. It eventually sold a million records (according to *Ebony*), put Jeffries's name before both the black and white public, and gave him the basis for his career as a soloist. "Most people arrive by stork," he's told a million club audiences, but "I came in on a flamingo." It also opened doors for Jeffries musically. Ellington described the young Jeffries as "inclined to the falsetto, but it was very well accepted." "When Herb Jeffries was first with my band, he used to sing high," Hines told Dance, "and we told him, 'You got to come down from there, because we don't know what the hell you are.'" Eckstine continued, "Billy Strayhorn was the one that got him to sing down when he did the arrangement of 'Flamingo' for Duke, got him down to a range. Before that he mostly used to sing falsetto."

Listening to Jeffries's records from the Ellington period on, one does indeed hear a man used to singing very high now exploring the lower reaches of his voice, and his enthusiastically pro-baritone comments in interviews also bespeak a sinner converted. Though corseted rhythmically, his tonal diversity

---

* He had also guest starred with Sidney Bechet on Victor in September 1940.

must have been what attracted Ellington to Jeffries, his four-octave range giving the master painter all the possibilities he relished. Ellington and Strayhorn's exquisite scores provide plenty of beautiful background to Jeffries's vocalizing, whether framing his voice in the conventional band-singer-band structure or experimenting with more adventurous forms, and their settings would be interesting even without a good soloist. But Jeffries's flights up and down the octaves supply the MacGuffin for all this activity. On "Flamingo," Strayhorn has Jeffries jump all over the place, from basso dives to flamingolike flights into falsetto as lyrics dissolve into wordless cries. It all contributed to the total picture: a swarthy, exotically handsome bronze man singing an exotic song in an exotic way. This octave jumping had also begun with Crosby, who did it to perfection on his 1934 "Someday, Sweetheart" (Decca), and Ellington claimed to be the one who convinced Jeffries to sound like Crosby. "Herb's imitation of Bing was the foundation until Herb's own singing self took over," Ellington explained. "I think he just forgot he was imitating Bing, and he has been there ever since."

"Everybody said I was crazy to leave Ellington [in 1942]—including him," Jeffries remembered. Even one as farsighted as Duke could not foresee a day when singers could actually compete with bands as box-office attractions. For a time, it looked as if Duke might have been right. Jeffries dislocated his pelvis in a car accident, and this added to his frustration as a pop singer trying to make it in a band-dominated business and as a black white man trying to make it in an Anglo world. For a year he thought he would never sing in public again, but then two sharp music businessmen got him back on his feet, manager Maurice Duke and A&R man–songwriter Leon Rene. For Rene's company, Exclusive Records, Jeffries rerecorded a Duke-less "Flamingo," which got both the singer and the label started, and then turned out any number of hits, including his theatrical but effective "Angel Eyes," a showoffy "Basin Street Blues," the boozy "After Hours" and "When I Write My Song," a well-thought-out swipe from Saint-Saëns's "My Heart at Thy Sweet

Voice." Meanwhile, Duke found more B-movie roles for Jeffries and booked him into both black and white nightclubs, where the singer convinced a few of the latter, like the Club Morocco in Hollywood, to open their doors to blacks. In the early fifties Jeffries earned more than any black entertainer after Cole and Eckstine, while his ten-inch LPs on Mercury (reissues of Exclusive material) and Coral kept him in the shops. He kept his popularity into the calypso era when he made movies like *Calypso Joe* (1957) and albums like *Flamingo* (Victor), *Say It Isn't So* (1957, Bethlehem, with Russ Garcia's classy string chart), and *The Devil Is a Woman* (Golden Tone), the latter an uneven balance of Belafonte-esque drivel and good ballads.

Unlike Eckstine, Jeffries's records as a band singer stand out more than his solo records because after leaving Ellington he never again found arrangers as determined to put him through the obstacle course. Instead, most of them ended up emphasizing his rather plain rhythmic sense and Jeffries comes across as stiff. As opposed to most singers of his generation Jeffries, who was owning and running his own club in California in the mid-eighties, has kept virtually all of his voice today, and his latest record, a set of Ellington songs using only Laurindo Almeida's guitar for accompaniment, strikes me as easily the best of his nonorchestral efforts. When this album does finally get released, we'll realize again what a terrific singer Herb Jeffries can be.

Eckstine, on some of his very first records, sounds a little like Jeffries; apparently the popularity of "Flamingo" encouraged him to adapt some of Jeffries's metrical immobility. On other Eckstine-Hines sides he assimilates the techniques of other black icons: On "The Jitney Man" (1941, Victor), the singer could easily be Cab Calloway ("I started by imitating Cab Calloway," Eckstine later wrote, "and won an amateur show that way") running through a nursery-rhyme lyric filled with interpolated scat sequences; "Water Boy," though in swing time, refers to Paul Robeson. Crosby and Russ Columbo, naturally, reappear time and time again, though even before his first records Eckstine had absorbed their influences to such a degree that their shadows never hang over him except—and this is important—in his repertoire: Tune after tune comes from Columbo's songbook and that of Crosby when Columbo was alive. Many of these tunes (see table) never became standards, so only someone very familiar with Crosby and Columbo's work would even know them; "True," in fact, comes from the Columbo songbook even though he sang it only on the radio and never recorded it.

Song Title	Original Artist and Year	Year Recorded by Eckstine
"Prisoner of Love"	Columbo, 1931	1945
"I Surrender, Dear"	Crosby, 1931	1947
"You Call It Madness"	Columbo, 1931	1945
"I've Got to Pass Your House"	Crosby, 1933	1946
"True"	Columbo, 1934	1949
"I Apologize"	Crosby, 1931	1950

The Eckstine-Hines hits, "Stormy Monday" (not to be confused with T-Bone Walker's "Stormy Monday Blues") and "Jelly, Jelly," come out of the country blues tradition that predates the big-band blues style of Rushing and Basie, but as well as that style's more contemporary descendants, as the electrified guitar behind Eckstine testifies. This would be the first of two incredibly significant contributions Eckstine made immediately to the developing black baritone school—the reinfusing of post-Crosby singing with the blues.

Eckstine has said in numerous interviews that he does not consider himself a blues singer (he told *Metronome* in 1947, "I hate blues, but they're commercial. You can't do anything with them"); however, his attitude pertains more to the social implications of the blues than the musical ones. I don't doubt that there's something of the traditional black middle-class attitude here that looked down on the blues. Lil Hardin Armstrong's mother warned her that the blues were "played by wuthless, immoral loafers expressin' their vulgar minds with immoral music." Milt Hinton told Ira Gitler that Cab Calloway "didn't believe in these blues, because these blues taught people to fight, and to get under, and to make them feel low and degraded." But even if you write off Eckstine's two hits with Hines, "Jelly" and "Stormy," and the bulk of the sides with his orchestra as being part of the fad that made hits out of the Rushing-Basie and the Walter Brown–Jay McShann numbers,* then why does Eckstine return to the blues at every single stage of his career, and why does his all blues collaboration with Count Basie, *Basie–Eckstine, Inc.* (1959, Roulette), remain one of the two or three greatest albums he ever made?† Because, while the blues may not be a foundation for everything Eckstine does, the way they were for Rushing, they are one of the many things Eckstine sings beautifully. But then, Eckstine can do so many things so well.

Just as Hines had first worked with Ellington's vocalist, Jeffries, Ellington first came across Hines's vocalist, Eckstine, when he was just a kid in Washington. He was born William Clarence Eckstine in Pittsburgh in 1914, but his family had moved to D.C. by the time he was old enough to go to Armstrong High School and then Howard University. "I started singing when I was about seven," he told Judy Spiegelman in 1974. "I didn't realize I was going to do it professionally, of course. It was just something I enjoyed doing." From singing to entertain himself and his family and then in amateur shows, Eckstine moved up to chorus boy work in local theaters and then in various small clubs. He gigged his way as far west as Chicago, when, in 1939, Budd Johnson recommended him to his boss, Earl Hines, who came into the Club De Lisa where Eckstine was singing and asked him if he wanted to join the Grand Terrace Orchestra.

Eckstine made his second major contribution to music after

---

* Not to mention Arthur Prysock and Buddy Johnson, Dinah Washington and Lionel Hampton, and, later, Joe Williams and Count Basie.

† Eckstine fans feel cheated that their only meeting on record should be devoted entirely to the blues, and clearly Eckstine and Basie should have reunited at some point for a second album, this time a collectiion of standards. According to Basie biographer Chris Sheridan, they were supposed to get together on Reprise in the mid-sixties, but it never came off.

he left Hines to form his own orchestra—partly because of his sense of responsibility as the most visible figure of the bebop movement and partly because in 1944 singers leading big bands (like Bob Crosby and Skinnay Ennis) seemed a better commercial bet than singers in solo acts. The Eckstine Orchestra itself, comprising as it did virtually all of the second-generation black modernists, rates as a major accomplishment, though it stayed together for only about three years. But Eckstine's most important legacy is his singing, specifically his merging of the baritone trend with the modern jazz movement itself. I don't mean scatting like Joe Carroll, though in the pre-MGM years he did sing quite a few "Rhythm in the Riffs" about "Jitney" men. Eckstine's incorporation of bebop into singing took place in far subtler ways at a very sophisticated level. And I don't mean, to bring up that awful misconception of what jazz singing involves, that he uses his voice like an instrument. Instead, he uses the advanced harmonic ideas brought to jazz by Parker and Gillespie in singing, thinking in terms of bop-oriented intervals as the basis for everything he sings: flatted fifths, tenths rather than tonic notes for conclusions, and original augmentations and diminishments that never occurred to singers before him. The bop scatters used many of these same devices in their wordless vocals, but it took considerable nerve to work them into "serious" ballad-singing. If you like, you can compare the two to, for instance, Spike Jones and Rahsaan Roland Kirk in the way that Kirk took many techniques that Jones used for comedy and made them work for "serious" jazz.

Rhythmically, Eckstine has the greatest empathy for post-Parker jazzmen when they play ballads, choosing to accentuate certain notes and syllables the same way as Gene Ammons playing "Travelin' Light" or Kenny Dorham doing "Like Someone in Love." However, since few jazz instrumentalists phrased their ballads this way until the modern era, and since Eckstine was doing this as early as his Hines period (and perhaps earlier), they most likely learned this approach from Eckstine—especially since most of them, including Ammons and Dorham, had been

sidemen in the Eckstine Orchestra. Just as Parker-era jazzmen
play ballads at incredibly slow speeds, Eckstine can sing extremely slowly, affording his voice further majesty and grand-
ness. The standard three-minute limit of the 78 record rarely
gives him time to do more than one full verse and refrain, so
instead of closing with a half chorus as most singers do, Eckstine
and his arrangers of the mid-forties came up with the idea of
writing original ending tags for some of these songs. It worked
most famously on his big-selling "Cottage for Sale" (1945,
National/Savoy), which he concludes with a five-line coda that
reprises ideas from the main text.* Even if these new tags tend
to sound similar from song to song, they still make Eckstine's
interpretation of a song more dramatic and more interesting
than anyone else's. Certainly Eckstine and Jerry Valentine, the
arranger and trombonist credited with the device, came up with
a way of getting around the AABA barrier, less radical than the
ninety-six-plus bar creations of Eddie Jefferson and his fellows
but a greater accomplishment aesthetically.

Eckstine sings more slowly than Bessie Smith, but her general attitude toward rhythm and harmony certainly informs his,
as Eckstine demonstrates a similar concern for individual notes
as opposed to the melodic lines that they form. Though he generally subdues this effect, his notes can have a tough, tearing
quality for all their smoothness, a quality that some of his protégés exploited more than he. At his most extreme, Eckstine
anticipates the vertical approach John Coltrane developed in the
late fifties, which perhaps explains Coltrane's fascination with
one of Eckstine's compositions, "I Want to Talk About You."
Coltrane recorded it several times beginning in 1958, and Eckstine, who hadn't touched it since his orchestra days, cut a new
version in 1962 for Mercury.

---

* Mel Torme came up with an Eckstine-ish tag for his 1947 Musicraft disc of "It's
Easy to Remember," and Sarah Vaughan sings one on her 1950 "It Might as Well Be
Spring" on Columbia, as does Ella Fitzgerald on her 1960 Verve of "Black Coffee" on the
album *Let No Man Write My Epitaph.*

During the three years he led his orchestra, Eckstine perfected the richest, ripest, and perhaps most beautiful voice of any male singer. You can hear it in his last sessions for National in April 1947 and in his first titles for MGM in May, and even more so in the LPs he recorded for Mercury and Roulette from 1957 to about 1964. His voice usually centers around the baritone range, but he often drops down to basso and occasionally soars into tenor. Have you ever noticed that some Eckstine impersonators sing very high and some sing very low? Eckstine sounds like he's singing both ways at once, every note dripping with a rich, juicy vibrato. These days, with off-key tremolos being so overdone by show-oriented belters, vibrato seems like a dirty word. Not so with Eckstine; his full, legato vocal gyrations add immeasurably to the total effect of his sound. Eckstine's voice has so much depth and muscle that he almost seems to sing harmony; not a harmonic *part,* as a member of a vocal group would sing, but the root, third and fifth of a chord all at once. Crosby and Sinatra, especially in the forties, leaned on their weaknesses—or rather the strength it takes to show weakness—for a certain part of their appeal. Their failings made them more like us, more identifiable. Not so with Billy Eckstine. Here was no Clark Kent next door but an honest-to-God vocal Superman soaring through clouds of aural ecstasy, lulling us all into a deep purple dream.

Those familiar with the characters appearing in *Superman* magazine will remember Bizzaro, a crazy, distorted funhouse mirror version of the original Superman. Eckstine had his Bizzaro in Al Hibbler. Here's how Eckstine might sound if he took out all the smoothness in his voice and exploited instead his potential for roughness and perverseness; how he might sound if he were drunk. Duke Ellington, who liked Hibbler enough to feature him with his orchestra for eight years, described Hibbler's way with a song as "tonal pantomime," and no one has yet to come up with a better term for it, though many people feel that Leonard Feather's "grotesque distortions" came close to the point. The idea of pantomime, dramatic movement without sound, must have seemed ironic to Hibbler, who was blind; one would expect he thought in terms of noise without visual movement. But Hibbler's blindness "never deterred his appreciation of good-looking girls," remembered Pat Willard, who should know, being part of Ellington's publicity crew and also a good-looking girl. Brooks Kerr, pianist and Ellington scholar who is blind himself, points out Hibbler's fondness for Spike Jones records and Hollywood cartoons. "I don't know what he sees in his head when he hears these things," says Kerr. "After all, he's been blind since birth."

Typically, Hibbler growls, rasps, and grunts almost like he's belching, and his diction sounds mysteriously like London cockney. Many an urban black I know has a slight cockney twang in his or her speech, and from time to time you can hear such a vocal gesture in the singing of Nat Cole, Della Reese, or even Eckstine, but only Hibbler made it the focal point of his work. He also tosses in Ethel Waters's style of rolling *r*'s (on "I'll Be Around," from *Torchy and Blue*) and Jewish mannerisms, from Eastern Europe by way of New York, resulting in combinations of mispronunciations like "I'd like ta get yez on a slew bewt to Choinah," as if he had his heart set on playing Fagin in some all-black revival of *Oliver!* Even the more conventional moments of "After the Lights Go Down Low" (on *Starring Al Hibbler*, Decca) contain grunts and grimaces galore, while in the last four bars of the first chorus (followed by a honking alto) he makes like an impatient pimp berating one of his bimbos, flailing her with harsh, rude snarls.

Hibbler replaced Jeffries in the Ellington orchestra and was in many ways his opposite. Jeffries could sound overcontrolled and stiff, with a taut tone reminiscent of Ellington's greatest trombonist, Lawrence Brown. Hibbler typically came off as out of control and crazy, and found his parallel in the earthy, emotional rip-snorting of Tricky Sam Nanton and in the blues-derived ballad style of Johnny Hodges. But Ellington obviously saw similarities in both of them, as he did not substantially alter the character of his arrangements for male singers when Hibbler

joined the band in 1943; furthermore, he had Hibbler sing at
least one of the songs Jeffries recorded for the band, "My Little
Red Book,"* and also made a point to write extended works for
each of them—Jeffries's "I Don't Know What Kind of Blues I
Got" and Hibbler's "Strange Feeling" (from "The Perfume
Suite") and "I Like the Sunrise" (from "The Liberian Suite").
Though they express it differently through their senses of dynamics, Jeffries and Hibbler have a thing about high and low
sounds. Hibbler, born in 1915 in Little Rock, started singing as
a boy soprano in the Arkansas School for the Blind, and when
later asked to name his influences, he chose Crosby and Columbo, like everyone else did, but also mentioned ultrahigh tenors
Pha Terrell and Arthur "The Street Singer" Tracy. Throughout
most of his Ellington tenure, Hibbler stayed up near the alto
range, which allowed Ellington to balance his voice with that of
alto saxophonist Johnny Hodges and alto vocalist Kay Davis (on
"Ain't Got Nothin' but the Blues" [1945, D.E.T.S. aircheck]).
By the fifties his voice settled down to a comfortable baritone,
though he often, as on the out-chorus of "After the Lights,"
crashes down into a guttural basso.

The one rule that Hibbler always adheres to is that there are
no rules. Generally his nuances have all the lightness of baby
elephant patter, but on "Believe It, Beloved" (with Johnny
Hodges and His Orchestra [1952, Clef]) he tiptoes into Chi-chi
Rose Murphy territory and does the same on "It's Love I'm In"
(with Ellington [1952, Columbia]), but there he's had a head
start since Ellington had instructed Harry Carney to demonstrate with his baritone sax how a heavy tone can achieve feather
lightness. Hibbler rarely scats, and when he does, the nonverbal
noises he improvises come out completely uninformed by the
two sages of scat, Armstrong and Watson. Instead, his scats have
the same wacky rhythm and playful pitch as his lyric singing. "It

---

* Ellington and Herb Jeffries recorded this Billy Strayhorn ballad just before the
1942 AAM ban, and Hibbler sang it with the band, and on dozens of broadcasts. He
recorded it twice with other groups but never with Ellington.

Don't Mean a Thing" (1948, Chess) has Hibbler paying tribute to the deceased Tricky Sam by quoting the tiniest but most appropriate fragment of Nanton's solo on "C-Jam Blues," while Tyree Glenn, Nanton's replacement, picks up on the idea and quotes "Ebony Rhapsody."

At the time of his Verve LP of Ellington songs in 1954, Hibbler gave an interview to *Downbeat* in which he announced that he intended to "unbend his swoop and scoop singing style," because from now on, he said, he would "sing straight." Then, with typical Hibbler perversity, he proceeded to do just the opposite when he signed his first big-label contract with Decca the following year, as his singles and LPs from that point on show even less respect for the lessons singing teachers drill you on. Whether planned that way or not, Hibbler's Deccas came loaded with unintentional humor, as the company conspired to conventionalize their star by saddling him with choirs and strings no end. Jack Pleis, a usually tasteful arranger who had the intelligence to recognize camp when it bit him on the butt, even introduced Hibbler's "Pennies from Heaven" (on *Here's Hibbler*) with the melody of "Holiday for Strings." Imagine this if you care to: a white choir even blander than most all cooing in perfect Caucasoid unison, "Do nothin', baby . . ."—not just dropping the "g," mind you, but quite literally singing the apostrophe!—Hibbler grunting over them all the while.

It wasn't the coming of the rock era that pushed Hibbler out of the pop market once he had made the long climb out of the jazz and band genre. Hibbler's career in mass-market pop didn't really begin until the mid-fifties, and his biggest seller, "Unchained Melody," got its push from the R&B marketers. Hibbler lost his career because of politics. He'd always been one to defy the status quo as readily as he denied the conventions of vocal music, whether hell-raising with Charlie Parker back on the Jay McShann band bus or finding the nearest bar in any town Ellington played through, without the aid of a guide or Seeing Eye dog. When the civil rights movement began to gather momentum in the late fifties, Hibbler marched. Armstrong, Ellington,

Cole, and the others offered their money and services, but Hibbler marched. In 1960, New Jersey police arrested him for being a "disorderly person" and allegedly breaking into a gas station while drunk (though not stealing anything), and in 1963 police arrested Hibbler in Birmingham for walking a picket line and leading fellow marchers in "You'll Never Walk Alone" as part of an antisegregation protest. As details of Hibbler's activities got in the news, it wasn't long before the major labels decided to have nothing to do with him. Frank Sinatra, a longtime friend and then a supporter of the movement, came to Hibbler's aid with the offer to do an album for his label, Reprise, *Monday Every Day*, the title being a reprise of a song Hibbler had done with Ellington.

Hibbler made his last worthwhile record in 1972, contributing four titles to a Rahsaan Roland Kirk session released as *A Meeting of the Times* (Atlantic). Kirk had wanted to do an Ellington-style album for some time, said producer Joel Dorn. But of all the Ellingtonians he could have picked, and many (including the Duke himself) were still alive at that point, he chose Hibbler. Their mutual blindness and commitment to civil rights certainly had something to do with it, but it seems more likely that Kirk recognized their shared ability to make the far-out seem down-to-earth and to make musical sense of what seem like the most unmusical of sounds. Furthermore, both get a mischievous kick of breaking rules established for them by sighted, white people; both can also turn on the sentiment in "This Love of Mine" and "Daybreak," and then defiantly stomp their way through "Do Nothing Till You Hear from Me."

Now over seventy and not getting as many opportunities to work as befits the best of all Ellington male vocalists, Hibbler lives in retirement except when offered the chance not to.[*] Even if chances seem slim that he'll get to participate in another meeting of the times, hopefully some of his classic sides with and

---

[*] When last we spoke, Hib mentioned an upcoming tour in tandem with Herb Jeffries. Now that will be something to hear.

without Ellington will soon be reissued. After all, as far as popular singing goes, Al Hibbler, the Boris Karloff of the blues, is also our Salvador Dali, our Luis Buñuel, and our Krazykat combined—our greatest surrealist.

While most of the black baritones started with Crosby, Johnny Hartman, the last important figure in this movement, came out of Haymes and early Sinatra in that the middle of his phrases has Sinatra's firmness but tends to go in different directions at the end like Crosby or Haymes. Hartman has little of the mannerisms of Eckstine and Hibbler; in fact, he has almost no mannerisms at all. He sounds so smooth and unfrivolous that unless he gets exactly the right kind of accompaniment his records can be like slipping on a patch of ice with nothing to hold on to. Conventional orchestral and string backing does Hartman no good, as on most of his first two sessions (1947, Regent/Savoy) and Bethlehem's 1956 *All of Me*. Not just any small group will do either, Erroll Garner's trio can't coax the best out of Hartman (1949, Mercury) and neither does a conventional modern jazz combo with several horn soloists, as on his final album, *Once in a Lifetime* (1980, Beehive).

Hartman's two finest recordings, *Songs from the Heart* (1956, Bethlehem) and *John Coltrane and Johnny Hartman* (1963, Impulse), demonstrate that Hartman needs a trio plus one instrumental master as foil to challenge him, inspire him, and keep him on the level. Coltrane, in what many people feel was if not his greatest period (the early Impulses) then at least the point in his career when he could appeal to the greatest number of people, serves as Hartman's dancing partner on the 1963 album, while Howard McGhee, at a peak of his own during his California sojourn of the fifties, takes the lead on the first Bethlehem. On both, Hartman's voice sounds, contradictingly, fullest when the space around it is emptiest, meaning they don't overload the background with strings or bongo drums but just let him resonate into the dry air. On the slicker Impulse, the engineer tampered with the reverberations of both Coltrane and Hartman to make them match a tad more, but the rougher Bethlehem uses a more honest, starker mix, proving that ballads can be more effective with a less sentimental hand on the dials. The Impulse, unfortunately, just whets your appetite for more John and Johnny, its six songs at about five minutes each could just about fill up a ten-inch LP and certainly finish too quickly for a twelve-incher, especially since one of the six, "Lush Life," offers the only example ever of Hartman actually beating Eckstine (though not Nat Cole), who had recorded the Strayhorn masterpiece on his live Roulette set, *No Cover, No Minimum,* four years earlier. Surprisingly, *Songs from the Heart* was all but ignored, much to Hartman's deep frustration, while *John Coltrane and Johnny Hartman* got the attention it deserved and revitalized the careers of both men. But for the already-bitter Hartman, it seemed too long in coming.

Hartman's responses to Leonard Feather's *Encyclopedia of Jazz* questionnaire reveal an obvious chip on his shoulder and resentment toward the music biz for making him suffer so long. Exact birth date: 7/3/26. Where born: Chicago. How did you get into the music business?: Special Services in the army. Bands or combos you have worked with: Earl "Fatha" Hines, 1947; Dizzy Gillespie, 1948–49. Ever won any magazine awards?: No. Who are your favorite musicians on your instrument?: Nat Cole, Frank Sinatra, Ella Fitzgerald. The kicker comes when the questionnaire asks Hartman to describe his recordings: "Goodbye" (1949, Mercury), he says accurately, was a "great record and arrangement on [a] Benny Goodman theme" but it received "no promotion." He also had the scoop on "Wheel of Fortune" early on, but Victor "let [his record] lay idle seven months before the Sunny Gale and Kay Starr release." He waxes optimistically about his latest release, the second Bethlehem set, which contained the song "I'll Follow You," claiming that the "album is beginning to move from continuous plugging of that particular song." Still nothing happened. Hartman did not record at all between the Victors of 1951 and the two Bethlehem LPs of 1956, and then, except for one even more obscure Roost album from the late fifties (unknown even to collectors and discographers), not again until 1963.

That 1963 album, *John Coltrane and Johnny Hartman,* finally landed Hartman the career and work that he wanted, including two additional Impulse albums—neither with Coltrane, hang the luck!—which try to soften his already willowy tone with guitars and flutes, as well as less successful pop-oriented projects for ABC and Perception. At the time of his death in 1983, Hartman had become, with Mel Torme and Joe Williams, one of the most highly regarded male singers in jazz. His most recent recording, on Beehive, had returned him to the jazz small-group format, and a session that he never lived to make was to have teamed him with his ex-boss Dizzy Gillespie in a quartet format of the kind where Hartman really shined.

There were other black baritones, too, several of whom held down Dizzy Gillespie's balladeer post both before (Earl Coleman) and after (Melvin Moore, Austin Cromer) Hartman. The perpetually returning Earl Coleman, best known for his records with Charlie Parker ("This Is Always" [1946, Dial]) and Sonny Rollins ("My Ideal" [1956, Prestige]), starts like a thinner-voiced Eckstine (who has been one of his greatest boosters for years) but applies enough of Hibbler's distortions of pitch and diction to reach the point where most reviewers can't figure out if he's doing it deliberately or not (I'm still not sure). Melvin Moore, who spent years with the territorial band of Ernie Fields, recorded a few numbers with Gillespie for his Dee Gee label in 1951; Austin Cromer toured with the great 1957 Gillespie orchestra and with it recorded one of the finest of all versions of "Over the Rainbow" (Verve).

By the sixties, the blues elements of the black baritone school were becoming part of pop without necessarily first passing through jazz: Arthur Prysock combined the deep sound of the Eckstine school with the static harmonies of rhythm and blues and soul (check out his album with Count Basie),[*] while Lou Rawls started as a far looser blues and ballads baritone with a terrific first album, *Lou Rawls–Les McCann Ltd.* (1962, Capi-

---

[*] Actually two, the familiar *Count Basie–Arthur Prysock* (1965, Verve) and Basie's guest appearance on one of Prysock's Old Town Records.

tol). Somebody named Frank Mignon made a crazy album for
Bethlehem that uses the black ballad sound much the way Mark
Murphy uses the cool sound, as a vehicle for jumping between
various genres, including Pleasure-able vocalese (for half the
album he translates Miles Davis's *Kind of Blue* into vocal terms),
jazz-and-poetry, calypso, and Louis Armstrong impressions. But
without question, the foremost exponents of the black baritone
movement were Eckstine and Sarah Vaughan.

Eckstine "discovered" Vaughan at an amateur show in 1942,
encouraged Hines to hire her, and then brought her along as his
own female vocalist when he launched the Billy Eckstine Orchestra (other versions of this story have Hines hearing her for
the first time at the Apollo and hiring her on the spot, but
Vaughan herself named Mr. B. as her discoverer in a 1957 *Downbeat* interview). Even at eighteen, Vaughan was already the
greatest thing ever to happen to Newark, New Jersey, where
she had been tinkering with both the piano and her voice since
childhood and sang around town with the fine trumpeter Jabbo
Smith. Even without the direct influence of Eckstine's presence, her first husband and manager, George Treadwell, who
took credit for her commercial success (describing himself as the
man who "stage-managed the fairy tale"), labored hard to package her as the female Eckstine. As the big Mr. B. hits started
pouring out on MGM, beginning with three from his first season
on the label—"Everything I Have Is Yours," "The Wildest Gal
in Town," and "Blue Moon"—Vaughan, soon to switch to big-
time Columbia from the humble indie Musicraft, recorded more
and more material patterned after the Eckstine MGMs.

Certainly Vaughan had a lot in common with Mr. B.'s other
followers, though her incredible musicianship beat most of
them at their own games. Vaughan has a range even wider
than Herb Jeffries's; she could probably sing half the piano if
she wanted, each note being as firm or as wobbly as she willed
it to be, and her ease in jumping up and down the octaves
serves her better than it does him, as she seems less ashamed
of it: Jeffries's arrangers buried his gift in the middle of their

orchestrations and he seems to have been too self-conscious to try it with a small group. Vaughan brought this technique and many others front and center and ran up and down the registers whenever she wanted, no matter how appropriate it was or wasn't to the song or to the accompaniment. Like Hibbler, Vaughan also uses distortion, but where Hibbler tilts his to the side of the grotesque, Vaughan alters the pitch and pronunciation of a note/syllable to make it more beautiful, coherence being a secondary consideration. She shares with Earl Coleman the knack for varying her lines from paintbrush thick to pencil thin but does a far better job of it, changing the weight of her lines so frequently that it achieves a mischievous kind of consistency in its constant variety.

But even before Treadwell started working his Svengali act on her, Vaughan owed the greatest debt to Eckstine,* whose singing provided the foundation for her approach to rhythm, pitch, and sound, not to mention style. Both made vibrato a key element of their work; in fact, the blur that follows a note assumes no less importance than the pitch of the note itself. But as stylistically close as they may be, Vaughan made a mistake in trying to duplicate Eckstine's popular successes. Eckstine, being not only a great pop singer but an archetype for a style of pop singing, could do virtually any song in any setting, making him a true descendant of Crosby; Vaughan perfected a quirkier, more idiosyncratic approach that suited certain types of material and accompaniment better than others.

Which isn't to say that there aren't Eckstine records that are better than others. He may have been at his summit in early 1947, at about the time he reluctantly broke up his orchestra and worked for a short time (at Billy Berg's in Hollywood, among other spots) with a small group that included Hank Jones, Sonny

---

* For an arresting example of Eckstine singing like a male Vaughan, refer to his 1950 MGM recording of "Body and Soul." He later named it his "best on wax" for *Downbeat*, even though, "A lot of people objected [and said] that I went too far out and didn't stick to the melody, and all that, but I liked it."

Criss, Pony Poindexter, and Al Killian. On his sessions for National, both with and without the orchestra, the modern minds of Budd Johnson, Jerry Valentine, and Tadd Dameron charted the course of Eckstine's accompaniment, even if they didn't write every score. As a result, his records from the spring of 1947 and earlier have, paradoxically, a far more modern sound than his MGMs of that point and onward, especially the creaking orchestrations of Hugo Winterhalter,* who also dispensed with one of Eckstine's most ingenious devices: the original tag extensions at the ends of songs (Jack Miller's chart on "Goodbye" being an exception). Later arrangers on both MGM and Mercury, including those hip to Charlie Parker thought, like Pete Rugolo, or at least originality, like Nelson Riddle, reflect better Eckstine's bop soul.

You couldn't ask for better vocal albums than Eckstine's first three for Mercury (in between MGM and Mercury he spent two seasons making disastrous singles for RCA, including the infamous "Condemned to Life with a Rock-and-Roll Wife")—*Sarah Vaughan and Billy Eckstine Sing the Best of Irving Berlin* (1957), arranged by Hal Mooney; *Imagination* (1958); and *Billy's Best* (1959) with Rugolo—and the three that followed for Roulette—*Once More with Feeling*, with Billy May; *Basie–Eckstine, Inc.*, with Count Basie; and *No Cover, No Minimum*, recorded live in Las Vegas with Bobby Tucker, Mr. B.'s working accompanist of forty years now. Though his records from the mid-sixties onward lack the consistent excellence of these, he does deserve credit for *The Prime of My Life*, the only decent product ever to be manufactured in the Motown foundry, and his current release, a set of standards wherein he splits a mike with Benny Carter.

Vaughan's Columbia and Mercury/EmArcy singles came out at the same time as these, but playing the 17 albums' worth of

---

* *Color* magazine, in a feature article on Eckstine in June 1948, referred to his conductor as "Hugo Winterbottom," a faux pas that actually seems more appropriate than his real name.

material she recorded at this time makes for a vastly different experience than listening to the 189 Eckstine MGM singles. Mr. B. gets deeper into his material than Sassy,* who gets more into her own voice. In recent months I've read the same comment construed as a complaint about Michael Feinstein, Bobby Mc-Ferrin, and Vaughan, that their love for their own voices exceeds their love for the material. In Vaughan's case, where's the crime? The simperingly square Feinstein (who makes Nelson Eddy look like Bobby Darin and who is mentioned in the same sentence with Vaughan strictly as a contrast) deals in unadulterated, mountainous narcissism (completely unfounded at that), while Vaughan's inner to outer journeys are devoid of all egotism.

Singers in the jazz area have to consider interpretation (already a no-no to Feinstein) and improvisation, and balance the demands of their own egos against the projected ego of the songwriter (that's what they mean by respecting the material), but that voice, as Vaughan would say if she were in a forties movie, is something bigger than both of us. Vaughan bathes in her own sound not to interpret a song but to use it as a diving board into a long, slow swim through honey-thick pools of aural euphoria. (In giving any sort of written description of Vaughan, you're not doing her justice unless you go overboard with metaphors.) It's not that Vaughan herself doesn't pay any attention to the words (it's that she gives you more interesting things to concern yourself with), or that she wants you to think that the composer's melodies are inferior, but her overhaul-like embellishments make you forget the original tunes. A million glissandi, a million arpeggios, a million swoops, dives, and modulations all add up to a sonic reverie.

Eckstine represents the farthest boundary of one specific ideal of the Crosby tradition—Crosby's concept of naturalism—and

---

* Eckstine's nickname, "Mr. B.," came from Fred Robbins, who also dubbed Torme "The Velvet Fog." Sarah Vaughan's tag, "Sassy," has been attributed both to Al Hibbler and John Malachi, one of her pianists.

Vaughan goes one step beyond that, to a definition of popular singing that has no connection whatever with any conventional idea of naturalism. Crosby and the entire army of jazz-derived pop vocalists that followed him hid their artistry under the carpet and tried to make it "look easy," as if, as Crosby said in what must be the most repeated quote in all of popular music (other than the opening line of Holiday's *Lady Sings the Blues* memoirs), to make the listener feel he can sing as well as the performer, and thus bring about a cathartic oneness between entertainer and audience. By going that one step farther, Vaughan defied all that. She brought her remarkable vocal mechanisms front and center, and made them part of the act itself. In attracting attention to what previously had been covered up, Vaughan created a new way to sing and to think about popular singing.

So why, then, did the black baritone school lose momentum in the early fifties, and how were Sinatra and his followers able to supersede them so effectively? Eckstine may have had far more hits in the late forties than Sinatra did ("My Foolish Heart" and "Caravan" to name two), and Vaughan's big sellers in the late fifties (among them the calypso novelty "Day-O," the million-selling "Broken-Hearted Melody," and "Passing Strangers," a duet with Eckstine that was his last big hit) certainly rivaled if they didn't surpass FS. But neither Eckstine nor Vaughan ever really mastered the twelve-inch LP form. They each did all the obvious ideas: collections of movie songs, show songs, and Vaughan responded to Ella Fitzgerald's *Songbook* series with a double-length Gershwin set of her own, but neither B nor Sass had the guidance or the inspiration to put together albums as meaningful *as albums* as Sinatra's *Songs for Swinging Lovers* or *Only the Lonely.*

Just the opposite: Vaughan did best when the record wasn't a literate, well-organized conception at all but an off-the-cuff outing with a small group, preferably a trio, as on *Swingin' Easy* (1954 and 1957, EmArcy), or with one or two great jazz horns, like Clifford Brown and Paul Quinichette on *Sarah*

Vaughan (1954, EmArcy), or, best of all, a live set, such as the fine *Live at Mr. Kelly's* (1957, Mercury) and the thrilling *After Hours at the London House* (another Chicago club [1958, Mercury]). In the days when it was possible for her to sell a million records, such directly jazz-oriented projects had to take second fiddle to her more commercial singles and LPs, but in the seventies such loose, small-group affairs became the norm when Vaughan made six generally stunning discs for Norman Granz's Pablo label.

Eckstine, who has recorded very infrequently from the late sixties onward, made his best album in over twenty years in his 1986 *Billy Eckstine Sings with Benny Carter* (Japanese Mercury/ Polygram). At seventy-five, he's become more a club experience than a purely acoustic one; catch him with a live audience and you'll get a better idea of what all the swooning is about. My greatest hopes are for future Vaughan records, though her post-Pablo recording career has yet to result in anything exciting. One of the instigators of the "symphonic date" trend in name jazz artists, Vaughan has so far only dipped into symphonic treatments of borderline pop-classical composers like Gershwin and Rodgers and uses the symphony merely as a slightly larger version of one of the big string orchs that backed her thirty years ago; I predict we'll see more of Vaughan going into directly European material. If she can treat "Send in the Clowns" like an aria (a hip aria, to be sure), how about "Un Bel Di" as a pop song? And the time is also right for an album of religious music. Why not some "Jesus Is a Rock"–type gospel, some "Rock of Ages"–type WASP hymns, some "Sweet Chariot"–type spirituals, and maybe even a separate disc of Ellington's sacred music, like "Come Sunday" or "Heaven," which almost could have been written with her in mind?

Owing to the onetime close proximity of jazz and popular music, it seems likely that modern jazz and singing would have gotten together anyhow, but never with any enduring excellence had not Lambert, Hendricks, Ross, Billy Eckstine, and Sarah Vaughan been there. They gave the new union of the two musics both form and direction and enriched their art immeasurably for both audiences and their fellow musicians. Perhaps one reason the art of both vocal boppers and baritones went out of fashion is that no one wanted to go up against them. Could there be such a thing as an artist greater than Sarah Vaughan or Billy Eckstine? I sure can't think of one.

Modernism 3

Torme, O'Day, and the Vo-Cool School

"I always liked his singing too. No matter what he was doing, he wasn't imitating anybody and he had that beat."
—Billie Holiday on Mel Torme

"All I know is that there are four beats to a bar and there are a million ways to phrase a tune."
—Anita O'Day, undated Downbeat *clip circa 1938–39, probably her first write-up*

Bix Beiderbecke was the grandfather of the "cool," and the precedent he set for lyricism as well as for bringing harmonic devices from "serious" music to jazz would not be fully appreciated until a generation after his death. Lester Young was the father of the cool, and the dozens of Prez-idential tenor players he sired would be its four dozen brothers. The "progressive"-minded bandleaders of the mid-forties—Artie Shaw (whom Budd Johnson described as having "the first cool band"), Stan Kenton, Woody Herman, Boyd Raeburn, Benny Goodman (for a time), and, in particular, Claude Thornhill—served as godfathers. A group of their former sidemen, led by Miles Davis, late of Charlie Parker's greatest band, gave birth to the cool at New York's Royal Roost in September 1948; they would later preserve snapshots of the newborn child at three sessions for Capitol Records spread over the next two years.

Cool jazzmen had a theoretical basis for their work, certainly, as had earlier hot players like Coleman Hawkins and Art Tatum. The first generation of boppers had temporarily minimalized the importance of ensemble playing and structure, and since the cool restored the use of form to its previous stature, many schools of jazz thought have continued to make it one of their primary considerations. Hot jazzmen played ballads, could swing and play the blues; cool jazz musicians did the same, as a listen to any of the major players in this genre—Chet Baker, Art Pepper, Hampton Hawes, Stan Getz—will reveal. In short, cool jazz meant no change in the degree or quality of emotion inherent in a jazz musician's individual statement; the only difference lay in the way he expressed it.

One of the most important ways to express cool jazz was to sing, and cool singers came out of the same bands, both large and small, that produced their instrumental counterparts. As an art form, however, the vo-cool style did not reach a point of fruitful maturity until the mid-fifties, roughly the time when cool instrumental jazz relinquished its critical and popular following to hard bop. In 1954 trumpeter Chet Baker recorded his first collection of vocals, and the following year Capitol released June Christy's first and finest album, *Something Cool* (she already had been doing vocal refrains and singles for a decade), and Anita O'Day and Chris Connor, both relegated to minor-league labels since their canary days, signed contracts with the big-time outfits of Verve and Atlantic. The following January, Mel Torme began his remarkable series of albums with arranger Marty Paich—which led to the masterpiece of the vo-cool era, 1960's *Mel Torme Swings Shubert Alley*—and other male singers influenced by him, such as Jackie Paris, Mark Murphy, and Matt Dennis, started to find opportunities to record at about this time.

The key word to their music is subtlety. Cool singers choose to imply rather than directly state. They prefer to understate, treating a song like an impressionist painter treats a subject, suggesting its outline with a brush stroke here, a patch of color there, letting the listener put it all together in his own head. Listeners can never be passive spectators here; they have to work at understanding these sounds. To be sure, some cool-oriented singers, like those in any other field, take it too far, and end up with a performance style so uncommunicative that only a few insiders sprinkled amid their small audiences can decode these cryptic inferences. Like the impressionists, they believe that the areas of the canvas you leave blank are just as important as the ones you cover with paint.

Vibrato, or absense of same, would become a crucial issue. Just as a deep, rich vibrato defined Billy Eckstine's black baritone followers, the vibratoless tone, which really begins in jazz with Lester Young, came to typify the cool school. Anita O'Day, foremother of the style, claims that a clumsy tonsillectomist forced her to sing in the short, staccato phrases we think of as vo-cool, but her story strikes me as apocryphal at best—like Louis dropping the sheet music on "Heebie Jeebies." In any event, she uses no vibrato even on her earliest recordings with Gene Krupa's Orchestra in 1941, and neither do her two closest "students," June Christy and Chris Connor. Mel Torme, for all the comparisons he suffered in his early years to various atmospheric conditions, used vibrato telescopically—that is, binding it tightly to him and never letting it grow beyond a certain low level. In more recent years, in accordance with his growth as an artist, Torme has relaxed his hold somewhat and occasionally will light upon a passing tone in between two notes that he will let vibrate with the grace and delicacy of a Ben Webster or the middle-aged Zoot Sims. But, as with O'Day, vo-cool was only one of many phases that Torme passed through, and neither singer could be contained by genres—not even those they had helped create.

Cool singers also put a high price on dynamics; the loudness or softness of a note counts for just as much as its pitch. Torme's volume inflections occasionally lead him to a line of spoken recitative, coming out of Torme the lyric interpreter whose goals are identical to those of Torme the musician. O'Day's constant pianissimos and fortes seem, on the surface, just as crazy as everything else she does, but on closer investigation they add an important piece to the jigsaw puzzle she makes of a number and then puts back together. Chris Connor often stays on a relatively consistent volume level, which makes a statement in itself, even when she comes dangerously close to monotone.

Furthermore, cool singers also share the belief that written melody is only the starting point for a performance. Though Sarah Vaughan may still stand as the greatest of melodic para-phrasers, neither Torme nor O'Day seems much influenced by her. On O'Day's "The Man I Love," from 1954, she alters the tune as she goes along, stretching notes, reconfiguring the tempo (the occasional triplet) to create a new melody without scatting but using the standard lyrics. But where Vaughan's lush voice demands the slow tempi associated with the Eckstine school, O'Day's new melody sounds starker, more jagged, and more directly boppish. Torme can also spontaneously recompose a piece much the same way, and often masterfully intermingles paraphrase with out and out improvisation, but, as we'll see later, his most effective performance pieces are not impromptu at all.

If Sarah Vaughan provides a comparison point for paraphrase, Ella Fitzgerald supplies the point of departure for scatting. In the late forties Fitzgerald had been the first to combine the tradition of Armstrong and Leo Watson with the new language of Parker and Gillespie and declared herself the finest vocal im-proviser jazz has ever had. So far, no one has ever given her any back talk. Only she could create solos that stand on their own without their originator; no other scat singer's works could be transcribed, performed instrumentally, or sung by other voices (as Torme has successfully demonstrated in his homage to Ella, "Oh, Lady Be Good") and not lose any of their power. But where Ella can depend on the sheer meat of her chops, Torme and O'Day have to consider the potatoes, the context in which the scat sequence appears. No matter how far out Ella may go harmonically—and she does get way out there—and no matter how brilliantly she may construct a solo, you always pretty much know where she'll end up. With Fitzgerald, a ballad is a ballad, a swinger is a swinger, a comic number is a comic number, and her scat features use only the barest of frameworks around her solos; "How High the Moon" always has a straight chorus, a "specialty" chorus designed to introduce the scat chorus, and then the scat itself.

With Torme and O'Day nothing is so simple. On O'Day's earliest extended wordless vocal, "Malagueña" (1947, Signature),* she abandons the lyric altogether, but deciding she likes the melody, keeps it (this before Thelonious Monk asked his famous question, "Why do we throw away the melody?"), only gently altering the Lecona tune, wordlessly interpreting it as she would on later pure scat specialties like "Four Brothers" (on *Anita Sings the Winners* [1958, Verve]), "Hershey Bar" (on *Cool Heat* [1959, Verve]), and "Slaughter on Tenth Avenue" (on *Incomparable!* [1960, Verve]). But more revealingly, on her own "How High the Moon" (also 1947, Signature) she first prefaces and then follows her scat solo with the lyric; however, she sets it to an interpretation of the tune transformed through bop rhythm and several tempo changes. Having developed the ability to use both the composer's melody with scatted lyrics or the original words with a new melody, O'Day, from the late forties on, integrated the two concepts.

Only a particular kind of person could be as unpredictable and spontaneous as O'Day, and only an even rarer breed of artist would choose to build an art form on these qualities. Early in 1946, shortly before O'Day left Gene Krupa's band for the last time, *The Hollywood Note* ran a brief story on her that included the observation, "Anita is completely frank. She says what she

* Recorded before either Vaughan's or Fitzgerald's most famous total-scat numbers "Pinky" (1950, Columbia) and "Ella Hums the Blues" (1955, Decca).

thinks, wears what she pleases, behaves as she prefers to be-
have." The comment has been made dozens of times about
O'Day, by every interviewer who has ever spoken with her and
every fan I know who's introduced himself to her at a show
(myself included). I'll wager that she didn't have to do a lot of
soul-baring to come up with her remarkably candid, unglamorous autobiography, *Hard Times, High Times;* she's already so
used to discussing her life with brutal honesty. And what works
in conversation applies equally to performance. As Jules Feiffer
once wrote, most of us would like to be more creative, but we
have editors and critics in our heads picking apart everything we
do. O'Day has no such barriers to thwart her self-expression.
Repression may ultimately keep society together, as Freud argues in *Civilization and Its Discontents,* but it would only cramp
O'Day's style. By removing this safety net, O'Day gives a high-
risk performance, sort of like a tightrope walker, with plenty of
chances to fall, and she creates a lot of suspense by getting the
audience to pull right along with her, wondering whether or not
she'll make it.

Mel Torme also takes chances and risks failing, but he never
falls off the tightrope. He's always struck me as such a perfect
example of what a jazz-derived pop singer should be that I find
it difficult to sound objective when writing about him. Torme's
music amounts to such an unshakably cohesive whole that it can
be analyzed and dissected element by element with no fear of
the sum of the parts ever distracting from the whole—just the
opposite. At close examination, the breadth and scope of Torme's
art multiplies in front of your eyes like Jack's beanstalk: Torme
is one of the greatest lyric interpreters in history; his ability to
breathe life into the words of a song rivals anyone this side of
Billie Holiday and Frank Sinatra. But if what he has said is true,
that to him lyrics represent 99 percent of a song, then what
incredible mileage he gets out of that remaining one percent!
Torme possesses one of the most highly developed senses of
rhythm in all music, reflecting the innovations of the great jazz-
oriented male pop singers that came before him (Armstrong,

Crosby, Sinatra, Cole, and Eckstine), while simultaneously finding his own way. Vocally, Torme works with the most beautiful
voice a man is allowed to have, and he combines it with a flawless sense of pitch that allows him to squeeze both musical and
dramatic effect by exploiting his ability to reach for head tones as
high as the end of "Here's That Rainy Day" or as low as the basso
profundo Jobim threw into "Wave." As an improviser, he shames
all but two or three other scat singers and quite a few horn
players as well, and he also has an intuitive flair for harmony and
tonal color, knowing what sounds align themselves most reward-
ingly with what other sounds. And that's not even mentioning
the matter of his gifts as a composer or an instrumentalist, though
both of these abilities figure in the overall "gist" of his singing,
and, beyond that, his accomplishments as an actor, writer, collector, and maven.

Individual elements are fine, but what earmarks Torme for
greatness is the way he puts it all together. Too often in "jazz
singing" (a term he questions), as one post-Torme singer, Mark
Murphy, said in *Cadence*, "Someone will write, 'Gee, he wasn't
singing jazz that night.' Then I come and I sing a tune here and
the reviewer says, 'Yeah, but he wasn't singing the lyric.' " Of
course the essence of jazz-derived pop singing, as with musical
comedy and opera, is the perfect marriage of musical and dramatic intentions. Far from there being a conflict between the
seemingly separate aims of interpretation, improvisation, and
composition, Torme has created an art form in which all three
are ultimately the same thing. His career can be summed up as
an eternal pursuit for better ways to bring this about, a quest for
a higher musical truth.

As early as his Artie Shaw period (and Shaw's influence on
Torme's music extends far beyond the dozen or so songs they
recorded together), Torme revealed a concern for structure fully
the equal of his other gifts, which passed through two distinct
phases: his recomposition method of the fifties, by which individual songs were deconstructed and rewritten in the image of
Torme and his collaborators (chiefly Marty Paich); and the ex-

tended multisong structures he began experimenting with in the mid-sixties, in which the backbone elements of music (again, emotional as well as musical) take precedence over the songs themselves.

After a child-prodigy period, Torme broke into the music industry as a songwriter and then as an arranger and lead singer for a vocal group. Both of these roles suggest a keener knowledge of harmony and the inner workings of music than most singers have. In working out his method for singing solo, Torme brought along this bank of knowledge and used it to catch up with Fitzgerald just as O'Day exploited her own special, individual qualities. As early as 1947 we find Torme looking for new ways to go with vocal improvisation: "Night and Day" (Musicraft) reverses the classic Armstrong model of solo structure (melody, routine, then routine-ing the routine) so that after a triple-time head statement, Torme flies into a solo that, instead of getting more and more abstract, starts off quite far out and gradually returns to the melody.

Through both methods Torme has always had a clearer sense of where he wants to go and how he's going to get there than O'Day. He improvises, but in a manner similar to Robert Altman directing a movie—the better rehearsed you are the more you can ad lib. Many Ellington sidemen operated in the same way (a point not lost on Torme, who describes himself as an "Ellington idolator"), working out a general pattern for their solos that, though they feel no obligation to follow it every time, gives them a frame of reference apart from the changes and the melody of the composition itself. Mature Torme, in performance with his trio, displays a sophistication unmatched anywhere in jazz, with the exception of the Modern Jazz Quartet, in terms of this incredibly articulate balance of prewritten and improvised material.

To put it another way, both O'Day and Torme change each song into a personal piece of music that would fit no other performer; the only difference is that O'Day emphasizes the deconstruction of the tune and Torme stresses its reconstruction. For instance, most of O'Day's classic set pieces have at their center very familiar standards, like "Sweet Georgia Brown" and "Tea for Two," which listeners know so well that O'Day can play with them all she likes and still not lose anyone. On the other hand, when Torme recomposes a song he wants you to forget about how it ever sounded before he took up with it. Thousands of people, in fact, know nothing about Dick Powell or the 1935 movie he made called *Broadway Gondolier,* and they think that "Lulu's Back in Town" must always begin with Torme's special introduction ("You've heard about Margie . . ."). If this reminds you of the way the Boswell Sisters reconstruct a song, it's supposed to.

O'Day tears a song apart in front of your very ears: Remember the line in *Amadeus* where Salieri remarks how Mozart's music is so perfect that to alter one phrase would destroy it? Well, O'Day alters much more than phrases. By pausing, stopping, and venturing out of the melody into improvisation just at the moment you least expect it, she makes the entire structure fall apart, but Lord, what a joyful noise she makes as the pieces break off and hit the ground.

Torme presents you with the finished product and nary a clue as to how he did it. If O'Day's strength is her frankness, Torme's is his intelligence; the line "Songbirds are not dumb" has been one that he intones with relish and obvious agreement. As one who has studied the glass of fashion and the mold of form since childhood, he must have been determined to create something new. The only method of jazz-derived popular singing before him was a linear method by which songs are interpreted on a piece-by-piece basis, or if you want to get particular, a phrase-by-phrase method in Armstrong and Crosby, word by word in post-Commodore Billie Holiday, and line by line in Sinatra. The linear approach has its limits, at least partially corresponding to those of the AABA song form, and at the same time, only Fitzgerald had found an audience that would permit her to get around the words and sheet-music melody for half her set. In response, Torme devised a holistic approach by which songs are not chewed up one bite at a time but devoured in their entirety, completely reshaped into all but completely new works that skillfully intersperse paraphrases of the original tune with all-new material by Torme and his arrangers. The Torme "Lulu" (first recorded in 1956 for Bethlehem) adds a whole new piece of music to the Warren-Dubin number, a chromatically rising vamp that Torme and Paich use as an introduction and later in the chart, as a vehicle for a key change.

We can look through at least two other windows into the adjacent rooms of Torme and O'Day, their shared concepts of vocal/orchestra placement and rhythm. They each agree on where the voice should go in relation to the orchestra, smack-dab in the middle. "I see no reason why arrangements can't be made which bring in the voice as part of the orchestra," O'Day explained in a 1950 *Downbeat* article, "and not the orchestra as something to back up a vocal solo." Torme has said pretty much the same thing, that he likes the voice scored right in the middle of the ensemble, and he tried it as far back as 1947's "Kokomo, Indiana" and "Boulevard of Memories" (both Musicraft). When the Miles Davis Nonet, the Gerry Mulligan Tentet, and then Shorty Rogers and His Giants perfected their constantly floating ensemble sounds, another earmark of cool style, they further encouraged Torme to find ways around the accepted though potentially restrictive format of solo and accompaniment. That Torme and O'Day want their voices positioned right where an instrument usually goes doesn't mean they're trying to sing like horns. Quite the opposite, it means they're trading on the uniqueness of the human voice and their own voices in partic-ular. Even in the middle of the highway of brass and reeds with no piano road map, as on most of the five-milestone Torme-Paich albums, or scatting through a wordless jazz instrumental, like O'Day's "Four Brothers" and "Hershey Bar," the voice can never register in the mind as anything but a voice. Like certain forms of Japanese theater in which male actors come incredibly close to becoming women or Walt Disney cartoons where ani-mated characters become so real you almost, but never quite, forget they're drawings, we can never lose the instant recognition of the human voice.

Rhythmically, Torme belongs to that borderline area of swing and bop that inspired many other white musicians who were working in the swing bands at the time of the bop explosion in the mid-forties, like Buddy Rich, Art Pepper, Gerry Mulligan, and all of the Brothers. Though six years older, O'Day has what Count Basie calls a "bop soul," and her clipped, staccato phrases of the early forties anticipate the bop movement in toto, not just its cool reaction.

Both Torme and O'Day stand unique in their use of rhythm. After Sinatra, pop singers in general formulated a very simple and effective way to work against the beat. Even Peggy Lee, to whom rhythm is so important that her touring backup group amounts to a five-piece rhythm orchestra, nearly always rides clear over the top of the beat they generate. Torme's use of rhythm owes much to the King Cole Trio and to his own experiences as a drummer, much as Cole's did to his piano playing. Cole and Torme *match* the beat rather than ignore it. Take the out-chorus of "Fascinatin' Rhythm" (on *Mel Torme and the Marty Paich Dek-Tette* [1956, Bethlehem]) where he and Paich rewrite the bridge as an out-of-tempo exercise that might go for baroque if they stayed with it any longer than eight bars, then slow down to ballad speed for the final A. Or the end of the bridge to "Nice Work If You Can Get It," which, as Gershwin wrote it, gets its charm from a couple of extra notes that the Gershwins used to syncopatedly delay the rhyme (made doubly cute by its reference to an earlier Gershwin Brothers' song, and who could ask for anything more?), so when Torme and Paich do it they go out of their way to make these odd notes even odder. The climax of "Malagueña" (on *Olé Torme* [1958, Verve]) makes for a textbook example of vocal-orchestra unity in terms of both harmonic and rhythmic empathy, as Billy May's screeching brass strain right through their upper registers into overblowing, and Torme blows his cool to deliberately crack his voice and keep up with them.

I could go on all night citing similar examples, but O'Day's approach to rhythm can be summed up with a single number, her "Sweet Georgia Brown," which she has recorded about as many times as Torme has done "Lulu," first for Verve in 1956 (on *Pick Yourself Up*), the chart probably being mapped out by O'Day first and then scored by Buddy Bregman. This "Georgia Brown" must come from the Middle East the way she shimmies to a snake charmer theme and bongo background, though the thrill comes from her putting on clothes rather than taking them off. She begins all but naked (or is it "all *butt* naked"?), doing the first chorus with only drum skins behind her, the second with a rhythm section and the horns slowly creeping up while she looks the other way, the third with the full band trying vainly to throw fig leaves on her, and each of the three in a whole new tempo. As on her other major polyrhythmic exercise, "Honeysuckle Rose" (on *Anita* [1955, Verve]), the beat goes off in several directions at once, first this way, then that way, but no matter where it runs it never gets away from her.

To be this rhythmically in tune you need to have a drummer playing constantly in your head; as Branford Marsalis recently said of a former employer, "[Art] Blakey taught me how to play the drums when I play." Marsalis told Kevin Whitehead, "Rhythm is it, it's what makes soloists different, what makes Sonny Rollins or Bird so great." No surprise, then, that Torme, in interviews, speaks as fondly of the days when he sat in as "second-chair percussionist" with Ellington, Kenton, Dorsey, Herman, and Krupa (yes, Gene Krupa!) as he does of his singing. Or that the single most important relationship in O'Day's life was not with a husband, parent, relative, lover, or even accompanist in the conventional sense, but her drummer of thirty-five plus years, John Poole.[*]

O'Day had been singing professionally since the late thirties when Carl Cons, then editor of *Downbeat* magazine, discovered

---

[*] Torme's drummer, Donny Osborn, is also the only unchanging and longest lasting musician in his entourage.

"the 19-year-old rhythm singer" sitting in at various musicians' hangouts in Chicago (including the famous Three Deuces) and gave her a gig at a new club he was opening, the Off-Beat. O'Day, born in that city in 1919, had only recently changed her name from Colton after starting in show business at a series of "professional" marathon dances she participated in largely to get away from her turbulent home life. Between various club dates, fellow Chicagoan Gene Krupa got to hear her, liked what he heard, and offered her the canary perch in his band as soon as his incumbent thrush, Irene Daye, vacated, which she did in 1941. O'Day made her name with the big bands, and vice versa: In the first of two separate tenures with Krupa's band, 1941–43 and 1945–46, she handed the drummer-leader his biggest hit in "Let Me Off Uptown" (1941, Okeh), and in between her Krupa periods she put Stan Kenton on the map with "And Her Tears Flowed like Wine" (1944, Capitol).

Since leaving the bands in the mid-forties, O'Day's moments in the spotlight have been few and far between.* She recorded only occasionally until the tail end of 1955, when Norman Granz, the producer she'd been working with for three years, formed his big-time Verve operation. Her stay at Verve outlasted his, though the post-Granz Verves include her only loser for the label in her mismatch with the consistently boring Three Sounds (you know something's wrong when even Roy Eldridge can't liven things up). So a combination of older band buffs and those who remember her from her sixteen musically excellent and generally good-selling Verves make up her audiences today. In the seventies and eighties she's gone back to the independent labels, mainly that most independent of indies, her own Emily Records. As opposed to the Verves—even *Live at Mr. Kelly's* (1958)—the Emilys replicate almost identically the kind of performance O'Day gives in the clubs, which rings appropriate as

---

* She got a little mileage out of the notoriety she achieved after admitting a few unsavory habits, just as Billie Holiday did. Musical talent has nothing to do with being asked to write an autobiography or getting on "60 Minutes." Just ask Torme: They wanted him on the show until he confessed to having *not* been a junkie.

more of these records get sold at gigs (and far more beyond U.S. borders than within them) than in stores. Reflecting a depressing trend of music today that I'll get to later on, it's more than possible for an artist to be a significant force and still be ignored in record stores.

Torme shares O'Day's Chicago background, though being born six years later, he missed the height of the band era, getting in only at its tail end. Like his colleagues Mickey Rooney, Buddy Rich, and Sammy Davis, Jr., he began as a child performer who grew up into a high-energy performance dynamo. Ben Pollack, the impresario-bandleader who was to Chicago whites what Fletcher Henderson was to New York blacks, put Torme in Chico Marx's all-juvenile orchestra when the pianist-comic fronted a dance band to pay off some gambling debts (and also toyed with the idea of building a similar kid band around Torme). Not long after Torme broke into pictures (he had previously played child parts on radio soaps) and a few months before his enlistment, he put together his first edition of the Mel-Tones and recorded with them on Jewell and Decca. After the war, Torme rejoined the group, got them on Musicraft Records, where they made a series of sessions with and without Artie Shaw (discussed in Brothers and Sisters), and brought the vocal group into modern jazz.

After "giving up the ghost" (Mel's term) with the Mel-Tones, Torme for a time seemed destined to become a "big-time bobby-socks idol" (*Look* magazine's term), when Carlos Gastel—who had helped make stars of Nat Cole and Peggy Lee, and put Kenton and O'Day together—moved him up to Capitol Records and MGM Pictures. He had hits, which incurred the resentment rather than the respect of the older showbiz community (prior to the baby-boom young adults rarely became singing stars) at his ill-planned New York debut at the Copacabana.

If anything, Torme's records for Musicraft and the much bigger Capitol Records were *too* successful: They led his managers and A&R men to think Torme could be converted, like so many other talented artists, into a mere cog in the hit-making machinery. But he had, in William Blake's words, learned what was enough by first learning what was more than enough. After a few years of bobby-sox idolatry, Torme decided to stick with smaller labels and classier music. His first long-playing record had also been the first Capitol LP, his own most spectacular stab at an extended composition, *The California Suite* (on Discovery DS-900), a thirty-five-plus-minute work that extols the virtues of the Sunshine State in eleven parts, all being songs but none fitting traditional thirty-two-bar AABA patterns. Torme made his first conventional album, *Musical Sounds Are the Best Songs* (1954, Coral), in which he says goodbye to the big-band era in a set of nonsensical but very hard-swinging rhythm numbers. He followed *Musical Sounds* with lush ones on *It's a Blue World* (1955, Bethlehem), which shows how much better his ballad singing had gotten since the Musicrafts and Capitols.

The vo-cool era, then, begins at its highest point, *Mel Torme and the Marty Paich Dek-Tette*, which leads to four other Torme-Paich collaborations, the second also on Bethlehem, *Mel Torme Sings Fred Astaire* (1956), and the others on Verve: *Torme* (1958), a flawless collection of unlush ballads with a small string section; *Back in Town* (1959), the Mel-Tones' reunion album; and the climax, not only of the Torme-Paich relationship but of the whole cool genre, *Mel Torme Swings Shubert Alley* (1960). Torme today dislikes the sound of his voice on these records and, in fact, once offered to remake them for the current corporate owners of the Bethlehem catalog. But even though his voice is a finer-tuned instrument in the late eighties, I doubt that anything could improve these records, especially the first and the last. The original *Dek-Tette* recording set the greatest diversity of tempo and on more adventurous works such as "The Blues"* in which he translates the multileveled Ellingtonian sound into multileveled Torme-Paich sound. On "Lullaby of

---

* This excerpt from "Black, Brown and Beige" fares better than any of the six Duke tunes he recorded as half of *I Dig the Duke! I Dig the Count!* (1960–61, Verve), with the exception of "Reminiscing in Tempo." On the strength of "Blues" and "Reminiscing," you could go so far as to call Torme the finest interpreter of Ellington's extended works outside the Ellington fold itself.

Birdland," Torme gradually flies farther and farther out, not by Ella-vating himself off the nearest chord progression but by building a scaffold of scat (and voice-horn interplay with the Dek-Tette) that he can climb as high as he wants.

All twelve songs on *Shubert Alley*, by contrast, come from the same source, the book-shows of post-*Oklahoma!* Broadway, and Torme and Paich reconfigure them all into the same medium-bright tempo. All have been thoroughly recomposed so that the familiar patterns of vocal-band-vocal and band-vocal-band are exceptions rather than rules, and only the closing chart, "Lonely Town" (the one track on *Shubert Alley* to use a piano), could have been sung by any other singer on any other album. On two numbers, Torme and Paich postulate on the possibility of blues devices in other kinds of material, as when Torme gathers momentum by repeating the penultimate six notes of "Just in Time," over and over without the final tonic, until it assumes the shape of a Count Basie–Joe Williams blues, and when in "Too Darn Hot" they have trombonist Frank Rosolino and altoist Art Pepper not wait for the "instrumental" second chorus to solo but instead take their eight-bar turns after each of Torme's opening A sections—in other words, shaping a standard as if it were Billie Holiday's "Fine and Mellow." Interpolations, of the kind that will eventually become a Torme perennial, figure on almost every track, though they're not usually made by the singer but by the band behind him, as on the second chorus of "Once in Love with Amy," where Torme sings the first A and the Dek-Tette plays "Makin' Whoopee," switching to "Easy Living" for the second A, and also when Torme sings the Latinate "Whatever Lola Wants, Lola Gets" and Paich and crew pay homage to Gerry Mulligan by way of "Bernie's Tune." Its virtues could be extolled ad infinitum, but the point is that the strength of the album does not lie in any of its individual elements, nor do certain tracks stand out above the others. Instead, from start to finish, *Mel Torme Swings Shubert Alley* is a masterpiece. Neither the vo-cool specifically nor vocalizing in general got any better than this, though a few contenders had come along in the interim.

Betty Roche, who sang with Duke Ellington in 1943–44 (in between Joya Sherrill's two stays) and again in 1952–53, seems to have been the first thrush to use O'Day as a starting point. She recorded only sporadically, making just two commercial discs with the band, and those only in her second tenure there, a blues and a standard, "I Love My Lovin' Lover" and "Body and Soul" (both 1952, Columbia), but extant airchecks and soundtracks of Roche from her first Ellington tour sound as if they could be O'Day-Krupa discs, while her fifties albums (on Bethlehem and Prestige) resemble O'Day's Verves. Most of us remember Roche for her "Take the 'A' Train," a prewritten set piece (after she left the band Ray Nance performed it nightly) that mixes a lengthy scat episode amid the title lines of nearly a dozen songs, among them "I Ain't Mad at You" (a blues-ish novelty that seems to exist only to be interpolated by scat singers),* "Stormy Weather," "I Cover the Waterfront," and so on, dropping them all off somewhere in the general vicinity of Strayhorn's theme. Though Roche doesn't have Fitzgerald's sense of improvisation or Torme's sense of structure, much of O'Day's sense of humor has rubbed off on her. By way of a negative example, if you want to hear Roche's shtick done without Roche's charm, sit through Babs Gonzales's "Cool Whalin' " and endure the title-line medley bit being done to death. "She had a soul inflection in a bop state of intrigue," Ellington said, "and every word was understandable despite the sophisticated hip and jive connotations." Betty Roche was also, quite easily, the best of Ellington's canaries after Ivie Anderson.

She was also the only O'Day follower to try to find her identity within O'Day's method of improvisation. Neither of O'Day's two major replacements, June Christy and Chris Connor, made much of an attempt, though the Kenton-Christy arrangement of "How High the Moon" included a prewritten scat line. One

* It occurs in numerous Fitzgerald ventures as well as Vaughan's "Shulie-a-Bop." Roche's "Route 66" contains "Horses, Horses," another Watson-Fitzgerald favorite.

other element separates Roche from Christy and Connor: She came out of O'Day-Krupa; they came out of O'Day-Kenton. Modern America's Man of Music, as the press agents called him, Kenton hired Christy and Connor because they sounded like O'Day, and had each record a remake of the hit "And Her Tears Flowed like Wine": For Christy it was "Tampico" (1945, Capitol); for Connor it was "The Bull Walked Around" (1953, Capitol)—each a novelty in an ABAB pattern, the B sections given over to repetitious band-chant episodes.

Coincidentally, each of them had recommended the other as a successor. When O'Day, ready to crack up after ninety-six straight one-nighters, decided to quit Kenton in 1945, she promised to find a new girl to fill her pumps. As O'Day tells the story, she came across Shirley Luster, singing a lot like her at the Three Deuces in Chicago, and said to her something along the lines of, "Hey little girl, how would you like to become rich and famous?" And months after Christy had left the band with a few hit singles under her arm and Kenton needed a replacement (neither Jeri Winters nor Kay Brown had worked out), Christy reminded him of Chris Connor, whom she'd heard broadcasting with Jerry Wald and had been, Connor told Ernie Santuosso, "actually frightened by the similarity in our voices." Not coincidentally, in their early Kenton days each of them could be mistaken for O'Day, but then O'Day, at age nineteen, had been touted as being indistinguishable from Billie Holiday, as supposedly Teddy Wilson had been unable to tell the two apart in a blindfold test.* "We all grew up together, so to speak," Raymond Chandler wrote, "and we all wrote the same idiom, and we have all more or less grown out of it. A lot of _Black Mask_ stories sounded alike, just as a lot of Elizabethan plays sound alike. Always when a group exploits a new technique this happens."

* The _Downbeat_ clip that describes all this is especially interesting as it refers to an O'Day disc several years prior to her first commercial waxing with Krupa, and spells Lady Day's name as "Ho*lli*day," apparently because she had not yet settled on the single "_l_" spelling.

Certainly by 1953, when Connor left Kenton to go out as a single, no one could fail to tell them apart. O'Day continued to perfect the imperfections that make her great, the total goofiness that to this day makes listening to her a ball. Christy took the high road to her own kind of long-form singing that, like Torme's recompositions, extended song and vocal arrangement patterns to encompass a greater range of dramatic possibilities. Connor reconventionalized the O'Day approach, making the waterfalls flow downward and the sky blue again. She attached less value to either keeping the audience guessing or enthralling them with programmatic drama, and instead developed a style entirely dependent on control and relaxation, tension and release.

Like O'Day, both changed their names: Christy had been born Shirley Luster in Springfield, Illinois, on November 20, 1925, while Connor, whose first name was originally Mary, was born just under two years later on November 8, 1927, in Kansas City, Missouri. Compared to the oft-married O'Day and Torme, both Christy and Connor have been relatively lucky in love, as these things go in the music business; since 1946, Christy has been happily married to Bob Cooper, the tenorist and arranger whose Kenton period coincided with her own, * and who quickly became one of the leading lights of West Coast jazz. Connor, too, has enjoyed a comparatively stable love life. Unfortunately, Christy and Connor have also shared their archetype's problems with addictions, in their cases alcoholism.

Christy grew up in Decatur and there, at age thirteen, sang with Bill Oetyel's local band. After graduating from high school she winged it to Chicago, where she barely got by, singing with society bands including Denny Beckner's, which convinced her that she couldn't stomach that "society stuff." She began to break through when she joined a dance unit led by Boyd Raeburn, whose regular warbler, Ginnie Powell (later Mrs. Raeburn), had taken a leave of absence. Raeburn had decided to build a jazz

---

* Christy and Cooper have enjoyed the only marriage in jazz of any duration, unless you count Pearl Bailey and Louis Bellson, or Lena Horne and Lennie Hayton.

orchestra. At the same time, he was getting better gigs—such as Chicago's Band Box—and radio exposure; an aircheck of Christy and Raeburn doing "Shoo Shoo, Baby" with the band in 1943 survives as her earliest extant performance.* Unfortunately, Christy contracted scarlet fever during the Band Box gig, and when the band left town to tour, it went without her. She worked with Benny Strong's band and at a few jazz joints like Ye Olde Cellar and the Three Deuces. It was at the latter club that O'Day claims to have heard Christy and recommended her to Kenton, though Christy (in various interviews) says she met Kenton in the office of a booking agency, General Artists Corp.

Leaving Kenton's orchestra took more time than getting into it, as from her first (May 1945) record, the hit "Tampico," Kenton wanted to build her up as a solo attraction. As early as December 1945, Kenton encouraged her to make vocal records, first for Transcription services and then, after she began placing heavy on the polls, on Capitol proper (starting with "Skip Rope," 1947). Her earliest sessions use Kenton sidemen, but as she started to take on club dates of her own, she used Johnny Guarnieri and the King Cole Trio as accompanists. (Though both Christy and Cole had contracts with Capitol, they only recorded together on Columbia as part of the Metronome All-Stars.) She stuck with Kenton for about six years altogether, through several complete overhauls of the band, and didn't leave him permanently until he broke up the "Innovations" orchestra in 1951. She then began a series of reunions with the band, including a tour of Europe in 1953 and of the States in 1959. Of the O'Day-Christy-Connor triumvirate, only Christy really lasted with the band, only Christy remained on Capitol afterward, and only Christy continued to explore the Kenton sound.

Pete Rugolo probably had a hand in these decisions. An ex-Milhaud student who began writing for Kenton at the same

---

* The sound quality is too poor for me to offer any judgment on what Christy sounded like in her pre-Kenton days.

time Christy joined, Rugolo created the sound of Kenton's greatest band (the Art Pepper–Eddie Bert–Shorty Rogers–Shelly Manne–Christy–Rugolo edition of the late forties) and then left Kenton in 1949 to replace Paul Weston as Capitol's music director. Though his tenure there lasted only a short while, in that time he inspired most of the modern jazz recording on the label, including the quasi-bop Barnet and Goodman records and the Modern Jazz Series with Tadd Dameron, Dave Lambert, Miles Davis, and Dizzy Gillespie, and even provided Kenton-esque bop-oriented backings for mainstream vocal dates by Jo Stafford, Mel Torme, and Nat Cole.[*] Of Christy's eighteen post-Kenton albums, Rugolo would arrange and conduct nine, as well as the majority of her singles, most after he and Capitol had otherwise parted company.

Recording on *Something Cool* began on August 14, 1953, with the title track, which Capitol released first as a single. By the end of the year, sales proved strong enough for the label to build an album around the song, and in 1954 they issued one, both as a ten-inch LP and 45 Extended Play set with six more songs recorded in December 1953 and January 1954. The good business it did justified rereleasing *Something Cool* as a twelve-inch LP when that format took over a year later, with four more songs (recorded at the end of 1954) for a total of eleven. By fall of 1956, when Capitol was about to release *The Misty Miss Christy*, the second Christy-Rugolo album, *Something Cool* had sold a walloping 93,000 copies. In the early sixties they converted the album to yet another new format, stereo, by having Christy and Rugolo re-create their 1953–55 performances note for note.[†] The remake edition, which sports a slightly different cover painting (four colors instead of one and June's eyes are open instead of closed) has been the only Christy album to weather the cor-

---

[*] Rugolo also did Capitol a major service in signing Nelson Riddle in 1950.

[†] According to some sources, the stereo *Something Cool* reuses the original voice track (though 1953 seems early for multitrack recording).

porate slashing of Capitol's nonrock catalog and remain in print to this day.

While the other ten tracks count for far more than filler, the main attraction of *Something Cool* is the title song itself,* which has opened the record in every one of its versions. Christy, Rugolo, and composer-lyricist Bill Barnes, known also for "I Stayed Too Long at the Fair," came up with a way to break through the limitations of pop-song structure that makes even the Rugolo–Nat Cole triumph "Lush Life" seem like a mere dress rehearsal. It creates its own shape—would you believe AABACDDEAA?—as near as I can count, that's somewhere around a hundred bars at four minutes and seventeen seconds.† Contextually, it could have been inspired by Tennessee Williams, and it simplifies Williams just as sung versions of Shakespeare (opera for the tragedies and musical comedy for the comedies) simplify the bard. "Something Cool" also evokes Eugene O'Neill's iceman, and the episode in Ray Bradbury's *The Martian Chronicles* in which madmen create illusions that are so real to them they actually become three dimensional, and even cast shadows. For a song to evoke one world so realistically is remarkable; for it to depict two is incredible.

The Blanche Dubois–like heroine of "Something Cool" at first seems quite sane as she tries to entice the gentleman on the adjacent stool to buy her a drink. As she talks (yup, it's one of those "half a bar-room conversation" songs, like "Angel Eyes" or "One for My Baby"), she begins by feigning innocence—pretending not to smoke or drink—and gradually falls deeper and deeper into her delusion, on an I-was-not-always-as-you-

---

* Other singers, such as Della Reese and the Mississippi piano-singer Dardanelle, have attempted "Something Cool," which is a mistake; it belongs more to Christy than any singer has ever possessed any song.

† Other notable attempts to create "long songs" for vocalists include the well-known "Soliloquy" from *Carousel* and other numbers on *The Concert Sinatra* (1963, Reprise), Torme's *California Suite*, Gordon Jenkins's *Manhattan Tower*, and less famous pieces of Tony Bennett's such as his "Glory Road" on *Live at Carnegie Hall* and the entire *Hometown, My Town* album with Ralph Burns.

see-me-now motif, until she conjures up grand illusions of a palace with too many rooms to count and more hunks hondling for her hand than Liz Taylor has ex-husbands. Her hallucination becomes complete when she gets around to describing a trip to Paris in the fall, and suddenly we are no longer in the bar listening to her babble but actually in her head visualizing Paris, seeing what she sees. The mood of the piece switches from impressionistic to expressionistic, as Rugolo builds up to Parisian street music to make her illusion three dimensional and put shadows on it. She snaps out of it after a few bars, remembers where and who she is, and we leave her where we found her, with just a guy who stopped to buy her "Something Cool." When Leonard Feather asked Christy to name her "best solo performance on record," she answered, "The album *Something Cool* is the only thing I've recorded that I'm not unhappy with."

None of the other June Christy–Pete Rugolo pairings goes as far out as *Something Cool*, but in all of their records together they succeed in their ambition to avoid the conventional. Obscure, often adventurous tunes that match her to a "T," startlingly original backgrounds that constantly vary in instrumentation and mood, as well as Christy's toned-down, honestly emotional singing, characterize all of the Christy-Rugolo's. As a team, Christy and Rugolo never cease to find melancholy in a joyful setting (*Fair and Warmer*, *Gone for the Day*, both 1957) or the optimism, if not the silver lining, in the darkest of clouds (*The Misty Miss Christy* [1956], *Off Beat* [1959]). Christy doesn't tour much these days, primarily because she's too much a band singer, and a trio just won't do for her what it does for O'Day, Connor, or Torme. Yet don't confuse this with overreliance on Rugolo; her albums with other arrangers hold up almost as nicely, particularly *June's Got Rhythm* (1958), the jazziest of three made with Bob Cooper, the other two being *Ballads for Night People* (1959), in which both Christy and Cooper pour their hearts out on a masterful "My Ship" (Cooper's solo here being worthy of even Stan Getz), and the more commercial Broadway show adaptation *Do-Re-Mi* (1961).

Then there's *Duet* (1955), the scariest of all vocal records. The latent harshness of Christy's voice comes to the fore in this battle of the bizarre with Stan Kenton's funereal piano. As a spare keyboardist, Kenton would have loved to be able to play like Ellington, Basie, or John Lewis; instead, his pounding recalls an odd distillation of Fred Chopin and Thelonious Monk. No matter, Christy, perhaps out of gratitude, matches him by exposing her own latent intonation problems (which were "one of my difficulties," she admitted in 1956), and they both have something more to offer than pitch. Kenton can't help being morbid, and provides such a bleak background for Christy that the cheerful becomes bittersweet, the slightly sad becomes downright depressing, and the sentimental becomes suicidal. Even the fleeting instances of comparative levity in "Baby All the Time," "Come to the Party," and "Just the Way I Am" come off like vain efforts to smile while the House of Usher collapses, and the deliberate downer, "Lonely Woman,"* makes you want to jump off the nearest bridge—and I don't mean an eight-bar bridge.

Chris Connor doesn't have that kind of tragedy in her—even her definitive female version of "Lush Life" doesn't pack the same emotional wallop as Cole's or Johnny Hartman's. Connor's records also reflect the East Coast, where they were recorded, just as Christy's and O'Day's reflect the West Coast—where you expect to find Bob Cooper, Art Pepper, Jimmy Giuffre, and Bud Shank. Al Cohn, John Lewis, Oscar Pettiford, and Joe Newman are Connor's most frequent studio companions.

But mainly, when you think of O'Day, think spontaneity; when you think of Connor, think control. Think also of an O'Day-ish voice whose shaping of lines and phrases owes more to Holiday, Sinatra, and Lee. Think understatement but not under-singing or "minimalism." Think of a warm, assured voice that wants to

---

* Two great altoist-composers, Benny Carter and Ornette Coleman, each wrote an extended ballad called "Lonely Woman," and each got recorded by one of the Kenton canary trio, Carter's by Christy (first with Kenton's orchestra and later with his piano) and Coleman's by Connor.

make sure she can trust you first and refuses to let go until then, as on "Get Out of Town" (on *Chris Connor* [1956, Atlantic]), wherein the taut low tones of the first chorus become a symptom of the heroine's frustration, and the up-tempo optimism that follows in the second chorus becomes a flashback to the rapture that preceded this anguish. Think also of a voice that values dynamics so much that it only uses them sparingly and meaningfully, rather like Popeye waiting until the very last minute before eating his spinach. Think, lastly, of an unbeatable sense of time and an ear perfect enough to guide her through—most of the time, anyway—this obstacle course she sets for herself.

The fifteen albums Connor recorded for Bethlehem and Atlantic constitute the essential body of her music, though were we to choose one single performance to represent Connor it would have to be "Follow Me," from her album *A Portrait of Chris* (1960). Arranger Jimmy Jones, in one of his best pieces of work, takes a tip from the song's title and turns the *Camelot* song into a duo concerto for voice and violin, as fiddler Harry Lookofsky follows her with what, in the jazz context, sounds like an improvised obbligato of the sort that goes back to Bessie and Joe Smith. But since Lookofsky never tries to give the impression of extemporaneousness, and because of his instrument (virtually the only time that the violin has filled this particular role in jazz), the piece has a heavily classical feeling. At one point it seems European in texture but Afro-American in rhythm, for Connor swings the most eloquently in slow-ballad time; you can hear it the way she sprinkles a topping of short chipped notes over the crust of slow, long pulses that Jones and Lookofsky bake. However, in the bridge, Lookofsky drops out and Barry Galbraith's guitar assumes his place as Connor's partner, though instead of loosening up, she pulls the reins in even tighter, changing the number's complexion entirely: The piece herewith becomes classical in rhythm but, because Connor's voice has so much of the stuff of the jazz-influenced vocalist (just as Roy Acuff has so much of the stuff of the country singer), "Follow Me" briefly becomes bebop in texture but classical in time.

Which gives us only one example of what Connor is capable
of: She creates the same kind of magic on "All About Ronnie"
(1953, Capitol), her feature with Kenton that first attracted attention to her, and "Lush Life" (1954, Bethlehem), a song still
associated with her despite dozens of renditions by other performers. Though neither is as finished as "Follow Me," each
shows her on the way. With her parents, she'd moved to Jefferson City at thirteen and later went to the University of Missouri
in 1945, where she sang with the college band. She returned to
Kansas City for a few months after graduating, there working
with a small group led by Bob Brookmeyer. Seven weeks after
landing in New York in Spring 1949 she fell in with Claude
Thornhill and would chirp with his orchestra for three different
periods in that many years. During down-time from Thornhill
she giggled with Herbie Fields's short-lived big band and Jerry
Wald's Orchestra, where Christy heard her and recommended
her to Kenton, prompting *Downbeat* to run a shot of her and
Stan on one cover with the headline, "DOES KENTON HAVE ANOTHER
JUNE CHRISTY?"

She worked far more with both Thornhill and Kenton than
her scanty discography with those two bands indicates, and she
didn't begin recording in earnest until a few months after leaving
the band when Murry Singer of Bethlehem Records happened
to catch her at Birdland and subsequently hired Sy Oliver to
assemble a big band to back her. Up to then, according to *DB*,
the label had tried and failed with pop singles, but when they
received advance orders to the tune of 16,000 (a figure far beyond that which any new Chris Connor album will sell today)
copies for the original ten-inch *Chris Connor Sings Lullabies of
Birdland*, they decided to concentrate on jazz. By 1955, Bethlehem had sold 40,000 copies of each of the first two Connor
albums and became, for a brief time, a force in the record biz.
These figures naturally brought the bigger labels in for a peek,
and Connor began recording for Atlantic in 1956. At the turn of
the sixties, Atlantic had reached sales of 100,000 with *Chris in
Person*, and at the big clubs where she played (Basin Street East

and the Village Vanguard were favorite spots), Richard Dyer remembered, "You had to stand in a line that circled the block if you wanted to hear her."

We won't dwell on her fall from this peak of popularity just yet, nor on Christy's or O'Day's; instead, for now we'll move on to two noteworthy cool crooners: Jackie Paris and Mark Murphy. Paris has one of the most appealing sounds in jazz, his raspy baritone carrying with it the same kind of catch, though not the same kind of syncopating mechanism, as Crosby. Just as his voice has far less range than Torme's, especially Torme today, his approach to the music has also been far simpler, and he generally remains true to straightforwardly structured renditions of the basic repertoire, ballads and swingers. Unlike most of the others in this idiom, he has no hang-ups about vibrato, and lets his hang like a tongue. Paris has so much charm you don't mind when his voice shakes or breaks; like the screeches he only narrowly avoids on "Everybody Needs Love" (on *The Song Is Paris*), these weaknesses provide a substantial part of his attraction. The scrapes and scratches he exposes in his throat also make him more of a bluesman in spirit, as does his forceful and ratty guitar work, which suggests a sort of white Tiny Grimes.

Paris has spent his career in a fruitless search for an audience, though his failure to find one reflects more on the music industry than his own talent. He started promisingly, having been born in Nutley, New Jersey, in 1926, and getting his first job, as he told Feather, through the Mills Brothers, who knew a good guitarist-singer when they heard one. After getting out of the service, Paris gigged around 52nd Street and MGM recorded him in 1947 with his working group, a trio inspired by King Cole's; he made his first "straight" vocal records for National in 1949, among them the premier vocal version of "Round Midnight." Throughout the forties and fifties it kept seeming as if the big break was just around the corner for Paris, who, in efforts to become more show-bizzy, gave up the guitar for a while, then started tap dancing (he told Dom Cerulli that he'd tapped professionally as a child, with no less than Bill Robinson) in his act.

But efforts to reach the mass audience somehow resulted only in his going deeper into the jazz underground; he toured with the Charlie Parker Quintet in 1949 (the only vocalist to do that) and then with the considerably better known orchestras of Lionel Hampton and Les Brown. He also recorded a blues with Charlie Mingus in 1952, a ballad with a Bob Thiele *Jazztime U.S.A.* show in 1953, and a bunch of wordless semi-improvised scats with the Don Byrd–Gigi Gryce Jazz Lab Quintet in 1957. Still, not even the jazz public came out to support him in sufficient numbers, and though Mercury/EmArcy (on their spinoff label, Wing), Coral, Brunswick, Atlantic (on their East-West subsidiary), Time, and Impulse each gave him a shot at an album (Capitol auditioned him on the insistence of booster Peggy Lee but didn't bite), none ever came back for a second. At the time of the Impulse album in 1962, Paris said to Bill Coss, "I've worked twenty weeks out of the last five years."

A British critic once wrote that the greatest compliment you can pay a jazz musician is to call him "underrated." Jackie Paris deserves that awful cliché more than even the most classically underrated jazzmen, like Kenny Dorham or Lucky Thompson. Reviewers sarcastically use the term as a compliment, but it's one that no one wants, least of all Paris. "I've got about seven or eight albums and they're all collector's items," he told me at a 1985 gig at New York's West End. "What the hell good does it do me?" How he'd love to trade the several dozen fanatics (myself included) who are dying to drop a week's salary to an out-of-print dealer for a copy of *Skylark* (the one on Brunswick) for a few thousand moderately interested consumers who'd be willing to part with $9.99 for one of his albums at Tower Records. In the sixties he tried a duet act with his then-wife Anne-Marie Moss, who served as interim vocalist with Lambert and Hendricks (in between Ross and Bavan) and who has had, if you can believe it, even worse luck than Paris, since her potential has not resulted in even one decent record. Today, Paris still sings like a dream, teaches, and works where he can. He made a low-key album for Audiophile and has said to have a terrific disc in the can if only he can interest a label in releasing it. I hope it's out by the time you read this, and I hope you'll spend ten bucks to get it. Paris deserves it, and so do you.

Mark Murphy has received precisely what Paris deserves: an audience that will come to see him in each of jazz's important cities, recording contracts with small but visible indies that will let him do what he likes and at the same time earn him dinner money, and respect from all corners of the music world, even the charlatans who give out Grammies. It's not a matter of under- or overrated (both Paris and Murphy made major New York gigs in 1988 at Fat Tuesday's), it's just that Murphy's "cult" is bigger than Paris's; he's a few steps closer to getting what he deserves.

Still, mass public acceptance seemed as unlikely thirty years ago as it does now. Even then Murphy devoted his career to exploring all genres known to jazz, long before terms like "eclecticism" and "neoclassical" became hundred-dollar secret words in the jazz press. He's the Woody Herman of vocalists, being too intrigued by whatever worthwhile movement comes along to limit himself to a single "house" sound. The streets are still littered with deep thinkers scratching their heads over whether or not Murphy is a "jazz singer," but while they ponder the "jazz" half of the term, he's unconcernedly experimenting with the "singing" half: letting his spiels and intersong patter seamlessly meander into the music, combining singing with recitations of text and poetry—Murphy switches techniques like other singers do songs, often segueing directly from one to another like numbers in a medley.

Perhaps all jazz styles come equally naturally to Murphy, because it's possible to imagine him, to use his own term, "before jazz." There's nothing the least bit forced or artificial about anything he does; still, Murphy comes off like a man who set out to be one of the most exciting jazz-derived performers around and achieved it, forcing himself to master jazz's infinitely tricky intricacies and nuances. As Malvolio in Shakespeare's *Twelfth Night* distinguishes among those born great, those who achieved greatness, and those who had greatness thrust upon them, Murphy gives the impression of having had to work to achieve natural swing, unlike, say, Nat Cole or Mel Torme, who were born jazz rhythm virtuosos. (Cole couldn't escape it, even when he rambled through roses in the lazy, hazy, crazy days of that Sunday that summer.)

So that's bad? The impression of distance between Murphy and his music is his greatest advantage: Murphy's genre-crossings don't argue for the eradication of familiar styles; they support their preservation. Sharper than the most astute critic, Murphy comments on the music. There may be lapses when singing "about" jazz is something less to aspire to than plain old singing jazz, especially when vocalese lyrics to milestone solos became recited résumés for their creators. Murphy is no less guilty on the only two dispensable tracks of the otherwise perfect *Bop for Kerouac* (1981, Muse), in which "Boplicity" becomes the ad slogan "Bebop Lives"—precisely the kind of patronizing, however sincere, that composer Miles Davis would detest (and unusual in that Murphy otherwise shows an astute affinity for the music of Davis and his sidemen).

Murphy's straight vocalese is nothing special, and his straight scatting thrills less than his straight ballads, but it's his ability to comment on the commentaries that's really riveting. All interpretation is an opinion: The performer stresses one aspect of the melody or lyric over another because he likes it better—King Pleasure's words to "Parker's Mood" comment on the solo (even though this particular lyric doesn't depict Parker directly), as does Kerouac's depiction of Bird in action in *The Subterraneans*. No matter that both Pleasure and Kerouac have dated badly while Parker hasn't, Murphy's re-reinterpretation surpasses both and combines the two like a good movie made from a mediocre book (I can't say it approaches the majesty of Parker himself, but what does?). The juxtaposition of an *On the Road* excerpt in the middle of "The Ballad of the Sad Young Men" produces an incredibly moving torch song on the level of "Something Cool," designed to salt the beer glasses of he-men from the generation after Billy Bigelow and dat ole man ribber.

Murphy was born in 1932 in upstate New York, where he sang with his brother's dance band and various other units at high school. After college, Sammy Davis, Jr., and Irene Daye encouraged him to keep singing, and he eventually got to open for Anita O'Day at a San Francisco club in 1954. Finally, as he told Hal Webman, a chain of introductions led him from Tony Scott to Nat Hentoff to manager Monte Kay and to Milt Gabler and his first records. After two albums for Decca, beginning with *Meet Mark Murphy* and *Let Yourself Go* (the first includes a very accomplished "Exactly like You" that has him emphasizing odd parts of the beat), Murphy switched to Capitol. He paid dues for his claim to an audience there, grinding out three forgettable albums that include a tasteless march-time arrangement of "The Lady Is a Tramp," where, despite the sarcasm intended in Lorenz Hart's lyric, the lady really *is* a tramp.

The two finest early Murphy albums are the two he made for Riverside in 1961 and 1962: *Rah!*, with Ernie Wilkins, which has the only non–Lambert, Hendricks, and Ross version of "Doodlin' " that's any good; and *That's How I Love the Blues*, with Al Cohn, which is particularly good. As an all-blues collection, it almost matches the Cole-Riddle *St. Louis Blues* in its triumphant translation of traditional material into a modern idiom. Nat and Nelson find everything they want in Handy's music; and Murphy, in an album apparently designed to dovetail with Cole's classic, covers everything but*: the whole spectrum of the form, like big-band blues à la Basie and Kansas City, or New York from Bennies Carter and Goodman, or Chicago like Earl Hines and Billy Eckstine, and stuff both more ancient, like Joe Turner and Pete Johnson, and modern, like Horace Silver. Murphy also makes the semi-blues sound convincing, as he may be the only one since Big Joe Turner to treat "Blues in the Night" as if it were a genuine blues, and scores one for the archeology depart-

---

* He later got around to Handy's "Memphis Blues" in the 1988 release *Beauty and the Beast*.

ment with "Everybody's Crazy 'Bout the Doggone Blues," an O.D.J.B.-type vaudeville number that Marion Harris sang back in pre-Harding days. And that's the *most* Tin Pan Alley–oriented of his albums, as he spends far more time chasing after jazz composers—like Benny Golson and Art Farmer and others who wrote songs (or compositions that could be sung which occasionally require him to write a lyric, for example, Oliver Nelson's "Stolen Moments")—and songwriters—like Fran Landesman and Bobby Troup, whose work rightfully belongs to the jazz canon. No singer, in fact, has ever valued jazz as highly as Mark Murphy.

At the height of the cool era, the labels went after dozens of Torme and O'Day types, with no consistent degree of talent or success, the most persistent and best known being Mercury's indecipherably cool Helen Merrill (I like her the least, yet have to concede that she made some terrific records in these years), whose Hellenic foremother was not Humes, Ward, or Forrest but Kane. Bethlehem, in particular, desperately wanted another Chris Connor, and ushered through their studio door chirpers as gifted as Betty Roche and as awful as Frances Faye. Julie London, who comes off today as something mighty appetizing to fill up all that cover space on those new twelve-inch LPs, took cool to mean minimal and parlayed a single hit into an entire career of mumbling in a monotone. The list, dwarfed only by that of post–Dinah Washington soul sisters, goes on: Jeri Southern, Johnny Pace, Bev Kelly, Beverly Kenney, Marty Bell, Lucy Reed . . . and too many soft-singing trumpeters and piano players to list. Then, one day in the early sixties, somebody looked around and noticed that it was suddenly uncool to be cool.

Pop music had been captured and recaptured by the youth brigade, and jazz, which hadn't dared to call itself cool since the mid-fifties, had gone and polarized itself into commercial funk on the one hand and anticommercial free jazz on the other. In 1962, Creed Taylor released both Anita O'Day and Mel Torme from their Verve contracts, and Atlantic did the same to Chris Connor. By 1965, June Christy had cut her last album for Capitol and both Mark Murphy and Jackie Paris had left the country. The vo-cool was dead; the artists who would survive it had to find something else. But every time a singer appears with a band billed as an octet or a nonet or reharmonizes or restructures a tune to go beyond thirty-two bars, or finds a new way to juxtapose the human voice with musical instruments, the cool lives.

Sinatra!

And Other Swingin' Lovers

● ────────────────────────────────────

"Being an 18-carat manic depressive, I have an acute capacity for sadness as well as elation."
                                    —*Sinatra to Pete Hamill*

"I'd just like to say thank you from the bottom of my heart. There's been quite a controversy out here as to whether or not I should appear here at the [Hollywood] Bowl, and I want to say that it seems as though those people who thought I shouldn't kind of lost out in a very big way. I have a comment to make about that: I don't see why there shouldn't be a mixture of all kinds of music in any bowl or in any public auditorium. Music is universal, whether you hear a concert singer with a philharmonic orchestra or a crooner with a jazz band, it doesn't make any difference."
                                    —*Frank Sinatra, 1943*

(At the final concert of his tour with the Los Angeles Philharmonic, perhaps the first such performances by a jazz or pop singer in a "legitimate" concert hall with a symphonic orchestra.)

Film critic Ethan Morden once described Bing Crosby as a "healer." His function in depression and wartime America was to soothe and to reassure. Frank Sinatra's mission has always been just the opposite. Sinatra shocks. Sinatra jolts. Sinatra arouses our anger and our passion by expressing his own. Sinatra gets our pulses to race and our brains to click. He achieves this partially through his politics: From the late forties, when he upset our cold war complacency by daring to suggest that there might be room for blacks and Jews in the country that just defeated Nazism, to the eighties, when pop stars slide out of limos to give up five minutes of their time so that the Third

World might eat cake, he ignores popular sentiment and turns up in South Africa. Children of the last few decades risk growing up thinking of him more as a political figure than a musical one.

Still, I can overlook the nonmusical aspects of the man Sinatra and still make my point, because Sinatra expresses most of his radicalism through performance; he desecrates the innocence of a ballad with an all-knowing gesture or inflection that suggests there is no innocence. He taints the most cheerful of up tunes with the melancholia of the angst that requires this release. When we cry for simple, black-and-white sentiment, he gives us instead a synthesis of reality—as channeled through an extraordinary perception and an extraordinary technique—that explodes in full color. Sinatra's most important contributions to his music should be viewed not as acts of revolution but as reformation, for he has implemented changes in vocal style that might have come about without him—but never with such force. Certainly his style would not have had enough power to virtually wipe out the memory of all styles before him, nor would it have been strong enough to maintain ground against the mass hysteria of the pop music that has come after him but has yet to outlast him.

One element of Sinatra's vocal style distinguished him from all contenders to Crosby's throne in the early forties: his elimination of the syncope. And since syncopation signified the single most important device of Crosby and his generation, removing it amounted to forging a new style. Ever since establishing the breaking up of meter as a defining element of American singing, Crosby had never felt obliged to stick with it religiously. His syncopation had always been a great deal subtler than, say, that found in Scott Joplin's music, and from the late thirties on he extends the phrase longer and longer until the time of "I'll Remember April" (1943, Decca), where he stretches his lines almost as far as Sinatra's. Crosby anticipates Sinatra on other occasions, too. On "When the World Was Young" (1951, Decca), Crosby picks a dramatic highpoint where verse and refrain connect and bridges the two sections by extending the last note

of the previous line so far that it dissolves into the first note of
the next; on "Old Man River" (on *The Concert Sinatra* [1962,
Reprise], but even better on the TV special *A Man and His
Music + Ella + Jobim* [1967]), Sinatra joins the bridge and the
last chunk of the refrain with a similar megalegato note, and
though he holds his a few measures longer, as you'd expect, both
provide some of the most breathtaking—literally—moments in
music.*

Sinatra has been quoted as calling his approach "much more
difficult" than Crosby's, but the earlier style was no lead-pipe
cinch either. Listen to one of Crosby's lesser devotees, Bob
Eberle,† on Jimmy Dorsey's "Only a Rose." Near the end of his
vocal chorus he falls into a trap: Unable to handle this kind of
rhythm as eloquently as Crosby, on the word "roses" he emphasizes the "zez" with a sore thumb of a high note, then makes
you question the validity of the whole technique.

Sinatra realized that vocal jazz could move beyond the broken
pulse into perfectly even 4/4, the completely "democratized
beats" that Gunther Schuller has spoken of. "You've got to get
up and sing but still have enough down here to make your
phrases much more understandable and elongated so that the
entire thought of the song is there." As he told Sidney Zion,
"You don't chop [phrases] up like some people, and I'm not
criticizing, but a lot of people could never do that, singers I
know. They'd sing, 'Don't forget tonight . . .' (breathes loudly)
' . . . tomorrow!'‡ You know, that kind of thing, and I'd say my
God, why do they do that? It's so simple to cure."

* He thereby connects "*l*" sounds ("rec*all*"; "j*ail*") with soft vowels ("*Ah!* The apple
trees . . ."; "*I* [pronounced "Ah"] gets weary . . .").

† Highly regarded in the early forties and considered one of Sinatra's main rivals by
FS himself, today Eberle comes off as square, cardboard, and something like Mighty
Mouse in a tuxedo.

‡ I'll never know what prompted Sinatra to use this of all songs to make his point. He
recorded "Don't Forget Tonight Tomorrow" for Columbia in 1945, and I'd assumed he
had immediately forgotten about it along with everyone else.

Sinatra would have made a pretty mediocre Crosby imitator anyway. He should have stayed away from "Sunshine Cake" (1949, Columbia), for example, because, even more than most of their songs, Burke and Van Heusen wrote it very specifically for Crosby's voice. Virtually all the rhymes depend on trills, and whereas Crosby could bend a single-syllable word like "bake" into two beats, when Sinatra tries it, he sounds like he's walking around a corner and stepping into an open manhole. (Crosby might be equally clumsy doing a song written for Sinatra's deep breaths, such as "Time After Time.") Conversely, on "If It's the Last Thing I Do" (on *Close to You* and *The Rare Sinatra* [1956, Capitol]), Sinatra successfully injects a Crosby-like pause into the concluding phrase ("thing . . . I do") which throws the audience, breathing along with him, completely off-kilter.

"Summer Wind" (1966, Reprise) provides a textbook case of mature Sinatra swing: the singer constantly surging ahead of the beat, the piece gradually rising in tempo and key (modulating from D flat to E flat to F), and Sinatra and the band in a perfect push me–pull you situation—is he pulling the band or is the band pushing him? The big thrills come on the final A when FS shifts gears into staccato and delivers "The autumn wind" and "The winter wind" in short, undotted triplets. The piece reveals arranger-conductor Nelson Riddle's mastery as much as it does Sinatra's, as the orchestra fills in the spaces around these words with response triplets of their own. Were either Sinatra or the band to be off by even a single beat they'd crunch down on each other's toes.

Sinatra heard this sound in his head before he was able to create it, and he has elaborated on particular inspirations to this effect—Tommy Dorsey's legato trombone solos, Jascha Heifetz's arco violin style—as well as on the training of his body to accommodate longer and longer breaths by swimming underwater and other methods (which gave him lots of wind, if never intonation on the same level as Crosby). However, the swing era's standard 4/4 time could also mean smoothness (as opposed to the stricter syncopation of the twenties), and Sinatra simply expanded on the long meter smoothness already inherent in Dorsey's melodic statements and some of Ellington's ballads (particularly the trombone features, like Juan Tizol's exotica, as in the sixty-four-bar AABA "Caravan"). Sinatra's music from the beginning, until say "My Way," has been an extension of swing-era ideals. He shows such commitment to big-band swing that other forms of music, even those closely related to swing circa 1940, only get in his way.

For one thing, Sinatra is not a good blues singer, but he isn't a bad blues singer either. He's just not a blues singer of any kind. Even on a number written for him, like "Lonesome Man Blues,"* his voice holds its place at the end of a line where a blues singer's is supposed to go down. Sonny Parker, Lionel Hampton's R&B vocalist in 1950, falls so far off at the end of a phrase that the concluding words of the last line become the first words of the next. Sinatra isn't interested in this. For me, "Blues in the Night" provides the closest thing to a weak spot on *Only the Lonely,* and another blues song, Billy May's "Lean Baby" (1953, Capitol), finds Sinatra incapacitated until the bridge— and, as if you didn't know, bridges are not exactly standard equipment on the blues. In 1945, when Columbia was trying to universalize Sinatra as Decca had done with Crosby, they had him record two spirituals with the Charioteers, the black vocal group from Crosby's radio show, and his voice turned out to be entirely unsuited to the material. The same thing happened when he tried his hand at Dixieland jazz for the soundtrack of the movie *The Joker Is Wild;* he just can't make his voice fit into that old-time two-beat pattern.

Perhaps because Sinatra has no empathy for pre-swing forms of jazz, some commentators have been tempted to surmise he has roots in classical singing. I just don't hear it. For one thing,

---

* Sinatra never sang this on a commercial record, with good reason, but in the movie *Meet Danny Wilson* (1952) and on television in a duet with Louis Armstrong.

he fares no better with earlier European song forms, such as the waltz, than he does with the blues. In trying to describe his work, Sinatra once used the term "bel canto," an Italian expression meaning "beautiful singing," and he felt compelled to amend this innocent-enough phrase by adding, "without making a point of it." Sinatra has nothing in common with any opera or classical styles of singing. Whenever he speaks of an opera singer he always goes out of his way to distinguish between their style and his by saying something like, "We of the jazz or popular world . . ." Certainly no opera buff would take seriously his single tryst with a genuine aria, his duet with Kathryn Grayson, "La Ci Darem" (from *Don Giovanni* by way of *It Happened in Brooklyn*, the 1947 MGM picture). His last name may end in a vowel, but he is not an Italian.* He is an American, and that makes all the difference. As he said to Sidney Zion, "I was never a great fan of classical music."

What's more, Sinatra lacks Crosby's generic diversity—which Columbia didn't learn after he couldn't bite off gospel and they proceeded to steer him toward pseudo-Latin ("Stars in Your Eyes," 1945), pseudo-western ("Sunflower," the inspiration for "Hello, Dolly!," 1948), and pseudo-bop ("Bop Goes My Heart," 1948)—and Torme's rhythmic diversity, since Torme really can handle waltzes, blues, and trad with no sweat. But that doesn't make him any less complete an artist, because if he puts all of his eggs in one basket he knows it's going to hold out, and Sinatra and 4/4 swing have served each other remarkably well all these years.

Because Sinatra swings so remarkably, for him to assimilate other musics would amount to mediocre eclecticism. Sinatra found everything he wanted in the big-band swing idiom. His instrumentation, for one thing: the sixteen-plus-piece dance orchestra has always provided the bread for the Sinatra sandwich

---

* He doesn't speak the language and has never sung in it other than phonetically. All of his movies have had to be dubbed for European release and most Italians have never heard his speaking voice.

while obliging obbligatists and soloing sidemen supplied the
mayonnaise. He usually beefs it up with strings—as did Artie
Shaw and Tommy Dorsey—in the bulk of the charts written for
him by Nelson Riddle or enlarges the string section to the point
where the horns function only as a sort of rhythm section for all
the assorted violas and cellos—as on his albums with arranger
Gordon Jenkins—or he may pare it down some for a session
designed to evoke the Red Norvo–Eddie Sauter band, or tour
with a Benny Goodman–inspired sextet of five rhythm (the usual
piano-bass-drums plus vibes and guitar) and one woodwind.

He also found the vocalists who influenced him most in the
swing era. We've already mentioned Crosby, though the similarities between the two men may seem obscure today. If there
is any one earlier vocal artist whom Sinatra reminds us of, it's
Billie Holiday, whom he named as his "single greatest musical
influence." Holiday toyed quite freely with the duration of her
phrases while Sinatra remains more faithful to the length of the
line, though within the course of each he can accentuate notes,
words, or syllables for both dramatic and musical effect without
ever losing the flow of the phrase. Early TV appearances reveal
a pretty clear visual demonstration of Sinatra waiting for the end
of each line before breathing, though you won't find him doing
this in movies where he lip-syncs to a prerecorded track or later
videos where he's too much the magician to give away his tricks
on camera. Sammy Cahn, the lyricist generally responsible for
most of Sinatra's "special material" over the years, once wrote of
how he and partner Jimmy Van Heusen "have written many
songs for Frank, his reaction is never over-enthusiastic. It is
always the most imperceptible nod." The Kester lyric to "Love
Locked Out," which Sinatra sings on *Close to You*, contains
another perfect summation of Sinatra in the phrase, "Love beats
its tiny wings no more." Like Holiday, Sinatra's art is all imperceptible nods and the beating of tiny wings.

Finally, Sinatra found tunes. The years 1935–45 also provided
Sinatra with much of his repertoire, because Sinatra all but invented the standard. Before Sinatra, the basic repertoire for

singers consisted of the latest plug tunes, good and bad, that their A&R men put in front of them. Previously, as one *Downbeat* commentator wrote in 1949, singers "rarely made much of melodies penned prior to six months ago." On one Lee Wiley broadcast in 1938, the announcer can't get over how the singer will actually perform a song from as far back as last season.* After Sinatra, singers did "The Song Is You," "Night and Day," "Come Rain or Come Shine," and maybe a few dozen others over and over until it got to the point where, as June Christy once discovered, customers were coming into record stores in search of albums that *didn't* have "My Funny Valentine."

I don't mean that Sinatra went out of his way just to sing old songs. Other people had done that. Lee Wiley had recorded albums of the music of certain Broadway composers for Liberty Music Shop, which was hardly a mass-market label but rather a musical comedy connoisseur's equivalent of what Commodore was for jazz specialists. Dick Haymes had sung old songs because they were old and sentimental, and in doing so, tapped into the public that went to see all those postwar musicals set in the 1890s, teens, and twenties who wanted nostalgia. Dean Martin, Spike Jones, and others camped up a lot of silly old-time tunes. In the years of Sinatra's rise to fame, he had lived through the deaths of three of the most important contributors to the art of the American popular song, George Gershwin, Lorenz Hart, and Jerome Kern. It must have occurred to him that songwriters of their echelon would not be coming along to replace them so quickly, and that their work would have to be preserved or else it would get buried under the mire of forgettable tunes pushed off the *Hit Parade* racks, especially since the average song of 1949 already wasn't up to the level of the average song from 1939. In picking out songs for his recording schedule, Sinatra codified the basic repertoire of adult popular music.

---

* The song, appropriately, is one that Sinatra would later "make much of," "I've Got You Under My Skin."

He must have done it at least partly out of ego, for in wanting to be the best singer in the world he realized he had to have the best songs in the world.* The actual quality of Sinatra's voice makes for a perpetual subject of debate among those who study singing in either rock, jazz, or classical (his chops and capacity for intonation and melody are hardly comparable to Crosby's), but all agree that his inflections and nuances count for more than actual vocal quality. Somehow, partly because of and partly in spite of the nature of his nonmusical activities, we believe Sinatra. I think it's something more than just having heard him all our lives and not having been there in the early forties when he first stuck his neck out from the pile of Crosby-imitating band singers. I can't say for sure, but Sinatra strikes me as having always had this quality.

His egotism, certainly, contributes, because so much of what he sings about is himself, and he doesn't try to hide his arrogance but instead makes it part of his performance: his casting of himself as the romantic lead of every love song he sings, for instance, and his dwelling on desire and want as opposed to self-sacrifice. Bob Eberle sings about love as if it were noble, heroic, and black and white—a cardboard cutout experience by no one in the real world. Sinatra is a realist: Though he may use an intensified, heightened reality, he makes love sound like something we all can relate to. And once he's got us respecting him for his honesty, partly because he admits potentially negative things about himself, he just about has us believing him. And also because he occasionally will kid a lyric that deserves it, we have all the more faith in him when he does come to a set of words that he can take seriously. He had built up such a bank of trust that both listeners and other singers took his decisions as gospel when he told us which songs would transcend their generations and which would not.

---

* Ever wonder why songs like "Because of You" and "Dedicated to You," hits that were enormously popular and covered by everyone in the fifties, never became standards? Because Sinatra never recorded them.

He began resurrecting oldies in the Dorsey band, in accordance with TD's policy of swinging ancient numbers; as a solo act on Columbia, he raised a few eyebrows by interspersing decade-old Gershwin tunes with new numbers pushed on him by the A&R men Manny Sachs and then Mitch Miller. The label ultimately got its comeuppance, because within a few years they began issuing their forties Sinatra singles on albums, and only chose the standards that he had selected, leaving it to outfits that both CBS and Sinatra's lawyers would like to know about to reissue "The Dum Dot Song" and "One-Finger Melody." Along the way, Sinatra also helped to turn new tunes into standards, as Armstrong, Crosby, and Fred Astaire had done in previous decades, among them songs from the new rage on Broadway, the book-shows of Rodgers and Hammerstein, Lerner and Loewe, and Irving Berlin.

Sinatra's new contract with Capitol Records, which began in 1953, happened to dovetail with the introduction of the long-playing record, and he and his coadjutant, Nelson Riddle, worked out a perfect system for the division of one-shot numbers and standards: singles for the new tunes that came along; albums for those that had already proven themselves. The 45 became the medium for singles as jukeboxes converted to the new speed, but higher-browed 33s appealed to a market far larger than the cognoscenti to whom they were presold (the liner to the first album describes it as being aimed at "our urban young people," though Sinatra is far too deep for contemporary yuppies). Ultimately, Capitol collected many—though not all—of Sinatra's singles on to LPs, and you can tell the difference in quality right away between these afterthought compilations and sets conceived originally as albums, even the first and exceptionally excellent singles collection. *This Is Sinatra,* which Sinatra recorded in his first few months at Capitol, before making that first album, *Songs for Young Lovers.*

On *Young Lovers* and its immediate follow-up, *Swing Easy* (1954), Sinatra and Riddle sound each other out. Previously, Riddle (a trombonist and vet of the Dorsey bone section) had

done right by Capitol with three important hits for the label, one
being Sinatra's "comeback" record "Young at Heart" (1953). On
one of their first tunes together, "South of the Border," Riddle
mimicked the sound of Capitol's very popular Billy May
Orchestra* as he had done for Nat Cole on "Teach Me Tonight"
and Heinie Beau had done for Sinatra on May's tune "Lean
Baby." Those first two ten-inch albums also set the pattern for
what was to follow, and while today they may sound similar in
instrumentation and mood, the differences between each esca-
lated over the six-year course of the first phase of Riddle and
Sinatra's miraculous collaboration. The wistful romance of *Songs
for Young Lovers* modulates into the film-noir bleakness of *In
the Wee Small Hours* (1955), which lead to the dark humor of
Close to You (1956), and ultimately to the suicidal mise-en-scène
of *Only the Lonely* (1958). At the same time, the cheerful *Swing
Easy* multiplies into the ecstatic *Songs for Swingin' Lovers* and
the euphoric *A Swingin' Affair* (both 1956).

Sinatra divided his other albums with other arrangers into
similarly polarized patterns. His exuberant *Come _____ with
Me* series with Billy May—which includes *Fly* (1957), *Dance*
(1958), and *Swing* (1961)—shows the predilection of both men
for ultrahard swing and of May's use of Fletcher Henderson–
inspired conflicting orchestral sections. Sinatra's trilogy of melodramatic ballad sets with Gordon Jenkins—*Where Are You?*
(1957), *No One Cares* (1959), and *All Alone* (Reprise, 1962)—
marks the most successful of Jenkins's attempts to Europeanize
the popular song with semisymphonic pitfulls, and sometimes
pitiful pitfalls, of strings. Sinatra apparently trusted his non-
Riddle arrangers only as far as individual moods; only Riddle
could handle sadness as well as elation.

As dj Jonathan Schwartz has pointed out, too many people
assume that Sinatra has already sung *all* the great songs. Such an

---

* May obviously enjoyed the tribute and repaid the kindness in his chart for "South
of the Border," and Mel Torme on Verve (1958) paid homage to the homage by reprising
some of Riddle's May-style brass figures.

assumption depletes Sinatra of a fundamental facet of his art. Ella Fitzgerald, three years younger but already a star when Sinatra was first turning professional, came to twelve-inch LPs at the same time he did and her most important collaborator, not an arranger-conductor but producer Norman Granz, devised a completely different method for organizing albums. For her *Cole Porter Songbook* they simply picked the thirty-two best-known Porter standards, and did the same for Rodgers and Hart, Irving Berlin, et al., until they got to the Gershwins, at which point Granz decided to forgo the selection process and just include *all* the songs of George and Ira Gershwin. Not only is it impossible for Sinatra to work this way, but when Capitol deconstructed his albums into collections of songs of Porter, Rodgers, Mercer, and Arlen, the entire content, beyond the form of the material, seemed completely altered (Sinatra sued and got them to cease and desist as their contract, it turned out, forbade it).

Sinatra's selection process operates on a far more intricate plane than Granz's "twelve Kern songs and you got your album" method, which rings appropriate since Sinatra's emotional involvement with his texts digs far deeper than Fitzgerald's. People have used the term "theme album" to describe them, but ever since *Sgt. Pepper's Lonely Hearts Club Band* this term no longer means what it once did, and even in the fifties it applied to a set of twelve songs about birds or with the word "blue" in the title or any of a dozen albums called *Jazz Goes Dancing* or *Jazz Goes to Correspondence School*. The classic Sinatra works, which unfold like Ellington's suites or Schubert's lieder cycles, would be lessened by the appellation of "concept album." Better to think of them as hieroglyphics, for like that preliterate form of writing, in which, for instance, a drawing of a cloud followed by a drawing of water is supposed to register in the head as rain, Sinatra's best music depends not on the individual songs themselves but in the way these songs are juxtaposed. Some individual songs had used hieroglyphic form like Porter's various "laundry list" numbers such as "Anything Goes" for comedy, Strachey's "These Foolish Things" for drama, or a combination of the two, like Robins's "Thanks for the Memory." Sinatra extended the process beyond songs into entire albums.

On *Only the Lonely*, to name the greatest, Sinatra and Riddle seek out the darkest moment of romantic despair, and, having found it, crystallize it into a solid object that they proceed to examine from twelve different angles. A few are metaphors; "Gone With the Wind," "Ebb Tide," and "Willow, Weep for Me" liken the loss of love to various natural phenomena. "Angel Eyes" and "One for My Baby," two boozy ballads that Sinatra has in mind when he calls himself a "saloon singer" (in actuality he's more of a "stadium singer"), use the milieu of the band itself to conjure up a setting—for example, the rinky-dink piano background behind most of "Baby." In his live *Sands* version of Arlen and Mercer's composition he even entreats his audience to "assume the role of a bartender." "It's a Lonesome Old Town" and "Spring Is Here" describe loss in the most painful way, by comparing experiences that occur with and then without love. "Good-Bye" is spoken to a departing lover and "What's New?" to that same person on a chance meeting. I can think of only a handful of singers who can actually sustain a mood for two or three songs but none who can keep exploring such a particular, subtle shade of a mood for an entire album, which, though reasonably long when clocked, seems far too short when listened to. Riddle also makes it hang together with recurring motifs, particularly a Chinese wind-chime *idée fixe* that he first introduced on "It Never Entered My Mind" (on *Wee Small Hours*) and, to further the idea of wind, here closes with "Gone With the Wind" (Sinatra also used it on "Willow, Weep for Me"—not the album version but a television performance of the Riddle arrangement).

The Sinatra-Riddle albums demolish, thematically at the very least, the songbook concept. For *Close to You*, the greatest of the ballad sets besides *Lonely*, Sinatra recorded fifteen numbers, only two of which come from the heavyweight show-tune composers whose work comes to mind when you talk about standards; the rest are by the likes of Burke and Van Heusen, Matt Dennis, Oscar Levant, and Walter Donaldson, whose "I've

Had My Moments" Gershwin apparently plagiarized for his own, later, "A Foggy Day." None of these men ever rated a Fitzgerald songbook, and by anthologizing their best and most appropriate numbers, rather than just digging into all of the music of a given major composer, Sinatra does a greater service to music. For this reason, *She Shot Me Down* (1981), the best of Sinatra's postretirement efforts, succeeds as a better album than his most recent and better advertised *L.A. Is My Lady*. *Lady* has a few superior songs ("Stormy Weather," "Mack the Knife") whereas most of *Shot* goes to hook-based quasi-rock, but Gordon Jenkins knows loads more about how to put albums together than the overrated Quincy Jones, and with Sinatra and one of his master aides-de-camp, the way you arrange and compile your songs is a lot more important than the songs themselves.

Good artists exploit their strengths like shoemakers sticking to their lasts. Only a great artist can dwell on his weaknesses and produce something that touches us and inspires us. Sinatra achieves this on "Wait Till You See Her," a Rodgers and Hart song inexplicably deleted from the original issue of *Close to You* (1956, Capitol, an album itself inexplicably deleted from the catalog for thirty years), in itself a masterpièce de résistance. The song comes from the long list of approximately thirty waltzes written by Richard Rodgers, and as I've suggested earlier, Sinatra rarely feels at home with 3/4 time. He tried them from time to time in "The Girl That I Marry" (1946, Columbia), "Lover" (1950, Columbia, also Rodgers), "I'm Walking Behind You" (1953, Capitol), "Weep They Will" (1955, Capitol), and so on. He even made a whole album of waltzes with Gordon Jenkins, *All Alone*,* thereby attempting the impossible: Anybody can be real with a Johnny Mercer or a Lorenz Hart lyric, but how do you take a text where you have to pronounce "again" as "a-gane" and not sound like Nelson Eddy? To make himself comfortable

---

* Reprise had originally intended to call the album *Come Waltz with Me,* but Capitol deemed it an infringement on their *Come whatever with Me* Sinatra albums, according to collector's lore, and sued until they agreed to change the title.

Sinatra gets around it by smoothing most of their melodies out into an even 4. So, if the time signature of "Wait Till You See Her" makes Sinatra uneasy, why not use that uneasiness in actual performance? Riddle's 3/4 waltz setting unbalances Sinatra's 4/4 symmetry, and his deliberately loosely concealed nervousness put the lyric over. Voice, song, and orchestra melt together exquisitely. Sinatra can move you even in a time signature that means nothing to him.

His believability, his rhythmic surefootedness, his eroticism, his vulnerability, his ability to give and take with his collaborators (as important as Torme's ability to do everything by himself), his unfailingly good taste (all the more interesting when it does desert him), his hats—all derive from a single trait of Sinatra's art, which immediately distinguished him from the generation of good singers that preceded him. Sinatra was the first to consciously think of himself as an artist, whereas even Crosby and Armstrong apparently thought their primary missions were to make a few bucks and have a few laughs on the way. More important than even his conception and perfection of the swingin' lover style, the dominant idiom of nonrock pop singing since the fifties, Sinatra sang and thought in long form, deliberately seeking to create music that would outlive him.

It's the same feeling you get from Shakespeare: There's no death, as Howard Dietz once said, like you get in *Macbeth*, but *Only the Lonely* is at least as profoundly moving an experience of romance undercut by tragedy as *Romeo and Juliet*, while *Songs for Swingin' Lovers* and *A Swingin' Affair* balance feel-good machismo with erotic tenderness as effectively as *Henry V*. It's led him to excesses of mountainous self-consciousness time after time, but the man and his ego have bettered both the business and the beauty of this art form almost as much as the man and his music.

"The leader," Sammy Davis, Jr.'s code name for Sinatra, is therefore apropos even outside the Rat Pack, however many of Sinatra's "followers" have proven themselves worthy of his fedora and bow tie. Sinatra has, in fact, inspired more imitations

than any other personality in adult pop, both the flattering and
the insulting kind. None of them could have made *Close to You*
or *A Swingin' Affair* any more than one of Louis Armstrong's
rivals could have made "West End Blues," but the best post-
Sinatra artists did add something to the style. Bobby Darin
brought a touch of the blues with him; Sammy Davis, a heavy
but often effective hand of old-time showbiz hoke; Vic Damone,
the prettiest voice in all of pop; and Buddy Greco, a Hibbler-
esque genuine flair for the ridiculous.

"I'm excited; they're grooming me as the new Sinatra," Vic
Damone told *The Melody Maker* in 1961. "[Capitol] tells me I've
got to be Frank's successor when he leaves to record for his own
Reprise label." Someone to fill Sinatra's shoes? Damone does
have a magnificent voice, and I don't doubt that he feels hounded
by the comment that "he doesn't know what to do with it,"
which Sinatra is supposed to have made.* Damone knows what
he's doing, all right; it's just that he chooses not to do all that
much. Beautiful? Sure, but it's a centerfold kind of beauty,
mighty pretty on the surface but nothing to indicate anything
going on underneath. I can't stop myself from buying fifties
Damone albums though, the two gutsiest being the Columbia
sets *That Towering Feeling* and *This Game of Love*, if only to
hear that lovely a voice singing such wonderful songs. One of his
Capitols, *Strange Enchantment*, does offer strong personality,
the source of which, you soon learn, is not Damone at all but
arranger-conductor Billy May. Damone is the perfect WNEW-
New York entity: pretty but uninvolving.

Sammy Davis, Jr., can be a gas, but it depends on whether or
not you get the right Sammy. If you're not careful, you may get
stuck with Sammy who records songs like "Candyman" and
writes thousand-page autobiographies that alternate intensely
personal episodes with empty name-dropping, patting himself

---

* Nonetheless FS wanted him on Reprise, though Damone thought Capitol could do
more for him, or so he says in the same *Melody Maker*.

so hard on the back he risks breaking his arm. This is the same Sammy who appears on "The Tonight Show," imparts an anecdote about never having had a formal education, then laughs hysterically at Johnny Carson's joke about that being why he never made anything of himself—and within a few months turns up on "Late Night" and laughs equally hard at the exact same joke when told to him by David Letterman, as if he had never heard it before. This is the same Sammy best known for an unfortunate photograph taken while hugging Richard Nixon (Billy Eckstine explains that Sammy wasn't *hugging* Nixon, he was *frisking* him).

But you might also get the good Sammy who made much worthwhile music, at least during his Decca and early Reprise periods (or roughly the years before he started appearing in Nehru jackets on "Laugh-In"). This Sammy made records with titles like *Sammy Swings* and *I Gotta Right to Swing*, which justify their titles; duet albums with Carmen McRae that are actually worthy of her (*Boy Meets Girl* and *Porgy and Bess*); and Broadway anthologies as good as anyone else's after Torme's like *Forget-Me-Nots for First-Niters* and *Sammy Belts the Best of Broadway*; and recorded daring if not entirely successful voice-guitar collaborations with Mundell Love and Laurindo Almeida. The Sammy who spiels endlessly about showbiz as if it were, to use a Sammy-ism, "Charley Messiah," seems a different animal entirely from the Sammy who sang "Bewitched" so beautifully (on *Try a Little Tenderness*).

The contradiction between the two Sammys keys into Davis's refusal to limit himself to any one particular way of doing things; Bobby Darin found a set routine that led to more exciting music, but he couldn't do as many different kinds of things within the adult pop–Tin Pan Alley genre as Davis and so, to find variety, had to leave class music for old folkie country and Nashville, as well as trips back to kiddie pop. Davis doesn't have a pattern to follow like "Mack the Knife," so his is more of a hit-or-miss operation. "That Old Black Magic," on *Sammy Swings*, represents for Davis what "Mack" was for Darin, though because it

wasn't the same kind of superhit (it was still a hit, though) it
didn't become the foundation for a dozen other numbers. Just
the same, it illustrates what the good Sammy does best: combining a modern sense of swing with old-time vaudeville hoke.
Does it sound racist or, worse, reverse racist that Davis should
bring to this style a characteristic normally associated with white
people, while Darin should excel Davis at blues and jazz, which
are normally thought of as black qualities? It shouldn't, because
if there's anything that these men prove, it's that these elements
transcend color boundaries—that is, blacks have been in vaudeville at least as long as whites have been improvising jazz.

"Old Black Magic" uses as its basis a Basie-cum-Sinatra-
Riddle-type crescendo "building" chart, which Davis relent-
lessly shticks up, intelligently exploiting his flair for impressions
as he refers to Torme, Cole, Eckstine, Ray Charles, and Jerry
Lewis along the way (on the album's previous track, "Don't Get
Around Much Anymore," he evokes Hibbler; on the succeeding
one, "Oo-Shoo-Be-Doo-Be," his attempts to scat like Joe Carroll
suggest Popeye the Sailor). The music doesn't start out slow and
build; it begins incredibly fast with a few choice bars of Khacha-
turian's "Sabre Dance," and then gets even faster. When we
begin to sense that the big, big climax is somewhere on the
horizon, Davis delays its arrival with unexpected stop-time interpolations: nonsense, children's sayings, and movie dialogue
clichés ("You four men go that way . . . the rest of you come
with me"). The satirizing of clichés has in itself become a cliché
in the post–Mel Brooks world—most of us have seen more parodies of Mountie operettas than we've seen Mountie operettas,
for example—but Davis's lines are fresh and witty. Davis has
also put over ballads very nearly this successfully, specifically his
"Blame It on My Youth" on *The Wham of Sam*, where his rising,
surging sound effectively sells Oscar Levant's song.

With the exception of Davis, who takes himself a great deal
too seriously at times, all of these Frank-entypes possess a gift
for intentional self-parody of the whole finger-snapping Vegas
vocal idiom. But this style never produced a funnier soul than

Buddy Greco, who predicted by thirty years the parodying of Vegas-isms by pseudo-comedians-turned-pseudo-crooners like Tony Clifton (the late Andy Kaufman) and Bill Murray, who in turn anticipated the unintentionally ludicrous parody-shaped insults leveled by Linda Ronstadt, Buster Poindexter, and others I'll get to in the last chapter.

Greco's art is all based on violated trusts, as in *Live on Stage* (Epic) where he warms us up with a few bars of "Moanin' " and then, just when he's got us ready for it, dispels the bluesy feeling and destroys the number as if to say, "You bozos thought I was gonna play 'Moanin',' didn't ya?" Or, in "Cheek to Cheek" on *My Buddy*, where he builds to a remarkably tender mood that he immediately destroys, like a Blue Meanie stomping a butterfly in *Yellow Submarine*. Shortly into any Greco performance he's got us, in turn, going, "Okay, Mr. Cocky Sonofabitch, let's hear what you really can do!" Greco knows he's not going to win any fans with his sunny personality (making him diametrically opposed to Davis, who perhaps tries a little too hard to be Charley Lovable), so instead he turns on the abrasiveness and makes it one of his *good* qualities. He's got to win us over with his music, not his charm, and sure enough he usually does. Greco is not only funnier than Murray or Kaufman, he's a genuinely satisfying musician who parodies constructively instead of just tearing down.

Unfortunately, Steve Lawrence never found as effective a way to creatively use his obnoxiousness. Sinatra can be a humble egomaniac and Greco a charming creep, but Lawrence's oily slickness renders him completely untrustworthy, where his smooth-voiced, post-Sinatra style and obvious intelligence should make him superreal. Lawrence functions best at extremes of low comedy: How can you not crack up at a Vegas lounge lizard who opens "Hello, Young Lovers" with the Kingfish (of "Amos 'n' Andy" fame) extending, "Well, hello 'dere!" or concludes "It's All Right with Me" with Señor Wences asking "S'all right?" "S'all right!" Lawrence's opposite—all singing from the heart and no put-ons—was Frank D'Rone, Nat Cole's protégé.

Mercury seems to have chosen him as their replacement for
Damone when the latter absconded to Columbia in the mid-
fifties, though the similarity was more in name than in style: On
albums like *Frank D'Rone Sings* and *After the Ball*, D'Rone has
a forties-type voice (touching off memories of Columbia-era Sinatra and trio-era Cole) in a fifties Capitol FS setting (Billy May)
and generates genuine warmth.

To reduce Bobby Darin's art to its barest essentials, start with
Sinatra's "I've Got You Under My Skin" (on *Swingin' Lovers*).
Almost all of Darin's best records have their point of departure
in this arrangement, performed without any of Sinatra's or Riddle's subtlety, but with a rock-hard swing that rolls heavily
enough to compensate for it. Think of Darin as a theoretical
cousin to the more recent Dianne Schuur in that he forged his
"style" out of a compendium of other people's approaches, with
Sinatra being his "No. 1 Favorite."* But where Schuur offers
only a directionless hodgepodge of hand-me-down ideas, Darin
has both vision and purpose, and while Schuur acts like she'd do
anything in the world to make you *like* her (making even superstar Sammy seem standoffish), Darin displays confidence enough
to simply do what he does and know that his people will come
around to him.

Rhythmically, Darin is the most successful of all fusionists, for
early on he found the *X* that marked the spot where swing and
R&B could meet. Darin essentially uses a rock beat but articu-
lates it loosely enough to interest those of us accustomed to more
sophisticated rhythms. After the career-establishing "Mack,"
Darin returned to the same formulas over and over again, rarely
varying his approach more than between very hard ("Beyond
the Sea," "All by Myself," "This Nearly Was Mine") and ultrahard ("Roses of Picardy," "Artificial Flowers," "Hello, Dolly!").

Some have even argued that Darin's "Mack" descendants can
be even more exciting than Sinatra's Swingin' Affairs; I don't

---

* The quote is from Darin as reported in *The Melody Maker*.

agree, but I do find it a respectable opinion. No one could deny that on straight ballads Sinatra leaves Darin as far behind as he does everyone else. On slower tempos Darin is a big, friendly dog who wants to jump on your lap when you're trying to do something else. You tell him to get off, and he extends a paw and looks at you like, "Can't I just touch you a little teensy bit?" just as Darin tries to make the rhythm move his way even when it's not appropriate. But who ever thinks of Darin as a slow-ballad singer? He has too many other identities that he assumes so successfully—finger-snapper, cowboy, rock icon—for us to dwell on his failings. Even his preliterate, teeny-bopper repertoire ("Splish Splash," "Queen of the Hop") has merit enough to suggest that this field might not be the wasteland every other doo-wopper's material so loudly insists it is. And we need only the continually popular and incessantly exciting "Mack" to remind us that Darin was easily, after Sinatra, the greatest of all Swingin' Lovers.

With one exception.

But look out, old Macheath is back. "Mack" was Darin's most popular record, and thirty years later, he and the song—despite worthy renditions by Louis Armstrong and others (Satch's having been cut long before Darin's)—are still inseparable. In the mid-eighties, however, Sinatra began performing "Mack the Knife." It didn't really take off on the official commercial recording (on *L.A. Is My Lady*), where a special-material chorus that drops the names of some of the all-star musicians backing him resorts to throwing an indulgent bone to any listeners who might have heard of these guys, but in concert, where he uses that segment to introduce his accompanists to the crowd, it's another story. By the time Sinatra finishes with "Mack," the audience hasn't forgotten that Darin ever sang the number but leaves the stadium in unspoken agreement that Sinatra has now claimed it for his own. Though the song is a display of pure energy, and in this department the seventy-year-old Sinatra can't really compete with the twenty-five-year-old Darin, the beauty part is that Sinatra doesn't have to erase the memory of Darin to take over the song. Darin's ghost can loom as large as it likes and it is still no match for Sinatra.

Comparing a Sinatra version of a number with anyone else's generally makes for a loaded dice proposition. I can't think of a single example where any of the Swingin' Lovers discussed here actually bests Sinatra at one of his own songs. It's been known to happen but never by a Sinatra imitator. I'm not talking about instances where Sinatra has covered another singer's hit; usually he expresses a reluctance to do so which comes through in the performance, as in his half-hearted chase after Nat Cole's "Nature Boy" and Tony Bennett's "San Francisco," the latter of which he felt so guilty about he had the single recalled almost immediately after release, but Cole and Bennett do best FS on "My Kind of Girl" and "How Do You Keep the Music Playing?," respectively. The black baritones like Eckstine and Vaughan provided an alternative to the Sinatra style for a short while, as did the cool school of Torme and O'Day, but none ever held up to the challenge of philistinism as strongly as Sinatra; he alone has had fortitude to outlast ever-changing trends in pop.

Who would have guessed that the next largest landmark in jazz-derived popular singing would be Peggy Lee? Listening to her early records only increases my admiration for her "discoverers," Benny Goodman and Johnny Mercer (and DeSylva and Wallichs of Capitol), for having spotted something in her that was worth recording, even when her whole first decade of 78s doesn't wholly support their faith.[*] I wouldn't call it a routine matter for the mature Lee to top Sinatra, but she does it often enough ("Call Me" being the most dramatic example) for it not to be an event each time it happens. Lee suffers from being compared to Billie Holiday too often, as vocally she owes more to Mildred Bailey and, especially, Lee Wiley, and any similarity

---

[*] She diminishes her forties Capitols through her insistence on singing too many of her own songs, which weren't always as wonderful as she'd like you to believe. For the best 78-era Lee, get *You Can Depend on Me* (Glendale 6023), an album of superior standards originally recorded for noncommercial transcriptions.

with Holiday is strictly philosophical, a shared belief in the primacy of individual expression. They also describe Lee as a "song stylist" too much, a backhanded compliment at best since it implies that she doesn't have any voice, and Lee's concept of style goes beyond songs. Operating in conjunction with her gifts for interpretation and rhythmic versatility, Lee is our all-time great neoclassical, pan-cultural music stylist.

Neoclassical because her singing embraces all that modern pop has to offer on a vertical plane, from Bessie Smith's time to the current Top 40 pieces, and in style as well as material. Pan-cultural because she extends herself horizontally to embrace world concepts of performance—some even beyond music—while keeping far too mobile for anyone to build a fence of genre around her. She doesn't even pass through phases, as most artists do; the same qualities I like about her work in the late sixties can be found, though latent, in the early forties. Lee has never existed on a conventional time line. She's apt to be singing the blues while everyone else is wailing about doggies in windows, and just as likely to do a Jerome Kern song in the middle of an album of soft rock.

Duke Ellington called her the Queen; I would describe her as the High Priestess of Alternative Music, in the sense that we use the term today.* To paraphrase Nietzsche's quote from Zarathustra, Sinatra asks how the music of the great songwriters is to be preserved while Lee asks how Tin Pan Alley is to be overcome. For nearly fifty years she's consciously and successfully sought out alternatives to adult pop's reliance on Tin Pan Alley (in terms of repertoire) and the standard dance-band format (in terms of instrumentation).

But any sort of quest away from the tried and true would be

* Spleen-venting Reactionary Footnote: I should say in the sense that some of us use the term today, since there are "seminars" devoted to "new music" that refer to only the same Top 40 rock bands; "alternative" music makers who sell only 100 million albums as opposed to 300 and "New Age" music makes Lawrence Welk and Guy Lombardo seem avant-garde by comparison.

futile unless Lee actually found something new to sing, and she does. To start with, she's always included the blues in her act, like "All Right, Okay, You Win" (Joe Williams commented, "Peggy Lee certainly did a better job on it than we [Basie and I] did"), "The Comeback," "You Don't Know," "See See Rider," and her income-earning demiblueses, "Fever" and "I'm a Woman." She's also made a specialty out of poetry recitations, as far back as a 1952 broadcast on which she used Yeats to introduce "These Foolish Things" to the early seventies when a part-spoken, part-sung, and part-droned piece of bargain basement Brecht called "Is That All There Is?" became her last major hit. She also took a hack at sixties modality for one song, an inspired reading of "Whisper Not" on the Benny Carter–produced *Mink Jazz*.

Furthermore, if Sinatra's adherence to the mainstream of the American pop tradition sounded the death knell for such frivolity as exotica, Lee has made it a staple of her act. After her first really big hit, the condescending "Mañana" (which convinced her to get back into show business full-time), and the mock-Italo-American "Who's Gonna Pay the Check?," Lee's Latin leanings have climaxed in her series of all mildly Latinized standard sets *Latin à la Lee, Olé à la Lee*, et al. If you were a Peggy Lee fan in 1955 you probably thought that she'd gotten as far away from Tin Pan Alley as she possibly could with *Sea Shells*, where she not only leaves behind show and movie tunes but the entire Western tradition to recite translations of Chinese poetry, but in the mid-eighties she went even farther when she performed Japanese material *in Japanese*.

All these extensions might be seen as compensation for her basically limited vocal vocabulary. Since she can do so little with her voice, you might think she wants to make up for it with interesting material and an original presentation. But in the forties, before Peggy Lee was really Peggy Lee, she used a more centered, heavier, and generally conventional kind of sound that she probably could have continued with; her decision to narrow her range and all but eliminate the middle of her voice to concentrate on the mist around its edges parallels Count Basie's paring down of his two-handed stride technique to just an incredibly appropriate "splank" now and then. Like Basie, Lee has almost no discernible technique, and when you compare her to vocalists who have so much technique that they can use it as a way of shielding what they really feel from their audiences (Streisand), even if you don't feel like reiterating the old truism that "less is more," you've got to admit that just enough is just right.

Sinatra has the choice between holding notes longer on ballads and making them shorter and faster on up-tempo performances. Lee has far less vocal equipment and instead had to develop a ballad style based on notes that aren't necessarily any longer than the ones she uses on swingers. So, if her options as to what she can do with the notes themselves are limited, she concentrates more on the spaces between them. Even when she holds a note beyond a beat or two, as on "My" at the end of the later Capitol version of "My Old Flame," she has no desire to sustain the pitch, and instead lets it rise or fall chromatically.

As an addition to the "dance band with strings" format that Sinatra has used as his basic accompaniment (he once said that he would never have left Harry James for Tommy Dorsey if Dorsey hadn't recently added a string section to his band), Lee's backing usually consists of a rhythm orchestra. She starts with the basic bop-era rhythm trio of piano, bass, and drums, and then adds guitar, vibes, Latin percussion, harp, and/or sometimes celesta, a setup she uses as either an alternative or adjunct to the backup bands in studios or bigger clubs where she sings (at Basin Street East, in one of the major gigs in her career, Neil Hefti backed her up with a ten-piece unit that included five brass, two pianos, and no reeds). You can hear this instrumentation most clearly on about half of *Dream Street* (1956, Decca) and also how she sings *over, ahead of,* or *behind* the beat, like Sinatra or Tony Bennett, as opposed to *on top of* it like Cole or Torme.

But Lee goes even farther away from it than anyone else; in

fact, her way of doing things has incredibly little to do with anyone else's—another reason I get so burned up when hack reviewers dismiss Lee as a white Holiday. Her use of counter-swing contributes to the general ellipticism of her singing, the knack for going in directions just slightly to the left of where the listener predicts she'll wind up. Lee differs from most other singers the same way Coleman Hawkins shapes his lines a drop more elliptically than Ben Webster, or the way Benny Carter differs from Johnny Hodges. I don't necessarily mean that Carter is *better* than Hodges, but in Lee's case it gives her a distinct advantage over the competition. She didn't always sing like this; in the forties, when she had a fuller voice, the way she phrased and paraphrased couldn't be distinguished all that easily from any other singer. One of the most rewarding aspects of eighties Lee, on the other hand, is her almost complete immersion into this kind of imaginatively offbeat approach to melody.

Even after Lee perfected this approach in the fifties she couldn't always stick to it. You get the impression that her producers and sometimes arrangers tried too often to take the choice away from her. No performance better illustrates the difference between Lee with her hands tied and Lee unbound than "Pass Me By." Cy Coleman had written it as a march-time follow-up to "Hey, Look Me Over," and, sung as originally written, a drab affair indeed. Even Lee's record has nothing to recommend it until the second chorus, when the tempo changes from 6/8 to 4/4 and all heck breaks loose. The number thereupon becomes as exciting as ten bars ago it was dreary.

Her two collaborations with Nelson Riddle, the upbeat *Jump for Joy* and the ballad collection *The Man I Love* (arranged by Riddle with orchestra directed by Frank Sinatra, his most notable conducting of another vocalist), made the same point in a different way. Lee made them after returning to Capitol following a few seasons away from her home-base label at Decca, a sojourn that had brought her a few more hits and served the same function as John Coltrane's brief departure from the Miles Davis Quartet in the mid-fifties to work with Thelonious Monk.

Upon returning, it seems as if arranger Riddle and conductor Sinatra, now the biggest attraction Capitol had, sought to teach her a lesson as to what the label expects from its prodigal. All through both albums you get the idea that another's sense of order is being imposed on Lee: Her lines are terser, less meandering, more centered, and a lot less Lee-like. *Jump for Joy* actually sounds less like one of Riddle's albums for Cole, Fitzgerald, or FS than one of his instrumental works (*Joy of Living* especially) with Lee's voice annexed; *Man I Love* could be a dry run for future Sinatra-Riddle ballad albums, "My Heart Stood Still" directly prefiguring *The Concert Sinatra*. The two Lee-Riddle albums also drive home the point that where Sinatra is an actor as much on a recording as on a picture and works best with a director—be he musical or visual—Lee loses interest when she subjugates her vision to someone else; her conductors do best when they execute or supplement her ideas. Lee has got to be her own auteur.

You can find examples of Lee coming off beautifully in conventional contexts. *Man I Love* contains the single most moving "Folks Who Live on the Hill" anyone ever heard, while on the essential *Black Coffee* she sticks with the classic vocal jazz format, voice with one horn (Pete Candoli working under the nom de plume "Cootie Chesterfield" and doubtlessly wearing a pair of Groucho-glasses besides) and three rhythms, though the near-blues "Gee Baby, Ain't I Good to You?" has her dropping the trumpet in favor of her familiar colleagues the guitar and vibes. On "Small Hotel" a triangle helps her keep the waltz time. The *Pete Kelly* album finds her in a traditional jazz setting and coming about as close as she ever would to Lee Wiley, while *Miss Wonderful* uses Sy Oliver's forties-style dance orchestra, and even here Lee is drawn to the unconventional. Long before *Miles Ahead* and the rediscovery of Gil Evans, Lee described him in *Downbeat* as "Another arranger I learned from. Not just musically, but in the man's thinking. That's a key, I believe, in all fields of art . . . a musician must start to *think* before he can become great." Accordingly, *Miss Wonderful* contains an Evansstyled "Where Flamingos Fly" waxed several weeks before Evans's first recording of the John Benson Brooks tune and four years before his superior remake (with Jimmy Knepper replacing Helen Merrill).

Lee also made beautiful music with some of the biz's heavyweight "name" arrangers. It's downright odd that Riddle should disappoint us in his writing for Lee, since the other two major Sinatra men, Jenkins and May, pass with flying colors. Jenkins had worked with Lee on her two most important Decca sides, therein revealing a hitherto unexplored fascination with exotic ethnicity: "Lover," which transformed Richard Rodgers's "Little Waltz" into an ecstatic polyrhythmic cacophony that started its staid stuffed shirt of a composer spinning in his grave even though he was still alive; and "I Hear the Music Now," the Jewish wedding song from the Danny Thomas remake of *The Jazz Singer*, which qualifies as the most gloriously schmaltzy piece of klez-pop ever shouted by a shiksa. May arranged the *Pretty Eyes* album for Lee, untypically string-heavy set but still excellent May, including a standout "You Fascinate Me So," with great sexy snake-lines for Lee to curl in and out of. Their greatest get-togethers came in the sixties on two May guest appearances on albums otherwise arranged by others, where May helps Lee fuse sixties trends with big-band swing, "The Girl from Ipanema" on *In the Name of Love* and "Call Me" on *Guitars à la Lee*. In both cases, Lee and May try to confine themselves to the "commercial" concept for a while, bossa nova on the first and watered-down R&B with too many electric guitars on the second, but soon capitulate to their own better judgment and atavistic inner urges. On "Call Me," especially, the difference between the wishy-washy soft rock in which the piece starts out and the high swing it modulates to is in itself invigorating; you can almost hear May shouting, "Screw the guitars! This clambake is going to swing!"

Partly through big triumphs and partly through "minor" albums that would be major events in anyone else's discography (most with lesser-known arrangers who could be trusted to place her style before theirs, like Jack Marshall on two minimarvels, *Things Are Swingin'* and *I Like Men*), Lee has kept a great deal of the massive audience she had in the fifties and sixties. She hasn't retained as much of it as Sinatra has, and hasn't had any hits since "Is That All There Is?," through which she might increase the number of attendees at her performances, but she can count on several weeks' worth of terrific business at practically any club in the world.

Still, her following in the eighties has the air of a cult; not that she builds her act around elements that only her faithful understand, as Nina Simone does, but in the way she presents herself: hiding her face and hair (covering them with a jeweled "helmet" and big shades), virtually hypnotizing one and all just in the way she shifts her weight—and those well-choreographed arm motions that one reviewer called a "hand ballet," keeping her audience guessing as to whether she's putting us on or not in her dizzy intertune spiels. It doesn't even hurt Lee's popularity that she hasn't made a really good record since the sixties.

Which only underscores the basic validity of the Swingin' Lovers style. Aesthetically, like any other kind of art, the genre is diminished by its lesser lights—and there are probably more bad Sinatra imitators further demeaning the already-shoddy "Feelings" at weddings and bar mitzvahs hither and yon than there are Mick Jagger or Elvis Presley clones in local bars—but redeemed by its nobility.

Box-office-wise, Sinatra and Lee still make sense, because they require comparatively little mental investment to be appreciated. The TV generation isn't willing to put any effort into appreciating art and can't be bothered to listen to scratchy old records to hear the great singers of the prewar period, or get past Louis Armstrong's gravel voice or to have explained to them what Eckstine is doing harmonically or unlock O'Day's method of improvising—in other words, to acquire acquired tastes. Sinatra and Lee happened to stay on top of the music world long after the appearance of Presley, Pat Boone, and the Beatles, and so, to millions of grown-up kids, they simply *are* adult pop. And much as I love Vaughan, Torme, Cole, Christy, Hartman, and Carter, perhaps that's as it should be. Because in the voluminous body of work that Sinatra and Lee are still creating, there's a kind of completeness, a kind of summation of everything that this music can be.

Singing Horns

Jack Teagarden to Chet Baker

"In New Orleans, all of us musicians could sing. It helped you to get a job if you could. Except the real good ones—take George Lewis, now he didn't have to sing."
—Percy Humphrey to Herb Friedwald, 1984

"Vocalizing gives me a break from having to blow my brains out all the time. It gives me a rest, and I'm entitled."
—Doc Cheatham to Francis Davis, 1987

"Have you ever heard someone who couldn't sing, but did something to you emotionally?"
—Ornette Coleman to Hank Bordowitz, 1987

Singing jazz musicians are—how you say?—*sympatico.* That's an Italian word whose English equivalent is, roughly, "sympathetic," though without the tinge of pitifulness that requires sympathy. Nonplaying singers also exploit their *sympatico* qualities; only a few—Sinatra, Lee—can afford to go above it, and even rarer is the Al Hibbler or Buddy Greco who can build a personality on being *antipatico,* which means what it sounds like. Singers like Tony Bennett who rely almost totally on their lovableness are far more common (though no one can match Bennett for sheer lovability).

Musicians who sing rely on the warmth, friendliness, and even cuddliness that they exude. They needed to in the taxi dance halls of New Orleans, in the novelty orchestras of the jazz age (Waring, Whiteman, Lopez), and later in the big swing bands, in the R&B-oriented jump groups of the forties, and even late into the modern era. You can almost take it as a fairly sure sign that a musician wants an audience when he starts singing, be it Archie Shepp or Benny Goodman. In their cases, and in a few others, sometimes it doesn't seem to matter if their singing is any good or not, we're supposed to appreciate the effort to reach us. At Barry Harris's Jazz Cultural Theatre one night when Jaki Byard's big band, the Apollo Stompers, was on the bill, Byard straight-facedly introduced his "boy singer—Billy *Sex*stine," who turned out to be Barry Harris himself, and then proceeded to sing a comic blues.

Many old-time jazz buffs claim that all horn players can also play piano and sing the blues, but just as Oscar Peterson supposedly criticized Charles Mingus's piano playing, we could probably find much to dislike in the work of most nonsinging singers—Peterson, for example, whose *With Respect to Nat* album (1965, Mercury) resulted in more of an insult than a tribute to King Cole, for the same reason that anyone who's ever taken a singing lesson resents the hell out of Bob Dorough for having the nerve to pass himself off as a vocalist. But sometimes we can also find something quite worthwhile in the singing of those whose training lies elsewhere. Ornette Coleman's ideas concerning another instrument also apply to the voice: "The thing that's amazing about saxophone music," he told John Zorn, "is that it's so hard to get away from the saxophone sound as your idea . . . every saxophone player [feels he has to] establish the fact that he's playing a saxophone." Some musician-singers work twice as hard to "establish the fact that" they're singing, as opposed to playing, and some don't. Many come to the "instrument" with a completely fresh, Ornette Coleman–like frame of mind, with no preconceptions of what a singer has to do. The music they make can be awful or it can be beautiful (rarely is it in between), and occasionally, it can result in something original and valid, whether by itself—like Lionel Hampton's "vibraphonic" piano style or Clark Terry's "Mumbles" routine (when they have the taste to restrict the use of these tricks to a few choruses)—or incorporated back into the mainstream, as in the case of Chet Baker's "soft" singing.

An examination of the hows and whys of jazz players who sing requires a broader look at exactly what we expect from them in general. To begin with, virtually all jazz musicians have incredible technique; you just can't get anywhere in this music unless you have some kind of virtuosity, whether you are lucky enough to be born with it or you achieve it—on at least one instrument, that is. Even if the Benny Carters, who exhibit equal fluency on both brass and reeds, are uncommon, most jazz musicians generally also play more than one horn, whether it's a saxist doubling on clarinet, a trombonist who can play valve or slide, or a trumpeter who'll switch to flügelhorn. And a great many can play the piano, too. Most jazzmen also write tunes—many no more than a new or renamed head for the blues perhaps—and quite a few arrange. A few also have talents for bandleading: putting together and conducting bands, coordinating tunes and charts, a talent not necessarily connected to their own abilities as players. And quite a lot of jazz musicians sing.

Still, in an art form given to doubling in all sorts of ways, its audiences never cease to be amazed that a given musician can do more than just play his instrument. To resist this notion, jazz listeners developed the idea that if so-and-so could do only one thing, he'd still be great. Sometimes they take it too far, like suggesting that if Benny Carter played only the alto sax he'd be better than he was and is, whereas Carter's career has proven that his greatest strength may well be his diversity. I think the most famous expression of the concept occurred in Patrick Scott's essay on Jack Teagarden. "Had he lost his lip twenty years ago," meaning his ability to play the trombone, Scott wrote in the liner notes to the *King of the Blues Trombone* set, "his voice alone would have ensured his greatness." Why can't we just accept that some men can do many things brilliantly rather than wondering how great they would be if they chose to concentrate on only one aspect of their talent? Perhaps something in the

American, especially twentieth-century American, mind-set embraces the idea of specialization too tightly. Certainly the musicians themselves don't encourage it. Jack Teagarden would never take good enough care of himself to outlive his ability to play the trombone. On Louis Armstrong's later albums, when he doesn't play trumpet, his singing sounds out-of-sorts, as if it's lost its purpose without a horn solo to keep it company. Thirty years ago, the followers of Al Cohn predicted the day when Cohn would grow too feeble to pick up his tenor and would settle down to writing and arranging; instead the opposite happened, and the sixty-two-year-old Cohn abandoned pen and paper to concentrate on blowing the horn.* And the only great jazz musician-singer who gave up his instrument (for health reasons) to sing, turns out to be Roy Eldridge, whose vocalizing was never a tenth as good as his playing.

Most singing horns fall into that pattern: We tolerate their singing only because they have already proven themselves on their instruments—we are aware of who they are. We have to put up with it more and more today, because the singing horn act makes for a surefire crowd pleaser, and in the eighties jazz has to constantly prove and reprove its ability to please crowds, and also because the surviving jazzmen of the forties and fifties (and occasionally earlier) are not young people today and they feel entitled to "take a rest," as Doc Cheatham says. With Cheatham as an example, the singing horn idea becomes the domain of the old-timers, the tried and the true who don't have to prove themselves anymore. Do Mulgrew Miller, Arthur Blythe, Bobby Watson, Tim Berne, or John Hicks ever get up there and sing? Is it only because they haven't become family favorites and earned the right to yet?

Louis Armstrong initially taught musicians both that they should sing and how they should sing, just as he had outlined the

---

* Buck Clayton has done it the other way around, having ceased trumpet playing to write.

basic principles of the jazz solo. Under Armstrong's spell, dozens and dozens of bandleaders all over the country and the world drafted sidemen from the ranks into doing Louis impressions, and dozens of players—especially trumpeters—studied Louis's vocal refrains as attentively as they did his solos. Though most of these men had little talent for singing, they provided a welcome alternative to the screechy vaudevillians who sang band vocals a few years earlier. By the start of the swing era, as we have seen, Armstrong and Crosby had become models for virtually all other male singers. Even before the end of the twenties, Armstrong had to contend with the singer-trumpeters thrown at him by other record companies looking for their own answer to Louis: Jabbo Smith on Vocalion, the nonsinging (pre-Louis) Johnny Dunn on Columbia, and Red Allen on Victor.

Allen and Smith in particular were around at a time when distinctly jazz small groups began to attract more and more attention in the music marketplace. Most bands big-time enough to record could afford at least one full-time vocalist, and even in the early years of the Crosby revolution, the results argue that they might have saved their money and made better music just by assigning the vocal refrain chorus to their trumpeters. The small bands of the thirties did this out of necessity, and so much of the best musician-singing can be found there, not so much in the satellite units of Goodman, Ellington, or Shaw, for example, but in recording or performing groups that owed no allegiance to any particular big band. I've already mentioned the series of sessions led by singers—Holiday, Bailey, Bullock, Robertson— the ones referred to here had player-singers for leaders and stars: Fats Waller, if not the founder then the most visible figure in the genre; Allen; Jabbo; Hot Lips Page; Wingy Manone; Frankie Trumbauer; Louis Prima; Lionel Hampton (who had no particular affinity for singing, but did so, I suspect, because it was expected of him as the leader of the session!); Johnny Davis; Emmett Matthews . . . even Louis Jordan's prototypical rhythm-and-blues organization, the Tympany Five, started life as one of these bands. Of the major singing musicians of the era, only Armstrong and Teagarden did their best work outside this format, and they, too, used it occasionally.

These groups occupy a unique place in the story of American music in being commercial pop and uncompromised art music at the same time, with neither faction detracting from the other. The music generally had a rough, polyphonic texture, and soloists could stretch out far longer than they could in big bands; the only concessions they made were ones that ultimately benefited the music itself: They had to play pop tunes and they had to play them in dance tempos. And quite often, though not every time, they had to squeeze in one chorus of vocal refrain amid the instrumental solos.

A few such groups, like Waller's Rhythm and Allen's orchestra, already had been making noise in the jukebox industry at the time Benny Goodman put big-band swing on the map. In fact, when Goodman broke into the movies, Warner Bros. tried to annex one of these men, Johnny "Scat" Davis (whom Goodman had already played with as a sideman),* to BG's band, much to the leader's chagrin.

Armstrong, in both his playing and singing, revealed a strong comic side as well as a gift for expressing the darker human emotions, and, importantly, both of these ways of looking at life came through in his vocals on both standards and blues-derived material. As with Crosby's imitators, the post-Armstrong vocal/instrumentalists don't display such three-dimensionality. Of the two greatest that followed him, Jack Teagarden and Fats Waller, Teagarden refined his art until he became one of the greatest blues singers that ever lived, and though he certainly had a sense of humor, comedy numbers (especially the novelties he sang in his big-band days) never suited him very well. Waller, on the other hand, immersed himself deeper and deeper in show business and grew into the funniest man in all jazz—Dizzy

---

* Or did he? Some discographers say he did, some insist he didn't. In any case, Davis cut his best pseudo–Pops vocals with Waring's Pennsylvanians.

Gillespie claims even funnier than Pops—but never let his serious side show.

None of Armstrong's trumpet-playing protégés quite reached their level; concentrating on one particular aspect of what Armstrong could do did not guarantee musical greatness. Jabbo Smith improvised scat vocal choruses à la Louis on the early Hot Fives; Red Allen had a fierce blues singing technique that came to the fore in the fifties and sixties when his slightly hostile attitude provided relief from the usual teddy bear–like musician/ singer; Hot Lips Page proved himself only second to Teagarden in his command of the blues, which he could intone with originality and humor; and most of Armstrong's white followers concentrated on comedy, each quite successfully: Wingy Manone, Louis Prima, Nat Gonella, and Scat Davis.

Jack Teagarden had a very limited range of notes he could hit but, as a vocalist almost as much as a trombonist, built what would have been a flat monotone in anyone else's hands into a virtually unlimited range of possibilities of expression. Teagarden also enjoys the distinction of having the only voice in jazz virtually identical to the sound of his instrument; sometimes I think he must have mapped out his throat into slide positions. Normally a pointless exercise and the musical equivalent of grooming your dog to look like you (and something few player-singers bothered with after Armstrong made "Confessin' " and "Sweethearts on Parade"), Teagarden nevertheless made it work in his favor, and it never bothered anyone that on a casual listen they couldn't really tell where his playing ended and his singing began. Unlike most horn players who take up singing, Big T didn't make himself cuter and cuddlier as he got older; instead he got his cute phase out of his system while still a very young man in the Ben Pollack Orchestra.

During his earliest glory years when he was the hottest trombone in town, Teagarden reworked material out of the jazz tradition through a series of very effective combinations of special vocal-and-trombone arrangements. In his definitive treatments of Spencer Williams's "Basin Street" and Handy's "Beale Street" blues, he strips off their pop-song veneers to find the folk-blues inspirations of each; on the first, Teagarden sings a phrase Rushing and Basie would later call "Goin' to Chicago" rather than the more familiar lyric Tea (not to mention Bing Crosby, Connee Boswell, Al Bowlly, Dinah Shore . . .) sang later which describes that infamous street where the dark and the light folks (later the elite) meet to eat food. Even better is "Sheik of Araby," where Teagarden uses an ingenious introductory vocal refrain to get the audience ready for an even better trombone solo. During his Whiteman tenure (1934–39), "The King of Jazz" featured him on only a few records, but he frequently spotlighted Teagarden on the radio. The program's writers tried vainly to create a white Stepin Fetchit persona for him ("Here comes lazy Jackson Teagarden ambling up to the microphone . . .") as did a series of less formal small group dates of Whiteman sidemen, led nominally by Frank Trumbauer (a delightfully lumpy player-singer himself) but giving the lion's share of space to Teagarden's voice and horn. In 1934, Teagarden also recorded for the first time strictly as a singer, with "orchestral accompaniment" and the same kind of "straight" vocal arrangements Crosby or Connee Boswell might get, complete with verses and even a string or two.

It was all only a warm-up. Later Teagarden, say from after the collapse of his big band (1946) to his death (1964), is the stuff you gotta watch. All of the qualities to admire in his early singing come to the fore, while anything you might not like about his voice withers and disappears. That woody, slight Texas drawl has aged and eroded beautifully, like good whiskey—in fact, *by* whiskey, oceans of it, both bad and good.* You might, at times, feel that the texture and sound of thirties bands suits him better than that of the fifties, especially as they had perfected elevator music by this time—as some of the men who arranged Teagar-

---

* Jazz buff Gus Kuhlman once spent a night at a New Jersey club with Teagarden when the trombonist was trying to get on the wagon and didn't touch a drop all night. I treasure this story because it's the only time I ever heard of Teagarden *not* drinking.

den's later records seemed bent on proving. But at least one album, *Think Well of Me* (1962, Verve), teamed Teagarden with a pair of writers who really knew where he was at: Russ Case, who had long admired Teagarden and used him on some of his dance records for Victor years earlier (letting him solo on "The Night Is Young and You're So Beautiful"); and Bob Brookmeyer, whose understanding of Teagarden can be summed up by the simple statement that he was a trombonist himself when not arranging. And just as Jimmy Owens said that "No one who played trumpet ever thought Louis was an Uncle Tom," anyone who ever played the trombone had to appreciate Teagarden. *Think Well of Me* would be a worthwhile record even if it were Teagarden rehashing "Basin Street" for the nine hundredth time (which he did beautifully on his previous Verve album, *Mis'ry and the Blues*), but this is an album of songs by Willard Robison, whose understated, bucolic tone poems so uniquely suit Teagarden's singing and playing that the finished disc ranks with any of the masterpiece albums made in the first decade of the LP.

Hot Lips Page's most famous record, "Uncle Sam Blues" (recorded during the draft in 1944), includes the line: "Uncle Sam ain't no woman, but he sure can take your man."* Though we're concentrating on Lips's talent as a singer rather than as songwriter (or trumpeter), the line exemplifies the strain of humor running through Page's work. That Page worked with one of Count Basie's earliest bands makes a difference, because as a blues-based singer with equal capacity for comedy and tragedy, Page takes a backseat only to Basie's blues giants Jimmy Rushing and Joe Williams. Even today, musicians sing the blues almost exclusively for comic purposes. Clara Smith or T-Bone Walker may be free to express the invective and the hostility inherent in the blues, but jazz musicians who make a specialty of the blues rarely show enough faith in their vocal abilities to trust listeners

---

* If it seems unpatriotic to suggest that women, "wringin' their hands and cryin' " should view the army as they would another woman, Page compensates by detailing how our boys have got "Fritz and Tojo all in a jam" and closing his trumpet solo with a respectful quote from the military theme "Reveille."

to regard their singing as anything but a joke. Page never played it cute; his voice was the equal of any full-time blues singer, and had he lived long enough to trade in his trumpet for an electric guitar (which would have been a shame), he would surely have become a celebrity on the blues circuit that has basked in reflected glory from the rock phenomenon. One serious drawback, however, does deter our enjoyment of Page's music: the scarcity of it. Where we have almost as much Armstrong and Teagarden as we can use, Page recorded so sporadically in his brief life that his performances are at a serious premium.

You might think that Manone, Prima, Gonella, or Davis would object to being labeled "white Armstrong imitators," but actually they'd probably take greater offense at the Jim Crow grouping of them in the "white" category than they would deny their adoration of Louis Armstrong—none more so than Gonella, who referred to Pops as his "inspiration" and "guiding star." (Tony Pastor called him "My idol, Louis Armstrong. Is there anybody better than that?") Prima and Manone had New Orleans in common with Armstrong and the same singing musician tradition of which he considered himself a part. Gonella and Prima reinterpreted Armstrong through their ethnic backgrounds: Prima's Neapolitan-American; Gonella's London cockney.

Through his gravelly lisp and cockeyed embouchure, Gonella captures the very serious, ascetic Armstrong of the early thirties, the Louis we know from "I Cover the Waterfront" as opposed to the sillier, more primal Louis of "The Lonesome Road." Gonella, a contemporary of Al Bowlly,* first served as a sideman with several major British dance bands before inaugurating a hot sort-of-small group nearly as successful musically as the better-known Quintet of the Hot Club of France (like the Hot Club, Nat Gonella and his Georgians played semiarranged charts at least as skillfully assembled as those written for Armstrong's thirties big bands). Gonella was also the first non-American to display a

---

* If I wanted to confuse you, I could say that Gonella played Armstrong to Bowlly's Bing Crosby, much as Prima did for Armstrong what Dean Martin did for Crosby.

genuine gift for the blues in his playing and singing. Valaida Snow, the other important trumpeter-singer working in thirties Britain, also mimicked Armstrong but hardly matched Gonella's talent on either instrument, and at times her biography (not just her being a black female trumpet player in the thirties, but her becoming a star in Europe and subsequent internment in a Nazi concentration camp) has threatened to attract more attention than her music. But by performing like Armstrong reincarnated in the body and voice of Adelaide Hall (according to Rosetta Reitz, they called Valaida "Little Louis" in Europe), Valaida broke down traditional notions of what male instrumentalists and female canaries are supposed to do over the course of several dozen very exciting records made with the cream of English and Scandinavian musicians.

Louis Prima had the most exclusively humorous slant of all trumpeters. By the time he made it to Las Vegas especially, he had worked out the details on a performance method completely devoted to breaking people up, as funny in its own way as Victor Borge or Spike Jones. Prima brought to banal novelties the same dedication of purpose that Toscanini brought to Verdi or that Leonard Bernstein brought to the Broadway musical, and "Hitsum Kitsum Bumpity Itsum" means just as much to Prima as "Body and Soul" does to Coleman Hawkins. His wonderfully flaunted irreverence, as when he "outlines" (feeds the lyrics of) the Neapolitan pop song "Oh, Marie" ("Maria Mari") in *Italian* for a chorus of Mitch Miller–inspired WASPs, has such an absolute purity to it that it becomes incredibly reverent.

It's got to be more than coincidence that the name Prima sounds so much like the word "primate," and that Prima's Vegas act was so wild he could easily have been confused with a gorilla: In fact, he supplied the voice for a cartoon ape in Walt Disney's *The Jungle Book*. Fats Waller also had all the physical accoutrements of a great funnyman: a comic bulbous body, flabby fingers that resembled bananas, big eyes designed expressly for rolling, and a grinning froglike face—when the Hollywood cartoonmakers caricatured Waller as a frog, they barely had to alter his physiognomy. Waller could be as tragic and mournful as the occasion called for when he played the piano, but as a singer he went strictly for laughs. In his case it was fortunate that he had extremely little voice for singing in the traditional sense, because it forced him to develop a remarkable gift for dynamics— whispers and shouts arranged with a master musician's sense of organization and texture. What "serious" singer could alternate between different voices as he did, poking fun at crooning baritones one line and whining in falsetto the next, sending up rolling *r* balladeers of the Edwardian music hall or weeping in mock-hysterics (as on "Somebody Stole My Gal")? Even if Waller should get through as many as twenty-four bars of a song without nudging you in the ribs at least once, like on "Sweet Sue" (both 1935, Victor), he'll then stop and leer at you with the most appropriate little "ah-ha!" just to make sure sentiment has no chance of seeping in like gas under the door. Don't bother to ask if Waller had never played the piano could he still entertain us? Rather, even if Waller had never created a note of music he'd still be remembered as one of the great clowns of his epoch. "Oh, mercy! Sweet apples and pink buttermilk!"

Waller's success, like Armstrong's, inspired lots of would-be Wallers, each with their own versions of "his Rhythm," on other labels, the most prolific being the pianist Putney Dandridge and the nonplaying Bob Howard (real name: Howard Joyner). Whereas Waller recorded with his working band, men who more or less stayed in his Rhythm, content to support their leader rather than develop their own names as big-band stars, collector labels have reissued much of the output of Dandridge and Howard for just the opposite reason: Being recording-studio-only bands, they contain such name musicians as Roy Eldridge, Artie Shaw, Teddy Wilson, Benny Carter, and Bunny Berigan. Vocally, though, Emmett Matthews outclassed both men by a considerable distance. In the two sessions on which his reputation rests (as opposed to the dozens churned out by Dandridge and Howard), Matthews's singing and soprano sax solos receive backing by a band of Waller sidemen, and he does the same kind of wonderfully esoteric songs Waller did. Matthews sings like Waller with a lot more vocal muscle, applied beautifully, or sort of like Cab Calloway when he exhibits taste. Like Page, we could use more records by Emmett Matthews.

A few generations of lady pianists who doubled on voice also marched in Waller's broad path, ranging in quality from the charming and polished Rose Murphy to the off-putting and un-communicative Nina Simone, with Nellie Lutcher, Blossom Dearie, Dorothy Donegan, and Shirley Horn falling in between. Murphy, known as the "Chi-chi girl" for an endearing if over-used little phrase that she threw into almost all of her vocals, as in "I Can't Give You Anything but Love (Chi-Chi)," recorded dozens of bright and peppy routines from the forties to the early sixties, some of her best bits (like her reprisal of the Cats and the Fiddle's line "If you're not too big and fat to remember" in the "When I Grow Too Old to Dream") comparing favorably to the King Cole Trio. Though she offered girlish giggles in place of Waller's knee-slapping yoks, Murphy came about as close as one can to being a female Fats Waller.

I never found Blossom Dearie as imaginative or as easy to take as Murphy, but lots of other people do; she's consistently found audiences for her soft, biteless style of singing since she began recording in earnest in the mid-fifties (during an earlier incar-nation she hung out with the Gil Evans Birth-of-the-Cool cote-rie, sang on records with Lambert and Stewart and King Pleasure, and formed a brief partnership with Annie Ross). To-day she has a following substantial enough to support a success-ful all-Dearie record company, a level she shared until recently with Anita O'Day, Betty Carter, and virtually no one else ("suc-cessful" being the key word here). There's not an awful lot of dynamic variety to Dearie's singing; like Bobby Darin switching between fast and very fast, Dearie doesn't vary her approach much more than between soft and very soft, and at times she creates the kind of performance designed to be in the back-ground and talked over. But no one can say that her singing is not pleasant. Nellie Lutcher came on lots stronger with a heavier two-fisted playing and singing style, specializing in double-entendre blues ("My Man Stands Out") and rhythm specialties ("Hurry on Down"). Dorothy Donegan sings naughty blues tunes, too, in the same kind of rhyming-couplet recitative as any number of Manhattan *boîte* drag queens, her vocals being more or less an adjunct to her regular set of Erroll Garner imitations performed beneath a layer of Garner–Keith Jarrett–like moaning.

If Donegan only bluffs you, Shirley Horn delivers the real thing: both vocals and piano alike coming from the heart, neither with much virtuosity but with just enough technique to get her feelings across. Waller, Dearie, and Murphy get the most out of their limited voices, but only for comic purposes; Horn uses the same ideas to make a dramatic point. She also has lots of smarts, which comes through in her performance as well as her choice of material in albums such as *Garden of the Blues* (1984, Steeple-Chase), made up entirely of songs (and one song cycle/suite) by a composer named Curtis Lewis. Like an updated and more urbane Willard Robison (and at times the comic-strip poet Don Marquis), Lewis wrote tunes that parallel Horn herself, a little obvious and willing to sacrifice cleverness for emotion, but *real*—even when couched in the artificial patterns of blank verse—and at times, deeply stirring.

Singing post-Armstrong trumpets and post-Waller pianos tended to dominate in the swing-era small groups and "vocadance" records; the big bands used them and plenty of singing saxophone and trombone players as well. The singing saxist line begins in the late twenties with Frank Trumbauer, who later made a fine foil for Teagarden in that the low moo of his singing approximated that of his C-melody sax solos, though without their haunting beauty and architectural mastery. On one record, "Get Happy" (1930, Okeh), Trumbauer adds cornet and clarinet to the usual doubling of C-melody and alto plus vocal, and the five instruments sound so much alike that you have to put your ear way up close to the speaker to determine exactly which one he's playing at a given time.

Tony Pastor, a star of the first great Artie Shaw band, typified the swing-era singing sideman, as millions of jitterbugs who sang along with his "Indian Love Call" (the flipside of Shaw's biggest hit, "Begin the Beguine") will testify. "Tony had a kind of nice beat when he sang," Shaw recently told Pat Willard. "He came right out of Louis," Shaw added, and might well have pluralized the Louis since Pastor owes as much to Prima as to Armstrong. All three of them could effectively give a piece of ethnic material the Satchmo treatment, as Prima did to dozens of Neapolitan and pseudo-Neapolitan airs and Armstrong later did with the German "Faithful Hussar." Pastor Satchmo-ized the Russian number "Prosschai" (most famously in one of the Shaw band's movie shorts) and prolonged his vocal to engage in some interplay with leader Shaw's clarinet and shout, "Oh play it, Arthur!" To Shaw's credit, he rarely used the standard boy crooners of the era in his bands, perhaps realizing that there were too few Sinatras, Eckstines, and Comos around for him to bother (at least until the Mel Torme–Artie Shaw collaboration of 1946), and preferred instead to use classy dames (Helen Forrest, Lena Horne, Paula Kelly, etc.) for the ballads and singing horns like Pastor, Roy Eldridge, and the great Hot Lips Page for the rhythm pieces. But even when musicians sang ballads straight in these years, vis-à-vis Basie's Earl Warren and Lunceford's Willie Smith (both alto players), they didn't necessarily sound any hipper than the full-time band singers. And just the reverse, when Pastor formed his own band in the forties, his vocals, so terrific in Shaw's great 1939 band, now sounded leaden and corny.

Other leaders less arty than Shaw developed gimmicks for singing sidemen, which they used quite frequently. Take Tommy Dorsey and the "Marie"-routine: While the boy singer does the number almost obnoxiously straight, the rest of the band sings a countermelody around him, with lyrics comprised of the titles of other songs.* After "Marie" (1937, Victor)—which

---

* While it's pretty much accepted that Dorsey got this idea from the Sunset Royal Entertainers, a black band (and they picked it up from Don Redman), neither Dorsey himself, writing in *Metronome*, nor Carmen Mastren nor Jack Leonard (interviewed by Mort Goode) could agree on how: Some say Dorsey bought it, some say he swapped "eight arrangements for one of theirs." It seems fairly certain, in any case, that the Dorsey arrangers added the lead voice and the idea of the song-title background.

went "Oh Marie, 'tis true . . . Just breakin' for me . . . Girl of my dreams, I want you, I need you . . . Have a little faith in me . . . tra-la-la-la-la . . . here I go cryin' again . . .")—they reprised the idea as kind of a running gag in the story of the Dorsey band, as in "Who?" (1937), "Sweet Sue" (1938), "Yearning" (1938), "East of the Sun" (1940), and so on almost ad nauseam (to use Dorsey's own term) as when Duke Ellington guested on TD's radio show and the band went into a "Marie"-style version of "Solitude." Dorsey also continuously reprised the original hit "Marie" long after the irritating Jack Leonard had been replaced by that harbinger of the new, Frank Sinatra. Glenn Miller had a similar device he used and used and used, consisting of a brief patter chorus exchanged between Miller himself and his singing saxist, Tex Beneke, which would then lead up to Beneke's vocal refrain, as recorded on "When Paw Was Courtin' Maw" (the 1938 aircheck, issued by Victor), "The Lady's in Love with You," "I'm Sorry for Myself," and "The Little Man Who Wasn't There" (all 1939, Bluebird). By the time Miller recorded "Chattanooga Choo Choo" (1941), his biggest hit using the "Hi there, Tex!" bit, he had hired a more professional quintet, the Modernaires, to take over his role in the dialogue.

At least a few other horn players–cum–rhythm singers deserve mention. The Bob Crosby band, despite credible but hardly sensational vocalizing from the leader, used individual voices for the standard rhythm-and-blues numbers almost as creatively as Jimmie Lunceford used group voices to rework standards. The first genuinely "neoclassical" jazz group, they mutually advocated a reexamination of the root materials of jazz, and accordingly played a lot of blues, like Kokomo Arnold's "It Was Only a Dream" (1941, Decca, today the property of Lou Donaldson), sung by tenor soloist Eddie Miller, and Will Weldon's "I'm Gonna Move to the Outskirts of Town" (on a 1942 transcription issued by Hindsight), on which guitarist Nappy LaMare cleans the lyrics up for the white public. In this version, the protagonist complains that he and his missus never get any privacy; in the original, he wants to move to get the little woman away from the iceman and grocery boy who are constantly *shtupping* her.

And let us not overlook Ray Nance, the one-man floor show whom Duke Ellington gave ample opportunities to display his gifts as trumpeter, violinist, rhythm singer, and eccentric dancer; or Bunny Berigan, with Red Allen, the greatest trumpeter of the thirties, who turned a lot of folks both off and on with his clumsy though endearing vocal on "I Can't Get Started" (1937, Victor), his best-known record, but could actually do a fairly credible Leo Watson imitation on "Mama, I Wanna Make Rhythm" (1937, Victor). Or how about those two singing trombonists; Joe Harris, a poor man's Jack Teagarden (or rather a Goodman's—Benny, to be specific); and Ford Leary, who growled bearlike on "All Dark People Are Light on Their Feet" (by Rodgers and Hart, believe it or not) with Berigan's orchestra and "Swingin' on Nothin' " (the rhythm singer's national anthem, having been done by Ford Leary with Charlie Barnet, Sy Oliver with Tommy Dorsey, Eddie Miller with Bob Crosby and Louis Armstrong)?

Louis Jordan, whose star rose as that of the big bands fell, may have gone down in history as the prototypical R&B comedian-altoist, but he came out of the same singing sideman tradition and failed to entertain only when removed from the familiar setting of his Tympany Five. Transformed into a would-be usurper to King Cole's crown when Decca appropriated Nelson Riddle, one of Cole's chief arrangers, to write some Cole-style orchestral ballad charts for Jordan, the results do neither Riddle nor Jordan justice. Another small-band-leading comic, Slim Gaillard, extended Watsonian stream of consciousness scatting into suitelike works and also used his rather smooth and attractive voice to put over an unending cycle of self-composed novelties on the subject of junk food.

Just as Woody Herman's bands have stayed on top of every wave in jazz from Dixieland to "Giant Steps," Woody's singing encompassed all the fashions of singing musicians of the thirties, forties, and fifties. Notoriously generous for giving the plum tunes to his canaries (who came in second only to Kenton's, Frances Wayne and Mary Ann McCall being the two best), Herman reserves the "off" numbers for himself, and subjects his own voice to lots of dumb comedy songs that no one else wants. Herman mainly sings the blues and its variants: serious blues ("Blue Downstairs"), funny blues ("I've Got News for You"), fast blues ("Fan It"), slow blues ("Panacea"), jump blues ("Yeah, Man"), rhythm and blues ("Caldonia"), pseudo-religious blues ("Noah"), novelty blues ("It Must Be Jelly ['Cause Jam Don't Shake like That]"), and quasi-blues ("I Ain't Got Nothin' but the Blues" and "Blues in the Night"). Herman also specializes in exotica ("Pancho Maximillian Hernandez," "My Pal Gonzales," "Cowboy Rhumba," which he sang with Duke Ellington's Orchestra, and the calypso "Down the Wishing Road") and makes a harmonious and gleeful duet partner, having shared the mike with Bing Crosby, Peggy Lee, Billy Eckstine, Dinah Shore, and Nat Cole (their attack on "Mule Train" is a crack-up).

Herman only rarely treats himself to a first-rate solo ballad, though when he does the results justify his trying more. After his vocal on "Laura" went Gold for Columbia (Herman modestly attributes this to CBS's issuing his version over Harry James's instrumental record of the song),* they began to take him seriously as a vocalist and scheduled him for some sessions as soon as he could fit them in. As if to show how bandleading would always be Herman's first priority, they had to wait until one of his relatively inactive inter-Herd periods. He doesn't quite have the equipment for a full album of ballads, unfortunately, and his one entire album of *Songs for Tired Lovers* affects me like the good friend you invite for a visit who sticks around too long. Because you like Woody so much you don't want to tell him to keep quiet for a little while and let us hear more of his backup group, the Erroll Garner Trio. Here, where ballads are the rule

---

* According to No. 1 Herman-iac George Hall, James's had been done before the tune had lyrics and Herman cut his; Mercer had only just finished the lyrics and had to read them to Columbia over the telephone.

for a change, varying to the blues or exotica would have been a welcome respite.

In the days before his big instrumental hit, "Woodchopper's Ball" (1939, Decca), Herman had been best known as a singer: His voice carried him through his salad days as a child star in vaudeville and then as a sideman with several of the major white dance bands of the early thirties: Tom Gerun(ovitch), Harry Sosnick (before his days as a studio house bandleader), Gus Arnheim, and biggest of them all, Isham Jones. After he formed his own "Band That Plays the Blues" with the hottest of Jones's soloists, his vocals gave that first Herman orchestra virtually its only distinguishing characteristic on records sanctioned by Jack Kapp, who used Herman as a "B" band for tunes he couldn't get anyone else to cover. Beginning in 1939, Herman's vocal hits kept pace with his instrumental sellers and, to a certain extent, like Billy Eckstine, his singing supported his band. Still, Woody's vocals have greater validity than his denture commercials; that familiar screechy baritone of his, so like a Milwaukee Bugs Bunny, helps the band musically as much as it does commercially. You can only express one regret concerning Herman's singing in his last years: He didn't do it often enough.

All jazz musicians who sing have a certain brotherhood through common goals and shared ancestry, usually Louis Armstrong (even Herman tends to shape his lines along Armstrong's). They also have relatives: singing songwriters and tap dancers. Not all of them use jazz (and then, not all singing jazz musicians use jazz when they sing), but some use it brilliantly, with just as much to offer as singing musicians or singing singers. Jazz-oriented singing composers go back as far as J. Russell Robinson of the Original Dixieland Jazz Band (he didn't sing with the O.D.J.B. but made plenty of records later on as a vocalist), Clarence Williams, and Willard Robison, all songwriter-bandleaders who made piano-vocal records, like most in this genre, usually singing their own tunes. Robison and Williams might have been the same person from the nearly identical texture of their untrained voices, though Williams's semicomic blues songs depict the daily life of twenties Harlem, a world far removed from the pastoral preachers and country concerns of Robison.

For years and years, Hoagy Carmichael epitomized the American singing songwriter, drenched in rustic ardor and at the same time producing remarkably urbane melodies, brought down to earth via his own extremely limited abilities as a performer and with a down-home twang that made him so much more appealing to middle America than any of the Eastern "Broadway" crowd. Carmichael's music opened the door for him as a vocalist and rather than being ashamed of this he reveled in it, never passing up an opportunity to remind the folks back home that he had written "Star Dust" and "Rockin' Chair." He even made it to pictures, usually playing himself (in one case of poetic justice, in *Young Man with a Horn* playing a version of himself based on a character based on himself from a novel), and subsequently, because of his movie exposure, landed a radio series and a regular recording contract that called for him, almost alone among all songwriters, to do songs by other people—though there was nothing about his often flat voice that really qualified him to (and the songs Decca gave him were generally pretty awful). Carmichael had one great album in him: 1956's *Hoagy Sings Carmichael with the Pacific Jazzmen* (Pacific), in which one side of the Bix legacy, Hoagy, meets a later generation of post-Bix post-cool jazz giants.

Harold Arlen, less rural but no less vigorous, had stronger chops than Carmichael both as a pianist and singer, as he had earned his living as a band vocalist in the years before his music really caught on, as did Johnny Mercer. Mercer, the only member of the "And then I wrote" bunch who didn't need the protection of a piano when he got up in front of an audience, is also the only one who could have made it had he never written a single song, so catchy was his Southern accent and so sure was his command of the beat. As his own A&R man at his own label for a few years, he got to record as many songs of his own or anyone else's as he wanted, but apparently Capitol never forgave his abrupt departure and punished him—and us—by never bothering to reissue any but a pittance of his excellent forties vocal records. Fortunately, transcriptions and broadcasts have been commercially issued to show that Mercer deserves his reputation as one of the great rhythm singers of all time. In due course, Mercer inspired other songwriters to sing similarly, some who shouldn't have bothered (Bobby Troup) and some who should have (Matt Dennis).

Musical events in the post–Tin Pan Alley world have produced two generations of jazz-oriented performers who are neither singers nor songwriters but strictly singer-songwriter-pianists, a little of this and a little of that. The fifties belong to Joe Mooney (aka "Nerd King Cole")—who graduated from the Paul Whiteman and Sauter-Finegan orchestras to his own quartet, a superb vehicle for his charming songs, light engaging voice, and noncorny accordion playing, the latter characteristic being remarkable enough—and to Mal Fitch—the Joe Mooney of the piano, who perfected what collectors call "stop singing," because his voice didn't have enough power to sustain a note for any but the briefest of durations, so Fitch had to constantly "stop." In the last two decades, Dave Frishberg has become jazz's definitive singer-songwriter-pianist, and his strengths and weaknesses typify the genre: Though he doesn't have Carmichael's gift for really great melodies, and his lyrics, while funny, don't compare with Mercer's (and unlike Mercer, his singing isn't strong enough to fill an album), his piano playing could (and did) stand on its own—but that isn't the point. What matters is that Frishberg puts it all together into a very entertaining package, which works as a whole partially because none of the individual elements *have* to stand on their own.

Succeeding singer-songwriters can be viewed as a gradual process of subtraction. Take a little talent away from Frishberg and you have Jay Leonhart, one of the great bassists of the eighties, whose comic songs should not be heard more than one or two in a row. Take something away from Leonhart and you get Bob Dorough, who at his worst falls into the Babs Gonzales trap—that is, playing, singing, and writing as an excuse to hang around and do drugs with musicians—and even at his best has charm that he hasn't used yet (why, I don't know) and makes you wonder why, when given the chance to reach the multitudes who buy Miles Davis records, he comes up with a piece of knee-jerk political twaddle like "Blue Christmas" and promptly eliminates any reason someone might have to want to hear him. Take a little away from Dorough and add a little attempt at blues feeling, copied from Percy Mayfield and inauthentic as the day is long, and you have Mose Allison. Take a little away from Mose Allison, go in the direction of comedy numbers that are unfunny on a grand scale, and you get Michael Franks. Take some charm away from him, until you have practically nothing left, and you get Ben Sidran, a very talented jazz broadcast producer who has also found an audience as a performer. You then find you can't take anything more away, though I don't doubt that someone will figure out a way.

Black entertainers had been making records since Bert Williams committed his musical monologues to shellac in the teens. Tap dancers did most of the good jazz-oriented singing, beginning with the great Bill "Bojangles" Robinson, who, on his first record, a thoughtfully paraphrased "Ain't Misbehavin' " (1929, Brunswick) that must have delighted his friend Fats Waller, defined the percussive style of singing, where syllables equal taps, that he passed on to most of the great black hoofers. John W. Bubbles, the original Sportin' Life in *Porgy and Bess* and at one point part of the fine team of Buck (song) and Bubbles (dance), continued the vocal-pedal partnership by dancing on sand and singing with a voice every bit as smooth as No. 12 sandpaper.

Perhaps the greatest flash act of all time, the Nicholas Brothers were polished and exciting singer-dancers even when they were six years old, like pint-sized Cab Calloways with a stronger, more convincing and probably pedal-derived sense of syncopation. Because of the aural nature of their footwork as well as the snappy singing that went with it, of all the famous dance acts of the thirties only the tappers got recorded, and even then record producers had questions about putting taps on wax. The Nicholases circumnavigate these reservations beautifully on their English recording of "Keep a Twinkle in Your Eye" (1936, HMV) by having brother Fayard make like Ted Lewis while brother Harold goes into his dance. For sixteen bars, Harold taps and Fayard informs the listeners, "He's my brother, folks, that's my brother." Then, after altoist Freddy Gardner improvises beautifully on the bridge and Harold reenters, tapping, Fayard informs us, "He's back again, ah, he's back again." The team worked in Hollywood movies and Vegas casinos for years and years, and these days Harold (the younger) plays the clubs almost strictly as a singer, the last chance we have to hear anyone using the thirties method of syncopated singing that disappeared in the wake of Sinatra.

The greatest singer-dancer of them all had nothing to do with Harlem; in fact, Fred Astaire's world of top hat and tails, Broadway revues, and Hollywood musicals seems so far removed from the mainstream of jazz culture that one wonders how he could understand it so well. Certainly none of the other major white dancers—Gene Kelly, Eleanor Powell, Dan Dailey—sang so well or with so much jazz feeling, yet all had the same basic tools as Astaire, a limited range and a pleasant though unspectacular voice. To appreciate Astaire's singing, get inside his head and try to imagine what might be going through it. Because he hasn't the technique to do whatever a trained singer might be able to do with his or her voice, Astaire is limited as to the kind of decisions he can make. Yet he inevitably decides in favor of what works for jazz: making a line go in a certain direction or to emphasize a pulse in a particular way that contributes to the syncopation or the swing of the phrase. Even the simple fact of his thinking in terms of phrases, groups of notes brought together in a way that may or may not match the way the composer chose to organize them, shows that Astaire is at heart a jazz artist. Even before it was customary to admit that whites had anything to learn from blacks, Astaire paid tribute to Robinson with his "Bojangles of Harlem" number in *Swingtime,* which succeeds as homage despite the potentially condescending minstrel-show milieu Astaire performs it in. Astaire recorded with the jazz-oriented bands of Benny Goodman and Bob Crosby and, as Stanley Green tells it, only consented to make the disastrous movie *Second Chorus* (which he later cited as the worst he ever made) so he could appear with Artie Shaw; later, he would bring Jonah Jones and Count Basie on his television specials.

He finally consummated his love affair with jazz in 1952 with *The Astaire Story,* in which producer Norman Granz backed him up with a Jazz at the Philharmonic sextet to rerecord a more than representative sample of the great standards he'd introduced in his career. Even on his earlier recordings, made with more "commercial" dance orchestras like Leo Reisman's or Harry Sosnick's, Astaire sounded great, and part of what makes *The Astaire Story* so special is that he doesn't necessarily "open up" any more because of the JATP accompaniment. He doesn't try to scat (he does hum exquisitely over Oscar Peterson's piano solo on "Lovely to Look At," though) or "sing like a horn" or any of the other things hack reviewers think "jazz singers" are supposed to do. Astaire just does what he usually does: sensitively interpret great songs through a dancer's sense of rhythmic style, with jazz backing—and it works like a charm. Astaire's singing, no less than his dancing, signifies one of the high points of American culture—a dancing man who left his footsteps on the sands of rhythm and time.

But nothing in the worlds of singing horn players, piano-singers, singing songwriters, or song-and-dance men could prepare the world for Chet Baker, who was, in his own quiet way, to have the last word. Singing horns appeared less and less in the modern age, though they never disappeared; in fact, it's been argued that if there had been more like Dizzy Gillespie, James Moody, or Lou Donaldson, all great modern musicians and great entertainers who encompass singing in their acts (Milt Jackson and Gerry Mulligan have also sung on records, but a more tactful writer would overlook this), modern jazz might have had a better chance of keeping its audiences.*

"My Funny Valentine" functions as a recurring motif in the relationship of jazz and popular music in the fifties: It was the number most of the cognoscenti felt—even thirty years ago— was the most overused, as June Christy wisecracked; it was the tune mentioned when the phone company stamped Miles Davis as a recognizable name (and make-out music maker) when they dropped said name in one of their ads; and it was the tune that made a celebrity out of Chet Baker, a star in the big world even before hardly anyone in the little world of jazz had heard of him. Baker recorded it three times in the years of his ascent, first with the Gerry Mulligan Quartet for Fantasy in 1952, then live in 1953 at the Haig with Mulligan, and lastly, and vocally, with the first of his own quartets in early 1954. The two instrumental Mulligan recordings take the same shape as the vocal version, with Baker exposing the melody at dirge tempo (the inherently light quality of the pianoless quartet keeps it from getting too heavy). He embellishes the tune on both trumpet solos, and briefly improvises on the live version (the 1953 one), but we focus on Baker's treatment of the melody itself, stated as simply and directly as he can. Once we have the tune and tempo in our heads, we can pretty much figure out where he's going to go, and his improvisations don't make a point of leading into unpredictable directions. Baker operates like one of Antonelli's or Kuleshov's actors in that he is typecast, put into a given situation not because of what he can do but who he is.

And who is he? Baker is the original sweet comic valentine that Larry Hart described, the naïf to whom everything happens, and the romantic bumbler who begrudgingly guesses he'll have to change his plan. He's never had the kind of talent that translates into virtuosity of any kind, but he has all he needs: the

---

* I disagree, because neither big bands, Louis Jordan–era R&B groups, nor singers held out against the rock inundation. For that matter, the Art Ensemble of Chicago boasts as much psychedelic paraphernalia as any heavy metal band.

basic vocabulary of chord changes, a few handed-down phrases for his trumpet, and the skill to hit about seven or eight notes with his voice, ranging from a little bit under "stands" on the bridge of "I'm Old-Fashioned" to almost as low as "gone" on "Travelin' Light." Many artists "make the most" of limited powers or work around or through their limitations, as Duke Ellington often stressed. Baker does neither: He communicates a wide range of feeling through such a narrow gateway (like trying to push tomatoes through a funnel), and expresses passion on a level that's profound both in and of itself and in the way that it is communicated. Profound in that Baker is strongest when he's weakest. Strong in that he has confidence to offer his real self, without defenses or barriers. The absence of recognizable technique doesn't necessarily account for this, just as Sarah Vaughan can use her mountains of chops to express her feelings and Barbra Streisand uses hers to cover them up.

The who-he-is also takes in the real-life Baker, a figure many find impossible to distinguish from Baker the performer, in fact, the worst case of an artist's life affecting the way his public perceives his music since Billie Holiday. To many people he was the James Dean of jazz, only that he had talent enough to justify the fascination people had for him, and not just good looks and an early death. To others he became the Bix Beiderbecke of the fifties, a comparison that works for me neither musically—like Bix he prides himself on pithy understatements, but where Beiderbecke works from a basis of harmonic and tonal mastery, Baker goes for a simpler and gutsier sound—nor personally—for as J. L. Collier perceives Beiderbecke's life, his short and tragic demise resulted from post-Victorian bourgeois WASP repressiveness, whereas the comedy that is Baker's life has roots in his complete lack of control. To some (Wim van Eyle for one), Baker's career works in cycles, in which high points alternate with nadirs; to me, Baker forever experiences climax and catastrophe at the same time—that is, the most successful European tour made by a jazz artist up till then interrupted by the death of the piano player from an overdose, or a four-star review of a new album running in the same magazine as a shot of the hand-cuffed Baker being dragged off to some Italian prison (he would never be State Department "Goodwill Ambassador" material). Neither triumph nor tragedy has been particularly good to Baker physically; as Alain Gerber has written, they have left him with "a smile which looks too much like an open wound," but his is the rare kind of art that feeds off both. Despite his spare machinery, he can transmit remarkably precise gradations of feeling. You keep wondering how Baker can possibly do so much with so little: On top of everything else, he also makes the most effective use of gender blur in all singing, as his unisexual tone conveys both yin and yang elements simultaneously as it does the good times and the bad.

Definitive Baker performances generally include both trumpet and vocals, though in the eighties Baker segregated the two. *Chet Baker Sings* (1954 and 1956, Pacific Jazz), the first album released of Baker vocals, contains the purest and most essential examples of Baker's art: Baker singing and playing (sometimes at the same time thanks to well-applied overdubbing) with a tight working trio, both star and sidemen committed to the absolute absence of wasted motion. Baker could win anyone over on "But Not for Me" and "That Old Feeling," wherein he prefaces his vocals of the choruses with an interpretation of the verses. Normally antisocial creatures never designed to swing, Baker puts them into tempo and makes them move. Later, Baker would make numerous strides both as an instrumentalist and singer but would never get it together as beautifully as he does on these fourteen tracks. On *Chet Baker Plays and Sings with Strings* (1955, Pacific) many of the selections come up to the level of the 1954 and 1956 tracks, though the strings now and then intimidate Baker to the point where he feels obliged to push his voice into directions it was not meant to go, fairly shouting on "I Remember You." *It Could Happen to You* (1958, Riverside) also hits the mark quite often, but Baker's attempts to scat as well as his New York unit's inability to match the cohesiveness of Baker's West Coast band bring the album down. *Baker's Holiday* finds Baker at peak level in homage to Billie Holiday's Decca period (and to Johnny Griffin's similar album, *White Gardenia*), but backing Baker with a forties-style reed section would be a one-shot idea. Even the postrecording tinkering with the original *Chet Baker Sings* perfectly matches the music by sticking Joe Pass's incredibly light acoustic rhythm guitar into the tiny ensemble and adding the most effective drop of warm reverb to beef up that scanty though endlessly appealing voice.

Baker served to climax and conclude the development of the singing jazz musician. Singing horns were strictly middle brow, and after the fifties jazz split into camps of both lower (fusion) and higher (avant-garde) social position, leaving Baker's generation as the last to have a direct connection with the public. In the fifties Baker touched off the last widespread vogue for singing musicians (which also included Don Elliott, the multi-instrumentalist whose singing conveyed an attempt to invent a white male Sarah Vaughan).

An anecdote from Billy Eckstine, which he offered upon spotting Dizzy Gillespie in his audience at New York's Blue Note one night two or three years back, underscores what is so remarkable about Chet Baker. Though singing had always been Eckstine's calling, he taught himself how to play valve trombone and trumpet during idle moments in his years on the road with Earl Hines. By the time he formed his own band, Eckstine had developed into a competent though hardly first-rank brass soloist. Long after his bandleading days he continued to produce his trumpet from time to time, on records and in his act; in the sixties he sometimes remarked upon such excursions with a line like, "Last time I looked Harry James's singing wasn't too good." In any event, at the Blue Note, Eckstine told of how for years he'd been pestering Gillespie for one of his special, custom-made trumpets with the upturned bell. When Dizzy finally relented, Eckstine tried the horn and was instantly disappointed that the instrument did not make him sound more like Gillespie. "I realized that Diz only gives these horns out to guys he doesn't worry about [outplaying him]," said Eckstine. "Next time I saw him I said, 'Now that you sent me the horn, when are you going to send me the lips to go with it?' " Eckstine didn't worry either; he might have heard Gillespie's record of "Something in Your Smile" (on *Swing Low, Sweet Cadillac* [1969, Impulse]), a mediocre Bricuse-Newley love song from *Dr. Doolittle* and virtually Gillespie's only "straight" vocal ballad rendition.

Examples of singers who have taught themselves to play (Maxine Sullivan on flügelhorn, Mel Torme on baritone ukelele) and players who *shouldn't* sing cram the annals of jazz: There's Zoot Sims, on *Tonight's Music Today* (1956, Storyville), seemingly determined to prove that not all jazz musicians can sing the blues; or Kenny Dorham, who made *This Is the Moment (Kenny Dorham Sings)* (1958, Riverside) for no apparent reason other than to make sure he'd have one really embarrassing record in his discography, as if he knew then that he was never to capitulate to what he would view as the fads of free-form, third stream, or fusion.

But the best singing musicians—Teagarden, Waller, Baker—possess an incredibly perceptive understanding of the nature of the relationship between the voice and other instruments in jazz: They both come from the same heart and the same mind; the trick is to figure which instruments you're best at—and overly specialized minds aside, you are allowed more than one. It's all a matter of talent and technique, regardless of whether you play or sing, or do both.

Revolt of the Philistines

Problems and Answers in the Sixties

"It's a shame that so many good records today of good old standard tunes done by really fine artists are bypassed for things like 'Sh'Boom.' I don't think it takes any talent at all to sing 'Sh'Boom,' but it takes talent to sing things by Cole Porter and Gershwin and Rodgers and Hart. The people today are on a different trend, and I guess there's nothing you can do but just bat your brains out. But I think any of us who delve into standards, or good original tunes, should stick by our guns."
—*Carmen McRae to Leonard Feather, 1955*

"In 1955 it changed. They started going for this obsolescence idea. They didn't want records that would last, they didn't want lasting artists, they wanted lots of [consecutive] artists. It became like a supermarket: Go with the next, the next. So they started discarding people like me and Duke Ellington and Leonard Bernstein. The marketing boys took over. It took a big walk away from melodic music. It suddenly became very professional to be unprofessional. Which was very neurotic."
—*Tony Bennett to Chet Flippo*

"The children of Israel are giving themselves over to the ways of their oppressors!"
—*Marc Connelly*, The Green Pastures

I don't like rock 'n' roll. To me it's all like the land somewhere east of Suez, "where the best is like the worst."* I say this

* For once the reference is to Rudyard Kipling, not Charlie Ventura.

at the beginning of this chapter to save the reader the trouble of inferring it. Not that this would prove all that difficult, for as far back as I bend over to avoid appearing reactionary, my prejudices in this area repeatedly insist on rearing their nappy heads.

Post–Andre Hodier and Martin Williams jazz criticism has focused on the idea that the history of jazz can be viewed as a continuum—that is, that the music of Jelly Roll Morton is essentially the same kind of music as that of Ornette Coleman, and that one kind of jazz is not any "truer" than any other kind. Some rock reviewers have more or less applied the same idea to pop music, a way of thinking that holds little water for me. Morton and Coleman, different as they may be, have far more common ground than, say, Nat Cole and Mick Jagger. If anything, the two musics only approach each other at their worst—or to be kinder, their most *extreme* points, say Al Jolson and Elvis Presley or Mitch Miller, inventor of the rock 'n' roll mentality, and Phil Spector.

The music businessman, as he had matured in the AFM and ASCAP wars of the forties, created the new pop of the fifties and sixties onward in response to demand, which he himself did much to create. For the first time, the taste of the average ten-year-old became the dominant factor in what everybody listened to—and had there been no ten-year-olds sired in the immediate aftermath of the war, there would never have been any "kiddie pop."

According to pop legend, the music supposedly begins with the observation by dj-superstar and purveyor of cultural genocide[*] Alan Freed that there was a small market for black R&B records among white kids. If this music could be simplified and reduced somewhat, Freed and his colleagues correctly theorized, and brought down to the level of a grade schooler, and then whitened through the use of Caucasian mimics to impersonate the black originals (who were largely unprotected by ASCAP or the AFM), the market would expand. Around the

* The term is Sidney Zion's.

same time, radio station owners were looking for something with which to fill their airtime, as the traditional staples of their programming deserted them left and right to go into the new medium of television. But though radio ceased to broadcast variety, dramatic, and comedy shows, it could still make hit records, providing some of its palms were stroked occasionally, that the hits required no mental effort on the part of the listener, and that the songs could be easily digested and even more easily mass-produced.

It seems that the decision to use R&B as a basis for this new commodity was an arbitrary one; the early rock producers could have just as easily picked on Hawaiians, Latins, or cowboys as they did Negroes. As a style, R&B, except at its greatest (say, Louis Jordan or Amos Milburn), rarely gets as musically interesting as even the average swing band, although its formulas were loose enough to accommodate a few broader talents, like Big Joe Turner, Gene Ammons, or Dinah Washington, just as the swing bands were able to showcase Lester Young and Charlie Christian. Still, big-band swing seems by far the more satisfying style, encompassing as it does everything from country and western (Bob Wills) to the blues (Count Basie, Woody Herman), even with its excesses—from the comedy bands of Kay Kayser or Tony Pastor to the avant-garde bands of Boyd Raeburn or Claude Thornhill. Chick Webb's great orchestra alone had even employed two of the founding fathers of other pop musics: rhythm and blues in Louis Jordan and Latin in Mario Bauza, not to mention Ella Fitzgerald. With the decline of the bands, music entered a period of segregation: Modern jazz went one way; country-western in another; comedy, waltzes, blues, and the others did the same. Bob Wills dropped his horns to begin a cowboy combo; Dizzy Gillespie's rhythm section left behind reeds and brass to become the Modern Jazz Quartet; Haymes, Sinatra, Lee, Eckstine, O'Day, and any other vocalist worth his or her salt got booked as singles; and all the categories that had previously been played by the big dance bands went off in their own directions.

As dance music with a great sense of humor, rhythm and

blues assumed several of the roles of big-band swing but far from all, leaving behind the big-band gift for adapting the great songs of the era as well as vocal and instrumental virtuosity on any kind of musical form other than the blues. Considering that the father of modern R&B, Louis Jordan, first established himself as a big-band sideman, and that his Tympany Five was only one of many small swing groups with a singing horn player for a leader when it began, it's possible to see R&B in some ways as a reduction of swing. But rather than expanding this style when they decided to use it as a basis for a whole new kind of pop music, the movers and shakers of early rock reduced it even further, limiting its range of possibilities until there was virtually no margin for individuality. Anyone who thinks rock is fundamentally the same music as R&B should compare Joe Turner's Atlantic singles in the early and late fifties: The loose free-swinging sound of "Oke-She-Moke-She-Pop" (1953) sounds positively avant-garde compared to the mechanical doo-wop of "Teenage Letter" (1957). Or contrast Dinah Washington's "Big Long Sliding Thing" with any of her later execrable exercises with the talentless Belford Hendricks and Brook Benton. All of which suited the "marketing boys" fine as creativity traditionally had a bad track record when it came to the ledger sheet.

What happened supports the argument that Luis Buñuel made in *The Phantom of Liberty*, that man will always choose chains over freedom, that he wants to have his decisions made for him by others. This became doubly clear by the mid-sixties, when the public bought so darn many Beatles records that they effectively trumpeted that they weren't interested in anyone else. Instead of twenty artists selling, say, a million records each, from the sixties on it became a matter of a single artist selling 20 million records while the other nineteen went unrecorded or got dumped into the cutout bins. It wasn't just rock style specifically. The same thing happened in the movie business with a most unrocky venture called *The Sound of Music* (reiterated years later with *Star Wars*), a single picture that generated the equivalent of what the entire industry was supposed to gross. And the results of thirty-five years of mass media without alternatives tell today more than ever, with kiddie pop still accounting for something like 90 percent of all record sales while jazz (instrumental and vocal), adult pop, and the entire European classical tradition divvy up the leftovers.

Given this attitude it seems impossible that even the established stars of jazz singing and adult pop have been able to stay in business, much less triumph market-wise and even advance their art, as Sinatra, Torme, Vaughan, Lee, Joe Williams, and others have done. It's even more remarkable that a few new stars, without the visible starting point of big bands or a battery of talent set up to help them (arrangers, songwriters), have managed to establish meaningful careers, as Tony Bennett and Carmen McRae have done.

No one has fought the philistines longer, harder, or more successfully than Tony Bennett. He was and is the perfect gladiator for adult pop to send out to fight the barbarians who were even then gathering at the gates. First, Bennett made a ceaseless apostle for "the tradition," never missing an opportunity to wave the flag for hard-core jazz, from Louis Armstrong to Miles Davis, on the one hand, and the Broadway showbiz world of Merman, Garland, and Durante on the other, with the jazz-pop faction of big bands and their singers running down the middle, all interacting in Bennett's own music. Second, Bennett had credibility with the kids: Though the endless spieling that the Columbia publicity division did about Bennett's youth following in the fifties may have been pure PR bs (grown-ups in age and mind-set have always comprised the bulk of Bennett's audiences), he had dished out enough singles with a kiddie-pop doo-wop slant so that his name meant something to the teenyboppers who were taking over the recording industry. He may have championed what became known as the "establishment," but as far as the basic values that the younger generation supposedly stood for, simplicity, creative integrity, and sincerity, Bennett made even the hippies and folkies of Haight-Ashbury look like Hollywood lawyers. There was nobody realer than Bennett, nobody who had less pretense, and nobody less capable of getting away with anything that wasn't completely on the level. Sinatra's decree that Bennett was "the best singer in the business" may adorn a million album jackets and concert programs, but an earlier quote from FS has greater relevance here: "You can only be yourself," he told Bennett in 1957. "But you're good at that."

Bennett's charm is his greatest gift; when it comes to heart, Bennett is a virtuoso, and has just enough technical ability as a musician to keep up with his soul. When he comes out only halfheartedly in a performance, maybe from not getting enough sleep or whatever, he can't keep it a secret, like a good friend who's let you down. As for his chops, they're a kind of medium-horsepower engine that takes his heart and mind wherever they want to go, and Bennett gets good mileage out of them particularly on one of his much-used "big" ballad endings (which also reveal where Judy Garland has had her influence on him). Bennett holds the last or second-to-last note for a few slow measures while steadily ascending, and while it seems like he must be climbing up the whole piano, when you analyze this movement pitch-wise it turns out he's gone up only an octave.

That endearingly rough voice of his functions as an extension of his soul, revealing his Italian lineage as much in Louis Prima as in the smoother-sounding Sinatra. Gravelly and incapable of sounding slick, Bennett also brings to mind Louis Armstrong, whom in 1964 he singled out as an influence: "Most people don't realize that Louis Armstrong has taught practically every pop singer of the day how to phrase correctly. Without this basic phrasing one cannot be a good pop singer." The inherent husk of his throat recalls Connee Boswell and an equally surprising similarity with an important singer whom I doubt Bennett ever heard of, Al Bowlly. Bennett's credo for interpretation, as told to the *Daily News* in 1964, might easily also be Bowlly's: "I like to sing . . . as if I just picked up the lead sheet for the first time and the tune struck me."

In 1973, *Variety* announced that Vittorio De Sica, the cele-

brated Italian film director, was planning a movie on the life of
Tony Bennett, with the singer playing himself in the lead as "a
first generation New Yorker with a tough exterior but a soft
center." It was never made, but they were to have shot it in
Brooklyn and Queens, with the young Anthony Benedetto probably being played by a child actor as he haunted local spots
looking for the chance to sing. They would have shown Bennett
getting drafted, returning to the door-knocking and pavement-
pounding routine after the war, and then his discovery, when
Pearl Bailey used him in her show at the Greenwich Village Inn.
Bob Hope hears him at said show, gives him his stage name, and
includes him in his troupe at the New York Paramount and a
minitour of six cities. Finally, Mitch Miller hears a Bennett
demo disc of "Boulevard of Broken Dreams" and, sight unseen,
signs him to Columbia in March 1950.

The fifties are shown as a montage of contradictions and close
calls with compromise. Bennett the crusader for class at first
gains and then loses the advantage over Bennett the cog in the
Miller machine. At the start of 1952 he was the biggest-selling
recording artist in the country with "Because of You" and "Cold,
Cold Heart," while "Rags to Riches" and "In the Middle of an
Island" weren't far behind. But his efforts on behalf of jazz seem
by far the more worthy undertaking, especially his two landmark
collaborations with Count Basie in 1958 and 1959 and his bringing the somewhat adventurous band from his *Beat of My Heart*
album (which included Herbie Mann and Candido) into the
Copacabana, where previously no hot artist dared tread.

The battle with the philistines goes on. In the beginning of
Bennett's recording career, his bosses were apparently unable to
tell the difference between him and talentless hacks like Frankie
Laine and Johnnie Ray, the other two most important male singers on post-Sinatra Columbia. In the sixties the new rock regime
at the label lumped him in the same category as Andy Williams,
whom Roger Miller might have dubbed "King of the Middle-
of-the-Road" and whose voice might be nice enough to make you
forgive the rotten songs and the Muzaky backgrounds he cov-

ered them in if only he didn't completely lack the gift of singing words as if they meant anything to him.

By this time, Bennett typifies the trend of the artist surviving in the marketplace by a kind of compromise that keeps him sane, like a jazz musician who plays as many jingle sessions as he can on weekdays while waiting for the chance to play the music he likes in a club on Saturday night. Before his really big hit, "I Left My Heart in San Francisco," he had drawing power enough to be granted the chance to do a few art records, and for a few years Columbia borrowed the Sinatra/Capitol pattern of making commercial music for singles while putting the classier stuff on LPs, so many of Bennett's first twelve-inch releases contained exclusively standards. Several also used adventurous jazz and small-group settings and one (*Hometown, My Town*) went so far as to experiment with song form itself. But Bennett had to pay for the opportunities to make these. "Before I recorded 'San Francisco,' " he said several years later, "I was advised to try out all sorts of tricks and gimmicks. Songs were offered to me which were supposed to be surefire, but they weren't my style."

In the twenty-five years since "San Francisco," Bennett has been kept on this same middle-brow level (even though "I Wanna Be Around," a decidedly meatier tune, also landed him a hit) and has only rarely gotten much farther out or farther in than the middle of that "San Francisco" road, with exceptions. Some of these exceptions have been for the worse, as when Columbia's rock-headed president tried to render him psychedelically commercial in a series of maneuvers that eventually caused Bennett to leave the label, and some have been for the sake of art, as when, on his own short-lived Improv label, he made a series of offbeat chamber jazz albums. "San Francisco" itself makes a perfect example of how low and high brows mingle in Bennett's music. It's a good, though hardly great, tune and words, infused with as much warmth as Bennett can muster— and as we've seen, that can be quite a lot—but the producer figured he had to cheapen it in some way, so the performance remains grounded by an especially tacky and out-of-place piano riff that transforms the number into only so much Muzak.

After the watershed year of 1962, which produced his two biggest sellers ("S.F." and "Wanna Be Around") as well as his triumphant Carnegie Hall debut, Bennett albums began to lose their identity, whether crass or artsy. "We had Bennett in the studio all the time then," one Columbia exec recently told me, "practically every day." CBS threw together Bennett LPs almost randomly, mixing up sessions from all over the place, throwing in single releases as well as material already released on other albums. Especially when a hit single came around and Columbia wanted to capitalize on it with an album, they seem to have grabbed whatever pieces of tape marked "TB" were nearest and threw them on the album master without rhyme or reason. Tracks from older Bennett albums, like his 1957 jazz set, *The Beat of My Heart*, kept turning up on later albums, and even dedicated Bennett buffs have a tough time remembering which songs are on which records. Sometimes the directionless mishmash of quality and crap even extends to individual tracks. "Take the Moment," on *If I Ruled the World*, interpolates thirty-two wonderful bars of Bennett swinging with the Ralph Sharon trio, but they've been sandwiched in between unbearable episodes of Bennett meandering in a field of choral corn.

Small wonder that Bennett's sales would eventually slacken in the age of the flower child. As with Eckstine's LP-era work, if Columbia had put together more conceptually interesting packages, Bennett would have been better able to compete with Sinatra. Both of the Ralphs in Bennett's career, Sharon, his accompanist, and Burns, one of the greatest arrangers to emerge out of the modern jazz big-band movement, had the potential to become his Nelson Riddle or Marty Paich; each possessed the capability to construct challenging album programs for Bennett. But after landing such an easy and unexpected hit with "San Francisco," Columbia just wasn't interested.

The only Bennett albums that work as well in toto as the classic Sinatra and Torme albums come from the pre–"San Francisco" period, beginning with the small-group session *Cloud 7* (1954) and continuing up to the magnificent *Carnegie Hall* (1962) double set. *Cloud 7* spotlights Bennett with guitarist Chuck

Wayne, his most frequent accompanist before Sharon, and a fine combo featuring the noted ornithologist Davey Schildkraut, backing that easily parodied early Bennett voice, which lisps, quivers excessively, and acts unsure of certain vowels ("Darn That Drum"). On *The Beat of My Heart,* the hippest of his small–jazz group records, Bennett and Sharon worked out the unique concept of pairing Bennett with six major jazz drummers on different tracks (most notably Papa Jo Jones and Art Blakey).

Four albums from the early sixties win the prize as Bennett's best, two very small band sets with Sharon, *Tony Sings for Two* (1959) and *When Lights Are Low* (1964), and two orchestral packages with Burns, *Hometown, My Town* (1958) and *My Heart Sings* (1961) ("My heart sings—that's what I'm trying to do," he said at the time). *Hometown, My Town* marks Bennett's most Sinatra-Riddle-like effort, consisting of six songs that Bennett and Burns use to describe life in New York on a conceptual level—that is, none of them include the words "New York" in the title. More remarkably, singer and arranger open up each of the six to "Something Cool"–like proportions, adding long instrumental portions (and jazz solos), verses, specially written melodies and lyrics, fitting each song together as if into a suite, which more effectively fulfills Gershwin's promise of a symphonically expanded jazz-pop fusion than any composition in between *Black, Brown and Beige* and *Skies of America.*

If pressed to select one single Bennett performance as definitive, it would have to be "The Gal That Got Away" from the *Sings for Two* set, which, as the title promises, is an album of duets with Sharon. We should be grateful for this alone, as it's the best chance we've ever had to revel in the full power of Bennett's miraculously phonogenic voice; the microphone loves his voice like the camera loves Hedy Lamarr's face. While "Gal That Got Away" is characteristic Bennett through and through, he does a couple of things differently here than we're used to. The same way that Bobby Darin can be said to have based most of his career on Sinatra's "I've Got You Under My Skin," Bennett has built much of his on Sinatra's "Where or When" (the

Capitol version, from 1958), meaning the ballad starts out small and gets progressively bigger and more dramatically intense, which is also as much of a Garland trademark as a Sinatra one (as of late, Bennett's most performed number in this format is "How Do You Keep the Music Playing?"). "Gal That Got Away" does not, however, use this format. Instead, it sets up a virtually unachievable balance of total control and total hysteria. Bennett also breaks his rule about scatting here. Where Mel Torme's scat choruses have all the grace of Fred Astaire dancing, Bennett's more closely resemble the pantomime bear on *Captain Kangaroo*, lots of "dot-deet-doots" but hardly the harmonic chutzpah necessary for improvisation.* The wordless passage works here because Bennett doesn't use it for musical purposes as much as atmospheric ones, the low moans that begin "Gal That Got Away" effectively putting the listener in a frame of mind to hear about bitter nights and glitterless stars.

Bennett also has a field day with dynamics, using superhard fortissimos and feather-light pianissimos perhaps partly to compensate for the lack of an orchestra, and showing an intelligence too few people are willing to give him credit for when he actually emphasizes a point by uttering it softly. He gets the same effect through his use of singspiel—spoken lines—especially his decision of which lines to speak and which to sing, and when he lets up and quietly whispers, "there's just no letup," it resounds as one of the most breathtaking moments in all of adult pop.

But the sixties weren't about heights so much as nadirs, and for every triumph of good music—*The Concert Sinatra*, Eric Dolphy and Booker Little's *At the Five Spot*, Benny Carter's *Further Definitions*, Stan Getz and Eddie Sauter's *Focus*, Duke Ellington's *Far East Suite* and *His Mother Called Him Bill*, Jack Teagarden's *Think Well of Me*, John Coltrane and Johnny Hartman, Miles Davis's *E.S.P.*, and Billy Eckstine and Sarah

---

* And Bennett is better at it than Al Jolson, whose scatting suggests terrible gas pains.

Vaughan's live albums on Mercury—the philistines landed another six blows: the British invasion, flower power, the rise of the rock singer–songwriter, folk rock, heavy metal, and Astrud Gilberto. The boom fell in the aftermath of the Beatles and Clive Davis's rise to power at Columbia; Bennett had been lucky enough to generate enough sales momentum, not only to keep going in the face of changing tastes, but also to land a couple of lesser hits like "If I Ruled the World" and "Maybe September." Though his concert attendance would never slacken, by 1969, Bennett had cause to worry about his recording career.

But more on that later. In the meantime comes the opportunity to reflect on an earlier skirmish. Gary Giddins has described a period in the late fifties, after Elvis's induction and his subsequent failure to "come back," when hard-core rock for a time took a backseat to an even less interesting kind of kiddie pop, one even more commercially prefabricated and dominated by the likes of Ricky Nelson, Pat Boone, and something called Fabian. It proved enough to turn many musically minded youths away from the pablum aimed at them and encourage them to take a look at the stronger stuff, like jazz, classical, and the better kinds of adult pop. During these years the reappearance on the charts of Sinatra, Bennett, Cole, Vaughan, and Louis Armstrong led to hope for grown-up music, as did the "crossing over" of the extremely talented Bobby Darin from the Presley kind of thing to the Sinatra kind of thing. Needless to say, the coming of the Beatles (and with them the end of the record business as it had existed up to that time) put an end to such aspirations. By 1963 the ever-fickle Darin, the Great Under-Thirty Hope and the only performer to concoct a listenable blend of adult and kiddie pop, had opened up his shirt Belafonte style and chosen "Michael Row the Boat Ashore" as his featured song on TV variety show appearances.

But Darin, who limited his importance to good music by deserting it so early and by his overdependence on Sinatra, turned out to be only the first of two crossovers that would prove important to this period; the second, Dinah Washington, would also be stopped short, not by desertion but death. Perhaps it's

naive to assume that Darin and/or Washington could have challenged the Beatles, but the ironic part is that Darin achieved his
crossover by doing good music and Washington achieved hers
through a combination of junk and material entirely unsuited to
her.

I've griped about the generally stifling, repetitive beat of
R&B, but when used creatively, as Washington (and Darin) did,
and perhaps loosened up for a little jazz shading and accenting,
it could be an invigorating, even thrilling experience. Washington, blessed with a searing, intense sound, an infectious swing
(which allowed her to expand upon R&B rhythmic style), and a
gift for the improvisational embellishments that are at the heart
of jazz, was easily the finest- of all blues artists, perhaps even
including Bessie Smith and Robert Johnson. It seems carping,
therefore, to complain that she could sing nothing as well as the
blues, sort of like griping that Horowitz could play nothing but
classical piano or that Bill Monroe can only produce bluegrass.

Nevertheless, the complaint stands, because Washington
didn't find her greatest commercial success until she "broke out"
of the black market into white songs, accompanied, though not
sung, in an overly white way. Of the major male blues singers of
the thirties and forties—Eddie "Cleanhead" Vinson, Big Bill
Bronzy, T-Bone Walker, Turner, Jordan, Joe Williams, Jimmy
Rushing—only the last two had interest enough in Tin Pan Alley
to develop a ballad style independent of blues conventions.
When Washington takes on "Love for Sale," "Making Whoopee," or even her crossover hit "What a Difference a Day Makes,"
it just doesn't work for me; her harmonic alterations and approach to melody and lyrics—deeply passionate but not the particular passion the words suggest—keep telling me that she'd
rather be singing the blues, which is exactly what I'd rather hear
her sing. That obscure though worthy category known as "blues
songs" tells a different story (an album of Harold Arlen would
have been terrific), as does that equally rarefied strata of conventional pop songs that have been picked up by blues artists,
like "I Wanna Be Loved" and "Teach Me Tonight." But of all the
phases Washington passed through in her twenty years of re-

cording before her death at thirty-nine in 1963, her postcross-
over period produced her weakest music.

Though none of the heirs to Washington's title of the Queen
could inspire pounding hearts and chilled spines the way Dinah
could, a few had better luck with standard material. Capitol's
initial two tries at replicating what Mercury and then Roulette
had in Washington, Donna Hightower and Dakota Staton, tempered Washington's flames with the softer lyricism of Mildred
Bailey and Helen Humes. Only Della Reese could keep up with
Washington in terms of harshness and bite, which can be at least
partially credited to her similar church background. In a terrific
vocal version of Mercer Ellington's "Things Ain't What They
Used to Be" on an early Jubilee LP, Reese gets downright mil-
itantly defiant. A little later, on RCA albums with Mercer Ellington and Neal Hefti, the strength and ferocity of her highly
stylized chomping up of song and scenery suggests a female Al
Hibbler—her shouting recast of the bridge to "I'm Beginning to
See the Light" (on *Della*) being even wilder than Hib.

Though Reese hit the biggest at first, with a big seller for
Victor on "Don't You Know?" (based on "Musetta's Waltz" from
La Bohème, it led a set of classical adaptations that marked
Reese's only really bad Victor album), Staton has proven herself
equally worthy. Her first batch of Capitol albums (if only they
had kept her instead of the less interesting Nancy Wilson), even
Dakota with the great Benny Carter, barely scratch the surface
of the vastly entertaining artist that has developed in the years
since, not least because she possesses a sense of humor almost as
compelling as Washington's.

None of which meant much at the cash register. By the mid-
sixties, neither lady had a major-label contract. Not even Reese,
who had reached a sales pinnacle in 1959, the same year as
Washington's "What a Difference . . . ," could get the time of
day from djs by 1963.* Still, despite the way the teeny-boppers

* Much of this data comes from the late Arnold Shaw, the very reliable chronicler
and "plugger" of black music.

bought Ricky and Fabian, all ears were tuned into the blues as a rediscovered source. Even as kiddie-pop producers looted R&B like juvenile delinquents stripping your car, both of jazz's new movements, hard bop and free jazz, claimed the blues for a foundation. The traditional blues form gave hard bop much of its energy, while R&B gave it most of its great soloists: Hank Mobley from Paul Gayten, Bill Hardman from Tiny Bradshaw, Blue Mitchell from "Red" Prysock, Benny Golson from Bull Moose Jackson, John Coltrane from Earl Bostic, and so on. And Ray Charles, the well-named "genius" of R&B, kept two of the decade's great improvisers with him in Fathead Newman and Hank Crawford.

Hard bop's effect on singing differed from "classic" bop in important, often ironic ways. The bop of Parker and Gillespie did not seem at face value a singer's music, yet it touched off at least three separate species of singing: Ella Fitzgerald and the new school for scat; Pleasure, Jefferson, and vocalese; and the modern ballad style of Eckstine and Vaughan (and that's not even mentioning later developments like the cool school). Hard bop, at heart a far simpler and more direct method of expression, at first looked like a music with greater potential for singers, yet few rose to its challenge. To make a further contrast, where the Charlie Parker–Gil Evans–Dave Lambert Singers session had been such a total flop, hard bop used choirs quite effectively.

Most notably Max Roach and Charlie Mingus, two venerable giants of bop into post-bop (and occasional collaborators), dabbled with voices for a variety of ensemble color, much as they flirted with strings. Roach affixed seventeen nasty, gnarrly voices to his sextet on *It's Time* (1961–62, Impulse) and the results could have been Gregorian chants scored for the soundtrack of an Alfred Hitchcock movie; Mingus's singers vocalize the most effectively on *Pre-Bird* (1960, Limelight), an orchestral album that includes much reworking of Ellingtonian material, and with it two pieces inspired by Duke's voice-as-band-instrument experiments with Adelaide Hall and Kay Davis. When used creatively, voices could bring to the fore positive qualities already inherent in a bandleader/soloist's music. Donald Byrd backed his hard-bop small bands (in 1963 and 1964) with Coleridge Perkinson's choirs to enhance their down-home churchy quality (and devised the modernist's answer to *Louis and the Good Book*), while the six bogus Rastafarians who chant behind Sonny Rollins on "Don't Stop the Carnival" and "Brownskin Gal" underscore the saxophone colossus's belly-laugh sense of humor. Unfortunately, voices—especially French ones—could still be ill-advised bows toward the mass market, as with the Modern Jazz Quartet and Dizzy Gillespie.

Around the same time, the hard-bop movement inspired a brief flurry of activity by black male singers, primarily those who had been around a while but had been given few opportunities to record. Take Ernie Andrews, for example: Here was a talented blues-and-ballads man and a fixture on the Central Avenue scene in black Los Angeles long before "bop" or "hard," who, like his friend Earl Coleman, had a hit ("Soothe Me") with an indie label on which he was never able to build a career. Then, in 1964, he made *Live Session! Cannonball Adderley with the New Exciting Voice of Ernie Andrews* for Capitol, and it's still the highlight of his forty-plus years of trying to be heard. On this album he makes the point vocally that Junior Cook and Curtis Fuller make instrumentally: that the funky and the fancy have a lot in common, blues style (as opposed to blues form) can be used to express ideas as sentimental or intellectual as the artist wants to shoot for. Much the same thing can be said about the work of Bill Henderson, both musically and commercially. Henderson's credentials alone are enough to justify calling him the definitive hard-bop vocalist, as he played Japan in 1961 with the greatest edition of Art Blakey's Jazz Messengers (with Wayne Shorter, Lee Morgan, and Bobby Timmons) and recorded jukebox singles for Blue Note with the Horace Silver Quintet. Like Andrews, he brings devices associated with the blues to standard material, and while Andrews uses a kind of shout with a catch in it, Henderson relies more on moans and stage whispers, done with a character voice of the kind singing musicians use—

and reminiscent, if you can imagine this, of a cross between Ray Charles and Johnny Hartman.

Oscar Brown, Jr., captured the limelight as the best-known jazz-oriented vocalist of the era, but in retrospect Brown's greatest talents were in his lyric writing. His most important album, *Sin and Soul* (Columbia), runs out of steam vocally about halfway through and like many another songwriter who sings, we keep being reminded of how much better his songs sound in the hands of full-time vocalists: "Dat Dere" by Sheila Jordan or Mel Torme, "Afro Blue" by Abbey Lincoln, "Work Song" by Bobby Darin, Earl Coleman, or another, more surprising Junior, Sammy Davis (with Count Basie). Brown might have made a real contribution to music had his show, *Kicks*, ever made it to Broadway, as it might have done something to improve disintegrating relations between jazz and the theater—and, for that matter, relations between "musical" comedy and music. By contrast, the shoddiest of all attempts to translate sixties jazz into vocal terms came from Leon Thomas, who had earlier established some credibility as one of Count Basie's better replacements for Joe Williams. Thomas fails because he doesn't think in terms of influence—like Billie Holiday learning a certain device from Buck Clayton or Lester Young—but in terms of imitation: Gargling and yodeling, in Thomas's work, is supposed to equate a "free"-period Coltrane tenor solo, but it just doesn't work. Thomas, like most singers who take the idea of instrument imitation too far, misses the point of singing by so much he makes me wonder why he just doesn't learn how to play an instrument.

Developing a repertoire of hard-bop songs, as Oscar Brown and Jon Hendricks were trying to do, would have been one way to make the jazz vocal tradition relevant to hard bop and modal jazz, but Abbey Lincoln, the most perfect singer of the era, achieved this by doing precisely the opposite. On *That's Him* (1957), the first of three sumptuously flawless Riverside albums, she selects material so out of date attitude-wise that it risks setting women's rights back thirty years. At a time when Dinah Washington and her followers evoked Bessie Smith and the classic blues genre, Lincoln summoned up the spirits of the other stream of black chanteuses of the twenties and thirties—Ethel Waters, Elizabeth Welch, and even the unrecorded Florence Mills—who were the first black women permitted dignity. *That's Him* takes on nine songs of romantic masochism, specifically black female masochism, which Lincoln, through her demeanor, her stance, her presence, and the relationship she sets up with an audience from the first note, deprives of their pejorative slants. She gets help from the music; on "Don't Explain," the absence of the piano keeps the proceedings unsentimental in the manner of the Mulligan-Baker Quartet, and on "My Man," Lincoln and accompanists rediscover the march idea at the song's core (Paul Whiteman, in one of the earliest American recordings of "Mon Homme," had treated it in strict 6/8) as a basis for their position of defiance. Lastly, on Kurt Weill's "That's Him," the most upbeat song on the album, Lincoln immerses herself in the lyric's refreshing bagels-and-lox view of love.

"Chicago-born, Kalamazoo-bred, jazz band–trained and honky-tonk-educated," in the words of songwriter Bob Russell, Lincoln had a whole other career before becoming Mrs. Max Roach (for twelve years) and the first lady of modern jazz. She had considerable success as a conventional pop artist who packed them in at the Hollywood nightclubs (especially Ciro's, L.A.'s equivalent of the Copa), recorded for Liberty Records (*not* their jazz division), and proved she had more sex appeal than Jayne Mansfield (no mean feat) in Frank Tashlin's absurd classic *The Girl Can't Help It*. After linking up with Messieurs Roach and Bill Grauer (of Riverside), Lincoln swung a radical 180 degrees in the other direction, joining Roach on the edge of political and musical campaigning (hers was one of the voices on the Roach choir album) and more recently adopting an African name.* But

---

* To me, "Aminata Moseka" sounds like something you order at a Greek coffee shop, but then she only took the name Abbey Lincoln in 1956 when she was twenty-six, having been born Anna Marie Wooldridge. She also worked as Gaby Lee (if you don't believe me, it's all in Feather).

she could no more give in to racial mushiness on *The Freedom Now Suite* than she would surrender to the temptations of melodrama on "Two Cigarettes in the Dark."

Lincoln recorded both before (*Affair* [1956, Liberty]) and after (the excellent *Talking to the Sun* [1983, Enja]) the three Riversides, but still they represent a singular pinnacle by virtue of uniformly excellent material (with outstanding contemporary writing—by Brown, Hendricks, Benny Golson, and Lincoln herself—mixed in with the standards), incredible sidemen (Kenny Dorham, Sonny Rollins, etc.), and Lincoln's miraculous gift for merging with her accompaniment, thanks partially to arrangements that, while never sounding anything like conventional arrangements, seamlessly mix voice, ensembles, and solos. "Afro Blue," the track that leads off *Abbey Is Blue*, the climax of the series, makes a good example. Using an ABABAB form that immediately establishes it as something separate from conventional AABA song shape, Lincoln organized her definitive reading in a set of alternating vocal and instrumental episodes,[*] connected by a beguiling minor vamp figure. It might sound slick were not the texture so grittily expressive. We can speak of the discrepancy between the literate (i.e., lyrics) and the musical aspects of singing, but Lincoln's battery of devices integrates the two: her habit of dividing up measures into the most off-center mathematical patterns and her African-influenced use of tone and pitch, both essentially technical stratagems that she uses to make a dramatic point.

Lincoln grabs us with her constant reliance on the unconventional in pitch, rhythm, and other elements of singing. Carmen McRae sounds much more conventional at first, but closer analysis reveals that on paper McRae could be as avant as anybody. Her sharp, occasionally biting tone approaches that of Billie Holiday; her method of altering melody lines has strong ties to

---

[*] The spirit of Max Roach's small bands lingers here, with trumpeter Tommy Turrentine (for my dough, *the* real talent of the Turrentine family) taking one of the pithiest solos of his career.

the Vaughan-Eckstine school, and the knowledge of harmonic practice (as opposed to theory) it requires to paraphrase lines as surefootedly as McRae does far exceeds that of your average scat singer. If you never noticed any of this, it's because McRae doesn't want you to. The central difference between her and Vaughan*—the singer with whom she has the most in common—lies not in music but in attitude, as McRae preaches a return to the Crosby ideal of hidden technique. When Bennett, for instance, pushes a note up an octave, he dramatically milks it for all it's worth and, as we have seen, can make it sound like six. When McRae does it, as on the end of her version of "Funny Valentine," you barely notice the octave jump at the end. One forever walks away from Carmen McRae records liking her tremendously but not being exactly sure why.

The fastidious musicianship lies underneath the surface, covered with a coat of real emotional involvement. And to further cloud the issue, she even understates *that*. On "My Man's Gone Now" (on *Porgy and Bess*), she never raises her voice, she resists the opportunities for histrionics that Gershwin wrote into the score via his wordless moans, and even when one moan rises up into a key change for a big payoff, McRae makes you feel as if she's earned it by saving up for it.

Earning and saving up figure in McRae's life story as well, for here is a woman who was virtually unheard of until her earliest major-label exposure, at age thirty-two in 1954, who within a few years came to be regarded as one of the finest singers in jazz, on the same level as Vaughan and Ella Fitzgerald. She had been born in Harlem in 1922 and her parents invested five years' worth of piano lessons in her. Though they tried to push a classical pianist's career, McRae instead applied the knowledge gleaned from this tutelage to jazz. As she told Art Taylor, "That experience of studying music is what put me where I am today.

---

* Among other similarities, McRae scats like Vaughan, as on "Devil and the Deep Blue Sea" on *After Glow* and "Yardbird Suite" on *By Special Request* (both Decca)

Without it I perhaps would not even be singing, or if I had become a singer, it might not be as impressive as whatever it is I do now." Like Vaughan and Fitzgerald (in fact, long closer to Fitzgerald's time than Vaughan's) she cites her first break as winning an Apollo Theatre amateur show, which led to an early association with Teddy Wilson, his then wife, songwriter Irene Kitchings, and Billie Holiday, who recorded a song of McRae's called "Dream of Life." (McRae returned the favor by reviving some of the obscurer songs in the Holiday pantheon such as "I'm Pulling Through" and eventually dedicating an album and night-club sets to her.) In the years that followed, McRae worked intermittently as a pianist-singer and very occasionally subbed as a replacement or interim vocalist with Benny Carter, Count Basie, and Earl Hines.

Her first regular important singing gig came with a band that would ultimately make no impact on the music world but would have great significance for McRae's own career, that of Mercer Ellington. The band didn't last long: Partly sabotaged by Ellington Senior (or so Mercer claims), they broke up in Chicago in 1948.* But at least McRae had gotten on records, married one of the leaders of the bop revolution in Kenny Clarke, and acquired a self-confidence that has never failed her. "I liked Chicago and wanted to stay," she told Arthur North in the *News* in 1962. "A girlfriend knew someone who was looking for a pianist-singer and talked me into auditioning for the job. I started with a two-week contract but stayed for seventeen." Furthermore, she remained in the city for three and a half years, returning only at the insistence of her parents. Not long after, "I was playing a small club in Brooklyn when I was offered a contract with a small recording company, and then things really started happening." McRae's first solo vocals are a weird lot, including eight tracks currently owned by Bethlehem, apparently produced by Chuck

* The year is 1948 according to *Current Biography;* it's 1949 according to Feather's entry under M. Ellington.

Darwin, using the same backup crew that he would later use on his Dawn and Seeco Records sessions (including Tony Scott, Herbie Mann, and Mat Mathews, the fifties' leading jazz accordionist), and, as with most Darwin productions, relying heavily on strange songs either written or published by Darwin.

McRae sounds out of sorts on these tracks, as if she doesn't know quite what to make of the bizarre material and accompaniment (clarinets, bass flutes, accordions, and so on); you can take her records completely seriously from her Decca and Kapp releases onward. Some of the Deccas fare no better than the Bethlehems though: On *Carmen for Cool Ones* (1957), assembled for her by the jazz-minded cellist Fred Katz (best known for his work in the Chico Hamilton Quintet), she never quite comes to terms with what seems like an attempt to record the weirdest arrangements ever written for a singer and also to cash in on magazine stories about McRae with titles like "New Cool Singer" and "McRae Profits by Training in Cool School"; and *Mad About the Man* (1957), where neither singer, arrangements, nor material (Noel Coward songs) have been formally introduced to each other.

For a record company to err on the side of trying to make good music seems an incredible event these days. Since the fifties the thrust of pop has been toward not taking chances, and taking the sleaziest commercial route to selling the highest poundage of vinyl. Even when the aim is to make good rather than commercial music, singers rarely get to delve any deeper than the most obvious tried-and-true ideas. But the uncredited producers and the A&R department at Decca might have all memorized Artie Shaw's creed in their determination to put together the best possible music for McRae.

Album after album from this period rates as a classic: *By Special Request* (1955) with the Bethlehem crew, including Mann, Mathews, and McRae's first husband, Kenny Clarke; *Torchy* (1955) with Jack Pleis and Ralph Burns; *Blue Moon* (1956) with Tadd Dameron and Jimmy Mundy; *Boy Meets Girl* (1957) with Sammy Davis, Jr., joining McRae at the mike and

Jack Pleis arranging and conducting; *After Glow* (1957) with three different piano trios, one of which featuring McRae at the ivories and all of which feature Ike Isaacs, McRae's second husband, on bass; *Something to Swing About* (1959) with Ernie Wilkins; *Book of Ballads* (1958) with Don Abney on piano and Frank Hunter conducting; *When You're Away* (1959). Even *Birds of a Feather* (1958), the McRae Decca with the tritest possible premise—twelve songs about birds—boasts anything but flighty arrangements by Ralph Burns while McRae and Ben Webster (incognito and identified on the jacket as "A. Tenorman") infuse so much soul into their performances that they threaten to scare the birds away.

As hard as she swings on "How Little We Know" (on *Something to . . .*) and the other up-tempo pieces, and as cute and charming as she gets on *Boy Meets Girl* (she also made singles with Sammy and guest starred on his *Porgy and Bess* album in 1958), the ballads make up the heart and soul of McRae's best work. As with her scatting, she reminds one most of Vaughan here. The tempos are still as slow as ballads tend to be after Parker's "Embraceable You," but the tone is far smaller than Vaughan, meaning it takes up less space vertically, resulting in there being a lot more room for McRae to play around in. Her melodic invention comes to the surface more readily than Vaughan's, who tends to cover hers in a sauce of technique. She almost never lets melodies remain exactly as written; nearly every line receives some kind of alteration, rhythmic or melodic, large or small. *Within* jazz, she makes the point that paraphrase and embellishment can be just as satisfying as out-and-out improvisation. Yet she makes an even greater point *for* jazz, concerning its relationship to other musics, because improvisational devices help her delve deeper into the narrative; she reiterates the message of Holiday and Sinatra that jazz can be the most important item in the toolbox for interpreting lyrics.

McRae's post-Decca career compares interestingly with that of Johnny Griffin. While the other leading saxes of his generation drifted into fusion (Wayne Shorter), free jazz (Jackie

McLean), and obscurity (Hank Mobley), Griffin is virtually the only one to remain true to the bop that suited him best, and while we prayed for the others to "come back" to their callings, that Griffin never strayed doesn't cause anybody to undervalue him. Of the major jazz-oriented singers, McRae is one of the few to keep recording good music straight through the sixties and seventies, although she, too, has given in to a smattering of the unavoidable Billy Joel, Lennon and McCartney, Stephen Wonder, Stevie Sondheim, M. Legrand, et al. As you can see from her two collaboration albums with Dave Brubeck on Columbia (1961), McRae has still worked on making good material sound terrific, but also had to waste time making mediocre material sound passable.

None of her colleagues fared as well. Peggy Lee had been looking for alternatives to Tin Pan Alley throughout the forties and fifties, and though she defended Porter and Gershwin as loudly as anybody, it was obvious that she would be the least harmed by the rock inundation, especially as she had the strongest ties to the blues. For a time the rock thing might have even helped her: "Fever" fit right in with the new pop, and Ray Charles's songs found a place in her act with little fuss. But by the end of the sixties, when Lee had reached her peak vocally, juvenilia had begun to command too great a portion of her time. It got so you could skim over the backs of album after album and not find one song worth her time or yours. Good as her voice got, that's how bad her material was, and you could scream that *Norma Deloris Egstrom from Jamestown, North Dakota* wastes her by-now formidable talents on trite rubbish, but those who invest time and money into digging up this dispensable disc will be rewarded by the presence of three credible tracks hidden on the B side, Lil Armstrong's reliable old blues song "Just for a Thrill" and two superb wartime standards, joined together as if in a medley, "The More I See You" and "I'll Be Seeing You." She had one last peak at the charts with "Is That All There Is?" in 1970, which probably did her more harm than good as it encouraged her to try entire albums of stuff by Jerry Leiber and

Mike Stoller, who proved that they could imitate European avant-gardists as commercially as they could Southern Negroes.

At least Frank Sinatra was able to continue sensibly dividing up music for the moment and music for all time: For every *Somethin' Stupid* or *That's Life* there was a corresponding *Francis Albert Sinatra and Edward Kennedy Ellington* and *Sinatra at the Sands;* and the runaway success of the discotheque-directed single "Strangers in the Night" led to an album of class material not cheapened in the least by its tacky little track. For at least ten years Sinatra could overlook the new pop. He had tried, once around the time that Elvis left Sun Records for RCA, to see how he would do with a couple of doo-wop numbers ("From the Bottom to the Top" and "Two Hearts, Two Kisses") with a doo-wop backup band, but the results convinced Capitol that this was not an avenue worth investigating. After all, Sinatra had no affinity for the blues that were early rock's only strength. As it happened, rock moved out of the blues and into those fragments of underdeveloped melodies called "hooks" just around the time that it put other kinds of pop to rest in the mid-sixties (roughly around the time that Clive Davis took over at Columbia). Sinatra waited until he didn't have to contend with the blues before he tried rock again, and then it was the soft, gutless kind still heard in elevators today, which he overpowers like Kirsten Flagstad would nursery rhymes.

But while rock-type material figures only marginally in the overall scope of his performance in the seventies and eighties, Sinatra is today more like a rock star than anything else. I don't mean so much in terms of music as in mentality: To stand in the crowds that flock to the sports arenas where he plays, to see the scalpers or the legions of security guards, and to sniff the air of reverential worship among the throng, it might as well be a heavy-metal event as a set from Torme, McRae, or Vaughan at the Blue Note or Michael's Pub. Still, those who have grown up going only to rock concerts, expecting only an exact reiteration of record hits, don't know what to make of Sinatra, who actually creates something every time he goes out there, who refuses to be what Billie Holiday and Lester Young call a "repeater pencil," and who may be showing them for the first time what real eloquence and passion are.

The sixties started beautifully for Mel Torme. Where he had been the dean of the cool school on the West Coast label Verve, he easily switched to hard bop with the home of the funk, Atlantic.* Torme's blues strengths even landed him in the Top 40 with a single called "Comin' Home, Baby," which led to one of the five or so greatest albums of Torme's career, the hit single bringing cash customers in to hear thoroughly thought-out vocal versions of instrumentals by Miles Davis, Bobby Timmons, Nat Adderley, Benny Golson, and Randy Weston, along with freshly hardened standards by Irving Berlin and Frank Loesser. But the gap between 1962 and 1967 might have been fifty years as easily as five, for all the while Torme continued to grow as a live performer, his records increasingly reflected some punk producer in guitar-shaped sunglasses and a Beatle wig. In clubs and festivals, among other venues, he kept refining "Comin' Home, Baby" until it became an excuse for an extended and usually brilliant blues improvisation, and he began to develop the multisong framework that would be his mettle in succeeding decades, as well as slowly building to the best voice of his career. But all that got on records (most infamously *Right Now*† on Columbia and *A Time for Us* and *Raindrops Keep Fallin' on My Head* on Capitol) constituted vain attempts to climb aboard the Andy Williams "If-it-moves-cover-it!" bandwagon. When pressured recently to comment on this period, Torme didn't mind so much that these tracks were rock and kiddie pop, but the fact of

* Don't think that the cool and the hard have so little in common. After all, each of the three leading pianists of black hard bop began with white cool bands: Horace Silver with Stan Getz, Bobby Timmons with Chet Baker, and Sonny Clark with the Lighthouse All-Stars.

† *Right Now* has one saving moment. At the end of "Strangers in the Night," when Torme modulates from Sinatra cover to Sinatra parody, he ridicules Old Blue Eyes' pseudo-scat closer.

their being regurgitations of other people's hits offended his individuality. The dichotomy continued into the seventies: At Carnegie Hall he sang with Basie, at Monterey it was Woody Herman, at Basin Street East, Ellington. In the studios, he recorded junk that, when compelled to perform live, he introduced with the wise-guy line, "Here are some of your favorites and I certainly hope they're also mine."

Torme seemed to sense it was only a matter of time before he could get back into a more sensible recording situation. On the other hand, poor Tony Bennett was left standing there with a stupid look on his face, wondering what in hell was going on. As Columbia president and philistine supreme Clive Davis tells it, by the end of the decade Bennett's album material remained as good and as bad as it was, say, in 1965, but his sales hardly reflected the boffo business he continued to do live all over the world. So, the reasoning goes, to get big sales, record whatever happens to be selling big. Bennett got as far as making a whole album of Davisian covers, and the notion of regurgitation was no longer metaphoric but concrete, as Bennett actually vomited before the session. He couldn't keep the stuff on his stomach beyond this one record, *Tony Sings the Great Hits of Today* (which came complete with a bogus Peter Max cover and "Eleanor Rigby" recited as if it were Gray's *Elegy*), so his sales continued to plummet. Davis's prodding for more great hits of today eventually caused Bennett to leave both the label[*] and the country; he relocated to England and Verve/MGM Records, neither association lasting long. When Bennett finally formed his own independent label, Improv Records, founded in conjunction with a wealthy hotel owner who felt, like Bennett, that neither adult pop nor its brother, jazz, was getting a fair shake from the rock-dominated majors, it was no surprise that folks didn't flock to buy the new Bennett albums as they had "I Wanna Be

---

[*] Bennett also insisted on recording an extended composition by Alec Wilder on the subject of world peace and took umbrage when Columbia turned him down.

Around" fifteen years earlier and "Because of You" ten years before that. What had happened?

Simply put, the record industry as Bennett had known it in 1952 no longer existed. In Bennett's time, record labels had endeavored to sell as much of their product as possible, by fair means but often by foul. Eventually the decision was made to eliminate choice on the part of the artist as well as the consumer. As tenor saxist Lew Tabackin once said in describing playing in sessions for Motown Records, "Everything had to be interchangeable. When one of the girls [the Supremes] would act up, they'd replace her with a new one and no one would know the difference. There was no room for jazz [i.e., individuality] in their thinking." So it'll always be, as long as the kiddies must have their pop and records remain one of the more profitable areas of the children's toy industry.

Present Tense

The Past Predicted, the Future Re-created

•

"After me, there are no more jazz singers. What I mean is that there's nobody scaring me to death. No young woman is giving me any trouble when it comes to singing jazz. I'm not even worried about it and that's a shame. It's sad there's nobody stepping on my heels so I can look back and say, 'I better get myself together because this little girl is singing her thing off!' They're all doing what everybody else is doing, and as I'm not doing what everybody else is doing I'm not even worried. It's a crime that no little singer is socking it back to me in my own field. To keep it going, to keep it alive, because I'm not going to live forever, I'm going to die eventually and I don't want it to die with me. I want it to live on."
— Betty Carter to Art Taylor

"I wish that one of these days somebody would learn to do [my art] so it doesn't die where it is."
— Frank Sinatra to Walter Cronkite

History, even a critical history, is generally set down in narrative form, and the mere act of using narrative to talk about something tells us two things: First, as Aristotle dictates, a story must have a beginning, a middle, and, this is important, an *end*; second, first-person fiction (novels or movies where one of the characters narrates) especially comes with the preconception that the mere act of telling a story signifies to the reader that the story is finished.

This story has no such neat *Time* magazine–style conclusion or summation, not only because the arbitrary selection of a concluding event would do a disservice to the vast diversity that is jazz singing, but because this art seems to have, at this writing, no present. I don't doubt that it has a future, and we've just spent some time looking at its past, but whenever I look around for a current generation in this music, all I find are polarized factions trying either to predict the past or to re-create the future. Even both of the artists that strike me as the closest thing jazz singing has to a present, and who have the most to do with the way people sing this music *today*, go back to the forties: Betty Carter and Rosemary Clooney.

Bluntly, Betty Carter is the best thing that's happening to jazz singing today. The reaction most people have to Carter can be likened to the reaction they have to Cecil Taylor or, for that matter, to August Strindberg or the Three Stooges, radical extremes of adoration or violent rejection, with little middle ground. True, Taylor has several times named her as his favorite singer (to which she has offered no comment), but there's little in Carter's personality or music to justify such a response. In the first place Carter, like many bop-era musicians, *deplores* the avant-garde, which, she said to Tony Schwartz, "alienated black audiences. They couldn't take it, so they just disappeared. Everybody's busy thinking he's the beginning of something. But when you got something new, you don't have to tell nobody." Musically, Carter today seems a perfectly logical extension of what came before her, specifically Ella Fitzgerald, in her use of extended improvisations; Sarah Vaughan, in her reconciliation of enormous technique with enormous warmth; and Mel Torme (whom she went out of her way *not* to "say anything bad" about in an interview with Leslie Gourse) in her masterful, MJQ-like approach to structure. And that's just musically. As an interpreter of lyrics she can match Carmen McRae or, occasionally, even Billie Holiday, while totally at different times, especially at earlier stages of her career, she seems the spitting image of both Rose Murphy and Anita O'Day.

Carter makes over her material from start to finish, with references to the techniques of both Vaughan (largely spontaneous) and Torme (partially prearranged by the singer). Her sense of structure, refreshingly asymmetrical, makes use of the virtues modern jazz offers in terms of freedom (with a small *f*) but none of its overused clichés: the head-solo-head formula, for example. Carter's "What a Little Moonlight Can Do" has two scat improvisations, one where you'd expect it to be in the middle of the arrangement, the other taking you by surprise at the end. "I Could Write a Book" opens with a scat sequence that is more than an introduction or prelude but rather becomes an integral part of her interpretation of the Rodgers song.

She also eschews standard forms for longer pieces, such as suites, sonata form, and symphonies; in fact, her longest composition-performance-improvisation yet, "Sounds Movin' On" (on *The Audience with Betty Carter* [1979, Bet-Car]), is also, paradoxically, her least structured. If I were to bandy the musical dictionary around a bit I might call it a "thematic suite," as it comes in sections; however, each of these varies the same basic material and chord sequence. Carter doesn't even wait for the introductory vamp to end before she makes her entrance, she leaps in wordlessly, then refuses us a conventional melody statement. She sings the brief lyrics with her trio, which plays a variation on the vamp rather than the expected comping. Using the ABAB format, she uses the bridge as a point of reference; in the first chorus the trio comes in behind her on the B sections, in the second chorus she ceases scatting and returns to the lyrics on these Bs. By the third chorus she dispenses with the words, which are of the inconsequential swing-era rhythm-tune variety (as in "Opus One") entirely, and the rest of the A side of the album gets turned over to scatting. Carter divides the piece into chunks, each at a different tempo, generally switching between slow and fast variants (as opposed to between fast and faster), each launched by Carter's literal declamation "Moooovin' on!"

If there's a problem with "Sounds Movin' On" it isn't that Carter doesn't have enough ideas to sustain nearly half an hour of improvising on the same material (none of the musicians solo, except briefly during her bow music); far from running out of things to do, she almost has too many. Within the shifting tempos, Carter varies the shapes of her lines and her approach to solo construction. At one point it's a series of riffs, each taken up and down the scale, whispered quietly, shouted loudly, elongated, shortened, examined from every possible angle and then discarded as Carter moves on to the next one. Later it's a series of short phrases, then a sequence of long, legato ones. Sometimes she packs these little pieces so close together that they look like a dizzying blur, then she'll restate them in such a way that their patterns become crystal clear. Carter's performance here derives as much from, say, one of Billie Holiday's thirty-two-bar minute-and-a-half vocal refrains of the thirties as do Rollins and Coltrane from one of Lester Young's solos on those same records. Her undiluted brilliance sometimes becomes too much to take in all at once, like certain periods of Coltrane and Rollins, especially as jazz by nature requires shorter forms than classical music, and vocal jazz works best in shorter forms than its instrumental counterpart. Carter has found a way to extend the role of the vocalist, but, as we'll see with much of contemporary vocal jazz, it's one that—and this takes nothing away from her—has little relevance for any singer beyond Carter herself.

Carter combines composition (music and lyrics), arrangement, performance, and improvisation into a single integrated statement. Take a track from the other side of *The Audience with Betty Carter*, "Tight." From every one of these angles it's a successful work, composed and arranged so that its verbal points of importance correspond exactly to its musical peaks. I can't imagine another artist doing one of her songs any more than I can imagine one of them singing any of her reworkings of songs by Rodgers, Porter, or even Rudy Vallee. She works them into something more than a style, more than an approach or a point of view, but an entire musical universe. Carter finds room for everything in this universe, feminism and femininity, slyness and naïveté, the very appropriate retaining—even strengthening—of a composer's original intention (as on "The Trolley Song" and "Everything I Have Is Yours," where she better serves the song by improving the ending that composer Burton Lane initially gave it), and the transformation of said original purpose from something flippant and frivolous to something quite meaningful, most remarkable on Neal Hefti's "Girl Talk," a patronizing and chauvinistic lyric she renders tender and loving.

Because this universe is so complete, in spite of how the discographies of Vaughan, Fitzgerald, and most of the others in her class so totally dwarf hers, it encompasses a few surprising elements, surprising even in light of the way Carter leads us to expect to be surprised. For one thing, her earliest solo recordings, where she does far less of this compositional reworking and far "straighter" run-throughs of the written melody and lyrics, fit just as neatly into Carter's universe as her more recent work. They don't sound like the work of an unfinished artist, but like a performer exploring a different facet of her music. Like Wynton Marsalis's album of standards or Arthur Blythe playing "in the tradition," it's not something Carter was forced to do because of either limited ability—not that singing a melody well is any less difficult than improvising (and Carter has a far better sense of how to put over a ballad than, for example, Clifford Brown)—or commercial pressure.

Carter was twenty-six when she recorded her first album, which went only partially released until twenty-five years later. She had been born Lillie Mae Jones outside Detroit in 1929,[*] and experienced her first contact with music in the church, where she sang, played piano, and did her first arranging. She grew up in exactly the right time and place (thirties and forties Detroit) to become absorbed by the bebop movement. In addition to the church, she played and sang at school, amateur nights at theaters, and bars and cabarets, gradually upgrading her professional status, in Detroit and the Midwest—she even sat in with the Charlie Parker Quintet in 1947. But she didn't officially leave her hometown until friends dared her to present herself to Lionel Hampton as a singer, and he took her up on that dare.

---

[*] Usually the date is given as 1930 (as in Feather and most other sources), but Carter herself admitted to the previous year in a 1982 interview with Whitney Balliett.

She and Hampton had their ups and downs during the two and a half years she canaried with his orchestra (many of their feuds settled by his wife, Gladys Hampton, who got into the habit of rehiring her whenever Hamp gave her the sack), but today she acknowledges Hamp for being the first to recognize her as a future heavyweight. She left the band in 1951, having gained the knowledge of how to lead a band from Hampton and how to arrange from the late Bobby Plater in the band's sax section, and having obtained her stage name, from a combination of noms de plume dreamed up by her and the Hamptons.

The one thing she didn't have when she left Hampton was a hit record as a calling card to help her find work.* In fact, it took her at least twenty years to get her act completely together and her career rolling. She turns up only intermittently in the fifties and sixties: replacing Blossom Dearie as the piano part on King Pleasure's "Red Top" in 1953 (Prestige), sharing an album with Ray Bryant on Epic in 1955, a bill with the Miles Davis Quintet at the Apollo in 1959, and a tour of Japan with Sonny Rollins a few years later. Interest in her from the R&B community led to a second album, on the Texas blues label Peacock (recorded in New York with a group of star bop sidemen) in 1958, and then Ray Charles took her into his entourage and pushed his current label, ABC-Paramount, to let her do a solo disc with Bobby Darin's fine arranger, Richard Wess, as well as an album of duets with Charles. *Ray Charles and Betty Carter* do sound well together, coming off better than Dinah Washington and Brook Benton but nowhere near as well as Billy Eckstine and Sarah Vaughan, though the presence of Charles's squeaky baritone-tenor forces Carter into her squirrelly upper register. It doesn't do her much good to spend the whole album up there; meanwhile the Jack Halloran Singers are also around to crap things up. Charles's next set of duets stoop down to that watered-down bargain basement Betty, Cleo Laine, while Carter's next album

---

* All of Hampton's great forties vocalists—Dinah Washington, Jackie Paris, Joe Williams, Little Jimmy Scott, Carter—went virtually unrecorded with the band.

would mark the lowest point, artistically, of her whole career. It doesn't bother me so much that the arrangements by Claus Ogerman and Oliver Nelson on her Atco album, *'Round Midnight*, are so bad—though bad they are—but that they're so entirely unsuited to Carter. How could anyone even remotely familiar with Carter's art have her debase herself with a "Wheel of Fortune"–type choir of overdubbed voices and assign her such turkeys as "The Good Life" and, believe it or not, "Theme from 'Dr. Kildare.' " Even her own composition, "Who, What, Why?," seems unworthy of her.

In different interviews, Carter has discussed the pros and cons of the mid-sixties rock inundation.* First, it took away all her chances to work, as she had little interest in performing rock or soul, but at least by this time the rockers were acknowledging their debts to the black innovators, she said. In a way, it worked to Carter's advantage, as it forced her up out of the pop market where at least she wouldn't have to contend with hacks like Ogerman anymore (which, in Carter's case, was worse than not recording at all). Her last "early" album, *Inside Betty Carter* (United Artists), was also her first "modern" one to capture much of Carter's contemporary vision, such as her dewaltzed chart of "My Favorite Things" and her long, luxuriant "Spring Can Really Hang You Up the Most," and was made with the same trio she worked with in the clubs. By the end of the decade, she was finally producing her own albums, first for Roulette and then for her own label, Bet-Car. She was bound to reach the point when she'd be appreciated on the same level as her peers, and in the early and mid-seventies one good break led to another: a highly successful tour of Japan in 1975 and then an important run at San Francisco's Keystone Korner later that year.

A few months later she starred in a now-forgotten Brooklyn

* Though she hasn't mentioned it since, a 1966 *Downbeat* feature on Carter mentions a concert with her in the company of Archie Shepp, Albert Ayler, Coltrane, and Sun Ra. As of late, the only thing she has in common with Ornette Coleman is an inflated sense of her market value.

show titled *Don't Call Me, Man,* which led to the first of about six major write-ups she has had in *The Village Voice* over the intervening ten years, far more coverage in that paper than any other musician I can think of. Since then, her career and her music have remained at a peak, she gets the big clubs now, as many of them as she wants, as well as college dates and even network and PBS television appearances. Her label, Bet-Car, went on to release nearly a dozen fine Carter albums, but then faded because as good a businesswoman as Carter is, she's not good enough to run an independent jazz label. In 1988, her first album on the reactivated Verve label was released, which doesn't bother me or any of her other fans as we know that these days she's too much Betty Carter to let anyone tell her what to do or how to do it.

Excepting Art Blakey, no bandleader has introduced more worthwhile musicians in the last ten years or so than Carter; to name just a few: John Hicks, Curtis Lundy, and her latest graduate, the truly remarkable piano prodigy Benny Green (who, as if to prove my point, has also toured with Blakey). Apart from Green, most of Carter's trios have been black. Similarly, Sheila Jordan has worked with many of the major white jazz musicians of the last thirty years, beginning with Lennie Tristano and his associates—George Russell (who gave her her first hearing on a record), Steve Kuhn, Harvie Swartz, and Steve Swallow. Also like Carter, Jordan traces her inspiration back to the early years of the bebop movement with her greatest thrill being that she sat in with Charlie Parker when he played her hometown.[*] Besides a common time and place of birth—Jordan was born in Detroit a year before Carter—the two women share a similar kind of warmth and eagerness to communicate, which, at the further risk of sounding reactionary, cannot be taken for granted either with singers as "far out" as they or considerably further in.

---

[*] Carter, Jordan, and Jon Hendricks all sat in with Bird. Earl Coleman, Dave Lambert, and Buddy Stewart either recorded or broadcast with him. Only Jackie Paris seems to have actually toured with Parker's group.

Carter may have the greater voice, ears, and imagination, but Jordan has much to recommend her.

Where Carter reteaches the importance of the trio as the primary accompaniment for the jazz soloist, Jordan advocates breaking it up into one-on-one duos, like Steve Swallow's bass in "Let's Face the Music" (she once said that she preferred bass to piano because she had a tough time finding pianos that were in tune) or over drummer Beaver Harris's brushes in the first chorus of "By Myself," leaving occasional spaces for a cappella passages. As pianist Steve Kuhn explained to John Wilson in 1981, "We're not accompanying Sheila. She accompanies us. We do duets, solos, trios—we mix it up." Jordan continued, "I can't get into a piece much if I sing two choruses, the piano player plays a chorus, and then it's over." Jordan loves to let her wobbly voice fly into the air with nothing to cover up its affable, friendly vibrato, her Appalachian accent (she grew up in a Pennsylvania coal community) forever perched on the edge of a blue yodel whenever a real high one comes along. Despite an occasional indulgence in scatting, like the six wordless choruses she squeezes out of Parker's standard-form original "Confirmation," Jordan's primary interest lies in reinterpreting (or, as Francis Davis astutely described it, reimagining) melodies and lyrics.

As a rule, Jordan's collaborations with notable composer-theorists like Russell (a very bleak "You Are My Sunshine"), George Gruntz (a 1987 tour with his all-star Concert Jazz Band), and Kuhn (the 1979 *Playground* album for ECM, which consists entirely of Kuhn's "songs") weigh in far heavier (as in serious) than her own efforts, which she intends as entertaining, fun affairs. Jordan's childlike quality refers back to forties Fitzgerald, Humes, and Rushing, and makes her "Dat Dere," on her first album (*Portrait of Sheila* [1962], Blue Note's only important vocal record) quite believable but at the same time renders the record's next track, the attemptedly decadent "When the World Was Young" quite unconvincing.

Confirmation (East Wind 8024), the Jordan album that affords me the most pleasure, has Jordan making practical use of her childlike demeanor. She dedicates the first side to "children all over the world," an introduction that would come off like Jerry Lewis on Labor Day coming from anyone else, and yet without any attempt at loading her phrases down with Orson Wellesian girth, many of these kid songs ("Inch Worm" especially) assume all the profundity of William Blake. This side works like a song cycle in that one track moves directly into the next without stopping, so "God Bless the Child" becomes "My Favorite Things," which goes into another Coltrane standby, "The Inch Worm." Jordan and her players certainly have Trane in mind during both tunes, but the homage is never explicitly stated until tenorist Norman Marshall solos and blows their cover, and as "Inch Worm" segues into "Because We're Kids," Marshall's sax over the background of bells and chimes recalls the Coltrane–Rashied Ali duos of *Interstellar Space*. *Confirmation* ends with the wackiest bit of business of all, a piece called "Pearlie's Swine," which opens with a rather funky stint of hog-calling and then moves into a really weird monologue on the delights of carnivorism—I mean really weird*—that's as silly and straight simultaneously as it is nonkosher ("Ham! / I love eatin' ham! / I don't give a damn!"). *Confirmation* demonstrates how perfectly Jordan matches her sixties postmodal Lydian cohorts, just as Billie Holiday matched her thirties and forties swing associates. For the listener, Jordan personalizes her idiom, gives us something to focus on; for the musicians, Jordan gives them a center to work around without once tying them down, and Kuhn and Swartz et al. never sound nearly as good elsewhere as when they work with Jordan.

Jordan's voice bears a faint resemblance to Anita O'Day and her followers, and *Confirmation* has tonal as well as programmatic qualities in common with June Christy's *Songs for Grown-Up Children*. The difference lies in her swaggering, unfettered vibrato, which shakes back and forth more than O'Day's,

---

* Kuhn retitled it "The Zoo" when he and Jordan rerecorded it in 1979.

Christy's, and Connor's combined. Similarly, Jeanne Lee, who once might have been viewed as the center of avant-garde jazz vocal activity in Europe, initially strikes one as an outgrowth of Abbey Lincoln. Like Jordan, though, the discrepancy between the records she makes on her own and those she makes playing Adelaide Hall for Marion Brown (*Afternoon of a Georgia Fawn* [1970, ECM]), Archie Shepp (*Blase* [1969, BYG]), Anthony Braxton (*Town Hall 1972* [Trio]), and her husband, Gunther Hampel (practically all of the releases on his Birth label, including *All the Things You Could Be If Charlies Mingus Was Your Daddy* [1980]) typifies the sixties. *The Newest Sound Around* (1961, RCA), Lee's first and so far only "conventional" vocal album, juxtaposes parallel relationships on a theoretical level: Warmth and sensuality exude so much from her voice no matter how monotonal she gets, and she has the substance of the avant-garde so deep in her bones that this never becomes threatened by her journeys into the tradition, wherein she points to Dinah Washington on "Evil Blues" and pays tribute to O'Day, Connor, and Christy through their school song, "When Sunny Gets Blue." Meanwhile, on "Laura," Ran Blake's Kenton-on-Valium piano reminds us that David Raksin originally wrote the tune both as a love song and a theme for a murder mystery. Blake makes a perfect partner for Lee, helping her to realign her selections melodically and rhythmically so seamlessly that you scarcely notice the difference.

Other singers in Europe (including some Americans) who have followed Lee and Jordan's example—collaborating with postmodern musician/composers and from time to time getting their own dates—include Lauren Newton and Kate Westbrook. The English Maggie Nicols most exemplifies the bunch. She seems the very essence of the avant pin-up girl: Completely devoid of bourgeois gratification, Nicols writes original songs, both with "straight" lyrics or setting up a whirling, swirling improvised mass of sounds that, when they drift into recognizable speech (cockney, however), use radical musical ideas to express radical social and sexual ideas.

Still, all of these are what you might call traditional radicals, rooted in sixties free jazz; newer vocal avant-gardists have come along to push things even farther out using "new age" thinking and electronics. It doesn't bother me so much that the two female voices in Ellen Christi's *Ménage* don't sound like voices since the three "rhythm" instruments backing them aren't used to sound like instruments; instead, all five participants are front liners in the manner, say, of the Albert Ayler–Sonny Murray groups, but with an amorphous blob of ECM-ish meditational seagull sounds instead of Ayler's tortured cat yowls. No, what bothers me is that they don't have the compositional strength to do anything interesting with the sound; by now we take it for granted that this kind of thing is going to get boring in about five minutes. *Fortune Teller* (1985, Leo Records) by the Russian Valentina Ponomareva also makes scatting seem conservative. She takes the music as far out as it possibly can go, skittering Oliver Messiaen-ically through a mass of real and test tube–created sounds, and even on the album's two standards she produces little we can recognize as a human voice. As arguable as the term "jazz singer" might be, traditionally the "jazz" part provides the controversy; today we can no longer take it for granted that this music qualifies as "singing." In saying that, we should remember that the verbal labels we ascribe to any kind of art have nothing to do with its quality, but in the twenty-five years since Jeanne Lee's first album (or, for that matter, Chris Connor's record of Ornette Coleman's "Lonely Woman") the avant-garde has yet to produce its own Betty Carter.

To be fair, no other recent movement has produced its own Betty Carter, which is as she intended. When she was coming up, she told Michael Ullman, "At the time we dared not imitate. It wasn't easy for us as black people to imitate other great stars and make it. A second Sarah Vaughan would never have the respect of the black community. In the white world, they imitated each other. Stan Getz had a lot of tenor players sounding like him, while he sounded like Lester Young. There were all those girls like Anita O'Day, June Christy, Chris Connor—and they all made it. There were never two Sarah Vaughans, or two Billie Holidays, or two Ella Fitzgeralds." She continued, "We [black people] all strived to be our own person. That was my whole background, my whole foundation." Carter's opinion has relevance here, even if her setting it up in terms of black and white is patently wrong. Stan Getz sounds no more like Lester Young than Ben Webster sounds like Coleman Hawkins, while Lester had at least as many black "vice presidents," like Wardell Gray, Gene Ammons, and Paul Quinichette, as he had white "brothers" like Getz, Zoot Sims, and Al Cohn. And that's not even getting into the dozens of black Armstrong, Crosby, and Eckstine impersonators.

Nevertheless, Carter's point hits home exactly where it should: in her own work. Her line of thinking, the influences upon her, her background and life story, and other factors contributed to the development of a method that works only for her. In recent years I've noted a few singers who can be described as "post–Betty Carter"—Carmen Lundy, Cassandra Wilson—only in terms of theoretical or conceptual parallels, specifically their approaches toward composition and arrangements.*

Carter's "arrival" in the mid to late seventies culminates the development of the most recent movement in jazz—namely, the end of movements. In the thirties and forties there was enough work in this field to support a dozen Bing Crosbys or five Roy Eldridges (remember Frank Humphries?), but after Sinatra's Swingin' Lovers school of the fifties (and, simultaneously, Chet Baker–derived "soft singing") we haven't had one new genre— in other words, a style that works for an entire group of musicians on the same instrument. From the sixties onward, we've had only one Tony Bennett, one Betty Carter, one Bobby Mc-Ferrin, and so on.

---

* Cleo Laine, who started as a British second-string Sarah Vaughan, has matured into a bottom-of-the-barrel Betty Carter, but only through approximating aspects of Carter's sound, completely ignoring her structural accomplishments, which may explain why Laine has been on major labels for so long.

Still, there are dozens of would-be Bettys. As she suggests, they'll never "make it," but in the early eighties you could hear them by the carload in New York's jazz performance spaces like the Universal Jazz Coalition and the now-defunct Jazz Cultural Theatre, as well as the lofts and new-talent clubs like the Angry Squire. Most are women and many are involved with this music primarily to be "part of the scene" (and not just only sleeping with musicians) and only secondarily to sing, though most have the mistaken idea that scat singing is the key to vocal jazz and try to do the same kind of superextended vocal improvisations that Carter does. I have no objections to this theoretically: New artistic styles are supposed to grow out of influences, but a talent like Carter's comes along only once in a millennium, and attempts to bring about the Second Coming have, scat-wise, thus far brought about only off-the-chord caterwauling.

This is where it gets dicey. I've said there are no more genres left, only uninformed glances forward and backward, but at this level, where perpetual amateurism has replaced up-and-coming talent, future and past blend together as if in a Cuisinart. Futurism eschews lyrics and written melody—even as an introductory head—and neoconservatism provides an equally shoddy excuse for camping up old songs and cultural cross-dressing (someone in the audience during Angela Bofill's 1986 JVC Jazz Festival appearance dubbed her "The Singing Lampshade"). Past and future become indistinguishable in their mediocrity. On the looking-backward side of the fence, standards have fallen so low in the type of music known as "standards" that many of those at the top, kiddie-pop stars trying to move up to adult pop (beginning with Linda Ronstadt), are on the same level of ineptness as the rankest beginner on the bottom rung of the musical/social ladder, supplying further proof that neither talent nor ability is necessarily an asset in the age of Bush and Madonna.

As the movement of futurists engaged in endless abstract exercises would name the unwilling Carter as their inspiration, Rosemary Clooney, the other great singer to emerge at the end

of the seventies, has also circumstantially inspired a largely negative movement that must embarrass her: revivalism and the
comeback trail. Especially as Carter for years recorded only
sporadically, and since Jordan and Jeanne Lee at their busiest
turn out new releases only rarely, revivalism, which encompasses a broad range of subjects, attracts the most attention to
any jazz–adult pop development of the current period. If only a
few of the other birds in this flock flew anywhere near Clooney's
heights there would be little to squawk about. As it stands,
Clooney inspires them not so much in terms of music and performance, but in terms of careers and would-be careers.

Starting as a band canary at the end of the forties, Rosemary
Clooney became a big pop star in the fifties, but got out of show
business in the sixties. She left for (mental) health reasons; most
of the others left for economic ones—in other words, the rock 'n'
roll revolt took away their opportunities to work, and when the
market got tighter, the lesser singers generally beat it (even with
little work around, the talented ones, including those who had
never made it, like Jackie Paris and David Allyn, generally managed to keep singing). They became plumbers or married
wealthy manufacturers or whatever.

Then, when Clooney, Torme, and others began to attract
attention again, generally on the jazz club and festival circuit,
doing new albums for jazz-minded independent labels (Concord
Jazz in both cases here), the others also decided it was time to
"come back." This mentality has had a staggering effect on the
music, not only in terms of forgotten-but-not-gone old-timers
who have tried to crawl back, but also on younger artists who
weren't around before the rock era and, more surprisingly, legions of fast-fading kiddie-pop stars in search of a new gimmick.

Such developments have led to acres of bad—or even worse,
useless—music, but you can't blame any of this on Clooney
herself, any more than you can blame Cleo Laine on Betty Carter
or Charles Lloyd on John Coltrane. Clooney's singing is so good
it has habitually pulled her through unfortunate circumstances,
from out of the frying pan of the slightly corny Tony Pastor band

to the great flaming corn of the Mitch Miller assembly line at Columbia during the nadir of Miller-ism. Her triumphant musicianship rescued her from potentially shallow recording situations in the fifties just as it does in the eighties when she works for a label that believes in cookie-cutter production—though in saying that I should clarify that Concord Jazz generally cuts out pretty terrific cookies. Singing came so naturally to Clooney that, if her autobiography, *This for Remembrance*, is accurate, she barely struggled at all to become the biggest-selling singer in the world and the first canary to perch on the cover of *Time;* the major battle of her life came with her breakdown in 1968. Still, I can't believe music means as little to her as this book suggests, what with her elaborating endlessly on the costumes the Clooney Sisters wore with the Pastor Orchestra while barely giving us word one about the kind of music she sang with that band.

Clooney's biography can be summed up rather quickly: Born in 1928 in Maysville, Kentucky, the product of a continually breaking and unbreaking home, Clooney grew up there and in several other towns on the Ohio River, eventually ending up in Cincinnati. In the days before television, radio stations still hired on-staff singers, and it was almost laughably easy for Clooney and her sister Betty to make the professional grade. The station, WLW, led to opportunities to work around Cincinnati and a forum to audition for Tony Pastor when he played through. After two years, with a bunch of band vocal refrains (some solo, some as half of a sister act) and some good reviews under her arm, she left Pastor, staying with Pastor's manager, Joe Shribman, and Pastor's label, Columbia. Despite an early duet disc with Sinatra and a summer replacement radio show with the up-and-coming Tony Bennett, nothing much happened with her career until Mitch Miller came to Columbia with his fresh, original ideas about how pop music could be made worse. He came up with new gimmicks for tacky orchestrations (ways of plucking electric guitar strings and harpsichords) and appealed to the urban white's inherently racist tendency to pooh-pooh ethnicities, whether Armenian ("Come On-a My House"), Italian ("Botch-a

Me," "Mambo Italiano"), or even regional American ("This Ole
House"), and also fashioned hits for Clooney out of good songs
like "Tenderly" and "Hey There."

All of Clooney's worthwhile early music came from her ventures outside Miller's sphere of influence at Columbia. She exhibited a healthy interest in jazz ever since her first write-up
compared her with Ella Fitzgerald, and this affected her music,
even in the Miller years, on individual tracks (like "The Lady Is
a Tramp," made with a trio, and three tracks from a 1955 session
where she sits in with the Benny Goodman Sextet) and entire
LPs (such as *Hollywood's Best* with Harry James and *Blue Rose*
[1960] where she overdubbed her voice to prerecorded tracks by
Duke Ellington and His Orchestra). Her best early work came
after leaving Miller and Columbia altogether, for example on her
1960 RCA albums like *Clap Hands, Here Comes Rosie* (where
Bob Thompson's arrangements throw a bone to Rosie's jazz fans
with the presence of Jimmy Rowles, Bud Shank, and others, but
take it away with the presence of an unwelcome choir of background voices and hand-clappers) and the straightforwardly hot
Rosie Solves the Swingin' Riddle—the Riddle being Nelson
(which includes a post-Basie "April in Paris" that suggests the
Bill Davis arrangement without swiping from it). Both albums
demonstrate that Clooney has little in common with the other
jazz-influenced white pop post-canaries of the era (Stafford, Day,
Shore, Whiting) and almost equally little with the great black
tradition of "purer" jazz vocalizing (Holiday, Fitzgerald,
Vaughan), but they do show a genuine affinity with the great
male icons of the jazz-and-pop mainstream: Sinatra, Bennett,
and, most of all, Crosby; her experiments with cowboy and
mambo formats indicate multistylistic leanings on the order of
Crosby and Sonny Stitt.

The solidest Clooney album of all, *Swing Around Rosie* (1959,
Coral), finds her surrounded by the organ trio of Buddy Cole
(who shouldn't be blamed for being chosen to play piano on Nat
Cole records over the King himself), who often plays his electric
instrument less like Jimmy Smith and more like Wollman's skat-

ing rink. When jazz folk discuss vocalists, they usually point out how the setting in which a singer operates affects a given performance; here's one example of a singer affecting her background, transforming a latently corny setup into a true jazz group.

Yet Clooney is a singer in the present tense, and as much as I enjoy her fifties and sixties sides, the great Clooney didn't come into being until nearly ten years after her crack-up. One earlier record will make my point, *Rosemary Clooney Swings Softly* (MGM). An average early Clooney album, remarkable in that it collates songs even I've never heard of, it switches between up-tempo and ballad-time numbers. And while you couldn't go so far as to attribute to Clooney the shallowness endemic of the Mitch Miller idiom, her ballads lack the authority of the faster pieces. At her worst (which is a lot of other singers' best), she comes off as sentimental, acting or faking it rather than feeling it. That stops in her later work. You can partially credit this to postcollapse therapy; she writes: "Under the care and guidance of [her psychiatrist] a very beautiful thing happened to me. I am today able to show my emotions, which I never could before." Though she doesn't make the connection (not in so many words at least) that this might affect her singing, it makes all the difference in the world. Combined with her rhythmic gifts and her tenor-saxy tone, it makes Clooney one of the best singers going today, and the essence of modern Swingin' Lover style: the knack for moving an audience both emotionally and musically.

Clooney's steady swing supplies the basic essence of what she does, but her tone attracts the most people to her in terms of both audiences and other singers. Traditionally, the most dependable kind of sound in vocal jazz, from Bessie Smith and Bing Crosby onward, can be described as a "black" sound— sometimes more directly African, as in the case of Abbey Lincoln. From Armstrong up, the other kind of tonal approach jazz often uses is "character" singing, the kind of voice that disciplines itself to sound undisciplined, which applies to singing musicians and regional accents, from Jack Teagarden's Texas drawl to Anita O'Day's Chicago slurs. The central difference between recent and older Clooney, aside from emotional weight, lies in her touching on "old" sound, which is one of the most important elements of the comeback movement. Old sound works in degrees from light (as in Clooney's case) to heavy (as with Billie Holiday, to isolate this from other aspects of her art, who managed to sound incredibly old before she was forty), and encompasses such technicalities as rasp, the sound of air breathing through old throats and lungs, and the gradual loss of the ability to control vibrato and pitch—though if anything the gift for keeping *time* becomes acuter. Especially with today's reverence of the very old, as indicated by, among other things, TV weathermen who report the birthdays of nonagenarians and talk shows where anyone nearing the century mark (even if they've achieved nothing else) is greeted with wild applause, "old" sound is somehow regarded as authentic. Someone who combines all three attributes—black, character, and old, like Jabbo Smith and Doc Cheatham—can count on delighting crowds wherever they sing.

Lesser comeback singers with "old"-sounding voices sometimes actually try to substitute dynamics for pitch; by getting louder and softer they bluff audiences and even critics into thinking they're hearing a melody line, which automatically separates them from the folk-and-rock-bred youngsters who moan everything in an emphasisless monotone. Old style has generally more negative points than positive, since it implies the loss of the ability to sing (it ruined Helen Humes), but it can also add dramatic credulity to a performance. In addition to Clooney, that rasp made better singers out of Fran Warren, Margaret Whiting, and a few others, and it made Maxine Sullivan an extremely good singer in the last few years of her life.

Sullivan had made her biggest noise at the start of her career with the softest style, an emotionless proto-cool style that attracted her to the proto-cool arranger-bandleader Claude Thornhill. Born in Pittsburgh in 1911, she worked around that town until the pianist with Ira Ray Hutton's all-girl band happened to catch her and recommend her to Thornhill. Thornhill's ideas as to how to use her voice were to soon do as much for his career as they would for Sullivan, and he concentrated on a gimmick that Sullivan had already been using for years. Thornhill matched Sullivan's "suave, sophisticated swing" with material from way out of the Afro-Jewish jazz and Tin Pan Alley lexicon, from Anglo-European folk sources, which paid off in the Sullivan-Thornhill hit "Loch Lomond." The novelty wasn't in swinging the old-time stuff—the English show singer Ella Logan had already been doing that*—but in hearing a four-foot-ten black girl sing it in a black-white way, swinging, certainly, but subtly and with unusual restraint.

Sullivan recorded extensively with and without Thornhill, and with and without her other major collaborator (and first husband), bassist–combo leader John Kirby. However, in spite of contracts with all three of the major labels in the years immediately following "Loch Lomond," and other triumphs such as movie and Broadway appearances and the first black-jazz series on major network radio, her career faltered from the 1942 AFM ban onward. She had coasted for too long on the folk-song gimmick, moving from Scottish airs to "Orchichonia,"† "My Yiddish Mama," and along the way initiated a brief vogue for swinging Shakespeare songs. Unfortunately, there was no building a lasting career in any of these brief vogues, and she couldn't get people to pay attention to her work with standards, and never had another hit. On the strength of "Loch Lomond" she continued to work and record occasionally for minor labels until 1958, at which point she decided to concentrate on her family and the community affairs that had already been occupying much of her attention.

---

* "Loch Lomond" was, in fact, part of her act; her niece Annie Ross (then known as Annabelle Logan) had swung it as such in an *Our Gang* movie short.

† In the 1939 musical *St. Louis Blues*, Hollywood gangster Allen Jenkins tells Maxine, "Sure there's black people in Russia. Ain't ya never hoid of the Black Sea?"

Sullivan stayed away from professional singing for only seven years or so, but that was long enough for her to qualify as one of the principal figures in the comeback movement. Gradually, at least two reliable groups of followers sprang up around her. The first were people from her neighborhood, dozens and dozens of them, who knew her as much as a nurse and community leader as a performer, and were rallied by the rock-steady determination and forcefulness it took to succeed at both; the second was the equally tight traditional jazz network of festivals and small labels, which gradually increased her work load until, in the months immediately preceding her death in 1987, she not only worked all the time but had new albums out virtually every month. Her followers also came to venerate her as the New Orleans purists of the forties had worshiped Bunk Johnson; in her they found an authentic relic of 52nd Street and the Onyx Club, a survivor from the golden age whom they interviewed countless times* and taped virtually every performance she gave.

The traddies celebrated Sullivan for the wrong reasons. After "coming back," she sang the dreaded "Loch Lomond" only when the money was big enough (at the dozens of occasions I saw her, I don't think I heard the tune once) and dwelt instead in the realm of Gershwin, Arlen, Carmichael, et al. Still, the biggest changes were not in repertoire but in texture: The familiar coolness remained, still anchored by her gentle swing, but both were now tempered with "old" sound, a rasp with slight pitch problems, that added immeasurably to her convincingness. Like Clooney, it gave Sullivan a whole new dimension. Especially in live appearances, the juxtaposition of her controlled bounce mixed with the hard-tack tenacity of her personality to create a depth unmatched in her "first career." Too many of those dozens of seventies and eighties albums put her in unrehearsed jam-session settings, which brought out more of the difficulties she

---

* They do the same thing to Doc Cheatham, who sings, in his version of "I Can't Get Started": ". . . Maxine Sullivan has had me to tea."

had at seventy-plus years at staying in tune, the kind of problems you would never notice in a club or concert set.

Inevitably, her best later albums require a collaborating arranger to come up with the same kind of well-constructed frameworks as her Thornhill and Kirby sessions, like Loonis McGoohan on *Good Morning, Life* (1983, Audiophile), Dick Hyman on *I Love to Be in Love* (Tono), and best of all, Bob Wilber on *The Music of Hoagy Carmichael* (Monmouth-Evergreen). It must be a source of frustration for the classic jazz fans who were to some degree responsible for her "second career" that her best albums were produced by two men with no experience and little interest in jazz, but instead approached recording Sullivan as they would a Broadway show. Ken Bloom and Bill Rudman, of Harbinger Records, in cooperation with the British arranger-pianist Keith Ingham, taped Sullivan "live" with a small band, and then meticulously overdubbed any sections where pitch or rhythm problems occurred. The resulting three albums, *Maxine Sullivan Sings the Great Cotton Club Songs of Harold Arlen and Ted Koehler* (1984, Stash), *Maxine Sullivan Sings the Music of Burton Lane* (1985, Stash), and *Maxine Sullivan Sings the Music of Jule Styne—Together* (1987, Atlantic),[*] make the most creative use yet of the overdubbing process and, more importantly, capture a fine singer at her all-time peak. Her talent took seventy-five years to completely mature, but it was worth the wait.

A few other older-fashioned-style singers deserve mention at this point. Carol Sloane and Marilyn Maye each tried to launch nonrock careers in the sixties when the industry had on its tightest rock-only blinders, but Sloane today has a comfortable enough coterie of followers in America (especially in North Carolina, where she lives) and Japan for her to make a living singing. She repels a lot of listeners at first because of her overwhelming

---

[*] In the interest of full disclosure, I worked on two of these Sullivan albums as well as the Anita Gravine album described later. In the interest of modesty, however, my only capacity was in postproduction.

tonal similarity to Ella Fitzgerald, but that only means she has to work a little harder to win them over. And her strengths as an interpreter (she's more into lyrics than Ella) are generally up to the task. Another comebacker, Jane Harvey, the 1945 entry in the Benny Goodman parade of vocalists, probably has enough talent and taste (and intelligence to change the opening line of "God Bless the Child" from "Them that's got" to "Those that have," which sounds more natural coming from someone who isn't Billie Holiday) to sustain a career but hasn't tried to. Reflecting a common opinion that says little for the music industry, Harvey classifies her singing as a "dilettante pursuit" and chooses to work only one important gig, in New York, each year. Even as a dilettante Harvey has more to offer than most professionals, but with both her attitude and the industry in such negative accord it seems unlikely that she'll ever become truly great.

Dilettantism is, in fact, the curse of the revivalist and the comeback movement, as is the idea of the "second career." No one can make a decent living; this music has become the property of those who can't sing it professionally. "It's not my fault I can't get a gig," they tell themselves. "It's the fault of the business." The admittedly nowhere state of the record biz then becomes an excuse for not trying. As I say, some of them used to be professionals back when there was a market for them, though generally of the jazzless pop variety rather than the harder kind of stuff. Clubs and record labels generally supplied audiences for singers then. Today, as a parallel to the increasingly popular Catch a Rising Star type of comedy nightclubs, unestablished singers have to dig into their pockets to be given an audience, in rooms that today are called "cabarets" where the performer (generally a singer) must guarantee to sell a certain number of admissions. The same thing goes on in the record business, where self-financed vanity albums range from privately pressed productions to independent labels that require a bankroll to subsidize a release all the way up to the ultimate vanity artist, Pia Zadora.

Even worse are the current pop stars who delve into this for one reason or another. Aside from the much-publicized Linda Ronstadt and the less successful Toni Tennille, Maria Muldaur, and Barry Manilow (who come out of the classic Eddie Fisher–Teresa Brewer–Johnny Mathis tradition of really bad singing), the eighties have seen a run of so-called soul singers trying the old stuff as a last resort to save a failing career—for example, Patti Austin and Angela Bofill, who presume that the only requirements for singing Duke Ellington and Billie Holiday songs are being black and being female. The dilettantes come from even more surprising places, such as the jingle business; the offspring of star jazz musicians, singers, and critics; and classical music, as in the case of Kiri Te Kanawa (who, like Ronstadt, hired Nelson Riddle to make her authentic), Eileen Farrell, and the vacuous Maureen McGovern, who has a background (meaning a "first" career) in pop but a classical sound.

Pretty soon we were bound to have a few full-time dilettantes, and our worst fears were realized with the rising career of the major idiot who calls himself Buster Poindexter and who massacres the great songs in brutally inane renditions that make even Bette Midler seem tasteful, and that both he and his audiences are too ignorant to realize are part parody and part insult. For years I've put down the white guitar groups who take black bluesmen as their models, but by comparison we've so far been unable to find a rock-pop artist who can "cover" Sinatra and Lee even as respectfully as the Rolling Stones covered Muddy Waters. This type of singing seems part and parcel of the "Saturday Night Live" school of comedy: Create a few obvious characters, have them repeat a given set of lines or catch phrases week after week, and pretty soon everybody will be going around parroting, "You look mahvelous!" The singers who have made it in the last twenty-five or so years all seem to operate on the same theory: Take a few obvious mannerisms (whether your own or borrowed) to use as substitutes for soul and swing, and string them together just as obviously; people who don't know any better will think they're listening to something. It becomes less a matter of music than a form of connect the dots.

Cleo Laine has traditionally worked this way, as has Dianne Schuur. That she's virtually the only "jazz singer" in the traditional sense (even granted that the term is undefinable, especially traditionally) to succeed commercially in the eighties is genuinely disturbing. Schuur is truly the Steven Spielberg of singing. After years of flagrant amateurism from the likes of Ronstadt and others, who can't even pronounce the words to the songs, let alone interpret them musically or lyrically, anyone who can strike people as being even halfway professional looks good. Schuur at least can keep a tempo, has clear diction, and stays in tune, and so no one seems bothered by her fashioning a style out of hand-me-down ideas she can't begin to do justice to, or her resorting to screaming as a cheap shot when she can't think of anything else to do, or her grotesque stage mannerisms, her vast unoriginality in terms of repertoire, arrangements (after Vaughan and Torme, do we really need another "Just Friends" where the singer harmonizes a wordless chorus with the orchestra?) . . . in short, the works.

But by far the *worst* thing to happen to jazz-pop in recent years, even including fusion, is Michael Feinstein. Movie director Herbert Ross once predicted that if we kept making ultra-bloody horror films for too long, there would eventually be such a backlash that censorship groups would spring up and prohibit anything more violent than *Bambi*. This is the only explanation I can come up with for something like Feinstein. Perhaps too many years of Sarah Vaughans and Billy Eckstines reharmonizing their material, or Frank Sinatras substituting phrases like "baby," "Jack," and "Ring-a-ding-ding" for the original words, or Louis Armstrongs doing the same with "chops" and "Swiss kriss," or Betty Carters and Mel Tormes (Mel*s* Torme?) coming up with their own time signatures and daring to combine one song with another have scared people off.

Perhaps they react along the lines of Brian Rust, master discographer and amateur critic, who deplores performances of "Body and Soul" where "the melody line is bent out of recognition," or classical crit Sergius Kagen, who feels that dotting notes or changing a sixteenth to an eighth is "an adolescent

affectation, but it may become most obnoxious if it is left un-
checked and allowed to become an integral part of one's way of
singing." Rust and Kagen might be right. Feinstein certainly
agrees with them, for his approach is the least interpretive and
the flattest, sheet-music-demonstration-ist imaginable. But you
can't justify him on the basis of preserving the composer's intentions, because for every supersquare Richard Rodgers or Ira
Gershwin who moans when you emphasize the wrong word,
there's a Harold Arlen, who felt honored when black jazzmen
played his songs and himself arranged a double-time version of
"It's Only a Paper Moon," or a George Gershwin, who wrote
"Variations" for his own "I Got Rhythm" and reworked his opera
Porgy and Bess into a suite that is quite similar, theoretically, to
what Miles Davis and Gil Evans would later do with the same
material. And you can't defend Feinstein on the basis of the
cabaret tradition, because even though cabaret king Bobby Short
doesn't swing,* he at least performs with the knowledge that
Duke Ellington and Bessie Smith once existed and that their
music is relevant to his. And even though Mabel Mercer held
lyrics sacred, she knew that the way to treat them most respectfully was to interpret and personalize them.

But it will always be easier to dwell on the negative, a trait
possibly endemic to all criticism and certainly to anyone writing
about jazz and singing today. As of late, there have been plenty
of positive happenings to report concerning this music, by artists
under forty even, which is free from the self-indulgences of
either dilettante reactionaries or, to paraphrase Gary Giddins,
Jackson Pollocks of the voice.

To a certain extent, unfortunately, so far these successes are
generally not commercial ones. In the previous chapter, I de-
tailed the record industry's gradual abandonment of non–kiddie
pop forms, and nothing has changed since the sixties. About the
kindest thing we can say about the record business—particularly

* To point out a critical failing in myself, it took Feinstein to make me fully appreciate Short.

the retail end of things—is that it's completely out of sync with what's happening in the clubs or wherever else the music is performed live. Anita O'Day, for instance, produces her own records, and while they accurately reflect her nightclub sets, she presses them to sell primarily at gigs, and neither distributors nor retailers give them the respect they deserve. Mel Torme records regularly at least, yet his Concord Jazz albums with George Shearing never live up to the excitement generated by his inspired East Coast trios with pianists Mike Renzi and, more recently, John Campbell.

For an established artist, it isn't so bad (Torme's records are always great at the very least); for an up-and-coming one, the discrepancy between what goes into the stores and what goes on in the clubs makes or breaks careers. Take the case of two other Anitas: Anita Moore and Anita Gravine. Moore, who was probably the last canary to work with Duke Ellington's band while Duke was alive and a fixture of the band under Mercer Ellington's direction ever since, impressed me tremendously with the scope and range of what she could do at a concert at St. Peter's a few years ago. She demonstrated ideas about the possibilities of a bridge between Ella Fitzgerald and Sarah Vaughan, which also incorporates the best that the Ellington girl-singer tradition had to offer, specifically Adelaide Hall's wordless sonorities (extended by Kay Davis and Alice Babs) and Joya Sherrill's danceband bounce. But as far as records go, so far Moore has come out with only a soporiferous attempt at breaking the black pop charts, full of meager originals, including a song called "It's Bad" that serves as an accurate description of the disc itself. (Though a bit more professional, the very promising Carmen Lundy's only album, *Good Morning Kiss*, suffered from the same problem, shallow black pop instead of the harder, swinging stuff her audiences are still waiting for.)

The problem also exists in reverse. Anita Gravine* has pro-

---

* For a time, Gravine was married to bassist Michael Moore, and so was legally named "Anita Moore."

duced three of the more satisfying vocal albums of the eighties, and yet she has never had the opportunity she wants to perform in front of audiences. *Downbeat* reviewer John McDonough once used Gravine to make the point that the degree of jazz in a vocal record depends upon the accompaniment, and if he couldn't find anything in Gravine's singing that matches his description of a jazz singer, then her backing might earn her the title. Although McDonough was discussing her first album, *Dream Dancing* (1982, Progressive), he could have also meant her second, *I Always Knew* (1984, Stash),* which features Tom Harrell, one of the current generation's most frightening trumpeters; besides which arranger-pianist Michael Abene fashioned string quartet charts for her that reflect the post-Bartók string textures currently fashionable in jazz. However, singer and accompaniment don't exist in capsules; as with Clooney's *Swing Around Rosie*, they affect each other. Gravine and Abene also re-reconcile jazz and pop singing on their duet, "Not for All the Rice in China," which recalls Thelonious Monk as much as Irving Berlin. It's not just the spaced-out Monk-ey phrasing that both singer and pianist employ, it's how they exploit the method Monk and Charlie Rouse devised to replace the customary horn solo and comping chords from the piano with a dual melody statement by tenor and piano in harmony—or heterophonic near-harmony. Whether or not Gravine would fare as well in live performance as she does on *Dream Dancing, I Always Knew*, and her third album, an as-yet unreleased songbook set of "*Road movie*" songs by Johnny Burke and Jimmy Van Heusen, remains to be seen.

The title of Vocal Summit's only album, *Sorrow Is Not Forever—Love Is* (1982, Moers Music), could serve as a motto for the state of vocal jazz today, and the album contains some of the most remarkable music our generation has produced. It's too small a compliment to call it the best vocal group jazz of the

---

* Another conflict of interest, I was involved with this record in postproduction.

eighties, since nothing else has come anywhere close. Significantly, Vocal Summit represents the sum of its members in important ways—only Urszula Dudziak does anything fundamentally different from her customary appearances, since here she uses a cappella and acoustic backings instead of her usual electronics. Jeanne Lee is, as usual, modestly content to remain away from the solo spotlight and rarely emerges from the ensemble. Jan Clayton, whose individual efforts are marred by too much of an "I-am-an-instrument!" attitude, contributed "Meet You There," which could be a four-hundred-year-old motet, reflecting her interest in formal art music, both the contemporary and the classical sort.

Lauren Newton brought along a piece called "Conversations Junior," which she recorded the same year on her solo debut album *Timbre* (1982, Hat Art), which nonverbally mimics and, at the same time, musicalizes human dialogue and digs deep into the fundamentals of jazz and singing. "Conversations" merges Clark Terry's "Mumbles," the comedian Cliff Nazarro's[*] semiverbal double-talk routine, Charlie Mingus's own "Conversations," and the whole vaudeville tradition of "talking" instruments, which seeped into jazz (for example, Harry Raderman's laughing trombone "conversation" with Ted Lewis on "When My Baby Smiles at Me").[†] On both appearances, Newton's pure pitch and her restless imagination and sense of humor prove that there is room today for at least one full-time scatter.

But Vocal Summit's most valuable benefaction is introducing to vinyl Bobby McFerrin, who, at the dawn of the nineties, would seem to be the one unqualified commercial *and* artistic

---

[*] His best-remembered role is probably that of Fred Astaire's sidekick in *You'll Never Get Rich*.

[†] There are other examples: King Oliver's trumpet "sermon" mentioned by Jim Collier in *The Making of Jazz*, Pee Wee Russell and Louis Prima's instrumental conversation in the 1936 film short *Swing It!*, Rex Stewart's *Chatter Jazz*, and Bob Effros, a respected jazz session man of the early thirties who specialized in approximating human speech on his muted trumpet.

success the jazz/pop-vocal tradition has produced this decade. Even considering that most of the Vocal Summit LPs make uniquely effective use of demanding a cappella settings, McFerrin simply amazes here. The duet with Dudziak, "New York Polka," opens with the two loosely approximating a piano, McFerrin riffing (or "comping") in the bass, Dudziak stating then improvising on a melody line in the treble. McFerrin's solo/ composition "Steam" has him doing both parts by himself, on one level like a piano, on another like a guitar (say, Kenny Burrell) or a horn (say, Sonny Rollins)* does when playing solo and making like a piano. Then, by the first track on his second and best own album, *The Voice* (1984, Elektra Musician), McFerrin has moved beyond the necessity of separating the bass and treble, melody and accompaniment lines, and "Blackbird," based on an infantile Beatles song, blends both lines together so that the lyrics get stated directly on top of the "background" figure as McFerrin wheezes it up and down. These lyrics come out at odd intervals, so that if McFerrin happens to be at a high point in the riff, they're high, if not, they're low; additionally, he mixes in whistling, birdcalls, and a vocal impression of echo-chamber resonance. McFerrin obliterates all doubt that he can sustain interest for a whole album without benefit of lyrics (they're only briefly heard on "Blackbird") or accompaniment; they only cramp his style, which explains why his first album, the overproduced *Bobby McFerrin* (1982, Elektra), was such a disappointment.

While McFerrin may have perfected an all-new framework for the voice to operate in—none at all—vocalist, arranger, and composer Cassandra Wilson has developed a more radical idea: Nearly twenty years after Tony Bennett's monologue on "Eleanor Rigby," she dares to suggest that recent pop may yet be relevant to vocal jazz. This isn't fusion, that slick, empty blend

---

* Rollins virtually invented the unaccompanied solo, but Phil Wilson's solo trombone performances could make the point equally well. For argument's sake I'm avoiding free jazz solo improvisers like Leo Smith, Anthony Braxton, and Albert Mangelsdorff.

of the worst of both worlds that does justice to neither. Rather than dwelling strictly on the surface, as fusers do, Wilson and her collaborators (most notably altoist and genre-builder Steve Coleman) build their textures from the inside out, using rock rhythm as part of their vocabulary and, for reasons more important than simply pacifying suspicious souls such as myself, mutating it at least as thoroughly as Benny Golson does his marches and Max Roach his waltzes. On her first solo album, *Point of View* (1986, JMT), Wilson achieves this by adding her voice to basically the same texture developed by Steve Coleman for his first album, *Motherland Pulse* (1985, JMT), an ensemble/compositional approach that grows out of his alto sound, which he described to Peter Watrous as a "fly-hang-fly-hang thing," inspired by martial arts moves, sixties soul (specifically James Brown), and the flying patterns of bees.

Affixing a voice to this makes sense, as Coleman and Wilson had previously proven when she contributed a guest vocal to *Motherland Pulse*. Coleman has come up with a particularly vocal, post-Ornette kind of texture in which vamps, of the sort that "traditional fusion" folks (e.g., Miles Davis) restrict to the bass, permeate the whole ball of wax harmonically, melodically, and structurally. Wilson, who deals in lyrics and melody more than scat and improvisation, characteristically stretches tunes over the fly-hang thing. The blending with soul music occurs nonaudibly, as Wilson's dry, livid tone has far more to do with Jeanne Lee than Aretha Franklin.

Point of View replaces the pianist from Coleman's band, Five Elements, with trombonist Grachan Moncur III, though otherwise it sounds pretty much the same. *Days Aweigh* (1987, JMT), Wilson's second album, supports her with backings more familiar—and in her music, background and foreground are ultimately indistinguishable—with a quartet (generally with one or two horns on top) that alternates between acoustic and lightly electric instruments, though occasionally with her voice multi-tracked in unheard-of ways. Coleman presides once more as co-producer and sideman, but other arranging voices participate besides those of Wilson and other Elements, such as Henry Threadgill and Olu Dara. On "Electromagnolia," Dara's delightfully schmaltzy cornet introduces Wilson while Jean-Paul Bourelly's guitar makes like a sea of electric mandolins, and when Dara and Wilson sing together they could be the avant-pop Louis Prima and Keely Smith.

Despite the more intriguing acoustic textures of the first album, *Days Aweigh* represents an advance, mainly in the deepening maturity of Wilson's own singing. Geri Allen, pianist with Five Elements, has spoken of the group's preference for developing their own repertoire as an alternative to learning everyone else's standards. The one familiar tune on *Point of View*, the Billie Holiday favorite "I Wished on the Moon," signifies the closest thing to a disappointment, as instead of getting inside the song, Wilson and company merely adapt it to their approach as an American abroad would convert his dollars into the local currency. "Let's Face the Music," on side one of *Days Aweigh*, gets a little deeper, while "Some Other Time," on side two, has Wilson, at last, meeting the song halfway. Three other standards recorded apart from Coleman and the Elements gang, guesting with a quartet of guitar (Jim DeAngelis), flute (Tony Sigma), bass, and drums (released 1987, Statiras), prove that she's learning to handle Tin Pan Alley as expertly as that composed by and for her.

I end with Wilson and McFerrin because their music is so filled with promise, and also because they are being heard (McFerrin is on a major label; Wilson's three albums and five guest appearances are, at least, distributed by one). In any event, this chapter has been written with a planned literary obsolescence. How many Wilsons and McFerrins are out there waiting to be found? And how many Kay Starrs and Jackie Parises await rediscovery? With the music's social and commercial status having almost nowhere to go but up, future rewrites of these last few pages will certainly stress the positive over the negative. Today the jazz-influenced pop vocal tradition can coast on what it has achieved in the last sixty years. When you can hear live, in the course of a single week in New York, Mel Torme, Sarah Vaughan, Joe Williams, and Betty Carter, surely there is little to complain about. And even if the music were to have no future, even if the philistines of the business were to succeed in banishing individuality in favor of "sedative culture," these six decades would still be valid.

Duke Ellington used to include in his sets a routine involving an inquiry as to what he thought jazz would sound like in the year 2000. "I have given great consideration to this matter," Ellington would say with great seriousness, "and I am convinced that in the year 2000, jazz will sound like this . . ." At this point, one of his trumpeters would jump up and go into an impression of Louis Armstrong singing "When the Saints Go Marching In."

Selected Discography

Further Definitions

●————————————————————————

When I first compiled this listing in 1985 and '86 (along with the rest of the book), I imagined that should I ever be lucky enough to be asked to update it, the situation would be completely different five years hence. It's therefore surprising to find how little things have changed in ten. With the CD now entrenched as a way of life, things have reverted to the scene of the early '70s. The major-label American issues generally amount to samplers and introductory issues; those seeking deeper reissues on CD are still advised to look overseas: to Europe for swing-oriented 78s and to Japan for '50s LPs.

One thing that has changed is the price: where $15 to $18 seemed like a lot to pay for a Japanese LP ten years ago, it's now customary to pay around $35 a pop for their digital equivalents. Another is the disappearance of many artists whose audience, or whose reissue producers, have apparently never made the technological leap to the digital domain. Quite a few are from the '20s, such as Ruth Etting, Annette Hanshaw, Cliff Edwards (then again, you don't see too many Red Nichols or Adrian Rollini CDs either), but that doesn't explain the low number or total absence of domestic discs by artists as major as Dick Haymes, Della Reese, or David Allyn. Go figure.

In the interest of progress, the current listing includes only compact discs. It follows that if the reader is interested enough to get out those old phonograph records ("the ones we used to play so long ago"), then it shouldn't be too much trouble to seek out the hardcover edition of this book, which contains extensive LP listings. A few CDs listed here are currently out of print, some having only been pressed in limited quantities to begin with (like Fresh Sound's pressing of Billy Eckstine's *Once More With Feeling*), some temporarily deleted from their corporate catalogues (like the CD of *Nat King Cole Sings for Two In Love*).

In any event, for these updates, I'm grateful to Bob Sixsmith, who provided nearly all of these current catalogue numbers—many from his own living room but also by shlepping all over New York.

May 1996

I. *Don't Show Up At A Desert Island Without 'Em*

The following are the absolutely essential discs for which Edison invented the phonograph. Of course, like the rest of this volume, that's only my opinion, since less than half of these are as yet on CD. Many, in fact, were only on LPs that haven't been available at all since their original release.

Louis Armstrong with Russ Garcia's Orchestra, *Louis Under the Stars* (Many individual tracks have been on various collections, but I look forward to the time when Verve does both this great set and its companion, *I've Got the World on a String*, as a single 19-track disc. In the meantime, the original LP was Verve MGV-4012).

Tony Bennett with the Ralph Sharon Trio, *When Lights Are Low* (Japanese CBS/Sony CSCS-5242).

Connee Boswell and the Original Memphis Five in Hi-Fi (last on a Japanese LP, RCA RJL-2628).

June Christy with Pete Rugolo and his Orchestra, *Something Cool* (Capitol Jazz CDP7-96329-2). 35 years ago, the original 10" LP was expanded with singles to fill a 12", and now the 12" has been doubled to 24 tracks with more Christy-Rugolo items circa 1953–'55. The original album tends to get lost in there, but it's still good to have it all.

Nat King Cole Sings St. Louis Blues, with Nelson Riddle and his Orchestra, reissued in the early '60s as *Nat King Cole Sings the Blues*. This is supposedly coming out on CD even as we speak.

Bing Crosby with Bob Scobey's Frisco Jazz Band, *Bing With a Beat* (unavailable since the original LP release on Victor LPM-1473).

Billy Eckstine with Pete Rugolo and his Orchestra, *Billy's Best* (Mercury 526 440).

Ella Fitzgerald with Paul Smith, piano, *Let No Man Write My Epitath,* now titled *The Intimate Ella* (Polygram 839 838-2).

Billie Holiday, *The Complete Decca Recordings* (GRP 601, 2 CDs).

Peggy Lee with Jimmy Rowles, Conte Candoli, etc., *Black Coffee* (Japanese MCA 25P2-2829).

Abbey Lincoln, *Abbey Is Blue* (Riverside/Fantasy OJCCD-069-2).

Jimmy Rushing, *The Jazz Odyssey of James Rushing, Esq.* (LP only: Japanese CBS/Sony 20AP-1506).

Frank Sinatra, arranged and conducted by Nelson Riddle, with the Hollywood String Quartet, *Close To You* (Capitol CDP-746572-2). Currently deleted, but hopefully soon to be restored.

Mel Torme Swings Shubert Alley, with Marty Paich and his Orchestra (Polygram Jazz, 821 581-2).

Sarah Vaughan with orchestra arranged and conducted by Quincy Jones, *Vaughan with Violins*, now released as *Misty* (846 488-2).

Lee Wiley with Ralph Burns and his Orchestra, *West of the Moon* (Japanese RCA R25J-1007), although most tracks are on the domestic *As Time Goes By* (RCA Bluebird 3138).

Notice two things: First, that I've arranged them in alphabetical order, not best-to-worse or whatever. Second, though many of the artists here go back to the '30s, I've limited the selections to LPs conceived as such, not 78 compilations, with the exception of the rule-defying Billie Holiday Deccas.

II. Heavy-Duty Alphabetical Listening by Artist

Conflict of interest department: In the interest of full disclosure, all items that have my name on them, whether in connection with production or annotation, have been indicated with a + sign. Also note that the following artists are thus far not represented on CDs, except possibly on anthologies: Russ Columbo, Cliff Edwards, Annette Hanshaw, Marion Harris, Bob Manning, Della Reese, and Buddy Stewart.

Louis Armstrong: Alright! We walks in the door, we rolls up our sleeves, and we gets to work:

No one has ever attempted to come up an anthology package that covers Armstrong's entire recording career, which lasted almost 48 years, but, in general, those that cover the early work use terms like "art" and "history," while those that cover the later years often incorporate the phrase "greatest hits."

'20s & '30s: The Smithsonian's 4-CD *Portrait of the Artist as a Young Man: 1923–1934* (Columbia / Legacy 57176) is as good a collection as one could hope for of the pivotal early work, including his key appearances with King Oliver, Fletcher Henderson, Maggie

Jones, Clarence Williams, and the best of his blues vocal accompaniments for Bessie Smith and others.

However, you will want to get, at the very least, all of Armstrong's Hot Fives, Hot Sevens, and early big band sides complete, and by far the best-sounding collection of these comes on four individual discs from the British JSP, *Hot Fives And Sevens, Vol. 1* (44049), *Hot Fives And Sevens, Vol 2* (313), *Big Bands Volume 1: 1930–31* (305) and *Big Bands 1931–1932* (306), all brilliantly remastered by the great John R. T. Davies.

American CBS has also covered these in a series of which critics cross-country continue to debate the sound quality, the more recent volumes generally being more palatable than the early entries: *Vol. 1, 1925–'25* (CK-44049), *Vol. 2, 1926–'27* (CK-44253), *Vol. 3, 1927–'28* (CK-44422), *Vol. 4, 1928* (CK-45142), *Vol. 5, 1928* (CK-46148), *Vol. 6, 1929–'30* (CK-46996). At the same time, the Classics people in Belgium have an Armstrong series primarily concerned with his big band work: *1928–'29* (570), *1929–'30* (557), *1930–'31* (547), *1931–'32* (536), *1932–'33* (529), *1934–'36* (509), *1936–'37* (512), *1938–'39* (523), etc.

'30s & '40s (Decca big band): US MCA also has several thematic issues: *The Singer, 1937–'56* (MCAD-31346), *The Composer, 1935–'57* (MCAD-10121), *Rhythm Saved The World* (GRP 602), and *Louis Armstrong of New Orleans* (MCAD-42328). Bluebird has issued Armstrong's Victor material from the '30s and '40s on *Laughin' Louie*, ain't no phooey (9759-2) and *Pops: the Small Band Sides* (6378-2). Other interesting RCA compilations: *Sings The Blues* (66244), *Sugar* (61068), *Young Louis Armstrong* (1930–1933) (66469).

Other recommended releases: there are the two classic Columbias, significantly altered for CD, *Louis Armstrong Plays W. C. Handy* (CK-46148) and *Satch Plays Fats* (CK-40378), and three Verve samplers (although not the classic Garcia album), *Compact Jazz* (833 293-2), *Jazz Round Midnight* (843 422), and *The Essential Louis Armstrong* (517 169 +) as well as the great *Louis Armstrong Meets Oscar Peterson* (825 713-2) (you haven't lived until you heard Louis sing the verse to "How Long Has This Been Goin' On," which includes the line, "when I trotted out in little velvet panties"). *The Silver Collection* (823 466-2) and *An American Songbook*

(Verve 843 615) sample the great Russ Garcia orchestral albums. (Pops's pivotal meetings with Ella Fitzgerald are listed later on.)

Also: two discs called *What a Wonderful World* (MCA MCAD-25204 and Bluebird 8310-2), appropriately capitalizing on the success of the song after its use in *Good Morning, Vietnam*; *Hello Dolly* (MCA MCAD-538); *The Real Ambassadors* with Carmen McRae and Lambert, Hendricks & Ross (French CBS 467140-2); *Live in '43: On the Sunny Side of the Street* (Jass J-CD-19); *Louis Armstrong's Greatest Hits* (Curb D2-77339); *Louis Armstrong at the Pasadena Civic Auditorium* (GNP Crescendo 11001); *Mack the Knife* (Pablo 2310 941-2); *Reunion with Duke Ellington* (of course you remember the original Armstrong-Ellington union!) (two Roulette LPs on one EMI CD, Blue Note B2-93844); *Chicago Concert, 1956* (French CBS 466439-2); and *Disney Songs the Satchmo Way* (two discs, Japanese Columbia 32C38-7753).

Mostly Live and Mostly All-stars: *16 Most Requested Songs* (Legacy 57900); *Basin Street Blues*; live All-Stars stuff from '56 & '57 (Black Lion 760 128); *The California Concerts* (Decca Jazz 4-613); an excellent 4-CD package containing two great shows from '51 & '55; *The Complete Town Hall Concert* (RCA 66541), an essential 2-CD concert from 1947; *The Essential Louis Armstrong* (Vanguard 91/92); *The Sullivan Years: Louis Armstrong & The All Stars—TV appearances* (TVT 9427); *Mack The Knife*, a 1957 concert (Pablo 2310-941); *Satchmo The Great* (Legacy 53580).

Would it be possible for the labels of the world to put out too much Pops? Not on your rice and red beans!

David Allen/Allyn: Alphabetically, as Portland Hoffa would say, actually precedes Louis Armstrong, but Pops always comes first on any list Mrs. Friedwald's little boy compiles. Also, there's painfully little to report: in the late LP era, virtually all of his (few) albums were available, but none of them has crossed the great divide over to CD. As of now all you can get are assorted band vocals on *Boyd Raeburn* (Echo Jazz EJCD-13), Boyd Raeburn: *Boyd Meets Stravinsky* (Savoy 0185), and *Jack Teagarden Vol. 1, 1941: It's Time For Tea!* (Jass J-CD-624). Three composer anthologies featuring one Allyn track each: *The Great Jazz Vocalists Sing The Gershwin Songbook* (Capitol/EMI 80506 +), *Great American Songwriters Vol. 2:*

Johnny Mercer (Rhino 71504), and *American Songbook Series: Jerome Kern* (Smithsonian Collection Recordings 048-4). None of the classic World Pacific or Warners albums have yet been CD'd; furthermore, his incredible band of the early '90s, which played great charts by Johnny Mandel, Bill Holman and others, went entirely unrecorded.

Fred Astaire: *Fred Astaire Rarities* (RCA 2337-2), guest-starring Adele Astaire and Ginger Rogers, collects everything Astaire did that the label could find, but *Starring Fred Astaire* (two discs, Columbia C2K-44233), aside from having muffled sound, frustratingly leaves off a couple of crucial Astaire tracks owned by CBS. Some of the same material is also on two releases from ProArte, *Cheek to Cheek* (CDD-431) and *A Fine Romance* (CDD-458), and a further two from England, *Crazy Feet* (Living Era CD AJA-5021-R) and *Shall We Dance* (BBC BBCCD-665).

The commercial Decca recordings of the *Holiday Inn* and *Blue Skies* scores are on, respectively, MCA MCAD-25205 & MCAD-25989, while the soundtrack studio masters are on Vintage Jazz Classics VJC-1012-2; MCA also has released *Fred Astaire Sings* (MCAD-1552). Later items include the essential *Astaire Story* with Jazz at the Philharmonic (from Verve, two CDs, Polygram 835 649-2), *Astairable Fred*, culled from the three "evening(s) with Fred Astaire" TV shows (DRG CDMRS-911), *Top Hat: Hits From Hollywood* (Legacy 64172), *Fred Astaire Volume 2* (Living Era 5123), *Steppin' Out: Fred Astaire Sings* (Verve 523 006), and *Steppin' Out: Fred Astaire At MGM* (Sony Music Special Products 47712, now out of print and eventually to be replaced by a Turner-Rhino package).

Mildred Bailey: The Old Rockin' Lady has the highest ratio of great music recorded to that reissued, but kudos to GRP/MCA and Columbia for becoming the first American majors to release Bailey discs: *Squeeze Me (1935–37)* (Decca Jazz 644) and *Red Norvo Featuring Mildred Bailey: Best of the Big Bands* (Legacy 53424). More: *Me And The Blues* (Japanese Savoy 0200), *Harlem Lullaby* (British Living Era ASV CDAJA), *Portrait of Mildred Bailey* (32DP-562), *Squeeze Me* (British Affinity CDAFS-1013), a title as long as La

Bailey was wide—*The Legendary V-Disc Masters: The Ol' Rockin' Chair Lady Sings Scrap Your Fat and other Hits*, (VJC 1006), *Red Norvo And Mildred Bailey* (Circle 3), and *The Rockin' Chair Lady (1931–1950)* (Affinity 1013, UK). Mrs. Swing also guest stars on four tracks on Columbia's *Benny Goodman, Vol. One: Roll 'Em* (CK-40588).

Chet Baker: Since he is easily the most digitally available of all modern jazzmen, just concentrating on Baker vocal-oriented projects gives us a handful. And that's even if we eliminate several discs of the "tampered" Pacific Jazz vocal masters with various overdubs. *Let's Get Lost: The Best of Chet Baker Sings* (from Pacific Jazz, Capitol CDP7-92932-2 +), *Chet Baker Sings . . . It Could Happen to You* (from Riverside, Fantasy OJCCD-303-2), *Chet With 50 Italian Strings* (Fantasy OJCCD-492-2), *Baker's Holiday* (from Limelight, Polygram 838-204-2), *Let's Get Lost* soundtrack (Novus 3054-2), *Chet Baker Plays and Sings* from 1964 (Spanish Jazz Junction JJ-205), *Baby Breeze Chet* (from Limelight, Japanese EmArcy EJD-3039), *Chet Baker Sings Again* (Dutch Timeless CD SJP-238), *Chet In Paris, Vol. 2—Everything Happens To Me* (Verve 837 475), *Grey December* (Blue Note 97160), *The Pacific Jazz Years* (Pacific Jazz 89292), *Chet Baker Plays The Best Of Lerner & Loewe*—instrumentals that will appeal to vocal fans (Original Jazz Classics 137). There's plenty, plenty more, and I'll tell you all about it on some snowy evening.

Tony Bennett: We start with another box, *Forty Years—The Artistry Of Tony Bennett* (87 tracks from 1952–'72 and 1986–'89 in a 4-CD boxed set, Columbia C4K-46843 +), which is both a greatest hits package and a collection of Bennett's own personal favorites (although we could have used more of the latter).

More samplers: the highly-recommended *JAZZ* (2 CDs, CGK-40424), *16 Most Requested* (CGK-40215), and *The Very Thought of You* (Sony Music Special Products, A13303).

Complete albums: *Movie Song Album* (CK-9272), *Snowfall—The Tony Bennett Christmas Album* (CK-9739), *I Left My Heart in San Francisco* (CK-8669), *The Good Life* (Sony Music Special Products, A21552), *In Person! With Count Basie* (Master Sound) (Legacy

64276), *Sings A String Of Harold Arlen* (Columbia Special Products 8359 or from Japan as CSCS-5244), *Snowfall: The Tony Bennett Christmas Album* (Columbia 66459), *Tony Sings For Two* (Columbia Special Products 8242), and *At Carnegie Hall Live! 1962* (Collectors Series 75012). Just out: *Something* (CK 64601), *Who Can I Turn To?* (CK 66503), and *I Wanna Be Around* (CK66504). Only forty or so more albums to go!

The Japanese affiliate, CBS-Sony, has done at least another six of the very best Bennett LPs on CD: *Alone Together* (32DP-568), *My Heart Sings* (CSCS-5245), *Tony Bennett Sings A String of Harold Arlen, Songs for the Jet Set* (25DP-5320), *A Time For Love* (CSCS-5243), *When Lights Are Low* (CSCS-5242). As Bennett says, "I just got back from Japan and I never saw so many happy people. They even sang their new national anthem for me. It goes like this: 'We'll take Manhattan...'"

As fate would have it, while only a smattering of his classic Columbia sessions are available, virtually ever single item Bennett ever recorded that is not controlled by CBS has come to light, including the Roulette *Basie Swings / Bennett Sings* (Capitol Jazz C27-93899-2), the *Tony Bennett / Bill Evans Album* (Fantasy OJCCD-439-2), the MGM/Verve albums pared down to *The Best of Tony Bennett* (Curb D2-77447), and the Improv sets on DRG, *The Special Magic of Tony Bennett* (CDMRS-801), *Tony Bennett and Bill Evans: Together Again* (CDMRS-901), *The Rodgers and Hart Songbook* (CDXP-2102).

Last but most, Bennett's renewed association with Columbia (now Sony Music) has brought forth the excellent: *The Art of Excellence* (CK-40344), *Bennett / Berlin* (CK-44029), *Astoria—the Portrait of an Artist* (45348), *Perfectly Frank* (Columbia 52965), *Steppin' Out* (Columbia 57424), *MTV Unplugged* (Columbia 66214), and the just-released *Here's To the Ladies*.

Personally, I think that Columbia should do with Bennett what Capitol and Reprise have always done with Sinatra: keep *all* of his classic albums in print, all the time.

Connee Boswell and The Boswell Sisters: Not much on CD, I'm afraid. The Sisters are represented by *Everybody Loves My Baby* (ProArte CDD-550), *Okay America!: Alternate Takes & Rari-*

ties (Jass 622), *Syncopating Harmonists From New Orleans* (Take Two 406), and *It's The Girls* (British Living Era AJA-5014). Connee solo: *An Evening with Connee Boswell* (from Design, PMTD-16008), now believed to be out of print.

Al Bowlly: Here's some class crooning guaranteed to bowl-ly you over! *Goodnight Sweetheart* 1931 (British Saville CDSVL-150), *Proud of You* 1938 (British Living Era AJA-5064), *The Very Thought of You* (British EMI CDP7-94312), *Just A Bowl Of Cherries* (Pearl 7003, UK), and two British budget issues, *Al Bowlly* (SMS-39) and *Stage Door* (SDC-8086).

With Ray Noble: *Ray Noble & Al Bowlly, 1931–'34*—one of the famous Robert Parker "stereo" projects (British BBC BBCCD-649), *1935–1936* (Jazz Band 2112, UK), and *The Very Thought Of You* (Living Era 5115, UK).

Plus: two titles on the German IRS imprint, *Classic Years* (970-649) and *Dance Bands USA* (970-650). (Time out for a S. Z. "Cuddles" Akall impression: "Ach! Der peoples dat blitzkrieged him, now dey reissue him! Gott in himmel!") Then there's Brit folk-rocker Richard Thompson's "Al Bowlly's In Heaven" (true enough).

Chick Bullock: Nothing notable on CD yet, but there is a good cassette available, *Chick Bullock and his Levee Loungers* (cassette only, Audio Archives #1004) by mail order from Audio Archives, PO Box 711, Oakhurst, NJ, 07755. He can be heard on the anthology: *The Great Depression—American Music In The '30s* (Columbia 57589).

Cab Calloway: Columbia currently has three Calloway CDs available, one showcasing Calloway the showman, *Best of the Big Bands* (CK-5013 +), one spotlighting the band's jazz capabilities, *The Best of the Big Bands: Cab Calloway Featuring Chu Berry* (Legacy 48901), and one concentrating on the band's proto-R&B aspects, *Are You Hep To The Jive?: 22 Sensational Tracks* (Legacy 57645). More complete: *1930–31* (516), *1931–32* (526), *1932* (537), *1932–34* (544), *1934–37* (554), *1937–38* (516). Still more: *Cab Calloway, 1930–'39* (Telecom Systems L'Art Vocal 6, French), *Kicking The Gong Around* (Living Era 5013, UK), *Cab Calloway & Co.*

(RCA 66496), *Cab Calloway And The Missourians (1929–1930)* (JSP 328, UK). Non-commercial: *Soundtracks And Broadcasts* 1944 (Jazz Anthology 550232), *Cruisin' With Cab* (Magic 52, UK). Still more: *Get With Cab* (West Wind Jazz 2403).

Betty Carter: In roughly chronological order: *Meet Betty Carter and Ray Bryant* (Japanese CBS/Sony ESCA-5056) and *Social Call* (Sony Music Special Products 36425) both offer her earliest own sessions, *I Can't Help It* (GRP 114), *Ray Charles And Betty Carter* (Digital Compact Classics 039), *Round Midnight* (#1) (Atlantic 80453), *'Round Midnight* (#2) (from Roulette, Capitol Jazz CDP7-95999-2), and *Finally* (from Roulette, Capitol Jazz CDP7-95333-2). Her own self-produced Bet-Car series is now available on CD from Polygram (who has also produced two new Carter albums in recent years): *The Audience with Betty Carter* (835 684-2), *The Betty Carter Album* (835 682-2), *Compact Jazz* (843 274-2 +), *Look What I Got* (843 274-2), *Droppin' Things* (843 991-2), *At The Village Vanguard* (519 851), *It's Not About The Melody* (513 870), *Feed The Fire* (523 600), and *Whatever Happened To Love* (835 683-2), which features the most capitivating performance of "Cocktails for Two" since Felix Unger and the Sophisticatos. Two foreign rarities: *Betty Carter with her Trio, Berlin 1985* (Japanese Wave 32WD-1007) and *Jazzbuehne 1985* (German Repertoire RR-4901).

June Christy: It's called *June Christy And The Stan Kenton Orchestra, The Complete Recordings* (Cema / Collector's Choice Music CCM 001) and even though it isn't complete, it is 22 of their best tracks together. More Kenton with Christy: *Kenton: Innovations In Modern Music, Concert, Seattle, 1951* (Mark 56 CD-860), *Stan Kenton / June Christy / The Four Freshmen: Road Show* (Capitol Jazz CDP7-96328-2), *Kenton-Christy: Duet* (Capitol/EMI 89285 +). There are also three CDs of Christy from the Kenton period—and in a roughly Kenton kontext, *The Uncollected June Christy, Vol. 1* accompanied by "The Kentones," 1946 (Hindsight 219), *The Uncollected June Christy, Vol. 2* (Hindsight 235), and more on *The Early Years* (Spanish Fresh Sounds FSCD-1011).

Post-Kenton: *Something Cool* (Capitol Jazz CDP7-96329-2) as mentioned above, with mucho bonus tracks also from 1953–'55, and also the 1960 stereo remake of *Something Cool* (Japanese Toshiba TOCJ-5316), with Art Pepper in for Bud Shank. *The Best of The Capitol Years* (British EMI/Capitol CDP7-92588-2), *The Misty Miss Christy* (Capitol/EMI 98452 +), *June's Got Rhythm* with Bob Cooper and very heavily recommended (Japanese TOCJ-5316). One sampler: *Spotlight On June Christy* (Capitol/EMI Records). The US Giants of Jazz release of '50s transcriptions, *A Lovely Way To Spend an Evening*, has come out on a British CD (Jasmine CD-2528), but this is a rare case where the LP is distinctly better than the irritatingly high and thin-sounding CD. More transcriptions: *The Uncollected June Christy, 1957* (Hindsight 235).

Buddy Clark: Columbia's main entry is *16 Most Requested Songs* (Legacy 48976); also recommended, *Band Vocals From The Thirties* (Take Two 402). The mail-order-only operation Special Music has issued *The Best of Buddy Clark* (no number available), which seems to be from his Carnation *Contented Hour* broadcasts circa 1946–'49. Also available is *Once and For Always, 1938–'49* (Jass J-CD-631), a collection of radio transcriptions from *Hit Parade*, V-Disc, *Contented Hour*, and other sources.

Rosemary Clooney: Old (meaning young) Rosie: *16 Most Requested Songs* (CK-44403) and *The Essence Of Rosemary Clooney* (Legacy 53569) contain most of her early hits for Columbia, while what may be her best album, *Blue Rose* with Duke Ellington, is available from French CBS (466444-2) with two bonus tracks. Also: *Tenderly* (Columbia Special Products 22542). A mess of the Columbia LPs are available from Japan, including *Clooney Tunes* (32DP-795), *Ring Around Rosie* with the Hi-Los, unfortunately (32DP-671), *Hollywood's Best* with Harry James, fortunately (32DP-670), *Rosie's Greatest Hits* (32DP-643). More '50s albums from Japan: *Swing Around Rosie* with Buddy Cole and two bonus cuts (MCA 25P2-2840), *Clap Hands! Here Comes Rosie!* (RCA R25J-1038), and *Rosie Solves the Swinging Riddle* (Nelson, that is) (RCA R25J-2840). Noncommercial: *Everything's Rosie 1952/1963* (Hindsight 255) and *Uncollected Rosemary Clooney, 1951–1952* (Hindsight 234).

The Concord Jazz albums just keep on coming. Like Fitzgerald's Verves, they can be pretty easily divided into two categories—songbooks and everything else: *Sings Irving Berlin* (CCD-4255), *Sings Rodgers, Hart & Hammerstein* (CCD-4405), *Sings the Lyrics of Ira Gershwin* (CCD-4112), *Sings the Lyrics of Johnny Mercer* (CCD-4333), *Sings the Music of Cole Porter* (CCD-4185), *The Music Of Harold Arlen* (4210), *The Music Of Irving Berlin* (4255), and *The Music Of Jimmy Van Heusen* (4308). Alas, we wait in vain for the Herman Hupfeld album.

Others: *Everything's Coming Up Rosie* (CCD-4047), *My Buddy* with Woody Herman (CCD-4226), *Show Tunes* (CCD-4364), *Sings Ballads* (CCD-4282), *With Love* (CCD-4144), *Do You Miss New York?* (4537), *Girl Singer* (4496), *Still On The Road* (590), *Tribute To Billie Holiday* (4081), *Demi-Centennial* (4633), and *For the Duration* (CCD-4444). Let us hope that the flow will continue unabated.

Nat King Cole: *Nat "King" Cole* (Capitol/EMI 99777 +) represents Capitol's gallant attempt to address the entire King Cole career, both trio and orchestral, in a coherent 4-CD package.

Trio, 1938–1951: for those who want just one representative CD of this great trio's best-known tracks during their prime years, try *Best Of The Nat King Cole Trio* (Capitol/EMI 98288). Mosaic's *The Complete Capitol Recordings of the Nat King Cole Trio* (M18D-138 +) includes all of Cole's own trio and small group sessions from 1942 onward (including the Capitol transcriptions), approximately 350 tracks on 18 CDs. Simply put, it is to die for. The only other studio recordings made by the trio are covered in the following packages: *Hit That Jive Jack* (MCA MCAD-42350), containing the complete Decca KC3 output (if you want the '36 Nat and Eddie Cole band sides, go to *In The Beginning*, Japanese MCA 25P2-2836) and *Birth of the Cole* (Savoy ZDS-1205 +). These latter two are just one disc each, but the second is apparently out of print as of 1996. The group also recorded a long series of studio transcriptions, which are covered on *Sweet Lorraine: The Complete Early Transcriptions of the King Cole Trio, 1938–1941* (4 CDs & 104 tracks, VJC-1026/29-2), and *The Trio Recordings* (5 CDs & 78 cuts, Laser Light 15-746/750) includes all the Trio's featured recordings for MacGregor transcriptions circa 1943–'45, though not the dates in which they accompany Anita Boyer, Ida James, and, believe it or not, the Barrie Sisters. The MacGregor material is also sampled on *WW II Transcriptions* (Music & Arts Programs of America 808), which contains several items not on the Laser Light box. Live Trio Material: *Crazy Rhythm: The Wildroot Shows, 1947–'48* (VJC 1011), live radio performances; *Any Old Time* (English Jasmine—Giants of Jazz GOJ CD 1031), duplicating some of the MacGregor material but also including the V-Discs; and *Straighten Up And Fly Right* (VJC 1044).

Later jazz-oriented items: Two small group sets, *The Complete "After Midnight" Sessions* (CDP7-48328) and *Penthouse Serenade* (Japanese Toshiba TOCJ-5363) (both part of the Mosaic set). *Big Band Cole,* (formerly *Welcome to the Club*) with the bands of Basie and Stan Kenton (Blue Note B2-96259 +), *Lush Life: The Pete Rugolo Sessions* (Capitol/EMI 80595), *The Billy May Sessions* (Capitol/EMI 89545, 2 CDs), and *The Piano Style Of Nat "King" Cole* (Capitol/EMI 81203).

Orchestral, 1951–1965 (all Capitol): Those seeking a quick fix of virtually all his number-one hits should quickly find his *Collector's Series* entry (CDP7-93590) and the 1992 *Unforgettable Nat King Cole* (99230), while *The Nat King Cole Story* (2 discs, C2-95129) is Cole's own more thoughtfully-considered autobiographical collection of his major numbers, most rerecorded in superior voice and sound. For original albums, check out the following: with Nelson Riddle, the deleted *Nat King Cole Sings for Two In Love* (46650) with bizarre bonus tracks, *Unforgettable* (CDP7-46736), *To Whom It May Concern* (31773), and *Wild Is Love* (28511). With Gordon Jenkins, *Love is the Thing* (CDP7-46648), *The Very Thought of You* (CDP7-46649), and the gospel *Every Time I Feel the Spirit* (C2 96263). With Dave Cavanaugh, *Cole Espanol* (CDP7-46489), which has a sequel in *Cole Espanol and More, Vol. Two* (CDP7-46482). More: there's the live *Nat King Cole at the Sands* (C2-93786), the country-styled *Rambling Rose* (CDP7-46649), and *Nat King Cole Sings / George Shearing Plays* (48332) with Ralph Carmichael's orchestra. Later live: *Early American* (A Touch Of Magic 5, UK) and *Live* (A Touch Of Magic 1, UK).

Earl Coleman: Earl, who died in 1995, still doesn't have an American CD to himself, although he can be heard on a number of anthologies and guest appearances. "This is Always" and "Dark Shadows" with Charlie Parker and Erroll Garner are currently on *Charlie Parker: The Legendary Dial Masters* (Stash ST-CD-523 +); others are on *Atlantic Jazz: Voices Of Cool, V.1* (Rhino 71748 +), Miles Davis: *Bopping The Blues* (Black Lion 760 102, UK), *The Gene Ammons Story: The 78 Era Compilation* (Prestige 24058), and Sonny Rollins: *Tour De Force* (Original Jazz Classics 095). Of his own albums, only the Xanadu *There's Something About An Old Love* was ever available on CD, and that only in Japan (Crown BRJ-544).

Perry Como: RCA's flagship Perry package is *Yesterday And To-day—A Celebration In Song* (66098), a three-CD box including 71 titles from 1943 to 1987, including most of his hits but very little selected with regard to quality—completely ignoring, for instance, Mr. C's best album, *We Get Letters*. The sound, however, is excellent.

Here's what else is available: *All Time Greatest Hits* (RCA 8323-2), *Today* (6398-2), *Pure Gold* (RCA 0972-2-R), *Easy Listening* (Pair PCD-1001), *Como's Golden Records* (RCA 53802), *Dream Along With Me* (Camden 403), *It's Impossible* (Camden 2651), *A Legendary Performer* (RCA 51752), *Pure Gold Compilation* (RCA 0972), *Round And Round And Other Hits* (RCA 52167), *Today* (RCA 6368); or from Japanese RCA: *And I Love You So* (R32P-1048), *Como Swings* (R25J-1004), *The Best of Perry Como* (R32P-1016), and *So Smooth*, containing Como's classic "Like Young" (R25J-1039). Well hot-ziggetty!

Chris Connor: All her commercially-recorded vocals with Kenton, as it happens, were arranged by Bill Russo, and are therefore available on *Stan Kenton: The Complete Capitol Recordings of the Holman and Russo Charts* (Mosaic 4CD-136 +). You have to buy four CDs to get about four tracks of vocals, but it's worth it! The three LPs worth of material on Bethlehem have generally been handy in the last few years, although the three most recent CD issues are, at this time, technically out of print: *Chris Connor* (BR-5001/BCP-56), *Lullabies of Birdland* (most recently as Bethlehem 3005), and *This is Chris* (BR-5017/BCP-20); one CD's worth of this material is currently gettable from England on *Cool Chris* (Charly 115).

Connor singlehandedly put Atlantic Records on the map as far as adult pop goes 35 years ago, and now only a couple of Connor sets are available from the company: *Chris Connor Sings the Gershwin Almanac of Song* (2 CDs, 601-2) and *A Jazz Date With Chris Connor/Chris Craft* (Rhino 71747). Japanese Atlantic has rightfully made available virtually everything she ever did: *Chris Connor* (AMCY-1050), *Chris Craft* (AMCY-1062), *Chris In Person* (AMCY-1063), *Double Exposure* with Maynard Ferguson (AMCY-1074), *Free Spirit* (AMCY-1077), *He Loves and She Loves* (AMCY-1059), *A Jazz Date with Chris Connor* (AMCY-1072), *A Portrait of Chris* (AMCY-1073), and the singles collection, *Misty* (AMCY-1078). And, out of force of habit, you might desire the Japanese issue of the *Gershwin Almanac* set (AMCY-1051-52).

Of her post-Atlantic recordings, you may want to try: *At the Village Gate* (Japanese Toshiba TOCJ-5332), *Weekend In Paris* (Japanese Toshiba TOCJ-5359), *Love Being Here with You* (Stash ST-CD-14 +), *Classic* (Contemporary CCD-14023-3), *New Again* (Contemporary CCD-14038-3), *Lover Come Back To Me: Live At Sweet Basil* (Evidence 22110), *This Is Chris* (Bethlehem 5017), *Sings Lullabys Of Birdland* (Bethlehem 3005), *Sweet And Swinging* (Audiophile 208), *As Time Goes By* (Enja 7061).

Bing Crosby: *His Legendary Years 1931–1957* (MCA 10887 +, 4 CDs) is MCA's attempt to come to grips with the complete Crosby career (with the exception of the earliest Whiteman stuff), sampling all the big hits and best known songs.

Pre-Decca: the Jonzo series, which covers the Whiteman and Brunswick years, has been covered almost over-completely (with lots of alternate takes) on a series of 13 LPs which take it up to 1932. After a long hiatus, supposedly, the series will continue on CD beginning in 1996. Columbia has sampled the same ground on the box *The Crooner: The Columbia Years, 1928–'34* (C3K-44229) and the single *16 Most Requested Songs* (Legacy 48974). Columbia Special Projects' *The Bing Crosby Story: The Early Jazz Years* (AS-201) goes over generally different tracks on the same ground; the BBC's *Bing Crosby* (BBC CD-648) does likewise but as one of Robert

Parker's controversial digital stereo experiments. RCA's *Paul White-man and his Orchestra* (9678-2-R) sports eight Crosby vocals. The British Living Era label has three CDs going from the Whiteman period into the Deccas, *Bix 'N' Bing* (CD AJA-5005), *Here Lies Love* (CD AJA-5043), and *On the Sentimental Side* (CD AJA-5072); and, of similar vintage, *Pennies From Heaven* (ProArte CDD-432), *Pocketful of Dreams* (ProArte CDD-457), *The Most Welcome Groaner* (Parade 2021, UK). The best of the many generally excellent British CDs covering the late '30s is *On Treasure Island* (JSP 703, UK).

Apart from collectors and fanciers of art deco music, it's clear that Crosby is generally taken more seriously today as a film performer than a musician, since his movies show up on the air and on video far more than his records do on CD. Accordingly, most of the CDs of his '40s and '50s work is movie-oriented: *Holiday Inn* (commercial recordings, MCA MCAD-25205), *Blue Skies* (commercial recordings, MCA MCAD-25989), *Holiday Inn & Blue Skies* (pre-soundtrack studio discs, VJC-1012-2), *Swingin' on a Star* (MCA MCAD-31367), *White Christmas* (British MCA DMCL-1777).

Also available: '40s & '50s: *Bing's Greatest Hits* (MCA MCAD-1620), *Bing Sings Again* (MCA MCAD-5764), *Twenty Golden Greats* (British DMCTV-3), *Bing Sings More Great Songs* (British Pickwick PWK-088), *The Christmas Songs* (VJC-1017-2), *The Radio Years Vol. 1* (GNP Crescendo 9051) and *Vol. 2* (9052), *Fancy Meeting You Here* with Rosemary Clooney (Japanese RCA 252J-1003). '70s: *Bing & Basie* (Polygram 824705-2), *Feels Good, Feels Right* (British London 820586-2), *Where the Blue of the Night* (British London 820552-2), *Out of Nowhere* (British London 820553-2), and the overdubbed orchestra set, *Tenth Anniversary Collection* (3 discs, British Warwick U1005).

Still more: *1927–1937* (DRG/ABC 836 172), *All-Time Best Of Bing Crosby* (Curb 77340), *At The Movies* (Laser Light 15411), *A Couple Of Song And Dance Men* with Fred Astaire (Curb 77617), *Big Band Days* (Echo 12), *Bing Crosby And Some Jazz Friends* (GRP 603), *Bing Swings Compilation* (Magic 48, UK), *Bing's Buddies* (Magic 41, UK), *Classic Bing Crosby 1931–1938* (DRG/ABC 838 985), *The Jazzin' Bing Crosby 1927–1940* (Affinity 1021, UK), *The Movie Hits* (Pearl 9784), *That's Jazz* (Pearl 9739). Lastly, *World*

War II Radio, a five-CD Box (Laser Light 15934) is a generous helping of the Crosby charm in ten complete mid-'40s radio shows, highly recommended.

Vic Damone: *The Best of Vic Damone Live* (Ranwood RCD-8204), *The Best of the Capitol Years* (British EMI CZ-197), *Portrait of A Song Stylist* (what style? They should have called it, "Portrait of Pipes at their Purest") (British Harmony HARCD-110), *The Magic of Vic Damone* (British Prima PXCD-108), *Vic Damone Sings the Great Songs* (British Pickwick PWK-134), *16 Most Requested Songs* (Legacy 48975), *Best Of Vic Damone* (Curb 77476), *The Glory Of Love* (RCA 66016), *Inspiration* (Laser Light 12327), *Let's Face The Music And Sing* (Pair 1303), and *Spotlight On Vic Damone* (Capitol/EMI Records 28513). Damone represents the triumph of substance over style.

Bobby Darin: Two box sets should give you the best overview: *As Long as I'm Singing: The Bobby Darin Collection* (Rhino R2 72206, 4 Cds) or *His Greatest Hits and Finest Performances* (Reader's Digest 134C, 3 Cds), although they duplicate each other so much that there's no need to buy both. More Darin: start with the self-narrated *Bobby Darin Story* (Atlantic 33131-2), *Two of a Kind* with Johnny Mercer and Billy May and perhaps the noisiest album ever made (Atlantic 90484-2), *Bobby Darin, 1936–'73* (Motown MOTD-5185), *Live at the Desert Inn* (Motown MOTD-9070), *Classic Darin* (Pair PCD-1189), *Collector's Series* (C27-91625-2), *Ultimate* (Warner 27606-2), *Greatest Hits* (D21K-77325), *25th Day Of December* (Atco 91772), *Bobby Darin* (Atlantic 82626), *Darin 1963–1973* (Motown 635 185), *Darin At The Copa* (Atlantic 82629), *Splish Splash: Best Of Bobby Darin, Vol 1* (Atco 91794), *Mack The Knife: Best Of Bobby Darin, Vol 2* (Atco 91795), *Spotlight On Bobby Darin* (Capitol/EMI 28512), and *That's All* (Atlantic 82627). Look out, old MacHeath is back!

Sammy Davis Jr.: In his last few years, bad imitations and putdowns of Sammy D. were considered far more chic than actually listening to his best music, but that may be gradually changing as Slacker Nation begins to embrace the ratpack. There's *Collector's*

Series (Capitol C27-94071-2), *The Decca Years* (MCAD-10101), *Best Of Sammy Davis Jr.* (Curb 77444), *Greatest Hits, Vol. 1* (Dunhill GRZ-018) and *Vol. 2* (DZS-055), and another *Greatest Hits* collection, this one from Curb (D21K-77272). Davis's most impressive efforts as a jazz singer are *The Wham Of Sam* (Warner Archives 45637 +) and *Our Shining Hour, with Count Basie* (from Verve, Polydor 837 446-2). Another classic is *Sammy Sings and Laurindo Almeida Plays*, in which Charley Showbiz becomes Charley Sensitive (which has been spotted as both Dunhill DZS-055) and Sandstone Music: 33081). These recordings are so good that they don't deserve to fall through the trap doors on *Laugh-In*.

Doris Day: The big news in the '90s for those of us who appreciate this most unsung of great American pop singers is the series of Doris Day box sets on the German Bear Family label, which will cover in toto all of her recordings for Columbia in four glorious boxes. So far, they are *It's Magic, 1947–50* (15609, 6 CDs), *Secret Love, 1951–1955* (15746, 5 CDs), while the third, *Que Sera Sera*, which takes the series up to 1959, has just been released.

Day's most jazz- and band-oriented efforts include *Doris Day and Les Brown: Best of the Big Bands* (Columbia CK-46224 +), the *Young Man with a Horn* original soundtrack with Harry James (Japanese CBS/Sony 32DP-911), and *Duet* with the Andre Previn Trio (Columbia Special Products 8552). Her single classiest job of singing ever may well be the *Love Me or Leave Me* soundtrack (Legacy 47503). Also available are domestic compilations, like Crosby's CDs, all with obvious "hooks": *Personal Christmas Collection* (Legacy 64153), *Day at the Movies* (CK-44371), *Hooray For Hollywood Vol. One* (CK-8066) and *Vol. Two* (CK-8067), and *Greatest Hits* (CK-8635). Two similar sets are also out in England, *Portrait of a Song Stylist*—as Hedy LaMarr would say, "I hate that cliche!"—(Harmony HARCD-101) and *Calamity Jane and The Pajama Game* (CBS 467610-2). But, as usual, the most of the best comes from Japan (all CBS/Sony): *Day Dreams* (32DP-916), *Christmas Album* (32DP-814), *Day by Day* (32DP-915), *Day by Night* (32DP-916), *Day In Hollywood* (32DP-914), and *Show Time* (25DP-5309). Also: *Sentimental Journey* (Hindsight 200); and *Doris Day Sings 22 Original Recordings* (Hindsight 411) is a generic title for what turns out to be a wonderful collection of Ol' Dodo getting re-laxed and groovy with the fine Page Cavanaugh Trio.

Billy Eckstine: Big Band years: All of his vocals with Earl Hines and his Orchestra are on *I Want To Talk About You* (Xanadu 207), but that's still only on LP if you can even find it that way, although five Eckstine vocals are included on *Earl Hines* (French Classic 567). Most of the Savoy recordings of the legendary Eck-stine Orchestra were available here as *Mr. B and the Band* (ZDS-4401) and have been reissued more recently on Japanese Denon. (There was also a French CD, *Gloomy Sunday* [Vogue 650145]).

The two-LP set of B's pinnacle as a pop star, *Everything I Have Is Yours: The M-G-M Years*, which simultaneously creams both B's biggest hits and his most jazz-oriented tracks (with Woody Herman, Lester Young, Sarah Vaughan, and others), has been ex-panded into a two-CD set (Verve 819 442). Polygram also asked me to compile two samplers of Eckstine, *Jazz Round Midnight* (Verve 521 652) from the MGM period and *Compact Jazz* from Mercury. Another sampler is *Verve Jazz Masters* (Verve 516 693).

Most highly recommended: *Billy Eckstine's Imagination* (Emarcy 514 075), *Billy's Best* (Mercury 526 440), *Basie/Eckstine, Inc.* (Rou-lette 28636), *Once More With Feeling* (Spanish Fresh Sounds FSR-CD-24), *At Basin Street East* with Quincy Jones (Polygram 832 592 +), *No Cover, No Minimum* (Roulette 98583 +), *The Irving Berlin Songbook* with Sarah Vaughan (Polygram 822526). Later: *Stormy/Feel The Warm* (Stax 88020). His two final albums are happily available, *I Am A Singer* (Japanese Phonogram 32JD-150) and the fine *Billy Eckstine Sings With Benny Carter* (Polygram 832011-2), concerning which one magazine actually listed the artist as "Billy Carter."

Cliff Edwards: Nothing yet, only appearances on two antholo-gies, *They Called It Crooning* (ASV 5026) and *The Crooners Com-pilation* (Legacy 52942), which is a recommended double-set in any event.

Ruth Etting: *Ten Cents a Dance* (British Living Era AJA-5008) and *Goodnight My Love 1930–37* (Take Two 403). She also appears on two anthologies on the same two labels, *Flappers, Vamps &*

Sweet Young Things (Take Two 407) and *The First Torch Singers,
V.1: The Twenties* (Living Era 5015).

Ella Fitzgerald: Decca: *75th Birthday Celebration* (Decca Jazz
619) is a beautiful sampler of the first 20 years of her recording career, selected by Milt Gabler, who produced many of the original
dates. Like many another major Afro-American artist of the '30s,
her works of this period (Chick Webb, Teddy Wilson and Benny
Goodman) have been collated most completely once again on the
Classics label: *Ella Fitzgerald, Vol. 1 1935–'37* (500), with Webb
and her own Savoy Eight on *Vol. 2 1937–'38* (506) and *Vol. 3
1938–'39* (518), with her own post-Webb orchestra on *Vol. 4 1939*
(525) and *Vol. 5 1939–'40* (566). American Decca has also so far issued three doubles of early Ella, which are neither complete nor
can be called highlights (they're almost complete, omitting only the
occasional track that the producer didn't like, such as "Melinda the
Mousie"): *The Early Years, Part I, 1935–39* (GRP 618), *The Early
Years, Part II, 1939–41* (Decca Jazz 623), and *The War Years*
(Decca Jazz 628). Also, *Pure Ella* contains two LPs worth of super-
lative duos with the great pianist Ellis Larkin.
   Verve: first the songbooks: *Duke Ellington* (three CDs, 87-035-2),
Harold Arlen Vol. 1 (817 527-2) & *Vol. 2* (817 528-2), *Rodgers &
Hart Vol. 1* (821 579-2) & *Vol. 2* (821 580-2), *Cole Porter Vol. 1*
(821 989-2) & *Vol. 2* (821 990-2), *Johnny Mercer* (823 247-2),
George and Ira Gershwin (three CDs, 821 024-2), *Jerome Kern*
(825 669-2), and *Irving Berlin Vol. 1* (829 534-2) & *Vol. 2* (829
535-2). Or just go whole hog and invest some salary in the 16-CD
box, *The Complete Ella Fitzgerald Song Books* (519 832).
   Live Sets: *Compact Jazz: Ella Fitzgerald Live* (833 294-2), *Ella
in Rome: The Birthday Concert* (835 454-2), *At The Opera House*
(831 269-2), *Returns To Berlin* (837 758), *The Complete Ella In
Berlin: Mack The Knife* (519 564) and *Ella at Juan-Les Pins* with
nine bonus cuts (Japanese Polydor POCJ-1925). Concerts from the
Verve years issued by companies other than Verve: *Ella Fitzgerald
& Jazz At The Philharmonic, Stockholm 1957* (Tax 3703), and two
with Duke Ellington from their 1966 tour, *Live at the Greek Theatre, Los Angeles 1966* (Status DSTS 1013, UK) and *The Stockholm
Concert* (Pablo 2308-242).

Team-Ups: *Ella & Basie* (Count, of course, 821 576-2), *Ella and Louis* (Armstrong, that is, 825 373-2), *Ella and Louis Again* (825 374-2), and *Porgy and Bess with Louis Armstrong* (once two LPs, now one CD, 827 475-2). Other: *These are the Blues* (829 536-2), *Ella Wishes You a Swinging Christmas* (827 150-2), and the masterpiece, *The Intimate Ella* (formerly released as *Let No Man Write My Epitath*, 839 838-2).

Ella and Great Arrangers: *Ella Swings Brightly With Nelson* (519 347) and *Ella Swings Gently With Nelson* (519 348)—Riddle, that is! Also: *Ella Swings Lightly* (847 392) with Marty Paich.

Other Verve albums: *Clap Hands, Here Comes Charlie* (835 646-2 +), *These Are The Blues* (829 536), *Ella Wishes You a Swinging Christmas* (827 150-2), and *Like Someone In Love* (511 524) with Stan Getz and Frank DeVol.

Verve Samplers: start with *First Lady Of Song* (Verve 517 898, 3 CDs), as a basic, 75th birthday sampler of the entire Ella–Norman Granz experience (there's also a one-CD sampler of highlights from this three-CD sampler, if you're not sampler'd out already). *Compact Jazz* has four Ella entries: *Ella Fitzgerald* (831 367-2), *Ella Live!* (833 294), *Ella & Louis* (835 313), and *Ella & Duke* (517 953). More samplers: *The Essential Ella Fitzgerald: The Great Songs* (517 170 +), *For The Love Of Ella* (841 765, 2 CDs), *The Best Of The Song Books* (519 804), *The Best Of The Songbooks: The Ballads* (521 867), *Jazz Round Midnight* (843 621), and *Jazz Round Midnight Again* (527 032).

Miscellaneous '60s & Early '70s: at one point Capitol had all three of their bafflingly undistinguished Ella albums on CD, the Gospel collection (almost as lame an idea as Ella doing Bessie Smith-style blues) *Brighten the Corner* (C2-95151), *Misty Blue* (C2-95152), *Ella Fitzgerald's Christmas* (Capitol/EMI 94452), and *Thirty By Ella* (C2-48333). Reprise has both *Ella* and *Things Ain't What They Used To Be* on one disc (Warner 26023-2). And Columbia's two-volume *Live at Carnegie Hall, 1973* is available on two single discs from CBS France (466 547-2 & 466 548-2) or one double set from Japan (CBS/Sony 50DP-565/566).

Pablo albums, currently available from Fantasy Records: *All That Jazz* (2310 938-2), *At Montreux, 1975* (2310 751-2), *The Best Is Yet To Come* (2312 138-2), *The Best of Ella* (2405 421-2), *A Classy*

Pair with Count Basie (231 132-2), *Dream Dancing* with Nelson Riddle (2310 814-2), *Easy Living* with Joe Pass (231 921-2), *Ella & Oscar Peterson* (2310 759-2), *Ella In London* (2310 711-2), *Fine and Mellow* (2310 829-2), *Ella and Joe Pass... Again* (2310 829-2), *Lady Time* (2310 825-2), *Nice Work if You Can Get It* with Andre Previn (2312 140-2), *A Perfect Match* with Count Basie (2312 110-2), *Speak Love* (2310 888-2), *Take Love Easy* with Joe Pass (231 0702-2), *Ella à Nice, Live* (OJCCD-442-2), *Ella Abraça Jobim* (2630-201), *Montreux '77* (231 0702-2), *Digital III At Montreux* with Basie & Pass (2308 223), and lastly, the spectacular live *Concert Years* box (4414).

Buddy Greco: The Don Rickles of song can currently be heard on *Movin' On* (USA CD-622), *Buddy's Back In Town* (Japanese CBS/Sony Epic ESCA-5054), *16 Most Requested Songs* (Legacy 53775), *For Once In My Life* (Project 3 5105), and *Round Midnight* (Bay Cities 2008). Let's hope someday the folks at Sony will get around to the rest of his nice 'n' gnarly Epic epics, like *Let's Love, I Like It Swinging, On Stage,* and *My Buddy* (LN 3660).

Annette Hanshaw: *The Girl Next Door* (Take Two 408).

Marion Harris: Take Two Records, which specializes in preswing personalities, has recently entered the CD forum and may eventually issue *The Artistry of Marion Harris* (Take Two LP: TT 217) on CD. In any case, it culls from her later, largely electric period (1924–34); someday we'll get the really red hot Harris sides of the teens.

Johnny Hartman: His first records, three vocals with Dizzy Gillespie, are on *Dizziest* (Bluebird 5785-2-RB) and his first solo sides are on *First, Lasting and Always* (Savoy Jazz ZDS 4405), while his last are on *Once in a Lifetime* (LP only: Beehive 7012). In between he made, among others, two Bethlehem albums which have been on CD several times, recently and at least definitively on *Songs from the Heart* (3003) and *All of Me* (3012), both with alternate takes. His sole Roost album came out briefly in Barcelona, *And I Thought About You* (Fresh Sounds FSR-CD-35), while all of the three classic Impulse! are also out, the too-short masterpiece *John Coltrane and Johnny Hartman* (157), *The Voice That Is!* (144), and *I Just Dropped by to Say Hello* (on the older 39105). Also: *Unforgettable* (Impulse! IMPD-152 +), which contains 17 out of his 23 ABC tracks, and *This One's For Teddi* (Audiophile ACD-181).

Dick Haymes: You can get very early Haymes with Harry James: *On The Jazz Varsity* contained all fourteen Haymes-James vocals over 2 LPs (Savoy SJL-2272) although the CD deletes four (ZDS 4406); Haymes also appeared briefly on James's *Best of the Big Bands* entry (Columbia CK-45341), and on his World transcriptions on *1941* (Circle CDD-5). You also can get late Haymes: the two heart-stopping Capitol LPs, *Come Rain or Come Shine* and *Moondreams*, combined in toto onto one disc, *The Best of the Capitol Years* (British EMI/Capitol CDP7-94563-2), while two American compilations, *The Best of Dick Haymes* (Curb D2-77479) and *Easy to Listen To* (Pair PCD-2-1228) offer highlights only. From still later, the *Richard the Lion Hearted* album is currently *Dick Haymes's Swingin' Session* (Starline CD-SG404) while *Oh, Look At Me Now* is *Dick Haymes—The Ballad Singer* (British Jasmine CD-2525) or, under the original title, if you can find it, from the Barcelonan Fresh Sounds (FSR-CD-119). But what about the classic Haymes of the '40s, the years when he was at his most popular and recording one great song after another for Decca? You should only live so long! Some are on the cross-label, mail-order-only anthology, *You'll Never Know* (Good Music Record Co., MSD-35197), also including a smattering of the Haymes–Helen Forrest duets. Airchecks: *Star Eyes* (Jass J-CD-631) and *Drifting And Dreaming With Jo Stafford* (VJC 1040). Old Dick: *Imgination* (Audiophile 79).

Woody Herman: His major works as a vocalist, the inter-Herd Columbia and Capitol singles, the Columbia album with Erroll Garner and the two Verve albums (one with Ben Webster), have been out of print ever since they were first issued. Here, however, are a few CDs where you can hear Woody sing: *The Best of the Decca Years* (MCA MCAD-25195), *Golden Favorites* (MCA MCAD-31277), *Best of the Big Bands* including "Laura" (Columbia CK-

45340 +), *The Hits of Woody Herman* (Capitol CDP7-91213), *The Best of Woody Herman* (Curb D2-77394), *The Thundering Herd: Blowin' Up a Storm* (British Charly CD Y-100), *Blues On Parade* (GRP 606), *Early Autumn* (Trend 944), *The Essence Of Woody Herman* (Legacy 57157), *Keeper Of The Flame: Complete Capitol Recordings of the Second Herd* (Capitol/EMI 98453), and two live collections on Jass, *Vol. 1, 1944: Woodchopper's Ball* (J-CD-21) and *Vol. 2, 1945: Northwest Passage* (J-CD-23). My all-time favorite Woody vocal record, *Woody Herman Goes Native*, a ten-inch LP on his own Mars label, on which he plays calypsos and sports a Carmen Miranda tutti-frutti hat on the cover, is unlikely to ever be reissued in toto.

Al Hibbler: Please Mr. Major-Label person, reissue more Hibbler records. Can't complain about his Ellington band vocals, though, since virtually all have been made available on various complete Duke packages, mainly *Black, Brown and Beige*, an LP Box containing about a half-dozen or so Hibbler vocals (three discs, 6641-2-RB), *Happy-Go-Lucky Local* (only one vocal, the gorgeous "This Shouldn't Happen to a Dream", Musicraft MVSCD-52), and *The Complete Duke Ellington, 1947–1952, Recorded Works in Chronological Order* (five CDs containing about 10 tracks with Hibbler, French CBS 46365-2). Hib also participates in four of the *Duke Ellington Carnegie Hall Concerts, December '44* (Prestige 2PCD-24073-2), *January '46* (Prestige 2PCD-24074-2), *January '47* (Prestige 2PCD-24075-2), and *November '48* (Vintage Jazz Classics VJC-1024/25-2). As for Hibbler's post-Ellington work, that's another story. So far, all you can get is three vocals on the out-of-print *Shoutin', Swingin' & Makin' Love* (Chess 9327) and all of *After The Lights Go Down Low* (Atlantic 1251-2 +), which is righteous, raucous, and recommended.

Billie Holiday: ARC: sampler time: *16 Most Requested Songs* (Legacy 53776).
As of 1991, Holiday's masterpiece 1933–'42 sides with Teddy Wilson and under her own name have received a semi-definitive compilation, in the form of nine CDs from domestic Sony Music: *Vol 1.* (CK-40646), *Vol 2.* (CK-40790), *Vol 3.* (CK-44048), *Vol 4.* (CK-

44252), *Vol 5.* (CK-44423), *Vol 6.* (CK-45449), *Vol 7.* (CK-46180), *Vol 8.* (CK-47030), *Vol 9.* (CK-47030). While the programming—the master take of every song—should likely satisfy both connoisseur and casual listener, everybody seems to have their own take on the sound quality. The earlier Japanese collection, *The Lady—Complete Collection* (CBS/Sony OODP-570-577) offered the extant alternate takes as well; but the sound varied widely and now you can't even find the thing.

Also: the entire Teddy Wilson output, everything both with and without Holiday, has also been made available on two preferable European series, from the Belgian Classics and the Scottish Hep. On Classics: *Teddy Wilson 1934–'35* (508), *1935–'36* (511), *1936–'37* (521), *1937* (531), *1938* (556). Classics has also launched a separate series of the Holiday titles originally issued under her own name, beginning with *Billie Holiday, 1933–1937* (582) and *1937–39* (592). Antoher good series is on the Italian King Jazz label, titled *The Complete Billie Holliday Mastertakes Collection, 1933/42: 1: 1933/36* (KJ 156 FS), *2: 1936/37* (157), *3: 1937* (158), *4: 1937/38* (159), *5: 1938/39* (160), *6: 1939/40* (161) etc.

Commodore: the basic 16 master takes can be found on *Lady Day, 1939–'44* (Pair/Commodore CCD-7001), while the Japanese *Complete Commodore Recordings* (King KICJ 43/44) includes all the alternates as well in 45 tracks.

Decca: here is the definitive '40s Holiday package: *The Complete Decca Recordings* (GRP 601, 2 CDs). Enough said.

Verve: you gotta have *The Complete Billie Holiday On Verve, 1945–1959* (Verve 517 658,10 Discs), even though there's too much mishegoss (rehearsals, breakdowns, repetitive alternates) along with the great stuff. The booklet, also, is impossible to read, but since part of it was written by Joel Siegel, it's just as well. Individual Verve discs and other collections: *The Billie Holiday Songbook* (823246-2), *Compact Jazz* (831371-2), *Compact Jazz—Live* (831434-2), the best-known Carnegie Hall concert on *The Essential Billie Holiday* (833767-2 +), *Songs For Distingue Lovers* (823449-2), *The Silver Selection* (815055-2), *Last Recording* (835370-2), *The Essential Billie Holiday—Songs Of Lost Love* (517 172), *The Essential Carnegie Hall Concert* (833 767), *First Issue: The Great American Songbook* (523 003), *Billie Holiday Story, Vol. 3: Recital By Billie*

Holiday (521 868), *Billie's Best* (513 943), *Body And Soul* (833 766), and *Stay With Me* (511 523).

Miscellaneous, mostly '50s: *Billie's Blues*, the 1942 Capitol side plus the Alladin session and the U.A. concert (Blue Note CDP7-48786-2), *The Sound of Jazz* LP, which is the rehearsal, is on Columbia (CK-45234), while the video is available under the original title (VJC-2004). Columbia also has released *Lady In Satin* (CK-40247) with bonus tracks, while the French Giants of Jazz folks have released two oddball sets with Tony Scott from 1955–'57, both titled *Billie Holiday* (CD-53038 and CD-53074); *In Rehearsal*, Las Vegas, 1954 with Jimmy Rowles (Mobile Fidelity); and two more live CDs, the deleted *At Monterey*, 1958 (Black-Hawk BKH 50701-2) and *At Storyville*, Boston, that is, 1951–'52 (Black Lion BLCD-760921). Probably from Boris Rose airchecks *Broadcast Performances Vol. 1* (ESP 3002).

Helen Humes: Two of her early "classic blues" vocals are on *The Slide Guitar: Bottles, Knives & Steel, Vol. 2* (Legacy 52725). Her Basie sides are covered on *The Complete Decca Recordings* (Decca Jazz 3-611) and both the Hep and the Classics complete Count Basie series. The Classics volumes currently available are: *Count Basie, 1938–'39* with four Humes vocals (504), *1939* with four more by Helen (513), *1939 Vol. 2* with eight vocals (533), *1939–'40* with four more vocals (563). Also *Sneakin' Around* (Black And Blue 233 083, French). Three Contemporary LPs have been OJC'd by Fantasy, *Songs I Like to Sing* (OJCCD-171-2), *T'ain't Nobody's Business If I Do* (OJCCD-453-2), and *Swingin' with Helen Humes* (OJCCD-608-2). More to come, hopefully. You know, she's always being rediscovered.

Eddie Jefferson: If you must, there are three Fantasy Original Jazz Classics replica reissues, *Come Along with Me* (OJCCD-613-2), *Body and Soul* (OJCCD-396-2), and *Letter From Home* (OJCCD-6013). Also around: *Godfather of Vocalese* (Muse MCD-6013), *The Jazz Singer* (Evidence 22062), two guest shots with Richie Cole—*Hollywood Madness* (Muse MCD-5207) and *New York Afternoon* (Muse MCD-5119)—and *Hipper Than Thou* (British Zu-Zass ZCD-2015).

Herb Jeffries: His two first vocals are on Classics's *Earl Hines and his Orchestra, 1932–'34* (514). All his Ellington band vocals (that I know of) are on the recent and easy to find *Duke Ellington: The Blanton-Webster Band* (three CDs, Bluebird 5659-2-RB) plus a couple of transcriptions on *Take The "A" Train* (VJC 1003). As with all the Duke's vocal department, Post-Ellington Jeffries is far scarcer; I'd be hard-pressed (get it?) even to find many twelve-inch albums—most of his LPs were ten-inchers—let alone compact discs. Anyhoo, here are two: *Say It Isn't So* from 1957 (Japanese Bethlehem COCY-6494) and *I've Got the World On A String* from 1989 (Discovery DSCD-957).

Al Jolson: *The Best Of The Decca Years* (MCA 10505 +) is a good primer for those who don't favor acoustic sound. *You Ain't Heard Nothin' Yet: Jolie's Finest* (Columbia Legacy 53419 +) is the best official compilation of the early years. And then there's *Mammy*—what else? (ProArte CDJ-436), *Stage Highlights* (British Pearl CD-9748), *The World's Greatest Entertainer* (British MCA DMCL-1734), *Twenty Golden Greats* (British MCA DMCTV-4), *Alexander's Ragtime Band (Irving Berlin Tribute)* (VJC 1010), *Volume 2: The Salesman Of Song 1911–1923* (Pearl 9796), *You Ain't Heard Nothin' Yet* (Living Era 5038), and *The First Recordings, 1911–1916: You Made Me Love You* (Stash 564 +) is the first volume of a projected complete Jolson series.

Sheila Jordan: *Portrait of Sheila*, containing her definitive "Baltimore Oriole" (Blue Note B2 89002), *Old Time Feeling* (Muse 5366), *Lost and Found* (Muse 5390), *Body and Soul* (Japanese CBS/Sony 32DP-687), *The Crossing* (Black Hawk 505), *Heart Strings* (Muse 5468), *One For Junior* with Mark Murphy (Muse 5489), *Sheila* (SteepleChase 31081), *Songs From Within* (M-A MUSIC 14), and George Russell's *The Outer View* with her classic "You Are My Sunshine" (Original Jazz Classics 616). Still my personal fave: *Confirmation* (Japanese East Wind EJD-3079).

Louis Jordan (no relation to Sheila): Here are the basic Decca packages for the young and the Moe-less: *The Best of Louis Jordan* (MCAD-4079), *Five Guys Named Moe: Decca Recordings Vol. 2*

(MCA 10503), and *Just Say Moe!—Mo' Of The Best Of Louis Jordan*, which samples the best non-Decca sides (Rhino 71144). The most recommended Jordan Package of them all, however, is the German box *Let The Good Times Roll* (Bear Family 15557) which contains all 219 of Jordan's Decca sides 1938–1952 on eight CDs. Like the big King Cole package on Mosaic and the Sinatra box on Columbia, this is a voluminous full day of music that you will actually listen to—and over and over. Non-commercial: *Louis Jordan & Tympany 5: 1944–1945* (Circle 53) and *Five Guys Named Moe* (VJC 1037).

Post-Decca: The Alladin sides on *One Guy Named Louis* (Blue Note 96804), the Victor sides on *Rock 'N Roll Call* (Bluebird 66145), and the Mercury material on *Rock 'N Roll* (Mercury 838 219) and *No Moe!* (Verve 512 523). Still later: *Louis Jordan & Chris Barber* (Black Lion 760156) and *I Believe In Music* (Evidence 26006).

Other imports: *Golden Greats* (British MCA DMCL-1631), *G. I. Jive* (British Jukebox Lil RBD-602), *Live Jive* (Magic DATOM-4), and *At the Swing Cats Ball: The Early Years, 1937–'39* (JSP 330, UK). That's all there is, there ain't no Moe.

Lambert, Hendricks and/or Ross (and Buddy Stewart):
Dave Lambert and Buddy Stewart: not much, merely one live guest appearance with the Charlie Parker Quintet (Savoy Jazz ZDS-1173). None of Buddy Stewart's own great vocals seem likely to be reissued anytime in the near future, and that includes either his refrains with Gene Krupa on Columbia and Capitol Transcriptions or his solo features with Al Haig on the Sittin'-in-With label. You can hear him guest-starring on *The George Wallington Trio* (Savoy 0136), *What's This?—1946, Vol. 1* with Gene Krupa And His Orchestra and Dave Lambert (Hep 26, import), and *Early Bebop: The Essential Keynote Collection 3* (Mercury 830 922).

Lambert, Hendricks & Ross: *The Swingers* (from Pacific Jazz, Capitol CDP7-46849-2), *Sing Along with Basie* with Count Basie and Joe Williams (from Roulette, Blue Note B2-95332), and *Everybody's Boppin'* (Columbia CK-45020). This last disc includes the complete *The Hottest Group in Jazz* LP (also reissued as *The Best of Lambert Hendricks and Ross*) and samples from their other two

Columbia albums, *High Flying* and *Lambert, Hendricks and Ross sing Ellington*. Also: *The Real Ambassadors* (Legacy 57663).

Annie Ross: *King Pleasure Sings/Annie Ross Sings* (Original Jazz Classics 217), *Sings a Song with Mulligan*—Gerry, 'natch (from Pacific Blue Note B2-46852), *A Gasser!* with Zoot Sims (B2-46854), *A Handful of Songs* (Spanish Fresh Sounds FSR-CD-61), *Gypsy* (Blue Note 33574), and several tracks of *In Hoagland* with Hoagy Carmichael and Georgie Fame (DRG 5197).

Jon Hendricks: *Recorded in Person at the Trident*, from close to the L, H & R period (Verve 510 601), then the more recent *Love* (Muse 5258), *Cloudburst* (Enja 4032), and *Freddie Freeloader* (Denon CY-6302). He also guests on Thelonious Monk *Underground* (Columbia 40785).

Jeanne Lee: with Ran Blake, *The Legendary Duets* (originally *The Newest Sound Around*) (Bluebird 64621-2 RB), *Archie Shepp & Jeanne Lee* (West Wind Jazz 2036), Carla Bley & Paul Haines: *Escalator Over The Hill* (ECM 23403), Andrew Cyrille, Jeanne Lee & Jimmy Lyons: *Nuba* (Black Saint 120030), Anthony Braxton: *Town Hall (Trio & Quintet) 1972* (Hat Hut Records 6119, Switzerland).

Peggy Lee: Official-Lee she's made made 59 albums including 631 different songs, almost more than anybody, which doesn't even include recent releases of airchecks and transcriptions, et al. She hasn't quite dominated the CD universe as thoroughly as she did the old world of LPs, thus, collecting all international-Lee known digital discs is not all that daunting a proposition.

With Benny Goodman: the most easily findable sampler of her big band work is *Benny Goodman Featuring Peggy Lee: Best Of The Big Bands* (Legacy 53422). She also may be heard on *Peggy Lee Sings with Benny Goodman* (Columbia CK-7005), BG's *Best of the Big Bands* entry (CK-40834 +), *Benny Goodman, Vol. II: Clarinet a la King* (CK-40834), *Benny Goodman Small Groups, 1941–'45* (CK-44437), and *Portrait of Peggy Lee, 1941–'42* (Japanese CBS/Sony 32DP-563), although between them they duplicate a lot of the same material.

Capitol First period: her *Collector's Series* (Capitol CDP7-93195-2) contains many gems and a few meaningless hits (I mean, "Ghost

Riders in the Sky?"), and is thus far the only disc of her first Capitol period. The A & R on the Macgregor transcriptions, available on *Jazz Collector Edition* (Laser Light 15742), is considerably more copasetic. Also: *The Uncollected Peggy Lee 1948* (Hindsight 220), *Live 1947 & 1952* with special guest Desi Arnaz (Jazz Band 2115, English), and the now-withdrawn *Why Don't You Do Right?* with Jimmy Durante (VN 158).

Decca: *Black Coffee & Other Delights: The Decca Anthology* (Decca 11122) is a good double sampler to start with. Seeing as it's unlikely that they'll do any complete albums, there's always Japan, where at one time you could get CDs of her three most important albums for the label, *Black Coffee* (25P2-2829), *Dream Street* (25P2-2830), and *Sea Shells* (25P2-2831). Non-commercial from the same period: *If I Could Be With You* (Jasmine 2534) and *The Uncollected Peggy Lee* (HSR-22).

Capitol Second Period: there are the samplers *Spotlight On Peggy Lee* which is mainly good stuff but also contains some filler, the ten-track *Fever and other Hits* (CEMA Special Products CDL-57358), *Seductive* (16 tracks at least, Pair PCD-2-1194), and from England: *The Best of the Capitol Years* (EMI/Capitol CDP7-90552-2) and *Portrait of a Song Stylist* (Harmony HARCD-116). Complete albums: Capitol at one point announced *Ps & Qs*, a double-length disc containing both of the Lee–Quincy Jones albums, but it doesn't seem to have ever been released. However, they have come out with *Beauty And The Beat!* with George Shearing (Capitol/EMI 98454 +), live at *Basin Street East* (32744), and *Christmas Carousel* (94450). From Japanese Toshiba: one sampler, *Peggy Lee—Best 20* (CP32-5297), and three for-real albums, *Mink Jazz* (TOCJ-5342), *The Man I Love* (TOCJ-5356) with Nels arranging and Francis making with the downbeats, and *If You Go*, sporting Quincy Jones's ballad charts (TOCJ-5393). Hey! It's a beginning!

More Recent: *Mirrors* (A & M CD-5268) is the all-original Lieber & Stoller album which introduced "Some Cats Know," *Close Enough For Love* (DRG 5190), *Peggy Sings the Blues* (MusicMasters MMD-60249K), *There'll Be Another Spring (Peggy sings Peggy)* (MusicMasters MMD-5034), *Moments Like This* (Chesky 84), *Peggy Lee Sings The Blues* (Musicmasters 5005), and last-Lee *Love Held Lightly: Rare Songs by Harold Arlen* (Angel 54798 +). Also recommended: Jeanie Bryson's tribute a la Lee, *Some Cats Know*, forth-coming from Telarc.

Abbey Lincoln: The three classic Riversides have been reissued digitally by Fantasy as part of their Original Jazz Classics series, thank the Lord: *That's Him* (OJCCD-085-2), *It's Magic* (OJCCD-205-2), and *Abbey Is Blue* (OJCCD-069-2). *Affair* (originally on Liberty, now Capitol/EMI 81199) serves as a prelude to the series, like *Rheingold* to the *Ring* cycle. If you need more, then go for *Straight Ahead* (Candid CCD-79015), *People in Me* (excuse me?) (now Verve 514 626), *Talking to The Sun* (Enja 4060), and *Abbey Sings Billie*, a live set that isn't quite as good as it should have been (Enja R21Y-79633). Her current line of Verve / Polygram CDs is also uniformly recommended, starting with *The World is Falling Down* (843 476-2) and particularly the collaborations *You Gotta Pay The Band* with Stan Getz (511 110) and *When There Is Love* with Hank Jones (519 697). Also: *Devil's Got Your Tongue* (513 574) with children's choir.

Bob Manning: At last a legit Manning reissue! It's *Spotlight On Bob Manning* (Capitol/EMI 89940) and it does feature the surreal "My Love Song for You."

Dean Martin: FS: "There's me, Tony Bennett, drunkie Dean and that's about it." There's also three sampler sets, *Capitol Collector's Series* (Capitol CDP7-91633), *The Best of the Capitol Years* (Capitol CDP7-90718-2), and *All Time Greatest Hits* (Curb D2-77383), and one real album, but it's a goodie, *Swingin' Down Yonder* with Dick Stabile and eight bonus tracks (CDP7-94306-2 but now unavailable). Also available: *Happy Hour* (wotta title) (Pair 1177) and *A Winter Romance* (Capitol 94306). It's not surprising that the reissue czars of the major labels, who are more rock-oriented individuals (if that's not a contradiction in terms), should dig Dino like the most; after all, Dean was Elvis long before Elvis was Elvis. *This Time I'm Swingin'* with Nelson Riddle, and *Sleep Warm*, conducted by the Sober Thin One, are both generously sampled on the newly-released *Spotlight on Dean Martin*. Here's hoping that we'll soon see the jazzier-than-usual *Pretty Baby* and all those great (if admittedly jazzless) early Italian singles soon. Now that's amore!

Red McKenzie: Finally there's an entire CD devoted strictly to this pivotal leader and proto-crooner: *Red McKenzie* (Timeless OJC; Dutch import) contains two mid-30s sessions with Bunny Berigan and other 52nd Street faves. He also may be heard with Benny Goodman on *Bill Dodge All-Star Recordings* (Circle 111) and on the Columbia anthologies *Charming Gents Of Stage & Screen* (Legacy 57712) and *The Crooners* (Legacy 52942).

Carmen McRae: The classic Kapp albums are only available as they should be (meaning complete!) from Japan, among them *By Special Request* (25P2-2824), *After Glow* (25P2-2825), *Something to Swing About* (25P2-2826), *Book of Ballads* (25P2-2823). There are a few samplers available stateside, just to whet your appetite: *The Greatest Of Carmen McRae* (MCA Jazz 4111), *Here To Stay* (GRP 610), and *Sings Great American Songwriters* (GRP 631).

Columbia Special Products at least keeps one of her great albums for that label available, *Take Five* with Dave Brubeck (A 9116, also on Japanese CBS/Sony 32DP-620). It's only a matter of time before they too get to the others, as the foreign affiliates have done: *Lover Man (Carmen Sings Billie)* (Japanese CBS/Sony 32DP-564) and *The Real Ambassadors* with Louis Armstrong & Lambert, Hendricks & Ross (French CBS 467140-2). There's also *Alive!* (Columbia Legacy 57887).

Mainstream has reissued *The Ultimate Carmen McRae* (MDCD-705) and *Woman Talk* (MDCD-706); or, from Japanese Century, *Live and Wailing* (32ED-5011), *Live and Doin' It* (32ED-5012), *Live at Sugar Hill* (32ED-5009). And from Groove Merchant: *Miss Jazz* (CD 2625022) and *A Whole Lot of Human Feeling* (CD 2625062). More recently, *The Ultimate Carmen McRae* comes from the more recent Columbia-Mainstream union (Legacy 57122).

Stop me if you've heard this before, but American Atlantic only has an abridged issue of *The Great American Songbook* album available (904-2), while Japanese Atlantic has issued that set in its full, two-disc incarnation (AMCY-1053), as well as *Portrait of Carmen* (AMCY-1053), *For Once In My Life* (AMCY-1064), *The Sound of Silence* (AMCY-1069), *Carmen "Live" at Century Plaza* with nine bonus tracks (!) (AMCY-1075), and *Just a Little Love* (AMCY-1079); *Bittersweet* (Japanese Phonogram PHCE-1013) is also from the Atlantic Period and *1961–69* (Hindsight 602) contains non-commercial tracks from across the whole decade.

Miscellaneous '70s: *Velvet Soul* (33038-7970), *Ms. Magic* (Dunhill DZS021), *As Time Goes By (Live at the Dug)* (Japanese Victor VDJ-1570), *Carmen McRae* (Dutch Sound of Jazz CLCD-5009), *Can't Hide Love* (Blue Note 89540). And '80s: *Live at Bubba's*, Ft. Lauderdale, 1981 (Japanese Crown BRJ-4049) or *Carmen McRae Live*, which is the Bubba's album plus a bonus track (Kingdom Jazz CD Gate-7001), *Any Old Time* (33CY-1216), *The Betty Carter— Carmen McRae Duets, 'Live'* (Great American Music Hall GAMHCD-2706-2), *Live At Ronnie Scott's* (DRG 91426), and *Live in Tokyo* (Lobster LFA-1055).

Elder stateswoman, on Concord Jazz: *Fine and Mellow, Live at Birdland West* (CCD-4342), *You're Looking at Me*, her great tribute to Nat Cole (CCD-4235), *Two for the Road* with George Shearing (CCD-4128), and *Heat Wave* with Cal Tjader (CCD-4189); and on BMG/Novus, all of which, coincidentally, are tribute albums: *Carmen Sings Monk* (3086-2) and the highly recommended *Sarah— Dedicated to You* (3110-2) and *For Lady Day* (63163). Consumer Guidism: if McRae's name is on the cover, buy it.

Mark Murphy: My personal favorites: *That's How I Love The Blues* (Fantasy OJCCD-367-2) and *Bop For Kerouac* (Muse 5253). Also on Muse: *Beauty and The Beast* (5355), *Stolen Moments* (Muse 9154), *Nat's Choice, The Complete Nat King Cole Songbook, Volumes 1 & 2* (on one CD, 6001), *I'll Close My Eyes* (5436), *Kerouac, Then And Now* (5359), *One For Junior* with Sheila Jordan (5489).

And furthermore: *Night Mood* (Milestone MCD-9145-2), *September Ballads* (Milestone MCD-5102), *Swingin' Singin' Affair* (Japanese Phonogram EJD-1011), *Rah!* (Original Jazz Classics 141).

His two latest are also two of his very best, *Mark Murphy & Nine: Very Early* (West & East Music CD 220 222-2, German) and *Mark Murphy & Metropole Orchestra: The Dream* (Jive Music JM-2006-2, Dutch). Unfortunately, they're both difficult-to-find imports, but they're worth seeking out.

Anita O'Day: '40s: With Gene Krupa: Japanese CBS/Sony has issued one all-O'Day-Krupa disc, *Anita O'Day Sings With Gene Krupa* (32DP-567), and, closer to home, she turns up on *Roy Eldridge with the Gene Krupa Orchestra* (Columbia CK-45448) and *Drummin' Man* (British Affinity 81). With Stan Kenton: nothing yet, but while we're on the subject of her four known Kenton vocals, let's also express the hope that Capitol will get around to her so-far-unissued 1945 premiere solo session. Signature: They're all on the horrendously-packaged *I Told Ya I Love Ya Now Get Out*, which Gary Giddins recently described as the most expensive music—in terms of the ratio of playing time to list price—ever released. She also guest-stars with the King Cole Trio on *Volume Four* of that group's Laser Light series of MacGregor transcriptions (15749).

Granz and Verve (Currently Polygram): Virtually all of her wondrously juicy Verves are seeing the light of day again in Japan, and a few have also been released here as well. Local product first: *Anita* (currently titled *This Is Anita* 829 261-2), *Anita Sings the Most* with Oscar Peterson (829 577-2), *Anita O'Day Sings the Winners* (837 939-2 +), and the *Anita Swings Cole Porter with Billy May* is available domestically with bonus tracks of Porter songs from other O'Day Verves, or from Japan in toto with *Anita O'Day Swings Rodgers and Hart with Billy May* (two LPs complete on one CD, Japanese Verve POCJ-1914). Also from Japan: *The Lady is a Tramp* (J25J-25140), *An Evening with Anita O'Day* (POCJ-1927), *Pick Yourself Up* (POCJ-1940), and *At Mr. Kelly's* (POCJ-1924). Also *Compact Jazz* (517 954 +)

'60s to '90s: Although the all-Anita Emily catalogue is currently up in the air, a number of items once available as Emily LPs have been CD'd: *Anita 1975* (Emily, Japanese Apollon BY30-5150), which is also titled *A Song for You* on a German release (Storyville STCD-04147), and *Live in Tokyo, 1975* (Emily, Japanese BY30-5140). Also: *Once Upon a Summertime*, her best post-Verve live album so far, with super-spacy solos from pianist Stan Tracy (British Jasmine JASM CD-2531), *Wave: Live at Ronnie's* 1986 (Castle ESMCD-019). *I Get A Kick Out Of You* seems to be the same as the old *a song for you* (Evidence 22054). New to me, both on the Italian label Moon Records: *Tea For Two* (023) and *That's That* (047). Still more: *In A Mellotone* (DRG CDSL-5209), *Live at Vine*

Street, Live In Person (Starline 9004 +), and, most recently, *Rules Of The Road* (Pablo 2310-950).

Jackie Paris: The best albums by this brilliant, overlooked bop-balladeer remain as unobtainable as ever, but you can pick up a few other worthwhile Paris efforts: from Audiophile, *Nobody Else But Me* (APCD-245), *Jackie Paris* (158); from Japan comes the vintage *Lyrics of Ira Gershwin* (from Time, Tokuma 32CT-105), and the more recent *Lucky to Be Me* (from EmArcy, EJD-2) and *Love Songs* (Phonograph PHCE-5020). Two guest shots with Charles Mingus: *Changes Two* (Atlantic/Rhino 71404) and *Debut Rarities, Vol. 4* (Original Jazz Classics 1829). The recent big band album, which had a version of "Small World" that brought tears to my eyes when he played a sample for me on his walkman one day when we ran into each other in Jimmy Dayton's out-of-print record shop, has still never been released.

King Pleasure: The following releases contain all the Clarence Beeks you need: *Sings*, half by Annie Ross (Prestige OJCCD-217-2), *Golden Days* (the Hi-Fi Jazz album, Fantasy OJCCD-1772-2), *Moody's Mood For Love Compilation*—the Aladdin and United Artists material (Blue Note 84463). Further performances by this artist may not necessarily yield you any more Pleasure. There you go, there you go, there you go . . .

Louis Prima: *Zooma Zooma: The Best of Louis Prima* (from Capitol, Rhino R2 70225) and *Capitol Collectors Series* (94072) sample the best-remembered New Orleans-via-Las Vegas R&B-flavored Prima of the '50s, with the equally great Keely Smith and Sam Butera. Even better, *The Capitol Recordings* on German Bear Family (15776) offers you the whole pizza pie, the complete Capitol output of Prima, Smith and Butera (together and separately) on eight glorious discs. Four further releases spotlight Prima's exuberant if occasionally out-of-tune big band of the '40s with Lily Ann Carol: his Majestic 78s on *Play Pretty For the People* (Savoy Jazz ZDS-4420) and live on *Louis Prima* (Echo Jazz EJCD-16), *Remember* (Magic 12, British), and *Angelina* (Viper's Nest VN-155), the latter with Smith. Going further back, *Louis Prima and his New*

Orleans Gang, Volume One, 1934 is the start of what will hopefully be a long series documenting Prima's complete '30s recordings, with Pee Wee Russell and others, on English JSP (339).
Zooma zooma!!

Della Reese: Probably the only major artist of the post-war period who is, as far as we can tell, completely unrepresented on
compact disc! (RCA has announced tentative plans for a DellAn-
thology in '96—well we'll just see about that!)

Betty Roche: Her best CD shots with Ellington are *Carnegie
Hall Concert, January 1943* (2 discs, Prestige 2PCD-34004-2) and
Uptown (Columbia 40836), not to mention *Earl Hines and The
Duke's Men* (Delmark 470). Solo albums, Bethlehem: the excellent
if slightly repititious album *Take the "A" Train* (from Bethlehem,
CY-3782), and, with Moody Marilyn Moore, *Sophisticated Ladies*,
both LPs apparently in toto (British Affinity CD AFF-763). On
Prestige: *Lightly And Politely* (Original Jazz Classics 1802) and
Singin' And Swingin' (Original Jazz Classics 1718).

Jimmy Rushing: Most of his records, like Mr. Five by Five
himself, have been here and gone. Fortunately, all of his Decca
Basie vocals can be found on the *Count Basie: Complete Decca
Recordings* box (Decca Jazz 3-611). A French three-CD series collates many of Basie's airchecks from the Rushing years, *The Gold-
en Years Vol. One, 1937* (French EPM Musique FDC-5502), *Vol.
Two, 1938* (FDC-5510) and *Vol. Three, 1940–'44* (FDC-5521);
Rush also appears on Basie's *The Legendary V-Disc Masters: Beaver Junction* (VJC-1018-2), *Count Basie, 1944* (Hindsight HSR-
224), *Count Basie 1947: Brand New Wagon* (RCA Bluebird 2292)
and *Count Basie at Newport with Joe Williams and Jimmy Rushing, 1957* with five bonus tracks (Polygram 833 776-2). Beyond,
Little Jimmy also guests on Duke Ellington's *Jazz Party* (Columbia
40712) and *The Indispensable Benny Goodman Vol. 3/4* (RCA
66470). Of his post-Basie work, there's only *The Essential Jimmy
Rushing* (Vanguard VCD-65), *The You and Me That Used to Be*
(Bluebird 6460-2), and the essential *Rushing Lullabies* (Columbia
Special Products 8196).

Dinah Shore: It's not surprising that none of her better jazz-oriented material is out—like the Chamber Music Society of Lower Basin Street sides or the album with Red Norvo. (Although *Dinah Sings—[Andre] Previn Plays, Songs in a Midnight Mood,* CP28-5689 and *Dinah, Yes Indeed!* with Nelson Riddle, CP28-5688, were available at one time from Japanese Capitol.) What is distressing is that there isn't any kind of comprehensive retrospective on this most popular of all popular female vocalists and TV stars. The best retrospective of her early material is *You and I* (Conifer 231, UK) which includes only one of the Basin Street tracks ("Dinah's Blues") but does demonstrate how boring most vocal orchestrations were before Strayhorn and Stordahl. Also currently available: *16 Most Requested Songs* (Columbia 45315), *Blues In The Night* (British ASV 5136), *Love And Kisses, Dinah* (RCA 66023), *Spotlight On Dinah Shore* (Capitol 28514), *The Best of Dinah Shore* (Curb D2-77459), and *The Best of the Capitol Years* (British EMI CZ-222). Vintage radio material: *When Dinah Shore Ruled The Earth!* (VJC 1052) and *Dinah's Showtime '44–47* (Hep 45). Sometimes she'll surprise you and sing something really well.

Frank Sinatra: After two editions of this discography, in which I tried vainly to list all releases of interest by this deservingly most-CD'd of all vocalists, I hereby throw in the towel. If you want a semi-complete list of Sinatra CDs, you are referred to my *Sinatra! The Song is You,* which will be issued in paper by Da Capo Press in 1997. Since *Jazz Singing* only offers a sampler examination of Sinatra's artistry, it makes more sense this time around to merely suggest three key multi-volume samplers of Ol' Blue Eyes's most crucial works.

Songs for Swinging Samplers: these sets are recommended for both the novice and advanced Sinatra collector. For the newcomer, they contain the major hits and the signature songs of the eras they cover. At the same time, the compilers also generally throw in a few rarities to make them desireable to the connoisseur. *The Best of the Columbia Years, 1943–1952* (C4K 64681 +, four CDs) concentrates on ballads and standards. These are the sessions in which Young Blue Eyes and arranger Axel Stordahl "legalized" passion, creating a vocal style far more romantic than any pop singer until that time. The sensuality of these fifty-year-old sides is still over-whelming. *The Capitol Years* (C2-94777 +, three CDs), from 1990, offers 75 tracks for 75 years, including most of Sinatra's hit singles and sampling his sixteen classic concept albums of the years 1953–1961, showcasing his work with Billy May, Gordon Jenkins, and especially Nelson Riddle. Since these years are generally regarded as the summit of the Sinatra career, this set is as perfect a starting point as a new listener could wish for. *The Reprise Collection* (926340-2, four CDs) picks up where *Capitol* left off. This package offers a generous and well-chosen sample of key singles and album cuts from 1960 to 1986. Virtually all the key later albums are represented, although the emphasis, justifiably, is on the classic early '60s work.

Songs for Swinging Completists: *Tommy Dorsey–Frank Sinatra: The Song is You* (RCA 07863 66353-2 +, five CDs): while a thought-fully-selected anthology of the best Dorsey Orchestra sides with Sinatra vocals would appeal to everybody, this complete accounting of their 83 tunes together is more specifically aimed at collectors. However, the sound is superb and the more often one listens, the clearer it becomes that the years 1940–'42 produced music no less remark-able than any other Sinatra era. *The Columbia Years 1943–1952. The Complete Recordings* (Columbia Legacy CXK 46873 +, 12 CDs): again, although principally for collectors, this 285-song selection is a treasure trove of famous and obscure treaures from Sinatra's first decade on top. You'll hear his only recording with a latin band and a gospel quartet as well those thankfully few Mitch Miller novelties like "Mama Will Bark." *Sinatra Concepts* (+) contains all sixteen of the classic Sinatra "theme" albums made for Capitol, but omits the singles compilations and soundtracks. *The Complete Reprise Studio Recordings* (Reprise 46013, 20 CDs) is a beautiful-sounding, bizar-rely-packaged mega-amalgam of everything Sinatra recorded for what was originally his own label, from 1960 to 1988. While you might not want to hear those carefully-sequenced concept albums decon-structed into chronological order, the set compensates with dozens of 45-only and completely unissued items.

Carol Sloane: Miss Sloane's stock has continued to rise, with new albums from Concord and others—now let's hope the majors will stick some of her earlier stuff on CD. Domestic: *Love You Madly* with Richard Rodney Bennett, 1988 (Contemporary CCD-14049-2), *The Real Thing* with Mike Renzi (Contemporary CCD-14060-2). From Japan: *Early Hours* with Larry Elgart, 1958–59 (CBS/Sony 32DP-794), *Out of the Blue* with Bill Finegan, 1962 (CBS/Sony 32DP-616), *Live at 30th Street* 1962 (CBS/Sony 32DP-617), *But Not For Me* with Tommy Flanagan, 1986 (CBS/Sony 32DP-681), *Subway Tokens* 1975 (Century CECC 0017), *Cottontail* 1978 (from Choice, Sohbi SHCJ-1007), *Midnight Sun* 1977 & '83 (Lobster LFA-3045), *A Night of Ballads* 1984 with two bonus tracks (Baybridge TECP-20465), *Live* with Joe Puma, 1982 (Baybridge 30CP-196), *Carol Sings* (Audiophile 211), and *As Time Goes By* (Baybridge TECP-20464). The big news is that Concord has finally found another first class femme chirper to keep Rosie Clooney company, on *Heart's Desire* (4503), *Love You Madly* (4049), *Sweet & Slow* (4564), *When I Look In Your Eyes* (4619) and, best of all, the tribute to McRae, *Songs Carmen Sang* (4663), which teams Sloane with the marvelous Phil Woods and Bill Charlap, the most exciting accompanists to emerge in recent years.

Jo Stafford: Anthologies and compilations: I recommend *The Portrait Edition* (a three-CD box from Sony Music Special Products 57836 +, but which covers stuff from her whole career, from Dorsey onward) for starters, as well as *Her Greatest Hits and Finest Performances* (Reader's Digest RBD 052). Also three Capitol collections, *Collector's Series* (CDP7-91638-2) and *You Belong to Me* (Pair CD-1225), and, from Britain, *Best of the Capitol Years* (EMI CDP7-95756-2). From Corinthian: *America's Most Versatile Singing Star* (1802), *The "Big Band" Sound* (112), *Broadway Revisited* (118), *G.I. Jo (Sings Songs Of World War 2)* (105), *Greatest Hits* (106), *Jo + Jazz* (yes! 108), *Jo Stafford Sings American Folk Songs* (110). Duets: *Down Memory Lane* (Memoir Classics 402, UK) and *Old Rugged Cross* (MFP 99140, UK), both with Gordon MacRae, and, from the radio, *Drifting And Dreaming* with guest Dick Haymes (VJC 1040). From Japan: Toshiba: *Starring Jo Stafford* (TOCJ-5362), *Autumn In New York* (TOCJ-5346), *Best Now* (CP32-9035), *Swingin' Down Broadway* (32DP-672), *Once Over Lightly*—everybody's favorite jazz accordion vocal record (32DP-673), and *I'll Be*

Seeing You (32DP-488). And lastly, *Jonathan and Darlene's Greatest Hits—Volume II* (Corinthian 103CD). How'd they get in here?

Kay Starr: Entire albums are super-scarce; locally there are just a couple of samplers, *Capitol Collector's Series* (C27-94888-2) and *Spotlight* (Capitol 29392), and several collections of transcriptions, *Moonbeams and Steamy Dreams* (Stash ST-CD-534 +), *The Uncollected—Kay Starr in the '40s* (Hindsight HSR-214), and its sequel, *The Uncollected Kay Starr, Vol. 2* (Japanese Hindsight only, R28J-3140). Two actual albums have been done overseas, *Movin'* (from Capitol, British Jasmine JAS CD-307) and *Rockin' With Kay* (Japanese RCA R25J-1006).

Maxine Sullivan: Band vocals and miscellaneous early stuff: *Maxine Sullivan and John Kirby, More 1940–'41* (Circle CCD-125), *Claude Thornhill: Tapestries* (British Affinity 82), *Benny Carter: All of Me* (Bluebird 3000-2-RB), and *Teddy Wilson: Everytime We Say Goodbye* (Musicraft MVSCD-59); the earliest all-Maxine albums available are *A Tribute To Andy Razaf* (from Period, DCC Compact Classics DJZ-610) and *1944 To 1948 Compilation* (Legend/Island 6004) an import which I've seen listed but never heard. Old and Great Maxine: *Great Songs from the Cotton Club* (Mobile Fidelity MFCD-836), *Sings the Music of Burton Lane* (Mobile Fidelity MFCD-773 +), *Together* (Atlantic 81783-2), *Uptown* with the Scott Hamilton Quintet (Concord Jazz CCD-4288), *Swingin' Sweet* (Concord Jazz CCD-4351), *Spring Isn't Everything: The Music of Harry Warren* (Audiophile DAPCD-229), and *I Happen to Be in Love* (Japanese 32DP-698).

Jack Teagarden: He rarely if ever did an all-vocal album, but here are some sets where you can glom onto Big Tea's gin-tinged crooning of blues and ballads: *That's a Serious Thing* (Bluebird 9986-2), *Jack Teagarden & Pee Wee Russell* (Fantasy OJCCD-1708-2), *Texas Trombone* live in '58 (Star Line CD-SG-403), *A Hundred Years From Today* live in '63 (Columbia Special Products CSP-4523-2-F), *Jazz Original* (British Charly 80), *I Gotta Right To Sing The Blues* (British Living Era CD AJA-5059), *This is Teagarden!* (TOCJ-5319), *Masters of Jazz, Vol. 10, 1941–'44* (German or Danish

Storyville, STCD-4110), *1934–1939* (Classics 729), *1939–1940* (Classics 758), *Jack Teagarden And His All-Stars* (Jazzology 199), *A Hundred Years From Today*—a 1963 concert with great guest stars (Memphis Archives 7010), *Live In Chicago 1960 & 1961* (English Jazz Band 2114), and three volumes of big band transcriptions, all heavy on the vocals, *Jack Teagarden Vol. 1, 1941: It's Time For Tea!* (Jass J-CD-624), *Vol. 2: Has Anybody Here Seen Jackson?* (637), and *Big "T" Jump (Vol. 3)* (643). We wait in vain for his three masterpiece Verve albums—so far I haven't heard of Polygram even issuing a *Compact Jazz* set.

Mel Torme: Mel-Tones, Musicrafts and other early items: two CDs just about cover the Musicraft period, both Mel-Tones and solo sides, *A Foggy Day* (MVSCD-54) and *There's No One But You* (MVSCD-60), while *Spotlight On Mel Torme* (Capitol 89941) spotlights the Capitol years 1949–1953. From the Coral period, *Mel Torme In Hollywood* (Decca Jazz/GRP 617) has a stupid title (I mean, he lives in Hollywood!) but smartly expands on the original 1954 *Mel Torme at the Crescendo* album.

I officially give up trying to keep track of the various permutations of the classic Bethlehem albums. Here's all that I could find out: *It's A Blue World* (Bethlehem 5015), *Live At The Crescendo* (Charly 60), *California Suite* (Bethlehem 5026), *The Complete Porgy & Bess* with Frances Faye, Ralph Sharon (Bethlehem 5014), *Mel Torme* (Bethlehem 5007), *Mel Torme Sings Fred Astaire* (Bethlehem 3008).

The great Tops album with Marty Paich, which has come out on more LPs than Carter has little liver pills, has thus far made it to two CDs, each difficult to find now: *Smooth as Velvet* (Pickwick PMTD-16009) and *Prelude to a Kiss* (FRS-CD-109). Miscellaneous live tracks and transcriptions: *'Round Midnight: A Retrospective* (Stash ST-CD-4 +), *Easy To Remember* (Hindsight 253), and on Laser Light: *Luck Be A Lady* (12224), *Round Midnight* (12223), *Smooth As Velvet* (15381), and *Swingin' On The Moon* (12222).

Verve, Polygram Jazz: *Compact Jazz* (833 282), *I Dig The Duke, I Dig the Count*—now titled *The Duke Ellington & Count Basie Songbooks* (823 248-2), *Torme* (823 010-2 +), *Swings Shubert Alley* (821 581-2), and *Back in Town* with the Mel-Tones and Art Pepper

(511 522) have been brought out over here. Two more can be found in Japan, *Ole Torme! Mel Torme Goes South of the Border with Billy May* (J25J-25136) and *Swingin' On the Moon* (J28J-25101).

'60s & '70s: *Comin' Home Baby* (Japanese Atlantic 30P2-2322) and *Songs of New York* (Atlantic 80078), *That's All* (Columbia Special Products 09118), *16 Most Requested Songs* (Columbia 53779), *Mel Torme and Friends, Live at Marty's* (two CDs, Japanese Finesse 30JD-20-21), *Live At The Maisonette* (Atlantic/Rhino 18129), *Mel Torme & Buddy Rich: Together Again—For The First Time* (Gold Disc UDCD01-00592), and *London Sessions* (Dunhill DCC-608).

Concord Jazz: with George Shearing, there are two studio sessions, *Top Drawer* (CCD-4126) and the new *Torme & Shearing Do WWII*, and a series of live "evenings," *An Evening with George Shearing & Mel Torme* (CCD-4190), *An Elegant Evening* (CCD-4294), *An Evening at Charlie's* (CCD-4248), and *A Vintage Year* (CCD-4341). More team-ups ala Torme: *Nothing Without You* with Cleo Laine (4515), with *Rob McConnell and the Boss Brass* (CCD-4036), followed by the brand-new *Velvet and Brass* (4667), and, with the Marty Paich Dek-Tette in the studio, *Reunion* (CCD-4360), and live, *In Concert Tokyo* (CCD-4382). Also live, in a set marking the equally long-awaited recording debut of his great trio with John Campbell, *Night at the Concord Pavilion* (CCD-4433). Also live: *Fujitsu-Concord Jazz Festival '90* (4481). More Concord: *Sing, Sing, Sing* (4542) and *A Tribute To Bing Crosby* (4614), the latter with string orchestra.

On Telarc: *The Christmas Songs* (83315) and *The Great American Songbook* (83328 +). Lastly, Rhino Records has announced a comprehensive four-CD set which will contain nearly a hundred tracks from over a dozen labels, sampling the entire Torme *ouvre*, which will be released later in 1996 (+). Get it? Got it! Good.

Rudy Vallee: *American Legends Series: Vagabond Lover* (ProArte CDD-459), *Heigh-Ho Everybody, This Is Rudy Vallee* (Living Era 5009, UK), and the imaginatively-titled *The Voice That Had Them Fainting* (Take Two TT405).

Sarah Vaughan: '40s: Danish Official gathered her *First 15 Sides* into a truly abysmal-sounding disc (83-003) which will have to do until the real thing comes along. The ever-generous Discovery label has managed to stretch their minimal Musicraft license of Vaughan into three CDs, would you believe it? *It's You Or No One* (MVSCD-55), *Tenderly* (MVSCD-57), *Time and Again* (MVSCD-61). On Columbia: *16 Most Requested Songs* (Legacy Records 53783), *Deep Purple* (Columbia 11318), *In Hi-Fi* (Columbia Special Products 13084), and *The Divine Sarah—The Columbia Years, 1949–'53* (C2K-44165). That latter double set contains most of her best work for the label, or roughly 50% of everything she did at the time. But the hell with that! The late and Divine one is one of those few super-prolific artists where you really have to have it all, which is precisely what you get in the next phase of her career.

Mercury (and EmArcy & Wing): Ta-da! Here it is! Polygram's *The Complete Sarah Vaughan on Mercury,* in four box sets, *Vol. 1: Great Jazz Years* (six CDs, 826 320-2), *Vol. 2: Sings Great American Songs* (five CDs, 826 327-2), *Vol. 3: Great Show on Stage* (six CDs, 826 333-2), *Vol. 4: '60s* (six CDs, 830 714-2). The same material is also available on a mess o' singles and doubles from Polygram: *Swingin' Easy* (Emarcy 514 072), *The George Gershwin Songbook Vol. 1* (846 895-2) and *Vol. 2* (846 896-2), *Golden Hits* (8244891-2 +), *In the Land of Hi Fi* (826 454-2), *Misty / Vaughan & Violins* (846 488-2), *No Count Sarah* (824 864-2), *The Rodgers and Hart Songbook* (824 864-2), *Sassy Swings Again* (814 587-2), *Sassy Swings the Tivoli* (2 CDs, 832 788-2), *Sarah with Clifford Brown* (814 151-2), *After Hours at the London House* (Japanese EmArcy PHCE-1015), *The Irving Berlin Songbook* with Billy Eckstine (Emarcy 822 526), *Vaughan And Voices* (846 506), *At Mr. Kelly's* (Emarcy 832 791), *Sarah Vaughan Sings Broadway: Great Songs From Great Shows* (526 464), and one of the all-time great live albums, *Sassy Swings The Tivoli* (Emarcy 832 788). More compilations: *Compact Jazz* (Verve 830 699), *Compact Jazz—Sarah Vaughan Live!* (832 572), *Jazz Round Midnight* (512 379), *Verve Jazz Masters 18* (518 199).

Roulette: *The Roulette Years Vol. 1* (94983) and *Vol. 2* (95331), *The Singles Sessions* (95331), *Basie-Vaughan* (59043), *Dreamy* (59051), *The Benny Carter Sessions* (28640), *Sarah Sings Soulfully*

(98445), *Sarah Slightly Classical* (95977), and the Japanese *You're Mine You* (Toshiba TOCJ-5394) and *The Divine One* (TOCJ-5387).

Mainstream: you definitely need *The Complete Sarah Vaughan in Japan* (two discs, Mobile Fidelity MFCD-2-844). You definitely don't need *with Michel Legrand* (Mainstream MDCD-702), or, in the same vein on Atlantic, *Songs of the Beatles* (16037-2). Also: *A Time In My Life* (Mainstream MDCD-704).

Pablo: they're all—yes!—available from Fantasy, sampled on *The Best of Sarah Vaughan* (231 211), *The Duke Ellington Songbook Vol. 1* (231 2111-2) and *Vol. 2* (231 2116-2), *Copacabana* (Pablo 2312125-2), *Crazy and Mixed Up* (231 2137-2), *How Long Has This Been Goin' On* (213 0821-2), *Send In The Clowns* (231 2130-2), and *The Best Of Sarah Vaughan* (2405-416).

Miscellaneous: *I'll Be Seeing You: The Sarah Vaughan Memorial Album* guest-starring Count Basie and Woody Herman (Vintage Jazz Classics VJC-1015-2); *Gershwin Live!* with Michael Tilson Thomas (Columbia MK-37277); *Brazilian Romance* with Milton Nascimento (Columbia MK-42519); *O Som Brasileiro De Sarah Vaughan* (Brazilian RCA CD-10027); *Jazz Festival Masters,* which is cheesily packaged but is an excellent live concert (Scotti Brothers / BMG 75244); *1961* (Hindsight 601); *Perdido* (Natasha 4004). Don't you love farce? Don't you approve?

Bea Wain: with *Larry Clinton and his Orchestra, 1937–38* (Hindsight 109). BMG does at last have an official Clinton-Wain compilation in the works, perhaps even for 1996.

Fats Waller: Here 'tis! Here's a sampling of Fatsy-Watsy's irresistible singing (not counting such strictly instrumental items as his great *Piano Solos* collection). With Waller, for once, it's the domestic corporations that are going for a complete series while the overseas independents issue a plethora of samplers.

On domestic BMG, one overview collection, *The Joint is Jumpin'* (6288-2) and a line of ambitious boxes, *Fats Waller And His Rhythm: The Middle Years, Part I (1936–38)* (66083), *The Last Years, 1940–'43* (three CDs, 9883-2). Also recommended: *The Indispensable Fats Waller Vol. 9/10* (66466).

Various samplers from Europe: *You Rascal You* (Living Era EVCJ-7023/24), *Fats and His Rhythm* (BBC BBCCD-684), *Jazz Classics Vol. 5, 1927–'34* (BBC BBCCD-598), and *Lounging at the Waldorf (1936)* (Saville CDSVL-213). As with Calloway, there's also a good French release offering 22 tracks concentrating on Fatsy-Watsy's highly serious crooning, so help me! It's *Fats Waller 1934–'39* (French Telecom Systemes, L'Art Vocal 4). So you like that mess? Well latch on!

Non-RCA material: two sets of Associated transcriptions and miscellaneous radio material, 1935–'39, *The Definitive Fats, Vol. 1: His Piano, His Rhythm* (Stash ST-CD-528 +), *Vol. 2: Piano and Vocal* (Stash ST-CD-539 +), and *Fats Waller In London* (DRG 8442).

Dinah Washington: Pre-history: *Mellow Mama* (Delmark 451) and *1943–'45* (Official 83004, from Demark).

The Great Mercury Years: the Mercury material has been issued in a complete and definitive series of seven three-fer boxes by Polygram: *Complete on Mercury: Vol. 1: 1946–'49* (830 700-2), *Vol. 2: 1950–'52* (832 444-2), *Vol. 3: 1952–'54* (834 675-2), *Vol. 4: 1954–'56* (834 683-2), *Vol. 5: 1956–'58* (838 952-2), *Vol. 6: 1958–'60* (838 956-2), and *Vol. 7: 1961* (830 960-2). Thank you, "Boxman!"

As with Sarah Vaughan, a bunch of the original albums are also available singly from Polygram: *Dinah Jams* (814 639-2), *The Fats Waller Songbook* (818 930-2), *In the Land of Hi-Fi* (826 453-2), *The Bessie Smith Songbook* (826 663-2), *What a Difference a Day Makes* (818 815-2), *Dinah* (Emarcy 842 139), *For Those In Love* (Emarcy 514 073), *The Two Of Us* with Brook Benton (526 467), *Unforgettable* (Mercury 510 602).

Polygram compilations: *Compact Jazz* (830 700), *Jazz Round Midnight* (514 363), *The Jazz Sides* (Mercury 824 883), *Dinah Sings Standards* (522 055), *A Slick Chick*—the R&B sides (Mercury 814 184), *The Essential Dinah Washington—The Great Songs* (512 905), *First Issue: The Dinah Washington Story* (514 841), *Verve Jazz Masters 19* (518 200), and *Compact Jazz: Dinah Sings the Blues* (832 573-2)

The almost-equally-great Roulette period, now part of Blue Note/Capitol Jazz: *Dinah '63* (94576-2), *The Best Of Dinah Washington—*

The Roulette Years (99114), and *Dinah In Love* (97273). Also in the same vein and highly recommended: Aretha Franklin's *Unforgettable—A Tribute To Dinah Washington* (Columbia Legacy 66201).

Ethel Waters: *On Stage and Screen* (Columbia Special Products A 2792, also spotted with the catalogue number 75018) and *Push Out, 1938–'39* containing the Bluebird tracks (French Jazz Archives Vol. I, Zeta ZET-747). From the Belgian classics label, where you takes your chances on the sound quality: *1925–1926* (672), *1926–1930* (688), *1929–1931* (721), *1931–1934* (735), *1935–1940* (755), and more will probably have been issued by the time you read this. Two discs are named after Waters's only starring role in a major Hollywood musical, *Cabin In The Sky*, the first a compilation of commercial sides (Milan 35626) and the second the first complete issue of the soundtrack music from that great film (Rhino 77245). It's surprising that Columbia hasn't done more on either their Roots and Blues series or their Art Deco line, and for that matter, where are Decca and Bluebird? More, please!

Lee Wiley: *I've Got You Under My Skin: The Complete Young Lee Wiley, 1931–'37* (Vintage Jazz Classics VJC-1023-2), *The Songs of George and Ira Gershwin and Cole Porter* (from Liberty Music Shop, Audiophile ACD-1), *The Songs of Rodgers and Hart and Harold Arlen* (from Music Box & Schirmer, Audiophile ACD-10), *Jess Stacy and Friends* (including two Wiley vocals, Commodore CCD-7008), *A Night In Manhattan* (Columbia Special Products A 656), *Duologue* (from Storyville, British Black Lion BLCD-760911 or Japanese Storyville 32JDS-141), *Lee Wiley Sings Vincent Youmans & Irving Berlin* (Japanese CBS/Sony 32DP-487). The two RCA albums have come out as they should in Japan, *West of the Moon* (R25J-1007) and *A Touch of the Blues* (R25J-1041) and have been ingloriously schmeared together, with a few omissions, on the domestic *As Time Goes By* (RCA Bluebird 3138). Two discs of collector's items: *Rarities*—like anything that she did wasn't a rarity!— (Jass J-CD-15) and *Look At Me Now* (Yadeon Music 503).

The Japanese *Lee Wiley with Eddie Condon All Stars, 1944-'45* (30CP-135) collates her vocal features from the famous Condon

Town Hall Concerts, but in so-so sound. Jazzology is issuing those concerts in complete, definitive form in excellent Jack Towers–level fidelity, as *Town Hall Concerts, Vol 5* (Jazzology 1009/10). Perhaps when they're finished we can start a grass-roots campaign to pressure them into likewise gathering all the Wiley numbers onto a single disc. *Eddie Condon: Dixieland All-Stars* (Decca Jazz 637) features three vocals by La Lee.

Joe Williams: The Pre-Basie material has been available as both *Every Day I Have The Blues* (Savoy Jazz ZDS-4405) and *Joe Williams Sings* (Savoy 0199).

With Count Basie on Verve: *The Greatest! Count Basie Plays, Joe Williams Sings Standards* (833 774), *Count Basie at Newport with Joe Williams and Jimmy Rushing, 1957* with five bonus tracks (Polygram 833 776), *Count Basie Swings—Joe Williams Sings* (519 852), *The Greatest* (833 774), and *Compact Jazz* (835 329-2). More Verve compilations: *Ballad And Blues Master* (511 354), *Every Day: The Best Of The Verve Years* (519 813), and *Jazz Round Midnight* (527 034).

With Basie on Roulette: *Count Basie: A Swingin' Night at Birdland* (Blue Note R2 9335) and in England, *A Man Ain't Supposed to Cry* (EMI/Roulette CZ-233) and *Memories Ad Lib* (Roulette 59037). All of the standard Basie Orchestra material, both with and without Williams, is also available on two highly-recommended boxes from Mosaic: *The Complete Roulette Recordings of Count Basie Live* (eight discs, 135) and *Live* (ten discs, 149). It would be terrific if all of Williams's classic solo albums on Roulette and RCA were to be so well-covered.

'60s & '70s: *A Man Ain't Supposed To Cry* (Roulette 59023), *A Night At Count Basie's* (Vanguard 8508), *Jump For Joy* (RCA Bluebird 52713), *Chains Of Love* (Natasha 4019, radio material), *Overwhelming* (6464-2), *Joe Williams with the Thad Jones/Mel Lewis Orchestra* (LRC CDC-9005), *Joe Williams Live* (Original Jazz Classics 438), and *Prez and Joe* with Dave Pell's Prez Conference (GNP Crescendo GNP-2124).

'80s & '90s: *Nothin' But the Blues* (Delos DCD-4001), *I Just Want To Sing* (Delos DCD-4004), *Having the Blues under European Sky* (Denon 33C38-7834), *Every Night: Live At Vine Street* (Verve 833 236), *In Good Company* (Verve 837 932), *Live At The Detroit Orchestra Hall* with the Count Basie Orchestra (Telarc 83329 +), *That Holiday Feeling* (Verve 843 956), and *Here's to Life* with Robert Farnon's orchestra (Telarc +). Big Joe's latest album, announced for the fall of '96, will be a tribute to the great and neglected lyricist Bob Russell.

Cassandra Wilson: Her albums divide up into three categories, guest appearances (of which there are many, mainly with Steve Coleman), the earlier "solo" works on JMT (currently on Polygram), and the more recent albums, mainly on Blue Note. On Polygram: *Point of View* (834 404), *Days Aweigh* (834 412), *Blue Skies* (834 419), *Jumpworld* (834 434), *She Who Weeps* (834 443), and *After The Beginning Again* (514 001). Also: *Cassandra Wilson Live* (Jazz Music Today 849 149 or video 084 359), *Dance To The Drums Again* (DIW/Columbia 53451), *Blue Light 'Til Dawn* (Blue Note 81357), and the latest, 1996's *New Moon Daughter* (Blue Note 32861).

Try Before You Buy: The following anthologies all offer a plethora of singers, making them good opportunities to sample various sounds before you invest in a full-length CD by any of them: *Jazz Club* vocals (Verve 840 029), *The Ladies*—Ernestine Anderson, Mary Ann McAll, Annie Ross (Savoy 1200 +), *Jazz Masters: The Vocalists* (RCA Bluebird 66072), *The Legendary Big Band Singers* (Decca Jazz 642), *Atlantic Jazz: Voices Of Cool, Volume One* (Rhino 71748 +) and *Two* (+), *Blue Vocals Vol. 1* (Blue Note 96582 +) and *Vol. 2* (Blue Note 96583 +), *Compact Jazz: Best Of Compact Jazz Vocalists* (Verve 845 466), *The 1940's: The Singers* (Columbia 40652), and various compilations of '20s and '30s pop that includes much of relevance: *The Lovely Ladies Of Stage & Screen* (Legacy 57711), *Art Deco: Sophisticated Ladies* (Legacy 52943), *Charming Gents Of Stage & Screen* (Legacy 57712), *The Crooners* (Legacy 52942), *They Called It Crooning* (ASV [Academy Sound & Vision] 5026, UK).

Miscellaneous

Jazz Vocal Styles of the Obscure and Neglected

Steve Washington: One record only, "We Were the Best of Friends" (backed with "Sing a Little Low Down Tune") with Benny Goodman as sideman reveals as hip a balladeer as one would ever hear in the thirties. Had Washington been part of any unit other than the Spirits of Rhythm where it was easy to be overshadowed by Teddy Bunn and Leo Watson, we surely would have heard more from him.

Teddi King: A Lee Wiley sound-alike whose short life was enough to encompass a first career (including records with George Shearing, Al Cohn, and fellow Bostonian Nat Pierce), a seventies "comeback," and a minor cult following.

Not of This Earth Department

If Pee-wee Herman could sing the blues, he would sound like **Frankie "Half-Pint" Jaxon.** Someone once asked James Baldwin if he was Jewish, and he responded with something along the lines that being short, gay, black, and ugly was bad enough. Half-Pint sings the blues for black midget transsexuals, and he has a groovy voice and infectious swing, and always works with the classiest black blues and jazz units. Here's to a Half-Pint Jaxon revival in the age of the postsexual revolution! In a similarly bizarre vein, Baby Rose Marie also has heavy-duty rhythm, and hence her Victor records with Fletcher Henderson sound less like a toddler and more like a groovy falsetto munchkin.

Blindfold Test Department

George Morton—who sings with the Mills Blue Rhythm Band on two 1931 titles (recorded under the pseudonym of "King Carter and His Royal Orchestra"), "I Can't Get Along Without My Baby" and "Moanin' " (on LP from the Italian Collector's Must M-8001)—sounds so much like Louis Armstrong that lesser mortals have actually speculated that he *is*, but if you pay close attention, you can hear that when he relaxes, his own natural voice sometimes comes to the surface. Then there's Ronnie Deauville, Tex Beneke's superb balladeer of the late forties who contemporaneously recorded solo singles for Mercury that fooled even diehard Sinatraphiles into thinking he really *was* Frank, circa the Dorsey period.

The same goes for the British Crosby clone Mike Holliday; singling him out makes him especially unique in his nonuniqueness since there were so many Crosby copycats (Jack Harris and Will Jordan each do frighteningly realistic Crosby imitations, too). Ah yes, he, too, could fool you (or me anyway) when he wanted. It was, however, to little avail: Rumor has it that he committed suicide out of frustration in being unable to establish any identity for himself. And don't forget: Mel Brooks's devastating parodies of "Boom Boom" Crosby (not to mention his "sour cream" version of "Dancing in the Dark") and "High Anxiety" Sinatra.

"Moody" Marilyn Moore looked like a Vegas chorine and sang like Billie Holiday—I mean exactly, close enough to fool Jimmy Rushing. In the course of studying Holiday, the two women became close friends, and when Leonard Feather gave Moore's Bethlehem album a good review, Holiday said that if he hadn't, "I'd've knocked him on his butt." Though she was Al Cohn's first wife (he never did marry Mary Ann McAll) and the mother of the fine guitarist Joe Cohn, she always professed a desire to marry James Moody so she could be known as "Moody Marilyn Moody."

Singing Movie Stars Who Sound Considerably Better Than You'd Expect Department

Gene Raymond ("Twinkle Twinkle"), Diana "Swinging" Dors, Jane Russell (the last two, like Marilyn Monroe, don't sound as good as they look, but it's an unfair comparison), and Tony Perkins, who made, among other records, a surprisingly good Epic album with Torme-collaborator Marty Paich. However, though pundit Francis Davis recently dubbed him "the ultimate shower singer," Perkins sang "Never Will I Marry" on Broadway in *Greenwillow*, not, as Mark Murphy claims, in a musical version of *Psycho*.

Lifetime Achievement Award Department

Billy Eckstine.

Really Square Guys Who Actually Sound, Well, Hip in the Thirties and Forties Department

Tony Martin, Perry Como, Frankie Laine.

Really Square Guy Who Never Sounds Hip Department

Andy Williams.

Underrated Award (The Highest Possible Honor):

David Allyn, Jackie Paris, Earl Coleman.

Must to Avoid Department

Cleo Laine, Teresa Brewer, Johnny Mathis, Harry Connick, Jr., Johnnie Ray, Linda Ronstadt, Michael Feinstein, Dianne Schuur, Toni Tennille, Vaughn DeLeath, Vaughan Monroe, Astrud Gilberto, Morton Downey (Jr. or Sr.), Manhattan Transfer.... The list could go on, but I've restricted it to those with major-label contracts.

Newcomers and Talent Deserving of Wider Recognition (1996)

Since Cassandra Wilson, I can recommend anything by Denise Jannah, Mary Cleere Haran, and Jeanie Bryson, as well as much of what I've heard by Paula West, Mary Stalling, Trudy Desmond, and, for those who like their eclecticism, Kurt Elling and Suzanne Cloud.

Most Unintentionally Silly Record

Al Jolson's 1932 Brunswick of "Rock-a-Bye Your Baby (with a Dixie

Melody)," backed with "April Showers," in which Mr. Mammy is accompanied by—are you ready for this?—Guy Lombardo and His Royal Canadians. Call Jolie anything you like, but he wasn't no wimp: While he belts and blusters, the Canadians quack and cluck quietly in the background, almost as if they're on another record. But fear not, the great Jolson is a swan among ducks.

Sources

I doubt that even the relatively recent and common releases listed here are obtainable from your local shop, even in New York (where the three best retailers are the J&R Jazz Marketplace, Vinyl Mania Jazz, and Tower Records). Here are a few mail-order addresses worth trying:

Cadence/North Country, Cadence Building, 345 Route One, Redwood, NY 13679.

Footlight Records, 113 East 12th Street, New York, NY 10003—international heavily show-oriented but with tons of vocalists.

The Record Centre, 45 Loveday Street, Birmingham B4 6NP, England—the best source for European imports.

Select Circles, P.O. Box 302, Riverside, CT 06878—a good provider of imports, independents, and secondhand material which specializes in vocalists.

Good Music, 352 Evelyn Street, PO Box 909, Paramus, NJ 07653-0909—more nostalgia than jazz-oriented, recommended for their own packages of Clark and Haymes.

Jazz M/O, 140 West 22nd Street, 12th floor, New York, NY 10011.

Specializing in Sinatra: Rick Apt, P.O. Box 343, Linwood, NJ 08221.

Acknowledgments

"ADDITIONS TO FURTHER DEFINITIONS"

● ──

So many people have served as surrogate ears for me that it's difficult to know where to start with the acknowledgments. First, to my father, who gave me my first Louis Armstrong record and showed me that one's true wealth isn't measured in money but in Louis Armstrong records. Along with my mother and dozens of friends and fellow mavens, he'll doubtless hear his own voice in these pages.

A few of the above-mentioned friends, in no particular order, are: Eve Zanni, Arthur Schell, Ron Sarbo, Dick Ables, the late Elliott Horne, Al Davis, James Gavin, Chick Wilson, Bob Sherrick, Dan Serro, Bernie Brightman, the late Herb Kurtin, Frank Driggs, Robert Altschuler, Ross Firestone, Marvin Longton, Richard Lieberson, David Weiner, John Leifert, David McCain, Dan Singer, Rich Conaty, and my two favorite jazz academics, Dr. Jack (from Hackensack) McKinney and Professor Lewis Porter. Eric Comstock deserves, at the very least, a sentence of credit all his own, for he supplied me with more than a few sentences.

Acknowledging my editors at Scribner's, Robert Stewart and Erika Goldman, and my agent, Robert Cornfield, and his assistant, Bruce Handy, almost seems redundant, as not only do they know and I know how essential they've been to this project, but so does everyone who knows the slightest bit about it.

I also tended to rely heavily on the staff, as well as the clipping file and record library, of the Rutgers Institute of Jazz Studies, which allowed me to romp through their brains like a kid in a candy store. Special thanks to John Clement, Vincent Pellote, Ed Berger, and especially Dan Morgenstern.

I flatter myself by calling the following men my colleagues (their first impulse, I'm sure, will be to make sure I credited them whenever I swiped facts or thoughts—just as mine would be): Francis Davis, Peter Watrous, Stanley Crouch, Chip Deffaa, Lee Jeske, Peter Keepnews, Don Schlitten, Michael Chertok and the late David Chertok, Bob Porter, Michael Cuscuna, the late Russ Sanjek, Ira Gitler, and Stanley Dance (who graciously read and offered comments on parts of the manuscript). My editors at *The Voice*, Robert Christgau, Tom Carson, and Doug Simmons, and also Gerald Gold at the *Times* have the right knack for giving me a real scare whenever I need it.

Gary Giddins gave me so many breaks, not the least of which was functioning as a role model and rabbi, that he not only made my whole career as a writer possible but desirable. If he finds this sentiment corny, I know he'll at least recognize it as "the real thing, straight from the fields."

Most of all there are the singers, starting with my friend Mel Torme and including Earl Coleman, Jackie Paris, Tony Bennett, and the late Maxine Sullivan and Annette Hanshaw. If not for them I'd probably be reviewing dog acts somewhere in Podunk, Kentucky.

W.F.
New York
October 1988

Index

Other titles of interest

AIN'T MISBEHAVIN'
The Story of Fats Waller
Ed Kirkeby
248 pp., 38 photos
80015-2 $11.95

AS THOUSANDS CHEER
The Life of Irving Berlin
Laurence Bergreen
704 pp., 51 photos
80675-4 $18.95

THE BIG BAND ALMANAC
Revised Edition
Leo Walker
476 pp., 540 photos
80345-3 $17.95

BILLIE'S BLUES: The Billie
Holiday Story 1933-1959
John Chilton
272 pp., 20 photos
80363-1 $13.95

BLACK BEAUTY, WHITE HEAT
A Pictorial History of Classic
Jazz, 1920-1950
Frank Driggs and Harris Lewine
360 pp., 1,516 illus.
80672-X $29.95

CALL ME LUCKY
Bing Crosby as told to Pete Martin
New introduction by Gary Giddins
384 pp., 64 photos
80504-9 $13.95

CELEBRATING THE DUKE
and Louis, Bessie, Billie,
Bird, Carmen, Miles, Dizzy
& Other Heroes
Ralph J. Gleason
Foreword by Studs Terkel
New introduction by Ira Gitler
302 pp., 9 photos
80645-2 $13.95

LOUIS ARMSTRONG
Hugues Panassié
149 pp., 32 pp. of photos
80116-7 $7.95

THE RELUCTANT ART
Five Studies in the Growth of Jazz
Expanded Edition
Benny Green
208 pp.
80441-7 $11.95

REMEMBERING SONG
Encounters with the New Orleans
Jazz Tradition
Updated Edition
Frederick Turner
189 pp., 21 illus.
80555-3 $12.95

SASSY
The Life of Sarah Vaughan
Leslie Gourse
327 pp., 21 illus.
80578-2 $13.95

SATCHMO
My Life in New Orleans
Louis Armstrong
220 pp., 20 photos
80276-7 $11.95

STOMPING THE BLUES
Albert Murray
272 pp., 127 illus.
80362-3 $13.95

SWING THAT MUSIC
Louis Armstrong
New foreword by Dan Morgenstern
200 pp.
80544-8 $12.95

TALKING JAZZ
An Oral History
Expanded Edition
Ben Sidran
535 pp., 20 photos
80613-4 $16.95

Available at your bookstore

OR ORDER DIRECTLY FROM 1-800-386-5656

VISIT OUR WEBSITE AT WWW.PERSEUSBOOKSGROUP.COM